SERVANTHOOD OF SONG

WORSHIP AND WITNESS

The Worship and Witness series seeks to foster a rich, interdisciplinary conversation on the theology and practice of public worship, a conversation that will be integrative and expansive. Integrative, in that scholars and practitioners from a wide range of disciplines and ecclesial contexts will contribute studies that engage church and academy. Expansive, in that the series will engage voices from the global church and foreground crucial areas of inquiry for the vitality of public worship in the twenty-first century.

The Worship and Witness series demonstrates and cultivates the interaction of topics in worship studies with a range of crucial questions, topics, and insights drawn from other fields. These include the traditional disciplines of theology, history, and pastoral ministry—as well as cultural studies, political theology, spirituality, and music and the arts. The series focus will thus bridge church worship practices and the vital witness these practices nourish.

We are pleased that you have chosen to join us in this conversation, and we look forward to sharing this learning journey with you.

Series Editors:
John D. Witvliet
Noel Snyder
Maria Cornou

SERVANTHOOD OF SONG

Music, Ministry, and the Church in the United States

Stanley R. McDaniel
Foreword by Wayne L. Wold

CASCADE *Books* • Eugene, Oregon

SERVANTHOOD OF SONG
Music, Ministry, and the Church in the United States

Copyright © 2024 Stanley R. McDaniel. All rights reserved. Except for brief quotations in critical publications or reviews, no part of this book may be reproduced in any manner without prior written permission from the publisher. Write: Permissions, Wipf and Stock Publishers, 199 W. 8th Ave., Suite 3, Eugene, OR 97401.

Cascade Books
An Imprint of Wipf and Stock Publishers
199 W. 8th Ave., Suite 3
Eugene, OR 97401

www.wipfandstock.com

PAPERBACK ISBN: 978-1-6667-5593-0
HARDCOVER ISBN: 978-1-6667-5594-7
EBOOK ISBN: 978-1-6667-5595-4

Cataloguing-in-Publication data:

Names: McDaniel, Stanley R., author. | Wold, Wayne L., foreword.

Title: Servanthood of song : music, ministry, and the church in the United States / Stanley R. McDaniel; foreword by Wayne L. Wold.

Description: Eugene, OR: Cascade Books, 2024 | Series: Worship and Witness | Includes bibliographical references and index.

Identifiers: ISBN 978-1-6667-5593-0 (paperback) | ISBN 978-1-6667-5594-7 (hardcover) | ISBN 978-1-6667-5595-4 (ebook)

Subjects: LCSH: Sacred music—United States—History and criticism. | Music—Religious aspects—Christianity. | Gospel music—History and criticism. | Hymns, English—History and criticism.

Classification: ML2911 .M50 2024 (paperback) | ML2911 (ebook)

VERSION NUMBER 052024

Title page images:

(Left) "A Negro Camp Meeting in the South"—Public Domain Image, Courtesy Library of Congress

(Right) "Camp-Meeting" by Hugh Bridport and Kennedy & Lucas after a painting by Alexander Rider. Public Domain Image, Courtesy Smithsonian.

In Memory of My Mother
Helen Elizabeth McDaniel
(1918–2016)

CONTENTS

Foreword by Wayne L. Wold | xvii

Prologue | 1

CHAPTER 1
BEGINNINGS—THE EIGHTEENTH CENTURY | 5
The Old Way vs. Regular Singing | 8
Singing Sermons and Lectures | 12
The Singing School | 19
Singing Masters and Their Methods | 24
William Billings and Church Song in Eighteenth-Century America | 27
Slavery and the Church | 31
The Revolutionary Years | 38
Resistance | 40
Concluding Remarks | 41

CHAPTER 2
TIME OF TRANSITION | 43
A Sea Change in Theological Outlook | 44
Perfectionism | 47
The Decline of the New England Singing School | 49
Choirs and the Church | 50
Instrumental Music in Churches | 51

CHAPTER 3
TWO GREAT RIVERS | 57
Public Education and the American Sunday School Movement | 61
Thomas Hastings | 64
Lowell Mason | 72

Musical Conventions | 81
Charles Grandison Finney and Worship at the Broadway Tabernacle | 84
W. B. Bradbury | 86
Hastings, Mason, and Bradbury Reconsidered | 90

CHAPTER 4
THE LITURGICAL CHURCH, PART 1 | 92
From Anglican to Episcopalian in the Eighteenth Century | 93
The Protestant Episcopal Church in the Early Nineteenth Century | 96
The Oxford Movement, Tractarianism, and Ritualism | 98
W. A. Muhlenberg | 100
Anglican Chant in American Churches | 103
Edward Hodges | 107
Anti-Catholicism in America | 110
Music and Roman Catholics from the Eighteenth through the Early Nineteenth Century | 113
Benjamin Carr | 116

CHAPTER 5
A MIGHTY SHOUT! | 120
Roots of Frontier Revivalism | 123
The First Camp Meetings | 126
Cane Ridge, August 6–13, 1801 | 129
Camp Meeting Song | 131
Baptists and Revivalism on the Frontier | 134
The Legacy of the Camp Meeting | 136
"Lining Out"—An Ancient Tradition Resurfaces | 137
Singing Schools and Shape-Note Hymnody in Pennsylvania and Beyond | 137
The Introduction of Shape-Note Notation | 142
An Affront to Cultivated Sensibilities | 146
A New Generation of Singing Masters and Compilers | 147
The Nineteenth-Century Singing School | 152
A Sacred Calling | 153
William "Singin' Billy" Walker | 154
The Southern Harmony | 156
Benjamin Franklin White and "The Sacred Harp" | 159
The Quest to Improve Musical Leadership through Musical Conventions and Certification | 161
Black Shape-Note Singing in the South | 161
Singing Schools, Tunebooks, and Shape Notes—a Living Inheritance | 162

CHAPTER 6

AFRICAN AMERICAN MUSIC AND WORSHIP | 164

Worship among the Slaves in Antebellum America | 166
Racial Bias in Antebellum Perceptions of African American Worship | 172
Confluence: A Merging of Musical Cultures | 176
Continuity versus Discontinuity | 178
The Sectional Crisis: The Church and Colonization versus Abolition | 186
The Contrabands | 187
The Port Royal Experiment | 190
Emancipation | 201
William Francis Allen | 203
Slave Songs of the United States | 205

CHAPTER 7

THE CIVIL WAR | 210

The Revival of 1857–1859 | 211
At the Brink of War | 213
The Chaplaincy | 216
Delegates, Missionaries, and Colporteurs | 220
The United States Christian Commission | 220
Tracts, Hymnals, and Songsters | 222
Worship and Revivalism during the Civil War | 223
Hymn Singing in the Camp | 230
Singing among African American Troops | 233
The Power of Sacred Song | 235
Wartime Advancement of Music in the United States | 240
The Importance of Sacred Music during the Civil War and Its Future Impact | 243

CHAPTER 8

THE CULTIVATED CHURCH AND ITS MUSIC IN POST-CIVIL WAR AMERICA, 1865–1885 | 244

The Gilded Age | 245
New Realities and Shifting Theological Currents | 246
Premillennialism and Postmillennialism | 248
The Church "Evolves" | 249
Sacralization | 250
The Reverend Henry Ward Beecher, Plymouth Church, Its Choir, and Congregational Singing | 252
The Plymouth Collection and Its Influence | 256
Birth of a Choral Tradition | 258

The National Peace Jubilee | 259
Choral Performance Becomes an Accepted Component
   of Protestant Worship | 260

CHAPTER 9

THE LITURGICAL CHURCH, PART 2 | 265

Ritualism, the Legacy of the Oxford Movement in America | 265
The Choir's "Priestly" Role | 268
The Choral Service | 269
Musical Reform at "Mother Church," Trinity Parish, New York City | 271
Henry Stephen Cutler | 271
Arthur H. Messiter | 275
Priest-Musicians in the Protestant Episcopal Church | 276
The New York Ecclesiastical Society and the Church Choral Society | 277
The Reverend John Ireland Tucker | 278
The Reverend John Henry Hopkins Jr. | 282
The Reverend Morgan Dix | 287
John Sebastian Bach Hodges | 291
The Boy Choir Movement in the United States | 294
The Exclusion of Women from Ritual Leadership: Theologically Defending the
   Indefensible | 299
Lutheran Worship in the Nineteenth Century | 304
The Church and Opera: Roman Catholic Worship Music in Nineteenth-Century
   America | 306
Early Efforts toward the Reform of Catholic Church Music | 308
The "Cæcilian Movement" in America | 310
The Broader Implications of Ritualism across Denominations | 311

CHAPTER 10

THE RISE OF PROFESSIONAL CHOIRMASTERS, ORGANISTS, AND SINGERS AS CHURCH MUSICIANS | 313

The Professional Church Singer | 316
The Quartet in Nineteenth-Century Worship | 327
Organ Manufacture in America | 336
Pump Organs, Reed Organs, Harmoniums, and Melodions | 337
The Rise of the Professional Organist and John Zundel | 340
A Perennial Problem: The Need for a Higher Standard of Training for
   Musicians | 344
Normal Schools of Music | 344
Choirmasters in the Late Nineteenth Century | 347
Dudley Buck, Organist, Church Musician, and Composer | 349

An Impediment to Progress | 359

CHAPTER 11
UNFULFILLED ASPIRATIONS | 362
Washington Gladden and Social Awareness in the Nineteenth-Century Church | 364
Social Reform Hymnody Prior to the Civil War | 366
The Social Christianity Movement | 368
Frank Mason North | 369
Five Classic Examples of Social Gospel Hymnody | 370
Rauschenbusch and the Social Gospel | 375
Social Hymns of Brotherhood and Aspiration | 377
The Legacy of the Social Gospel Movement for the Church and Its Music | 378
The Black Church | 380
A Younger Generation Turns Away from the Songs of Slavery | 381
Seeking a Musical Bridge Between Race and Class—The Spiritual | 382
Fisk University and the Spiritual | 385
The Tour | 389
Aftermath | 397
Reconstruction and Reform in the Late Nineteenth Century | 398
Booker T. Washington | 400
W. E. B. Du Bois | 402

CHAPTER 12
"THE GREAT URBAN REVIVAL" OF MOODY AND SANKEY | 405
Shoe Salesman Turned Evangelist—Moody in Chicago | 407
Evangelist in Wartime | 412
Re-envisioning Revival for the Late Nineteenth Century | 413
A Standardized Formula | 414
Moody and the Music of Revival | 415
Philip Phillips, the "Singing Pilgrim" | 417
Eben Tourjée and the "Praise Meeting" | 419
The Preacher and Pitch | 421
Ira David Sankey | 422
A Moody-Sankey Partnership Is Born | 425
Philip Paul Bliss | 426
Stebbins, McGranahan, and Towner | 429
Late Nineteenth Century of White Gospel Hymnody | 430
Gospel Songs, 1–6 | 433
Reassessing the Gospel Hymn Repertoire | 438

CHAPTER 13

BARBERSHOPS, BALLYHOO, AND BLUE NOTES | 440

Chicago and Bronzeville | 441
Urban Blacks Find Their Voice | 443
Sherwood's Hymnal | 445
Tindley, the Progenitor | 446
The Holy Spirit Sings! Sanctification, Holiness, and Pentecostalism | 451
Black Gospel Music and the Storefront Church | 454
The Storefront Church in Chicago | 456
White Urban Revivalism after Dwight Moody: The Preachers and Their Musician Associates | 457
Billy Sunday | 461
Homer Rodeheaver | 465
Traditional Evangelism and the Rise of Fundamentalism | 470
The Dilemma: Confronting Divisions of Class and Caste | 472

CHAPTER 14

A NEW CENTURY FOR MUSIC AND WORSHIP IN THE CULTIVATED CHURCH | 474

A Time for Optimism | 474
Sacred Music and Mainline Protestantism: Hymnody and Hymnals | 477
Reed and Pipe Organs in Turn-of-the-Century America | 480
The Second New England School of Composers | 483
Arthur B. Whiting and Arthur Foote | 484
Amy Marcy Cheney (Mrs. H. H. A.) Beach | 486
George Whitefield Chadwick | 488
Horatio Parker | 489
Dvořák Inspires a Dialogue on the Need for Music Uniquely "American" | 493
Choral Music Becomes a "Cultivated Commodity" | 496
The St. Olaf Lutheran Choir | 496
John Finley Williamson and the Westminster Choir | 500
"The Great War" and the End of an Era | 501

CHAPTER 15

THE *MOTU PROPRIO* OF 1903 AND ITS AFTERMATH | 504

Father Finn | 514
The Aftermath of the Motu Proprio | 517

CHAPTER 16
SACRED MUSIC EDUCATION AND THE FLOWERING OF MUSIC AS A MINISTRY IN THE UNITED STATES | 520
Waldo Selden Pratt | 520
Archibald T. Davison | 527
The American Guild of Organists | 530
Music Ministry Education | 532
The Founding of Westminster Choir College | 537
Clarence Dickinson | 539
Union Theological Seminary | 544
The UTS School of Sacred Music | 546
"Minister of Music," a Title and a Concept | 547

CHAPTER 17
GOSPEL METAMORPHOSIS | 551
Gospel Music in the Twentieth Century | 553
James Vaughan and the Southern Gospel Tradition | 554
The Vaughan and Stamps-Baxter Normal Schools | 558
The Publisher/Church Connection: A Formula for Success | 559
Virgil O. Stamps and the Stamps-Baxter Music Company | 560
Singing Conventions and Commerce | 561
Male Quartets and White Southern Gospel Music | 562
Black Gospel Music, the Developing Years | 565
The Great Migration—A Collision of Cultures | 568
Thomas A. Dorsey—the Early Years | 569
The Influence of African American Preaching | 570
Dorsey and Chicago | 572
Dorsey, Frye, and the Birth of the Black Gospel Chorus | 574
Black Women and Gospel Music | 579
Arizona Dranes | 581
Sallie Martin | 582
Roberta Martin | 583
Mahalia Jackson | 584
Breaking Boundaries: Sister Rosetta Tharpe | 585
From Spiritual Business to Show Business | 587
Emergence of Independent Gospel Recording and Performing Artists | 588

CHAPTER 18
COLLAPSE AND CONFLICT | 590
The Church in the Great Depression | 590
H. Richard Niebuhr on "Culture Protestantism" and Denominationalism | 593
Archibald Davison and "Protestant Church Music in America" | 596
Winds of Change | 599
Church Music Reform and the Episcopalians during the Depression Era | 600
The Hymnal 1940 | 609
The Broadman Hymnal, a Milestone for the Evangelical Wing | 610
Depression Era Advancement of Sacred Music Education | 612
The Coming of War | 618
Evangelism in World War II | 621
Wartime and the Manufacture of Organs and Keyboard Instruments | 623
The Long-Term Impact of the Second World War on Church Music in America | 625

CHAPTER 19
SACRED MUSIC IN THE POST-WAR ERA, 1946 TO 1965 | 626
Return to Peacetime, 1945–1950 | 626
Charles C. Hirt, a Choral and Sacred Music Giant of the Post-War Era | 627
Cultivated Church Music in 1950s America | 629
A "Golden Age" for Sacred Choral and Organ Music | 630
Traditional Mainline vs. Evangelical; Cultivated vs. Populist—Southern Baptists Occupy the Middle Ground | 635
Introducing the Evangelistic Cantata | 638
Shea, Barrows, and the Billy Graham Crusades | 639
Billy Graham and the Media | 643
Radio and Recording Become the Engine Driving White and Black Gospel Music in the Mid-Twentieth Century | 644
Black "Crossover" Artists and Sam Cooke | 646

CHAPTER 20
A TIME OF TURBULENCE | 651
The Church at Mid-Century | 652
Hymn Explosion | 653
The Promise of Vatican II | 654
Discordant Voices | 661
Sacred Troubadours, Guitars, and the Rise of the Folk Mass | 666
Baby Boomers and the Folk Revival | 673
The Origins of "Praise and Worship" | 675

The "Jesus Movement" | 677
Calvary Chapel | 680
Sacred Pop Goes Mainstream | 684

CHAPTER 21
THE DECLINE OF THE CULTIVATED TRADITION IN AMERICAN CHURCH MUSIC | 686
The Maturation of Contemporary Christian Music: Calvary Chapel and Maranatha! Music | 691
The Vineyard | 693
The Megachurch and the Church Growth Movement | 698
The Church Growth Movement | 703
Bill Hybels and Willow Creek Community Church | 705
Rick Warren and Saddleback Community Church | 706
Issues Raised by the Megachurch and Church Growth Movements | 709
Contemporary Worship Music and Mainstream Protestantism | 710
Toward a New Century in African American Church Music | 712
The White Protestant Church Choir in Decline | 714
Music Ministry Education and Professional Standards, a Dream on Hold | 715
Music Merchandizing | 718
The King of Instruments | 721

CHAPTER 22
LEARNING FROM THE PAST—HOPE FOR THE FUTURE | 723
Missed Opportunities for Consensus | 725
The Congregational Singing Dilemma | 726
Music Ministry Education | 728
Dualism and Postmodernism in the Twenty-First Century | 729
The Crucible of Perfectionism, Elevation of Musical Taste, and Sacralization | 732
"The Call" | 733
Hopeful Signs | 735
To Revitalize Artistic Expression in Church Music—A Challenge for the Twenty-First Century | 739
The Tyranny of Labeling | 740
A Final Word | 741

EPILOGUE | 742
BIBLIOGRAPHY | 749
INDEX | 797

FOREWORD

"I have tried with *Servanthood of Song* to write the book I wish I had had in mentoring church musicians at a critical time in our history," wrote author Stan McDaniel as he shared his manuscript with me. I love his choice of the word "mentoring," as it implies so much more than merely teaching. Mentoring encompasses teaching, yes, but also the sharing of one's experiences, the challenging in areas needing growth, the struggling with difficult topics, the gaining of perspective, the building of relationships, and all done in a caring, collegial manner.

"A little learning is a dangerous thing" wrote Alexander Pope in 1774. Although the saying has morphed into "a little knowledge . . . ," it still rings true when those who are educated and experienced in their particular field encounter questionable claims that come from a place of insufficient insight. Great teachers want to turn a "little learning" into so much more—not mere information but ultimately a spirit of curiosity and the tools to think and to apply what they learn.

But such a point of view can also betray an attitude of elitism, a one-way vision of education, characterizing a student as an "empty vessel" needing to be filled by the all-knowing teacher.

Perhaps a better paradigm comes from Maya Angelou, who advises us, "Do the best you can until you know better. Then when you know better, do better." I believe that is a more accurate picture of the type of education and experience that takes place in the field of church music.

When considered cumulatively, there is more music happening in houses of worship on a weekly basis than anywhere else. Worshippers come together by the millions, and, with rare exceptions, each gathering requires someone to lead the music. This need accounts for the wide range of expertise to be found in the hundreds of thousands of worship spaces across America alone. Many of us were called to be music leaders long before we had the requisite skills; yet God was praised and continues to be praised;

the gospel was proclaimed and continues to be proclaimed; the people were edified and continue to be edified. We do what we can, until we can do better. We must commend all those individuals who, throughout history to the present day, have stepped forward as music leaders, often feeling underqualified, yet learning by trial and error, success and discovery.

The history of sacred music is as broad and wide as the history of all music in Western culture. In fact, sacred music is at the very core of Western music history. Our system of tonality originated in the chants of the Jewish synagogue, which in turn became the earliest music of the Christian church; the church created the system of music notation that we still use today; the teaching of music reading and performance skills were strongly promoted and enabled by the church; and much of the music we now think of as "secular" has deep roots in sacred music.

Yet, those of us who are drawn to church music are seen as being in a specialty subgroup, and often thought to be second-rate musicians at best. "I don't have a very good piano background," stated an incoming college student during an interview with a few members of the music faculty where I teach. When asked to explain further, she said, "My teacher was just a church organist." She was shocked by the laughter that followed that explanation, for among the keyboard faculty in that group were four church organists, all well-trained and highly experienced, including one with a DMA in organ performance! She laughed, too, when we explained our response. But there was irony in our laughter; we all understood where her comment came from.

What is unique to those of us who are drawn to use our training, musicianship, and energy in the field of church music? Why do we seek positions where we know we often will be working with untrained musicians and under nonmusical supervisors? Why do we shy away from using such terms as "gigs" and "jobs" when discussing our church music positions? It often comes down to the sense of calling that we feel, something we experience strongly but cannot really explain. Dr. McDaniel's decision to title his book *Servanthood of Song* comes from such a sense of calling. Hundreds of authors have written about the spiritual and pastoral side of being a church musician, myself included. McDaniel certainly does not downplay this aspect of music ministry, as his copious footnotes and extensive bibliography profess. But here he focuses on a different facet of being an effective church musician—the importance of knowing the history behind our vocation.

Having knowledge and having good intentions are often pitted against each other in our churches. Poorly presented music often is accepted because the musician "did their best" and "their heart was in the right place." Too much musical or theological education can be seen as a detriment in some churches, fearful of an elitism that will divide the musician from the aesthetic of the congregation. And sometimes those perceptions are all too accurate. McDaniel begins with the conviction that mind and heart are intertwined, that both are important, and that they enrich each other. And he then he sets out to teach the reader about *our* profession, *our* history, and *our* present situations.

What can the reader learn from these pages? That church music and church/denominational history are closely entwined; that varying theologies and pieties are highly influential; that the cultural situations and realities outside the church's walls always make their way inside those walls, no matter how hard people may try to keep them out; that musical styles and practices that are vilified in one generation are often embraced in another generation. We can learn about numerous musical traditions and repertoire that might enrich our current programs. And perhaps the most important thing we can learn from pondering all that is contained in these pages is perspective—that most problems and concerns that we encounter in the modern-day church are not all that new after all. They are all part of the ministry into which we are called.

Through numerous examples, McDaniel recounts the swing of the pendulum. Each new generation has encountered tensions between the traditional and the progressive; the desire to return to "purer worship" and "holier music," whatever that is perceived to be at the moment; the ever-present tension between "high art" and vernacular styles; the conflicting philosophies regarding the goal of worship, whether it is to worship God or to attract new members. And he lays out for us the oft-recurring circular pattern of 1) wanting to improve congregational singing; (2) establishing systems to train singers to read and lead better; 3) the professionalizing of these singers into soloists, quartets, and choirs; 4) resulting in less congregational participation in the worship service; 5) lamenting that congregational singing is not good and "something must be done"; 6) starting the process all over again.

McDaniel could have gone back even further in history to present examples of these recurring pendulums and circular patterns. Such examples exist from the earliest years of the church, through the medieval era, the Reformation and Counter-Reformation, the various strands of Protestantism, the rise of the operatic style in the baroque era, and the tensions our beloved J. S. Bach had to deal with as he strove to create "well-regulated" church music in his day. Although I am sure McDaniel is just as knowledgeable about these examples—and would encourage you to learn about them, too—his focus in this volume is on church music as it has taken place on American soil since the first Europeans settled here.

Many histories of church music in America focus primarily on choirs and organs. McDaniel does not ignore this side of church music, but he spends more time on congregational singing than other authors have done. From the New England meeting house, to the singing school, to the impact of immigration and migration, slavery and emancipation, McDaniel supplies much important material on the music styles that have been birthed in America. And his recounting of religious and musical movements of the twentieth century helps the reader understand where we find ourselves in the first quarter of the twenty-first century.

We dare not reduce anything as important and complex as church music to a matter for mere knowledge, but we have to admit that more knowledge is much better than just "a little learning."

I close with these important words from Dr. McDaniel, words that you will encounter again near the end of these several hundred pages of helpful history and thoughtful insight:

> The challenge for the church musician of today is one of ministry—to know and embrace the diverse musical and liturgical needs of the community to which he or she is called and revel in that diversity. To do that effectively, musicians in ministry in the United States need broad training, both in sacred music and worship-oriented studies—clear-eyed training which recognizes the musical landscape in the twenty-first-century American church and puts forth positive avenues to work within that landscape.[1]

Wayne L. Wold, DMA, AAGO
Director of the Church Music Institute and Adjunct Associate Professor of Music at Shenandoah University, Winchester, Virginia
Professor Emeritus and College Organist at Hood College, Frederick, Maryland
Director of Music Ministry at First Lutheran Church, Ellicott City, Maryland
Author of *Preaching to the Choir: The Care and Nurture of the Church Choir*, 2nd ed., Augsburg Fortress, 2023

---

1. McDaniel, *Servanthood of Song*, 724.

PROLOGUE

WE ARE NOW IN the second decade of the twenty-first century. Clearly, it is an unsettled time in American church music. There is a dearth of young people seeking careers in church music. Some churches have discontinued choir programs, and, in many cases, traditional hymnody is being replaced with contemporary Christian "praise music." Full-time, career positions in music leadership are often being replaced with part-time or multiple part-time help. The classically trained church musician is likely to ask, "Why is this happening? What can be done?"

To gain perspective on the current state of American church music, I believe we must look at the historical record. In doing so, we will soon see that the problems we face are not new. The so-called "worship wars" have occurred under different guises throughout America's past. Where mainline traditional churches are concerned, for example, we have seen incredible progress made in the administration and direction of church choirs, in the development of the modern hymnal, in the acceptance of music ministry as a career choice, and in the technological advancement of pipe organ manufacture. At the same time, we've seen missed opportunities: the allowing of racial and gender discrimination to limit potential for ministry, the worship of "tradition" taking precedence too often over the pursuit of a "living faith," the seeming inability from one generation to the next to achieve robust congregational singing of hymns, and the unwillingness of many on either side of the divide between contemporary and traditional worship to listen and learn from each other.

This is not the time, however, to throw up one's hands in despair. Looking at the historical record, we can plainly see that none of this is new. Our forebears faced the same problems. Emotions ran high. Tempers flared. But out of it came a better understanding of how the art of music could best serve God's people. We can learn much from their successes and their mistakes.

Servanthood of Song was conceived based on several core beliefs arising out of years toiling as a music ministry professional, a teacher of American music history and sacred music studies at the graduate level:

- That music in the church must be understood as a ministry largely different in focus from that of secular society;
- That music in the church, without sacrificing either artistic or theological integrity, must minister to all segments of the worshipping community;
- That sacred music must be recognized for its unique power to comfort, to lift up in praise, and to exhort in worship;
- That the church and its musicians must return to the ancient understanding of community and what that means for servanthood;
- And, finally, that music ministry professionals must be grounded in American church music history to understand the challenges and promise of church music in the present.

Inclusivity: I believe that the great challenge of the twenty-first century for churches and for church musicians is not a contest pitting advocates of evangelical praise and worship music against supporters of classic hymns and anthems by master composers. In fact, that contest only serves to overshadow the real challenge. Demographic studies show that neither Mendelssohn nor Michael W. Smith can claim credit for reversing the decline in church membership! Music is not the antidote. Divisiveness must be replaced with a welcoming of diversity in musical styles focused on theological and artistic integrity—a holistic approach, reaching out to the people we serve, understanding their wants and needs, serving and teaching. That is inclusivity in church music.

Ministry: I titled this book as I did because I believe music must be understood as a ministry of the church. All ministry is servanthood. All ministry is pastoral. A theme in American church music history that keeps appearing from the 1830s onward is the idea that music in the church must be viewed as a ministry. Unlike his or her secular counterpart, the minister of music is equal parts musician, pastor, and teacher. In modern usage, when ministry is discussed, it is usually in reference to the ordained ministry—individuals "set apart" so to speak by calling, training, and profession to witness and to shepherd their flock. Pope John Paul II touched on the pastoral servant role of ministers when he said:

> In shepherding the flock and leading its worship, the priest lifts up to God and ennobles the Christian vocations of all the

faithful, whose servant he is. It is important that priests be both "set apart" and "servants," and that one be the condition of the other. If the priest is not clearly set apart, then he will not provide the service which the Church requires; and if he is not a true servant, he will end in a self-absorbed and sterile remoteness which is alien to an authentic shepherd.[1]

Ordained ministers are indispensable in providing needed leadership and an example of righteousness to contemporary Christians. But viewing ministry as the exclusive provenance of the ordained does not square with the Gospels.

But Jesus called them to him, and saith unto them, Ye know that they which are accounted to rule over the Gentiles exercise lordship over them; and their great ones exercise authority upon them. But so shall it not be among you: but whosoever will be great among you, shall be your minister. (Mark 10: 42–43, KJV)[2]

The role of servant is central to any worship leader: priest, minister, lector, acolyte, choirmaster, organist, song leader, and so on. Closely related is the Reformation concept of a "Priesthood of all Believers."[3] In 1520, Martin Luther wrote:

It has been devised that the Pope, bishops, priests, and monks are called the spiritual estate . . . This is an artful lie and hypocritical device . . . all Christians are truly of the spiritual estate, and there is no difference among them, save of office alone. As St. Paul says (1 Cor 12), We are all one body, though each member does its own work, to serve the others. This is because we have one baptism, one Gospel, one faith, and are all Christians alike; for baptism, Gospel, and faith, these alone make spiritual and Christian people. Thus we are all consecrated as priests by baptism, as St. Peter says: "Ye are a royal priesthood, a holy nation" (1 Pet 2:9).

Community: Another core belief underlying this study is my unshakable belief in the church as "community." We, as a church and as church

---

1. Pope John Paul II, "Address of the Holy Father to the Bishops of Canada."

2. "Universal priesthood" is generally associated with Protestantism and, in some circles, still regarded as a challenge to the holy orders of the Roman Catholic faith, by which ordination is intended to "set apart" the priesthood. This is unfortunate. The servant role, which Christ modeled so beautifully, was intended for all his followers, and in no way conflicts with administrative and priestly duties and authority of the priesthood.

3. Luther, "Address to the Nobility of the German Nation."

musicians, must continually aspire to minister to the entire worshipping community, and that means we need to know and embrace the entire community. It is so disheartening, I think, to review our history of repeated attempts from generation to generation to shape worshipping communities by setting arbitrary standards of musical taste. The effects on ministry have been devastating.

Understanding our heritage in American church music: It is my experience that very few church musicians, whether trained classically or in contemporary worship idioms, have a solid grounding in the history of American church music. I find that shocking. We all, I believe, have accepted a call to serve the communities in which we labor. How can we serve those communities in a holistic way if we don't know our history? The history of American church music, I believe, must be viewed as a marvelous, multihued quilt. Knowing something of its complexity gives us context to understand and respect the diverse and unique needs of individual worshipping communities.

Admittedly, this book attempts to address a huge and complex subject. Each of America's Protestant denominations has its own musical history about which, I suspect, much needs to be written. I devote chapters to the music of African Americans and how the church's dealing with slavery affected it; the place of music within Roman Catholicism; the fascinating drift from folk hymns to white and Black gospel music, to pop; the list goes on—but one might seek out other sources in each of these areas for a more comprehensive treatment. Out of necessity, I have chosen to focus only on mainstream Christian religious practice in our country. This required passing over or giving little mention to some very important and influential sacred music traditions, such as those of the Mormons, the Bohemian Brethren, and the Moravians. Without question, each of these deserves scholarly attention. What I have tried to do, however, is create a cross-denominational study from which church musicians and churchgoing Americans, whatever their race, gender, or religious preference, may learn about the historical and theological trends that have brought us to where we are in the twenty-first century.

Chapter 1

BEGINNINGS—THE EIGHTEENTH CENTURY

There is no better evidence of the importance of music in worship than the passion with which worshippers over the centuries have railed against change or supported it. Nearly every generation from the eighteenth century to the present has had its *worship wars*. That music should be viewed as a ministry, its leadership pastoral, is a view put forward by leaders in every Christian denomination as well as nondenominational groups. It was a point made unequivocally in *A Manual for Clergy and Church Musicians*, published in 1980 by the Standing Commission on Church Music of the (Protestant) Episcopal Church:

> Because the Church musician is inevitably put into the position of being a pastor and teacher, ideally this person should be well trained in the Scriptures, the liturgy, theology, and pastoral care, in addition to having high competency in music.[1]

To fully understand the great controversy that would erupt over what would be called *regular singing*[2] and the singing school movement which followed, one must first understand the context. The total population of Caucasian New Englanders in 1720 has been estimated to have been about

---

1. Hatchett, *Manual for Clergy and Church Musicians*, 39.

2. The term "regular singing" was probably *not* coined by Thomas Symmes in his *Reasonableness of Regular Singing* (1720), but was likely in common use well before that. It has been suggested that it was simply another way of describing *regulated* singing, that is, singing by note rather than improvised "by ear." There was no doubt also a connection to John Calvin's "Regulative Principle of Worship" as stated in the Westminster Confession of Faith. It was the Calvinist principle to forbid the use of any music in worship other than the singing of psalms.

406,200 people.[3] Already in 1700 approximately 106,000 of those identified themselves as Puritans or related Reformed denominations. Leaders on both sides of the controversy identified as Puritans or Congregationalists. The Puritans were not strict Calvinists. Their understanding of predestination, original sin, and other core teachings of John Calvin was nuanced from one community to another. They shared, however, vivid memories of the English Civil War and the hardships that led them to come to the new world. Anglicanism (or any overarching institutional church that threatened to inhibit their ability to worship as they chose) was regarded with fear and suspicion. In the late seventeenth and early eighteenth centuries, the colonial meetinghouse was the religious, governmental, and social center of the town. New England Puritans treasured the freedom to worship as they chose. Worship was central to everything for these folk—not some institutionally mandated style of worship, but their own very individualistic approach. They sought jealously to protect it from outside and *foreign* influences. Given the context of the times, we can appreciate how many Puritan communities viewed regional efforts to reform congregational singing as an unwelcome intrusion into the most deeply coveted part of their devotional lives.

Yes, we can point to examples of ignorance and superstition among adherents to the old way, but we should also point out the elitist rhetoric of their critics. Both sides in the argument shared a passion for vital and authentic worship but could not agree on how best to achieve that. While reformers defended *regular singing* as necessary for progress, there was never a real truce. Hard feelings and animosity cropped up now and again as late as the 1830s.

Music thought to be appropriate for worship by American Protestants[4] in the colonial era was rather narrowly confined to congregational psalmody and hymnody. Church leaders viewed music with ambivalence. Certainly, the importance of congregational song was recognized, but it was feared the sensual attraction of the art could distract from the pure and holy. This was not a new conundrum. Pope John XXII in 1324 railed against composers of the *Ars nova* and their early experimentation with polyphonic writing. "They intoxicate the ear without satisfying it; they dramatize the text with gestures; and, instead of promoting devotion, they prevent it by creating

---

3. "Colonial Population Estimates," https://www.infoplease.com/us/population/colonial-population-estimates

4. While Benjamin Carr had published some liturgical music for Roman Catholics (see chapter 4), a broad-based desire to incorporate music into Roman Catholic worship would have to wait until the 1840s.

a sensuous and indecent atmosphere."[5] Some members of the Council of Trent in the sixteenth century advocated abolishing polyphony entirely from Roman Catholic worship, based on the same rationale.

The influence of John Calvin and other non-German leaders of the Reformation was very strong during the eighteenth century in all English-speaking churches in America, including the Anglican. Calvin did not propose restricting congregational singing to the Psalms in his *Institutes of the Christian Religion* (1559), but *did* state:

> And surely, if the singing be tempered to that gravity which is fitting in the sight of God and the angels, it both lends dignity and grace to sacred actions and has the greatest value in kindling our hearts to a true zeal and eagerness to pray. Yet we should be very careful that our ears be not more attentive to the melody than our minds to the spiritual meaning of the words.[6]

While Calvin's attitude on the subject seems sensible and moderating, he nevertheless allowed only unison singing of psalm tunes in the churches he served.[7]

The early years of the eighteenth century were a time of transition and ferment in New England. Following the Salem witch trials in 1693, there was a desire among younger, more progressive clerics to move away from the superstitions of the past toward a faith based more in reasoning, and not so antithetical to developments in mathematics and scientific learning. The new generation of ministers sought to simplify ritual and expand the leadership in the meetinghouses to include leaders from the community.[8]

To understand the role of music in colonial America in the eighteenth century, one need only peruse writings from the period. Titles tell a great deal about shifts in cultural attitudes toward church music. John Cotton's treatise, *Singing of Psalms a Gospel Ordinance,* written in 1647, as the title implies, emphasized a rigid definition of propriety for singing in the worship service, requiring it be restricted to religious texts, and that all should approach it as a *holy duty*. He advocated restricting church song to the singing of metrical psalms. This became the general practice in both Anglican

---

5. Pope John XXII, Papal Bull (1324)

6. Calvin, *Institutes,* 895.

7. Ellinwood, *History of American Church Music,* 15. Actually, John Calvin enunciated his position on the singing of psalms much earlier. In 1537, he wrote, "it is a thing most expedient for the edification of the church to sing some psalms in the form of public prayers by which one prays to God or sings His praises so that the hearts of all may be roused and stimulated to make similar prayers and to render similar praises and thanks to God with a common love." See Reid, ed., "Articles," 48.

8. Turner, "Earwitness to Resonance," 27.

parishes and Congregational meetinghouses throughout the eighteenth century.[9]

When it came to music in worship, colonial Americans struggled with conflicted values. On the one hand, music had always been a significant force in the worship of God. On the other, its impact upon the emotions was a problem. The preface to *The Whole Book of Psalms Faithfully Translated into English Meter*, printed by Stephen Day in 1640 and better known as *The Bay Psalm Book*, stated the problem thus:

> The singing of Psalms, though it breathe forth nothing but holy harmony and melody; yet such is the subtlety of the enemy, and the enemy of our Lord, and his ways. . .[10]

The Rev. Thomas Symmes, in his *The Reasonableness of Regular Singing*, asked:

> Is there not great reason to fear that you mistake the *Pleasing Impressions* made upon your *Animal Spirits*, by the tune, [for] the Melody you ought to make in your heart to the Lord?[11]

The Old Way vs. Regular Singing

The congregational singing of metrical paraphrases of the psalms was central to Reformed worship from the arrival of the pilgrims forward. The English parish church practice of *lining out* was brought with these first immigrants from England. Congregations often lacked in literacy. *The Bay Psalm Book*, the first book published in British North America, "contained no music (probably for lack of anyone capable of engraving woodblocks for printing it) and, in fact, restricted the use of psalm tunes to only those tunes which conformed to its six meters."[12] The problem and an approach to solving it are described in John Cotton's treatise:

> We for our parts easily grant, that where all have books and can read, or else can say the Psalms by heart, it were needless there to read each lined of the Psalm beforehand in order to sing it. But if it be granted, which is already proved . . . that the Psalms are to be sung by the body of the congregation. Then, to this end, it will be a necessary help, that the words of the Psalm be

---

9. Ellinwood, *History of American Church Music*, 16.
10. Playford, *Whole Book of Psalms*, 1.
11. Symmes (attrib.), *Reasonableness of Regular Singing*, 18.
12. Wolfe, *Early American Music Engraving*, 14.

openly read beforehand, line after line, or two lines together, that so they who want either books or skill to read, may know what is to be sung and join with the rest in the duty of singing.[13]

Cotton was describing the practice of *lining out*. In practice, after the deacon lined out one or two verses of text, a *precentor* or church officer would *set the tune*. Each precentor had the freedom to ornament at will and sing at whatever pitch and tempo seemed right at the moment.[14] Tunes were passed down orally from one generation to the next, each adding changes as the spirit dictated. One needed only to approximate the tune. To ornament it with flourishes, slides, and imaginative roulades was regarded as the usual and most desirable way of presentation.

> Little slidings and purrings, risings and lowerings, as the heart inclined. Thereby was the singing made individual and thereby was the Lord pleased . . .[15]

Finally, when the deacon and precentor had completed their assigned tasks, the congregation could respond with singing, only to have the entire process repeated for the next verse or two of the psalm.[16] This extended and laborious process, commonly referred to as the "*old way*," naturally tried the patience of progressive worship leaders who saw it as an interruption and a deterrent to the effectiveness of the worship experience. They wanted to see it replaced with a more enlightened practice—*regular singing*.[17]

It is important to note that the regular singing controversy was initiated by clergy, not church musicians. John Tufts (1689–1750) was a ministerial candidate with a degree from Harvard. In 1715 he published *An Introduction to the Singing of Psalm-Tunes in a Plain and Easy Method, with a Collection of Tunes in Three Parts*. Tufts's book was basically similar to volumes, then familiar in the colonies, by the Englishmen John Playford and Thomas Ravenscroft. It was soon followed by the Reverend Thomas Symmes's *The Reasonableness of Regular Singing* (1720), the pamphlet forever identified with the movement and the one which gave it its name.

Recent research suggests that Symmes's book simply reflected the more liberal, cosmopolitan attitudes of the 1720s.[18] It was the age of reason.

---

13. Cotton, *Singing of Psalms, a Gospel Ordinance*, 65.
14. The office of precentor was not open to women.
15. Winslow, *Meetinghouse Hill*, 152.
16. Irwin, "Theology of Regular Singing," 176.
17. Urban churches typically had both a deacon and a precentor. Smaller and rural parishes often assigned both tasks to the same individual.
18. Irwin, "Theology of Regular Singing," 181.

A secular spirit was present, and Symmes's emphasis on regular singing with its focus on training in musical fundamentals was evidence of it. Common to the writings of all the reformers was a view that the old way was mainly being held onto by "rustics" and less-educated rural communities; that the old way was being favored mainly by older church members, while regular singing was the music of the future and therefore should be encouraged among youth.

The term *regular singing* might better have been called "regulated singing." Our twenty-first-century understanding of music in all its complexities was a far cry from the views of these gentleman amateurs of the eighteenth century. The improvisatory style of psalm singing in rural parishes was offensive to their rational sensibilities. They felt that if more worshippers understood basic concepts of music reading—in other words, were taught to sing the correct pitches and note values as they appeared in print—unity would be achieved over chaos. Psalm singing would no longer interrupt the flow of worship. Churches near and far, wherever they might be, would sing the psalms the same correct, uniformly regulated way.

Singing in the old way, of course, was not simply due to ignorance. Its adherents valued their independence and felt that the Reformation had entitled each person to be creative in praising God. They feared regular singing, seeing it as an effort "to strip praise of all flavor of individuality and to return to the formalism from which the Reformation had delivered them. Sung regularly, the Psalms would be mere ceremony."[19] Precentors or clerks adhering to the old way treasured the freedom they had to sing improvisationally. Teaching congregations to sing by note, they believed, would lead inevitably to a loss of this freedom. Moreover, the tradition of setting the tune and then lining it out did not originate in America. It had been used for over a century in the British Isles. The practice was designated the approved mode of congregational singing by the Scottish Presbyterians at the Westminster Assembly during the English Civil War.[20] The Assembly's *Directory of Public Worship* for that year decreed the following:

> That the whole congregation may join herein, every one that can read is to have a psalm book; and all others, not disabled by age or otherwise, are to be exhorted to learn to read. But for the present, where many in the congregation cannot read, it is convenient that the minister, or some other fit person appointed

---

19. Irwin, "Theology of Regular Singing," 181.
20. Irwin, "Theology of Regular Singing," 181.

by him and the other ruling officers, do read the psalm, line by line, before the singing thereof.[21]

That conflict over worship practice should not be seen as simply a squabble between Anglicans and dissenters. It was a conflict between commoners who wanted to retain the Calvinist worship practices in local parish churches and wealthy royalists who sought to embrace the great art music of cathedrals on the continent. A key issue was the common folks' desire for full congregational participation in singing, and full participation included ornamenting and improvisation by song leaders.[22]

The reformers believed that if there were to be any resolution to the problems involving congregational singing, churches needed to seek instruction in the basics of music reading for their members. Symmes, in his pamphlet, insisted that regular singing or "singing by note" was the true old way, while lining out the Psalms was the new and *wrong* way.

> There are many Persons of Credit now Living, Children and Grand-Children of the first settlers of New England, who can very well remember that their Ancestors sang by Note, and they learned so to Sing of them, and they have more than their bare Words to prove that they speak the Truth; for many of them can Sing Tunes exactly by Note which they learnt of their Fore Fathers.[23]

He noted that singing by note was supported by Scripture, citing passages in both the Old and New Testaments. In Psalm 33, he noted, reference was made to playing instruments "skillfully." The appointment of a skilled singing master was mentioned in 1 Chronicles 15:22–27.[24] Symmes also pointed out that one of Christ's last acts, as told in Matthew, chapter 26, was to join the disciples in the singing of a hymn or psalm.[25] To underscore his point in the most caustic possible way, Symmes observed that singing in

---

21. Campbell, "Giving Out the Line," 241.

22. According to Sammie Ann Wicks's "Life and Meaning," as of 1983, there were approximately 255 churches in the Appalachian region still using words-only hymnbooks and singing in a highly ornamented fashion akin to the old way so reviled by eighteenth-century reformers.

23. Symmes, *Reasonableness of Regular Singing*, 6.

24. 1 Chronicles 15:22: "And Chenaniah, chief of the Levites, was for song: he instructed about the song, because he was skillful" (KJV).

25. Matthew 26:30: "And when they had sung a hymn, they went out to the Mount of Olives."

the old way was bad enough to make a serious churchgoer wish to join the "papists." "They sing so much better than one finds now," he warned.[26]

Old way adherents responded that:

1. The old way was good enough for past generations and there was no good reason to change it;
2. The names of the notes were blasphemous, and to name notes, a return to formalism and popery;
3. Offering instruction in music reading was just another contrivance to get money;
4. Singing by rule would soon bring musical instruments into the church;
5. No one could learn the new tunes anyway.[27]

Singing Sermons and Lectures

While Symmes's pamphlet and the year 1720 are often cited as the beginning of the regular singing controversy, efforts to improve congregational singing began much earlier, and continued into the 1760s. The period from 1720 through 1722 is critical, though. Boston in the 1720s was perhaps the most cosmopolitan city in New England, a place where new ideas could be expounded and allowed to flourish. It was predictable then that Boston's more progressive and forward-looking clergy would support a reform of congregational singing. Because of this, an important step in introducing regular singing to a congregation was usually the "singing sermon" or "singing lecture" by clergy seeking reform. Most were published in pamphlet form and thus exerted influence well beyond the actual presentation. Two of the most prominent examples:

"The Accomplished Singer"
by the Rev. Cotton Mather

[1663–1728]

(INSTRUCTIONS FIRST, HOW the PIETY of SINGING WITH A True DEVOTION, may be obtained and expressed; the Glorious GOD after an uncommon manner Glorified in it, and His PEOPLE Edified. AND THEN, HOW the MELODY of *REGULAR SINGING*, and the SKILL of doing it, according to the RULES of it, may be easily arrived unto.)

---

26. Wienandt and Young, *Anthem in England and America*, 171.
27. Earle, *Sabbath in Puritan New Englan*d, 208.

"The Sweet Psalmist of Israel"
by the Rev. Thomas Walter
[1698–1725]

(A SERMON Preach'd at the Lecture held in BOSTON, by the SOCIETY for promoting *Regular & Good* Singing, And for Reforming the Depravations and Debasements OUR PSALMODY labours under, In order to introduce the proper and true *old way* of SINGING.)

Like Tufts and Symmes, both Mather and Walter were clergymen and esteemed graduates of Harvard. They were regarded as among the intellectually elite of the colonies. Their sermons addressing issues related to music in worship were widely read and suggest a biblical mandate that congregations sing with piety and skill. They also stressed the need for training and instruction for the sake of future generations:

> BUT in the pursuance of this Holy Intention, it would be very desirable, that people, (and especially our YOUNG PEOPLE, who are most in the Years of Discipline), would more generally Learn to SING and become able to Sing by RULE, and keep to the NOTES of the TUNES, which our spiritual Songs are set . . . It has been found accordingly in some of our Congregations, that in length of Time, their Singing has degenerated, into an Odd Noise, that has had more of what we want a Name for, than any *Regular singing* in it; whereby the Celestial Exercise is dishonoured; and indeed the Third Commandment[28] is trespass'd on. . . . The Skill of *Regular singing*, is among the Gifts of GOD unto the Children of Men, and by no means unthankfully to be Neglected or Despised. For the Congregations, wherein 'tis wanting, to recover a *Regular singing*, would be really a Reformation, and a Recovery out of an Apostacy, and what we may judge that Heaven would be pleased withal. We ought certainly to Serve our GOD with our Best, and *Regular singing* must needs be Better than the confused Noise of a Wilderness.[29]

Thomas Walter was the pastor of the congregational meetinghouse in Roxbury, Massachusetts, and Cotton Mather's nephew. The older Mather was likely Walter's mentor, and his Puritan theology is certainly reflected in Walter's writing. Mather's sermon was an extended biblical/theological

---

28. Exodus 20:7: Mather is referring to the commandment: "You shalt not take the name of the Lord your God in vain."

29. Mather, "Accomplished Singer," 22–23.

discourse replete with scholarly Latin interjections and very little about singing despite its title. Walter's "Sweet Psalmist," however, reads much more like the work of a musician minister.

Walter begins his address by referencing 2 Samuel 23, the last words of David:

> THE last and dying Words of Men use to be of Weight and Importance with the Survivors; and by them are wont to be esteemed awful and full of Authority. . . . THE four Verses following my Text are worthy to be transcribed as such and may serve as a glorious introduction to our Discourse upon the Sweet Psalmist of Israel; viz. David's Character as a sweet Singer, the Honour done him by God in the Record hereof, and the blessed End a Servant of God, famous for this Skill, may be able to make. THIS sweet Psalmist of Israel said with a more than mortal eloquence—
>
> The Spirit of the Lord spake by me, and his Word was in my Tongue. The God of Israel said, the Rock of Israel spake to me: He that ruleth over Men must be just, ruling in the Fear of God; and he shall be as the light of the Morning, when the Sun riseth, even a Morning without Clouds; as the tender Grass springing out of the Earth by clear shining after Rain. Altho' my House be not so with God, yet he hath made with me an everlasting Covenant.
>
> HERE we have verified the Fable of the expiring Swan singing her own Elegy; but with this Difference, that our dying Psalmist tunes his Voice to Notes of Joy and Triumph, and not to the Keys of Mourning and Sadness. These are David's last Words, this his dying Song, which better than a Monument of Brass, will consecrate his deathless Fame to all Posterity.
>
> BUT who and what was he, that composed and sung this divine Song?—It was David the Son of Jesse, and the Man who was raised up on high, the anointed of the God of Jacob . . . The last Words of so great a Man, and so distinguished in the Honours conferred upon him by Heaven, must command in us the most serious Attention and the highest Regard imaginable. They are the rich Legacy of a dying Prince, and to be received and laid up as an inestimable Treasure.[30]

Walter portrays David in the role of minister, a musician/poet thoroughly committed to the quality, integrity, and spiritual importance of his

---

30. Walter, "Sweet Psalmist of Israel," 2–3.

Beginnings—The Eighteenth Century

art. It is the earliest writing to be cited in this study that envisions a ministerial role for church music.

> The Title of Psalmist carries in it not only that of a poet, but of a Musician also. Not only the Psalms, but the Tunes to which they were to be set and sung, were his . . . His skill both in vocal and instrumental music were famous . . . But that he had a thorough Understanding of this sweet and divine Science is a matter beyond all doubt.[31]

Repeated references to *sweetness* and *science* run throughout Walter's dialogue:

> MUSIC considered alone and in itself, is a sweet and pleasant Science. The Charms of Music are a most celebrated Subject among the best Writers. . . . There is scarce anything in the whole Creation of God, so wonderful and astonishing, as the Doctrine of Sounds and Harmony. . . . There is, in the first Place, a Natural or Physical Sweetness in the Notes of Music. When a single Voice or String of an Instrument so equally and justly vibrates the Air, as to give forth a Sound agreeable to the Organ of the Ear, being free from all Jarr or Asperity, it strikes the Auditory Nerves in such Manner as one Unison String percuss'd or struck, causes the other to shake and tremble. When the external Air is thus vibrated, the same or a like Vibration is effected in the internal Air reposited in the Cavity of the Organ, and this communicates its even and just Motion to the Nerves aforesaid.
>
> BUT then Secondly, there is a Mathematical Sweetness and Pleasancy in Sounds. This is none other than the Doctrine of Concords, to which there are required more Sounds than one, so proportioned and distanced in certain Intervals, as to create a pleasant Harmony and Agreement.[32]

And now, to Walter's central point: "But let us come to the Theological Consideration of the Point, and show the blessed influence and effects of harmony upon the Soul, as it is helpful to Devotion . . ."[33]

> MUSIC happily serves to fix the Mind upon religious Objects, abstracting the Soul from every Diversion. It sweetly fixes the

---

31. Walter, "Sweet Psalmist of Israel," 5.

32. Walter, "Sweet Psalmist of Israel," 6–7. Here Walter, in discussing the relationship between science, mathematics, and music, shows himself to be among the younger, more progressive clergy in the reform movement.

33. Walter, "Sweet Psalmist of Israel," 11.

wand'ring Spirit, making us retire within ourselves, and be wholly employed in the present holy and delightful Exercise. It reduces the Mind to such a sweet Composure, as that all our Attention is fastened upon the Subject of our Devotion. This Fixedness of Soul is a necessary Preparation for our Entrance upon any Religious Employments, especially those of the Temple. So we find holy David addressing himself to the Worship of God. (Psalm 57:7, 8) "My Heart is fixed, [or prepared; a fixed Heart is a prepared Heart.] O God, my Heart is fixed; I will sing and give Praise. Awake my Glory, awake Psaltery and Harp."[34]

To move regular singing forward from a far-off dream and the subject of impassioned sermons, much would be required. First, one needed educational material, designed for use in a classroom format—this, at least in America, where the printing of notated music was still in its most primitive stage. One must remember that in the first decades of the eighteenth century, music for congregational singing printed in the American colonies was limited to "thirteen crudely engraved tunes in The Bay Psalm Book."[35]

It should not be surprising that New England clerics, when faced with the dilemma of how to move forward, should have looked to England and the efforts there to address problems in congregational singing in the parish churches. The English publishing company established by John Playford (1623–1687) produced some of the most influential musical collections and texts of the early eighteenth century. Playford's *An Introduction to the Skill of Music* (1655) and *The Whole Book of Psalms, Composed in Three Parts* (1677) were well known in the colonies. Included with *Introduction to the Skill of Music* were twenty-six psalm tunes.

Thomas Walter and John Tufts, both of whom we have already met, saw the immediate need for suitable training primers and labored to provide them. Walter's *The Grounds and Rules of Musick Explained or an Introduction to the Art of Singing by Note*[36] and Tufts's *Introduction to the Singing of Psalms* were both published in 1721. They modeled their primers on English models, and both based their teaching on the eighteenth-century preference in Britain for the *gamut*, where, in place of the common European scale of the nineteenth century (i.e., *do-re-mi-fa-sol-la-ti-do*), only four solemnization syllables were used (fa-sol-la-fa-sol-la-mi-fa), mi being used exclusively for the seventh-scale degree.

---

34. Walter, "Sweet Psalmist of Israel," 17.
35. Lowens, "John Tufts' 'Introduction,'" 89–102.
36. Walter, *Grounds and Rules of Musick*, ii.

Walter's *Grounds and Rules,* his regular singing sermon "The Sweet Psalmist of Israel," and Tufts's *Introduction*, all published between 1721 and 1722, were certainly groundbreaking. Walter, a product of the age of reason, appreciated the scientific and mathematical symmetry of music, while at the same time preaching its power as an aid to worship. Walter's tunebook included only sixty-four representative hymn and psalm tunes—music only, no text. The music portion was intended for class exercises in music reading and dealing with text may well have been viewed as merely distraction.

But progress was slow. By 1725, regular singing was the proclaimed goal of all eleven Boston churches,[37] but churches outside of that colonial center took much longer to come around. In 1733, the Congregational Society in Hartford agreed to try regular singing from September through December, and then to take a vote on whether to resume the practice. In Glastonbury, Connecticut, during the same year, the society threw up its hands and agreed to regular singing for one-half of each service, while old way advocates had sway during the other half.[38] The First Church of Windsor, Connecticut, voted down this new way of singing, deciding to continue in "the way that Deacon Marshall usually sung in his life time, commonly called the '*Old way*.'"[39] Clearly, dissension among the older congregants was very great regarding cherished traditions of congregational singing.

> In some congregations, the advocates of the *old way* were permitted to leave the assembly before the last singing in the afternoon, which followed the new fashion. The commotion made by the departing malcontents as they tramped along the aisles and down the gallery stairs was long remembered as an emphatic example of how vigorous can be the protests of an exasperated conscience . . .[40]

It must be noted here that during the colonial era, Presbyterians, Congregationalists, and Anglicans were all closely allied to Calvinist theology. Like them, most other Christian sects at the time restricted congregational singing to the Psalms. This was certainly true of Holy Trinity or "Old

---

37. Stevenson, *Protestant Church Music,* 22.
38. Stevenson, *Protestant Church Music,* 22.
39. Earle, *Sabbath in Puritan New England,* 209–11.
40. Porter, "New England Meetinghouse," 23.

Swedes" Church in Wilmington, Delaware,[41] and Dutch Reformed churches in Delaware and Connecticut.[42]

Jonathan Hehn did an in-depth study of colonial-era Presbyterian worship in 2013. From copious documentation he was able to construct a fictional depiction of worship, as observed by a participant, at the First Presbyterian Church or "Old Buttonwood Church" of Philadelphia in the first decade of the eighteenth century:

> All stood for the singing of a psalm as the precentor held his book high. It took some time for the man to find the tune, for this morning's psalm was of an uncommon meter.
> After a time, the first line was called out, and the people replied, in the usual fashion. This singing was chaotic; some sang faster, some slower, some with a decorous and rather vain trill.[43]

The "chaos" to which Hehn refers was, no doubt, common to much colonial worship. Regular singing advocates attempted to address it through educating congregants in the basics of music. Singing school classes were called in to "lead" the congregation, while vainly attempting to avoid the appearance of a choir. Tuning forks and primitive pitch pipes were acquired but starting on the right pitch did little to quell the cacophony that often followed. Despite a deep discomfort with the use of musical instruments in worship—particularly among dissenting churches—cellos, bassoons, clarinets, and other instruments were brought into church galleries to support the singing of psalms. But these too presented problems. There was no standardized instrumentation. Participation could be haphazard, depending largely on who was present on a given Sunday morning. Most important, fully harmonized settings of psalm tunes written out for a consort of instruments were nonexistent. The little organs, being used by the Anglicans and played by trained musicians, came to be viewed as a viable alternative to solve a vexing issue. By mid-century, even Congregationalists and Presbyterians were taking notice.

---

41. From *Records of Holy Trinity (Old Swedes) Church,* 196: "The congregation were reminded to be attentive, to have the music of the church performed in a proper, decent and devout manner, and that all who have received God's gift to be capable of singing with a pleasing voice, and with psalms to praise their God, ought by no means to neglect the gift and stand silent . . ."

42. Leaver, "More than Simple Psalm Singing," 74.

43. Hehn, "American Presbyterian Worship," 20.

Beginnings—The Eighteenth Century

The Singing School

The most efficient means of training members of the congregation to sing was to hire an itinerant musician to organize and lead a singing school. In return, the instructor received room and board and the opportunity to sell to the class the tunebook which he was using. As early as 1714, one James Ivers advertised his services in the *Boston Weekly News* as a teacher of singing classes for churches. The earliest documented singing school in the Northeast was held in Boston in 1721.[44]

A typical advertisement for a singing school in Philadelphia appeared in the *Pennsylvania Gazette* in 1760:

> Notice is hereby given that the Singing school, lately kept in the Rooms over Mr. Williams' School in Second Street, will again be opened on Monday Evening, the 3rd of November next, at the same Place; where the ART OF PSALMODY will be taught, as usual, in the Best manner, on Monday and Friday Evenings, from Six to Eight. And that, if any Number of Ladies and Gentlemen incline to make up an exclusive Set, to Sing on two other Nights, they may be gratified by making application in time.[45]

The tunesmith Daniel Read (1757–1836) summed up the role of the singing school in his *American Singing Book:*

> That the singing of Psalms, hymns, and spiritual songs is a duty incumbent upon all denominations of Christians is clearly evident from Sacred Writ. This opinion is so prevalent among us that to offer argument to support it is unnecessary and superfluous.
>
> Scripture also informs us that all the duties of the Christian church should be performed with decency and in order; and singing, being an important part of divine worship, claims particular attention and ought to be conducted with great propriety. This, however, will be impracticable unless the rules of psalmody are well understood and closely adhered to.[46]

A typical singing school curriculum consisted of ten to fourteen sessions over a two- to three-week period. While the idiosyncratic primers in tunebooks suggest a thorough grounding in the basics of music as it was perceived by the singing master, it must not be assumed that most schools

---

44. Stevenson, *Protestant Church Music*, 53. The year, 1721, followed by just one year the publication of Symmes's *Reasonableness of Regular Singing*.

45. Chase, *America's Music*, 184.

46. Read, *American Singing Book*, 2.

were able to offer anything like comprehensive musical training. "The singing school teacher's function was to reverse thoroughly entrenched and well-loved singing habits that the reformers declared were unacceptable."[47] They hoped idealistically that prospective singing school masters would have a thorough grounding in the theology of the Psalter, but obviously the essential qualification was musical literacy. Thomas Walter expressed the need for literacy this way:

> We don't call him a reader, who can recite (from memory) a few pieces of the Bible, and other authors, but . . . cannot tell ten words in a page. So is not he worthy of the name of a singer, who has gotten eight or ten tunes in his head, and can sing them like a parrot by rote, and knows nothing more about them, than he has heard from the voices of others; and show him a tune that is new and unknown to him, can't strike two notes of it.[48]

One "Mr. Ruggles" gives this description of the singing school at Christ Church, Poughkeepsie, in 1829:

> The organist of the church (in those days) was Abel Gunn, a youthful genius, with sunken cheeks and a consumptive tendency, while a lank New England singing master of the name of Stoughton exercised the youths and maidens of the congregation in psalm singing. He used to walk up and down before the class, and, as they sang; he waved his arms and beat time with both hands at once, reminding me of some picture I had seen of a sorcerer performing an incantation.[49]

As one reads the many singing lectures and sermons of the era, nearly all have in common references to the importance of involving young people. In a 1723 tract, the Massachusetts Congregationalist minister Peter Thatcher wrote:

> God bestows these choice talents on Young Persons as well as Elder Persons, and persons in their youth do learn the Art of Musick with greater ease and speed than such as are aged.[50]

The Rev. Nathaniel Chauncey of Durham, Connecticut, said the following in a 1727 singing sermon:

---

47. Gates, "Music Education's Professional Beginnings," 43.
48. Walter, *Grounds and Rules of Musick*, 2.
49. Reynolds, *Records of Christ Church*, 149–50.
50. Buechner, *Yankee Singing Schools*, 37.

> They [youth] are generally more free from prejudice than Elderly people ... and their present age disposes them to mirth ...[51]

Observers of everyday singing school activities in New England nearly always made mention of young people—older children and adolescents—being predominant among the students. The social opportunities offered were not lost on the scholars. Singing school classes were often the only nighttime activities held at meetinghouses, which required candlelight for illumination—a rare opportunity for boys and girls to be in the same space without parental supervision. The nineteenth-century humorist Henry Wheeler Shaw (1818–1885), who wrote and performed under the pseudonym "Josh Billings," wrote the following "Advice to Young Ladies" attending singing schools. While written much later than the period in question, it accurately reflects the chauvinism that was common and the carefree demeanor of youthful singers.

> Deer Miss—This is an important epoch into your life. The 1st thing to make a good quire singer is to giggle a little. Put up your hair in kirl-papers every Friday night, soze to have it in good shape Sunday morning. If your daddy is rich you can buy some store hair; if he is very rich, you can buy some more, and build it high up onto your head; then git a high-priced bunnit, that runs up very high at the high part of it; and git the milliner to plant some high-grown artifishalls onto the higher part of it. This will help you to sing high as soprano is the highest part.
>
> When the tune is giv out, don't pay attenshun to it, but ask the nearest young man what it is, and then giggle. Giggle a good eel. Whisper to the girl next to you that Em Jones which sits on the third seat from the front, on the left-hand side, has her bunnit trimmed with the same color exact as she had last year, and then put up your book to your face and giggle.[52]

It needs to be emphasized that before the mid-eighteenth century, the purpose for which singing schools were organized was generally limited in focus to strengthening congregational singing. They were to provide basic instruction that would allow students to be a strong core of singers and music readers in the pews. Typically, students were not grouped by section as in a choir. When classes took place in the gallery[53] of a meetinghouse, as

---

51. Buechner, *Yankee Singing Schools*, 37.
52. Brooks, *Olden Time Music*, 219–20.
53. In traditional meetinghouse architecture, the altar or chancel is placed on the east end of the sanctuary with worshippers symbolically facing the rising sun and, by extension, the risen Christ. The main entrance to the sanctuary is on the west end with

they often did, it was common to line singers up along the rail, men to one side, women to the other, the youngest students at the end, the older, more experienced in the middle. The singing school was not intended to be a chorus. The relationship between singing school master and his charges was one of teacher and student, not ensemble and conductor. Singing school masters did not conduct.

The focus of singing school repertoire began to change with newly imported collections from England and their colonial spin-offs in the 1750s and '60s. Boston musician Josiah Flagg's *A Collection of the Best Psalm Tunes' . . . to Which Are Added Some Hymns and Anthems, the Greater Part of Them Never Before Printed in America* was issued in 1761. William Tans'ur's *Royal Melody Compleat* of 1755 was especially popular in America in an edition published by Daniel Bayley of Newburyport, Massachusetts, in 1767. Retitled *The New Harmony of Zion*, Tans'ur's collection went through seven editions and was an important influence on William Billings. Aaron Williams's *Universal Psalmodist* (1763) was brought to America by Bayley in 1769.

One sees a change in the focus of singing school curricula in the second half of the eighteenth century. Singing schools had now become a staple of community life in New England. A typical school served forty to sixty scholars over a three-month period with two to three classes or meetings per week.[54] By 1750, the schools had become so prolific and successful that there was a hunger for new music and new types of music in addition to metrical psalms. The new collections being imported from England provided that, with far greater numbers of new tunes as well as anthems[55] and set pieces intended for the young singers to show off what they had learned. It became common for students to be grouped into established ensembles (for all practical purposes, choirs). After much resistance, meetinghouses began permitting them to sit together, usually in the gallery. To be sure, the singing scholars still provided leadership for the singing of psalms in worship, but now they were likely to embark on a busy schedule of non-worship-related singing opportunities. Because of their newfound independence, and to avoid that bugaboo word *choir* (thought by many to smack of "popery"),

---

the "gallery," a long narrow balcony-like structure, suspended above it. Galleries were often added sometime after the original construction and were often used to locate singers or instruments and keep them segregated from the congregation.

54. Buechner, *Yankee Singing Schools*, 60–61.

55. The intended purpose of anthems in colonial tunebooks is open to question. Were they for choral performance or idealistically conceived for singing by an entire congregation? Or, were they simply provided for exercises in music reading?

many churches labeled these ensembles *singing societies*. The former singing school master was employed as an outside resource to lead them.

There can be no question that singing schools sparked a great interest in group singing in the post-revolution years, but how successful were they in teaching the fundamentals of music reading? Despite the singing school's acknowledged goal of making singing scholars trained readers of music, it was not unusual to find them not singing from music, but rather repeating exercises from memory. Tunebooks were expensive and traditionally were purchased by the singers themselves. Because of this, shortages of tunebooks in the choir gallery were common. Samuel Gilman in *Memories of a New England Choir* recalled that:

> Accordingly, in our choir, among the men, the proportion of books was scarcely more than one to four or five performers, so that you might often hear some ardent and confident individual, who was stationed too far from the page to read distinctly, attempting to make out the sentence from his own imagination—or, when he despaired of achieving that aim, filling up the line with uncouth and unheard-of syllables, or with inarticulate sounds.[56]

Even when tunebooks were available, many students simply sang the music by rote. This was particularly true if the singing master had his class replace *solfeggio* singing[57] with words before they were ready. Daniel Read alluded to this when he wrote:

> After acquiring a good understanding of the rules, the learner may proceed to some plain tune . . . but should not attempt to sing any tune in words until he has first perfectly learned it by note.[58]

Solomon Howe (1750–1835), a preacher, tune composer, and singing master associate of William Billings, echoed this sentiment:

> The Master should *never* let his scholars sing a tune by word 'til they can sing the notes accurately from memory. Many masters ruin their schools by such foolish license.[59]

---

56. Gilman, *Memories*, 34.

57. *Solfeggio* or *solfège* was a core teaching technique of the singing school. It is a general term referring to the assignment of certain syllables to pitches based on where they are in the musical key. It would be further refined by adding distinctive shapes to each pitch/syllable. In theory, by recognizing shapes and intoning the related syllables, students did not have to understand the complexities of keys, key signatures, and intervallic relationships.

58. Read, *American Singing Book*, 22.

59. Howe, *Farmer's Evening Entertainment*, 6.

Of course, more demanding courses of instruction, more activities, and a long-term commitment to these programs, meant more expense. Local churches that chose to sponsor their own singing society often did it through a subscription plan. In other cases, the singing school might be completely independent, funded entirely through an enrollment fee which had to cover the singing master's allowance, materials, rental of a hall, heat, etc. It was common for independent singing schools to be held in a local tavern or hostel. Singing schools in their heyday often drew students from numerous churches and the community at large. Funding was even budgeted by some town governments as a community arts endeavor.

Singing Masters and Their Methods

The significance of the local singing master in the tapestry of New England village life was evidenced by Washington Irving's choice to make one the central character in one of his most famous stories:

> In this by-place of nature, there abode . . . a worthy wight of the name of Ichabod Crane; who sojourned, or, as he expressed it, "tarried," in Sleepy Hollow, for the purpose of instructing the children of the vicinity . . . In addition to his other vocations, he was the singing-master of the neighborhood, and picked up many bright shillings by instructing the young folks in psalmody. It was a matter of no little vanity to him, on Sundays, to take his station in front of the church gallery, with a band of chosen singers; where, in his own mind, he completely carried away the psalm from the parson. Certain it is, his voice resounded far above all the rest of the congregation; and there are peculiar quavers still to be heard in that church, and which may even be heard half a mile off, quite to the opposite side of the millpond, on a still Sunday morning.[60]

By the mid-eighteenth century, the intermingling of church and singing school activities resulted in changes to the job titles used by music instructors. In some churches where the precentor, a church officer and lay reader, was asked organize a choir to lead congregational singing, he was referred to as the "chorister."[61] Mostly, however, singing masters continued work in churches as "outside help." In any case, the work they did was much the same.

We can intuit much about the early singing masters and their goals from the writings of Tufts and Walter and from anecdotal information. By

---

60. Irving, "Legend of Sleepy Hollow," 89.
61. Andrus, *Century of Music in Poughkeepsie*, 3.

the 1760s, with singing school participation approaching its height, there is much more documentation from those who were involved. Moses Cheney (1776–1856) was a Vermont singing master for over fifty years. At the age of twelve in 1788, he attended his first singing school. Later he was able to vividly recall the experience:

> ... and it came to pass when I was about twelve years of age, that a singing school was got up about two miles from my father's house. In much fear and trembling I went with the rest of the boys in our town. I was told on the way...that the master would try every voice alone to see if it was good. The thought of having my voice tried in that way, by a singing master too, brought a heavy damp to my spirits...
>
> ... the good master began, "Come boys, you must rise and fall the notes first and then the gals must try." *[I.e., They were asked to sing a scale up and down after the example of the instructor to determine pitch and interval awareness.]* So he began with the oldest ... "Now follow me, right up and down." So he sounded (the scale), then the boy sounded ... More than one half could follow the master. Others would go up two or three notes, then fall back ... To see some of the large boys, full twenty years old, make such dreadful work, what could I do? Great fits of laughing, both (among the) boys and gals would often occur. This scared me, and I was at my wit's end ... And I had only time to draw a long breath and blow out the flutter of my heart, when the master came to me. "Well, my lad, will you try?" "Yes, sir." I looked him in the mouth and as he spoke *[i.e., sounded]* a note, so did I, both up and down ... The master turned away, saying "This boy will make a singer." I felt well enough ...[62]

While by the late eighteenth century one could expect to see an organized group of singers with their leader in the meetinghouse gallery on Sunday morning, the singing master was still viewed as hired help. Generally, the leader would sit on the front row of the gallery facing the pulpit. As leader, while directing, he would sing the "air" or melody and would be surrounded by the most experienced singers who would join him on this part.[63]

---

62. Buechner, *Yankee Singing Schools*, 43–44.
63. See Gould, *Church Music in America*, 109.

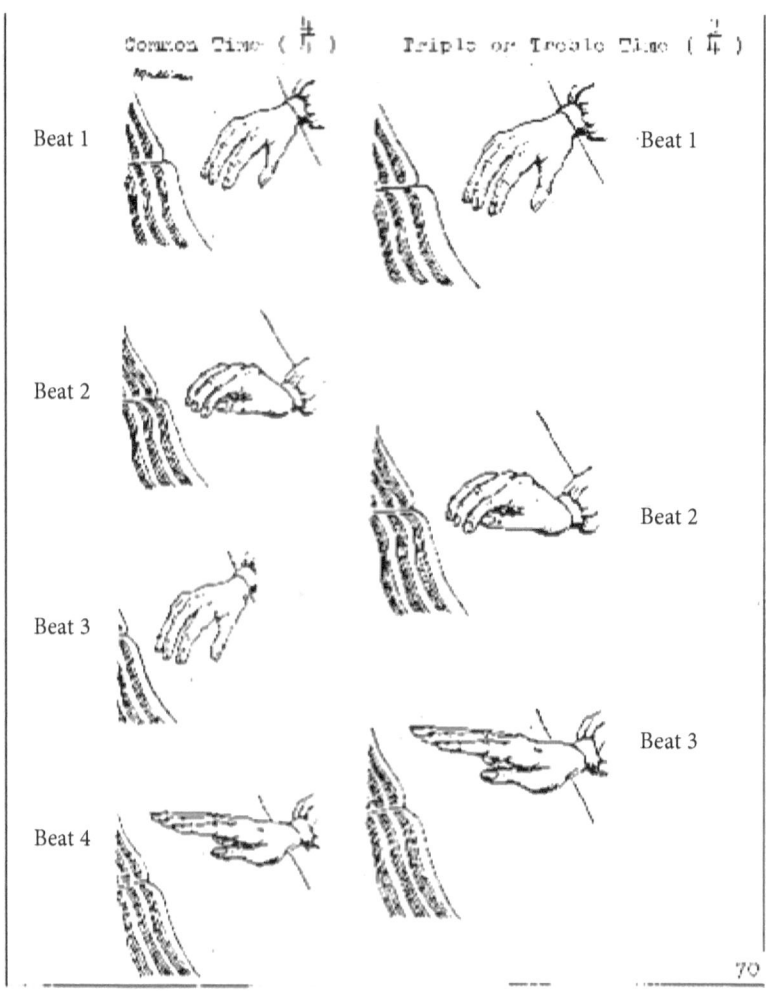

"Conducting" as described in Farmer's Saturday Evening Entertainment (ca. 1800). Line drawings by Susan Mulliner, Redondo Beach, California. Used by permission.

The singing master was expected to sound the "key note" and then to give the pitch successively to each part. Prior to the 1780s this had to be done without the aid of any pitch-giving instrument.[64] Early psalm books contained directions as to which level of pitch should be set for each tune. "When a compass of the notes was but five or six above the first, it was stated

---

64. Gould, *Church Music in America*, 111.

that a high pitch should be taken; when the compass extended to eight or nine notes above the first, the tune should be pitched low."[65]

The leader also was expected to beat time in some fashion. An article in *Farmer's Saturday Evening Entertainment* outlines one primitive system of beating time for use when the singers and leader were seated around a "square pew" or horseshoe gallery. To beat quarter notes in 4/4 or common time, the leader would "let the fingers fall on the table, then bring the heel of the hand down gently, then, raising it a little higher, throw open the fingers to begin the next bar." Triple time was done by omitting the third step and lifting the entire hand, with fingers out. Whether this method of keeping singers together was much used cannot be ascertained, but it does provide insight into one available means of beating time. Its main advantage was that the leader's motions could not be seen by and offend the worshippers below.

Of the many colonial singing masters, five of the most prominent were William Billings (1746–1800), Justin Morgan (1747–1798), Benjamin Dearborn (1754–1838), Jacob French (1754–1817), and Joseph Funk (1778–1862). By far the most well-known of those names today is that of William Billings.

William Billings and Church Song in Eighteenth-Century America

Billings is remembered today primarily for his work as a composer. He studied the work of English parish church composers and then originated a uniquely American choral style that inspired contemporaries like Daniel Read. His music stands to this day as a landmark in American music. Much has been written about Billings as a composer, but we must also remember that in his lifetime, he was New England's most famous and sought-after singing master. We first see him identifying himself professionally as a singing master in the copyright petition he submitted to the British government for his collection, *The New England Psalmsinger* (1770).

Fortunately, William Billings also felt the need to put his teaching philosophy into writing. He left us copious notes on his approach to teaching, on music in general, and the times in which he lived—all in the rough, inimitable style of a Boston yeoman tanner.[66] Billings offered rules for the

---

65. Gould, *Church Music in America*, 36.

66. Like other singing school masters, teaching music was not Billings' principal source of income. He learned the tannery trade in his teen years, worked as a tanner his entire life, and actually came to own a tannery near the Boston Common in the 1790s. Similarly, Daniel Read operated a general store. Timothy Swann was a hatter. Justin

operation of a singing school in his *The Singing Master's Assistant*. Among them was the following dictum, which clearly shows that, in Billings mind, the singing school was a sacred and churchly endeavor:

> I enjoin it upon you to refrain from all levity, both conduct and conversation, while singing sacred words; for where the words God, Christ, Redeemer, etc. occur, you would do well to remember the third commandment, the profanation of which is a heinous crime, and God has expressly declared he will not hold them guiltless who take his name in vain, and remember that in so doing you not only dishonor God and sin against your own souls, but you give occasion and very just grounds to the adversaries or enemies of music to speak reproachfully.[67]

Once the singing master had evaluated the singing potential of each student, it then fell to him to distribute voice parts among the singers. The modern concept of voice classification did not exist. More often, parts were distributed according to tradition and seniority rather than vocal range. The male leaders of the choir would sing the "air" or melody and this part was referred to as the "tenor." Harmony parts were typically labeled *cantus*. Having less status, they were sung by novices and at the octave by the women. Almost as important as the tenor was the bass line. Billings preferred it be doubled by a cello or bassoon when available.

The present practice of four-part mixed choirs being made up of women's voices singing soprano and alto, and men singing tenor and bass, had not begun to be standardized in America until Lowell Mason arrived on the Boston scene in the late 1820s. According to H. K. Oliver, "the altos were men's voices exclusively" in Boston choirs as late as 1810.[68] When it was suggested by Oliver and other choirmasters of the early nineteenth century that the men give over the singing of the "air" or melody to female sopranos, it was regarded as "an interference with the rights of man and contrary to Scripture."[69]

There continues to be the perplexing question of whether the many anthems written by colonial Americans and English parish composers were truly church music. While they were seldom heard in Sunday worship, choirs of singing school scholars often sang for Fourth of July celebrations,

---

Morgan, Supply Belcher, and Jeremiah Ingalls were all innkeepers.

67. Billings, *Singing Master's Assistant*, 3.

68. Oliver, "Lecture on Church Choirs," 93.

69. Hubbard, ed., *American History and Encyclopedia of Music: American Music*, 165. The role of women in sacred music or any other aspect of church life has continued to be a flashpoint for controversy almost to the present day.

Beginnings—The Eighteenth Century

election day gatherings, special holiday observances, and of course singing school commencement programs. It was also common for students who had matriculated through the singing school curriculum to join together as a choir to promote a new school when it was being announced.

In this way, choirs became an established and common part of New England life. The New Brick Church in Boston had a choir of "more or less trained voices" as early as September 1722, when a program of choral music was presented and possibly repeated in Dorchester and Reading, Massachusetts. The program is mentioned in a letter of one Joseph Green (1701–1800) to the Reverend Stephen Williams, a minister at Long Meadow, Massachusetts, dated October 1, 1722.

> On Fryday last was ye delightfull exercise of singing performed at ye New Brick Church. Mr. Coleman [preached] from Rev. 5:9 and they sung a new song & ye Singing was managed only by ye masters of it, viz. men & women, seated in the front gallery on purpose for it; they sang four tunes, all which were performed with a great dexterity and pleasancy . . .[70]

John Adams's diary mentions visiting the meetinghouse at Middletown, Connecticut, in 1771:

> Went to meeting with Dr. Eliot Rawston and heard the finest singing that I ever heard in my life. The front and side galleries were crowded with rows of lads and lasses, who performed all their parts in the utmost perfection. I thought I was wrapped up. A row of women, all standing up, and playing their parts with perfect skill and judgement, added a sweetness and sprightliness to the whole which absolutely charmed me.[71]

Around three hundred anthems were composed by American tunesmiths in the eighteenth century. Billings was by far the most prolific, with at least thirty-three anthems to his credit.[72] Other New England composers included Amos Bull (1744–1825), Oliver Holden (1765–1844), Jacob French (1754–1817), Daniel Read (1757–1836), Justin Morgan (1747–1798), and Supply Belcher (1751–1836).

When compared with the choral style of nineteenth-century composers, Daniel points out that "Neither the coloristic possibilities of the mixed chorus nor the expressive resources of dynamic shading or contrast and of

---

70. Green, "Letter to Stephen Williams," 391.

71. Brooks, *Olden Time Music*, 70.

72. Kroeger, ed., *Complete Works of William Billings,* lists thirty-three anthems or set pieces by Billings published between 1770 and 1790.

dramatic rests are exploited."[73] This was very characteristic of eighteenth-century musical style in general. It may also have been indicative of the kind of function anthems served; they were intended as "occasional music" to teach sight-reading skills. Beginning in the 1760s, however, newer "fuging tunes" and set pieces began to appear. As composers progressed beyond the simple, straightforward homophony of the early psalm tunes to canonic and polyphonic techniques a new level of expertise in choral training was required. The interest in longer, more complicated pieces was symptomatic of larger changes taking place. Gradually, singing schools were transitioning into established singing ensembles. While restricted to psalm singing in worship, they more and more identified themselves as "choirs" and strived at any opportunity to sing chorally.

Were the anthems of Billings and his contemporaries really choral music? Certainly, they were not choral music in the same sense that the term is used today. The singing school was viewed not so much as a musical ensemble but as an extension of the congregation, specially trained to lead fellow congregants toward better singing. Psalms tunes and set pieces were not intended to be listened to so much as participated in. Congregational song was the *raison d'être* of the entire enterprise. Billings's suggestions to double the parts at the octave, for example, tended to obscure the melodic outline of the composition for the listener. At the same time, this procedure enhanced the singing experience for the participants by lending additional resonance to the parts.

> When it was composed, this music was experienced rather than heard because it was not written for an audience's appreciation or to tickle an ear—it was written to be experienced by the performers. How it "sounded" to a non-participant was of very little importance. This is no novel concept; it is one of the essential pre-conditions of genuine church song. Clearly a basic function of congregational song within the service should be to enable members of the congregation to participate actively in worship through music. This active participation in worship is, of course, one of the foundation stones of Protestantism, a democratization of religion that was one of the great achievements of the Reformation. If congregational song is to fulfill this function, it is obvious that no performer-audience relationship is possible . . . Thus, congregational music must make its impact felt, not through the hearing experience, as with choir music, but through the performing experience.[74]

---

73. Daniel, *Anthem in New England*, 51.
74. Lowens, "American Tradition of Church Song," 283.

This concept was no doubt idealistic at best. Daniel states that "it is impossible to ascertain when, and to what extent, anthems first became regular and commonly accepted parts of New England church services."[75] The appearance of anthems in tunebooks that were labeled "for church use" meant little, he wrote. Such a prefix may have only indicated a hoped-for goal of the compiler. On the other hand, it may have served as a rather devious way of saying to the purchaser that the collection was a respectable one and bore the church's stamp of approval.

It would be a mistake to assume that psalmody and singing school anthems were the totality of sacred vocal music in eighteenth-century America. The Great Awakening[76] no doubt inspired singing. And what of folk hymns? Musicologist Irving Lowens speculated that folk hymnody existed and was thriving by the mid-eighteenth century. It was simply not written down.

> As early as the 1730s, folk hymnody appears to have flourished, prospering under the impetus of the "Great Awakening," when Jonathan Edwards, George Whitefield, and other inflammatory preachers seared the religious conscience of New England. It is highly probable that folk hymnody was an omnipresent phenomenon during the second half of the eighteenth century, although it is difficult to cite concrete written evidence to that effect. . . . Despite their popularity and widespread diffusion among the populace as a whole . . . [they] do not seem to have achieved the permanence of print much before the beginning of the nineteenth [century].[77]

Slavery and the Church

We must at this point put aside discussion of church music to focus on the issue of slavery. While we know African Americans, both free and enslaved, worshipped and sang in the colonial era, documentation is limited. We know more about the years following the American Revolution. How the

---

75. Daniel, *Anthem in New England*, 34.

76. For clarity, the "Great Awakening" as referenced here was a religious revival between approximately 1720 and 1740 in colonial America, led by Jonathan Edwards, George Whitefield, and others. It sought to counteract the growth of secularism with a return to Calvinist theology and a new emphasis on conversion. The "Second Great Awakening," running roughly from 1793 to 1835, was led principally by evangelicals among Methodists, Baptists, and Presbyterians who sought to energize soul-winning on the frontier, in small towns, and in rural areas.

77. Lowens, "John Wyeth's 'Repository,'" 114.

American church dealt with slavery during colonial times is a sad narrative. Understanding that narrative is necessary to follow the trajectory of African American music and worship in the century following.

In the year 1619 about twenty Africans in servitude debarked at Point Comfort, near present-day Hampton Roads, Virginia. They were technically not slaves, but indentured servants, since slavery was a legal status and statutes taking a position on enslavement had yet to be written. Slavery was part of life throughout British Colonial America, as it was in Great Britain itself, prior to the American Revolution. While often thought of as an issue primarily associated with the southern colonies, slavery was well established in New England during the seventeenth century.

Cotton Mather, one of the most prominent religious leaders of his time, was a respected Puritan preacher, theologian, scientific thinker, and prolific writer. He served first as assistant pastor and then pastor at Boston's original North Church from 1678 until his death. He is also known to have had at least one slave, Obadiah, serving him as a household servant, and his congregation included slaves, slave sellers, and owners. Like most church leaders of his time, Mather regarded the institution of slavery as a political issue and chose not to address its morality or the issue of racial equality. Rather, he stressed converting or "Christianizing" the enslaved African Americans.

Around 1693 Mather began a series of Sunday evening classes aimed at Blacks seeking conversion. As part of this process, he created and published his *Rules for the Society of Negroes*, a pact between prospective students and teacher which needed to be agreed upon in order to participate. The flavor and overall substance can be gleaned from the opening declaration:

> WE the Miserable Children of *Adam,* and of *Noah,* thankfully Admiring and Accepting the Free-Grace of GOD, that Offers to Save us from our Miseries, by the Lord Jesus Christ, freely Resolve, with His Help, to become the Servants of that Glorious LORD. And that we may be Assisted in the Service of our *Heavenly Master,* we now Join together in a SOCIETY, wherein the following RULES are to be observed. It shall be our Endeavour, to Meet in the *Evening* after the *Sabbath;* and *Pray* together by Turns, one to Begin, and another to Conclude the Meeting; And between the two *Prayers,* a *Psalm* shall be Sung, and a *Sermon* Repeated.[78]

The eighteenth century began somewhat hopefully with sincere missionary efforts to evangelize and educate enslaved Blacks. By 1700 slaves,

---

78. Mather, *Rules for the Society of Negroes,* 1.

Beginnings—The Eighteenth Century

mostly originating from the coast of West Africa, had been arriving in the colonies for over sixty years. It has been estimated there were 27,817 enslaved Africans in British North America. The growth in tobacco production in the Chesapeake and Virginia colonies during the seventeenth century produced an inevitable need for slave labor, far exceeding demand in New England. The demand skyrocketed with the development of the rice industry along the South Carolina coast in the 1690s. By the mid-eighteenth century, the slave population had increased to about 150,000, with that number tripling over the next thirty years. When the American Revolution began, about one-fifth of the total colonial population was enslaved and fully 35 percent of the population below the Mason Dixon line was African.[79, 80]

A major impetus to develop a ministry directed at African Americans was the establishment by the Church of England of the Society for the Propagation of the Gospel in Foreign Parts (hereafter referred to as the SPG) in 1701. The SPG's charter stated that:

> plantations, colonies and factories beyond the seas are wholly destitute and unprovided of a maintenance for ministers and the public worship of God, and for lack of support and maintenance for such, many of our loving subjects do want the administration of God's word and sacraments and seem to be abandoned to atheism and infidelity.[81]

A central focus of the SPG was to provide missionaries to Blacks in colonial America.

Despite the work of the SPG and Anglican missionary priests, the Church of England's mission to the slaves was challenged by several factors. First, there was the liturgy itself, which was complicated and born out of a British and Western European culture totally foreign to the enslaved African Americans. Moreover, the number of missionaries was inadequate for the burgeoning number of slaves on southern plantations and their outreach limited to areas in the immediate vicinity of established Anglican chapels.

The famous Anglican evangelist George Whitefield traveled widely in the Southern colonies, preaching revivals in Georgia, Virginia, and North and South Carolina. On January 23, 1740, based on what he had seen,

---

79. In 1808, owing largely to the vast and growing population of slaves in the southern sector, a federal law was passed, sponsored by Thomas Jefferson, prohibiting further importation. This, however, did not put an end to the influx of slaves as they were still being smuggled in through Florida and Texas, which had not yet become states. In 1820, slave trading was made a capital offense, further limiting the number of cases, but some illegal importation continued through the outbreak of the Civil War.

80. U.S. Census Bureau, "Historic Census Statistics."

81. "Letters from the Clergy," 2.

Whitefield published a caustic critique in an open letter addressed to the Southern colonies and their slave masters regarding their lack of interest in the welfare and spiritual development of their enslaved charges:

> As I lately passed through your provinces, in my way hither, I was sensibly touched with a fellow-feeling[82] of the miseries of the poor negroes. Could I have preached more frequently among you, I should have delivered my thoughts to you in my public discourses: but, as business here required me to stop as little as possible on the road, I have no other way to discharge the concern which at present lies upon my heart, than by sending you this letter. How you will receive it, I know not; whether you will accept it in love, or be offended with me, as the master of the damsel was with Paul for casting the evil spirit out of her, when he saw the hope of his gain was gone, is uncertain: but whatever be the event, I must inform you, in the meekness and gentleness of Christ, that I think God has a quarrel with you, for your abuse of and cruelty to the poor negroes. Whether it be lawful for Christians to buy slaves, and thereby encourage the nations from whence they are brought to be at perpetual war with each other, I shall not take upon me to determine; but sure I am it is sinful, when bought, to use them as bad as, nay worse than brutes . . .
>
> And though I heartily pray God, they may never be permitted to get the upper hand; yet, should such a thing be permitted by providence, all good men must acknowledge the judgement would be just. For is it not the highest ingratitude, as well as cruelty, not to let your poor slaves enjoy some fruits of their labor?[83]

Whitefield was particularly touched by the attendance of Blacks at his lectures, some of whom traveled many miles on foot to attend, and he frequently wrote in his journals of the desire to erect schools for them. Whitefield indeed pursued his "Negro School" idea in establishing an orphanage in Georgia, Bethesda. African American children were baptized, taught to read, and received training in skilled trades. According to Methodist historian William A. Sloat, because of his activities between 1739 and 1740 both in Philadelphia and the South, Whitefield had become the foremost advocate for African Americans in the colonies.[84] Unfortunately, Whitefield's work at Bethesda also resulted in criticism due to inconsistencies in

---

82. I.e., sympathetic sense or feeling.
83. Whitefield, "Letter to the Inhabitants," 35, 41.
84. Sloat, "George Whitefield, African Americans, and Slavery," 3.

his stance on slavery. While he forcefully condemned abuse of the enslaved, he took the position that only negroes could do field work in the hot climate of the South.[85] His reputation was to be considerably tarnished when he complained in 1747 that Georgia law prohibited his orphanage, Bethesda, from using slave labor to tend its fields.[86]

John Wesley (1703–1791) was an ardent opponent of slavery in the British Isles. Unlike the aforementioned Anglicans in the American colonies, he was outspoken in his condemnation of the institution of slavery itself. "Long and serious reflections upon the nature and consequences of slavery have convinced me," he wrote, "that it is a violation both of justice and religion; that it is dangerous to the safety of the community in which it prevails; that it is destructive to the growth of arts and sciences; and lastly, that it produces a numerous and very fatal train of vices, both in the slave, and in his master."[87]

Wesley's passionate condemnation did not go unheard in the colonies.

> The Methodist Episcopal Church (in America) was built on the rejection of Calvinism, works of piety and sanctification before God through Jesus Christ. Spiritual equality among people was a fundamental belief in the early Methodist church, whether male, female, Black or White. Methodists embraced Galatians 3:28 which says, "There is neither Jew nor Gentile, neither slave nor free, nor is there male and female, for you are all one in Christ Jesus." Slavery was antithetical to both the political ideals of the new nation and the "soul liberty" of the Methodist church.[88]

The evolution of the American Methodist views on slavery can be divided into three distinct periods. For much of the period before 1800, John Wesley was still alive and able to provide some guidance to his American followers. The church's principal leaders, Thomas Coke and Francis Asbury, were handpicked by him and shared his views on slavery.

Francis Asbury (1745–1816) was truly one of John Wesley's most unflagging followers. At just twenty-two years of age, he was tapped by Wesley to represent him and Methodism in the American colonies. Asbury sailed from England in August of 1771, arriving in Philadelphia on October 27. A month later he was preaching in New York City, when he made the following note in his journal:

---

85. Tesch, "Reception Accorded George Whitefield," 26.
86. Sloat, "George Whitefield, African Americans, and Slavery," 6.
87. Wesley, *Thoughts Upon Slavery*, 79.
88. Lawrence, "Relationship Between the Methodist Church," 2.

> I think the Americans are more ready to receive the word than the English; and to see the poor Negroes so affected is pleasing,[89] to see their sable countenances in our solemn assemblies, and to hear them sing with cheerful melody their dear Redeemer's praise, affected me much, and made me ready to say, "Of a truth I perceive God is no respecter of persons."[90]

Asbury's sympathy for enslaved Blacks only grew in depth over his many years of service. He was outspoken in his support of immediate emancipation and risked bodily injury numerous times during his evangelizing in the South. Discouraged, on June 10 of 1778 he wrote:

> I find the more pious part of the people called Quakers, are exerting themselves for the liberation of the slaves. This is a very laudable design; and what the Methodists must come to, or, I fear, the Lord will depart from them. But there is cause to presume, that some are more intent on promoting the freedom of their bodies, than the freedom of their souls; without which they must be the vassals of Satan in eternal fire.[91]

The official position of the Methodist Society in America[92] echoed Asbury's concern. In their 1780 Annual Conference Discipline recording actions of the assembly appears the following:

> Ques. 16. Ought not this Conference to require those traveling preachers who hold slaves to give promises to set them free?
>
> Ans. Yes.
>
> Ques. 17. Does this Conference acknowledge that slavery is contrary to the laws of God, man, and nature, and hurtful to society; contrary to the dictates of conscience and pure religion, and doing that which we would not have others do to us and

---

89. There were African Americans active in New York's Methodist Society from its birth. Peter, a converted slave, was the sexton at Wesley Chapel. When his British owner returned to England during the Revolutionary War, Peter was permitted to "work off" the sum of his indenture and freed. He would become one of the founders of the African Methodist Episcopal Church.

90. Asbury, *Journal and Letters*, 54.

91. Asbury, *Journal and Letters*, 562.

92. The Methodist Episcopal Church, as a denomination, did not exist until the formal break with the Church of England in 1784. The "Methodist Society" was a conference of traveling itinerant ministers serving the Methodist wing of the Church of England. Nevertheless, the position taken on slavery was courageous, given the fact that slavery was legal in Great Britain at the time.

ours? Do we pass our disapprobation on all our friends who keep slaves, and advise their freedom?

Ans. Yes.[93]

Baptists were the other evangelical group in the eighteenth century in a position to exert a missionary influence among the slaves. A wing of the Baptist church—the "Separate Baptists," led by the Reverend Shubal Stearns (1706–1771) in Virginia—sought to evangelize the slaves, welcome them into their congregations, and even give them positions of leadership as exhorters, deacons, and elders. While a message of God's love for the slaves was expounded by the Separates, it rarely became a critique of the institution.

A paternalistic but biblical view that slaves were to be cared for as one would care for one's own children was typical.[94] Emancipation it was thought would likely leave slaves both unconverted and destitute. In 1807 the Elkhorn (Kentucky) Baptist Association was asked to address the question, "[Were] Baptist preachers . . . authorized from the Word of God to preach emancipation?" After deferring the question for a month, the association responded that Baptists should not *publicly* oppose slavery, and that it was improper "for ministers or churches to 'meddle with emancipation.'"[95] The Baptist leader Richard Furman provided one of the earliest comprehensive statements defending biblically the peculiar institution.

> That the holding of slaves is justifiable by the doctrine and example contained in Holy writ; and is therefore consistent with Christian uprightness, both in sentiment and conduct. . . . Slavery, when tempered with humanity and justice, is a state of tolerable happiness; equal, if not superior, to that which many poor enjoy in countries reputed free. That a master has a scriptural right to govern his slaves so as to keep it in subjection; to demand and receive from them a reasonable service; and to correct them for the neglect of duty, for their vices and transgressions; but that to impose on them unreasonable, rigorous services, or to inflict on them cruel punishment, he has neither a scriptural nor a moral right. At the same time it must be remembered, that, while he is receiving from them their uniform and best services, he is required by the Divine Law, to afford them protection, and such necessaries and conveniences of life as are

---

93. Purifoy, "Methodist Anti-Slavery Tradition," 3.

94. Deuteronomy 16, for example, suggests that slaves be treated as part of one's extended family. (See Morrison, " Religious Defense of American Slavery.")

95. Kidd and Hankins, *Baptists in America*, 98.

proper to their condition as servants; so far as he is enabled by their services to afford them these comforts, on just and rational principles. That it is the positive duty of servants to reverence their master, to be obedient, industrious, faithful to him, and careful of his interests; and without being so, they can neither be the faithful servants of God, nor be held as regular members of the Christian Church.[96]

Presbyterians viewed literacy as the best pathway to freedom for all—enslaved or free, Black or white—and worked to establish schools for both Blacks and whites on the frontier. David Rice (1733–1816), the so-called Presbyterian "Apostle to Kentucky," exemplified the typical Presbyterian stance. Rice was an early advocate of emancipation and was active in the Kentucky Abolition Society, which was established in 1808 by David Barrow and Carter Tarrant. Rice favored gradual abolition of slavery in Kentucky. In 1792 he published a pamphlet he called *Slavery Inconsistent with Justice and Good Policy*. In it he enunciated how he saw slavery as an affront to the goals of the War of Independence:

> As creatures of God we are, with respect to liberty, all equal. If one has a right to live among his fellow creatures and enjoy his freedom, so has another. If one has a right to enjoy that property he acquired by an honest industry, so has another. If I, by force take that from another which he has a just right to according to the law of nature (which is a divine law) which he has never forfeited and to which he has never relinquished his claim, I am certainly guilty of injustice and robbery; and when the thing taken is the man's liberty . . . it is the greatest injustice . . .
>
> A slave claims his freedom; he pleads that he is a man, that he is by nature free, that he has not forfeited his freedom nor relinquished it. Now, unless his master can prove he is not a man, that he was not born free, or that he has forfeited or relinquished his freedom, he must be judged free; the justice of his claim must be acknowledged.[97]

The Revolutionary Years

The spirit of revolt (among newly arrived slaves) gradually died away under the untiring energy and strength of the slave masters. By the middle of the eighteenth century the Black slave

---

96. Furman, "Exposition of the Views of the Baptists."
97. Rice, *Slavery Inconsistent with Justice*, 4.

Beginnings—The Eighteenth Century

had sunk, with hushed murmurs, to his place at the bottom of a new economic system and was unconsciously ripe for a new philosophy of life. Seemingly nothing suited his condition better than the doctrines of passive submission embodied in the newly learned Christianity. Slave masters early realized this and cheerfully aided religious propaganda within certain bounds. The Negro, losing the joy of this world, eagerly seized upon the offered conceptions of the next, the avenging Spirit of the Lord enjoining patience in this world, under sorrow and tribulation, until the Great Day when he shall lead his children home—this became his comforting dream.[98]

Up until now, our focus has been on the relationship of missionaries to African Americans in the eighteenth century, but both slaves and freed Blacks were spiritual beings and worshipped as they were able. The first African American churches were established in the last thirty years of the century.

The first Black Baptist church in America was established in 1773 on the plantation of slaveholder George Galphin on Beech Island, South Carolina. Inspired by the evangelistic tenor of the times and with the encouragement of missionaries like Whitefield, Galphin wanted his slaves to have a church of their own in which to worship. To accomplish this, he enlisted the help of the Reverend Walt Palmer, a white Connecticut preacher, and George Liele,[99] a recently freed slave. Palmer assigned an empty barn on his property as a meeting place and called it the Silver Bluff Church. Liele in turn baptized and trained a slave, David George, who eventually became the congregation's pastor. Conflicting sympathies between British loyalists and supporters of independence, however, tore the congregation apart during the revolutionary years. The area around Savannah was in the direct path of hostilities between the British and colonials. Further complicating things, the British army offered emancipation to any slaves who would join their ranks. Galphin, who supported independence, fled South Carolina. Meanwhile, George, a British loyalist, and his followers fled across the Savannah River behind enemy lines to win their emancipation and freedom in Nova Scotia. Leadership of the congregation remaining at the Silver Bluff church fell to the slave and itinerant Baptist preacher Jesse Peter.

---

98. Du Bois, *Souls of Black Folk*, 199.

99. In 1775, Liele was ordained, making him the first ordained African American to preach in the Baptist Church. During the war, he was befriended by Colonel Moses Kirkland of the British Army, who assisted him in immigrating to Jamaica. In 1782, he became the first Baptist missionary in Jamaica.

Prior to the Revolutionary War northern Blacks commonly worshiped with whites, usually in a segregated area of the sanctuary. As the war drew to a close in the 1780s African Americans took seriously Jefferson's stirring words in the Declaration of Independence, viewing them as a promise of equality. In Philadelphia, Black members of Old St. George's Methodist Episcopal Church, no longer content to be shunted into the church gallery, broke away in 1792 to form the African Episcopal Church of St. Thomas. Two years later a larger group left to form Bethel African Methodist Episcopal Church, the historic birthplace of the AME denomination. A similar rupture occurred in New York City at John Street Methodist Episcopal Church. Peter Williams, an indentured servant, was purchased by the church in 1783 to work off his debt as the building sexton. Despite the promises declared in the Declaration of Independence, John Street continued to relegate its Black congregants to the church gallery. They had no vote in the church's administration nor could they be ordained to preach or serve as deacons. Finally, Williams and James Varick, along with much of the Black membership, left to form the African Methodist Episcopal Zion denomination—known as the Freedom Church. Frederick Douglass was a licensed AME Zion preacher, and the church claimed Harriet Tubman and Sojourner Truth as congregants. Another member, Rev. Jermain Loguen, would become a bishop of the AME Zion denomination after the Civil War.

Resistance

Factors making the work of evangelists painfully slow were bubbling just below the surface throughout the second half of the eighteenth century. By the 1790s while northern colonies had abolished or committed themselves to abolishing slavery, those to the South had become economically dependent on the peculiar institution. The number of enslaved people in the South had burgeoned to over one-third of the total population. In addition, there was the element of fear: fear of the biblical promises of freedom and equality before God; fear that large assemblies of slaves would result in uprisings; and fear that education and literacy would cause slaves to recognize their full human potential and the unacceptable injustice with which they were faced. Slave revolts, rebellions, and insurrections were not a fantasy dreamed up by slaveholders. They were reality, occurring from the mid-seventeenth century forward with ever increasing frequency.

Concluding Remarks

The regular singing movement was the first organized effort to provide music education in America and gave us a huge body of uniquely American music that is still being explored and studied. For all of that we should be grateful. The period, however, also created divisions that remain with us to the present day. The vociferous rejection by reformers of a budding folk music tradition in New England smacked of elitism. The colonial reformers sought to bring change by mandate instead of from within, and resistance was inevitable. The wedge thus driven between a less sophisticated but still music-loving populace and the educated elite would help shape much of the history of American church music to follow.

It was essential to provide in this chapter a brief overview of the British and American church's interactions with slavery. The writings of Mather, Whitefield, Asbury, and others document the church's awareness of the great scourge and efforts made to both educate and evangelize those in bondage. Implicit also in their writings was a desire for the slaves to be exposed to Christian teachings and experience worship in some form. Their work led to the establishment of the first Black churches in the South. While music is not mentioned, it can be said without hesitation that singing had to be a part of the slaves' daily life in the eighteenth century. It was central to the African culture from which they came. What we do know, and what will be touched on later in this narrative, is that white America first became aware of slaves singing on the cusp of the nineteenth century. Blacks had a significant presence in the earliest camp meetings, and the folk hymnody that arose out of that era was undoubtedly shaped in part by their participation. All of this may be seen as setting the stage for the emergence of a uniquely African American legacy of sacred song in the nineteenth century.

One must also note that the first "professional" church musicians appeared in the eighteenth century in the guise of itinerant singing masters and immigrant organists. With little training and under the most inhospitable of circumstances, they played an essential role in keeping music a vital component in worship.

> What has escaped notice about this process is the profound change it brought to local religious authority. For the first time in the long history of New England Congregationalism, non-ordained persons exercised significant control of a major aspect of parish life. Ministers traditionally held complete cultic control, designing and leading the Sunday services. The only possible countervailing authority was that of deacons, who, while they did lead the performance of psalmody, were hardly ritual

specialists. Indeed, it was their failure to achieve even minimal performance standards that provoked the singing school reform in the first place. The emergence of singing masters as lay ritual specialists sharply challenged this traditional authority structure. The singing master provided training for a highly visible dimension of public religious culture. Skills requisite to proper liturgical performance had been relocated beyond the competence of ministers and deacons, whose authority now rested in their certification of outside ritual specialists rather than in the performance of that specialty.[100]

The years following the American Revolution were a time of transition. In regard to church music, the seeds planted by the proponents of regular singing and singing masters would begin a maturation process that would lead ultimately to the "better music" movement in 1830s New England and rich source of religious folk music in the South and on the frontier. Meanwhile, though the smoldering debate over slavery continued, African Americans embraced Christian worship as pivotal to their existence. In the North, and to some extent even in the South, they began to establish their own churches, and with them, musical traditions.

---

100. Marini, "New England Singing School," 2–3.

Chapter 2

TIME OF TRANSITION

THE BATTLE OF YORKTOWN, the last major battle of the American Revolution, ended with the surrender of British General Cornwallis on October 19, 1781. The formal end of the war came two years later with the Treaty of Paris in 1783. While the conflict had ended, debate had only begun about what form this new experiment would take. In 1777, in the midst of the war, the Continental Congress adopted the first constitution of the United States, the Articles of Confederation. It created a loose confederation of the colonies in which each maintained its sovereignty under a weak central government. When peace was declared, problems immediately emerged. The new country, deeply in debt from the cost of the war, had no power to insist each state uphold its share of the burden. There was a need for a standing military now that state militias had gone home to their farms and villages, but there was resistance from individual states who saw it as infringement on their liberty. As a result, the United States Constitution was adopted and went into effect on March 4, 1789.

The transition from the Articles of Confederation to the US Constitution was not without controversy. While many leaders in government saw it as a practical necessity, others viewed it as a threat to individual freedom. Indeed, the balance between federal and states' rights continues to be a contentious issue to the present.

> How then to control selfish factions, oppressive local majorities, popular follies and passions? [James] Madison's answer went straight to the heart of the grand strategy of the men who would come to be known as Federalists. The solution was not to try to remove the causes of faction, for a free society would always

produce differences among men and a good republican must respect those differences. The solution was to dilute the power and passion of local factions by enlarging the sphere of government into a nation of many regions, interests, and opinions.[1]

The quest to achieve "a more perfect union" would include aspiring to the heights of scientific and artistic progress in Europe. It could not be limited to the narrow confines of the New England meetinghouse. The rationalism of the Age of the Enlightenment and other influences, both positive and negative, were at work broadening the worldview of Americans and their perspectives on religion and the arts, including sacred music.

> There was, moreover, something quite contradictory between the freedom and independence fostered by the new republic and the tyrannical character of the Calvinist God. Nothing could have been more alien to the Puritan notion of sinful and puny man than the optimism and self-confidence of democracy.[2]

A Sea Change in Theological Outlook

During the waning years of the eighteenth century a sea change in American theology was in progress. Powered by the progress in science and mathematics, critical thinkers like Thomas Paine, and the massive influence of an evangelical revival, many American Christians came to believe that human beings *could* affect their relationship with God and personal salvation through their own efforts. While expressed in many ways, depending on religious persuasion, American theology was on the cusp of a new day. It would be marked by a particular definition of progress, and, sadly, in the case of sacred music, a knee-jerk condemnation of much that had gone on before. We'll call this developing approach to theology "perfectionism."

For most of the previous century the theology and doctrines of John Calvin (1509–1564) or their influence permeated New England life, regardless of one's denominational persuasion, and had a direct effect on the progress of music as a ministry. Traditionally, Calvin's theology has been summarized in five central points or doctrines:

1. *Doctrine of Total Depravity*: Calvin believed that, as a consequence of the fall of man into sin, every person is enslaved to sin. People are not

---

1. Burns, *American Experiment*, 802.
2. Rugoff, *Beechers*, 7.

by nature inclined to love God, but rather to serve their own interests and to reject the rule of God.

2. *Doctrine of Unconditional Election*: Calvin asserted that God chose from eternity those whom he will bring to himself, not based on foreseen virtue, merit, or faith in those people; rather, his choice is unconditionally grounded in his mercy alone. God has chosen from eternity to extend mercy to those he has chosen and to withhold mercy from those not chosen.

3. *Doctrine of Limited Atonement*—Calvin preached that Jesus's substitutionary atonement was definite and certain in its purpose and in what it accomplished. This implies that only the sins of the elect were atoned for by Jesus's death.

4. *Doctrine of Irresistible Grace*—According to Calvin the saving grace of God is effectually applied to those whom he has determined to save (that is, the elect) and overcomes their resistance to obeying the call of the gospel, bringing them to a saving faith. This means that when God sovereignly purposes to save someone, that individual certainly will be saved.

5. *Doctrine of Perseverance of the Saints*—Calvin also asserted that since God is sovereign and his will cannot be frustrated by humans or anything else, those whom God has called into communion with himself will continue in faith until the end.[3]

The sticking point for New England progressives was Calvin's firm belief in predestination. Calvin was responding viscerally to the corruption he saw in the Roman Catholicism of his day, which he felt had degenerated into a religion of salvation by works. Calvin's "Doctrine of Unconditional Election" made it clear that one could not purchase or, in any other way, earn salvation. God alone determined who would be among his "elect." The "Doctrine of Irresistible Grace" suggested that those among the elect were *irresistibly* pulled to lives of charity and good works. Old-school Calvinists in the American colonies embraced Calvin's view of a truly omnipotent deity who "governed the world through both natural causation and supernatural intervention."[4] By the 1700s more progressive clergy, including many in the Puritan camp, found Calvin's views rigid and unbending. In the previous chapter, we saw that Tufts and Walter, in keeping with the age of reason, cited science and natural law as an argument for regular singing.

---

3. "What is Calvinism?"
4. Holifield, *Theology in America*, 79.

It goes without saying that Calvin's theology had its detractors from the very beginning. Among the most significant of them was Jacobus Arminius (1560–1609). Arminius, influenced by his understanding of Paul in Romans, passionately opposed Calvin's emphasis on election and predestination. He espoused a theology of salvation by faith rather than works. He also "proposed that God decreed to save all believers and that Christ died for all people, so that grace sufficient for faith was given to all . . ."[5] The sinner, he preached, bore responsibility for the sin. These views were regarded as a direct challenge to Calvinism, and the Synod of Dort in Holland (1618–1619) condemned Arminius of heresy, setting the standard for Calvinist orthodoxy outlined above. "Arminianism" was considered an always lurking threat by conservative Calvinists throughout the seventeenth and eighteenth centuries who accused more progressive clergy and theologians of Arminian influence.

Arminian ideas were brought to the colonies by Methodists and other evangelicals during the eighteenth century. Those who espoused the Arminian point of view differed with strict Calvinists on the issue of original sin, and thought that individuals could, by their own acts and choices (and empowered by the Holy Spirit), win salvation or lose it. It was a matter of personal choice. As a result, churches on the eastern seaboard became embroiled in a growing controversy between supporters of traditional Calvinism and those who found agreement with thinkers like Isaac Newton and John Locke, who espoused the more liberal Arminian view. The liberal group believed that strict adherence to doctrines of total depravity and predestination was "an affront to common sense which tended to undermine all humanity."[6]

The rise of Unitarianism in New England signaled that another earthshaking shift was in progress. Proponents celebrated Jesus's humanity but denied his divinity. It cast off the dogmas of the Trinity and original sin. Unitarian theology, which can be traced back to seventeenth-century Poland, first appeared in the colonies when in 1785 the pastor of King's Chapel, James Freeman (1759–1835), revised the church's prayer book to include a Unitarian-inspired worship liturgy. Other progressive Boston clerics soon followed: Joseph Stevens Buckminster at Brattle Street Church; Henry Ware, professor of divinity at Harvard; and William Ellery Channing (1780–1842), pastor at Federal Street Church, who would ultimately become the leader of the Unitarian movement in America. The movement would lead to the catastrophic 1825 split in the Congregational Church

---

5. Holifield, *Theology in America*, 37.
6. Hudson, *Religion in America*, 79.

resulting in a new American religious denomination, the American Unitarian Association.

Finally, we must consider the evangelical revival movements that swept across America in the eighteenth and early nineteenth centuries. During the First Great Awakening in the 1730s and '40s, revivalists such as George Whitefield and Jonathan Edwards espoused a variety of positions on aspects of Calvinist doctrine, but they shared a theology of revival and salvation that transcended denominational boundaries and helped create a common evangelical identity. They stressed providential outpourings of the Holy Spirit. In their often extemporaneous preaching, they encouraged commitment to a new standard of personal morality. They viewed confidence in the assurance of salvation as a normal expectation in the Christian life. A Second Great Awakening captured the attention of the new nation beginning in the 1790s and continuing into the 1820s. The changing theological spectrum was reflected on the more moderate side by the Reverend Lyman Beecher, who believed that individuals were free agents and able to determine their own salvation. Beecher, however, was a critic of the outspoken Arminianism of his archrival, the famous evangelist Charles Grandison Finney, an avowed believer in regenerative or "born-again" theology. The nondenominational, nonsectarian character of revivalism, as personified in Beecher and Finney, would become a paradigm for future generations.

Perfectionism

If the individual was indeed able to chart his own way and was not doomed by original sin, it was only a small step for those influenced by Arminianism to adopt a "Doctrine of Human Perfectibility."[7] The idea, thought scandalous by Calvinists, may have been contemplated in the mid-eighteenth century but had rarely been articulated openly. After 1800, when it was put forth in the preaching of such powerful clerics as Lyman Beecher and Theodore Parker, its influence began to grow. It was reflected in the educational reform rhetoric of Horace Mann and a host of other nineteenth-century reformers. Thus, the concept of perfectionism came to be a major force in American life. William Ellery Channing clearly elucidated the perfectionist approach to Christian theology in his remarkable sermon "Likeness to God" in 1828.

---

7. The concept of human perfectibility originated in the late eighteenth century both in Europe and America as theological barriers were being relaxed that had said only God could bring change to the human condition. Enlightenment writers such as Condorcet, Godwin, Kant, and Rousseau embraced this concept, which became a driving force of the era inspiring scientific and artistic progress, as well as the French and American revolutions.

> I affirm, and would maintain, that true religion consists in proposing, as our great end, a growing likeness to the Supreme Being. Its noblest influence consists in making us more and more partakers of the Divinity. For this it is to be preached. Religious instruction should aim chiefly to turn men's aspirations and efforts to that perfection of the soul which constitutes it a bright image of God . . . In proportion as we approach and resemble the mind of God, we are brought into harmony with the creation; for in that proportion, we possess the principles from which the universe sprung; we carry within ourselves the perfections of which its beauty, magnificence, order, benevolent adaptations, and boundless purposes are the results and manifestations . . . It is to approach God as an inexhaustible fountain of light, power, and purity. It is to feel the quickening and transforming energy of his perfections. It is to thirst for the growth and invigoration of the divine principle within us. It is to seek the very spirit of God. It is to trust in, to bless, to thank him for that rich grace, mercy, love, which was revealed and proffered by Jesus Christ, and which proposes as its great end the perfection of the human soul . . . I conclude with saying, let the minister cherish a reverence for his own nature . . . Let him hold fast, as one of the great qualifications for his office, a faith in the greatness of the human soul . . . Let him strive to infuse courage, enterprise, devout trust, and an inflexible will into men's labors for their own perfection. In one word, let him cherish an unfaltering and growing faith in God as the Father and quickener of the human mind, and in Christ as its triumphant and immortal friend.[8]

A generally accepted premise of American intellectuals at this time was that perfectibility was not to be achieved by legislating it, but through a new stress on the virtues of hard work, the importance of the family unit, and of education.[9] All of these received attention equally from the pulpit, the political stump, and popular literature of the day. Horace Mann offered public school education as the only hope of American society and his view was taken up by the well-known Boston preacher, theologian, and abolitionist Theodore Parker. Parker believed that "a shared sense of the divinity

---

8. Channing, "Likeness to God," 228, 234, 241–42, 245, 254.

9. All of these virtues, of course, were nothing new. They were also espoused by seventeenth-century Puritans who felt members of the elect would be irresistibly drawn to lives of learning, hard work, charity, and family values. The difference was that nineteenth-century perfectionists passionately believed that *humans could aspire to perfection through their personal effort.*

of [the] individual held society together; without it, no true community was possible."[10] This shared sense could only come through education.

> Looking around him at antebellum America, Parker found only the wrong kind of individualism, the kind that said, "I am as good as you are, so get out of the way." The right kind, the individualism whose motto was "You are as good as I, and let us help one another," was to be the work of Parker's spiritual revolution. He explained the method of revolution as one of "intellectual, moral, and religious education—everywhere and for all."[11]

This emphasis on education as the way forward to Christian and societal improvement inspired the budding Sunday school movement and later, the *Christian Nurture* theology of Horace Bushnell, each expressing a growing concern for the family and childhood learning.

The Decline of the New England Singing School

The changing theological drift at the turn of the nineteenth century had a direct effect on singing master/tunesmiths. Calls for education and self-improvement were coming from all sides, including from the pulpit. And for New England's middle and upper classes, self-improvement required embracing European culture and advancements. This Eurocentric view was particularly noticeable in changing attitudes regarding sacred music.

William Billings's contemporary Andrew Law (1749–1821) borrowed extensively from Billings's *Singing Master's Assistant* for his very popular *Select Harmony* (1778). Like Billings, he was a highly respected and much-in-demand singing master. Yet, in the preface to the second edition of his *Musical Primer* (1804), he included the following *mea culpa*: "A considerable part of American music is extremely faulty (while) European compositions aim at variety and energy."[12] Daniel Read (1757–1836), one of Billings's most celebrated successors, had been the composer of some of the most enduring music of the period. By the 1790s, however, he was trying to disavow his previous work despite its popularity. Inspired by exposure to the music of Handel in the 1790s, Read claimed a "growing preference for the more 'correct' style of voice writing proposed by the scientific musicians . . ."[13] This preference would eventually lead him to revise, as editor, many

---

10. Thomas, "Romantic Reform in America," 673.
11. Thomas, "Romantic Reform in America," 673.
12. Law, *Musical Primer*, 8.
13. Letter Draft to Joel Read, September 8, 1804, cited in Sims, "Dissonance Treatment," 23.

of his tunes that appeared in the *New Haven Collection* (1810). In the same year, Read wrote the following in a letter to a friend:

> Some of the tunes I should be ashamed to print in so incorrect a form had they not already appeared in print and gained a degree of popularity. But you will consider that I do not consult my own taste, so much of that of the publick; If I had consulted my own Taste solely you may be assured the book would have been a very different thing.[14]

One also senses that, during the opening years of the nineteenth century, there was a widespread feeling that singing schools had been ineffective in addressing the problem of congregational singing.

Choirs and the Church

Choirs, of course, were an anathema to the original reformers of regular singing. Churches attempted to thwart the seating of an ensemble by insisting singers be spread out through the hall to better lead the singing from among the general congregation. As singing schools became popular, however, it became unavoidable that singing scholars would seek to sing together. Some churches then chose a stopgap measure: if the singers insisted on being seated together, they were shunted off to less desirable side pews. The reason given was that the church could not afford to sacrifice the rental income generated from the choice center pews.

Once singers were seated as an ensemble, of course, it was inevitable that they would want to sing as a choir. The year 1802 brought forward a landmark collection, *The Columbian and European Harmony*, better known as *The Bridgewater Collection*, by Bartholomew Brown (1772–1854) and published in Boston. Brown's collaborator in producing this remarkable collection was Nahum Mitchell (1769–1853). *The Bridgewater Collection* was important for being one of the first collections to emphasize choral music intended to be performed by a choir for passive listeners. Instead of choosing works by native Americans, Brown and Mitchell looked to English parish gallery choir music represented by such composers as Kent, Calcott, Clarke, Madan, and Capel Bond. Perhaps even more significant was the inclusion of edited excerpts from the large works of Haydn and Mozart.[15]

Two other collections of choral music for churches quickly followed: Benjamin Carr's *Masses, Vespers, and Litanies*, written for Roman Catholic

---

14. Letter Draft to Joel Read, September 8, 1804, cited in Sims, "Dissonance Treatment," 23.

15. McDaniel, "Church Song and the Cultivated Tradition," 100.

parishes, and *The Salem Collection of Classical Music*, both published in 1805. Part of Carr's preface dealt with his methods for working with choirs—one of the earliest published discussions of choral techniques in this country. That Carr would feel it necessary to include these remarks is another indication that church choirs were evolving. That being said, choirs as regularly rehearsing performing organizations would be a long time coming.

The shift to choral and solo singing was alarming to many. This was particularly well portrayed in a passionate speech to the American Musical Convention by the Reverend Raymond Seely, a pastor in Bristol, Connecticut. "Our aim is this," Seely declared. "A piece should be sung, at least once each season of divine service in which the whole congregation should unite with the choir. For this purpose, such pieces should be selected as are well known to the congregation, and intimation, in some way, given that all are expected to take part." Seely complained that choirs, were becoming "performers for, rather than leaders in the worship of the people . . . The congregation," he said, had become "so entirely dependent on the choir, that it rests with a few leading singers to decide whether the church shall have any music at all in its services. In this way, some churches, have, at times, been forced to omit this part [i.e., congregational singing] of public worship altogether."[16]

How could choirs have become such a problem when so much effort over the previous century had been directed at avoiding having them? Many churches seemed to be giving up entirely on congregational singing, in some places replacing it with choral music, in others, dispensing with it entirely in favor of hiring paid professional singers.

Instrumental Music in Churches

At no time were American gallery choirs any more akin to their English parish church counterparts than when the bass viol and later a wide variety of other musical instruments were being introduced into American church galleries in the late 1700s. While the Puritans did not disavow instrumental music altogether, as was once thought, the early colonial attitude toward instrumental accompaniment for congregational singing approximated the distaste of the prophet Amos:

> Take thou away from me the noise of thy songs;
> for I will not hear the melody of thy viols. (Amos 5:23, KJV)

---

16. Wienandt and Young, *Anthem in England and America*, 302.

The development of choirs brought with it a need for musical instruments that could both give the pitch and sustain the singers with an accompaniment. By the end of the eighteenth century, twenty churches in New England had installed pipe organs, but these were mostly Episcopal churches. Dissenting churches such as the Congregationalists and Presbyterians[17] were more apt to consider organs as papist or a secular influence to be damned. It is significant that the first known American church organ was willed by Thomas Brattle in 1713 to Brattle Street [Congregational] Church in Boston, which, still adhering to Puritan prohibitions of instrumental music in worship, refused the gift.[18] It was then placed in King's Chapel, an Anglican parish. The first New York City church to install an organ was Trinity in 1739. The first known dissenting church to have an organ was First Congregational Church of Providence, Rhode Island, installed on July 10, 1770. Presbyterian churches tended either not to have organs or to have them only because they were put in the church building by a previous owner. New York's First Presbyterian Church did not install an organ until 1889. Brick Church, also in New York, installed one in 1858. The first organ in an American Methodist Church appears to have been the one installed in Chestnut Street Methodist Church, Portland, Maine, in 1836.

What were churches to do that either would not have or could not afford an organ? The first major breakthrough in the effort to establish instrumental music in many American churches was the introduction of the pitch pipe in the 1750s and '60s.[19] Pitch pipes were generally constructed in the shape of an oblong box, six or eight inches in length, four inches wide, and one inch thick. A small mouthpiece protruded from one end. Inside the box was a slide with the letters of the octave printed along one side, which could be used to adjust the pitch.

Alice M. Earle, in *The Sabbath in Puritan New England* (1892), referred to the pitch pipes as "comical little apple-wood instruments that looked like mouse-traps." The oblong shape of these devices made it convenient to disguise them as books.

---

17. The term "dissenting church" is of English origin and referred generally to groups who opposed any sort of state interference in their religious practice. In England, dissenting churches excoriated the Church of England, both for its exclusiveness and its connection to the monarchy. The term "dissenting church" refers then to a variety of Protestant religious groups, all of whom refused to conform to the dictates of the Archbishop of Canterbury, but who otherwise had very little in common. .

18. Owen, "Eighteenth-Century Organs and Organ Building," 656–61.

19. During the eighteenth century and as late as 1820 in New England, pitch pipes were considered musical instruments and therefore many churches viewed them as inappropriate for use in the house of God.

> Great pains were taken to conceal them as they were surreptitiously passed from hand to hand in the choir. I have seen one which was carefully concealed in a box that had a leather binding like a book, and which was ostentatiously labeled in large gilt letters, "Holy Bible"; a piece of barefaced and unnecessary deception on the part of some pious New England deacon or chorister...[20]

The tuning fork caused less dissension among the deacons but was also less useful. Forks, when struck, sounded usually G, A, or C, but there was always the problem of psalm tunes requiring pitches other than those. Not all choir leaders had a sufficient understanding of intervallic relationships to find E or E flat, for example, if the pitch struck was G.

The introduction of the bass viol was "the grand entering wedge that opened the way for all other instruments..."[21] The cello, or bass viol, as it was erroneously called in late-eighteenth century America, had already been in use in English parish churches since the 1760s. They found their way into colonial meetinghouses via the singing schools. There, the use of the bass viol appears to have started at the beginning of William Billings's career. Because classes were often held away from the church, there was no objection to instrumental accompaniment for the singing. In addition, many of the students were young people who were not predisposed to criticize the instruments for their secular associations. The support lent to the choir's bass line by having it doubled by such a rich-sounding instrument was not lost on the singers, and soon there was agitation to bring bass viols into the church gallery. It was a logical choice in churches without organs to keep singers on pitch.[22]

> Some, at the sound, would run out of the meetinghouse; others, immediately [would] dissolve their connection with the church and congregation; others lay their grievances before the church or town, praying to have the idol-instrument banished, asserting that it was of the same form as the fiddle they danced after when young, only a little longer.[23]

---

20. Earle, *Sabbath in Puritan New England*, 224.
21. Gould, *Church Music in America*, 170.
22. Kimberling, "American Bass Viol."
23. Gould, *Church Music in America*, 171.

One deacon at the Congregational Church in Stratham, Massachusetts, upon seeing the newly acquired cello, remarked to a friend that "they had got a fiddle into the church as big as a hog's trough."[24]

During its heyday, the bass viol was alternately referred to as a Godly Viol or a Lord's Fiddle by its admirers, and a Dagon, for the god of the Philistines, by its detractors. The origin of the term Lord's Fiddle, according to Nathaniel Gould, was that a certain recently immigrated cello player, upon arriving at an unidentified New England church, claimed to be a professor of religion in the old country. After leading the choir for a time, he spirited his cello into the gallery one Sunday morning, surreptitiously hiding it under a pew; reaching down he was able to play it during the singing and yet keep the instrument out of sight. Unfortunately, despite these efforts, the musical visionary was caught. After a fiery vestry meeting a committee was sent to discuss the matter with him. To their angry accusations,

> He mildly answered that he thought they were laboring under a mistake in regard to the instrument—that he had it made in his own country for the express purpose of playing church music and had used it for many years. And he had named it a "Godly Viol" and thought that he could satisfy them of the fact that it was not like other viols. He brought the viol forward, played and sung several tunes, which he was capable of doing in the most touching manner. The committee felt the power of the music, and looking at each other, said, "There can be no harm in that, I am sure"; and consequently reported that it was a "Godly Viol"—and, however incredible the account may seem, it worked a perfect cure for the prejudice.[25]

Bass viols were introduced in Portland, Maine, at Second Parish Church in 1787,[26] whereas they did not make their first appearance in Augusta, Maine until 1802.[27] In 1804, the Congregational Church in Quincy, Massachusetts granted its singers the sum of $25 to buy a bass viol for use at meetings, but a church in Wareham, Massachusetts, had a running debate about the issue from 1784 until 1829.

> They voted that a bass viol was "expedient," then they voted to expel the hated abomination; then was obtained "Leave for the Bass Viol to be brought into ye meetin' house to be Played On every other Sabbath & to Play if chosen every Sabbath in the

---

24. Pichierri, *Music in New Hampshire,* 34.
25. Gould, *Church Music in America,* 172.
26. Cole, "Music in Portland, Maine," 16.
27. Edwards, *Music and Musicians,* 28.

intermission between meetings & not to pitch the tunes on the Sabbath that it don't Play." Then they tried to bribe the choir for fifty dollars not to use the "bars vile" but being unsuccessful, many members in open rebellion stayed away from the church and were disciplined therefore. Then they voted that the bass viol could not be used unless Captain Gibbs were previously notified (so he and his family need not come and hear the hated sounds); but, at last, after thirty years, the choir and the "fiddle player" were triumphant in Wareham as they were in other towns.[28]

And so the controversy went. When the bass viol was admitted to the Roxbury (Massachusetts) Church, one of the deacons "stood for a long time outside the church door stridently caterwauling at the top of his lungs." When a disturbed fellow member asked what the old gentleman was doing, "he explained that he was only mocking the banjo."[29] The Reverend Brown of Westerly deplored the new "catgut and resin religion."[30] When James Marble was appointed "chorister" at the Methodist Church at Poughkeepsie, New York, in 1834, he found much prejudice against the use of violins and bass viols.

> On the first Sunday when they were used, it happened that Presiding Elder Rice, who was one of the opposing party, preached at the church. At the beginning of the service he solemnly said, with fine sarcasm: "We will (now) fiddle and sing the forty-ninth Psalm."[31]

After the bass viol was introduced, other instruments were soon to follow. Violins met the staunchest opposition, but even here compromises eventually had to be made. Some New England meetinghouses would allow the fiddle if it were played wrong end up, the church elders reasoning that an inverted fiddle "was no fiddle at all, but a small bass viol."[32] Of the wind instruments commonly used in churches around 1800, flutes, oboes, clarinets, and bassoons were very popular. The flute was favored because it was cheapest, and the fingering resembled that of the familiar fife.[33] The bassoon, on the other hand, was popular because it blended well with both the cello

---

28. Earle, *Sabbath in Puritan New England*, 227.
29. Wood, *History of the First Baptist Church*, 308.
30. Earle, *Sabbath in Puritan New England*, 226.
31. Andrus, *Music in Poughkeepsie*, 12.
32. Earle, *Sabbath in Puritan New England*, 226.
33. Gould, *Church Music in America*, 173.

and the bass voices of the choir.[34] The following excerpt from Washington Irving's *Sketchbook* gives an accurate, if somewhat capricious, description of the gallery choir in all its glory:

> The orchestra was in a small gallery, and presented a most whimsical grouping of heads, piled one above the other, among which I particularly noticed that of the village tailor, a pale fellow with a retreating forehead and chin, who played on the clarionet [sic], and seemed to have blown his face to a point; and there was another, a short pursy man, stooping and laboring at a bass viol, so as to show nothing but the top of a round bald head, like the egg of an ostrich. There were two or three pretty faces among the female singers, to which the keen air of a frosty morning had given a bright rosy tint; but the gentlemen choristers had evidently been chosen, like old Cremona fiddles, more for tone than looks; and as several had to sing from the same book, there were clusterings of odd physiognomies, not unlike those groups of cherubs we sometimes see on country tombstones.
>
> The usual services of the choir were managed tolerably well, the vocal parts generally lagging a little behind the instrumental, and some loitering fiddler now and then making up for lost time by traveling over a passage with prodigious celerity, and clearing more bars than the keenest foxhunter, to be in at the death. But the great trial was an anthem that had been prepared and arranged by Master Simon, and on which he had founded great expectation. Unluckily there was a blunder at the very outset—the musicians became flurried; Master Simon was in a fever; everything went on lamely and irregularly, until they came to a chorus beginning, "Now let us sing with one accord," which seemed to be a signal for parting company: all became discord and confusion; each shifted for himself, and got to the end as well, or, rather, as soon as he could; excepting one old chorister, in a pair of horn spectacles, bestriding and pinching a long sonorous nose; who, happening to stand a little apart, and being wrapped up in his own melody, kept on a quavering course, wriggling his head, ogling his book, and winding all up by a nasal solo of at least three bars' duration.[35]

---

34. Gould, *Church Music in America*, 173.
35. Irving, "Christmas Day," 250–51.

CHAPTER 3

TWO GREAT RIVERS

The Cultivated and Vernacular Traditions in American Music

The passage of the Patowmac *(sic.)* through the Blue Ridge is perhaps one of the most stupendous scenes in nature. You stand on a very high point of land. On your right comes up the Shenandoah, having ranged along the foot of the mountain a hundred miles to seek a vent. On your left approaches the Patowmac, in quest of a passage also. In the moment of their junction, they rush together against the mountain, rend it asunder, and pass off to the sea.
[Thomas Jefferson, 1788.][1]

AS A YOUNG MAN I remember visiting Jefferson Rock, also called the Point, at Harpers Ferry, West Virginia. It overlooks the confluence of the mighty Potomac and Shenandoah rivers. It is a sight that takes your breath away, as I am sure it did for Thomas Jefferson when he visited there in 1785. Jefferson knew, I'm sure, as he was standing there, that he and America were entering a new epoch, full of hope and risk. I would like to think of these two rivers as a metaphor for the state of American church music—American music in general for that matter—at the beginning of the nineteenth century.

As noted in chapter 1, a growing divide among Americans regarding musical culture had been present long before the war for independence. It directly paralleled the changes in the new nation's religious life and the

---
1. Jefferson, *Notes on the State of Virginia*, 143.

pursuit of "perfectionism." The eminent American musicologist H. Wiley Hitchcock referred to these opposing viewpoints as the "cultivated" and "vernacular" traditions.[2] To quote Hitchcock:

> I mean by the term *cultivated tradition*, a body of music that America had to cultivate consciously, music faintly exotic, to be approached with some effort, and to be appreciated for its edification—its moral, spiritual or aesthetic values. By *vernacular tradition*, I mean a body of music more plebian, native, not approached self-consciously but simply grown into as one grows into one's vernacular tongue, music understood and appreciated simply for its utilitarian or entertainment value.[3]

Those on the cultivated side viewed European art music as the *ne plus ultra* that Americans should aspire to. For them, the homegrown fuging tunes and rough-hewn harmonies of the colonial tunesmiths had to be abandoned in favor of more elevated, more scientific European art. In a letter written in 1778, Thomas Jefferson spoke his views of the superiority of art on the continent.

> If there is a gratification which I envy any people in this world, it is to your country its music. This is the favorite passion of my soul, and fortune has cast my lot in a country where it is in a state of deplorable barbarism.[4]

Music that did not fit into this rigid perspective was viewed as tasteless, inappropriate, or worse.

Conversely the vernacular contingent valued homemade, often sentimental art beyond any import. Musical originality and theological integrity were viewed as secondary in importance to emotional fervor. For them, the focus on high art was viewed as elitist and out of touch with the mass of Americans. The cultivated tradition, quite naturally, was most firmly rooted in older and wealthier congregations along the eastern seaboard. Smaller churches, urban or rural and often more evangelical, gravitated to the vernacular side of the argument.

We have already seen how the gradual insertion of choral music into public worship was warmly received by some while others saw only its defects and felt it was a deterrent rather than a help to corporate piety. In the early years of the nineteenth century, there was a fast-developing critical view that could not tolerate the imperfections inherent in most group

---

2. Hitchcock, *Music in the United States*, 54.
3. Hitchcock, *Music in the United States*, 54.
4. Jefferson, "Letter to Giovanni Fabbroni."

singing. The prevailing view was that congregational singing was defective and listless. Of necessity, it needed to be reformed or replaced by either the music of a well-rehearsed amateur choir or that of professional singers. The reasoning seemed perfectly logical: If the individual was to be reformed, the cultural aura of the church needed to be as cultivated to provide the proper example. It would be a lengthy process requiring both time and patience.[5] Joseph Bartlett, in an 1841 speech before the Handel Society of Dartmouth College, acknowledged this, declaring, "the day may come, and though a distant, it will be an auspicious one for music, when its science and its art shall be understood, that the voices of the great congregation shall rise as one man."[6]

Running as a thread through many of the arguments against congregational singing was the dogma of perfectionism and the unstated rule that music was only worthy of a place in worship to the degree that it approached perfection. Writing much later, the Boston clergyman James Hewins perfectly expressed the position of generations before him that perfection of musical rendition must be sought and that only those trained to sing well should sing at all.

> Congregational singing is eminently and notoriously a Puritan institution.... Calvin's music was intended to correspond with the general parsimonious spirit of his worship. Sensible that his chief resources were the rabble of a republic, and, availing himself of the natural propensity which prompts even vulgar minds to express their more animated feelings in rhyme and music, he conceived a mode of universal psalmody fitted to please the populace.[7]

The new emphasis on cultivating, reforming, and educating American musical taste had a direct effect on the music heard in the sanctuary. That which was foreign was thought to be exemplary. While church music was

---

5. While taking congregational singing away from the people and assigning it to a select few, even temporarily, was antithetical to the reformed ideal of *corporate* worship, it seems not to have troubled those seeking a cultivated ideal.

6. Bartlett, *Music as an Auxiliary*, 19. It should be understood that the modern concept of American church choirs was still in a formative stage during the first half of the nineteenth century. There were differing opinions about the need for choirs and their purpose. For most, if a church had a choir, its primary focus was on the leadership of congregational psalm singing. Stand-alone performing was infrequent and reserved for special observances. Choirs were still viewed with suspicion by many Protestants who saw them as step toward liturgical complexities and Romanism. There was also a general distaste for anything smacking of "performance," à la the theater or the music hall.

7. Hewins, *Hints Concerning Church Music*, 159–60.

not supposed to be tainted by secular art, tunes were still extracted from operas of the day. Choruses were often arranged from concert masses of symphonic composers such as Mozart and Haydn, then being heard in American concert halls for the first time. Often the educational value of the music was placed above its spiritual appropriateness. The value of a certain collection was often gauged on its ability to elevate the taste of the worshippers or cater to cultivated sensibilities. Such attitudes naturally tended to favor that music that was performed for a listening audience. The decorative aspects of church music were favored over corporate participation. Many viewed music as simply part of the veneer that was needed to create an atmosphere in the sanctuary.

Into this contentious epoch in American church music appeared two colorful and hugely influential personalities, Lowell Mason (1792–1872) and Thomas Hastings (1784–1872). Both were highly successful entrepreneurs, fabulously market savvy and in-demand compilers of tunebooks who built reputations as respected composers of a new "more tasteful" church music. As a result of their success, Mason and Hastings were sought-after lecturers, headliners for an ever-increasing number of "musical conventions," and prolific writers on every aspect of the church music of their time. In all of these areas, including publishing activities, they were mostly genial competitors. Theologically, Mason and Hastings represented two poles of nineteenth-century evangelism. Mason, like his mentor, the Rev. Lyman Beecher, represented the more conservative revivalism of Jonathan Edwards. Hastings, meanwhile, as we shall see, fell under the influence of the more radical evangelist Charles Grandison Finney.

One of the most powerful driving forces behind the success of Mason, Hastings, and others was the American Sunday school movement. It had a monumental influence and affected aspects of American sacred music for generations. It is of critical importance to understand that Sunday schools originated as a vehicle for public education and were usually administered independently from the churches where they often met. As an independent entity, the Sunday school had the freedom to incorporate a variety of music that at the time would not have been deemed appropriate for worship. Simple hymns easily learned by young children as well as recreational songs, folk songs, and teaching songs were all part of the mix. The Sunday school, or Sabbath school, like the singing schools before it, was a common source for basic music instruction, and the first exposure to singing for many a nineteenth-century singing master. A range of songs, sung in the Sunday school, became so well-known and well-loved, even among nonchurchgoers, that they could be heard around Civil War campfires on both sides throughout the conflict. The Sunday school movement, the American missionary movement, the YMCA, and the great urban revival of Dwight Moody and I. D. Sankey—all critical to an understanding of American church music during the nineteenth century—were utterly intertwined.

Public Education and the American Sunday School Movement

During the colonial era, the bulk of childhood and youth education was provided either in the home or in the church. There were, of course, various types of schools. *Dame schools* were loosely run operations run by women in their homes, somewhat akin to modern daycare. *Town schools*, funded through local taxes and focused on basic literacy skills, were rare, as were *subscription schools*, generally funded by subscription through church benevolence programs. Teaching methods were generally primitive and there was no coordination or government oversight of education.

In America in the late eighteenth century, what we know as public education was nearly nonexistent. In 1779, Thomas Jefferson had proposed "A Bill for the More General Diffusion of Knowledge," which outlined a detailed plan for taxpayer-funded public education in Virginia, but it was denied passage.[8] In 1790, Pennsylvania required free public education for children in families that could not afford to pay for an education. The New York Public School Society in 1805 set up schools for poor children that had a school master to teach the older children on a premise that they would teach younger siblings and classmates. It wasn't until 1827 that Massachusetts legislated free public education for all. Making education compulsory in the state had to wait until 1851.

The first "Sabbath schools" began to appear in England the 1790s. They were schools for the rudimentary instruction of poor children based on a concept originating with Robert Raikes and other evangelicals. Raikes, owner of the *Gloucester Journal* and a philanthropist, was concerned about the endless cycle of poverty in the slums and sought to address it through childhood literacy education. In a 1783 *Journal* column, Raikes recalled:

> Sir,
> My friend the Mayor has just communicated to me the letter which you have honored him with, inquiring into the nature of Sunday Schools.... I was struck with concern at seeing a group of children, wretchedly ragged, at play in the street. I asked an inhabitant whether those children belonged to that part of the town and lamented their misery and idleness. "Ah sir," said the woman to whom I was speaking, "could you take a view of this

---

8. Jefferson, "Bill for the More General Diffusion of Knowledge."

part of the town on a Sunday, you would be shocked indeed, for then the street is filled with multitudes of these wretches—who, released on that day from employment, spend their time in noise and riot, playing at chuck, and cursing and swearing in a manner so horrid as to convey to any serious mind an idea of hell rather than any other place."

. . . I then inquired of the woman if there were any decent, well-disposed women in the neighborhood who kept schools for teaching to read. I was presently directed to four . . . and made an agreement with them to receive as many children as I should send on Sunday, whom they were to instruct in reading and the Church Catechism. For this, I engaged to pay them each a shilling for their day's employment.[9]

With England in the throes of the Industrial Revolution and poverty in factory cities escalating, Raikes's idea, as promoted in his *Journal*, soon caught on. Hundreds of urban Sunday schools were established across Britain, and by 1785 it has been estimated that 250,000 children were enrolled, five thousand in the schools in Manchester alone.

The British Sabbath school concept was eagerly assimilated in America in the 1790s. From the beginning, there had been unanimous agreement that America's "future citizens needed to be honest, hardworking, trustworthy, and selfless. However, moral education had always been closely associated with religion, and many people distrusted the idea that Christian virtues could be inculcated in a secular setting."[10] Among the first schools modeled after the Sabbath school concept was one established for the children of textile mill workers in Pawtucket, Rhode Island. In Philadelphia, a mix of clergy, physicians, and businessmen joined together to organize a "First Day Society." The society was formed to set up schools to teach reading and writing on Sunday afternoons, using the Bible as their only textbook. The schools were independently administered and were funded through benevolent donors. Teachers were paid, and facilities for classes were rented.

Few First Day schools lasted into the nineteenth century. By 1800 they were being replaced by charity schools, which were operated by individual Protestant congregations and religious societies, often by subscription. Francis Asbury, the Methodist bishop, had advocated in 1796 that church-affiliated schools be established "wherever practicable, for the benefit of the children of the poor."[11] As in Britain, the schools met on Sunday afternoon and were tasked with teaching basic reading, writing, and Christian

---

9. Power, *Rise and Progress of Sunday Schools*, 37–38.
10. Reuben, "Patriotic Purposes," 4–5.
11. Reuben, "Patriotic Purposes," 9.

education. Also, as in Britain, the schools were evangelically oriented. "Teaching reading and writing was only a means to a greater end, not an end in itself."[12] That end was the indoctrination of children with a conservative evangelical interpretation of Scripture, highlighting innate depravity, future punishment, and need for conversion or regeneration.[13]

While the church-based schools were staffed by volunteers and were largely seen as a ministry to the poor, tuition-based private schools were available only to those who could afford them. As the inequality of opportunity became more and more pronounced, pressure mounted in the 1830s for free and universal public education. The trend was enthusiastically supported by Sunday school advocates because it freed them to focus purely on religious instruction.

During the first decades of the nineteenth century, communities with multiple Sunday schools operating in different areas formed Sunday school unions, and in 1834 these localized organizations were formed into the American Sunday School Union. The objective was, through combined resources, to publish textbooks, teaching manuals, and curriculum manuals. The union's founders, evangelical Presbyterians and Episcopalians in the Philadelphia area, were convinced that the scourge of poverty in most cases, wherever it appeared, could be eliminated by evangelical conversion.

The American Sunday School Union was focused not only on publishing religious literature but also music. According to one of the union's chroniclers, it "sought to displace the rollicking and ribald songs by cleaner and purer lyrics set to attractive music."[14] As music was seen to be an important component in Sunday School curricula, the union set about producing teaching methods. *A Manual of Instruction in the Art of Singing* was published in 1831, followed a year later by *Manual of Instruction in American Sunday School Psalmody*, both by Elam Ives (1802–1864). Ives also published one of the Union's first song collections, *American Sunday School Psalmody; or, hymns and music, for the use of Sunday Schools and teacher's meetings* (1832). Included was a section devoted to teaching methods. The following example is a typical melody, range limited to a minor third, intended to introduce singing from notation.

---

12. Reuben, "Patriotic Purposes", 9.

13. Note: "Regeneration", as a theological term, refers to God's interaction with humanity to bring new life to believers—literally to be "born again."

14. Rice, *Sunday School Movement, 1780–1917*, 147.

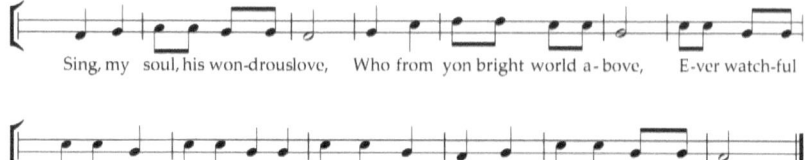

"Sing My Soul His Wondrous Love," p. x ("Example no. 19"), in *American Sunday-School Psalmody; or Hymns and Music: A Manual of Instruction*. Elam Ives, arranger. (Philadelphia: American Sunday School Union, 1832; https://s9.imslp.org/files/imglnks/usimg/6/64/IMSLP192979-PMLP331867-americansundayscooives_bw.pdf)

Thomas Hastings

Thomas Hastings was born in Washington, Connecticut, October 15, 1784. At the age of twelve in 1798, a young Hastings and his family moved to Clinton on the frontier in New York State. The fact that the move was accomplished by ox sledge gives some idea of the roughness of life at the time. Most of Hastings's career was based in Utica and Oneida County, New York, at that time, a fairly undeveloped part of the state. He and his three siblings suffered from albinism[15] and, as a result, Hastings had very poor eyesight requiring heavy, thick-lensed spectacles. Not much is known of his formative years except that he studied in a local singing school and in 1802, at the age of eighteen, was serving as a singing master in Clinton, New York, just outside of Utica.

Hastings's singing school work was well received, his reputation burnished, and soon he was called upon to lead sessions beyond Oneida County in Herkimer, Augusta, Vernon, Onondaga, Skaneateles, Auburn, and Seneca Falls. In 1815, Hastings published what would ultimately become one of the most well-known and popular collections of psalmody, *Musica Sacra, a Collection of Psalm Tunes, Hymns, and Set Pieces*, written for the Oneida County Musical Society. The collection was so well received that less than a year later Hastings collaborated with Soloman Warriner to publish a new, expanded and enhanced version.[16] Yet another enlarged edition followed a year later.[17]

---

15. Albinism is a congenital disorder characterized by the complete or partial absence of pigment in the skin, hair, and eyes. It is associated with a number of visual defects.

16. Williams, *Thomas Hastings*, 9–26.

17. *Musica Sacra* was revised and enlarged again by Hastings in 1818, and ultimately

Thomas Hastings (1784–1872)
from *The Story of the Hymns and Tunes*, Hezekiah Butterworth and Theron Brown. (New York: American Tract Society, 1906). Panel following p. 142. (https://archive.org/details/storyofhymnstuneoobuttuoft/page/n178/mode/1up)

Hastings was intelligent, articulate, and able to express his views engagingly. These traits set him apart from other singing masters of his time. In 1822, he published his *Dissertation on Musical Taste*, a two-hundred-page manifesto, declaring his views regarding the aesthetics of sacred music. Hastings's *Dissertation* was so widely read and quoted that it became a defining document for his generation and the next. His influence is obvious in Lowell Mason's 1826 *Address on Church Music*.[18]

The idea that church music needed to improve the hearers, not simply entertain them or aid in their worship, was prominent in Hastings's thinking. The best way for music to do this was to stay out of the way. Music that distracted from rather than enhanced the worship experience could not lead to edification of the believer and was therefore inappropriate. Music that tried to enliven worship, as Hastings thought the fuging psalm tunes had, was annoying and vulgar. The purpose of worship, Hastings said, was to put the soul "in harmony" with God's divine plan and any discord or musical complexity that diverted attention from this principal aim was out of place.

---

went through ten editions before 1840.
 18. Williams, *Thomas Hastings*, 69.

The ideal church music, then, was that which was eminently unobtrusive, a sort of heavenly background music that never drew attention to itself.

In *Dissertation*, Hastings used his opening words to distinguish the aesthetic he aspired to from the workmanlike teaching through repetition of basic music reading skills, characteristic of most eighteenth-century singing schools:

> Expression is one of the most important musical requisites: and it has been defined to be that quality in a composition or performance from which we derive a sentimental appeal to our feelings.[19]

It is important not to load our twenty-first-century negative connotations associated with the word *sentimental* onto the word as it was used in the 1800s. For Hastings, *sentiment* referred to human emotion—something felt but not seen. Music, he was saying, and we would agree, was an ideal vehicle to express sentiment.

> ... though we may be disposed to impute much skill to a musical composition or performance, yet if it universally appears to be unexpressive ... it ceases to deserve the name of musick.[20]

Hastings saw the teaching of his singing master predecessors as too focused on the mechanics of basic music reading. If one's goal was simply to achieve barely adequate congregational singing, one denied the very power of music to move the heart spiritually. He objected strenuously to the sameness he saw in many of the psalm tunes of his time. For Hastings, church music could not be viewed as simply a component of congregational singing but an essential exercise of devotion in itself. Church music, he wrote, "is a divine institution [and] must sufficiently prove that it is an important one, and it is equally evident that it was designed for the express purpose of assisting the devotions of the pious."[21] Music, he declared, should not be viewed as simply a warm-up exercise in preparation for the sermon, but an act of devotion in its own right.

> A question here naturally presents itself, whether musick should be considered as a mere preparative for subsequent devotional exercises, or whether it is to be employed in direct exercises of devotion. The latter is undoubtably [sic] its principal office ...[22]

---

19. Hastings, *Dissertation on Musical Taste*, 5.
20. Hastings, *Dissertation on Musical Taste*, 6.
21. Hastings, *Dissertation on Musical Taste*, 15.
22. Hastings, *Dissertation on Musical Taste*, 15.

Hastings felt the door should be opened widely to all manner of musical invention—anthems, set pieces, instrumental accompaniments, and so on—which might assist in the devotions of worshippers. He sought to divest himself entirely from the rigid prohibitions of earlier generations:

> Some well-meaning persons, we are aware, are for discarding everything in social worship that makes an appeal to the passions; for they imagine that in proportion as these are wrought upon, genuine devout exercises will be necessarily diminished, and hence, they contend that everything like expression in church musick is to be condemned.
>
> But that this is not the philosophy of the sacred scripture is evident . . . Poetry and musick have ever been considered the appropriate language of feeling . . . [T]he poetry of the scriptures is highly impassioned, abounding also with instances of the sublime and beautiful . . .[23]

Churches of Hastings's time, he felt, seemed hidebound. To him they appeared to be focused exclusively on universal participation in congregational singing, even if it meant a more elevated approach to musical art would never be achieved. He took the injunction in Psalm 5 seriously: "Let all who take refuge in you rejoice; let them ever sing for joy," and saw it as the duty of singing masters to teach all worshippers to sing who were open to instruction. He had to admit, though, "There is a class of individuals, who are willing indeed to admit, that their musick is indifferent . . . Their voices [they feel] do not need cultivation, for they can now sing in such a manner as to satisfy themselves."[24]

For Hastings, encouraging such people to sing despite their lack of skill and disinterest was injurious to artistic progress. He also decried the lack of standards set by many singing masters of his time, the lack of seriousness taken in their cause, and the social, recreational character of many schools. In short, he declared that the traditional singing school was not equipped to move church music forward:

> The more aged of the community . . . have all their lifetime neglected the cultivation of their voices [and] will not be likely to undertake the task in the decline of life; and a change of style would consequently leave the management of the singing too exclusively to the young, many of whom are light minded . . .[25]

---

23. Hastings, *Dissertation on Musical Taste*, 17.
24. Hastings, *Dissertation on Musical Taste*, 19.
25. Hastings, *Dissertation on Musical Taste*, 19–20.

Such pupils, after a few winters' attendance at school, where their tastes are necessarily vitiated, and their bad habits of execution confirmed, become, at length, too indifferent . . . to pay any further attention to the subject, and, of course, they relinquish their seats . . . to another young and equally giddy class who succeed them.[26]

Here Thomas Hastings is alluding to a new music for use in worship. It is a music accessible to average singers in a choir or congregation that is structured around common-practice (i.e., European) harmony. It avoids both the rough-hewn folk style with its open fifths and occasionally jarring dissonances of the colonial psalm tunes, and what he viewed as the frivolity of fuging refrains. An example of his approach to hymn tune writing and harmonization can be seen in his setting of the Watts hymn, "Come, Holy Spirit, Heavenly Dove."

"Come Holy Spirit, Heavenly Dove." (Text, Isaac Watts; tune, Newmark, Thomas Hastings), p. 29 in *Musica Sacra, or the Springfield and Utica Collections United* (Utica, NY: William Williams, 1819).

All things considered, Hastings spoke for many of his time in saying that "the congregational method of singing, either with or without accompaniment, was radically defective." He wrote, "A well-disciplined choir has, at once, every opportunity and facility for maintaining good execution. Safe from the disturbance of untutored singers, they are sufficiently remote from

---

26. Hastings, *Dissertation on Musical Taste*, 75.

each other, to lend an attentive ear to their own manner of execution."[27] We should not assume that here Hastings has given up hope for congregational singing. Rather, it is an issue of expediency, how best to solve the problem of painful congregational singing in the short term by substituting a choir's singing for it.[28] In fact, for the next thirty-four years, he would devote all his energy to encouraging more active congregational participation through his teaching and many compositions.

And what of the need for competent instructors in music? Hastings speaks bluntly:

> The art of singing is generally considered among us as a thing of so little difficulty, and so little importance, that almost any instructor, who will labor for a small compensation, can readily find employment. If he possess an agreeable voice and understand well the nature of a pitch-pipe, and a six-penny gamut,[29] he may readily pass for a competent man. A few giddy youths, perhaps, are wishing to spend their winter evenings together, and recourse is therefore had to a singing school . . . An insignificant . . . instructor is employed without the least hesitation. He, of course, supports neither order nor dignity in his school— his pupils are permitted to sing the most sacred words in the midst of unrestrained levity, without ever being reminded of their import. No real progress is made, either in the theory or practice of their art, but, on the contrary, a few indifferent pieces are committed to memory and executed in the most wretched manner, without the least reference to the real nature of the song or subject.[30]

Near the end of this seminal work, the author states, possibly for the first time in a widely disseminated and published document, that European art must be the model for Americans in the future. This mindset will drive American church music for over a century thereafter.

> When America . . . from her extensive cultivation and patronage of the art, shall have been equally prolific in the production of artists, and equally successful in disseminating a taste for the art, then, and not till then, may her professors hope to succeed in fully seconding the projects of her transatlantic brethren in

---

27. Hastings, *Dissertation on Musical Taste*, 69.

28. Hastings, *Dissertation on Musical Taste*, 77.

29. With "a six-penny gamut," Hastings is referring to an inexpensive instruction book on music reading.

30. Hastings, *Dissertation on Musical Taste*, 75.

the rapid march of refinement. We are the decided *admirers* of modern German musick. We delight to study and to listen to it. The science, the genius, the taste, that everywhere pervade it, are truly captivating to those who have learned to appreciate it.[31]

In his *Dissertation on Musical Taste*, Thomas Hastings provided a literal compendium of musical knowledge on music theory, form, and analysis, correct singing technique, and so on. While obviously a fine and well-read musician, some of his pronouncements seem dated or ill-informed. His seemingly rigid views on congregational singing should be painful to modern ears. They run counter to historical and biblical views on worship and singing as a communal activity that surely we all have come to accept. That being said, we must consider the time and context in which the document was written and appreciate Hastings's fervent desire to develop a better and more devout worship music for future generations.

The publication of *Dissertation* was a milestone in American music and made Hastings famous. From 1823 to 1832, he was employed as editor of *The Western Recorder*, a publication of the Western Education Society of the State of New York, based in Utica. In 1826 the evangelist Charles Grandison Finney preached at First Presbyterian Church in Utica, where Hastings was serving as church musician. Thus began a long-term relationship between the two men. Hastings's appointment to a lectureship at Princeton in 1829 was further evidence of the respect he had achieved.

Three years later, Hastings moved to New York City, where he would live for the rest of his life. It was there, in 1835, that Hastings founded *The Musical Magazine*, a monthly periodical featuring articles on music theory, upcoming performances, visiting artists, sacred music, and opinion pieces by Hastings himself. In October of that year Hastings set down his thoughts on the scarcity of qualified instructors in the field of music:

> At this season of the year great inquiries are made for teachers of devotional music; teachers who thoroughly understand their business, and can in every respect, be well recommended. The demand for such teachers is constantly increasing. If one hundred of them could now be obtained, there would be no difficulty in finding them employment . . . But what is to be done? How shall the neglected work be prosecuted? Where shall the right teachers be found? These are questions not the most easy of solution. A few suggestions are all that we can offer in reply:
>
> Good teachers have not hitherto been sufficiently encouraged in a pecuniary point of view. In a country like ours, men are

---

31. Hastings, *Dissertation on Musical Taste*, 194.

prone to seek their own advantage, in the choice of some lucrative employment: and the compensation for teaching music, has scarcely been found adequate to the comfortable support of a small family. The consequence is, that the best teachers in the land, almost without exception, turn their hand ultimately, to some other employment. The same kind of perseverance which has enabled them to excel as teachers of music, has placed within their reach, other occupations more lucrative and less perplexing and laborious. Some who were trained for eminent usefulness in this employment, have become merchants and manufacturers. Some physicians, lawyers, and even speculators. Others for better reasons have gone into the ministry...

If it be said that men who have the necessary qualifications ought to exercise some self-denial in this respect; we fully admit the justness of the remark. It is a blessed work to cultivate the praises of God, as a branch of Christian effort; and pious musicians who see this good work beginning to prosper in their hands, must answer it to the great Master of Assemblies, if they leave such an important employment through improper motives.

At the same time, it may be in season for the churches to bring such a charge against them, when they are ready to make pecuniary appropriations sufficient for their comfortable subsistence. This is reasonable. The workman is worthy of his hire; and if there is no alternative for him but starvation, the churches have not a word to say. They must expect him to seek other methods for the support of his rising family.[32]

In the November-December issue, Hastings wrote of the need for courses of study in church music:

We have among linguists, for example, our French, our Spanish, our Italian and our Greek teachers; our professors of the Oriental languages; and our translators and lexicographers. In philosophy, we have a natural, a mental, and a moral department; in history, a civil and an ecclesiastical department; and in rhetoric and *belles lettre*, we have our critics, our poets, and our writers of prose. In painting, also, there are various departments...

And who, that knows anything about the subject of music, can fail to observe ... the operation of the same principle.... In Europe, one man devotes himself to the flute, another to the violin or violoncellos, a third to the horn, a fourth to the drum, a fifth

---

32. Hastings, "Want for Teachers," 160.

a sixth and a seventh severally to the harp, the piano-forte, and the organ . . . And . . . there is a sacred and a secular department, too often blended in practice it is true, yet perfectly distinct in theory: and of sacred music there is the oratorial school, and the school of devotional music, which are totally different in their design and influence.

For ourselves, we shall rejoice to see the day, when this country will furnish the means of a thorough musical education, adapted to its own special wants and peculiarities as a Christian nation. Till then, nothing remains but to make the best of everything; and to manage, as well as may be, on the sound principles of Christian prudence and liberality. Let us do this, in everything which relates to the music of the church; and then we may safely look to the great Master of Assemblies for his presence and blessing.[33]

Thomas Hastings produced two highly popular Sunday School song collections. *Juvenile Psalmody* (1827) was written for the Western Sunday School Union, based in Utica, New York. *The Union Minstrel*, published in 1834, was highly popular, selling 250,000 copies before 1846.

Lowell Mason

Lowell Mason has been referred to as both the "Father of Music Education in America" and the "Father of American Church Music." Alternately, he has been labeled a talented salesman with no more than average musical talent who understood the cultural sensibilities of his time and parlayed that knowledge into fame and wealth. He did that by publishing immensely popular tunebooks, teaching, lecturing, and developing a larger-than-life persona while overseeing singing conventions attended by thousands.

---

33. Hastings, "Divisions of Labor," 210–13.

Lowell Mason
(1792–1872).
Portrait from William Mason, *Memories of a Musical Life*
(New York: The Century Co., 1901). Panel after p. 276 in biographical sketch by
William S. Tilden (1892), "Early Life of Lowell Mason." (https://archive.org/details/
memoriesofmusicaoomasouoft/page/275/mode/1up)

Mason was born in 1792 in Medfield, Massachusetts (near Boston), the son of the town clerk and treasurer. His was a musical family, steeped in the New England singing school tradition. Johnson Mason, his father, played several musical instruments, most particularly the cello. Grandfather Barachias Mason (1723–1795) was a graduate of Harvard. He taught singing schools and sang bass with a local singing society into his seventies.[34]

The young Lowell Mason was also greatly influenced by the neighborhood in which he lived. The nearest neighbor in Medford was the Reverend Thomas Prentice, who sent four sons to Harvard. Next up the road was George Whitefield Adams, who built organs, played clarinet, and conducted the local band.[35]

Lowell predictably became a singing school scholar himself, studying under the local singing master, Amos Albee (1772–1823). Joseph

---

34. Keene, *History of Music Education*, 109.
35. Tilden, "Early Life of Lowell Mason," 281.

Buckminster, pastor of Boston's Brattle Square Church, ca. 1805, also influenced Mason. Buckminster played several instruments, including flute, cello, violin, and organ, and had a chamber organ in his home. He was deeply concerned about the state of congregational singing and compiled a popular tunebook, *Psalms and Hymn Tunes for Public Worship*, which was commonly known as *The Brattle Square Collection*. Mason was a frequent visitor at the Brattle Square minister's home, probably to discuss musical topics or possibly to play on Buckminster's organ.[36]

At the age of seventeen Lowell was hired as organist/music director for the First Parish Church (now Unitarian) of Medfield, but three years later he struck out with George Adams for Savannah, Georgia, where he first worked in a dry goods store and then a bank. Soon he accepted the post of organist/choirmaster at the Independent Presbyterian Church. There he helped to organize and oversee Savannah's first Sunday school, one of the first in the nation. By 1817, Mason's choir was presenting public concerts of works by European masters, often arranged by Mason himself. The repertory for those years suggests a very capable choral group.[37] One concert by the choir on May 16, 1826, included selections from Haydn's "Creation," as well as choruses attributed to Croft, Gardiner, and Mozart. It was during the Savannah years that Lowell Mason became acquainted with Thomas Hastings's *Dissertation on Musical Taste*. He studied it thoroughly after it was published in 1822.[38]

Gilbert Chase, who was particularly critical of Mason, suggested he only went into music when he was sure a profit could be had by it.[39] Mason did indeed say that he "did not wish to be known as a musical man, and . . . had not the least thought of making music my profession." This statement reveals, more than anything else, the commonly held view at that time that church music was properly the enterprise of talented amateurs. Music was "not looked upon as a particularly reputable profession."[40]

We must remember that most of the Yankee singing masters earned only part of their livelihood teaching music. Therefore, was it any wonder that Mason, for some time during his younger years, chose to consider music not as a profession but as an avocation? The greater surprise would have been had he done things differently. Using Chase's terminology, "progress

---

36. Pemberton, *Lowell Mason*, 8.
37. Pemberton, *Lowell Mason*, 11.
38. Pemberton, *Lowell Mason*, 130.
39. Chase, *America's Music*, 152
40. Lowens, *Music in America*, 5.

and profit" were certainly motivating Mason during his Savannah years.[41] But to portray him solely as a profiteer is unfair.

While in Savannah Mason undertook the formal study of composition and harmony with F. C. Abel, a musician recently immigrated from Germany. With Abel's help and using the British William Gardiner's *Sacred Melodies* as a model, Mason decided to compile a collection of psalm and hymn tunes that he felt met the standard of "better music." Mason was intrigued by Gardiner's adaptations of melodies by Viennese classicists like Haydn and Beethoven into singable tunes for congregational use. Mason's entrepreneurial instincts told him that, using the Gardiner model, he could produce a profitable collection. The end result, *The Boston Handel and Haydn Society Collection of Church Music,* would radically change the trajectory of Lowell Mason's life and probably the whole trajectory of American church music. What made the collection revolutionary for its time, and set it apart from all other American tunebooks, was Mason's borrowing of fragments of tunes by well-known European composers and repackaging them in simple melodic and harmonic formats accessible to choirs and congregations.

With the unexpected success of his publishing venture, Lowell Mason made the decision to leave Savannah and return to Boston in 1827, beginning the life of a successful, much-in-demand musician. A year earlier he had received an invitation to deliver an important address on the subject of church music. Mason's *Address on Church Music* enunciated a philosophy of music to which he remained true, and with which he was generally consistent, throughout his life. It would prove to be, like Hastings's *Dissertation on Musical Taste*, one of the most influential writings on church music of the era. The lecture, given at Hanover Street Church in Boston on October 10, 1826, was well attended, and the hearers included the Reverend Lyman Beecher. Beecher was obviously moved by Mason's statements and afterwards headed a committee to have the lecture published. With Beecher's support and enthusiastic endorsement of his passionate mission to save and improve church music, Mason became a rotating director of music at three churches. Beecher's Hanover Street Church was one of them. Mason seemed to be everywhere at once. In addition to his organist duties and continuing to do some work in banking, he organized singing schools for children, some classes with as many as six hundred in attendance.

The pastor/musician collaboration Mason shared with Lyman Beecher is illustrated in a reminiscence he provided for Beecher's *Autobiography*:

> I was accustomed to go to Dr. Beecher before the time for the commencement of the public worship on Sunday morning.

---

41. Chase, *America's Music*, 153.

> Such calls are often annoying to the minister, engaged, perhaps, in preparation for the services of the day . . . One day I went as usual; it was very near the time for the commencement of the service, and just as I entered the room the bell began its call. He looked up, and, with a smile, said, "I can't give you the hymns now; I don't know what I shall preach about yet, so I wish you to select any you think proper." I left him to choose his subject and prepare his sermon while I went to select the hymns; probably in ten minutes afterward he came into the church. The hymns being of a general character, and adapted to direct worship, answered the purpose well, as such hymns always will. After this he requested me always to make the selection, and to send the numbers to him.[42]

As Mason continues, one can easily sense the underlying affection which the two shared:

> Very often, for years afterward, did Dr. Beecher allude to the admirable effect produced in the carrying out of this principle [i.e., Mason's assignment to choose the hymns]. "You seemed to take up," he would say, "the subject where I left it, and to carry it on beyond where I had the power to do." Yes, blessed old man; but this cannot be done unless the preacher has done his work somewhat as you used to do it. Unless the preacher awakens emotion, it cannot be intensified by any hymn power. I used to tell the doctor, in reply to such remarks as the above, "Sir, you laid the train, and there was nothing left for me to do but to apply the fuse."[43]

In his "Address on Church Music," Mason first defined the parameters of church music. Like Hastings, he emphasized music's subservient role. "That there is no religion in music," he said, "is readily admitted, but music is capable of subserving a religious purpose. Were it not so, it would never have been introduced by divine appointment."[44] He characterized music as having the unique powers to "move or melt, or rouse an audience," and said it "ought therefore to be made a powerful auxiliary to the faithful preacher."[45]

Again following Hastings's lead, Mason stated that anyone concerned with making music a more effective aid to worship must deal with the reform of musical taste. "Taste," he said, "is much more intimately connected

---

42. Beecher, *Autobiography*, 151–52.
43. Beecher, *Autobiography*, 152.
44. Mason, "Address on Church Music," 6.
45. Mason, "Address on Church Music," 6.

with religious feeling than is generally supposed. It cherishes on the one hand, or destroys on the other, those pious emotions which public and social worship is designed to call into exercise."[46] Assessing the current situation, Mason said that psalmody that was poorly done and dull was "calculated to excite disgust in the man of musical taste."[47] Furthermore, he felt that poor execution musically of psalm tunes and hymns diverted attention away from the biblical texts, which were of critical importance.

To state Mason's view in other words, good church music had the power to benefit people who heard it. Reforming the public's musical taste was not only a religious and spiritual issue but intimately connected with reforming the entire person for a new and better world. It was this power to reform that was music's chief object in worship, not art for art's sake, not to be an activity for congregational participation, and certainly not to be one for the edification of the performers. Mason saw music as a powerful tool and not one to be misused. He also objected to the use of music for any purpose other than ministerial. Music, he said, which simply provides a break or variety in the worship experience—like a musical interlude at the theater—"has nothing to do with religion."[48]

Both Hastings and Mason went to some length to express a growing concern for the quality of music being sung in American churches. Some wealthy New York and Boston churches had already hired professional vocal soloists to replace their choirs. Music calculated to appeal to the popular taste was being used to attract church members instead of to enhance the liturgy and make its message more powerful. The fact that some professional church singers tended to be associated with theatrical pursuits inflamed old prejudices in the minds of many, and so Mason's characterization of them is germane:

> The principal reason for the present degraded state of church music, seems to be, that its design has been forgotten, and its cultivation as a religious exercise neglected.... Hence it is often given up, almost exclusively, into the hands of those who have no other qualifications than mere musical talent; and who, being destitute of any feelings of piety, are almost as unfit to conduct the singing of the church as they would be the preaching or the praying. Having been furnished by nature with an ear to appreciate the melody of sweet sounds, such persons take up church music as a mere amusement and pursue it solely with reference

---

46. Mason, "Address on Church Music," 7.
47. Mason, "Address on Church Music," 8.
48. Mason, "Address on Church Music," 10.

to the tasteful gratification it affords them. In proportion, therefore, as they are able to delight themselves and to draw forth the applause of others, by communicating the same feelings to them, in the same proportion they succeed in accomplishing the object of their exertions.[49]

Mason drew a bold line dividing church musicians from their secular counterparts. The church musician was a reformer, using the reformative powers of music to help build a better, more cultured society. Those who performed mainly for the approbation of an audience were tainted and not fit for church work. Worse still, such musicians would communicate shallow secular views of music to the congregants and create among them an appetite simply to be entertained, not lifted up.

What was the responsibility of Christians as far as music was concerned? It was the sacred duty of Christians, Mason and Hastings said, to cultivate an interest in good sacred music. In contrast, John Cotton, almost two centuries earlier, had said it was the holy duty of all to sing, regardless of their vocal attributes. *Mason and Hastings, however, were saying that the real sacred duty was to become cultivated.* This perspective was entirely consistent with the perfectionist climate of the time. If fellow humans really wished to be reformed, they had first to forswear old ways and then cultivate new, more tasteful ones. During this reform process, having full vocal participation in the worship service was less important than the long-term goal: that the church, in all its worship, was to serve as a kind of remote sanctuary from secular life where ideal religion, ideal social commentary, and ideal music could be provided for the cultivation of the congregants.

> Shall the whole congregation be encouraged to join promiscuously in this exercise or shall it be committed to a select choir?[50]
>
> If it be said that it is the duty of every man to sing the praises of God and make melody *in his heart* unto the Lord—it is granted . . . [but] it is no more obligatory upon him to *sing aloud* in public worship, in the one case, than it is [for him] to pray aloud in the other . . .[51]
>
> May not the whole assembly be engaged in spirit in singing, although none but the choir perform audibly?[52]

---

49. Mason, "Address on Church Music," 8–9.
50. Mason, "Address on Church Music," 15.
51. Mason, "Address on Church Music," 16.
52. Mason, "Address on Church Music," 17.

It is only fair to Mason to understand that for him, denying any congregation its voice was a terrible choice, possibly necessary in some situations but not something he relished. Repeatedly throughout his career he undertook to improve and strengthen congregational singing, not dispose of it. An innovation Mason brought to Boston was the Congregational Singing School. Whereas traditional singing schools of the past had concerned themselves with the basics of music reading, the congregational singing school restricted itself to making group singing pleasurable. Rehearsals were well publicized and open to the participation of all who wished to come. According to an article in *The Musical Visitor*, Boston, February 12, 1841:

> Several new Congregational Singing schools have been raised on the plan of free general instruction. Mr. Hill, organist of the Baptist Church which worships at the Melodion, has just opened one, which is well attended. Mr. Allen, organist at the New Church in Bowdoin Square, has convened one on the same plan. The Handel and Haydn Society, under the direction of Mr. Webb and the Association of City Choirs under the direction of Mr. Mason are holding occasional meetings for public rehearsal of church music.[53]

Mason's commitment to congregational singing remained strong for the rest of his life. In May of 1853 he was appointed music director of New York's Fifth Avenue Presbyterian Church and immediately took the radical step of dismissing the church's choir and orchestra and embarking on a mission to strengthen singing in the pews. A much larger organ was installed, and strong voices were placed near the front on each side. A new choir formed specifically to lead was "spread through the room," and the singing was described as "marvelous . . . there is no church in the city where so many join in the singing."[54]

In terms of this study, perhaps the *most important* view shared by *both* Thomas Hastings and Lowell Mason was a belief that those who would lead the Christian community through music must have a deep abiding faith, an understanding of the seriousness of their role. Hastings felt that members of a church choir, tasked with leading congregational singing, must be persons of faith to effectively minister:

---

53. "Congregational Singing Schools," 2.
54. *Noble Landmark of New York*, 33–34.

> In relation to the *duty* of devotional singing, there can be but one opinion ... to perform with external piety if others are to be benefitted by our exertions ...[55]
>
> If, then, the members of a choir were to be sufficiently instructed [in the spiritual importance of their role] and perfected in their art ... and especially if the pious portion of [the] community were also to do their duty in relation to this part of the service, it appears evident that church musick would soon be performed, in some measure, as it ought to be.[56]

Mason addresses this ministerial requirement while suggesting that churches need to employ music leaders of faith, piety, as well as musical expertise:

> Every choir, thus formed, should have a competent leader—if possible—a pious man ... One who is acquainted with the whole subject of Church Music, and who is capable of instructing others ... Such a laborer is worthy of his hire; and although, like the minister, he should be influenced by nobler motives, yet it is proper he should receive a suitable compensation; for much time and exertion he must necessarily devote to the duties of his office. The services of such a leader have not generally been properly appreciated or rewarded.[57]

He was also probably the first of his time to propose seminary training in music for clergy:

> Everything connected with the interests of the church is a proper subject of attention and study at a seminary for educating the guardians of the church. If it be important that the praying and the preaching in public worship be performed suitably, it is also important that the singing should be performed suitably. And if ministers will not watch over this part of the service, who will? But proper attention will not be given to the subject in our theological institutions until they are furnished with professors of music. Let this be done and we shall witness a new era in the sacred music of our country.[58]

George Frederick Root, who would become famous both for his church compositions and his parlor and patriotic songs, recalled his initial contact with Mason soon after his return to Boston with this tribute:

---

55. Hastings, *Dissertation on Musical Taste*, 72.
56. Hastings, *Dissertation on Musical Taste*, 74.
57. Mason, "Address on Church Music," 25.
58. Mason, "Address on Church Music," 41.

Not many years before, a singing school had been held in the old red schoolhouse, where "faw, sol, law, sol, la, me, faw" were the syllables for the scale—where one must find the "me note" (seven) to ascertain what key he was singing in, and where some of the old "fuging tunes," as they were called, were still sung. I well remember how, shortly after, we heard that a new system of teaching music had been introduced into Boston, in which they used a blackboard and sang "do-re-mi, etc." to that scale. But how silly "do" sounded. We thought it smart to say that the man who invented that was a "doughhead," and how flat were "fa" and "la" in comparison with the dignified "faw" and "law."

Later, however, when some of the tunes connected with the new movement came, we changed our minds about the man who was at the head of it. Nothing before, so heavenly, had been heard as the melody to "Thus Far the Lord Hath Led Me On" (Hebron), and one of the great things in going to Boston was that I should probably see Lowell Mason.[59]

Musical Conventions

There is some question as to the actual origin of musical conventions,[60] but the idea of a three- or four-day convention of singing masters and choirs, for the purpose of learning techniques of musicianship, was born in 1835 out of the music classes that Mason and Webb were teaching at the Boston Academy of Music.[61] Lowell Mason and Thomas Hastings, while the most prominent early leaders of such gatherings, were certainly not the only ones promoting a new church music in the first half of the nineteenth century. The Englishman George James Webb (1803–1887), William Batchelder Bradbury (1816–1868), and George Frederick Root (1820–1895) frequently appeared on convention platforms. Two of the most prominent American teachers and composers of sacred music prior to the Civil War, both

---

59. Root, *Story of a Musical Life*, 9.

60. The first gathering to be called a "musical convention" was sponsored by the Central Musical Society of Concord, New Hampshire, in 1829, according to Ritter, *Music in America*, 201. Concurrent with Mason's efforts in Boston, the same designation was being given to meetings led by Moses E. Cheney in Montpelier, Vermont. H. C. Lahee, in his article, "Century of Choral Singing in New England," quotes a letter from Cheney stating that he led such gatherings in Montpelier in 1839, Windsor in 1841, Woodstock in 1842, and Middlebury in 1843. Cheney's conventions, however, differed from Mason's in that the entire time was devoted to choral singing. There were no lectures and the emphasis was on the performance of music rather than teaching.

61. John, "Origins of the First Music Educators Convention," 209.

students of Mason, Benjamin Franklin Baker (1811–1859) and Luther Orlando Emerson (1820–1915), continued the convention tradition through the 1850s. These gatherings, at their height in popularity in the 1840s and '50s, served to carry the message of a new and improved church music far beyond Boston and New York City to Chicago, St. Louis, and innumerable points in between.[62]

The concept fell neatly into Mason's master plan for the dissemination of ideas. The first four-day musical convention, attended by fourteen church musicians, was held at the Odeon Theater in Boston in 1836. Thereafter it became an annual event. In 1840, enrollment for the convention had exceeded a thousand, and Mason elected to move it to New York City and rename it the National Musical Convention. Smaller regional conventions would become commonplace throughout the Midwest and major cities in the Southeast.

Musical conventions as initially conceived were intended to be a time of intensive concentration on the fundamentals of music for singing masters and teachers of music. Classes typically began at eight each morning, consisted of lectures on harmony (including thorough-bass), the rudiments of music reading and composing, voice cultivation, and various chorus workshops and rehearsals. Conventions always culminated in the presentation of a concert. The emphasis in all classes was on teaching techniques so the material could be taken home and conveyed to others. While musical conventions were not usually promoted as being church-music related, the music that was sung, and the fact that the majority attending sang in church choirs or directed them, leaves little doubt where they exerted the most influence.

Mason's colleague George James Webb, at the 1838 convention, made clear that the role of the choir was no less important than the minister's in leading the congregation in prayer. Webb told the convention that the choir singer's duty was not only to God, but to the pews below. "As the minister should teach the congregation their duties, so should the choir teach them the importance of music, with which they would be more and more impressed, as the choir became more and more perfect in performance."[63]

When viewed in retrospect, Lowell Mason's idea that the church choir should be a formal body of singers that rehearsed and had a sense of duty and responsibility was ahead of its time. Repeatedly enunciated by Mason

---

62. W. B. Bradbury oversaw one of these gatherings in Austinburg, Ohio, in October of 1858 and returned for another convention in the nearby town of Andover the following spring, as he reported in "Special Notices," *New York Musical Review and Gazette*, 327. Austinburg and Andover are both villages in Ashtabula County in northeastern Ohio, this author's home.

63. "Selections: Proceedings of the Musical Convention Assembled in Boston," 259.

at conventions across the eastern seaboard and in middle America, it represented a complete break with the rationale behind the more informal singing societies that had proliferated around the turn of the nineteenth century.

To be sure, the musical convention was not an ideal platform for substantial teaching. Lectures presented to large audiences tended to be built on colorful generalizations and pungent paraphrase rather than hard facts. The atmosphere was festive. Most sessions could be expected to do little more than whet the interest of those present. A class in "The Cultivation of the Voice" led by Benjamin Franklin Baker was described as follows in *Dwight's Journal of Music*:

> [I]n these few brief opportunities the teacher could do little more than point out a few of the most essential principles of a true method ... [Baker] reduced the great mysteries of the art to a few (we might almost say to one very little formula)—just a couple of 4/4 measures, which stood almost always written on the blackboard, filled by one long note, with the sign of the swell and diminuendo over it.[64]

While the original objectives of musical conventions were admirable, by the 1850s the character of these enterprises had shifted frequently to gross commerciality. John Sullivan Dwight, the editor of *Dwight's Journal*, excoriated them for being pawns of an industry devoted solely to publishing the ever-increasing number of tunebooks. He referred to the conventions as "Singing-master's and Book-Maker's Fairs in Boston," and bemoaned the fact that the public's "quest of general appreciation of art music" was being ignored by the hucksters and tunebook sellers who made the conventions their headquarters.[65] The musical ideas, which were presented from the convention platform, often went unheard by those attending due to the din of the booksellers among them. The great evening chorus rehearsals, according to Dwight, were frequently marred by accompaniments poorly rendered on out-of-tune instruments, tempos too fast for learning, and too many raw recruits among the singers.[66]

Whatever the shortcomings of musical conventions though, they were an important influence in American church music. Conventions brought new ideas and new perspectives on worship and sacred song. They also brought the sound of choral music produced by vast numbers of voices to rural communities as far west as Ohio, Illinois, and Wisconsin.

---

64. "Musical Convention," *Dwight's Journal of Music*, August 21, 1852, 157–58.
65. "Musical Convention," *Dwight's Journal of Music*, August 28, 1852, 165–66.
66. "Musical Convention," *Dwight's Journal of Music*, August 28, 1852, 165–66.

Luther Orlando Emerson (1820–1915), one of the youngest of Lowell Mason's followers and, for a time, organist at Bullfinch Street Church in Boston, conducted over three hundred musical conventions. Recalling Dwight's criticisms, Emerson penned the following rather touching reply:

> So, it was *Dwight's Journal of Music* that said Lowell Mason and other psalm-tune writers were degrading and cheapening music? Well, we could not have expected anything better from that source, for Mr. Dwight was not in sympathy with the good work we were doing. In reality, we were doing more to help his cause than he himself was doing. His Journal was a good one, the best published at that time. It stood for the highest and best music of all kinds. It did not have a large circulation. It did not go abroad among the masses of people. He could talk about the musical giants of the past and of his own time, if there were any, criticize the performances of their music, the soloists, etc., which was all very well.
>
> While he was doing this, we were carrying the best choral music of the various kinds, from church music to the oratorio and opera, and also the best soloists obtainable to thousands and thousands of musically hungry singers and people all over the country . . .
>
> If this kind of work was degrading and cheapening music, then revive the convention and musical festival and let the good work go on, for it is needed. If the thousands of singers who attended the festivals, and the greater number of thousands who attended the concerts, could speak with one voice, they would send up a shout in their favor that would be heard across the continent. When Lowell Mason organized the Musical Convention in Boston and carried it from thence into the country, he set in motion an influence that for forty years or more did more to make this nation a musical one than any one thing (anyone) else has done.[67]

Charles Grandison Finney and Worship at the Broadway Tabernacle

In 1827, Charles G. Finney and Lyman Beecher, the two great evangelists, met to debate at the Convention of the Congregational Church at New Lebanon, New York. It was a face-off between titans of the pulpit and generated

---

67. Quoted in Metcalf, *American Writers and Compilers*, 216.

much interest among the public and in the press. Both men saw revivalism as an important witness. While both bristled at any suggestion their views were Arminian, both believed that humans could affect their salvation by choices made and actions taken. For Beecher, redemption required first a willingness to turn away from sin, and the reform of society's ills was key. He spoke out forcefully advocating abstinence, moral purity, and an end to dueling. For Finney, conversion was the key. He preached that any reform of society or of the individual sinner was impossible without a deliberate and visible turning away from sin and acceptance before God and one's peers of Jesus Christ as Savior.[68] Finney's opposition to "lukewarm religion," which he voiced at the convention, led to an invitation from a group of influential New York City Presbyterians to lead a series of evangelistic worship services and revivals there.[69]

Between 1830 and 1831 there were many attempts to find a church large enough to house such meetings, but each that was chosen proved to be too small for the crowd.[70] With the financial backing of dry-goods store owners, Arthur and Lewis Tappan, silversmith Isaac M. Diamond, and others, land was purchased from the P. Lorillard Estate in 1832. Finney devised the interior himself to seat 2,500 persons and personally planned everything— "interior decoration, acoustics, window lighting, the deep pulpit platform, the organ and choir seating and the side rooms."[71] The large sanctuary of the Tabernacle had a circular arrangement of pews with a large circular gallery and a platform in the center. The pulpit, when used, rested on the platform with large choir, organ, and sometimes orchestra behind it.[72]

Richard Hoffmann, a brilliant English pianist, gave his premiere American recital at the Tabernacle,[73] and his description of the surroundings gives much insight into the kind of place it was.

---

68. Finney's views on the abolition of slavery provide an excellent example of this. His writings reveal a deep revulsion for the institution, and yet he refused to openly endorse the abolitionist movement because he felt the only way to end the practice came with conversion of the slave holders and masters.

69. Nichols, *History of the Broadway Tabernacle*, 43–45.

70. Nichols, *History of the Broadway Tabernacle*, 48. At first, an effort was made to divide the congregation into smaller groups or free churches, each meeting simultaneously with the others. By 1834 five free churches had been organized. Nevertheless, Finney still felt a need to build an auditorium that could hold large audiences.

71. Nichols, *History of the Broadway Tabernacle*, 59.

72. Finney himself was pastor of the Broadway Tabernacle only until 1838, when he was succeeded by Joel Parker.

73. One of the most notorious events held there was a laughing gas demonstration in 1843, but it was also the site for meetings of the New York Bible Society, various anti-slavery groups, the New York Hymn Society, and temperance groups. The New York

> It was the only large room available for public concerts or meetings except Castle Garden (then used for the opera) and its acoustic properties were very good. It was, however, a dismal, badly lighted place and the entrance could only be reached through a long narrow alley on Broadway. The New York audiences of today would revolt against the inconveniences which were cheerfully endured by their grandparents in 1848.[74]

The fine acoustics at the Tabernacle caused P. T. Barnum to seriously consider it for the American debut of Jenny Lind in 1850. He finally decided on the Castle Garden opera house because it could hold a few more people.[75]

Thomas Hastings had a relationship with Finney and so it is not surprising that the Tabernacle adopted Hastings's *The Christian Psalter* (1836) for use as its first hymnal. Hastings was then living in New York and, while not serving at the Tabernacle, had a direct hand in training its first choirs.[76]

The first formally organized Tabernacle choir appears to have been started in 1840 and was directed by one George Andrews. It was an all-volunteer ensemble for four years, but beginning in 1845, money was budgeted to pay a professional nucleus for the group. The first professional "leader" employed to direct the choir was J. L. Ensign, then conducting the New York Philharmonic Society. He was hired in 1845, and in 1848, he was promoted to the post of organist/director when Andrews retired.

W. B. Bradbury

William Batchelder Bradbury was already well known to New Yorkers as the accomplished organist from 1841 to 1847 of the First Baptist Church (later renamed the Baptist Tabernacle).

Philharmonic made its first home at the Tabernacle.
   74. Hoffman, *Some Musical Recollections*, 95–96.
   75. Erskine, *Philharmonic Society of New York*, 12.
   76. Ward, *History of the Broadway Tabernacle*, 166, 168.

W. B. Bradbury.
Public domain image courtesy of the Library Company of
Philadelphia. (https://digital.librarycompany.org/islandora/object/
Islandora%3A64028?solr_nav%5Bid%5D=f00899baad0ea342bbb7&so
lr_nav%5Bpage%5D=0&solr_nav%5Boffset%5D=0)

During the years 1847 to 1849 Bradbury took an extensive study tour in Europe, and during that time, had an epiphany regarding the relative merits of choral excellence versus corporate participation in congregational singing. As we have seen, this was a conundrum with which Mason, Hastings, and many others had struggled. "Good congregational singing did not mean cultured voices, singing together," Bradbury declared, but "an active participation by the congregation."[77] Conscious of the trends of the times, which were decidedly away from corporate participation in singing, he warned "that if church musicians wait until they have a congregation of artists or even of good singers . . . the task of leading music in the church will be taken from their hands."[78] This willingness to acknowledge there was more to music ministry than the cultivation of musical taste was radically forward thinking for the time and suggests post-Civil War thinking on the subject.

While in Europe, Bradbury studied briefly in Leipzig with Moritz Hauptmann (1792–1868) and Ignaz Moscheles (1794–1870), both closely associated with the younger Felix Mendelssohn (1809–1847). Bradbury's

77. Wingard, "Life and Works," 54.
78. Wingard, "Life and Works," 55.

stay in Leipzig coincided with the very end of Mendelssohn's reign as the leading musician in that city. It was Mendelssohn who shaped the musical thinking of the Leipzig Conservatory and Bradbury was thrilled to see the great composer actually conduct his oratorio *St. Paul* in 1847. It would turn out to be his last performance at the Leipzig Gewandhaus.[79] Bradbury remained in Leipzig and was there at the time of Mendelssohn's death on November 4. He was among the hundreds of mourners who lined up to see the composer's body at the Mendelssohn residence. In his letter to the *New York Tribune*, Bradbury wrote:

> I shall never forget the sweet expression of his countenance. His death was peaceful as his life was pure.[80]

While Bradbury was greatly moved by what he characterized as the life, work, and tragic death of a fallen hero, he also saw it as an opportunity to produce a new collection of hymns and choral music under the master's name. Shortly after arriving back in the United States in 1849, Bradbury enlisted the help of Thomas Hastings to co-edit *The Mendelssohn Collection*. He used Lowell Mason's borrowings of melodic snippets from European master composers in *The Handel and Haydn Society Collection* as a model.

Unlike other American composers of later in the century who traveled to Leipzig for study, one can find little evidence of German influence in Bradbury's music. His most enduring hymns were all marketed for Sunday school use as well as for formal worship. "Jesus Loves Me," "He Leadeth Me," "Just As I Am Without One Plea," "Sweet Hour of Prayer," "Savior Like a Shepherd Lead Us," and "My Hope Is Built on Nothing Less"—all share a simple, tuneful quality and are immediately accessible for congregational singing.

In 1850, William Batchelder Bradbury became "vocal leader" at the Broadway Tabernacle. While he was only officially employed by the church for two years, Bradbury exerted vast influence on New York church music. As noted, he did not maintain an aloofness from secular music. One Tabernacle choir activity under Bradbury, which served to draw members and to keep choral music at the church in the public eye, was the staging of elaborate concerts once each year. These were called Annual Music Festivals

---

79. Following Mendelssohn's death, Leipzig became the center of a sort of "Mendelssohn cult." Brahms frequently visited, and his presence reinforced the conservative tendency among musicians there, as did the presence of Robert Schumann. Ultimately, Leipzig and Berlin would be viewed as meccas for musical learning, drawing scores of aspiring American musicians, including Dudley Buck, George Whitefield Chadwick, and John Knowles Paine.

80. Musselman, "Mendelssohnism in America," 341.

and the receipts from the programs helped to finance the church's music. The 1852 Annual Music Festival consisted of the following selections:

Glee Chorus, "Pleasures of Spring"

Kreutzer Chorus, "When Morning First Dawns"

Rooke Solo and Chorus, "Flora and the Forester"

Hewitt Chorus, "The Maying Party"

Atterbury, A Solo on the concertina by Prof. A. Sedgwick

Glee Chorus, "The Ramble" by W. B. Bradbury

Solo, "The Old Arm Chair" by H. Russell

Chorus, "The Linden Tree" by C. Loewe

Solo "Johnny Sands" by one of juveniles

Chorus, "The Switzer Boy" by W. B. Bradbury [81]

Bradbury also composed a *Lecture on Music*, the manuscript of which is in the Library of Congress. The following "church music creed" speaks eloquently of the composer's beliefs:

1st. I believe it the privilege and duty of all to unite in singing as an act of worship.

2nd. I believe that, from the congregation at large, a number possessing more musical talent than the rest, should be organized into a separate body with a competent leader and occupy a place by themselves.

3rd. That this choir, so organized, should not only serve in the capacity of leader to the congregation but that a part of each service may and should be performed entirely and exclusively by themselves—the congregation at such times being silent listeners. That in such services, new and beautiful music appropriate to the occasion may be performed with as much taste and skill as by attentive study and practice they can command.

4th, and lastly, that for Congregational Singing, only such tunes as are simple in their structure and very easy of execution should be introduced, and that these should consist chiefly of old and familiar tunes such as the congregation generally can sing; that in each service, one such congregational tune should be selected, and when introduced by the choir, all people should arise and sing it to the best of their ability,

---

81. "The Annual Musical Festival of the Broadway Tabernacle Choir," 247.

without reference to art or musical effect, but simply and solely as an act of worship before their Maker.[82]

Hastings, Mason, and Bradbury Reconsidered

For all of the nineteenth century and well into the twentieth, Lowell Mason was lionized by historians as the "Father of American Church Music." To a somewhat lesser extent, Hastings and Bradbury were celebrated as composers of classic and regularly sung congregational hymns in this country. Hastings's *Dissertation* tended to be viewed as *the* watershed manifesto—comparable to Luther's *Ninety-five Theses* on the Castle Church door—dividing a century of artistic progress from a dark age of ignorance. Composers of the colonial New England school and fuging tunes were either forgotten or thought of as primitives.

Those views began to change in the 1930s and the music of eighteenth-century tunesmiths came to be accepted as an example of prized American folk art, crafted by self-taught amateurs who eschewed the basics of European art music in favor of a rough-hewn style that was natural to pioneers in a new world. With the approach of the American bicentennial celebrations in 1976 and the appearance of musicologists specializing in American music, a long-needed reappraisal finally took place. Recordings by professional singers of the music of Billings, Read, Holyoke, and others opened eyes to a new, exciting, visceral, and historic group of choral and organ music, heretofore unknown to most Americans.

Along with these exciting revelations came condemnation of Mason and his colleagues for what was viewed as their short-sighted elitism. They were accused of promoting "cultivated taste" in European art over a genuinely original art form being born in their midst. They were blamed largely for the demise of the singing school movement and assailed for their crass profiteering in the sale of tunebooks. Through those collections, it was justifiably charged that they had disingenuously produced and marketed much mediocre but easily singable hymnody, using the names of European masters to encourage sales.

With the passage of time perhaps a more nuanced view of the contributions of Hastings, Bradbury, and Mason is called for. The music of the colonial and federal period tunesmiths may now be seen as the birth of a uniquely American musical style, but that was not nearly so obvious in the 1820s. Hastings and Mason were not seeing the singing school from the

---

82. Ellinwood, *History of American Church Music*, 209.

perspective of historians two centuries later, but from their own direct experiences. Both had received all of their early training in such schools. Their views on singing schools, singing masters, choirs, and every related subject were shaped exclusively through the prism of church music within the cultivated tradition. The poor state of congregational singing—despite a century of reform efforts—rankled them. They saw and sought to emulate the more advanced state of choral singing in Europe. More importantly, one can see in their writings a developing view of church music as a ministry. They proposed that singers and directors have a faith-based underpinning to their work. One can intuit from their writings also a feeling that choirmasters and organists had a calling separate from their secular counterparts and should be employed as church staff rather than journeyman outsiders. With regard to the uneven quality of selections in their tunebooks, Mason, Hastings, and Bradbury were all very open about trying to fill a need for easily accessible music for inexperienced choirs and congregations while hoping that future generations would be ready for more substantial literature.

Finally, one can only marvel at the huge impact these gentlemen and dozens of others like them had through their leadership. While the singing school movement's influence, by its nature, was limited to the local community, musical conventions brought a vision for artful church music to the nation at large which was rapidly expanding beyond its roots in New England and New York.

Chapter 4

THE LITURGICAL CHURCH, PART 1
Recovery, Reconsecration, and Recalcitrance from the Colonial Era to the Civil War

The gradual transformation of cultivated American church music in the first half of the nineteenth century was not limited to Calvinist and reformed congregations. Liturgical churches also experienced a gradual transformation, though change came incrementally and without much of the controversy surrounding such topics as regular singing and the cultivation of musical taste.

First, a word about terminology: The word "liturgical" can be used generically in reference to any set order of worship. In that sense, it can be said that "nonliturgical" Presbyterian, Congregational, and Methodist churches routinely follow an order of worship prescribed by their denomination. Those worship orders can properly be referred to as "liturgies." In this study, however, I will be referring primarily to the Roman Catholic and Protestant Episcopal communities as liturgical. Many if not most denominational groups draw elements of their worship practice from historic liturgy—parts of the mass, the Lord's Prayer, and the Nicene Creed, for example. The principal difference between these liturgical and nonliturgical churches is not so much the content of the liturgy as how it is viewed and experienced. For the liturgically oriented, the faithful weekly acting out of the liturgical drama is more central to their identity than any sermon. It is a source of comfort and a link to past and future generations.

Worship in Roman Catholic and Protestant Episcopal parishes in America was, and is, controlled by historic and doctrinal precedent, and attempts to modify or improve worship practices were not really a factor in the years prior to the Civil War. Prior to 1800, whether talking about Episcopalians or Roman Catholics, when it came to music in worship the problems and ways of dealing with them were similar. Congregational singing was generally poor and singing schools were the preferred method of addressing the issue.

In general, the Protestant Episcopal Church—seriously hurt by the Revolutionary War and subsequent rupture of relations with England—was a denomination at war within itself just trying to survive. Powerful contingents of traditionalists and evangelicals threatened to rend the fabric of the denomination beyond repair.

On the other hand, Roman Catholicism was a small minority religion in early nineteenth-century America that faced withering prejudice from many sides. Immigration of Catholics from Ireland and Germany in the 1830s and '40s would begin to change the denomination's minority status, and, following the Civil War, Roman Catholicism would become the largest religious sect in America. Nevertheless, it continued to be viewed as a primarily working-class and immigrant religion and anti-Catholic bias continued until after the Second World War.

From Anglican to Episcopalian in the Eighteenth Century

George E. DeMille, in his seminal work *The Catholic Movement in the American Episcopal Church*, referred to the state of the Anglican/Protestant Episcopal Church in eighteenth-century America as "A Church in Ruins." During the British colonial years, Anglicanism consisted of widely scattered parish churches "tied together in the loosest possible way by the common and extremely nominal oversight of the Bishop of London and the rather more effective aid and supervision of the Society for the Propagation of the Gospel (SPG)."[1]

While the Church of England was Mother Church to the American colonies during most of the eighteenth century, Anglican chapels tended to exist only in major population centers and were small. Clergy had to be trained and ordained in England and were in chronically short supply. In addition, the Anglican chapels suffered from a kind of malaise. Churches were funded through local taxes rather than member contributions and, having a governmental role as well as a religious one, set policies affecting all citizens. The local parish was generally controlled by local elites and wealthy landowners. There was little incentive for change or creativity. There

---

1. DeMille, *Catholic Movement*, 1.

was also a dogmatic malaise fueled by lackluster leadership from the pulpit and the intrusion of Enlightenment thought and Deism. DeMille speaks of a doctrinal vagueness that was reflected in a proposed 1785 *Book of Common Prayer*, which omitted the Nicene Creed and deleted "descent into hell" from the Apostles' Creed.

The most notable advancements related to music in colonial Anglican worship were in major population centers—New York, Boston, Philadelphia, and Charleston. Like dissenting churches, the Anglican chapels sought ways to improve the quality of congregational singing. Many chose to organize singing schools or encourage their congregants to attend ones being offered nearby. In New York another approach borrowed from parish churches in England was tried, the training of "charity school children." In eighteenth-century England, some parish churches had established "charity schools" in which children were organized into choirs and taught the music of the church. They were wards of the church and thus were required to participate in Sunday services. Some parishes had the children interspersed throughout the congregation while others grouped them together in a gallery or some other area. Using charity children for musical leadership was not a practice universally appreciated, as the following criticism in John Jebb's *The Choral Service of the United Church of England and Ireland* (1743) indicates:

> Our parish system has been to compel [sic.] all our children to sing, and that at the very top of their voices without the slightest regard to the antiphonal system, in such numbers effectually to drown such of a congregation as attempt to throw in a harmony. . . . [D]uring the whole Sunday they are on drill; and they are considered not as the children of Christian parents, and as members of families, but as No. 1, 2, or 3, in such a class in School . . .[2]

The music of the charity children also served to support and reinforce English class consciousness. The children were usually uniformed, which underlined their subservience to the church and the wealthier donors who supported the system. The purpose of the charity children was to lead congregational singing. It was hoped that the people would join in singing, thus elevating the quality of the music generally known. Instead, the effort was self-defeating. Choirs tended to monopolize the music while the people listened mutely.[3]

Choirs of charity children were no solution to the problem of poor congregational singing. Even so, singing children appeared to be an attractive and promising alternative to the church musicians then working

---

2. Long, *Music of the English Church*, 325–26.
3. Temperley, *Music of the English Parish Church*, 124–25.

in America. In 1741, when the first organ was installed in Trinity Church, New York, children of the Charity School that had been established in 1709 were asked to lead the psalm singing.

The British organist William Tuckey (1708–1781), who had received his training at Bristol Cathedral, appeared on the scene at Trinity in 1753. Tuckey was well acquainted with English parish church practices and the use of charity children.[4] He was an accomplished organist, teacher of singing, and composer, and one of New York's most prominent musical figures in the decades prior to the Revolution. He would serve Trinity in different capacities: for a time as organist but long term as the musical director of its charity school. On January 15 of 1761, a memorial service for George II was held with Tuckey as the organist. Notably the service included singing by boys from the charity school. The number of girls enrolled in the charity school had always been small and, given the British predilection for choirs of men and boys, it may well be that Tuckey decided to exclude girls entirely from singing. At any rate, the 1761 service was one of the earliest examples of boy choir use in an American church.[5]

Tuckey, like other immigrant musicians, came to America hoping to cobble together a comfortable living from a variety of activities involving music.

> **CONCERT OF CHURCH MUSIC,**
> WILL be performed at Mr. Burns's Room, on Tuesday the 9th of January, 1770.
> For the Benefit of Mr. TUCKEY.
> *First Part.* Some select instrumental Pieces, chosen by the Gentlemen who are performers: Particularly a CONCERTO on the French Horn. By a Gentleman just arrived from Dublin.
> *Second Part;* A SACRED ORATORIO, on the Prophecies concerning CHRIST, and his Coming; being an Extract from the late Mr. HANDEL's GRAND ORATORIO, called the MESSIAH, consisting of the Overture, and sixteen other Pieces, viz. Airs, Recitatives and Choruses.
> Never performed in America.
> The Words of the ORATORIO will be delivered *gratis* (to the Ladies and Gentlemen) who are pleased to patronize and encourage this CONCERT, or may be purchased of Mr. Tuckey, by others for six Pence.
> As it is impossible that a Performance of this Sort can be carried on without the kind Assistance of Gentlemen, who are Lovers of MUSIC and Performers on Instruments; Mr. Tuckey will always gratefully acknowledge the Favour of the Gentlemen who assist him.
> TICKETS to be had of Mr. Tuckey, at eight Shillings each. To begin precisely at 6 o'Clock.

Original advertisement from the *New-York Journal*, January 4, 1770. Image courtesy of the Archives, Trinity Church Wall Street, New York.

---

4. Ellinwood, *History of American Church Music*, 51.

5. Ellinwood, *History of American Church Music*, 51.

In addition to his work with the charity children he established a singing school and was very active in the theater, playing the leading role of "Mr. Peachum" in a 1769 production of John Gay's *The Beggar's Opera*. Tuckey also coordinated and conducted several concerts of vocal and instrumental music independent of his work in the church. He is most remembered today for the first two American performances of a large portion of Handel's *Messiah*. The first was given on October 3, 1770, in a private concert hall, and was followed, in April 1772, by a performance at Trinity Church.

With the signing of the Treaty of Paris in 1783, American independence became a reality. While three quarters of the signers of the Declaration of Independence were Anglican, much of the population viewed the Church of England in America as a haven for Tory sympathizers. Anglican clergy, all of whom had to swear publicly their allegiance to the king, were especially reviled. Following the Revolution, a large percentage of Anglicans fled into exile in Canada. Localized efforts to establish a new American church began almost immediately, but the prospects were dismal. When independence was declared, most public funding of religion ceased and many chapels and the property on which they stood were confiscated. "This, then, was the American Church at the end of the century; barely tolerated in some sections and distrusted as half-disloyal in all; despoiled of its endowments, with its churches in ruins and its clergy scattered."[6] The population of the United States of America in 1790 was approximately four million, of whom only ten thousand claimed membership in the newly minted Protestant Episcopal Church. The transition from highly influential, elitist sect to struggling minority religious group presented challenges that would plague Episcopalians well into the nineteenth century.

The Protestant Episcopal Church in the Early Nineteenth Century

At the turn of the nineteenth century the Protestant Episcopal Church had to not only confront debilitating financial and leadership issues, but also to determine its very identity. Was it to be a church of the Reformed faith with the preached word and scriptural teaching as central, or was it to be an evangelistic denomination following after the success of the Methodists? Was it to be the keeper of traditional British Anglicanism? Was compromise possible, and if so, what form was it to take?

Because of American Anglicanism's isolation from the Mother Church, its identity had been shaped in part by other more dominant religious

---

6. DeMille, *Catholic Movement*, 5.

groups. New England Calvinism was a prime influence with its innate conservatism. Architecturally, the typical Anglican chapel was practically identical to a Congregational meetinghouse with its huge, imposing central pulpit and communion table against the wall behind it and barely visible to the congregation.

> Yet in spite of their faithful adherence to the Book of Common Prayer and for all the Anglican traditions to which they were heir, the musical and ceremonial level in most Episcopal churches was undistinguished. The usual service was Morning Prayer, followed immediately by the litany and ante-communion,[7] all leading to the sermon. Congregations sat mute or murmured while clerks made their responses for them and choirs did their singing, even when the setting was a Tate and Brady metrical psalm to a familiar congregational tune.[8]

At first the denomination had to be concerned primarily with shoring up individual dioceses and parishes rather than building a strong national presence. Influential early bishops in the East included William White (1748–1836) of Pennsylvania, John Henry Hobart (1775–1830) of New York, and John Henry Hopkins (1792–1868) of Vermont. Also important were Bishops Philander Chase (1775–1852) and Charles P. McIlvaine (1799–1873), both of whom served on the western frontier that encompassed present-day Ohio and Illinois. Initially, these early bishops focused their ministries on establishing new churches and strengthening older ones within their respective territories. Hobart, Hopkins, and McIlvaine would become the most influential in forging a path for the Protestant Episcopal faith during the first half of the nineteenth century.

---

7. Regarding the term "ante-communion": In medieval Roman liturgy, the Mass was divided into three distinguishable parts. The first two, the "Introductory Rite" and "Liturgy of the Word" were intended for the entire worshipping community. Following the Liturgy of the Word, those who had been baptized but not yet confirmed into the faith were dismissed. Part 1, the "Introductory Rite" included the entrance of priests, a hymn of praise, and an act of penitence (the *Kyrie eleison*, for example, and time of corporate prayer). Part 2, which followed, was the "Liturgy of the Word," which was comprised of reading of Scripture (selections from the Old Testament, the Psalms, the New Testament epistles, and the Gospels); the homily or sermon; the reading of the Nicene Creed; and confession. The third and concluding section, the services' high point, was the "Liturgy of the Eucharist." The "ante-communion" is the Episcopal and Anglican equivalent to the Catholic "Liturgy of the Word." In the early nineteenth century, before liturgical renewal had taken hold, the typical Episcopal parish celebrated the "Service of Morning Prayer" (the ante-communion) on a weekly basis. Celebration of the Eucharist generally occurred monthly or was reserved for special occasions.

8. Ogasapian, *Church Music in America*, 143.

The Oxford Movement, Tractarianism, and Ritualism

A pivotal event in both Anglican and Protestant Episcopal history occurred on July 14 of 1833. John Keble, an Anglican priest and poet, preached an inflammatory sermon at Oxford entitled *National Apostasy*. The address was in protest of the British Parliament's reorganization of the Church of Ireland, reducing the number of its priests from twenty-two to twelve. What, Keble was asking, was the nature of the church to be—Christ's church or a church of the state; the Church of England, or the religious pawn of the monarchy? Inspired by Keble's words, other Oxford clergy began to seriously and deeply reflect on the true nature of the English church and its roots both from the Reformation and before. Their studies and deliberations went far beyond the political crisis of 1833. How, they reasoned, might the Church better restore and practice the true and universal—"catholic" with a small "c"—faith? John Henry Newman (1801–1890) and Edward Bouverie Pusey (1800–1882) were key figures in those studies and deliberations. From 1833 through 1841, Newman, Pusey, and a coterie of other divines produced a series of theological writings. Some were small pamphlets while others were book-length. The whole was called *Tracts for the Times*. In all, ninety tracts would be published, based around the historical theme that the heritage of the Anglican Church from the time of its founding, aside from the use of English language and answering to the papacy, was tied to Roman Catholicism.

Histories of American music often use the term Oxford Movement as a blanket designation for developments in liturgical Protestantism in the late nineteenth century. The Oxford Movement was actually a political protest movement beginning in the 1830s within the Anglican Church in England and had little to do with the Protestant Episcopal denomination in America. Tractarianism, which drew its name from the *Tracts for the Times*, was important in America, where the *Tracts* were widely read. The Tractarian effort occurred simultaneously with the Oxford Movement, but it was based at Cambridge. The *Tracts for the Times* helped to bolster and support Episcopal polity as well as the power and authority of the episcopacy in America. Just as important, the *Tracts* advocated reviving and prioritizing certain key rites of historic liturgy that had been de-emphasized or fallen into disuse (examples include baptism, confirmation, regularity of serving communion, etc.).[9]

---

9. Tractarianism should not be confused with the movement to restore *ritualism* in the Anglican Church. While related, ritualism concerned itself with the trappings of historic worship—processionals, placement of the altar/communion table, vestments, choirs, architecture, and so on. The subject of ritualism in the American church will be discussed in chapter 9.

Many of the *Tracts for the Times* dealt specifically with polity and governance within the English church, but others dealing with the forms, theology, and substance of worship were eye-opening for Americans. Among them: the validity or invalidity of transubstantiation, the use of a common lectionary, the observance of liturgical seasons and high holy days including saint's days, the liturgy of baptism, the weekly celebration of the Eucharist, and *mysterium*[10] in worship. While "ritualism" was not a titled theme in *Tracts for the Times*, the tracts on aspects of liturgy and worship forms inspired heated controversy in England and in America. High church leaders saw in the tracts a guide to enrich worship. Conservatives and evangelicals saw them as a pernicious tool to advance popery over Protestantism.

In America, Bishop John Henry Hobart (1775–1830) oversaw New York State—the largest, wealthiest, and most influential diocese in the nation. He would be critically important to the future of church music in the Protestant Episcopal Church for two reasons: He was one of the founders of the General Theological Seminary (GTS) in New York in 1817 and became a professor of pastoral theology there in 1821. Also, Hobart took it upon himself—which many of his contemporaries did not—to study and digest the voluminous work of the British Tractarians. Sympathetic to their reformist goals, he became a founder of the high church movement in the United States.[11] Joining Hobart on the faculty of GTS was Benjamin T. Onderdonk (1791–1861), professor of theology and church polity. Onderdonk was also a strong advocate for Tractarian ideas and would follow Hobart as bishop of New York in 1830. As a result of Hobart's and Onderdonk's leadership, GTS would become a hotbed for liturgical innovation. Among its graduates would be Morgan Dix, future pastor of Trinity Church, New York City, and John Henry Hopkins Jr.

---

10. *Mysterium* comes from "*mysterium fidei: Qui pro vobis et pro multis effundétur in remissiónem peccatórum*" in the memorial acclamation of the Tridentine Mass, which comes after the consecration of the bread and wine (referring to Christ's blood of the new covenant: "the *mystery* of faith which shall be poured out for you and for many for the remission of sins"). In the Protestant Episcopal Service of Communion, it is followed by the eucharistic acclamation, "Christ has died, Christ has risen, Christ will come again", after which the officiant speaks or intones, "Therefore we proclaim the mystery of faith." *Mysterium fidei* therefore means "a mystery of the faith," a Christian theological term for an article of faith or doctrine that defies human ability to grasp fully.

11. The high church movement was a predecessor to, but not the same as, the Anglo-Catholic movement in the United States. Hobart supported restoring the rites of pre-Reformation liturgy. At the same time, he sternly opposed aspects of Roman Catholic doctrine such as deification of the Virgin Mary and transubstantiation.

W. A. Muhlenberg

The person credited with lighting a spark that would eventually lead to ritualistic reform in the Protestant Episcopal Church in the United States of America was not a graduate of GTS. William Augustus Muhlenberg (1796–1877) was the great-grandson of Henry Melchior Muhlenberg, considered the father of Lutheranism in America. His father was a member of the First and Second Continental Congresses. Though raised in a Lutheran family, upon graduation from the University of Pennsylvania in 1817, Muhlenberg was ordained a deacon in the Protestant Episcopal Church and to the priesthood three years later. While at the university Muhlenberg also received training in music and became the director of music at St. James Church in Philadelphia in 1818.

William Augustus Muhlenberg.
The Life and Work of William Augustus Muhlenberg (New York: Harper & Brothers, 1880). (https://archive.org/details/lifeworkofwillia00ayre/page/n9/mode/1up)

One of Muhlenberg's first acts at St. James was to organize a choir of boys to lead the congregation in the singing of psalms in place of the parish clerk. This colorful description underlines the challenges he faced in making changes in a bitterly contentious atmosphere:

> There, too, he had his first singing boys, having, at the request of Bishop White, taken the direction of the music. He found rather a bad set in possession of the "organ loft", and it was on his reporting their ill-behavior to the bishop, who was also rector, that he

received full power to affect a reform. The clerk, who had hitherto been supreme, was naturally, very jealous of Mr. Muhlenberg's interference, and resisted it. At the practisings [sic.], as a first step in reformation, it was arranged that this functionary should simply lead the Bass: but when Sunday morning came, he took his place at the center desk and sang out as precentor as heretofore, the organist and he understanding one another, for they were equally opposed to the "revolution" as they deemed it. As long as the clerk did his old part of leading the responses and giving out the psalm, it was impossible to keep him in the necessary subordination. Mr. Muhlenberg stated this difficulty to the bishop . . . [and] indeed he was very glad of such cooperation in a reform which was beyond his power; for with regard to the organist and singers, the good bishop had often said, "Forty years long was I grieved with this generation!" On the strength of this, Mr. Muhlenberg went the next Saturday afternoon to the organ gallery, and, assisted by his brother, chopped away the clerk's desk, and sewed together the curtains in front of it, thereby reducing the clerk to the level of the other singers. The amazement of the poor man on Sunday morning, at finding himself thus disposed of may be imagined. And who now would give out the *metre* psalm? To the surprise of the congregation as well as the clerk, the bishop, who officiated that morning, did it himself.[12]

This early confrontation tells us much about Muhlenberg. His willingness to face head-on an entrenched tradition that he saw as destructive to effective worship would typify his career.

Muhlenberg was immensely talented in a variety of ways. He was a master teacher who believed fervently in the importance of education. As such, he founded the Flushing Institute for Boys in Flushing, Long Island, in 1828. As part of the school's charter, it was agreed that one in every ten students would be admitted at no charge, based on need. The school would become a model for church-sponsored Christian education for future generations. A significant part of student life at Flushing was worship in the school chapel. There, Muhlenberg endeavored to expose students to all the symbolism, color, and pageantry of cathedral worship.

> He made the chapel the center of his school . . . [and] had the imagination and flexibility to make the services of the Church rich, solemn and glowing. He laid great emphasis on the Church Year. Christmas and Easter were both spent at the school with much preparation in which all took part. He felt that if the

---

12. Ayres, *Life and Work*, 45–46.

drama of the Christian Year was a truly corporate undertaking and was not allowed to degenerate into mere formalism, there was much to be gained from it.[13]

In his dedicatory speech at the laying of the cornerstone for St. Paul's College, Muhlenberg alluded to his liturgical mindset, saying, "Such marking of the times and seasons . . . is admirably suited for the young, by keeping the objects of the faith before their minds in a natural way, and without repressing the proper cheerfulness of their years."[14] The weekly routine of college life reflected this:

> On Sundays, following the intention of the Book of Common Prayer, Morning Prayer was said before breakfast; at eleven o'clock, preceded by Bible study, came the Litany, Ante-Communion and sermon (the Holy Communion was celebrated once a month and on festival days); at four-thirty, Evening Prayer was read. The Epiphany season was marked by emphasis on the mission of the Church; Lent and Holy Week played an important part in the life of the school and college. On the other hand, "fasting and abstinence to any extent," he wrote, "is not . . ."[15]

A number of future leaders in the movement toward ritualistic reform were mentored by Muhlenberg at the Flushing Institute. In the 1840s, Muhlenberg had the rare opportunity, as pastor, to literally shape a church's ministry, worship practice, and music based on his own ideals. He tapped his family's wealth to purchase property in the Flatiron district of New York City for what would become the Church of the Holy Communion in 1846.

Threading throughout Muhlenberg's career was a love of music. From early on, he was a strong advocate of congregational singing and the use of hymns in worship.[16] Like Lowell Mason over at Fifth Avenue Presbyterian, he initiated weekly congregational rehearsals and his Church of the Holy Communion became known for the strength and vigor of its hymn singing. He wrote both texts and music for over twenty-five published hymns. Following his "boy choir experience" at St. James in Philadelphia, he went on to develop a similar program at the Flushing Institute, and—most prominently—at the Church of the Holy Communion. Because of

---

13. Ayres, *Life and Work*, 200.

14. Quoting from W. A. Muhlenberg, "Ceremony and Address at the Laying of the Cornerstone of St. Paul's College" (New York, 1837), in Woolverton, "William Augustus Muhlenberg," 200. St. Paul's College was an outgrowth of the Flushing Institute.

15. Woolverton, "William Augustus Muhlenberg," 200.

16. Woolverton, "William Augustus Muhlenberg," 163.

his pioneering work with boys' voices, Muhlenberg is often referred to as the "father of the American boy choir movement."

In regard to boy choirs, Muhlenberg saw them strictly as an effective means to lead and support congregational singing. He felt that teaching the young men the psalm tunes and hymns of the church not only provided leadership but also insured better singing and participation of future congregations. Vested boy choirs, trained to sing anthems and deliver the sung liturgy by themselves, were not part of his vision.

> Looking back many years later upon some distinctive features of his church, Dr. Muhlenberg said: "I never thought of myself as much of a musician. Had I been more of one, I might not have been satisfied with the kind of music I have been mostly concerned for as suitable for the worship of the church. I have always desired the chorus of the congregation, not however to the exclusion of more elaborate music by a trained choir. My abhorrence of a quartette is sufficiently recorded in my "Lecture on Congregational Singing." I was the first to introduce boy choirs in New York, but I reflect on that with less pleasure when I see how they have since been used, not to lead, but to be heard alone; their voices too often shrill and unpleasant from the want of culture. I fear also the effect upon the poor boys themselves.[17]

Anglican Chant in American Churches

The use of Anglican chant had rarely been embraced by colonial American parishes and practically disappeared after the revolution. An early nineteenth-century tunebook that contained music for chanting set for four-part mixed voices was Jonathan Wainwright's *A Set of Chants Adapted to the Hymns in the Morning and Evening Services of the Protestant Episcopal Church* (1819). Even so, chanting was considered a rather exotic practice in the time of Mason and Hastings.

Experimentation with more elaborate service music in 1830s was spearheaded by Unitarians, Presbyterians, and Congregationalists, not the liturgical denominations. In 1835, Thomas Comer (1790–1862) published *Music of King's Chapel* for the Unitarian assembly he served as organist. The music, edited and largely composed by him, included anthems and responses.[18] Thomas Hastings published collections around this time that included many short, simple pieces for use as introits and responses. W.

---

17. Ayers, *Life and Work*, 223–24.
18. Ellinwood, *History of American Church Music*, 69.

B. Bradbury wrote short pieces designated as "sentences, introits, and responses," and even included a few actual chants in his collections published during the 1840s and '50s.

Lowell Mason was particularly interested in the harmonized Anglican chant style. Mason's background was in the Congregational and Presbyterian Churches, not Episcopalian, but he viewed the Anglican style of chant as an ideal form of sacred music. The music, he noted, although correct harmonically, was totally subordinate to the text.[19] The following setting of the *Venite* appeared in Mason's *Handel and Haydn Collection*. Chants by Vincent Novello and other British composers were also included.

---

19. The view of chant expressed by N. E. Cornwall in *Music: As it Was, and As it Is* was probably typical of Mason's time. Cornwall perceived harmonized chant as an "improvement" over the ancient monophonic variety. Unison singing (as in Gregorian chant), he stated, was mainly a device to help people who could not read understand the texts of the day. Moreover, he suggested, chanting in unison was not effective in the English language.

The Liturgical Church, Part 1

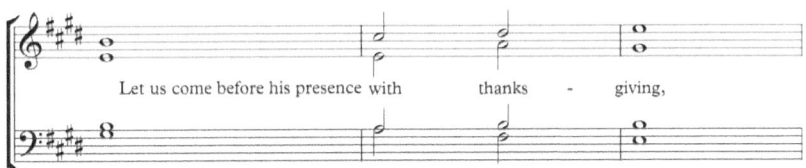

Chant, "O Come, Let Us Sing unto the Lord", (attributed to William Boyce) in Boston Handel and Haydn Society Collection of Church Music, eighteenth ed. (Boston: Wilkins & Carter, 1838) p. 351.
(https://s9.imslp.org/files/imglnks/usimg/7/72/IMSLP242919-SIBLEY1802.22980.a7a0-39087011256015.pdf)

Mason often included chant sections in his anthems and this practice was picked up by his followers. "The Earth is the Lord's and the Fullness Thereof" (1841) is labeled to be sung in "chanting style." We can assume by this that, while rhythms are written out, Mason would have choirs follow the natural accentuation and stress syllables of the text.

The Earth Is the Lord's

Lowell Mason, "The Earth is the Lord's and the Fullness Thereof," no. 294 in *The Modern Psalmist, A Collection of Church Music* (Boston: J. H. Wilkins and B. K. Carter, 1841).

Mason also published a *Book of Chants* (1846) on the pretext that chanting was an excellent way to heighten the worship experience and an effective technique for setting many nonmetrical scriptural texts musically. It contains 170 single chant harmonizations (i.e., each a six- to seven-measure setting to be applied to each verse of Scripture). In the Preface to *Book of Chants*, Mason opined that chant was ideal for congregational singing.

The simple harmonizations and repetitiveness made it more accessible to untrained singers than metrical psalmody. In chant also, text was key with harmonic setting of secondary importance, which, in Mason's view, made it especially effective for use in worship.[20] He saw the teaching of chant to a congregation as best accomplished through the leadership of a well-trained choir.

> Perhaps the best general direction that can be given in relation to the time in which a chant should be sung, is this: "Sing about as fast as a good reader, under similar circumstances, would deliver the words." Many well-taught choirs sing much faster than this; but it is believed that an adherence to the above rule will be found the most favorable to devotional effect. It is gratifying to know that choirs at the present time are turning their attention more to this excellent form of church music than in former years. It is hoped that the time is not distant when chanting will be generally introduced into public worship.[21]

Finally, during the 1840s, Trinity Church, New York—"Mother Church" to American Episcopalians—began to embrace the trend toward more elaborate worship in the Anglican tradition. This would culminate in a transplanted tradition of English cathedral music. It would be ushered in by British emigrant composer, organist, and church musician Edward Hodges.

Edward Hodges

The arrival in New York City in 1839 of the English organist Edward Hodges (1796–1876) was an auspicious event. Hodges, an 1825 graduate of Cambridge University, came to America after being rejected in favor of George Elvey for the position of organist at St. George's Chapel.[22] The sheer amount of work expected of Hodges when he was first hired must have been staggering. The parish budgeted $4,500 for him to hire, train, and provide music for choirs at the three parish chapels—St. John's, Trinity, and St. Paul's. Though it was a sizable task to organize three music programs, Hodges's pay for the work was miniscule. The budgeted funds had to cover the purchase of sheet music, salaries for two organists and several paid singers, and an allowance

---

20. Mason, *Book of Chants*, iii. Mason used a vertical line or *caesura* to indicate syllables assigned to each chord for verses of text not under the music. The later practice of "pointing" text came in the 1870s.

21. Mason, *Modern Psalmist*, 3.

22. St. George's Chapel at Windsor Castle is the traditional worship place of Britain's royal family.

for Hodges as well! The experiment was unsuccessful and was abandoned after one year. This plan seems to have been indicative both of the slighting attitude church administrations had toward choirs and the ignorance as to the amount of work required to establish and maintain a church choral program.[23]

Edward Hodges.
Engraved portrait facing cover page in *Edward Hodges, Doctor of Music*, by Faustina Hodges (New York: G. T. Putnam's Sons/Knickerbocker, 1896).
(https://archive.org/details/edwardhodgesdoc00hodg/page/n8/mode/1up)

Hodges's choir at St. John's Chapel was a double mixed quartet of paid professional singers such as were becoming fashionable in New York churches. The singers were hidden from view by curtains of purple velvet.[24] Once ensconced in the newly finished Trinity Church, Hodges set about attempting to establish a tradition of English cathedral music. Both anthems and composed services were looked on with disdain by some members who feared popery, as well as by many who wanted a style of choral music with more popular appeal. Indeed, after Hodges introduced the singing of anthems in the weeks following the dedication of the new Trinity Church, such a furor developed that they were banned from use by the vestry for two years.[25]

---

23. Like Hodges, Lowell Mason and Thomas Hastings were both contracted to develop choirs in programs that involved working with several churches simultaneously. In each case the endeavor proved to be a failure and was curtailed after a short time.

24. Messiter, *History of the Choir*, 41.

25. Messiter, *History of the Choir*, 321.

While Mason and others in the 1840s frequently cited a positive benefit to using chant in worship, many Americans had grave reservations, and Episcopalians shared this reticence. Chanting had disappeared in New York Episcopal churches after the revolution. While the practice was resumed at Christ Church as early as 1805, a warden at St. George's echoed the typical New Yorker's sentiment: "Away with your Jew gibberish, we want no such nonsense in the House of God!"[26] At Trinity, chanting was not permitted until 1859, whereas it had been allowed at the Church of the Ascension, also in New York, much earlier.

Edward Hodges's goal was ultimately to establish an all-male vested choir[27] in the English tradition at Trinity. The quality of young boy singers available to him however simply did not permit it at the time. In 1843, anticipating the needs of the new cathedral church, the parish music committee established the New York Protestant Episcopal School, a school for boys set up primarily to provide Trinity Church with a continuous source of treble voices.[28] Nevertheless, Hodges found it necessary to bring with him his mixed voice double quartet from St. John's, to which he added "twelve or fourteen boys with whom he had been working at the school," and a few adult volunteers.[29]

Anthems were sung regularly at Trinity Church only after the ban on such singing was lifted in 1848. Hodges was not only among the first to introduce anthem singing as a regular worship practice in an American church, he was also among the first to introduce the American public to some of the best literature of the English cathedral composers. A contemporary of Hodges recalled the music in the following way: "In the days of old Trinity's musical prosperity (never to be forgotten), there was a large and efficient choir who sang the grand old Anthems and Services of Gibbons, Boyce, Purcell, Croft, and Hodges; and for the first time in America, we heard the music that has been listened to with wonder and delight in the daily Cathedral Services of the Church of England."[30]

Edward Hodges's role was an influential one because, with the dedication in 1846, Trinity became the unofficial cathedral church for all of America. He was among the first in America to make elaborate choral music

---

26. Allwardt, "Sacred Music in New York City," 23.

27. The term "vested choir," in this and the remaining chapters, will refer boy choirs and choirs of men and boys.

28. Messiter, *History of the Choir*, 41.

29. By the time Hodges retired due to an immobilizing paralytic stroke and returned to England in 1859, only two women remained in the Trinity Choir. See Dix, *History of Trinity Church*, 274–75.

30. Dooley, "Thomas Hastings," 284.

an integral element in the ordinary weekly liturgy. One of the finest organists in America at that time, he was probably the first to play the Bach organ literature regularly in a mainline Protestant American church.[31] Among his first responsibilities was to design the new organ that would be installed in Trinity after the consecration. It was to be built by Henry Erben, had 2,169 pipes, and, according to Ellinwood, was "the first American organ of modern recital proportions."[32]

Anti-Catholicism in America

The idea that the Puritans came to the New World in the name of "religious freedom" is a myth. The truth is that in the seventeenth-century, English-speaking world, no single group was more religiously intolerant than the Congregationalists who made up the bulk of the Puritan settlements in early colonial America.[33]

Any discussion of Catholic music in the colonial era or nineteenth century must begin with a recognition that rampant anti-Catholicism existed. Catholicism in colonial and early America was a struggling, much-maligned minority sect. It has been estimated that of the roughly 4.5 million in the American population at the time of the War for Independence, only 25,000—about half of 1 percent—were Roman Catholic. Limited resources and an understandable desire to remain inconspicuous made music in worship low on Catholics' list of priorities.

The colonists, most of whom were Protestant, largely opposed anything that smacked of Catholic doctrine. This was a trait inherited directly from Britain where anti-Catholicism held sway throughout the seventeenth century.[34] The Church of England itself was fulminated against by the colonists because it was thought to be perpetuating popish ideas.

---

31. Ellinwood, "English Influences in American Church Music", 7.

32. Ellinwood, "English Influences in American Church Music", 8.

33. Farrelly, *Anti-Catholicism in America*, 2.

34. Note: The English Civil War, the Protectorate, and the "Glorious Revolution" of 1688, all were fomented in part by anti-Catholicism. The 1646 defeat of the Royalists in the English Civil War led to stringent laws banning the establishment of Catholic churches and schools.

Cartoon: "The Hand that Would Rob Us of Our Freedom." Public domain image from *Guardians of Liberty*, 1943 by Bishop Alma Bridwell White, illustrations by Rev. Branford Clarke. Published by the Pillar of Fire Church in Zarephath, NJ. (https://commons.wikimedia.org/wiki/File:Poperob.jpg)

The historian Mark Massa noted three reasons for the near universal prejudice against Catholics in America. First, the antipathy was cultural. From the beginning, American democracy was deeply rooted in Protestantism. Catholicism represented an Old World faith embedded in monarchies such as in France and Spain. Moreover, memories of Catholic persecution in England under Bloody Mary and the Gunpowder Plot were fresh.[35] A

---

35. Mary I or "Mary Tudor," a daughter of Henry VIII and Catherine of Aragon, ascended to the throne of England in 1553. A devout Roman Catholic, she reinstated Catholicism as the official state religion of Britain, an act which would be reversed just five years later when her sister Elizabeth I became queen. During Mary's reign, the English Parliament passed anti-heresy laws by which Protestants refusing to convert to Catholicism could be burned at the stake. In total, 283 people died and Mary was given the sobriquet "Bloody Mary," although she herself had never favored forced conversions. The "Gunpowder Plot" came fifty years later, a continuation of the animosity between English Catholics and Protestant. In 1605 conspirators under the leadership of one Guy Fawkes (1570–1606) attempted to blow up the British Parliament with thirty-six barrels of gunpowder in hopes of restoring Catholicism as the national church.

second cause, according to Massa, went to the nature of Catholicism itself. As the War for Independence had demonstrated, Americans valued their independence, both political and spiritual. Calvinism stressed personal freedom to study and interpret Scripture and Americans were deeply suspicious of an institution and a pope that might limit that freedom. A third cause for enmity was intellectual. The Church of Rome had historically been resistant to scientific exploration and the free exchange of ideas, both of which were fundamental pillars of the Enlightenment.[36]

Anti-Catholic sentiment was seen as practically a requirement to be truly British and colonial New Englanders were proud to say, "they were just as [English] as anyone who'd been born and raised in London."[37] Seven of the original thirteen colonies had some variety of anti-Catholic legislation. Persons of the Catholic faith were often denied the right to vote or to hold public office. In Massachusetts, Irish immigrants were often forced to adopt English surnames to hide their Catholic roots. In 1647 it was decreed that "any Jesuit or priest coming within the colony was to be banished and, if he return, executed."[38] During the colonial period American Catholics were viewed with suspicion by the Protestant majority. It was maintained that they were in league with the French in the French and Indian War (1754–1763). In general, they were thought to be enemies of liberty and patriotism, and New York City held an annual Guy Fawkes Parade in which the pope was burned in effigy.[39] Anti-Catholicism has even been cited as a justification for the War of Independence. The so-called Intolerable Acts passed by the British Parliament in 1774 included a guarantee to residents of Quebec that they be able to practice their Catholic faith openly. That was viewed by many Americans, including members of the Continental Congress, as an indication that George III intended to "establish the Romish religion and IDOLATRY" throughout North America.[40]

Anti-papist views, of course, continued throughout the nineteenth century. In 1827, a council of Episcopal bishops published a pastoral letter warning of papist perils. In the years following, over thirty Protestant newspapers and journals were in circulation, most of which featured articles

---

Fawkes was hung on January 31, 1606, and November 5 came to be celebrated as "Guy Fawkes Day" with a symbolic burning of Fawkes's effigy.

36. Massa, *Anti-Catholicism in America*, 7.
37. Farrelly, *Anti-Catholicism*, 9.
38. Massa, *Anti-Catholicism in America*, 19.
39. O'Donnell, *Jesuits in the American Colonies*.
40. Farrelly, *Anti-Catholicism*, 69–71.

"devoted to fighting the idolatry, cruelty, and blasphemy of the Church of Rome."[41]

In 1834 the British writer Harriet Martineau, on a two-year tour of the United States, was shocked at the amount of religious intolerance: Presbyterian clergy preaching hatred, convents burned, and nuns banished.

> The question "where is thy faith?" might reasonably have been put to the Presbyterian clergyman who preached three long denunciations against the Catholics in Boston, the Sunday before the burning of the Charlestown convent.[42]

Martineau was likely referring to a fiery sermon delivered by none other than Lyman Beecher, in which he declared that "the principles of this corrupt church are adverse to our free institutions from the contempt and hostility they feel towards all Protestants."[43] In response to Beecher's preaching, the next night an angry mob made up largely of Scots Irish workmen descended upon the Ursuline Convent, burning it to the ground.[44]

Music and Roman Catholics from the Eighteenth through the Early Nineteenth Century

The Roman Catholic presence in North America grew from a tiny minority population, mostly in Maryland and around Philadelphia in the eighteenth century. In 1633 Cecil Calvert (1605–1675), an English Roman Catholic nobleman, presented the largely Puritan English Parliament with a pamphlet entitled, *Objections answered touching Mariland* [sic]. Calvert's goal was to establish a colony "providing refuge for English Catholics" and to bring the Christian faith to native Americans living in the region.[45] In the last months of that year, Calvert and a small contingent of Jesuits set sail from Britain in two ships he had purchased and renamed as *The Ark of London* and *The Dove of Maryland*.

The earliest reference to music in the colony involved a baptismal ceremony in which the Tayac Chief Kittamaquud was confirmed as a Christian.

> [O]n July 5, 1640, when he was sufficiently instructed in the mysteries of the faith, he was solemnly baptized in a little

---

41. Farrelly, *Anti-Catholicism*, 151–52.
42. Martineau, *Society in America*, 226.
43. Massa, *Anti-Catholicism in America*, 24–25.
44. Massa, *Anti-Catholicism in America*, 24–25.
45. Grimes, "Emergence of Catholic Music," 7. Robert R. Grimes, a Jesuit priest with a PhD in ethnomusicology, is a dean emeritus of Fordham University.

chapel, which, after the manner of the Indians, he has erected out of bark for that purpose and for Divine worship. . . . In the afternoon the King and Queen were united in matrimony after the Christian rite; then the great Cross was erected, in carrying which to its destined place the King, the Governor, Secretary, and others, lent their shoulders and hands; two of us in the meantime—Fathers White and Gravener—chanted before them the Litany of Loretto in honour of the Blessed Virgin.[46]

Congregational singing was not a dominant aspect of Roman Catholic worship in colonial America. What was sung was handed down through oral tradition. Bishop Benedict Fenwick (1782–1846), bishop of Boston from 1782 until his death, was a descendant of the original Jesuits who settled in Maryland. In his journal he provided these notes regarding a typical Catholic baptism in late eighteenth-century colonial Maryland:

> The Litany of the Blessed Virgin was usually sung, in which all the people joined, by way of preparation for the ceremony. Then followed Baptism; and after this, Mass. During the celebration of this august mystery, a number of hymns and canticles were sung. Some of these were translated into the Indian tongue for the better understanding of the converts, who were not backward in joining in the chorus.[47]

The "Litany of the Blessed Virgin" or, as it was often called, the "Litany of Loreto" included a repeating *kyrie* refrain sung by the worshippers. Fenwick included this harmonization in his *Catholic Church Service Book* of 1833.

"Kyrie eleison" (Litany of Loreto) as realized in *The Catholic Church Service Book* (Boston: Bishop Benedict Fenwick, 1833). According to Grimes, variations on this tune appeared in most early Catholic service book collections including #17c in John Aitken, *A Compilation of the Litanies and Vespers, Hymns, and Anthems as They Are Sung in the Catholic Church* (Philadelphia, 1788).

---

46. Acosta, "Annual Letter of 1639," 378.
47. Fenwick, "Brief Account," 169.

Jesuit priests/missionaries soon gave up their idealistic plan to evangelize the native Americans and turned their attention to Catholics of European descent living in Maryland, Pennsylvania, and New York.

The circumstances did not lend themselves to elaborate, attention-getting worship celebrations nor did the far-flung separation between Catholic communities. Priests were required to travel between gatherings on horseback and to bring with them all ritual necessities. Mass was often celebrated in homes without music. The singing of one verse of the *Veni creator spiritus* before the preaching of a sermon became a tradition that spread to the other colonies. While there is little documentation beyond this regarding Catholic music in eighteenth-century Maryland, Robert Grimes postulates that it must have been simple (easily learned and repetitive), unaccompanied, produced by amateurs, and orally transmitted.[48]

With the Treaty of Paris in 1783 ending the American Revolution, the punitive anti-Catholic British laws no longer applied. While prejudices still existed, Roman Catholics were free to establish churches and a denominational hierarchy in the United States of America. Maryland's Catholic population was the largest of all the colonies. The colony's missionaries and clergy petitioned Pope Pius VI to appoint Father John Carroll as Superior of the Missions and, in 1790, as bishop. The Diocese of Baltimore became the first Catholic diocese in the United States.

From the founding of the colony, Pennsylvania's Quakers had tended to be tolerant of practicing Catholics and did not forbid the establishment of a Catholic parish and house of worship in Philadelphia. Old St. Joseph's Church, established in 1733, was for many years the only place in the English colonies where Catholics could worship openly. The church had to be enlarged in 1757 and a second chapel, Old St. Mary's, was built in 1763. (By 1808 the city had four Catholic churches.) The organist Stephen Forrage, a friend of Benjamin Franklin and a skilled performer on Franklin's "Glass Harmonica," was at St. Mary's Church. During the Revolutionary War, Philadelphia was the capital of the "nation to be." With France and Spain—both Catholic countries—as important colonial allies, worship services at St. Mary's Chapel were attended by the French and Spanish ambassadors as well as John and Abigail Adams, and George Washington himself. A *Te Deum* sung at St. Mary's on July 4, 1779, was described as follows:

> [The] throbbing of the sweet-toned violins, a rustle of silk as the congregation arose to its feet . . . the first notes of the "Te Deum laudamus" were intoned, by the celebrant at the altar.

---

48. Grimes, "Emergence of Catholic Music," 27.

The organ's opulent tones and the swelling volume of the goodly choristers rejoiced in the melody.[49]

From the 1750s forward, church music in Philadelphia's Anglican/Episcopal churches had been led by gentleman amateurs.[50] Francis Hopkinson (1737–1791), designer of the first official American currency, signer of the Declaration of Independence, musician, and composer, was organist at Christ Church. The English organist and composer Raynor Taylor (1747–1825) was at St. Peter's Church. It would soon become evident that a professional church musician was needed to advance Roman Catholic music in the City of Brotherly Love. Appearing on the scene to fill that need was Benjamin Carr.

Benjamin Carr

The arrival of Benjamin Carr (1768–1831)—pioneer of American music publishing, distinguished composer, and church musician, who immigrated to the United States in 1793 and took up residence in Philadelphia—was auspicious indeed. Born in London of a musical family, Carr studied with Samuel Arnold, then the organist at Westminster Abbey and Charles Wesley Jr., son of the famous hymnwriter and cleric. Before coming to America, he had already established a favorable reputation in London musical circles as the principal tenor and harpsichordist at the Academy of Ancient Music, and had even composed a pastoral opera, *Philander and Silvia, or Love Crown'd at Last*, which debuted at Sadler's Wells in 1792.

---

49. Higginson, "John Aitken's Compilation," 73.

50. The concept of the "gentleman amateur" arose in the late eighteenth century in Britain and America to describe men of excellent education and social breeding who contributed to the arts and literature as personal enjoyment rather than as a professional pursuit. It reached its high point in the Victorian era. See Stone, "Deconstructing the Gentleman Amateur."

Benjamin Carr.
Public domain image. (https://commons.wikimedia.org/wiki/File:Benjamin_Carr_by_John_Sartain.jpg)

In Philadelphia, Carr soon rose to the forefront of musical life in the city. Initially he worked closely with Raynor Taylor and Alexander Reinagle,[51] composing for and performing in the theater. When St. Augustine's Catholic Church was opened in 1801, Carr was tapped to be its organist and director of music. The church had a manuals-only pipe organ built by local organ builder Charles Taws. The choice of Carr was surprising since he was a committed Anglican/Episcopalian and was associated with the theater, but it gave St. Augustine's one of Philadelphia's most distinguished musicians.[52]

Carr immediately set about training a choir and, often in collaboration with Raynor Taylor, composing music for it as well. This included a *Mass for Three Voices*, which was performed by St. Augustine's choir for Christmas 1804. The mass would be published in a landmark collection of music for Catholic worship, *Masses, Vespers, Hymns, Psalms, Anthems and Motetts* (sic.) *composed, selected and arranged for the use of the Catholic Churches in the United States of America* (Baltimore: J Carr, 1805). Prior to

---

51. Raynor Taylor (1747–1825) and his younger student, Alexander Reinagle (1756–1809), were both British emigrants who were prominent in Philadelphia musical circles during the late eighteenth and early nineteenth centuries. Both were very active as teachers, composers, and theatrical impresarios. Taylor was organist at St. Peter's Church from 1795 until 1813.

52. Grimes, "Grand Selection," 21.

Carr's collection, the *only* previous collection of Catholic music for worship published in America was John Aitken's *A Compilation of the Litanies and Vespers Hymns and Anthems as They are Sung in the Catholic Church* (Philadelphia, 1787). Carr detested the Aitken collection:

> ... that dull, disagreeable, horrid monotony of all singing the same tone, alike disgusting to the hearers, and disgraceful to those who indulge in so idle, vulgar, and childish a method.[53]

Carr's *Masses, Vespers* bore little comparison with Aitken's, and the fact that Carr's *Mass in Three Voices* included music composed in Philadelphia set it apart.

In December 1807 Benjamin Carr was employed as organist/choirmaster at nearby St. Mary's Chapel while continuing to serve at St. Augustine's. Church records indicate that St. Mary's trustees, while aware of his commitments, felt desperately in need of the leadership Benjamin Carr could bring to their choir program.

> Resolved and agreed to that Mr. Benj'n Carr be ... hereby appointed Organist of St. Mary's Church, and that the whole and intire [sic] Arrangement, Management, and Conducting the Choir as he may Judge most proper for the benefit of the Church, be solely rested in him, also with power to Appoint or reject any of the members composeing [sic] the Choir heretofore or hereafter.[54]

Carr accepted the position but serving two churches simultaneously presented problems. He apparently chose to prioritize his work in worship at St. Augustine's on most Sunday mornings, while serving St. Mary's primarily as a choir trainer. To aid in the latter, Carr visualized having the choirs of the two churches rehearse together in preparation for a gala concert, hoping in the process to build the confidence and musicality of the St. Mary's singers.

The 1810 concert was billed as "A Grand Selection of Sacred Music" and was intended to be "the most sophisticated concert the city had ever seen or heard."[55] For it Carr amassed a fifty-three-piece orchestra and thirty-four singers. Choruses from Handel's *Messiah* and Haydn's *Creation* were sung. A writer in the *Federal Republican and Commercial Gazette* enthused:

> [W]hen the full Band and Chorus thundered harmony upon our astonished ears, then it was that fear and joy, hope and

---

53. Carr, *Masses, Vespers, Litanies*, vi.
54. *Minute Book of St. Mary's Church*, 381.
55. Grimes, "Grand Selection," 31.

reverential awe, gratitude and thanksgiving, had each, in their turn, full and entire possession of every individual in the congregation.[56]

The concert was a major success, though it did not yield a marked improvement in the St. Mary's choir as Carr had hoped. Discouraged, he wrote to Michael Egan, pastor at St. Mary's, "After a fair trial of two years and a half and gradual decrease in members and talent, my best hope lay in the Oratorio—I must confess tho' it was my *last* . . . my *best* hope of renovating the choir . . ."[57]

Benjamin Carr continued his service at St. Augustine's where his choir was known as one of best in the country. More repertoire from Handel oratorios was added, and a second "Grand Selection" concert was staged in 1814, this time with "over a hundred performers." He remained at St. Augustine's to the time of his death in 1831. Unfortunately, as a result of anti-Catholic violence, St. Augustine's Church was burned to the ground on May 8, 1844, and all records of Carr's activities in the 1820s were lost.

Carr was an Episcopalian, not a Roman Catholic, in an era when Episcopalians had yet to embrace ritualism. His approach to building a music ministry at St. Augustine's and St. Mary's was not by way of Catholic ritual but by choral performance. In doing so, he did much to raise the standard of music in Philadelphia, but also set a performance-based rather than worship-based example, which Roman Catholic church musicians would strive to emulate for the rest of the century.

---

56. Grimes, "Grand Selection," 31.
57. Grimes, "Grand Selection," 32.

Chapter 5

A MIGHTY SHOUT!

Frontier Revivalism, Shape-Note Singing, and the Second Great Awakening

"I look upon all the world as my parish; thus far I mean, that in whatever part of it I am, I judge it meet, right, and my bounden duty to declare unto all that are willing to hear, the glad tidings of salvation."

JOHN WESLEY IN HIS *JOURNAL* ENTRY FOR JUNE 11, 1739[1]

We now turn to the frontier revivalism that saw its peak in the early years of the nineteenth century[2] and a new singing school tradition that

---

1. Wesley, *Journal,* 74.

2. The history of American evangelical revivalism includes several periods loosely referred to as "awakenings." The "Great Awakening" of the 1730s and '40s encompasses the ministries of George Whitefield and Jonathan Edwards, as well as the beginnings of Methodism in the American colonies. The period from 1790 to the 1840s is often referred to as the "Second Great Awakening" and includes the evangelical ministries of Lyman Beecher, Charles G. Finney, and the camp meeting movement exemplified by Cane Ridge and Gasper River. The period from the Prayer Meeting Revival of 1857–1859 through the revivalist activities of Dwight Moody, through the post-World War I preaching of Billy Sunday to Billy Graham in the 1950s is generally referred to as the "Third Great Awakening." The Jesus Movement of the 1960s and the Contemporary Christian movement that followed has been referred to as a "Fourth Great Awakening." Frontier revivalism of the "Second Great Awakening" will be the focus of this chapter.

grew up beside it. Both had theological and musical ramifications for music ministry in the church.

Why, one might ask, devote a chapter to revivalism and music-making on the frontier, activities largely outside the church and nonsectarian? *It is my feeling that revivalism on the American frontier for the first time demonstrated the spiritual power of congregational singing as an act of corporate worship and brought awareness to the need for trained musical leadership for populist sacred music as it began to filter into rural worship in the South and West.* The singing was simple, spontaneous, and creative, an outpouring by worshippers of diverse backgrounds coming together and vitally involved in the act of sung praise.

At the beginning of the Second Great Awakening in the 1790s the dominant religious denominations were the Presbyterian, Congregationalist, and Episcopal. Increasing in number and influence were Baptists, Methodists, and evangelical breakaways. In the early decades of the nineteenth century, the evangelists Lyman Beecher (1775–1863) and Charles Grandison Finney (1792–1875) introduced a "new school Calvinism"[3] that saw revivalism as the key to successfully evangelizing America. Beecher's revivalism was focused on spiritual renewal within established Presbyterian and Congregational churches. Finney's, on the other hand, was outward focused and less concerned with rigid adherence to the worship practices of the mainline denominations. Finney had been sternly criticized for worship innovations such as dramatic delivery of sermons from outside the pulpit, use of "mourner's benches,"[4] more participation by women, and music provided by choirs or professional singers—things he referred to as "new measures." He encouraged any innovation that might invigorate the worshippers he ministered to both in and outside the established church and addressed his critics in an 1835 lecture delivered at Chatham Street Chapel (predecessor to the Broadway Tabernacle).

> In discoursing from these words, I design to show that God has established no particular system of measures to be employed and invariably adhered to in promoting religion . . . Under Jewish dispensation, there were particular forms enjoined and prescribed by God himself, from which it was not lawful to depart . . . But it was never *so* under the gospel. When Christ

---

3. Finney was nominally a Presbyterian.

4. The "mourner's bench" or "anxious seat" was actually a concept dating back to John Wesley's Methodism. It was a bench or pew set aside for individuals seeking a conversion experience to gather, confess sins, and receive forgiveness leading to sanctification. In mammoth camp meetings like Cane Ridge the concept was expanded to a large corral separating mourners from other worshippers.

came, the ceremonial or typical dispensation was abrogated, because the design of those forms was fulfilled, and therefore themselves of no further use. THE GOSPEL was then preached as the appointed means of promoting religion; and it was left to the discretion of the church to determine, from time to time, what measures shall be adopted, and what forms pursued, in giving the gospel its power.

We are left in the dark as to the measures which were pursued by the apostles . . . We do not know how many times they sung [*sic*] and how many times they prayed in public worship, nor even whether they sung or prayed at all . . . And when the apostles preached, . . . their commission was, "Go and preach the gospel, and disciple all nations" . . . No person can pretend to get any set of forms or particular directions as to measures out of this commission. Do it—the best way you can—ask wisdom from God—use the faculties he has given you—seek the direction of the Holy Spirit—go forward and do it. This was their commission.[5]

From a historical, theological, and liturgical standpoint, Finney's words were providential. In them, there was affirmation for the freewheeling worship of the camp meetings springing up across the frontier. Finney's endorsement of the freedom to do worship "the best way you can" under the "direction of the Holy Spirit" would be reflected in populist worship throughout the nineteenth and twentieth centuries—from Moody and Sankey through Billy Graham and the megachurch movement.

While important, Charles Grandison Finney and Lyman Beecher were northern preachers/theologians. The greatest manifestation of the Second Great Awakening, however, would be in lands yet to be fully settled beyond the boundaries of New England and the eastern seaboard. The rush to populate fertile land in the South and to settle the frontier would end once and for all the dominance of Congregationalism and Puritanism across the American landscape.

---

5. Finney, *Lectures on Revivals of Religion*, 232–33. One area where Finney and Beecher differed was on the subject of congregational singing. Finney supported Bradbury's work to build the large choir at the Broadway Tabernacle and designed the platform with its rear wall dominated by the organ pipe facade and choir area. That being said, hymn and psalm singing were de-emphasized in services he presided over. Lyman Beecher, on the other hand, gave his enthusiastic support to Lowell Mason's efforts to encourage congregational singing in Boston.

A Mighty Shout!

Roots of Frontier Revivalism

Throughout the eighteenth century there had been a constant push to expand to new territories. By 1750, colonists had settled all of the tidewater region, the eastern portions of Virginia, Maryland, and the Carolinas, and had also begun to spread out to the west. By the end of the French and Indian War in 1763 this westward expansion had reached the Blue Ridge Mountains and a few adventurous colonial traders had traversed the Appalachian Mountains.

The size and diversity of this mass migration would be of historic proportions. Roads were choked with wagons, loaded to overflowing with families and supplies.

> Old settlers in central New York declared that they had never seen so many teams and sleighs loaded with women and children and household goods passing through to the West, as in the very midst of the winter of 1814. From Lancaster, Pennsylvania, came the report that a hundred families had passed through that town in one week; at Zanesville, Ohio, fifty wagons crossed the Muskingum in one day. Nor was this stream of population movement sporadic; it continued day after day, week after week, month after month, and year after year.[6]

Initially many Catholics took up residence in the Maryland back country, while others—Catholics and Protestants alike—settled in Pennsylvania with its religious tolerance and abundant farmland. Unfortunately, by the 1780s land in those areas was becoming scarce and prohibitively expensive, and so for many the trek continued south or west. German settlers formed a large community in the Shenandoah Valley of Virginia. Many Scotch-Irish or "Ulster Scots" took up residence in the mountains of western North Carolina. A nonconformist and fiercely independent religious faith was common to most all of these pioneer settlers.

Presbyterians, Baptists, and Methodists, because of their shared evangelical bent, would exert the greatest influence in the spread of Christianity during these early years of frontier revivalism. Presbyterians took the lead in the first great camp meetings at Gasper River and Cane Ridge and, no doubt, had much to do with introducing the concept on the frontier.[7] The

---

6. Sweet, *Revivalism in America*, 41.

7. The Presbyterian Church's relationship to camp meetings was complicated. The two principal leaders at Gaspar River and Cane Ridge, Barton Stone and James McGready, were not traditional Presbyterians. McGready's fiery sermons on the wages of sin recalled similar ones of Jonathan Edwards, and yet his confidence that every person could have "new birth" through repentance was decidedly un-Calvinistic. After Cane

Methodists, working in the background at those meetings with their lay preachers and commitment to congregational singing, would ultimately be the group most identified with camp meetings.

The Scots Presbyterians, many of whom were based in western North Carolina, brought with them the tradition of "Holy Fairs." In the sixteenth century, the Protestant reformer John Knox, founder of the Presbyterian Church of Scotland, sought to distance his church from Catholicism. One way he did that was by reimagining the Eucharist with lay participation in the breaking of bread and the sharing of wine. He also hoped to balance more equally the importance of the service of word, corporate prayer, and sacrament where the Eucharist had traditionally been predominant. The sacrament of communion would be celebrated as the climax of a four- to seven-day "Communion Season" or Holy Fair, usually held in the summer months.[8]

> Farmers, workers, domestics, and artisans gathered in camps for a week of worship, self-scrutiny, and socializing. Special sermons prepared believers to approach the Lord's table. Individuals retreated at the end of the day for secret, night-long prayers. Ministers distributed lead tokens to those who deemed themselves fit and ready to commune. In the midst of these intense, introspective rituals, some people had visions, others found assurance, and a few collapsed in the ecstasy of emotional conversion or renewal of their faith.[9]

Enter the Rev. James McGready (1763–1817). While not really the father of the American camp meeting, as some have claimed, McGready was certainly instrumental in organizing the Cane Ridge camp meeting and was one of its most colorful characters. A Presbyterian of British descent, McGready was born in Pennsylvania and received his theological training at Log College in Neshaminy, Pennsylvania, as well as schools in North Carolina. All of McGready's education had an evangelical focus on the necessity of conversion.

In 1796 McGready left North Carolina, probably by the Wilderness Road. After spending a few months in Tennessee, he traveled north to Kentucky, where he was invited to pastor three small congregations in Logan

---

Ridge, the Presbyterian denomination—embarrassed by the emotional excesses and lay preaching—distanced itself from such meetings. Both McGready and Stone would be castigated by the Presbyterian Church for their theological leanings, and Stone would join Alexander Campbell in founding a new denomination, the Disciples of Christ.

8. Curtis, "Scottish Communions, American Revivals," 21.
9. Curtis, "Scottish Communions, American Revivals," 22.

County—Gaspar River, Red River, and Muddy River. There he found souls athirst for the reformed Calvinism of his preaching:

> God declares that we must be converted or be forever damned; that we must be born again, or never enter the kingdom of heaven. But the sinner by his conduct says, God is a liar ... I expect to be saved in a better way; I am for a rational religion, altogether upon philosophical principles, with very little praying and no feeling, one that will take along with it the sinful pleasures of the world, at least upon a polite scale, and that will not expose me to contempt, reproach and persecution, but will be popular among the polite and respectable members of society.[10]

A second important Presbyterian in early years of frontier revivalism and the Cane Ridge camp meeting was Barton W. Stone (1772–1844). Stone was born in Maryland, but his family moved to Virginia when he was five years old. In 1790, Barton enrolled at the Caldwell Log College in Greensboro, North Carolina. It was there that he first heard James McGready preach.

> He rose and looked around the assembly ... Such earnestness—such zeal—such powerful persuasion, enforced by the joys of heaven and miseries of hell, I had never witnessed before. My mind was chained by him ... Never before had I comparatively felt the force of truth. Such was my excitement, that had I been standing, I should have probably sunk to the floor under the impression.[11]

Stone was ordained in Greensboro, North Carolina, in the spring of 1796. In his autobiography he wrote plaintively of his being licensed to preach: "A venerable old father addressed the candidates, standing up together before the Presbytery. After the address, he presented to each of the candidates the Bible ... with this solemn charge, 'Go ye into all the world, and preach the Gospel to every creature' [Mark 16:15]. He [i.e., Stone] took the biblical mandate to heart and soon felt the call to 'seek some distant country.'"[12]

---

10. McGready, "On the Nature and Consequences of Sin," 38.
11. Stone, *Biography of Barton Stone*, 88.
12. Stone, *Biography of Barton Stone* 131.

The First Camp Meetings

In eastern and central Kentucky of 1800 "most of the settlers were ignorant and illiterate."[13] Novelists have romanticized these souls as hardy, self-reliant, and brave. In truth, many were of coarser stock. They were "relatively uncouth, being subject to the brutalizing and almost dehumanizing effects of the wilderness . . . Existing in close proximity to nature did not foster the growth of a benevolence and inward security often imagined by idealists. On the contrary, these early people were encumbered by the constant struggle for survival."[14] There was a definite class structure pitting landed aristocracy against poor homesteaders. "Each group was suspicious of the other and spent the greater part of its energies striving for self-advancement."[15]

Many Kentucky pioneers were unreligious. Some, called "opposers to religion," were openly hostile to the organized church. At the other end of the spectrum were Scotch-Irish Presbyterians who regularly worshipped as a family in their homes.[16] Others, who seemed indifferent to religion, had been active church members in the past but having gotten used to the freedom of the frontier they had fallen away.[17] What all of these pioneers shared was the deadening isolation, the fear of attack, the ravages of nature—inevitable corollaries to frontier life. Clearly there were universal needs as well: to find fellowship and community with far-flung neighbors, to find purpose in the midst of doubts and fears, to recognize and deal with the improprieties so typical of unruly life on the frontier, and—most important—to find hope and affirmation. It was a time ripe for revival!

In June of 1800, James McGready gathered the congregations of his three churches—Gasper River, Muddy River, and Red River—a total of about four hundred people, to conduct a communion season in the Scottish tradition at the Red River Church.[18] It was a four-day event culminating in the celebration of the Eucharist. Thirteen wagonloads of parishioners appeared for the gathering.[19] McGready would recall the scene at Red River:

---

13. Klein, "Public School Music in the State of Kentucky," 12.
14. Klein, "Public School Music in the State of Kentucky," 12–13.
15. Klein, "Public School Music in the State of Kentucky," 12–13.
16. Hiemstra, "Early Frontier Revivalism," 154.
17. Hiemstra, "Early Frontier Revivalism," 154.
18. One is immediately struck with the similarity of Holy Fairs to American camp meetings. All the most prominent leaders of the Cane Ridge event were Presbyterian and had ties to North Carolina with its Scottish heritage. The central and western parts of the state had been the scene of revivalist activity since the 1790s.
19. Ferguson, *Organizing to Beat the Devil*, 125.

> A dreadful, striking solemnity overspread the whole assembly—the multitude were all in tears—awakened sinners were struck with such keen, piercing convictions, that many of them fell to the ground, and roared out in extreme anguish, "What shall I do to be saved?" Some of God's children were filled with a sense of the love and goodness of God in Christ to their souls, like bottles filled with new wine, till their bodily strength was almost gone. It was truly affecting to see little boys and girls, of nine, ten, and twelve years of age, and some younger, lying prostrate on the ground, weeping, praying and crying for mercy, like condemned criminals at the place of execution.[20]

With its success, McGready scheduled a similar event in July at the Gasper River Church. This time, an enormous crowd appeared: twenty-two wagons with hundreds more arriving on foot.[21] Many brought camping gear while others slept in their wagons. Each day, there was continuous preaching from morning until dusk provided by McGready and two other prominent Presbyterian clergy, William Hodge and William McGee. Other similar gatherings began to pop up throughout the next year, and the stage was set for what has been called the greatest event of its kind.

Meanwhile, Pastor Barton Stone had received a call in 1798 from the Transylvania Presbytery in Kentucky to be pastor of the Cane Ridge and Concord churches. Arriving there, he found his congregations to be listless and apathetic.[22] In the spring of 1800, he heard of the faith gatherings in Kentucky and Tennessee being led by James McGready and other Presbyterian clergy. Curious, he attended what he heard called a "camp meeting" at the Gasper River Church in Logan County. What he encountered struck him as "new and passing strange. It baffled description."[23] He witnessed violent physical manifestations as well as worshippers rising up and shouting their deliverance.

> With astonishment did I hear men women and children declaring the wonderful works of God, and the glorious mysteries of the Gospel. Their appeals were solemn, heart-penetrating, bold and free.[24]

After the Logan County revival, Stone returned to his Cane Ridge and Concord churches with a new fire in his vision. He preached his Sabbath sermon

---

20. "1800 Revival at Red River and Gasper River."
21. Ferguson, *Organizing to Beat the Devil*, 125.
22. Stone, *Biography of Barton Stone*, 153.
23. Stone, *Biography of Barton Stone*, 154.
24. Stone, *Biography of Barton Stone*, 154.

on the very text from Mark's Gospel which so impressed him during his ordination:

> I ascended the pulpit and gave a relation of what I had seen and heard; then opened my Bible and preached from these words: "Go ye into all the world and preach the gospel to every creature. He that believeth and is baptized shall be saved . . ." The congregation was affected with awful solemnity, and many returned home weeping.[25]

A five-day prayer vigil was organized (Stone referred to it as a "protracted meeting"). "The whole country seemed to be in motion," he recalled. ". . . Multitudes of all denominations attended . . . Party spirit, abashed, shrunk away."[26] The time was right, Stone decided, to organize an even more magnificent camp meeting.[27] The result was an immense and historic gathering on a strip of land between two creeks in north central Kentucky—the place, a little-known postal way station called Cane Ridge.

---

25. Stone, *Biography of Barton Stone*, 36.

26. Stone, *Biography of Barton Stone*, 37.

27. While ordained as a Presbyterian minister, Stone, even before Cane Ridge, had developed serious doubts regarding Calvinist positions on total depravity, unconditional election, and predestination, as well as more generally accepted beliefs such as the Trinity. "Calvinism," he wrote, "is among the heaviest clogs on Christianity in the world . . ." (Stone, *Biography of Barton Stone*, 30). "[I had] believed and taught that mankind was so depraved that they could do nothing acceptable to God, til His Spirit, by some physical, almighty, and mysterious power . . . had regenerated the heart . . . From reading and meditating upon it, I became convinced that God did love the whole world. And that the reason He did not save all was because of their unbelief." (Stone, *Biography of Barton Stone*, 33). In the years after Cane Ridge, he would break completely with the Presbyterian denomination, embrace an Arminian view of theology, and become one of the founders of the Christian Church (Disciples of Christ).

A Mighty Shout!

Cane Ridge, August 6–13, 1801

"Camp-Meeting"
Lithograph drawn on stone by Hugh Bridport (ca. 1829). Public domain. Library of Congress Control #96510018; Digital ID ds 03095//hdl.loc.gov/loc.pnp/ds.03095
https://www.loc.gov/resource/ds.03095/.

It was probably the largest revival event of the nineteenth century and, for future generations, the event most associated with the term "camp meeting." It encompassed all of the most colorful aspects of the human condition, from examples of profound spirituality to revelations of scandalous excess. It spawned an ongoing debate played out in newspapers and periodicals between those who viewed Cane Ridge as the miraculous beginning of a new Jerusalem, and those who condemned it as a sham and cheap grace bestowed on the unsophisticated and vulnerable.

During the first week of August 1801, masses descended upon the Cane Ridge Meeting House near Lexington, Kentucky for a week of evangelical preaching climaxing in the service of communion. While it is unlikely more than ten thousand could have been on the grounds at any one time, it was estimated by militia policing the site that from twenty to thirty thousand people were in attendance over the course of the week.[28] Stone

---

28. The entire population of the state of Kentucky in 1801 was about 220,000.

recalled in his memoirs that "The roads were literally crowded with wagons, carriages, horsemen and footmen … Many had come from Ohio and other distant parts."[29] Every aspect—the encampment set-up, the preaching, the bodily manifestations of worshippers in the throes of "enthusiasm," and the music—was covered in detail in the press and written about by participants.

One of the striking things about the Cane Ridge camp meeting was the breaking down, at least temporarily, of many barriers existing in American life and, in particular, the American church at that time.

> There was a remarkable degree of cooperation between Methodists, Baptists, and Presbyterians, all united in the goal of evangelism. Factional differences were set aside. Women as well as men were urged to join in exhorting the crowds at Cane Ridge, a full 25 years before Finney scandalized proper northern churches by doing the same in New York State. Perhaps most poignant in light of the sectional enmity just beyond the horizon, Blacks were allowed "almost" equal participation.[30]

Charles Ferguson, who studied Cane Ridge and dozens of revivals afterward, wrote:

> Among the first sights to catch the eye of a voluble observer at Cane Ridge was that of an assembly of Black people being exhorted by a man of their own color, some of whom appeared deeply convicted and others converted. There was room for all on the grounds under the stars. In both slaveholding and non-slaveholding states and territories, Blacks were allowed to attend the meetings, setting up their own camp behind the preacher's rostrum.[31]

---

29. Stone, *Biography of Barton Stone*, 38.

30. From the mid-seventeenth century on, fear of a slave revolt among whites in the South shaped many aspects of the relationship been slaves and their masters. There was a general concern that a Christian belief system might encourage those in bondage to seek freedom. As a result, where worship participation was permitted, Blacks were usually expected to attend their master's church. There, seated in a restricted area, they could expect to hear only messages favoring their continued enslavement. Slaves were usually forbidden from worshipping independently or preaching. Cane Ridge, and the wave of revivalism following it, did encourage some slaveholders to relax these prohibitions, however fear of rebellion was only to intensify, fueled by the Nat Turner Slave Rebellion in 1831. Turner himself was a preacher and as a result, several southern states enacted more draconian laws limiting free speech and outlawing the teaching of reading and writing to slaves. In light of the above, the camp meetings of the early nineteenth century were a remarkable ray of light in an otherwise very dark period in American history.

31. Ferguson, *Organizing to Beat the Devil*, 129. Sadly, the racial inclusivity at Cane

The historian Charles Johnson described the scene as follows:

> Because of the close proximity, their services often merged with those of the whites, adding no little to the general confusion and emotional excitement. The Negro housing area, with its crazy-quilt tents after the fashion of Joseph's coat, was a picturesque affair.[32]

On the last day of the encampment, the barriers were torn down as a ritual act of unity allowing "the two peoples to join together in a song festival and 'marching ceremony.'"[33] That the separation between the two groups was not a permanent one says something regarding the egalitarian soul of the camp meeting.

Cane Ridge and many of the camp meeting revivals that followed it were four-day affairs, usually beginning on Thursday and climaxing with communion served on Sunday. Due to the success of Cane Ridge, efforts immediately followed to improve on and systematize the camp meeting and numerous manuals were issued.

Camp Meeting Song

In camp meeting parlance, singing was one of several activities referred to as "exercises." It was not seen as a performance medium or as a pleasant entertainment to occupy the time, nor was it viewed as simply a way to inject variety into a long and intense period of worship and prayer. Rather, the revivalists saw singing as essential if there was to be full physical, intellectual, and spiritual involvement of attendees. Both the singing and its leadership had a spontaneity to it. It was led, depending on the situation, by preacher, exhorter, or simply by someone in a group joined in prayer. None were professional musicians.

The leadership at Cane Ridge, as we have seen, was largely Presbyterian, but many Methodists were assisting, and singing was a central part of their heritage.

> They succeeded in introducing their own stirring hymns familiarly, though incorrectly, entitled "Wesley's Hymns"; and, as books were scarce, the few that were attainable were cut up, and the leaves distributed, so that all in turn might learn them by

---

Ridge did not carry over to later meetings. Typically, an area, set apart with a plank partition, was reserved for Blacks to camp and worship.

32. Johnson, *Frontier Campmeeting*, 46.
33. Johnson, *Frontier Campmeeting*, 46.

heart. By those who have ever reflected how great are the effects of music, and how probable it is that the ballads of a nation exert more influence than their laws, this will be acknowledged to have been of itself a potent engine to give predominance to the Methodists, and to disseminate their peculiar sentiments.[34]

The singing was likely almost always in unison and without instrumental accompaniment of any kind. There were no hymnals or songbooks. Leaders, if they had any resource at all, might have had a pocket "songster." It was a little book with texts only containing material thought appropriate for revival use. Music chosen had to be easily and spontaneously communicated to a large gathering of people from far-flung places and differing experiences.

Louis Benson, one of the foremost hymnologists of the twentieth century, wrote that spontaneous song was a marked characteristic of camp meetings. "Rough and irregular couplets or stanzas were concocted out of Scripture phrases and everyday speech with liberal interspersing of hallelujahs and refrains. Such ejaculatory hymns were frequently started by an excited auditor during the preaching, and taken up by the throng, until the meeting dissolved into a 'singing ecstasy' . . ."[35]

To do this effectively, some variation on the age-old call-and-response approach was required. Those already accustomed to the lining out of hymns and psalms in worship would have been already comfortable with it, and others could easily fall in behind them. Repetition was also essential. It facilitated quick learning, and with each repeat of a passage, the fervor of the singers was increased. Melodies were chosen on the fly from popular and folk melodies many in attendance would know.

---

34. Davidson, *History of the Presbyterian Church*, 141. By "Wesley's Hymns," Davidson is referring to the *Pocket Hymnbook*, 23rd ed., a songster published in Philadelphia in 1800.

35. Benson, *English Hymn*, 292.

"Together, Let Us Sweetly Live (Bound for the Land of Canaan)." Melody line as it appears in no. 100 of *The Mozart Collection of Sacred Music,* Elam Ives, ed. (New York: Pain & Burgess, 1846).

A leader would sing a stanza of a line or two. The melody would be familiar enough that some could join in. Then, what Dr. Ellen Jane Lorenz Porter referred to as a "stanzaic extension" would be added, the melodic material drawn from what had already been sung, and this would be repeated. By now, all were joining in. A variation on this was what Lorenz Porter called the "interlinear refrain." This is an interjection of easily learned material unrelated to the stanza being sung: "Hallelujah," "Glory, glory," etc.[36]

> The song leader and the congregation form the two structural elements of the performing group. The leader guides the progress of the song and introduces the verses in the order he *(or she)* chooses, while the congregation responds to him by picking up his cues and singing the rest of the verses he begins (if they know it), and providing the refrains at the end of lines . . .
>
> Historical accounts tell us that this was not only the way spiritual songs were learned, but also the way they were created—new verses and new tunes being assembled on the spot with congregational refrains liberally applied as the glue to hold the entire structure together.[37]

---

36. Lorenz, "Treasure of Campmeeting Spirituals," 133.
37. Caswell, "Social and Moral Music," 70.

To maximize group participation, the person leading would often add an easily learned refrain or chorus at the end of each or selected stanzas. The text for the chorus could be drawn from the opening stanza or be a completely independent exclamation of praise or faith. This component, called the "camp meeting chorus," while not used universally, is the characteristic most frequently cited by hymnologists.

At this point it must be repeated that camp meeting singing was a classic *oral* tradition, spontaneous music created as needed at a particular moment in time.[38] It was not written down at the time of its origins, and so much of what we know has been intuited from recollections of people who were there. We do know that many such songs were roughly cobbled together to serve a purpose. When no longer needed, they were forgotten and, perhaps deservedly, have vanished from memory.

We cannot depend on published tunebooks, though they are frequently cited as sources for camp meeting melodies, as an indication of how they might have been sung. John Wyeth's *Repository of Sacred Music, Part Second* (1813), for example, drew melodies from the camp meeting tradition, but we have no way of knowing if he actually ever attended a camp meeting. He likely acquired the tunes second- or thirdhand. The two-, three-, and four-voice settings of these songs, important as they are in their own right, are *arrangements* created for people who read or were learning to read music. They are not what the songs would have sounded like in their original format, sung by people in unison in the throes of evangelistic ecstasy, most of whom probably could not read music. Indeed, were the tunes ever sung the same way twice? It is unlikely.[39]

Baptists and Revivalism on the Frontier

The Baptists gave critical leadership in the development of revivalism in the rural South and on the frontier. They embraced the evangelical zeal

---

38. Worship music, sung and experienced orally rather than notated and read from the printed page, is a significant aspect of our American sacred music heritage that tends to be passed over or de-emphasized by church music historians. One can only understand the improvisational component needed to sing camp meeting hymnody and the shape-note tunes that followed with a realization of its origin in an oral tradition. The same is true for the African American spiritual and wealth of music descended from it—all born out of an oral tradition that mixed elements from both Africa and the new world.

39. That being said, we are fortunate to be able to study copies of some of the words-only "songsters" many a preacher carried in his saddle bag. We also can refer to the 1868 collection *The Revivalist,* which contains the largest, text-only listing of camp meeting choruses from which the song leaders probably drew.

of Pastors McGready and Stone, but refused to share in communion with non-Baptists, a key component of the Methodist and Presbyterian camp meetings. In the background too were long-standing divisions over infant baptism versus believer (or adult) baptism and baptism by immersion. Instead, Baptists had revivals of their own—not cross-denominational camp meetings in the wild, but meetings organized by the Baptist preachers and centered around their new or growing congregations.

Unlike the Presbyterians, the Baptists welcomed lay preachers who had experienced conversion. Theological training was not a requirement. They are often referred to by historians as "farmer preachers" because preaching was often a part-time occupation coupled with farming, mercantile, or some other pursuit. As a result, rather than thinking of evangelism regionally, as we will see with the Methodist circuit riders, they tended to be localized in their thinking. Instead of securing a campground to which worshippers would travel great distances, the Baptists established churches where they were and where they worked. When a preacher moved, it was common for many in the congregation to follow, and thus the "traveling church" was born. Traditionally, these Baptist preachers were the leaders of congregational singing for the communities they led. Notable in John Spencer's *A History of Kentucky Baptists* (1885) is the number of early nineteenth-century preachers known for their singing skills.[40]

A pioneer in the Baptist frontier revival was Pastor Lewis Craig (1737–1825). Craig was called to lead the Upper Spotsylvania Baptist Church near the Rappahannock River in Virginia in 1770. His preaching and evangelical zeal were well received, and the church immediately began to grow exponentially.[41] Finally, in 1781, Craig resolved to move west to Kentucky.

One of the largest of the Baptist revivals was led by the Rev. John Shackleford, who had been one of Craig's disciples and who also made the trek from Virginia west. When Craig elected to leave the pastorate at the South Elkhorn Church, which was near the Kentucky River and just a few miles from Cane Ridge, it was Shackleford he tapped to follow him. The South Elkhorn congregation was small, about 125 members. Between 1800 and 1801, Shackleford's revival at South Elkhorn netted over three hundred new congregants.[42] So successful was the Baptist revival in Kentucky that 113 new churches and nearly five thousand new converts were added in the state.

---

40. Spencer, *Black Hymnody*.
41. Taylor, "Lewis Craig," 82–88.
42. Spencer, *Black Hymnody*, 540.

The Legacy of the Camp Meeting

At the end of the day, aspects of the "'what" and the "how" of camp meeting hymnody remain an intriguing mystery. What we do have is a treasury of folk melodies born out of contagious revivalistic fervor. It is of little use to speculate on how closely the written-out melodies we have inherited resemble the musical outpourings of the camp meeting. For the treasured repertoire bequeathed to us, we are indebted to the inveterate singing masters and tunebook publishers of the South in the early nineteenth century.

Why then was Cane Ridge important beyond its size and aspects of notoriety? Its power and message for the church—and church musicians of the twenty-first century—is in the courage of its leaders to embrace diversity and minister to all in attendance. Musically, I think, we can learn by example from the revivalists' creativity to find and utilize music ideally suited to the time, place, and witness needed. It is certainly important to recognize that the music was integral to the worship and not an interruption.[43]

The historian Ellen Eslinger has written eloquently on the egalitarianism of Cane Ridge:

> The new style of religious worship evident at Cane Ridge in 1801, soon to become known as camp meeting revivalism, profoundly enhanced the sense of fellowship . . . It had the effect of reducing the contrast between rich and poor and creating a special, if temporary, community. Second, the high point of the Cane Ridge proceedings, participation in the sacrament on Sunday, was not restricted to church members but rather open to all. Third, in sharp contrast to contemporary forms of religious worship, the event strived to embrace all society, regardless of denomination or spiritual status.[44]

---

43. The site of the Cane Ridge Revival is now a designated historical site. Stone chose the location simply because the grounds were adjacent to the Cane Ridge Meetinghouse where he pastored. That edifice, built in 1791, still stands. The original meetinghouse had a slave gallery as was typical of many churches of the period. However, Barton Stone viewed slavery as contrary to Christian principles and his congregants supported that view. The Cane Ridge experience proved to be a turning point in Stone's life. He felt that open communion among people of diverse faiths and backgrounds was a powerful witness he was drawn to though it ran counter to the Baptist rigidity around him. Ultimately, he would leave the denomination and help to form a new one. The Cane Ridge Meetinghouse became a founding church for the Disciples of Christ. In 1829, Stone's congregation removed the slave gallery so whites and Blacks had to worship together in the same pews.

44. Eslinger, "Notes on the History of Cane Ridge," 22.

"Lining Out"—An Ancient Tradition Resurfaces

The actual practice of lining out was detailed in chapter 1 and has been described in numerous other studies. It changed little from eighteenth-century colonial New England meetinghouses to the primitive Baptist chapels in rural Georgia and Kentucky of the nineteenth century. For this study, with its focus on music ministry, perhaps the most important thing we have inherited from the old way was its dependence upon a skilled songleader. Over the decades, this individual was give many names—precentor, chorister, deacon, *Vorsinger* in the Pennsylvania Dutch tradition, and singing master—but they all reflected a need for leadership in the music of worship.

In less populated rural areas established churches were predominantly Methodist, Presbyterian, or Baptist. For the Presbyterians, congregational singing tended to be restricted to psalm tunes sung in the old way: in unison, with a precentor. The Baptists and Methodists sang hymns of Watts and others from words-only hymnbooks or "songsters." Congregations, whether singing metrical psalms or hymns, learned them by rote as they were "lined out."[45]

Many hundreds of Scottish Presbyterians had settled in North and South Carolina and Georgia during the eighteenth century. According to Nikos Pappas, in his brilliant and encyclopedic dissertation, *Patterns in the Sacred Music Culture of the American South and West (1700–1820)*,[46] Primitive Baptists and others brought with them a tradition of lining out hymns and psalms, often in an improvisatory manner. Many churches at country crossroads and rural hollows embraced those traditions and still do today, lining out hymns and psalms just as it was done in the days before regular singing. Taken *in toto*, Pappas refers to the practice of lining out and the style of worship music associated with it as "ancient style." He makes the point that the common settlers on the frontier were not ignorant and antiprogressive; rather, they were fiercely determined to retain a musical and spiritual heritage precious to them.

Singing Schools and Shape-Note Hymnody in Pennsylvania and Beyond

The shape note tunebooks and singing schools of the South, which would be a seminal development in the history of American sacred music, were not universally welcomed by church folk. Just as rural New England meetinghouse

---

45. The development of the modern hymnal with music and words on the same page will be discussed in chapter 8: "Music in Post-Civil War America."

46. Pappas, "Patterns in the Sacred Music Culture."

congregants resented the dictates and judgmental attitudes of regular singing proponents a century earlier, so too Primitive Baptists, among others, viewed the singing school as a threat. For them, it challenged their "religious value system"—a system steeped in fundamental reading of Scripture; a system which "compelled them to 'walk in the old paths' and live in the '*old way*.'"⁴⁷

> Thus saith the Lord, Stand ye in the ways, and see, and ask for the old paths, where is the good way, and walk therein, and ye shall find rest for your souls. (Jer 6:16, KJV)

Itinerant singing masters, a New England tradition for years, began springing up farther west in the 1790s, first in Pennsylvania, then in western Maryland, Virginia, Tennessee, and Kentucky. They were to become commonplace throughout the region by 1820 and were extremely popular as a community resource for musical knowledge and fellowship. Schools were established following much the same format as their colonial predecessors but incorporating the new "shape note" or "patent note" systems of notation to facilitate music reading. Unaccompanied singing was the rule.

Thanks to the work of Wiley Hitchcock, Gilbert Chase, Irving Lowens, and others in the mid-twentieth century, the music of colonial tunesmiths has come to be recognized for its unique place in the history of American music. However, when the singing school movement in the urban centers of New England and New York began to wane around 1800, it was not simply transplanted to the South and West. Yes, the music of Billings and some of his contemporaries appear in later tunebooks, but alongside it appeared music of different origins. Whereas many of the colonial collections were published in Boston, the newer ones were often published in Pennsylvania, Maryland, and Kentucky.

Much of what historians of the last generation knew and wrote about regarding church music in the southern United States during the early nineteenth century was based on the foundational study, *White Spirituals in the Southern Uplands* (1933), by George Pullen Jackson (1874–1953). Jackson's study of shape-note music and the "Fa-Sol-La folks," as he called them, is a classic in American musicology, though more recent research has pointed up some misconceptions and faulty conjectures in Jackson's work. It was Jackson who implied that the southern shape-note tradition originated in New England and that there was little in the way of a musical tradition in the South before it.⁴⁸ Further, Jackson wrote, "The earliest singing schools and their successors for over a century used no songs but those which could

---

47. Wicks, "Belated Salute," 621.
48. Norton, "Who Lost the South?," 396.

be transferred to the 'meetinghouse' without offense."[49] Such generalizations ignored the characteristic rebelliousness and disdain southerners had for any denominational authority and the South's already well-developed heritage of folk music.[50] The latter misconception was further stressed in an article by Jackson in the *Musical Quarterly* where he called the singing school movement in New England "about the only strong domestic (development) in music for over one hundred subsequent years."[51]

We know now that, as singing schools fell out of favor in New England, some singing masters did set out to the South to ply their wares. Many others did not have ties to the Northeast. They too made their mark. For the earliest of these itinerants, Pennsylvania was their destination. Stephen St. John, for example, came from Norwalk, Connecticut, where he likely was a descendent of Mattias Sention (later respelled, "St. John"), a Welshman, and one of the founders of the town. Stephen arrived in southeastern Pennsylvania around 1810 and taught singing schools in Chester, Montgomery, and Lancaster counties.[52] Aaron Burt Grosh (1803–1884)[53] recalled St. John as a popular performing musician as well as singing school master:

> I once heard him, at an "apple boiling" at my father's, sing from about 8 o'clock in the evening until 2 or 3 o'clock in the morning—a continuous flood of songs and ballads, without a repeat or a pause except to eat or drink! . . .
>
> I mention our singing schools—the earliest of which was taught by Mr. St. John. They were well-attended throughout, by pupils and spectators. The former generally filled all, or nearly all the writing desks, and the latter occupied most of the benches usually used by the smaller scholars at the pay-school—the desks and benches being so arranged that the singers formed an open quadrangle or "open square" with the teacher in the middle, while the audience was arranged outside—on the west side of the room. Here were the singers duly instructed in all the mysteries of "the heavenly maid" as far as "patent notes" were concerned, in a few "quarters'" of one evening a week, they were able to sing "'Canon Four in One," "Masonic Ode," "Easter

---

49. Jackson, *White Spirituals,* 5–6.
50. Norton, "Who Lost the South?," 396.
51. Jackson, "Buckwheat Notes."
52. Shoemaker, "Stephen St. John," 3.
53. Grosh attended St. John's singing schools in his youth. He would later become a well-known Universalist preacher and writer.

Anthem," and "Denmark" when led by the teacher—after which, to use an old-time phrase, "they were lernt out!"[54]

"Canon Four in One" from the cover of Stephen St. John's tunebook, *The American Harmonist* (Harrisburg, PA: Stephen St. John, 1821). Learning canons or rounds was a typical way to introduce part singing in nineteenth-century singing schools much as it is today.

Pennsylvania was founded upon Penn's religious ideology, which he verbalized in his 1701 "Charter of Privileges":

> That no Person or Persons, inhabiting in this Province or Territories, who shall confess and acknowledge One almighty God, the Creator, Upholder and Ruler of the World; and profess him or themselves obliged to live quietly under the Civil government, shall be in any Case molested or prejudiced, in his or their Person or Estate . . .[55]

Like the Primitive Baptists of Appalachia and the Scots in North Carolina, Germanic and Dutch groups found less-settled portions of the Keystone State congenial places to build communities. There, ethnic traditions could be maintained. The newcomers were anxious to guard their customs and heritage from contamination by the many different nationalities and religious traditions in their adopted country. For many, the church was the focal

---

54. Shoemaker, "Stephen St. John," 3.
55. "Charter of Privileges," 3077.

point of the community and the nexus for all relationships. Congregational singing was typically in unison and lined out. The leader was often called the *"Vorsinger"* because his singing preceded that of the congregation's. The church "Schule" guaranteed the proper training for their children. Music education for children was typically part of the curriculum and was viewed as an aid to the development of language skills and a way to build understanding and appreciation for worship practices.[56]

> The people felt enormously the responsibility of training their children in the ways of the Spirit, and believed music to be one of the ideal media for the learning of the mother tongue [in order to read the Scriptures] and for the learning of traditional forms of the church service.[57]

School days usually opened with prayer and the singing of a hymn. Singing lessons were incorporated into regular classroom instruction throughout the day to facilitate memorization of Bible passages, the rules of arithmetic, or any other area that melody might aid in teaching. In order to teach the hymns of the church and instruct students in the intricacies of note reading, classes focused strictly on music were often initiated—a singing school within the school. An important piece of paraphernalia given every singing class student was his or her copybook. This was an oblong blank notebook in which students, using quill and ink, laboriously drew staff lines and lessons the singing master had put on the chalkboard.[58] As musical skills and expectations increased, quite often the *Vorsinger*—usually a church member with little musical training—was found to be inadequate to the church's needs and outside help was needed. Enter the professional singing master.

By the late 1780s, itinerant singing masters soon began arriving in central Pennsylvania, often by way of Philadelphia and Baltimore, where they had tunebooks published. Joel Harmon (1772–1833) was typical of them. Like St. John, he was born in Connecticut.[59] Harmon served as a major, fighting in the Battle of Sachetts Harbor on Lake Ontario, an important victory in the War of 1812. In 1825 Harmon purchased a hundred acres of land near Andover, New York, and set about becoming a farmer. In Pennsylvania, he led singing schools in Carlisle, Harrisburg, York, and Gettysburg. He also led schools as far afield as Washington, DC and Petersburg,

---

56. Rosewall, "Singing Schools of Pennsylvania," 20.
57. Rosewall, "Singing Schools of Pennsylvania," 22.
58. Rosewall, "Singing Schools of Pennsylvania," 24.
59. Greene, "Joel Harmon's Home."

Virginia.⁶⁰ "Subject to the ravages of weather . . . the teacher furthermore ran the risk of coming into a territory, unannounced, only to find the inhabitants overcome with an influenza epidemic or involved in a community effort of a magnitude to preclude singing school attendance for months."⁶¹ Such were the hazards to the itinerant, and they were borne out in Harmon's own career. He died from exposure in 1833, traveling from school to school during the punishing snow and cold of a Pennsylvania winter.⁶²

The trek of many singing masters did not end in Pennsylvania. The mass of settlers moving south would need singing schools and tunebooks. An enterprising teacher could provide more efficient and easier-to-comprehend ways to learn the fundamentals of music reading. Itinerant singing masters seeking new domains were aware of those needs.

The practice of church music in the South and West would differ significantly from that in New England. What congregations sang, whether there were choirs or instrumental accompaniments—these things varied widely depending on religious persuasion and whether the community was rural or urban. Nevertheless, a common desire seemed to be to embrace traditions, some from colonial times but many also from an even earlier time in the British Isles. Participation in singing schools became an extremely popular community activity. The more popular tunebooks were treasured resources of sacred song. Whether or not they had any official recognition from the local church, they often found their way into clergy libraries and precentors' desks, where they helped to shape what their congregations sang for future generations.

The Introduction of Shape-Note Notation

In the early eighteenth century Tufts had explored the use of the four-note tetrachord combined with symbols of various kinds to simplify music reading. It was believed by him and others that the seven-pitch Guidonian scale was too complicated for efficient use in teaching.⁶³ Fast forward to the nineteenth century. Within just a year of each other, two competing systems appeared that promised to further simplify music reading by adding a visual

---

60. Greene, "Joel Harmon's Home."

61. Rosewall, "Singing Schools of Pennsylvania," 53–54.

62. Greene, "Joel Harmon's Home."

63. This is significant and goes to the root purpose of the reformers, then and later, to facilitate congregational singing. Using the four-note tetrachord as a teaching device did indeed simplify the teaching of basic music reading skills that a congregation would need. However, it was designed for diatonic music. It was not effective for the more complex and chromatic music of Europe.

A Mighty Shout! 143

representation of pitches within the scale. One was patented by the Connecticut tunesmith Andrew Law (1749–1821) in 1802 and used in his 1803 *Musical Primer*; the other was William Smith and William Little's *The Easy Instructor or a New Method of Teaching Sacred Harmony* (1801).

According to Richard Crawford, Law "was the most ambitious American psalmodist of the eighteenth century."

> The achievements of his musical career, which spanned half a century, are impressive. He traveled the length of America, establishing singing schools in eleven states . . . Yet, as considerable as Law's accomplishments may seem, they did not satisfy his hopes. Law's ambition may be measured by his goals, which were to attain national distribution of his tune books and to reform American taste in sacred music. Law worked tirelessly to extend his musical influence outside his native New England to the new nation as a whole, and he seems to have been the first musician to realize that America, now a single country, could become a gigantic market for his collections. Law was unable to exploit this market with consistent success, but his attempts marked him as a man of vision.[64]

The cover of Law's *Select Harmony* (1812) boldly announced that all music was notated according to Law's "new plan" with "easy lessons for learners." In Law's system, four distinct shapes were assigned to the noteheads of the tetrachord—the square, the oval, the triangle, and the diamond.

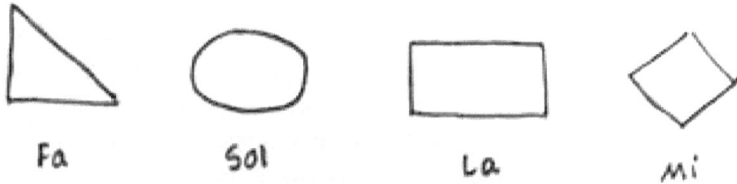

The notes could be moved up or down to indicate the shape of the melodic line.

---

64. Crawford, *Andrew Law*, xv–xvi.

Unfortunately, Law's four-shape system was ungainly and not received well. A competing collection—William Smith and William Little's *The Easy Instructor or a New Method of Teaching Sacred Harmony* (1801)—became extremely popular, running through multiple editions into the 1820s.[65] Its importance to the understanding of sacred music as it was sung and practiced outside of New England cannot be overstated. Robert Stevenson explained the importance the book well when he wrote, "The stigmata of all the more characteristic tune books in the South and West in the forepart of the nineteenth century were the shape notes introduced in William Little and William Smith's *The Easy Instructor*."[66]

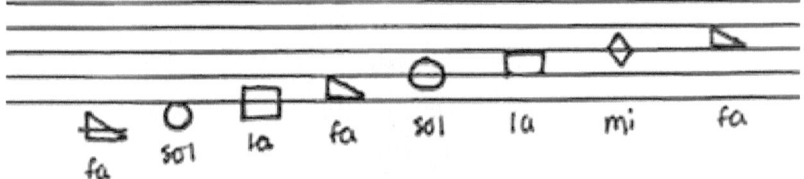

Shape-note scale comprised of two tetrachords as used in Smith and Little's *The Easy Instructor*.

The concept behind shape note/tetrachord systems, as used by both Law and Smith and Little, was that, by giving each of the four pitches of the tetrachord a unique and consistently used shape and matching that shape up with the four solfège syllables, the novice singer could quickly and easily learn to read music. A skilled singer experienced in shape notes was expected to instantly perceive a three-way connection between note of the scale, shape, and syllable. With practice, singers could navigate not only stepwise melodies, but also basic diatonic intervals such as thirds, fourths, and fifths.

While the shapes assigned to pitches by Smith and Little were quite similar to Law's, the choice of repertoire differed significantly. The focus of *The Easy Instructor* was on music of American-born composers.[67] The col-

---

65. More recent scholarship indicates that Smith and Little did not invent the shape note system used in *Easy Instructor*. The Philadelphia merchant John Connelly designed the system and signed it over to Smith and Little in 1798 to be used in their tunebook. (See Hall, "Philadelphia, Birthplace of Shapes.")

66. Stevenson, *Protestant Church Music*, 86.

67. This shift in focus from folk style revivalist psalmody and hymnody to cultivated, Eurocentric worship music is obvious with even a cursory look at other collections from the period. Many quote Lowell Mason ("Professor Mason") in the rudiments section. The title page of Aikin's *Christian Minstrel* proclaims "selected from the Most Popular Works in Europe and America," and the contents include twenty Mason tunes

lection helped to enshrine the music of New England tunesmiths like Billings, so roundly dismissed by the cultivated New England elite, and make it available to future generations. The musicologist Irving Lowens wrote:

> Of the 105 compositions included . . . , only five are of European origin; even these were old American favorites which had appeared in almost every New England tunebook . . . The American compositions, among them forty-one claimed as "never before published," are excellent examples of the characteristic native idiom of the time.[68]
>
> The omission of any reference to "European Music" on the title page and absence of any in the collection itself bear out the idea that Smith's preference was for music in the American idiom.[69]

In addition, while the *Easy Instructor* retained the eighteenth-century practice of keeping the melody in the tenor, the scoring was in four parts, SATB.

---

as well as three by Thomas Hastings. Swan's *Harp of Columbia* (1848) lists no fewer than twenty-five pieces by Lowell Mason. Walker's *Christian Harmony* includes ten by Mason and also pieces by members of the Mason circle: Bradbury, Hastings, Luther Orlando Emerson, and George James Webb.

68. Lowens and Britton, "'Easy Instructor,'" 37.
69. Lowens and Britton, "'Easy Instructor,'" 38.

Windham L.M.

for SATB Voices *a cappella*

Tune: "Windham" ("Broad Is the Road that Leads to Death," Isaac Watts) #41 in William Smith, *The Easy Instructor* (Trenton, NJ: 1803).

An Affront to Cultivated Sensibilities

It is impossible to ignore the outright disdain with which Lowell Mason and Thomas Hastings regarded Smith and Little's shape-note system. In 1835, in his *Musical Magazine,* Hastings wrote:

> Little and Smith, we regret to say, are names which must stand in musical history, closely connected with wholesale quantities of patented "dunce notes." Probably no other book in the country had ever such an amount of purchasers as theirs; or did so much, in the day of it, to hinder the progress of taste. This, however, was to be attributed, chiefly to the enterprise of money-making publishers. The compilers, we believe, were never the richer for their undertaking. Had there been no such practice as literally forcing books into the market, the work last mentioned, we are bold to say, would have never come into general notice. And yet the fact, that some fifty thousand copies of any book,

can, within a few years, in this manner, be palmed upon the public, is triumphantly quoted, as evidence of its great utility.[70]

While Mason and Hastings defended their opposition to shape notes because they ran counter to European common-practice notation and therefore were a stumbling block to teaching, it is difficult not to detect a measure of class elitism. Irving Lowens writes:

> Shape notes came to be regarded in urban centers as the musical notation of the country people, the naïve, simple people who sang for their own enjoyment songs in a strange, almost primitive native idiom. Leaders of fine city choirs, busy with Pucitta and Neukomm as well as Handel and Haydn, would have nothing to do with such music nor with such notation. Inevitably, the city choir leaders became the first music teachers in the public schools. Shape notes were never admitted to the classroom.[71]

A New Generation of Singing Masters and Compilers

In 1810, a creative and savvy book publisher, John Wyeth (1770–1858), stepped into the breach to supply a potential new market for tunebooks. Born and raised in Cambridge, Massachusetts, he served an apprenticeship with a printer. While living in Cambridge, Wyeth no doubt would have been aware of the burgeoning popularity of singing schools, and, through his apprenticeship, may well have been introduced to advances in the moveable type needed for music publication.[72]

---

70. Hastings, "Musical Authors and Publications," 87.
71. Lowens and Britton, "'Easy Instructor,'" 32.
72. Steele, "John Wyeth."

John Wyeth.
Public domain image in *History of the Counties of Dauphin and Lebanon,* by W. H. Egle (Philadelphia: Everts & Peck, 1885). Panel preceding p. 555. (https://www.google.com/books/edition/History_of_the_Counties_of_Dauphin_and_L/bMIpRoF UIgYC?hl=en&gbpv=1&bsq=Wyeth)

By 1792, Wyeth had taken up residence in Harrisburg, Pennsylvania, and had become the publisher of a local newspaper, *The Oracle of Dauphin*. In 1810, an advertisement appeared in *The Oracle* announcing the coming publication of a new collection of sacred music. Its eventual title would be *Wyeth's Repository of Sacred Music*. Wyeth's *Repository* was not formulated to appeal to cultivated progressives in the East. It contained all the most popular fuging tunes of the colonial era. The hymnody chosen stressed texts of Isaac Watts to appeal to evangelicals who were then active in Pennsylvania and farther south. Moreover, Wyeth took the controversial step of publishing his collection using the new system of "patent notes" or "shape notes" rather than standard notation.[73]

It was a well-chosen formula, and *Repository* sold over 120,000 copies. So popular was it that Wyeth decided to publish a sequel, *Wyeth's Repository of Sacred Music, Part Second*, in 1813. *Part Second* was equally revolutionary in its own way. It included a completely new repertoire of folk-based spiritual songs and hymns inspired by the rise of evangelical religious communities in the South and the camp meeting. For pioneer singing masters, *Part Second* would be a far greater influence than Wyeth's first volume. While John Wyeth's importance was as a tune collector and publisher, he was not a

---

73. Steele, "John Wyeth."

singing master. Hundreds of singing masters were active during this period, and we can only mention a few.

The brothers Chapin, Lucius (1760–1842) and Amzi (1768–1835), came from a family of singing masters who were active in the last decade of the eighteenth and well into the nineteenth centuries.[74] Lucius and Amzi were among the first singing masters to organize singing schools west of the Allegheny Mountains. The Chapins were gifted composers. Five of their tunes, "Ninety-Third," "Rockingham," "Twenty-Fourth," "Vernon," and "Rockbridge," which it is unlikely they ever profited from, appeared first in Wyeth's *Repository* and later in William Walker's *Southern Harmony*, classic collections of the era.

Singing masters, tunesmiths, and compilers like John Wyeth, the Chapins, and Ananias Davisson lived at a time when the rich treasure of American folk songs, spirituals, and folk hymns was just being discovered. A tantalizing rough rendering in Lucius's handwriting of a very famous hymn melody that he doubtless heard on his travels appears on the back of an envelope dated 1828.

"New Britain" hymn tune with ornamented melody as notated by Lucius Chapin (1828).

The tune, "New Britain," now inextricably coupled with Newton's hymn "Amazing Grace," was first published in the 1829 collection, *Columbian Harmony*, leading naturally to speculation that Lucius Chapin might have written it.[75] The pentatonic nature of the tune suggests it had a folk origin. The melodic ornamentation in Chapin's rendering suggests he may have heard it sung in his travels and jotted it down exactly as it was performed.

Ananias Davisson (1780–1857), like John Wyeth, was a tunebook publisher. He was also a well-known itinerant singing master, organizing schools throughout the Shenandoah Valley and in neighboring Tennessee. Davisson lived in Rockingham County, Virginia, from 1804 until he died in 1857. Methodists and evangelical Presbyterians were most active in the

---

74. Hamm, "Chapins and Sacred Music," 91.

75. Hall, "Did Lucius Chapin write the Amazing Grace tune?" "Amazing Grace" with its familiar text coupled with the New Britain melody first appeared in William Walker's *Southern Harmony* and will be discussed later in this chapter.

area.⁷⁶ Two collections published by Davisson were enormously important to the spread and encouragement of sacred song in the region, *The Kentucky Harmony* (1816) and *Supplement to the Kentucky Harmony* (1820).⁷⁷ The influence of Wyeth's *Repository* is obvious in the first edition of *Kentucky Harmony*, which seems to have been the source of much of the content. However, in the four succeeding editions and a *Supplement*, he included more and more of his own tunes and arrangements.⁷⁸ Davisson was an active and successful singing master. He taught not only in the Shenandoah Valley, but also made a number of trips over the Blue Ridge Mountains to Tennessee to teach. The first of those visits was announced in the *Knoxville Register* of May 26, 1818.⁷⁹

Joseph Funk (1778–1862) was born in Berks County, Pennsylvania, a grandson of Bishop Heinrich Funck, the first Mennonite bishop in America.⁸⁰ While still a child, his family moved to Rockingham County in Virginia, where he was destined to spend the rest of his life. Twice Joseph was married, and twice he was widowed, ultimately raising fourteen children.⁸¹ A talented musician with a passion for congregational singing, Funk, and later his sons, were extremely active teaching singing schools across the Shenandoah Valley. Funk developed his own tunebooks/primers and teaching aids for use in the schools he taught, many of them attended by German-speaking Mennonites.

Ein allgemein nützliche Choral-Music (1816) was unique among tunebooks of the period. The title, translated *Generally Useful Choral Music*, contained musical selections, entirely in German, but with shape notes utilizing the Smith and Little system. To further simplify score reading for learners, Funk eliminated most accidentals, assuming for example that, where needed in minor keys, the seventh scale degree would be raised without the need to notate it. Johannes Braun, a leader of the Virginia Mennonites, provided a foreword for *Ein allgemein,* in which he wrote:

> It is to be regretted that we Germans, especially in these parts, are so backward in the practice of the vocal art. Nowhere is this more noticeable . . . than in public gatherings and, more or less, in all religious organizations. There are many, and with the

---

76. Harley, "Ananias Davisson," 2.

77. The use of "Kentucky" in the title was probably a marketing ploy since there is no record of Davisson ever visiting that state.

78. Music, "Ananias Davisson, Robert Boyd," 73.

79. Music, "Ananias Davisson, Robert Boyd," 73.

80. The Funck name was apparently changed to "Funk" by Joseph's parents.

81. Eskew, "Joseph Funk's *Allgemein Nützliche*," 38.

scarcity of singing schools more and more, who do not open their mouths to sing at all; and there are others who cause, by unsuitable sounds, such discords that both the song service and the devotional service are disturbed if not entirely broken up.[82]

The collection contains eighty-seven pieces including chorales, psalm tunes, and folk hymns for two-part unaccompanied voices. German chorales are in the majority and include such well known ones as *"Jesu meine freude."*

Joseph Funk's *Ein allgemein nützliche Choral-Music* only received one printing. It was followed in 1832 by his *A Compilation of Genuine Church Music*, considered to be his masterpiece. By its fourth edition in 1842 it had sold over 28,000 copies. Now in its twenty-second edition, this collection is still in use today under the title *Harmonia Sacra, A Compilation of Genuine Church Music*.[83]

There are several key differences between it and the earlier *Allgemein*: It contains 271 tunes, over twice the number in the older book; it is entirely in English; only a few German chorales remain, the rest being replaced with British and American music; and many more American folk hymns are included. Eskew has suggested that Funk's transition from German to English and chorales to folk hymns parallels the broader integration into American society of the German-speaking population in the Shenandoah Valley, which was occurring in the early nineteenth century. It also accounts for the collection's long-standing success.[84] As a direct result of his publishing success, Funk established the first Mennonite printing and publishing house in the United States at Mountain Glen, Virginia (renamed "Singers Glen" in 1860).[85]

Allen D. Carden (1792–1859) was one of the most well known and successful singing masters and tunebook purveyors west of the Mississippi River. His *The Missouri Harmony* (1820)[86] became one of the most popular

---

82. Funk, *Die allgemein nützliche Choral-Music*, 11; translation quoted from Jackson, *White Spirituals*, 32–33.

83. Eskew, "Joseph Funk's *Allgemein Nützliche*," 44.

84. Eskew, "Joseph Funk's *Allgemein Nützliche*," 44.

85. Joseph Funk died in 1862. He left his publishing enterprise, Joseph Funk and Sons, to his grandson, Aldine Kieffer, and his granddaughter's husband, Ephraim Ruebush. In 1878 the company moved to Dayton, Virginia, and in 1890 it was renamed the Ruebush-Kieffer Company. Following Joseph Funk's legacy as a singing school master, Ruebush-Kieffer established the Virginia Normal School of Music in 1874 in New Market, Virginia. It was a key force in promoting the singing of gospel music in the South in the late nineteenth and early twentieth centuries.

86. Carden, comp., *Missouri Harmony*, 10–11.

collections of its time and was known to Abraham Lincoln. Carl Sandburg notably mentions the tunebook in his *American Song Bag*:

> A famous oblong song book of the pioneer days in the middle west was *The Missouri Harmony*, published in 1808 by Morgan and Sanxay of Cincinnati. Young Abraham Lincoln and his sweetheart, Ann Rutledge, sang from this book in the Rutledge Tavern in New Salem, according to old settlers there . . . The pages from the "Missouri Harmony" . . . contain at least two songs with which Abraham Lincoln had close acquaintance. Dennis Hanks, a cousin of Lincoln, has related that in Spencer County, Indiana, the song, "How Tedious and Tasteless the Hours" (Greenfield) was well known, and New Salem, Illinois, residents have told how Lincoln parodied "Legacy."[87]

The Nineteenth-Century Singing School

Nineteenth-century singing schools in the South and on the frontier differed in key ways from their colonial predecessors. Most schools were promoted and organized by the singing master and usually operated independent of church sponsorship. The schools were financed through an agreed-upon tuition, payable at the start of the session. They were nonsectarian but generally Christian, as is made clear by copious references to worship and congregational singing in virtually all the tunebooks of the period. Singing masters did continue to sell tunebooks (especially if they were marketing their own), but that was not their principal source of funding. Virtually all classes based their instruction on the four-note tetrachord and most used Smith and Little's shape-note system or one influenced by it.

Sessions of the singing school likely began with prayer. To preserve the egalitarian nature of the instruction, older youth and adults often addressed each other as "brother" and "sister," and children addressed adults as "uncle" and "aunt."[88] Frontier singing masters were focused on part singing as a communal activity. While there is little evidence that singing school choirs sang in worship, their musical repertoire was almost exclusively sacred. The enthusiasm for making music the schools generated certainly carried over to the churches nearby. Furthermore, the fact that shape-note singing continues to

---

87. Sandburg, *American Song Bag*, 152.

88. Sacred Harp Associations in the United States have scrupulously maintained these practices at their annual "sings." They can be dated back to the 1840s, and likely were institutionalized from singing school traditions in the region originating much earlier. See Smith, "Southern Folk-Hymn," 23.

the present day as an intergenerational, cross-denominational practice would suggest that the singing schools in the South and West were far more successful in achieving their goals than their New England predecessors.

A Sacred Calling

The sales and promotion of tunebooks was certainly a secular enterprise, and singing schools functioned independent of the church. That being said, singing masters/compilers never lost sight of the fact that those buying their books viewed singing as a spiritual act. Virtually all tunebooks of the period emphasize this. In his preface to *The Missouri Harmony,* Allen Carden declared, "The great Jehovah, who implanted in our natures the noble faculty of vocal performance, is jealous of the use to which we apply our talents in that particular lest we exercise them in a way which does not tend to glorify his name."[89] Smith and Little in *The Easy Instructor* were even more robust in their declaration:

> Music not only decently expresses, but powerfully excites and improves the devout affections; it is the prerogative of this noble art to cheer and invigorate the mind—to still the tumultuous passions—to calm the troubled thoughts, and to fix the wandering attention. And hereby it happily composes and prepares the heart for the exercise of public worship. But it further boasts a wondrous efficacy in leading to that peculiar temper which becomes the subject of praise, and is favorable to religious impression. It can strike the mind with solemnity and awe or melt with tenderness and love—can animate with hope and gladness, or call forth the sensations of devout and affectionate sorrows. . . . It is peculiarly agreeable as a social act, and that in which every person may be employed. Nor is it the least of its benefits, that it associates pleasing ideas with divine worship, and makes us glad when we go into the house of the Lord. It is also a bond of union in religious societies, promotes the regular attendance of their members, and seldom fails of adding to their numbers . . . Is there not every reason to expect that persons who frequent the house of God with this view alone, will not be uninterested in the other services of religion?—That they who come to sing may learn to pray—that they whose only wish it was to be entertained, may find themselves instructed and improved? Such is the happy tendency of well-regulated song in the house of God . . .[90]

---

89. Carden, comp., *Missouri Harmony,* 11.
90. Little and Smith, *Easy Instructor,* 5–6.

William "Singin' Billy" Walker

William Walker was born in the village of Cross Keys in Union County, South Carolina on May 6, 1809.[91] His father had immigrated from Wales while his mother was the daughter of Ralph Jackson, a well-known political figure in the county. From earliest memory, William had shown a precocious talent for music.

"Minister's Farewell," no. 14 in *The Southern Harmony and Musical Companion* (Philadelphia: Thomas, Cowperthwait & Co., 1845).

It is said that his mother taught him the above camp meeting spiritual and a couple of other songs before he reached the age of five. According to Jackson there were other William Walker's living in the area at that time. He was assigned the nickname "Singin' Billy" to differentiate him from "Hog Billy," who allowed local swine breeders to corral their pigs in his yard while on their way to market. A second William Walker, "Pig Billy," owned the local stockyard.[92]

---

91. Card, "William Walker's Music," 6.
92. Jackson, *White Spirituals*, 55.

A Mighty Shout!

William Walker.
Public domain image courtesy of Wikimedia Commons.
(https://commons.wikimedia.org/wiki/File:William_Walker,_American_
composer.jpg)

As one of the region's most famous and active singing masters and teachers, Walker traveled extensively. In the Preface to his *Christian Harmony* (1866), he wrote:

> Since publishing the Revised Edition of the *Southern Harmony*, we have traveled thousands of miles in the Middle, Southern, and Western States, and taught a number of singing schools—all the time consulting the musical taste of the clergy, music teachers, and thousands of others who love the songs of Zion—and all the time trying to ascertain the need and wants of the Church, in a musical point of view.[93]

E. W. Miller, the Philadelphia publisher of Walker's *Southern Harmony*, recalled his "tremendous energy . . . in leading classes."[94] Walker's belief in the importance of education and training carried over to his music teaching

---

93. Walker, *Christian Harmony*, iii.
94. Jackson, *White Spirituals*, 60.

activities and his training of local singing masters that would be left in charge after his departure.[95]

The Southern Harmony

And so, we come to one of the most important and influential tunebooks of the nineteenth century, William Walker's *Southern Harmony and Musical Companion* (1835). *Southern Harmony* was extremely popular, selling almost 600,000 copies between 1835 and 1866.[96] Since church hymnals of the era were words-only, tunebooks were the essential means by which hymns and hymn harmonizations were made known. In that capacity, *Southern Harmony* was highly significant because for the first time, much American folk hymnody, now standard in church hymnals, was introduced. The 1835 edition was among the last generation of tunebooks to use the traditional three-part, bass-tenor-treble voicing, using Smith and Little's shape-note system.

We have seen that Lucius Chapin encountered the "New Britain" melody, commonly associated with "Amazing Grace," around 1828. The first time, however, John Newton's text appeared with that tune was in Walker's 1835 *Southern Harmony*. The text had appeared as early as 1779 in William Cowper's *Olney Hymns*, and the melody had appeared in other American tune books but coupled with other texts. [97]

---

95. Jackson, *White Spirituals*, 60.
96. Eskew, "William Walker."
97. Eskew, "William Walker."

A Mighty Shout!

"Amazing Grace" with melody in tenor as it is set and harmonized in *The Southern Harmony* (1840 edition), p. 8.

Another folk hymn, appearing for the first time with well-known text and melody partnered together, is "Wondrous Love." The melody again appears in the tenor.

"Wondrous Love" as it is notated in *The Southern Harmony* (1840 edition), p. 220.

The text to this beloved folk hymn appeared in words-only pocket hymnals on the frontier as early 1811 in Mead's *A General Selection of the Newest and Most Admired Hymns and Songs in Use* (Lynchburg, Virginia), however it wasn't until Walker's 1835 *Southern Harmony* that text was wed with the familiar tune.[98]

---

98. Eskew, "William Walker."

A Mighty Shout!

Benjamin Franklin White and "The Sacred Harp"

> It is claimed that White taught more people to sing than any other man who ever lived in the South; not that he taught all of them himself, but he was instrumental in putting the ball in motion.[99]

The formative years of Benjamin Franklin White (1800–1879) and William Walker seem strangely intertwined. Ben, like "Singin' Billy," was born near the village of Cross Keys, Union County, South Carolina. His mother died in 1807, leaving his father, Robert White, widowed and left to care for five children under the age of sixteen. Ben was passed to the care of his older brother, Robert Jr., and his wife, Polly, who were members of the Lower Fairforest Baptist Church.[100] According to George Pullen Jackson, the boy—his musical aptitude already having surfaced—was recruited as a fifer during the War of 1812.[101]

Benjamin Franklin White.
Public domain image. (www.hymntime.com. http://hymntime.com/tch/bio/w/h/i/t/e/white_bf.htm)

William J. Reynolds speculates that White and Walker may well have met at church meetings or singings, but regardless, they soon became fast

---

99. Jackson, *White Spirituals*, 85.
100. Reynolds, "B. F. White," 1.
101. Jackson, *White Spirituals*, 82.

friends with a love for communal singing. Together they resolved to put together a collection of tunes, some from earlier tunebooks, others they had heard sung, and a few originals of their very own.[102]

The project in which William Walker and Benjamin Franklin White partnered would of course become the hugely successful *Southern Harmony*, but there is disagreement as to the nature and extent of White's contribution to the enterprise. He apparently felt he was an equal partner, but when the book was published in Philadelphia, under Walker's direct supervision, White's name did not appear on the cover, nor would he receive any royalties from sales. The result was a complete break in the relationship. White moved with his family to Hamilton in Harris County, Georgia. According to Jackson, the two never spoke again.[103]

Despite his bitterness toward Walker and the *Southern Harmony* experience, Benjamin Franklin White dreamed of creating a tunebook of his own. He made it a practice to create new tunes and arrangements of others, which he introduced in his singing schools, noting how each was received. In one of those schools, he taught one Elisha James King (1821–1844). Though barely out of his teens, King was already a respected singing master and had shown a creative spark in tunes he had composed or arranged.

King proved to be an excellent and precocious student, and the two soon decided to partner in White's dream—the tunebook that would become *The Sacred Harp*. Elisha was the son of a well-to-do cotton farmer in Wilkinson County, Georgia, and it is possible that his family help subsidize the collection's initial publication in Philadelphia. At any rate, *The Sacred Harp* was accepted for publication in 1844 with an initial run of 1,500 copies. E. J. King did not live to see it. He died prematurely in August of that year.[104]

Like William Walker, B. F. White was committed to collecting and disseminating the regional folk music he encountered in his travels. "He solicited compositions from local singers for the book. When the stock of books was exhausted, he assembled a committee of prominent singers to revise the book—three times in his lifetime—adding regional compositions and better accommodating regional tastes."[105] *The Sacred Harp* would become arguably the most successful musical publication in American history. After its initial publication in 1844, it has gone through at least ten editions.[106] After

---

102. Jackson, *White Spirituals*, 2.
103. Jackson, *White Spirituals*, 84.
104. Reynolds, "B. F. White," 2.
105. Bealle, "Sacred Harp," 327.
106. These include editions in 1847, 1859, 1860, 1884, 1911, 1936, 1960, and since.

a brief decline in popularity in the late nineteenth century, the number of annual Sacred Harp singings have risen, with hundreds participating.

The Quest to Improve Musical Leadership through Musical Conventions and Certification

Singing masters during the first half of the nineteenth century in the rural South were either self-taught or learned their craft attending singing schools. Advanced training, if available, came from the mentoring of other singing masters. Public schools in general were a rarity in the South, and the option of a collegiate degree in music was nonexistent until after the Civil War. Though the musical conventions discussed previously offered some opportunities for instruction, a two- or three-day convention could not provide the sort of in-depth training aspiring singing masters needed. Glimmers of change did appear on the horizon, however, beginning in the 1840s and '50s.

In the spring of 1845, just one year after the initial publication of *The Sacred Harp*, Benjamin Franklin White organized the first *permanent* musical convention in the United States, the Southern Musical Convention. Up to that time, musical conventions had been organized sporadically in locations where tunebook sales would be most profitable. White's concept of a permanent convention put education first. A binding commitment was made to have the gatherings annually in a central and accessible location, and White had amassed a broad contingent of teachers from across Georgia to lend their support. Also, in contrast to Mason's efforts to promulgate the music and techniques of Europe, it was focused exclusively on *The Sacred Harp* and traditional shape-note singing. Perhaps the most important aspect of White's Southern Musical Convention for us here is that specialized training and certification would be offered to singing masters. Such certification would gradually become a requirement for anyone aspiring to teach.

Black Shape-Note Singing in the South

During the early years of Reconstruction and prior to Jim Crow there was at least some commingling of Black and white culture. One example was a

---

Following B. F. White's death, various efforts were made to update the repertoire to suit contemporary tastes. This resulted in the "Cooper editions" of 1907 and 1909. They were not embraced by traditionalists in Alabama, however, resulting in the publication in 1909 and subsequent editions of the so-called "Original Sacred Harp" or "Denson edition."

number of Sacred Harp conventions in Alabama. William Walker actually advocated for joint participation of whites and Blacks at such events.[107]

While the white southern gospel singing conventions morphed more and more toward entertainment, the African American conventions remained squarely focused on congregational singing. The style of singing also differed significantly. Whole congregations learned to sing in full harmony by listening and by instinct. The tunebook or hymnal was a mere starting point to launch a song. Where white singing school students and convention-goers were taught to sing gospel tunes exactly as written, Black congregations improvised ornamental flourishes and added passing tones. Phrases were lengthened to allow for call-and-response and emotional outbursts so typical of traditional Black culture—"screaming, wailing, and walking the floor."[108] Individual expressions of joy, pain, or devotion were encouraged. The cultured preference for finely balanced and blended ensembles was foreign to these Spirit-filled singers. This was a musical tradition many southern Blacks would bring with them on the journey north.

Singing Schools, Tunebooks, and Shape Notes—a Living Inheritance

The singing school movement in the rural South was incredibly successful. It gave generations of rural southerners a basic understanding of music reading and, perhaps more important, encouraged a widespread interest in singing in general and sacred song in particular. Because of the singing schools, it was inevitable that first tunebooks, then hymnals, hymn singing, and choirs would become a common part of church life in urban as well as rural areas. Additionally, the southern singing schools and their tunebooks would preserve an invaluable piece of American musical culture—the folk hymn and a homegrown style of choral writing that was unique to the culture.

Conversely, the singing schools could be said to have been victims of their own success. As singing scholars grew in musical knowledge and ability, there followed a need for more thoroughly trained instructors. Transitioning to common-practice rounded notation would need to be a gradual process, but it was inevitable if musicians were to receive a comprehensive education in their art. Timothy Mason, in Cincinnati, for example, partnered with his brother Lowell to produce a tunebook named *The Sacred*

---

107. Fox, "African American Practice," 40.
108. Fox, "African American Practice," 46.

Harp[109] that was released in two separate editions, one with shape notes, the other with standard common-practice notation. Clearly there was among singers a need for both styles of notation.[110] The need for musicians with training only intensified as public schools with music in their classrooms were introduced. This scenario created the entrée for proponents of "better music" that reformers in the north had sought for years. With George Frederick Root and other similar leaders in the relatively new discipline of music education leading the way, music in the southern United States would be forever changed.

To be clear, Sacred Harp "singings" still occur on a regular basis, and not just in the rural South. Regional gatherings in many parts of the United States still sing from collections such as *Southern Harmony, Christian Harmony*, and Funk's *New Harmonia Sacra*. We should celebrate this! Through such events an important part of American musical culture and the history of sacred music in this country is being preserved.

There is, nevertheless, a poignancy, as shape-noters speak of remembering times passed, which is best illustrated from the words of the singers themselves. I include this touching tribute to North Carolina singing master, Stewart Hayes:

There was a gentle man
With softest silver hair
He raised his hands toward heaven
And led Mt. Lebanon choir
His voice was soft and tender
As the notes began to flow
This choir was filled with grandeur
And soon everyone would know
The songs upon their lips
Was given just to show
They served the Living One
And in His love did grow

This strong but patient leader
Stood for some sixty years
To lead this choir with joy
Along with pain and lots of tears
Years did come and years did go
Time just slipped away
Then one day in early Spring
The angels took this man away
Sometimes on Sunday morning
When the choir sings sweet and low
If you listen very quietly
You might hear a voice
You once did know

It's that of Brother Stewart
Whose body is now gone
But his presence will be with us
As we sing out in song[111]

---

109. Generally referred to as the "Ohio Sacred Harp" to avoid confusion with the famous B. F. White collection discussed earlier.

110. Jackson, *White Spirituals*, 18.

111. Hodges, "Evolution of Sacred Music," 75–76.

> As the reader has no doubt already noted, this is a "loosely chronological" study. For the sake of continuity in this discussion of African American worship and the spiritual, I found it preferable to continue the narrative through the period of the Civil War and beyond to the publication of Slave Songs in the United States (1867). A more general discussion of music, ministry, and American religion during wartime will follow.

CHAPTER 6

AFRICAN AMERICAN MUSIC AND WORSHIP
The Federal Period through Reconstruction

ANY STUDY OF AFRICAN American music as a ministry within the church requires dealing head-on with the tragedy of slavery in more than the cursory manner required in broad overviews of American music. Gilbert Chase, in his masterpiece, *America's Music*,[1] devotes several pages to "The Negroes and the Gospel," surveying Black musical activities in the eighteenth century, examining primarily styles and influences, but slavery—arguably the elephant in the room[2]—is barely discussed.

The church musician seeking to understand the development of music ministry in the United States, cannot ignore slavery. The experience of enslavement and the racial antipathy that continued long after emancipation played a central role in shaping the development of African American music and music in the Black church in particular in the last quarter of the nineteenth century. As Sydney Ahlstrom has written:

---

1. Chase, *America's Music*, 78–83.

2. The symbolism of the "elephant" in American colloquialism is interesting. The phrase "elephant in the room" is used metaphorically to refer to a subject of obvious important, of which all are cognizant, but which isn't discussed, the subject being an uncomfortable one. It likely originated in an 1814 fable, "The Inquisitive Man," by Russian novelist Ivan Krylov. The phrase did not, however, come into common American usage until the 1950s. A century earlier, in the American Civil War, soldiers referred to experiencing the horrific violence of battles like Antietam, Fredericksburg, and Gettysburg as "seeing the elephant."

[Slavery's] origins go back at least to Europe's almost simultaneous discovery of the African Gold Coast and the New World. Its aftermath still constitutes the country's chief moral challenge. Nowhere in Christendom was Negro slavery more heavily institutionalized, nowhere was the disparity between ideals and actuality so stark, nowhere were the churches more deeply implicated. Few subjects, if any, are so fundamental to American religious history.[3]

In the decade leading up to the Civil War, mainline Christian denominations had resisted government mandated social reform. The typical defense was that true reform could only come through a spiritual awakening, not legislation. Both Protestant Episcopalians and Roman Catholics, for example, had refused to acknowledge the peculiar institution of slavery as sinful. They said that since it could be defended on a biblical basis, it was a social problem to be addressed legislatively and not by the church. Perhaps the most graphic example of this was the fiery debate between southern and northern clergy which was eagerly covered in the press. It questioned not the rightfulness or wrongfulness of slavery but whether it could legitimately be called a "sin." Some Christian congregations favoring abolition challenged their denomination's neutral stance on slavery by choosing to leave the fold. The Wesleyan, Free Methodist, Free Presbyterian, African Methodist Episcopal, and African Methodist Episcopal Zion churches, and the Baptist Missionary Convention all came into being because of the Christian abolition movement.

While slavery had mostly been outlawed in the North by 1820, racial prejudice was far more widespread. It caused a barrier, severely limiting multi-cultural worship in the North and inhibiting racial reconciliation even between Blacks and abolitionists, at a time when it was most needed. Also germane is the mainline church's initial condemnation of the institution and later retreat from those values. On the positive side, separation of racial entities in the North resulted in the founding and flourishing of America's oldest African American Protestant denominations and the cultivation of worship styles unique to Black heritage and experience. If we are to learn from the past and develop a "radically inclusive" approach to music ministry in the future, we must have a grasp of that history.

---

3. Ahlstrom, *Religious History*, 94.

Worship among the Slaves in Antebellum America

While a few Black churches were founded in the South during the first half of the nineteenth century, they were exceptional. Slave owners were divided in how they viewed Christian ministry to the slaves. Some viewed any activity bringing Blacks together in numbers with suspicion and questioned the wisdom of teaching them principles of the faith. Others required some or all slaves to attend Sunday worship with the owners' families. In small rural communities, churches were often not large enough to seat the number of slaves required to attend. Therefore, it became common for congregations to schedule special afternoon or evening services just for Black congregants, sometimes with Black leadership. In many cases, household staff attended worship with the family while field hands received what instruction there was out on the plantation. It was through these experiences that many enslaved were first exposed to the hymns of Isaac Watts, which they would embrace, alter, and paraphrase to become a significant influence on the development of the African American spiritual.

Praise house at Sapelo Island, Georgia.
Photograph by Muriel and Malcolm Bell ca. 1939.
Public domain image from the Library of Congress, call no. 593. (https://www.loc.gov/pictures/collection/cph/item/2011645376/)

Contemporary historical accounts suggest that, for most of the slaves, Christian worship, wherever it occurred, was not viewed as a hardship. When attending a white church, they were especially drawn to the singing of psalms and hymns. But Blacks also wanted opportunities to worship with their fellow slaves and draw upon cultural elements they shared. If Sunday morning was to be devoted to their white master's church, perhaps they might worship among themselves on a weeknight somewhere? Initially, in the eighteenth century slaves were sometimes permitted to leave the plantation to gather at a central location for worship. This, however, resulted in security concerns because of the large gatherings and the risk that some would simply run away. Thus, with the blessing and encouragement of white missionaries, the "praise house" was born.

Where slave owners were amenable to it, praise houses (or *prays* houses) were set up on the plantation for this purpose. These were small, rectangular buildings, often built by the slaves themselves, where they could retreat on a weekday evening to have their own worship and were generally erected near the slaves' living quarters. They were small, often with an interior dimension of just ten by twelve feet, the size being intended to restrict the number of worshippers at any one time. Praise houses were not intended by slave owners to replace worship in the local white church, but rather to supplement it. Historian Kym Rice speculates that the term "praise house" was used instead of "church" because white overseers questioned the validity of what Blacks did there as worship.

> For Whites, praise houses did not have the same kind of authenticity or power as a church, but were necessary to keep slaves content and allow them to worship throughout the week . . . During services with Whites, or overseen by Whites, slaves would listen to sermons that taught that heavenly rewards could be attained only if they were obedient to their masters and dutifully performed their work. Within the praise houses, slaves practiced a Christianity that identified the Black slaves with the ancient Israelites, a chosen people led by Moses out of bondage. Through identification with Israel, slaves were able to make sense of their suffering and maintain hope that justice ultimately would be done.[4]

Praise house worship was traditionally in two parts and could last well into the night. First came a more formal service with call-and-response singing, lining out of hymns, prayer, sermons, and exhortations led by a specially appointed slave or freedman. Call-and-response hymns and songs

---

4. Rice, *World of a Slave*, 113.

were a staple of praise house worship and this, no doubt, played a part in their enthusiastic response to the camp meetings just over the horizon. The lining out of hymns in the praise houses of the late eighteenth and nineteenth century was the start of a tradition which continues today.

> Although lining out may have been necessary at first because of the illiteracy of the congregations and the scarcity of hymnbooks with printed music, the practice lingered long past the stage when it was essential for congregational singing. It became a stylistic convention in the Black churches . . . Renditions of the hymns became something distinctly different from what was heard in the White churches . . . Thus, the lined hymn in the present-day Black church represents the fusion of two musical cultures—the African and the European.[5]

Perhaps the single act of worship that more than any other was written about and preached about, yet seldom understood by whites was the *ring dance* or *ring shout*. The origins of the shout are still in dispute. While there is no definitive record of it in America before the 1840s, it is known to have been practiced much earlier by slaves in the West Indies. Some scholars have suggested African origins, citing similar worship dances among the Yoruba and other west African tribes. Others have suggested that the ritual may have originated among West African Muslims as an imitation of the mass procession around the Kaaba that is an essential part of the Islamic pilgrimage to Mecca. If so, the word "shout" may come from the Arabic, "shawṭ."

Following the formal segment of the service in the praise house, benches or chairs were pushed to the side, and worshippers would engage in the exuberant and spiritually charged ring shout. As with so many aspects of praise house worship, the ring shout was embraced by slaves to merge their Christian teachings with forms of expression from their African past. The gradual acceleration of the dance, often lasting hours, incorporated ecstatic shouting, fainting and falling to the floor, and spirit possession—all common to tribal worship in West Africa. "In the praise house, such syncretic religious expressions were performed without judgement or fear from Whites."[6]

Worship opportunities for the slaves varied by region and even by the individual plantation or slave owner. Not all slaves had such prospects. But even among those who were able to participate in religious rituals with their master's approval, there was discontent and mixed messages. Charlie Van Dyke,

---

5. Bailey, "Lined-Hymn Tradition," 4.
6. Rice, *World of a Slave*, 114.

an Alabama slave, described what must have been a generally held feeling: "Church was what they called it, but all that preacher talked about was for us slaves to obey our masters and not to lie and steal. Nothing about Jesus was ever said, and the overseer stood there to see the preacher talked as he wanted him to talk."[7] The Georgia slave Frank Roberson recalled an even more flagrantly paternalistic diatribe from the pulpit:

> You slaves will go to heaven if you are good, but don't ever think that you will be close to your mistress and master. No! No! there will be a wall between you; but there will be holes in it that will permit you to look out and see your mistress when she passes by. If you want to sit behind this wall, you must do the language of the text "Obey your masters."
>
> Now don't you steal your master's chickens, turkeys; don't you steal your master's hogs, and don't you run away; don't talk about your mistress and master. If you do, you will not get a chance to go to heaven and sit behind the glorious wall, because here is the language of the text—on these points—then he would reach upon the porch and get a long steel strap or bullwhip and show it to the slaves saying, that is what you will get if you disobey.[8]

Even when special services with Black preachers were offered, the controlling hands of the slave owners could be evident behind the scenes. "On a Bowie County, Texas, farm, slaves were allowed to hold church services on Wednesday nights, Sunday and Sunday nights. They were not allowed to preach or sing loud for fear of disturbing their mistress. The old master would read the Negro Parson a chapter in the Bible, select his text, and give him some instructions about handling the subject."[9]

The African American preacher Peter Randolph (1825?–1897) described in his memoirs what may be presumed to be a typical worship experience for slaves in Prince George's County, Maryland (near Washington, DC).

> In Prince George County there were two meetinghouses intended for public worship. Both were occupied by the Baptist denomination. These houses were built by William and George Harrison, brothers. Mr. G. Harrison's was built on the line of his

---

7. *Slave Narratives (Alabama)*, "Mary A. Poole with Charlie Van Dyke," 51.

8. Cade, "Out of the Mouths of Ex-Slaves," 329. John Cade (1894–1970), a professor at Southern University between 1929 and 1961, instituted a program to interview ex-slaves, pre-dating the WPA slave narrative project.

9. Cade, "Out of the Mouths of Ex-Slaves," 327.

> brother's farm, that their slaves might go there on the Sabbath and receive instruction, such as slaveholding ministers would give. The prominent preaching to the slaves was, "Servants, obey your masters. Do not steal or lie, for this is very wrong. Such conduct is sinning against the Holy Ghost, and is base ingratitude to your kind masters, who feed, clothe and protect you." All Gospel, my readers! It was great policy to build a church for the "dear slave" and allow him the wondrous privilege of such a holy instruction.[10]

A hugely important factor in slave life, particularly in the waning years of the antebellum period, is what has been called the "invisible institution." Enslaved African Americans needed a way to meet and worship in secret beyond the scrutiny of their white overseers

> but sometimes the slaves would steal away at night and go into cane thickets and pray for deliverance; they always prayed in a prostrate position with the face close to the ground so that no sound could escape to warn the master or the overseer.[11]

> "Us niggers used to have a prayin' ground down in the hollow and sometime we come out of the field, between 11 and 12 at night, scorchin' and burnin' up with nothin' to eat, and we wants to ask the good Lawd to have mercy. We puts grease in a snuff pan or bottle and make a lamp. We takes a pine torch, too, and goes down in the hollow to pray. Some gits so joyous they starts to holler loud and we has to stop up they mouth. I see niggers git so full of the Lawd and so happy they draps unconscious."[12]

Clandestine meetings were not without risk. By the early nineteenth century, particularly in the lower South, slaveowners had tightened their control considerably. Leaving a plantation typically required a written pass even to attend worship at a white church, and there were stringent time limitations. A slave returning home late was in violation and subject to beatings and other punishments. A common practice was to hire poor whites in the area to serve as slave patrols. They were tasked with verifying that any African American encountered off the plantation had proper paperwork and to mete out punishment as the situation required. The Georgia Penal Code laid out the role of slave patrols as follows: "To establish patrols, etc.... for the establishing and regulating patrols, and for preventing any person from purchasing

---

10. Randolph, *From Slave Cabin to the Pulpit*, 197.
11. Cade, "Out of the Mouths of Ex-Slaves," 330.
12. *Slave Narratives (Texas)*, interview with ex-slave Richard Carruthers, 199.

African American Music and Worship

provisions or any other commodities, from or selling such to any slave, unless such slave shall produce a ticket from his or her owner, manager, or employer."[13] Former slaves recalled the slave patrols when interviewed for the *Slave Narratives* in the 1930s.

> Whenever Massa sont any de slaves offen de place he had to gib 'em passes so de patterollers wouldn't ketch 'em and whip 'em foh runnin' away.[14]

> After de White folks got thro' preachin', den de cullered preacher would preach. Sumtimes de cullered folks would hab church when de White folks didn't an' den de slaves would hab tuh get a pass from his owner, 'ca'se dere would be some mean folks what would beat de niggers ef dey didn't hab a pass from dere owners or bosses.[15]

> There was a group of men, known as the "Patter-Rollers," whose duty it was to see that slaves were not allowed to leave their individual plantations without passes that they were supposed to receive from their masters. "A heap of them got whippings for being caught off without these passes..."[16]

Historical accounts of abolitionism in America tend to focus on the "invisible institution" as primarily an opportunity to plot escape to the North. Certainly, the pursuit of freedom from enslavement was in the forefront of many a slave's mind, but even a cursory reading of the slave narratives and recent scholarship reveals that the "brush arbor" meetings[17] were also the result of a need—a need for authentic and vital worship, solace and affirmation in a time of utmost injustice.

---

13. Hotchkiss, ed., *Codification*, 94.
14. *Slave Narratives (Alabama)*, interview with Eliza White, 223.
15. *Slave Narratives (Alabama)*, interview with "Aunt" Annie Stanton, 180.
16. *Slave Narratives (Georgia)*, interview with Jennie Kendricks, 5.
17. Brush arbors were rough, open-sided shelters set up in wilderness clearings and fields for primitive camp meetings and frontier revivals. They were constructed of vertical poles driven into the ground with additional long poles laid across the top as support for a roof of brush, cut branches or hay, hence the name "brush arbor." Similar structures were often used for the clandestine nighttime meetings often referred to as the "invisible institution."

Racial Bias in Antebellum Perceptions of African American Worship

Ruth Bader Ginsburg wrote that "The burden of justification is demanding . . . and it must not rely on overbroad generalizations about the different talents, capacities, or preferences of males and females."[18] I suspect that few would question the danger of overly broad generalizations, and yet, it seems to me that all historical writing is balanced somewhere on a tightrope between generalization and specificity. One might say for example that the best way to avoid unfounded generalizations is to rely on *prima facie* sources. But in truth, even the most objective contemporary observation of an event or movement will be limited by the perspective of the observer. In 1667, the British Parliament passed an Act to Regulate the Negroes on British Plantations based on generalized perception that Blacks had a "wild, barbarous, and savage nature, to be controlled only with strict severity." The act also stated that killing a slave engaged in rebellious acts could not be punished as a crime.[19] Education, preconceptions, background, and environmental factors helped shape how white Americans in both the North and the South viewed the enslaved Black. Those white preachers, already predisposed to racial profiling of Blacks, based their views on a wholly distorted understanding of biblical teachings.

> Biblical defenses of slavery were derived first from Genesis 9:18–29, taken largely out of context from the whole of the scriptural narrative. Using this as a justification, Negroes were labeled "children of Ham" whom God singled out to be Black because of Noah's curse. Aristotle, in order to justify Greek superiority, theorized that the moderate climate of Greece produced people of exceptional intellect and leadership ability, while unusually hot or cold climates produced inferior human beings who lacked the capacity to live freely or govern themselves. It was he who labeled Africans as "burnt faces," the original meaning of the Greek, "Ethiopian."[20]

Prior to the Civil War, most northern whites knew little of the slaves, and nothing of their worship practices or their music. Even some who should have been knowledgeable were not. Annie Bowen, for example, was the daughter of a noted Charleston writer who had written

---

18. Ginsberg, *United States vs. Virginia* (1996).
19. "Slavery Law and Power in Early America."
20. Kendi, *Stamped from the Beginning*, 22–23.

about slave life, and she had even collected a few songs she had heard. When Annie was contacted prior to the publication of *Slave Songs of the United States*, however, she replied: "I received your letter with regard to the 'Spirituals,' and I shall be very happy to do anything in my power towards furthering your project . . . (but) I do not see how an essay can be written, because I believe they have no history or a very short one."[21] Where preachers and others encountered Blacks in worship it was either viewed negatively or as strangely exotic. "Those that were aware frequently confused authentic African-American music with popular minstrel songs."[22] Though possessing little understanding the African American perspective on the role of music in worship, white observers shared their views regularly in print.

Frances Trollope, an English woman touring America in the 1820s, recorded her impressions of an Indiana camp meeting:

> One tent was occupied exclusively by Negroes . . . One of these, a youth of coal-Black comeliness, was preaching with the most violent gesticulations, frequently springing high from the ground, and clapping his hands over his head. Could our missionary societies have heard the trash he uttered by way of an address to the Deity, they might perhaps have doubted whether his conversion had much enlightened his mind . . .

> But how am I to describe the sounds that proceeded from this strange mass of human beings? I know no words which can convey an idea of it. Hysterical sobbings, convulsive groans, shrieks and screams the most appalling, burst forth on all sides. I felt sick with horror . . .[23]

This discomfort was not restricted to white observers. Pioneering Black Bishop Daniel A. Payne (1811–1893)[24] and the Reverend Richard Allen (1760–1831), two of the more influential shapers of the African

---

21. Epstein, *Sinful Tunes and Spirituals*, 322.
22. Epstein, *Sinful Tunes and Spirituals*, 242.
23. Trollope, *Domestic Manners of the Americans*, 223, 227.
24. In addition to being a bishop in the AME denominations, Payne was a veteran educator. He was born free and raised in Charleston, South Carolina. In 1829, at the age of eighteen, he established a school for slaves and free people of color. In 1835, after the Nat Turner rebellion, when it became illegal to teach literacy to slaves in South Carolina, Payne moved to Philadelphia to continue his education. There he became acquainted with Richard Allen and the pioneering ministry at Bethel Church. Probably because of his English ancestry, Payne saw worship in the white-dominated Protestant Episcopal Church as more to be emulated than that of the Methodists.

Methodist Episcopal Church, found the heightened emotions and physicality of evangelical worship inappropriate and distasteful.

The Reverend Richard Allen was born a slave known as "Negro Richard" and owned by Philadelphia lawyer Benjamin Chew. He, along with his family, was sold to a Delaware farmer, Stokely Sturgis, in 1768. He experienced conversion and became a Methodist as a result of a revival at the Sturgis farm in 1777. Six years later, Payne was able to purchase his own freedom and became a Methodist circuit rider.[25] It was Richard Allen who founded the first church of the AME denomination in Philadelphia, and in 1801 published the first Black songster, *A Collection of Spiritual Songs and Hymns Selected from Various Authors*. It was a text-only collection with hymns drawn mainly from Watts and the Wesleys, but none from the African American folk tradition. Having been a slave himself, Allen was sensitive to the religious folkways of his people as well as their music, but saw emulating the worship practice of white Methodism as progressive.[26] Far less tolerant was the younger Bishop Daniel Alexander Payne.

Daniel A. Payne had been born in Charleston, South Carolina, the son of London and Martha Payne, free Blacks who were part of the city's "brown elite." Self-taught in mathematics, physical science, Latin, and Greek, at the age of eighteen Payne opened a school for free people of color and slaves, but it had to close after the Nat Turner rebellion and the outlawing of education for blacks which followed. In 1835, Payne moved north, studying theology at the Lutheran Seminary in Gettysburg, Pennsylvania. In 1840, Payne joined the still-new African Methodist Episcopal Church and would become its sixth bishop in 1852.

Payne recorded the following observations after an 1878 visit to the South:

> In May it was my privilege to visit the Sunday-school of Old Bethel, in Philadelphia, and at a meeting of the Sunday-school ... I showed them how England had become great by habitually making her people read the Scriptures on Sunday in the great congregations; and how the colored race, who had been oppressed for centuries through ignorance and superstition, might become intelligent, Christian, and powerful through the enlightening and sanctifying influences of the word of God ...
>
> The strange delusion that many ignorant but well-meaning people labor under leads me to speak ... About this time, I attended

---

25. McCreless, "Richard Allen and the Sacred Music of Black America," 201, 207–9.
26. O'Connor, "Hymns, Songs, and the Pursuit of Freedom," 234–36.

a "bush meeting," where I went to please the pastor whose circuit I was visiting. After the sermon they formed a ring, and with coats off sung, clapped their hands and stamped their feet in a most ridiculous and heathenish way. I requested the pastor to go and stop their dancing. At his request they stopped their dancing and clapping of hands but remained singing and rocking their bodies to and fro. This they did for about fifteen minutes. I then went and taking their leader by the arm requested him to desist and to sit down and sing in a rational manner.

I told him also that it was a heathenish way to worship and disgraceful to themselves, the race, and the Christian name. In that instance they broke up their ring; but would not sit down and walked sullenly away. After the sermon in the afternoon, having another opportunity of speaking alone to this young leader of the singing and clapping ring, he said: "Sinners won't get converted unless there is a ring. The Spirit of God works upon people in different ways. At camp-meeting there must be a ring here, a ring there, a ring over yonder, or sinners will not get converted."

I have been strongly censured because of my efforts to change the mode of worship or modify the extravagances indulged in by the people . . . but by the ignorant masses, as in the case mentioned, it was regarded as the essence of religion. So much so was this the case that, like this man, they believed no conversion could occur without their agency, nor outside of their own ring could any be a genuine one.[27]

He who could sing loudest and longest led the "Band," having his loins girded and a handkerchief in hand with which he kept time, while his feet resounded on the floor like the drumsticks of a bass drum. In some places it was the custom to begin these dances after every night service and keep it up till midnight . . . Someone has even called it the "Voodoo Dance." I have remonstrated with a number of pastors for permitting these practices . . . but have been invariably met with the response that he could not succeed in restraining them, and an attempt to compel them to cease would simply drive them away from our Church . . . And what is most deplorable, some of our most popular and powerful preachers labor systematically to perpetuate this fanaticism. Such preachers never rest till they create

---

27. Payne, *Recollections of Seventy Years*, 253–54.

an excitement that consists in shouting, jumping, and dancing.[28]

Payne and Allen viewed the worship of African Americans through a very limited prism that sought to gain respect by emulating the worship practices of white denominations in the North. Influenced by Mason and the better music movement, theirs were among the first churches to introduce choirs to African American worship. Payne was proud to have introduced the first concerts of sacred and secular music featuring chorus and orchestra by a Black church in Baltimore and Philadelphia.[29] Allen was outspoken in his preference for traditional Wesleyan hymnody and viewed many traditional spirituals as inappropriate within the context of worship. It was not within Payne's purview to appreciate or even understand the rich cultural and folk heritage that African American worship and sacred music in the South represented.

Confluence: A Merging of Musical Cultures

Considering the wealth of circumstantial information, it seems hard to deny there was at least some confluence of West African traditions with the worship and music of nineteenth-century African Americans. In Africa religions tended to be community focused rather than tightly dogmatic, and natives moving from one location to another could easily absorb or blend into the religious activity of the new home. This flexibility helps to explain the willingness and even eagerness of many slaves to embrace Christianity when it was presented to them by missionaries in America. The Russian artist and secretary to the Russian Consul General Pavel Svinin, provided both a colorful description of worship at Bethel AME in Philadelphia in 1811 and a watercolor of the experience. Accustomed to the quiet, devotional atmosphere of Russian Orthodox worship and with no experience at all with worship steeped in West African tradition, Svinin was understandably taken aback by the heightened emotionalism of a pioneering Black church in the City of Brotherly Love.

---

28. Payne, *Recollections of Seventy Years*, 255–56.
29. Payne, *Recollections of Seventy Years*, 235–236.

African American Music and Worship

177

Pavel Petrovich Svinin (watercolor illustration), "Black Methodists Holding a Prayer Meeting." Metropolitan Museum of Art (public domain).

He wrote:

> We entered a large hall or chamber, lighted very dimly by torches. Walls Black with smoke, dilapidated benches and broken windows made at the outset a disagreeable impression upon us. We went up close to the platform and sat down on a bench in the third row. The hall was full of Blacks; the men were on the right, the women on the left. The frightful countenance and the sparkling eyes of the Africans, staring at us in the dim light, filled us in spite of ourselves with a dread which increased even further when they began to howl with wild and piercing voices. I believed myself to be in Pluto's kingdom, amongst all the monsters of hell, and, when the doorman, greatly resembling Cerberus, locked the door, lest anyone depart, I secretly repented my curiosity.
>
> On the platform a terrible Black skeleton was reading psalms from Holy Writ. At the end of every psalm the entire congregation, men and women alike, sang verses in a loud, shrill monotone. This lasted about half an hour. When the preacher ceased reading, all turned toward the door, fell on their knees, bowed their heads to the ground and started howling and groaning with sad, heart-rending voices. Afterwards, the minister resumed the

reading of the psalter and when he had finished sat down on a chair; then all rose and began chanting psalms in chorus, the men and women alternating, a procedure which lasted some twenty minutes. Then silence fell, a deep, terrible silence such as precedes a storm, when all things grow mute and when the air trembles in expectation of something dreadful and inexplicable.

In an even, hoarse voice the preacher began his sermon, expatiating in a high-flown style upon the terrors of hell and the wrath of God. At first all was fairly calm, but little by little the preacher warmed up and by means of terrible pictures and gestures fired the imagination of his hearers. Soon the groans of penitents were heard on every side, and the outcries and ejaculations of the possessed; finally, when in a strong impressive voice the preacher spoke of the destruction of the Universe, pointed to the Black cloud pregnant with all-shattering thunders and described the tortures and sufferings awaiting the sinners, they loosed such a howl that the very foundations of the hall shook and the vaulted ceiling trembled. I confess, at the moment I myself feared the destruction not of the universe, but of the gallery under which I sat and which threatened momentarily to collapse with the convulsions of the possessed, who leapt and swayed in every direction and dashed themselves to the ground, pounding with hands and feet, gnashing their teeth, all to show that the evil spirit was departing from them.[30]

Continuity versus Discontinuity

While the colorful, even disturbing, phraseology reflects Svinin's narrow view of worship appropriateness, Eileen Southern points out that his observations are useful. They provide one person's view, albeit distorted, of African influence in Black worship practice among free Blacks in the North in the first decades of the nineteenth century. According to Southern, the general passion—shouts and moans of the assembled worshippers, the antiphonal singing between men and women, and the physicality which included leaping, swaying, falling to the ground, and pounding of hands and feet—all point to a heritage extending back well before the Middle Passage.[31]

---

30. Yarmolinsky, *Picturesque United States*, 20.

31. Southern, *Music of Black Americans*, 14. The "Middle Passage" is a commonly used figure of speech referring to the triangular Atlantic slave trades. Ships left Europe loaded with manufactured goods destined for Africa. There goods would be traded for enslaved natives who would be transported to the Caribbean and America to be sold. Slave traders frequently used their profits to purchases hides, tobacco, sugar, rum, and

How shall we define that heritage? Frederick Douglass, in his biographical memoir *My Bondage and My Freedom* (1855), remembered vividly the close relationship between the singing of spirituals and the Black quest for freedom:

> We were, at times, remarkably buoyant, singing hymns and making joyful exclamations, almost as triumphant in their tone as if we had reached a land of freedom and safety. A keen observer might have detected in our repeated singing of "O Canaan, sweet Canaan, I am bound for the land of Canaan" something more than a hope of reaching heaven. We meant to reach the *North*—and the North was our Canaan.[32]
>
> > "I thought I heard them say,
> > There were lions in the way,
> > I don't expect to stay
> > Much longer here.
> > Run to Jesus—shun the danger—
> > I don't expect to stay
> > Much longer here."
>
> was a favorite air and had a double meaning. In the lips of some, it meant the expectation of a speedy summons to a world of spirits; but in the lips of our company, it simply meant a speedy pilgrimage toward a free state and deliverance from all the evils and dangers of slavery.[33]

W. E. B. Du Bois, the noted sociologist and historian, the first African American to receive a doctorate from Harvard, speaking of the Black spiritual, wrote:

> The Music of Negro religion is that plaintive rhythmic melody, with its touching minor cadences, which, despite caricature and defilement, still remains the most original and beautiful expression of human life and longing yet born on American soil. Sprung from the African forests, where its counterpart can still be heard, it was adapted, changed, and intensified by the tragic soul-life of the slave, until, under the stress of law and whip, it became the one true expression of a people's sorrow, despair, and hope.[34]

---

raw materials to be sold upon their return to England and Europe. Hence, the metaphor of the triangle with the Africa-to-America leg known as the "Middle Passage."

32. Douglass later explains that "Canaan" was often used as code for Canada.
33. Douglass, *My Bondage and My Freedom*, 278–79.
34. Du Bois, *Souls of Black Folk*, 191.

In contrast to Du Bois's reverential evocation of the "African forests," another respected African American sociologist suggested a *theory of discontinuity*. E. Franklin Frazier minimized any direct relationship between Black religion in America and its practice in the African diaspora. "Because of the manner in which the Negroes were captured and enslaved, they were practically stripped of their social heritage . . . In the New World the process . . . was completed. . . . From the available evidence . . . it is impossible to establish any continuity between African religious practices and the Negro church in the United States."[35] The writings of Frazier and Du Bois reveal a dichotomy of views existing to the present day with regard to the origins of the African American culture. Some ethnomusicologists have viewed African heritage as central to the African American experience while others have declared that heritage was lost due to the holocaust we refer to as slavery. I suspect the truth lies somewhere between those two polemics.

Putting aside the question of ethnic origins, there can be no question that distinctive characteristics of African musical culture and worship traditions existed also in the devotional practice of the slaves. Christianity and Islam are the dominant religions in present-day West Africa, but in the seventeenth through nineteenth centuries hundreds of traditional tribal religions were practiced. There were, however, traits common to most:

- Over one thousand religious belief systems were present on the African continent during the period being considered here. In virtually all of them, no distinction was made between the sacred and the secular.[36]

- African worship was not centered around shrines, temples, or altars. Rather, religion pervaded all aspects of everyday life. Worship occurred wherever people were and simultaneously with whatever they might be doing.[37]

- The "community of faith" was not limited to a particular church or congregation, but the actual *community*. For example, while an individual might bring forward an idea, that idea if accepted becomes the property of the community, and the community must embrace it. The community then comes together to facilitate it and make it work. "No individual exists in isolation from others."[38]

---

35. Frazier, *Negro Church in America*, 1–2.
36. Costen, *In Spirit and in Truth*, 1.
37. Costen, *In Spirit and in Truth*, 7.
38. Costen, *In Spirit and in Truth*, 6.

- While belief in spirits and minor deities were common among tribal religions, so also was a belief in a supreme being or creator God. Creation stories built around direct action of a creator God are common among African religions. Frequently, the creator God is viewed as all-powerful and remote, only to be communicated with by humans through an intermediary (not unlike the common views of Abraham, Mary, or Jesus acting as an intermediary to God in European and American religious culture). "The continuity of the African heritage is facilitated and enhanced by the African primal belief system grounded in an understanding that the Supreme Being sets all things in motion. One's identity is never conceptualized nor enacted in isolation from the heartbeat of the community, the rhythm of nature, or the divine harmony of creation established at The Creation."[39]
- Death in West African culture was generally not viewed as an end to existence, but a transition to a parallel existence. One's ancestors eternally watch over their earthly family and the land, guiding, warning, and protecting.

Here are characteristics shared between West African and African American sacred music:

- "Art" in West African culture is utilitarian, something to be used for a practical purpose, not simply appreciated for its aesthetic beauty. Africans use music to teach, to comfort, to inspire, to persuade, convince, or to motivate.[40]
- African music points to a central attribute in the slaves' struggle to survive—adaptability. In African tradition, music transcends contradictory concepts or opposites: body vs. spirit, sacred vs. secular, individual vs. community. Music serves to "reach toward unification and synthesis."[41]
- In West African tradition, music served to assemble the faith community at a common place and to engage in something transcendent over day-to-day non-spiritual concerns.[42]
- Music creation was a communal process, not attributable to an individual.[43]

---

39. Costen, *In Spirit and in Truth*, xi.
40. Bowman, "Gift of African-American Sacred Song," 215.
41. Bowman, "Gift of African-American Sacred Song," 214.
42. Lincoln and Mamiya, "Performed Word," 40.
43. Costen, *In Spirit and in Truth*, xi.

- The music of West Africa is and was primarily diatonic.
- Various forms of antiphonal singing are common, particularly those that involve alternation between leader and chorus.
- Singing is often extemporaneous and improvised, and commonly is a form of storytelling.
- Vocal embellishment is a prerequisite. These could include musical as well as nonmusical sounds.
- Like much folk music the world over, the "call-and-response" format is common. Typically, the music of the chorus is repetitive while the leader or soloist is free to improvise at will.[44]
- Music of the soloist or leader may range from identifiable melody to a form of heightened speech, "sung preaching" for example.[45]
- Rhythm, including an emphasis on the use of percussion, is featured prominently. Complex rhythmic structures are commonplace. "This element [the importance of rhythm] differentiates it from the music of all other cultures."[46]
- Rhythmic movement and dance are interrelated in African culture. Dance was a means of communication with God. The highest level of worship was reached when spirits (or the Holy Spirit) entered the body and took control.
- Song, dance, and gesture are all integrated in the act of worship through music. In 1737, the British naval surgeon and slaver John Atkins provided a description of ritual dancing he witnessed in Sierra Leone, a principal outgoing port for the slave trade: "Dancing is the diversion of their evenings: Men and women make a ring in an open part of the town, and one at a time shows his skill in antique motions and gesticulations, yet with a great deal of agility, the company making music by clapping their hands together during the time, helped by the louder noise of two or three drums made of a hollowed piece of tree, and covered with kid-skin."[47]

Among the first recorded references to a unique type of spiritual song being sung by Blacks was that of the lawyer, teacher, and congressman George Tucker (1775–1861), writing in 1816:

---

44. Baker, "Periodization of Black Music History," 148.
45. Costen, *In Spirit and in Truth*, 12.
46. Baker, "Periodization of Black Music History," 149.
47. Atkins, *Voyage to Guinea*, 53.

Here I rambled about for some time thro' the vacant streets, as my fancy led me, till I came to the courthouse. It was court day, and a large crowd of people was gathered about the door. I had hardly got upon the steps to look in, when my ears were assailed by the voice of singing, and turning round to discover from what quarter it came, I saw a group of about thirty negroes of different ages and sizes . . . As they came nearer, I saw some of them loaded with chains to prevent their escape, while others had hold of each other's hands, strongly grasped, as if to support themselves in their affliction . . . They came along singing a little wild hymn of sweet and mournful melody, flying, by a divine instinct of the heart, to the consolation of religion, the last refuge of the unhappy, to support them in their distress.[48]

Levi Coffin (1798–1877) recalled an experience when teaching Sunday school in South Carolina in 1821:

In the summer of 1821, my cousin Vestal Coffin, suggested to me that we should organize a Sabbath-school for the colored people, and endeavor to obtain the consent of the slaveholders in the neighborhood to teach their slaves to read . . .

Among them was one of Thomas Caldwell's slaves, called Uncle Frank. He was a gray-haired old Negro who had all his life been kept in ignorance, but his heart was full of love for God, and he was thankful for this opportunity of learning to read the Bible. He was quite a preacher in his way, and frequently exhorted the slaves in the neighborhood. On this occasion, he made a long and fervent prayer: . . . "Oh, Hebbenly Fader, we tank De for makin' our massas willin' to let us come to dis school, and oh, Lord, do bress dese dear young men you has made willin' to come heah and larn us poor slave niggers to read de bressed word from de mouf of God. Oh, Lord, teach us to be good sarvents, and touch our massas' hearts and make 'em tender, so dey will not lay de whips to our bare backs, and you, great Massa, shall have all de glory and praise. Amen."

Then the negroes broke out with one of their plantation songs or hymns, led by Uncle Frank; a sort of prayer in rhyme, in which the same words occurred again and again.[49]

A most distinctive type of Black sacred song was documented by Peter

---

48. Tucker, *Letters from Virginia*, 6.
49. Coffin, *Reminiscences of Levi Coffin*, 69–70.

Neilson, a Scot living in Charleston, South Carolina, from 1822 to 1828. Neilson was able to observe the Southern slave system firsthand and wrote about it:

> The coloured people chiefly attend the Methodist and Baptist meetings; and, in general, the Word seems to have a very powerful effect upon them . . . and upon the evening of a Sunday, the song of praise may frequently be heard to issue from the hovel of the Negro, whilst all is quiet in the mansions of the wealthy. I may, however, remark by the way, that the religious fervor of the Negroes does not always break forth in strains the most reverential or refined . . . A few lines recollected at random may serve as an example:
>
> "Sturdy sinners, come along! Hip and thigh we'll pull him down, Let us pull old Satan down. We shall get a heavenly crown!"
>
> Or,
>
> "Old Satan, come before my face to pull my kingdom down. Jesus, come before my face, to put my kingdom up.
>
> Well done, thank you, Massa Jesus. Hallelujah, etc."[50]

The tendency of early frontier evangelists, as reflected in the camp meetings they initiated, was to offer conversion without regard to race. It was a radically inclusive movement—whether white or Black, educated or illiterate, rich or poor, slave or freedman, landowner, sharecropper, or common laborer—it made no difference. Unfortunately, this aspiration to all-embracing Christian witness was short-lived. The Reverend William D. Watley (bn. 1947)—author, educator, and senior pastor of St. Philip AME Church, Atlanta—has written: "The tragedy of U.S. religious history is that the equality of the conversion experience was not strong or lasting or far-reaching enough to withstand the mores of the times, which pressured the church and the individual White believer to conform to racist social norms rather than transform them."[51] The creation of music as a communal activity squares directly with documentary evidence of how the camp meeting spirituals originated.[52]

---

50. Neilson, *Recollections*, 258–59.

51. Watley, *Singing the Lord's Song*, 34.

52. And what exactly was a "camp meeting spiritual"? In modern parlance, one hears references to "African American spirituals" and "white spirituals," the latter often being hymns originating out of early nineteenth-century camp meetings. In truth, the early camp meeting spirituals were neither Black nor white but the musical response of all those attending. It was later generations that would give certain hymns and songs a racial identity by the manner in which they were performed.

Most Black and white spirituals were true American folk art—music formed communally, not written down, adapted, and improvised to suit the situation and the song leader. Blacks were significant participants in that process. The diatonic nature of American folk hymnody and the frequent use of call-and-response technique in camp meeting song leading would certainly have been a familiar and comfortable format for the slaves. Other musical factors, however, had roots in African tradition: improvisatory singing, heightened speech, a strong emphasis on rhythm, ornamentation often so subtle it cannot be effectively notated, and the intimate relationship between sacred song and dance. These have become an indelible part of the African American musical persona to the present day.

The famed educator and scientist Booker T. Washington (1856–1915) certainly recognized the slaves' African heritage, yet he left no doubt that, in his view, the spiritual arose from nineteenth-century revivals initiated by whites:

> Negro music is essentially spontaneous. In Africa it sprang into life at the war dance, at funerals, and at marriage festivals. Upon this African foundation the plantation songs of the South were built. According to the testimony of African students at Tuskegee there are in the native African melodies strains that reveal the close relationship between the Negro music of America and Africa, but the imagery and sentiments to which the plantation songs give expression are the outcome of the conditions in America under which the transported children of Africa lived. Wherever companies of Negroes were working together, in the cotton fields and tobacco factories, on the levees and steamboats, on sugar plantations, and chiefly in the fervor of religious gatherings, these melodies sprang into life . . . The plantation song in America, although an outgrowth of oppression and bondage, contains surprisingly few references to slavery. No race has ever sung so sweetly or with such perfect charity, while looking forward to the "year of Jubilee."[53]

Edmund S. Lorenz in his *Practical Church Music* (1909) voiced similar views of the spiritual's origins: "The Jubilee songs, in so far as they have had their origin among the coloured people, are the direct offspring of the White man's 'spiritual.' Indeed, many of the songs sung by them are spirituals borrowed from their White brethren, the rhythmical swing being somewhat emphasized."[54] The African American scholar and researcher Newman I. White amplified on this perspective in his *American Negro Folksongs* (1928):

---

53. Washington, preface to Coleridge-Taylor, *Twenty-Four Negro Melodies*, viii–ix.
54. Lorenz, *Practical Church*, 92.

> At this point, at least in my own mind, the last element of doubt concerning the origin and development of the Negro spiritual vanishes. The identity of the word "spiritual" with the "spiritual song" of the White people, the identity of the religious background of the two in practice, the presence today of revival songs in both groups which have been in both groups from the first, the peculiar use of hymn fragments in the spirituals, the continued existence in the spirituals of fragments from old revival songs of the White people, the sporadic cases of old spiritual songs of the Whites that have survived in the Negro spirituals after being forgotten by White people—all these facts lead to the inevitable conclusion that the Negro spiritual is simply a continuation and development of the White spiritual.[55]

That the African American spiritual might have originated from the camp meeting experience is a logical consideration, given that the word "spiritual" did not come into use until well into the nineteenth century. Nonetheless making that a definitive judgement ignores the fact that songs of a spiritual type were known and sung by African Americans long before they were written down.

African Americans did, however, embrace camp meetings in both North and South, often outnumbering whites at those gatherings. Both Black and white scholars have sparred over the influence of the camp meetings. Were the spirituals Black reinterpretations of the white hymns heard and sung there? Or, was the reverse true? When whites at the camp meetings heard the ebullient singing of the slaves and freedmen, did it influence how and what *they* sang? Or, were camp meeting spirituals a unique and precious example of interracial harmony and praise? My guess is that the latter comes closest to the truth.

The Sectional Crisis: The Church and Colonization versus Abolition

The American Civil War began in April of 1861. Shortly thereafter, General Benjamin Franklin Butler was assigned command of Fortress Monroe at the southern tip of the Virginia Peninsula near Hampton Roads. It was Butler who initiated the "Fort Monroe Doctrine." At this early stage in the war, Federal policy was focused entirely on preserving the Union and not the abolition of slavery. Fleeing slaves were crossing into Union lines in alarming numbers, and there was no policy in place to deal with it. Since Southern slaveholders viewed their slaves as property, and there was plenty

---

55. White, *American Negro Folksongs*, 50.

of historical precedent for invading armies to confiscate enemy property as contraband, Butler refused to return fleeing slaves to their owners, instead putting them to work where possible in service to the Union. Butler's policy came to be known as the "Fort Monroe Doctrine" and would lead the US Congress a year later to enact the Confiscation Act of 1862, which made Union policy regarding seizure of property, including slaves, uniform across all the armed services. Almost immediately, the plight of the escaping African Americans was picked up by the northern press and it became a rallying point for abolitionists in the North.

The Contrabands

In August of 1861, the American Missionary Association (or AMA) contacted General Butler with a proposal to bring relief to the fleeing slaves who had been dubbed "contrabands" in the press. That September, the Reverend Lewis C. Lockwood, a Presbyterian minister, was sent to Fort Monroe. An anonymous observer—possibly Lockwood himself—reported on what he witnessed at Fort Monroe in the September 7, 1861 issue of *Dwight's Journal of Music*:

> "Contraband Singing"
>
> It is one of the most striking incidents of this war to listen to the singing of the groups of colored people in Fortress Monroe who gather at their resorts after nightfall. Last evening, having occasion to visit an officer of the garrison sick in his tent, I passed around by the fortress chapel and adjacent yard where most of the "contraband" tents are spread. There were hundreds of men of all ages scattered around. In one tent they were singing in order, one man leading as extemporaneous chorister, while ten or twelve others joined in the chorus. The hymn was long and plaintive, as usual, and the air was one of the sweetest minors I ever listened to. It would have touched many a heart if sung in the audiences who appreciate the simple melody of nature, fresh and warm from the heart. One verse ran thus:
>
> "Shout along, children! Shout along, children!
> Hear the dying Lamb.
> Oh take your nets and follow me,
> For I died for you upon the tree."
>
> There was no confusion, no uproar, no discord—all was as tender and harmonious as the symphony of an organ. Passing into the yard, I found a large company standing in the open air

around a slow fire. One young man sat on the end of a rude seat with a little book in his hand. It had been much fingered, and he was stooping down towards the dim blaze of the fire to make out the words, as he lined them out for the singers. Where he learned to read I know not . . . I caught the words:

"Could I but climb on Pisgah's top and view the promised land,
My flesh itself would long to drop at my dear Lord's command.
This living grace on earth we owe to Jesus' dying love;
We would be only His below and reign with Him above."

. . . Who shall dare say that these fellow-inheritors with us of the image of the Father and the love of the Son are fit only to be slaves?[56]

Shortly after Lockwood's arrival at Fortress Monroe, he heard the contraband slaves singing a spiritual song he was unfamiliar with and jotted down the words:

The Lord, by Moses, to Pharaoh said:
Oh! let my people go!
If not, I'll smite your first-born dead—
Oh! let my people go!

Oh! go down, Moses
Away down to Egypt's land
And tell King Pharaoh
To let my people go.

The song continued with nineteen additional stanzas, all of which Lockwood recorded. Sensing its significance to the slaves in their ongoing struggle for freedom, Lockwood sent the text to AMA headquarters, which forwarded it to Horace Greeley for publication in the *New York Tribune*. The Oliver Ditson Company quickly published an arrangement by Thomas Baker, with music and text copyrighted in December of 1861, called "Oh, Let My People Go—the Song of the Contrabands." This was the first publication of an African American spiritual song marketed to the American public. Lockwood himself stated the song was not new but had been sung by the slaves for decades.[57] Unfortunately, he was not a musician. While the text he recorded is similar to the spiritual we now know, he assigned the task of notating it to an English violinist/composer who had never heard it sung, and who tossed it off in the style of a British folk tune.

---

56. "Contraband Singing," 18.
57. Guenther, *In Their Own Words*, 334.

Song of the Contrabands (1861)

"Song of the Contrabands."
**Words paraphrased by the Rev. L. C. Lockwood; music arranged by Thomas Baker
(New York: Horace Waters, 1861).**

At any rate, the spiritual we now know as "Go Down, Moses" took on a mystique of its own. Sarah H. Bradford in *Scenes in the Life of Harriet Tubman* (1869) described Harriet Tubman using songs including "Go Down Moses" as signaling devices when she was a conductor on the underground railroad in the 1850s:

> At nightfall, the sound of a hymn sung at a distance comes upon the ears of the concealed and famished fugitives . . .
>
> "Hail, oh hail ye happy spirits,
> Death no more shall make you fear,
> No grief, nor sorrow, pain, nor anguish
> Shall no more distress you there . . ."
>
> I give these words exactly as Harriet sang them to me to a sweet simple Methodist hymn. "Dey don't come out to me", she said, "til I listen if de coast is clear; den when I go back and sing it again, dey come out. But if I sing,
>
> "Moses go down in Egypt,
> Till ole Pharo' let me go,
> Hadn't been for Adam's fall,
> Shouldn't hab to died at all."
>
> Den dey don't come out, for dere's danger in the way.[58]

---

58. Bradford, *Scenes in the Life of Harriet Tubman*, 26–27.

Whatever the date of its origin, after Lockwood's discovery of the song and its publication it became an anthem in the struggle for freedom. On September 22 of 1862, President Lincoln issued his Preliminary Emancipation Proclamation, declaring that as of January 1, 1863, all slaves in rebellious states "shall be then, thenceforward, and forever free."[59] On New Year's Eve, hundreds gathered in the contraband camp in Washington, DC to sing "Go Down, Moses" repeatedly as midnight approached.

The Port Royal Experiment

At virtually the same time General Ben Butler was addressing the problem of contrabands in coastal Virginia, another important development to our study was occurring farther south along the coast. On November 7, the Union Navy and an Army amphibious force liberated Port Royal, South Carolina, and over one hundred Sea Islands off the coasts of South Carolina, Georgia, and Florida. They would remain in Union hands throughout the four remaining years of the conflict. The Sea Islands had been home to lucrative rice, indigo, and vast cotton plantations, but white landowners tended to stay inland for long periods of the year to avoid malaria. The population of the islands—939 whites to 33,339 Blacks—reflected this.[60] The island slaves, as a result, had been allowed an uncommon degree of independence and had been able to establish communities and traditions not possible in other areas of the South.

The identification of fleeing slaves as contrabands was the beginning of a growing African American presence in Union-held territories and the Union army itself. Given the Union's need for additional troops in the early months of the war, there was a growing call to recruit Blacks and raise an African American regiment. Union General Rufus Saxton had been stationed in occupied Port Royal, South Carolina, serving as quartermaster for the troops there. On April 29th of 1862 he was appointed military governor of the Sea Islands with one objective—to raise such a regiment.[61]

---

59. The concept of a worship service closing out the old year and welcoming the new was not novel. John Wesley designed his famous "Covenant Service" for New Year's Eve, so many Blacks were accustomed to such a yearly observance, which was referred to as "Watch Night." The practice gained much greater significance, however, on New Year's Eve 1862 as enslaved African Americans as well as freedmen celebrated the Emancipation Proclamation becoming the law of the land. Watch Night is now an annual tradition in African American churches, tied inextricably to the struggle for freedom.

60. Epstein, *Sinful Tunes*, 253.

61. In 1863, the US War Department issued General Order Number 143, establishing a Bureau of Colored Troops to recruit African American men to fight for the Union.

Captain John Emory Bryant of the Eighth Maine Infantry, who deployed to Hilton Head and the Sea Islands in October of 1861, served under Saxton. During his stay Bryant observed that "Nearly all Negroes in this part of the South are religiously inclined," and that a Black prayer meeting "can beat a Methodist meeting out and out."[62] Describing a worship and praise meeting among the local Blacks, he wrote:

> The leader would repeat a few lines then all would sing—for Negroes are natural singers. They were just beginning to get up steam—some of the old coves [sic.] kept a constant swinging of their bodies and clapping of hands. I could see they were warming up and by the time the singing closed there was considerable excitement.[63]

Bryant recalled a leader then calling out, "God loves we!" and "God died for we!" The assembled worshippers then sang the eighteenth century hymn, "Come, Ye Sinners Poor and Needy."

The Sea Islands, while separated by only a few miles of inland waterway from the Confederacy, were firmly under Union control with a minimum threat of attack. Abolitionists, particularly those who supported the educational mission of the AMA, saw this as a unique opportunity—a laboratory, in a manner of speaking—to prove that freed African Americans could function as a successful and productive community.[64] Within months national organizations had been set up to move forward with what was referred to as the "Port Royal Experiment." During the first two years of its existence, the Port Royal Relief Committee expended nearly $50,000 in its relief effort. It also distributed thousands of dollars' worth of clothing and other items.

In the early months of the war, as Northerners found their way into the newly freed areas, their eyes were opened. For many of them, their journeys into the South were a voyage of discovery to another continent—another planet, exotic and alien. For the first time they saw slaves in the flesh, not just as vague figures they had imagined from what they read in the newspaper or from crude drawings they had seen in illustrated journals.[65]

The "United States Colored Troops" (USCT) ultimately numbered 175 regiments with nearly two hundred thousand men serving. While the vast majority were African American, Native Americans, Pacific Islanders, and Asian men also served.

62. McDaniel, *Carpetbagger of Conscience*, 28.
63. McDaniel, *Carpetbagger of Conscience*, 28.
64. Epstein, *Sinful Tunes*, 256.
65. Charters, *Songs of Sorrow*, 74.

Despite the unhealthy climate where malaria was common, the Port Royal Experiment persisted. It would prove to be a critical point in the history of American sacred music. For the first time, Northern Whites were receiving objective reports of African American worship practice by observers genuinely committed to justice and equality for the freed slaves and sympathetic to their African heritage.[66]

Fortunately for scholars, there was of huge interest in the American public and activities were regularly reported in newspapers and magazines. A number of these idealistic relief workers, teachers, and missionaries, or "Gideonites,"[67] as they were called, also published diaries and memoirs of their work on the islands. As one reviews these writings and recollections, one is immediately struck with the impression made on the observers by the slaves' music and worship practices. Descriptions of singing styles, character of tunes and texts that were heard, the ring shout—all were written about often and extensively. Among these island visitors and observers were Lucy McKim Garrison (1842–1877), Charlotte Forten Grimké (1837–1914), Laura M. Towne (1825–1901), Charles Pickford Ware (1840–1921), Colonel Thomas Wentworth Higginson (1823–1911), and William Francis Allen (1830–1889).[68]

When the first band of relief workers arrived by ship from the North, they were almost uniformly struck by the omnipresence of singing among the slaves. Charlotte Forten, a Black teacher from Philadelphia, arrived at Beaufort, South Carolina in October of 1862 on General Rufus Saxton's[69] ship, *Flora*. She then transferred to a small barque in which to be rowed across the waterway to one of St. Helena's sister islands. She described the crossing in her journal:

> The row was delightful. It was just at sunset—a grand Southern sunset; and the gorgeous clouds of crimson and gold were

---

66. Towne, *Letters and Diary*.

67. The designation "Gideonite," which was frequently used in reference to the Port Royal missionaries comes from the story of Gideon in the sixth and seventh chapters of the Old Testament book of Judges. There, the military leader, judge, and prophet Gideon is chosen by God to free the people of Israel and condemn their idolatries.

68. Lucy and Charlotte were both unmarried during their time at Port Royal. Lucy would later marry the editor and author William Garrison, and Charlotte would wed Francis Grimké, a Presbyterian minister. Lucy and Charlotte will hereafter be referred to by their maiden names, McKim and Garrison, respectively.

69. Rufus Saxton (1824–1908) was a brigadier general in the Union Army and a recipient of the Medal of Honor. In late 1862, he was appointed quartermaster of the South Carolina Expeditionary Corps headquartered at Hilton Head and was responsible for supplying the Contraband colonies at Port Royal and the surrounding islands. He would later be appointed Military Governor of the Department of the South.

reflected in the waters below, which were smooth and calm as a mirror. Then, as we glided along, the rich sonorous tones of the boatmen broke upon the evening stillness. Their singing impressed me much. It was so sweet and strange and solemn. "Roll, Jordan, Roll" was grand, and another:

"Jesus make de blind to see
Jesus make de deaf to hear
Jesus make de cripple walk,
Walk in, dear Jesus,"

And the refrain, "No man can hinder me."[70]

Laura Towne,[71] a Caucasian traveling from Pittsburgh, also disembarked at Beaufort. Before crossing to St. Helena, she spent time at a coastal plantation manor house near the water. She recalled Black boatmen sailing by regularly, their songs floating over the water:

Boats frequently pass by, the negro rowers singing their refrains. One very pretty one this morning Moses told me was:

"De bells done rung
An we goin' home—
The bells in heaven are ringing"

Every now and then they shout and change the monotony by several quick notes, or three or for long-drawn-out ones. One man sings a few words and the chorus breaks in, sometimes with a shout or interjectional notes.[72]

Religious faith seemed to permeate the daily lives of the slaves, as indicated by this almost rhapsodic descriptive passage from the foreword to Towne's diary:

Low-lying cotton fields, with here and there a sentinel palmetto; roads arched by moss-clad oak boughs; stretches of unclaimed timber and undergrowth; wide-sweeping marshes reflecting the moods and colors of the sky; the salt breath of the sea . . . Here, a woman, a bright bandana wound turban-like about her head,

---

70. Grimké, *Journals*, 388–89.

71. Born in Pittsburgh, Laura Matilda Towne was an educator and abolitionist. She originally studied homeopathic medicine at Women's Medical College in Philadelphia, and her medical training, no doubt, made her an attractive candidate to serve in the Sea Islands. Of all the relief workers, Towne was among the longest serving. Along with her Quaker friend Ellen Murray, she founded the Penn Center of St. Helena Island to minister to the freed slaves, provide medical care, teach them to read and write, and aid them in the struggle to protect their land rights. She made the center her life's work and remained on the island until her death in 1901.

72. Towne, *Letters and Diary*, 4.

looks from her door; yonder the patriarchal figure of a man toils over the ploughed field. It is a land of great distances in a small compass, of soft colors, of a people utterly dependent on the soil and weather, primitive in their faith and courage, long-abiding, and wonderfully patient. Gratitude comes easily to their lips. Thankfulness for what they have received still seems the keynote of their lives.[73]

Charles Pickard Ware, a recent graduate of Harvard University, was a third early arrival at Port Royal. While not a musician, Ware came from a musical family. Like Forten and Towne, "Charley" was immediately intrigued with the singing of the slaves. Though trained to be a schoolteacher, Ware had studied piano and played a great deal for enjoyment.[74] While headquartered at Seaside Plantation on St. Helena Island, he set about transcribing texts and words of the songs he heard in a notebook, eventually accumulating around fifty. These transcriptions would form a significant initial corpus for the seminal collection *Slave Songs of the United States* (1867).

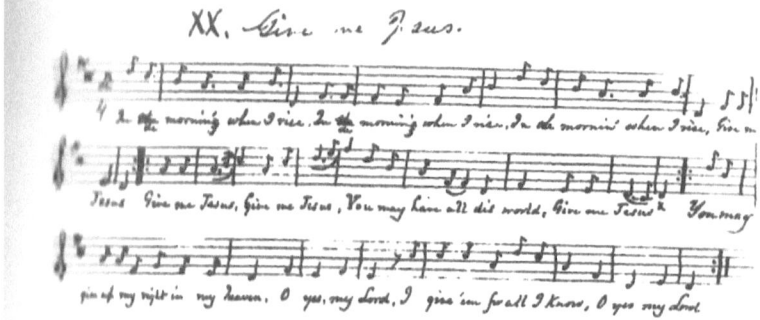

Handwritten transcription by Charles Ware of the spiritual "Give Me Jesus." This was one of several spirituals collected by him, but not selected for inclusion in *Slave Songs*. Charles P. Ware Papers, Howard University.

The fourth and arguably most influential visitor was Lucy McKim, firstborn child of one of Philadelphia's most prominent abolitionist families. McKim was one of the few semiprofessional musicians present during the Port Royal Experiment and was the daughter of James Miller McKim, a well-known abolitionist lecturer. On June 2, 1862, James McKim, accompanied by his twenty-year-old daughter Lucy, arrived in Port Royal. It was a short visit, but one that was life-changing for Lucy McKim. Her upbringing in a progressive, Unitarian, abolitionist family predisposed her to be

---

73. Towne, *Letters and Diary*, 4.
74. Epstein, "Documenting the History," 153.

sympathetic to the plight of the slaves, and her musical training naturally stimulated her to want to learn more about music in this exotic destination.

Many of the early relief workers who attended worship services held by the slaves, were moved by them, and wrote about them. McKim recalled a service she attended just prior to her return north:

> After dinner we went down to the "praise," which was held in the biggest and cleanest cabin—Aunt Phyllis's. Boards were laid across for seats, and an end of a tallow candle stuck in a Black bottle stood on a shelf in a corner and gave the only light. The little space was quite crowded, but room was made for us. The services were nearly over when we entered, there remained only two interminable hymns and a prayer. For the prayer we all knelt down and—well, I just cried, all through it. A prayer so simple, touching, and eloquent—I never heard. The preacher was an old Black man whose work was to supply the table with fish, figs, and vegetables . . .[75]

Lucy McKim left the Sea Islands on June 23, 1862, less than a month after her arrival, and was back at home in Philadelphia on July 3. Immediately upon her return, Lucy began arranging songs she had heard in Port Royal for voice with piano accompaniment.[76] Several months later, she wrote to *Dwight's Journal of Music*. Included with her letter was her arrangement of the song "Poor Rosy, Poor Gal." Both Lucy's letter, which appeared in the November 8, 1862 issue, and her arrangement have historic importance. Appearing under the headline "Songs of the Port Royal 'Contrabands,'" Lucy's letter is now regarded as the first serious acknowledgment by a trained musician of the African American spiritual as a unique and important example of American folk art. In it she made several observations about the music she had come to love. She noted that one could not accurately describe spirituals divorced from their textual substance and the style in which they were sung:

> It is difficult to express the entire character of these negro ballads by mere musical notes and signs. The odd twists made in the throat; and the curious rhythmic effect produced by single voices chiming in at different irregular intervals, seem almost impossible to place on score, as the singing of birds, or the tones of an Aeolian Harp. The airs, however, can be reached . . . Their striking originality would catch the ear of any musician . . . The wild, sad strains tell, as the sufferers themselves never could,

---

75. Charters, *Songs of Sorrow*, 113.
76. Charters, *Songs of Sorrow*, 118.

of crushed hopes, keen sorrow, and a dull, daily misery which covered them as hopelessly as the fog from the rice swamps. On the other hand, the words breathe a trusting faith in rest in the future—in "Canaan's fair and happy land," to which their eyes seem constantly turned.[77]

A frequent criticism of the slave songs by whites had been their repetitiveness, but, as Lucy explained, this was due to a lack of understanding of call-and-response singing:

> A complaint might be made against these songs on the score of monotony. It is true that there is a great deal of repetition of the music, but that is to accommodate the leader, who, if he is a good one, is always an improviser . . .[78]

What Lucy did not say, but certainly knew, was that this music was an act of corporate worship. It was an essential means by which the slaves were able to express their spiritual lives, their suffering, and their confidence in redemption. Repetition, leading often to a state of near euphoria, was indispensable. Like the shape-note singing of rural whites, also in the South, this was music that had to be experienced as a singer/believer/participant. Those hearing and evaluating it as passive listeners/nonparticipants could not hope to understand its powerful spirituality.

In African tradition, worship was not an activity restricted to a single day of the week or time of day. It permeated everything. One worshipped whether at work, at play, or in prayer. The same spirituals might be heard in each of these, but the interpretation could vary widely, depending on who was singing or how it was being used. McKim cited her arrangement of "Poor Rosy, Poor Gal" as an example. In her letter to *Dwight's*, McKim explained the improvisatory and extemporaneous quality of African American singing as she had experienced it:

> As the same songs are sung at every sort of work, of course, the tempi are not always alike. On the water, the oars dip "Poor Rosy" to an even andante; a stout boy and girl at the hominy mill will make the same "Poor Rosy" fly to keep up with the whirling stone; and in the evening, after the day's work is done, "Hea-b'n

---

77. Garrison, "Songs of the Port Royal Contrabands."
78. Garrison, "Songs of the Port Royal Contrabands."

African American Music and Worship

shall-a be my home" peals up slowly and mournfully from the distant quarters. One woman—a respectable house servant, who had lost all but one of her twenty-two children, said to me: "... I likes 'Poor Rosy' better dan all de songs, but it can't be sung without a full heart and a troubled spirit."[79]

Poor Rosy, Poor Gal

Traditional

Traditional, arr. Lucy McKim (1862)

---

79. Garrison, "Songs of the Port Royal Contrabands."

"Poor Rosy, Poor Gal" (traditional song of the freedmen at Port Royal) as transcribed by Lucy McKim Garrison (Philadelphia: by the author, 1862). Courtesy of Lester S. Levy Sheet Music Collection, Sheridan Libraries and Museums, Johns Hopkins University. (https://levysheetmusic.mse.jhu.edu/collection/024/097)

Three things stand out about Lucy McKim's arrangement from prior efforts. First, she endeavored to retain the simplicity of the songs she heard. The harmonization utilizes only primary chords and likely was modeled after the simple, improvised harmonies she would have heard at Port Royal.

Second, she indicates the need for a soloist or song leader and, in the accompanying letter to *Dwight's*, makes it clear the passage would have been sung in an improvisatory manner. Third, unlike the earlier publication of "Go Down, Moses," she retains the slave dialect. Of course, transcribing a spiritual for voice with piano accompaniment itself could be seen as a deviation from authenticity, but it was a means by which Lucy could bring awareness of an important example of folk art to a receptive public in the North.

Colonel Thomas Wentworth Higginson arrived in Port Royal in the fall of 1862. Higginson, a Massachusetts abolitionist and Unitarian minister, had been appointed a colonel leading the First South Carolina Volunteers, the first authorized regiment recruited from freedmen for Union military service. A graduate of Harvard and confidant of Emily Dickinson, Higginson was himself an accomplished writer, poet, and pioneer advocate of both racial and gender equality. Like so many others arriving before him at Port Royal, Higginson was taken by the slaves' singing, and his journals are peppered with snippets from the songs he heard. He was intrigued by the improvisational nature of the music and the ability of the Blacks to adapt new and appropriate lyrics, seemingly "on the fly," whatever the situation might be. He expanded on this in an 1867 article in the *Atlantic Monthly*:

> And I always wondered, about these, whether they had always a conscious and definite origin in some leading mind, or whether they grew by gradual accretion in an almost unconscious way. On this point I could get no information, though I asked many questions, until at last, one day when I was being rowed across from Beaufort to Ladies' Island, I found myself, with delight, on the actual trail of a song.
>
> One of the oarsmen, a brisk young fellow, not a soldier, on being asked for his theory of the matter, dropped out a coy confession. "Some good sperituals," he said, "are start jess out o' curiosity. I been a-raise a sing, myself, once."
>
> My dream was fulfilled, and I had traced out, not the poem alone, but the poet. I implored him to proceed. "Once we boys." he said, "went for tote some rice, and de nigger-driver, he keep a-callin' on us . . . Den I made a sing, just puttin' a word, and den anudder word." Then he began singing and the men, after listening a moment, joined in at the chorus as if it were an old acquaintance, though they evidently had never heard it before. I saw how easily a new "sing" took root among them.[80]

---

80. Higginson, "Negro Spirituals."

Higginson was quick to seize upon songs clearly adapted by the slaves to the war around them, recruitment, and related subjects.[81]

> The Gospel Ship
>
> De gospel ship is sailing,
>   Hosann—san—
> O Jesus is de Captain,
>   Hosann—san—
> De angels are de sailors,
>   Hosann—san—
> O is your bundle ready?
>   Hosann—san—

He was also moved by the prayers he overheard:

> Let me lib wid my musket in one hand and de Bible in de oder—dat if I die at de muzzle of de musket, die in de water, die in de land, I may know I hab de blessed Jesus in my hand, and hab no fear.[82]

Over the months he was in the Sea Islands, Higginson attempted to transcribe the melody and lyrics to dozens of songs. He described the process thus:

> Often in the starlit evening I have returned from some lonely ride by the swift river, or on the plover-haunted barrens, and, entering the camp, have silently approached some glimmering Ore, round which the dusky figures moved in the rhythmical barbaric dance the negroes call a "shout," chanting, often harshly, but always in the most perfect time, some monotonous refrain.
>
> Writing down in the darkness, as I best could—perhaps with my hand in the safe covert of my pocket—the words of the song, I have afterwards carried it to my tent, like some captured bird or insect, and then, after examination, put it by. Or, summoning one of the men at some period of leisure, Corporal Robert Sutton, for instance, whose iron memory held all the details of a song as if it were a ford or a forest, I have completed the new specimen by supplying the absent parts. The music I could only retain by ear, and though the more common strains were repeated often enough to fix their impression, there were others that occurred only once or twice.[83]

---

81. Higginson, *Civil War Journal and Letters*, 62.
82. Higginson, *Civil War Journal and Letters*, 65.
83. Higginson, "Negro Spirituals."

Emancipation

On September 17, 1862, the bloodiest single day in US military history, 26,000 men were lost at the battle of Antietam in Maryland. Despite the horrific toll, it was regarded as a Union victory and provided the needed opportune moment for President Abraham Lincoln to issue his historic Preliminary Emancipation Proclamation. Dated September 22, it read:

> That on the first day of January in the year of our Lord, one thousand eight hundred and sixty-three, all persons held as slaves within any states, or designated part of a state, the people whereof shall then be in rebellion against the United States shall be then, thenceforward, and forever free; and the executive government of the United States, including the military and naval authority thereof, will recognize and maintain the freedom of such persons, and will do no act or acts to repress such persons or any of them, in any efforts they may take for their actual freedom.[84]

The news took time to reach Port Royal, but on October 1 of 1862, Laura Towne wrote the following jubilant entry in her diary:

> Today the news came that Lincoln has declared emancipation after the 1st of January 1863. Our first victory worth the name![85]

The promise of freedom created an atmosphere of joy and anticipation among slaves and relief workers alike that would be remembered for years to come. On the Sunday before Thanksgiving, Charlotte Forten was attending church when the preacher, after his sermon, read General Rufus Saxton's *Thanksgiving Address*:

> I hereby appoint and set apart Thursday, the twenty-seventh day of November, as a day of public thanksgiving and praise; and I earnestly recommend to the Superintendents of Plantations, Teachers, and Freedmen in this Department, to abstain on that day from their ordinary business, and assemble in their respective places of worship, and render praise and thanksgiving to Almighty God for the manifold blessings and mercies he has bestowed upon us during the past year; and, more especially, for the signal success which has attended the great experiment of freedom and the rights of oppressed humanity, inaugurated in the Department of the South . . .

---

84. Preliminary Emancipation Proclamation, 1.
85. Towne, *Letters and Diary*, 92.

> You, freedmen and women, have never before had such cause for thankfulness. Your simple faith has been vindicated. "The Lord has come" to you and answered your prayers. Your chains are broken. Your days of bondage and mourning are ended, and you are forever free. If you cannot yet see your way clearly in the future, fear not; put your trust in the Lord, and He will vouchsafe, as He did to the Israelites of old, the cloud by day and the pillar of fire by night, to guide your footsteps "through the wilderness" to the promised land.
>
> I therefore advise you all to meet and offer up fitting songs of thanksgiving for all these great mercies which you have received, and with them, forget not to breathe an earnest prayer for your brethren who are still in bondage.[86]

Saxton's speech, Charlotte Forten wrote in her journal, was "the very best and noblest that could have been penned."[87]

The anticipation only grew over the next month. General Saxton issued a second proclamation on New Year's Day, 1863, which underlined the significance of the celebration.

> When in the course of human events, there comes a day which is destined to be an everlasting beacon-light, marking a joyful era in the progress of a nation and the hopes of a people, it seems to be fitting the occasion that it should not pass unnoticed by those whose hopes it comes to brighten and bless. Such a day to you is January 1, 1863 . . . Let all your voices, like merry bells, join loud and clear in the grand chorus of liberty—"We are free! We are free!"[88]

In response, over three thousand freed men, women, and children from Hilton Head, from Beaufort, and from the surrounding Port Royal plantations gathered, some arriving by steamer and others on foot.

One particularly memorable moment in the ceremony occurred as Colonel Higginson, the principal speaker for the day, rose to address the crowd. His journal entry described it as "an incident so simple, so touching, so utterly unexpected and startling that I can scarcely believe it when I recall it, though it gave the keynote to the whole day."[89] Higginson had just been handed flags to be borne before the newly organized Black regiment he was organizing.

---

86. Saxton, "Proclamation," 205.
87. Grimké, *Journals*, 401.
88. "Interesting from Port Royal," 2.
89. Higginson, *Civil War Journal and Letters*, 76.

> There suddenly arose, close beside the platform, a strong but rather cracked and elderly male voice, into which two women's voices immediately blended, singing as if by an impulse that can no more be quenched than the morning note of the song sparrow—the hymn
>
> "My country 'tis of thee,
> Sweet land of Liberty..."
>
> People looked at each other and then at the stage to see whence came this interruption ... firmly and irrepressibly the quavering voices sang on, verse after verse; others around them joined ... I never saw anything so electric; it made all other words cheap; it seemed the choked voice of a race, at last unloosed ...[90]

William Francis Allen

When William Francis Allen arrived in the Sea Islands the following November (1863), much had changed on the war front. The high tide of the Confederacy was past, and Lincoln and his cabinet had begun to seriously plan for peacetime and Reconstruction. Allen, a Massachusetts Unitarian, had considered entering the ministry but opted instead for teaching. He graduated from Harvard in 1851, after which he spent time in Europe, studying the classics in Berlin, Göttingen, and Rome. He loved music and was an accomplished flutist. Sponsored by the New England Freedman's Aid Society, Allen established a school for freed slaves where he taught from November of 1863 until July of 1864. He had been intrigued with the exotic songs of the slaves for some time.

One thing that fascinated Allen and all of his predecessors on the islands was the transcendent, even ecstatic, character of worship among the Blacks. Allen's eyewitness evocation of a Christmas Day shout in 1863 on St. Helena Island is a classic:

> The "shout" is a peculiar custom of these people ... Perhaps it is of African origin, with Christianity engrafted upon it just as it was upon the ancient Roman ritual. At any rate, it arises from that same strange connection between dancing and religious worship which was so frequent among the ancients ... These people are very strict about dancing [i.e., as a secular, social activity], but will keep up the shout all night. It has a religious significance, and apparently a very sincere one, but it is evidently [also] their recreation ...

---

90. Higginson, *Civil War Journal and Letters*, 77.

> At last [after an extended evening prayer and praise meeting] they cleared the room and began, and a strange sight it was. The room is no more than ten feet square, with a fire burning on the hearth . . . On one side of the room is a table, and in front of it stood young Paris (Simmons), Billy, and Henry who served as [the] band. Billy sang, or rather chanted, and the others "based" him as they say, while Jimmy, Lucy, Joan, Dick, Anacusa, and Molsy moved round the room in a sort of shuffle. This is the shout. Some moved the feet backward and forward alternately, but the best shouters—and Jimmy I was told today "is a great shouter"—keep the feet on the floor and work themselves along over the floor by moving them right and left . . .
>
> The shouters seldom sing or make any noise except with their feet . . . while the singers clap their hands and stamp the right foot in time . . . When they had shouted in this way for several minutes, they stopped and walked slowly round while Billy sang a sort of recitative interlude; then, when he began a new tune, they started off again . . .[91]

Allen's interest only grew as the months went by. When "he could take time from his duties in the classroom and chores of woodcutting, water drawing, and rough furniture making for the derelict house where he and Mary were quartered, he spent hours listening to the singing around him."[92] Over the spring and summer of 1864, Allen transcribed in his journal lyrics and melodies for twenty-one songs. Cousin Charles Ware contributed over fifty songs to Allen's growing collection, while dozens of others were obtained from Higginson, McKim, Forten, Towne, and other sources.

April 1865 brought both the end of the Civil War and the assassination of Lincoln. William Lloyd Garrison's fire-breathing abolitionist newspaper *The Liberator* ceased publication in December of that year, but its popularity had already been eclipsed by another popular weekly, *The Nation*, which went into circulation the previous July.[93] Coincidentally, Lucy McKim had married Wendell Phillips Garrison, the literary editor of *The Nation* that same December. Though long since departed from Port Royal, Lucy had lost none of her commitment to the cause of racial equality, the plight of her fellow relief workers in the islands, or the music of the freedmen. William Francis Allen, now a sought-after educator and speaker on Reconstruction efforts in South Carolina, was frequent contributor to *The Nation*.

---

91. Allen, *Yankee in Coastal South Carolina*, 66–67.

92. Charters, *Songs of Sorrow*, 200.

93. *The Nation*, still in circulation, is the longest continuously published weekly magazine in American history.

It is evident that Lucy's dream of publishing a collection of Black spirituals began seriously percolating in the offices of *The Nation* during 1866. We know that Allen met with Garrison in February of 1867, at which time, no doubt with Lucy's encouragement, he likely pitched the idea. Shortly after that Allen wrote to Charles Ware, requesting access to the songs he had collected; and additional meetings in New York were held to fine-tune the project. On May 30, 1867, the following announcement appeared in *The Nation*:

> We are able to announce a collection, based on the Port Royal hymnology, and including the songs of as many Southern states as are obtainable, which will be published either in the course of this year or at the beginning of next. The words and (whenever possible) the music will be carefully reproduced, and it is the aim of the editors to make the volume complete in both respects.[94]

While the collaborative efforts of McKim, Allen, and Ware resulted in the publication of the collection, they were by no means the only contributors. Among those contributing were one Annie M. Bowen, a South Carolina resident, Colonel Higginson, and other members of the military stationed in various parts of the South, and numerous teachers associated with the Freedmen's Bureau.

Slave Songs of the United States

O Black and unknown bards of long ago,
How came your lips to touch the sacred fire?
How, in your darkness, did you come to know
The power and beauty of the minstrel's lyre?
Who first from midst of his bonds lifted his eyes?
Who first from out the still watch, lone and long,
Feeling his ancient faith of prophets rise
Within his dark-kept soul, burst into song?
Heart of what slave poured out such melody
As "Steal away to Jesus"? On its strains
His spirit must have floated free,
Though still about his hands he felt his chains.
Who heard great "Jordan roll"? Whose starward eye
Saw chariot "swing low"? And who was he

---

94. Charters, *Songs of Sorrow*, 5.

That breathed that comforting melodic sigh,
"Nobody knows the trouble I see"?
Not that great German master in his dream
Of harmonies that thundered amongst the stars
At the creation, ever heard a theme
Nobler than "Go down, Moses." Mark its bars:
How like a mighty trumpet call they stir
The blood. Such are the notes that men have sung
Going to valorous deeds; such tones there were
That helped make history when time was young.
There is a wide, wide wonder in it all,
That from degraded rest and servile toil
The fiery spirit of the seer should call
These simple children of the sun and soil.
O Black slave singers, gone, forgot, unfamed,
You—you alone, of all the long, long line
Of those who've sung untaught, unknown, unnamed,
Have stretched out upward, seeking the divine.
You sang not deeds of heroes or of kings;
No chant of bloody war, no exulting paean
Of arms-won triumphs; but your humble strings
You touched in chord with music empyrean.
You sang far better than you knew; the songs,
That for your listener's hungry hearts sufficed,
Still live—but more than this to you belongs:
You sang a race from wood and stone to Christ.

EXCERPTED FROM JAMES WELDON JOHNSON, "O BLACK AND UN-KNOWN BARDS" IN FIFTY YEARS AND OTHER POEMS (PHILADELPHIA: CORNHILL COMPANY, 1917), 6.

Initially the editors sought publication with the larger, better known Scribner publishing house, but they were turned down. Oliver Ditson, the largest music publisher in the United States, also declined. The fruit of the McKim, Allen, Ware triumvirate, *Slave Songs of the United States*, was published in November of 1867 by A. Simpson & Company. The collection opens with an extensive preface by William Allen in which he described the goals of the compilation and the challenges its authors faced. It was the intention of the editors to produce (insofar as was possible) the music as it was performed and as they heard it. As Allen explains,

> The difficulty experienced in obtaining absolute correctness is greater than might be supposed by those who have never tried the experiment, and we are far from claiming that we have made no mistakes. I have never felt quite sure of my notation without a fresh comparison with the singing, and have then often found that I had made some errors. I feel confident, however, that there are no mistakes of importance. What may appear to some to be an incorrect rendering, is very likely to be a variation; for these variations are endless . . .[95]

Wherever possible the editors inserted as alternative melodic material labeled as "variations" in the manuscript of the song. This appears in the opening song of the collection, "Roll, Jordan, Roll."

"Roll, Jordan, Roll," no. 1 in *Slave Songs of the United States* (1867).

The improvisatory quality of singing was hardly the only challenge faced by the editors. "The best that we can do, however, with paper and types, or even with voices, will convey but a faint shadow of the original," Allen wrote. "The voices of the colored people have a peculiar quality that nothing can imitate; and the intonations and delicate variations of even one singer cannot be reproduced on paper."[96] Regarding the reproduction of the

---

95. Allen et al., *Slave Songs of the United States*, iv.
96. Allen et al., *Slave Songs of the United States*, iv.

songs unharmonized and unaccompanied, Allen wrote "There is no singing in parts." He goes on to describe the song leader/unison chorus approach allowing for much freedom of interpretation by both the leader and the base singers responding. One senses from Allen's description that the music was not devoid of harmony, but that it was the unplanned result of the improvisatory singing.

Allen, Ware, and especially Lucy McKim hoped for publishing success with *Slave Songs*, and they worked tirelessly to bring that about. They contributed articles on the spirituals in national magazines and lectured frequently. It was unfortunately a book ahead of its time. Northern elites were conditioned to evaluate all forms of musical expression through the prism of European art music. They viewed most forms of folk music as primitive. Respected reviewers labeled the songs of the contrabands "trash," "ugly," and "barbaric." The following excerpt from a review of *Slave Songs* appearing in *Lippincott's Magazine* is sufficient to illustrate:

> We do not believe that the negro, in his native state, knows what music is, if the term applies to melody or tune . . . He loves music dearly, however, when he hears it and readily appropriates a portion of it when he has been brought within its sphere . . .
>
> As regards the collection of tunes and words in the book under notice, we have played many of them on the piano, but have failed to discover melody in any of them, except where the idea of the tune was clearly traceable to some old hymn tune, to the composition of which no negro could lay claim. As to the words of the (so-called) hymns, they are generally so absurd and unmeaning, and often so absolutely profane (though not so intended), that it would be well for the teachers in the schools and meetinghouses where they are sung to commence, as speedily as possible, the destruction of the entire lot . . . It was hardly worthwhile to try to perpetuate this trash, vulgarity, and profanity by putting it in print.[97]

Such vituperative comments aside, *Slave Songs of the United States* did have its shortcomings, which the editors themselves were quick to acknowledge. The bulk of the songs and scholarship behind it all originated from the Port Royal Experiment, but Port Royal was not typical of the greater South. In an area isolated from the mainland, residents spoke in a Gullah dialect and had retained singing and worship traditions from the West Indies, Jamaica, and West Africa to a far greater extent than on the mainland. While the mostly white relief workers were idealistic and passionate in their

---

97. "Slave Songs of the United States," 341–42.

determination to create a better world for the now freed slaves, they generally came away regretfully admitting only a vague understanding of Black culture.

Nevertheless, it was a *first* effort to produce a true record of the African American folk spiritual. It was a work of ethnomusicology, before that term even existed. As Dena Epstein wrote:

> They produced a book of permanent historical value . . . There was no academic discipline of folklore in the 1860s. In the United States, there were no musicologists either, and what passed for anthropology at that time would not be accepted today. The systematic collection of European folk music had barely begun, while non-European musics were ignored or misunderstood, being considered exotic manifestations of the primitive mind, barbaric and strange.[98]

An understanding and appreciation of the African American spiritual in its simplicity and poignancy—and in particular its place in Christian worship—would have to wait until well into the twentieth century. For the newly freed African Americans, singing of spirituals was a sad reminder of their great tribulation and so they were often not passed down to the next generation. The melodies of course did not disappear but rather were dressed in new clothing, which brought them the popularity denied them earlier.

---

98. Epstein, *Sinful Tunes*, 303.

Chapter 7

THE CIVIL WAR
Music and Ministry in Wartime

In studying the history of any epoch, one soon becomes conscious of certain defining points—often catastrophic watershed events that separate one era from another leading, ultimately, to a radical new reality. The Civil War, four bloody years from April 1861 to April 1865, was such a defining point with regard to ministry in the American church and its music. Before the Civil War the average American's reality was bounded by the community in which he or she lived. His or her religious outlook, regardless of denominational activities and pronouncements, was driven by the local church, its particular sequence of pastors, and local worship and musical traditions. With regard to music, we have seen throughout the previous pages how outside forces seeking to initiate change were often met with fierce opposition on the local or regional level.

The world in which American church music and ministry would find itself in 1870 was *significantly* different from that of the antebellum years. Older elite Protestant churches that had resisted the use of anything other than text-only songsters (with the occasional tunebook for reference) were now exploring newly published "hymnals" featuring text and melody on the same page. Professional musicians, always viewed with suspicion because of their relationship to the iniquitous theater and musical hall, were finding greater acceptance. Organists and singers were routinely being hired by churches in larger population centers—not just as behind-the-scenes support, but visibly promoted as evidence of the church's good taste and vibrant worship life. The church choir, once the bane of nearly all clergy—Protestant *and* Roman Catholic—had become *de rigueur* in the 1870s. Post-Civil War America would see a virtual transformation to Victorian elegance in the form of heavy curtains and cushioned pews. Dark-hued woodwork, overwrought with gingerbread trim, spoke of wealth, excess, and sophistication. A yawning chasm separating the wealthy from the working classes would become evident. Evangelicals would make it their mission to reach out to a population that the mainline churches had chosen to ignore. The national crisis brought with it a time of fervent evangelical revival that would extend far beyond Appomattox. The great crusades of Dwight L. Moody and Ira David Sankey were inspired in large part by Moody's missional experiences during the conflict. From this perspective, it is fair to say that the one of the Civil War's greatest impacts was to create a flowering of populist/vernacular sacred music that would only expand and heighten for a century and half into the future.

The Revival of 1857–1859

The great religious revivals of America each arose out of intense intellectual, social, and theological ferment. By the year 1850, much of this innovation and ferment was past, both musically and in terms of spiritual vitality. The sectional feud over slavery and emancipation had reached a boiling point and engulfed the nation.

In September of 1857 the United States was in the midst of one of the most divisive and rancorous periods in American history. To make matters worse, a month later the country was to enter into the worst financial panic in its history up to that time. There appeared, however, a fleeting window of hope. Known at first as simply "the Fulton Street Prayer Meeting," its progress was followed in the national press, which renamed it, "the Businessman's Revival" and "the Great Prayer Revival." Soon it became the countrywide movement that church historians now refer to as "the Revival of 1857–1859." Over the next year, similar revivals sprang up in Ontario, Canada, Pittsburgh, Cincinnati, Philadelphia, Boston, and as far west as Chicago.[1]

To summarize general characteristics of the Revival of 1857–1859:

- First, it was a layman's movement. Ordained clergy had minimal involvement.

---

1. "Revival Born in a Prayer Meeting," 65.

- Second, it was strongly supported by the YMCA, which would also provide critical advocacy for the United States Christian Commission (the USCC).
- Third, the meetings themselves, much like evangelistic activities during the war itself, would focus more on Scripture reading, prayer, reading or hearing prayer requests, and the singing of hymns. A first generation of gospel songs by William B. Bradbury, Fanny Crosby, and others gained a national following because of the Revival of 1857.
- Finally, this was an evangelistic crusade and, as will be true in wartime, the prime movers will be Methodists and Baptists, with Presbyterians, Congregationalists, Episcopalians, and Roman Catholics involved to a lesser degree.

The flame of evangelistic zeal had been lit. Revivalistic activity would continue in both Northern and Southern armies throughout the coming conflict. Radical abolitionists, inveterate defenders of slavery and secession, and many in between all engaged evangelistic witness to support their causes. Lemuel Moes, writing shortly after the war in the Annals of the United States Christian Commission, explained the importance of the 1857–1859 Revival to ongoing missionary and relief efforts during the conflict:

> It is hence impossible not to recognize the immediate influence [of the revival] . . . upon the shaping of events which preceded the war, as well as upon the character of the troops sent to the field, and the volunteer agencies organized for the temporal and spiritual welfare of the army. We should not otherwise have been ready for the conflict . . . [The] wonderful religious interest which pervaded the [Union] army during the whole of the war was the continuance of the previous revival.[2]

Harriet Beecher Stowe, already famous throughout the land for *Uncle Tom's Cabin*, referenced the revival then going on in an 1858 article in the *New York Independent*.

> We believe in no raptures, in no ecstasies, in no experiences that do not bring the soul into communion with Him who declared He came to set at liberty them that are bound and bruised . . . We say, therefore, to our friends, that the period of great religious impulse has come; that there will be revivals all over the land,

---

2. Moss, *Annals of the United States Christian Commission*, 67.

either false or true—either of a Christian or a heathen type; and by their fruits we shall know them.[3]

Like many leaders within the institutional church, Harriet's father, the Rev. Lyman Beecher, was reluctant to forcefully condemn slavery, fearing it could cause a schism. For Harriet Beecher Stowe, that desire to preserve unity whatever the cost was indefensible. She did not believe that the curse of slavery rested solely on churches in the South, but churches throughout the nation. "She realized that northern Presbyterians like her father had refused time and time again to speak out against slavery for fear of shattering the unity of the Church and thereby weakening the evangelical effort."[4] She powerfully expressed that idealistic hope with revivalistic passion in the closing words of *Uncle Tom's Cabin* (1851).

> O, Church of Christ, read the signs of the times! Is not this power the spirit of Him whose kingdom is yet to come, and whose will to be done on earth as it is in heaven? "But who may abide the day of his appearing, for that day shall burn as an oven: and he shall appear as a swift witness against those that oppress the hireling in his wages, the widow and the fatherless, and that turn aside the stranger in his right: and he shall break in pieces the oppressor." Are not these dread words for a nation bearing in her bosom so mighty an injustice? . . . Both North and South have been guilty before God; and the Christian church has a heavy account to answer. Not by combining together, to protect injustice and cruelty, and making a common capital of sin, is this Union to be saved,—but by repentance, justice and mercy; for, not surer is the eternal law by which the millstone sinks in the ocean, than that stronger law, by which injustice and cruelty shall bring on nations the wrath of Almighty God![5]

At the Brink of War

In August of 1859 a local newspaper proudly described the up and coming town of Chambersburg, Pennsylvania, as follows:

> the destiny of Chambersburg is something beyond the ordinary lot of inland towns, if we are to judge by the piles of brick, lumber, etc., with which our streets have been blocked up, since early

---

3. Murison, *Politics of Anxiety*, 107–8.
4. Hovet, "Church Diseased," 174.
5. Stowe, *Uncle Tom's Cabin*, 252.

in the spring, materials for new brick buildings in the course of erection. Nor does it appear likely to cease, from the indications we have, until cold weather shall put a stop to the busy hum of the mason hammer and carpenter saw.[6]

Chambersburg was like hundreds of other small but growing towns across the American heartland. The railroad passing on the north side of town connected it to the rest of the country and helped ensure its robust economy. At the time Franklin County was among the largest wheat growers in the nation. It was to Chambersburg that area farmers brought and marketed their harvested crops. Still, it was 1859. Dirt streets and board sidewalks were the rule. By necessity it was a small, compacted universe where people's day-to-day lives were limited to that which could be done on foot or horseback.[7]

Such was the worldview of many a young Civil War recruit. Almost half of all soldiers in the Union Army came from farming families. Significantly more from rural areas enlisted to fight with the Confederates. Over 50 percent of the total force in both armies was between the ages of eighteen and twenty-five. A substantial number of recruits on both sides had only basic literacy skills. Church membership in Chambersburg, like much of rural America, was about one in four, but this can be misleading. Local churches were the centers for much of community life, and pastor/preachers often had the most influential voices for all inhabitants—church affiliated or not. Also, whether or not one belonged to a church, there was a near universal belief in God and a pre-Darwinian conviction that Providence controlled every aspect of living—nature, crops, financial success or failure, war, peace, and death, where, when, or how it might occur.

The process of enlistment in the opening months of the Civil War was similar across the nation. An important promotional tool was the war meeting. Prominent civic leaders and veterans of previous wars would speak, a military band and often large choirs would deliver patriotic songs such as "Rally 'round the Flag." As John D. Billings, a veteran of the Army of the Potomac in the Civil War, recalled:

> Sometimes the patriotism of such a gathering would be wrought up so intensely by waving banners, martial and vocal music, and burning eloquence, that a town's quota would be filled in less

---

6. Ayers, *In the Presence of Mine Enemies*, 10.

7. Ayers, *In the Presence of Mine Enemies*, 10. The idyllic life in Chambersburg would be forever changed during the coming Civil War. Located just fifty miles north of Harpers Ferry and forty miles east of Gettysburg, it would play a central role in the coming conflict. Twice, Confederate raiders would appear, creating havoc and frightening local residents.

than an hour. It needed only the first man to step forward, put down his name, be patted on the back, placed upon the platform and cheered . . . as the hero of the hour, when a second, a third, a fourth would follow, and at last a perfect stampede set in to sign the enlistment roll, and a frenzy of enthusiasm would take possession of the meeting.[8]

The hyper-patriotism of the first months of the war did not last. As it became clear to both sides that it was not to be a quickly won engagement, enlistment signings tapered off. Consequently, the Confederacy initiated conscription in 1862 with the North following a year later.

Once enlisted, the new recruit along with the rest of his company was transported to training camps in various locations. Unlike American armies in the twentieth century, there was no consistent level of battlefield training across the Confederate and Union armies. It was not uncommon for highly trained regiments to serve in combat alongside poorly trained or inexperienced ones. Life or death for the individual recruit often depended on the training he would receive, or the lack of it, and the quality of leadership offered by his superiors—factors over which he had no control.

Death from disease, accident, or old age was certainly no stranger to persons living in the nineteenth century. But the exorbitant loss of life experienced during the rebellion due to violence, weapons more sophisticated than their users, primitive medical knowledge, and out-of-control diseases and contagions challenged the emotions and psyche of most within the ranks. Into this virtual carnival of horrors came a woefully naïve generation of young men, many still adolescents. Our present ability to identify, diagnose, and treat "post-traumatic stress syndrome" or PTSD did not exist in the 1860s. Even for those who had seen death up close, there would be nothing to equate with the sheer tidal wave of pain, maiming, death, and destruction of which they would find themselves in the center.

The Civil War soldier found himself dropped into a new and unfamiliar world when recruited into the military. While regiments were drawn from individual states and were identified that way, the likelihood that an individual recruit would remain among his hometown friends was slim. Military discipline, and his very survival, depended upon sacrificing some of his individuality, being subservient to superiors, and being willing to blend into the larger regimental unit. In all probability that regimental unit

---

8. Billings, *Hardtack and Coffee*, 50. While Billings was referring to recruitment practices in Massachusetts at the beginning of the war, they were common to other parts of the nation as well.

would have a far greater variety of personalities, national origins, and religious backgrounds than he had ever encountered before.

The Civil War represented not only a constitutional, sectional, and moral crisis, but a *spiritual* crisis as well. The fact that, as the war ground on, more and more soldiers embraced and even demanded worship in the field with brothers of differing backgrounds, believers and nonbelievers alike, heralded a new openness to religious pluralism. Worship was largely nondenominational so the common soldiers often needed to discard rigid denominational views on how it should be practiced. The same applied to much dogma associated with particular sects.

An important—even critical—source of comfort for believer and nonbeliever alike was religion and music associated with it. Music was omnipresent in the camps of both Union and Confederate armies. Military records, diaries, and memoirs of the time are peppered with references to bands and band music, popular and patriotic songs, and especially singing—informal recreational singing, singing on the march, and singing in worship. Soldiers were known to sing hymns when meeting in small groups to pray. At larger prayer meetings and revival gatherings, the entire content might be limited to singing and prayer. In addition, the singing of hymns was an essential component of formal regimental worship services on the Sabbath, and a stanza or two of a familiar spiritual song was often incorporated into Sunday afternoon dress parades in both North and South.

The Chaplaincy

On May 4 of 1861, the US War Department, acting in response to the firing on Fort Sumter, issued General Orders No.'s 15 and 16, which authorized the organization of a 75,000-man volunteer army. To be included was a regimental chaplaincy:

> There will be allowed to each regiment one chaplain, who will be appointed by the regimental commander on the vote of field officers and company commanders on duty with the regiment at the time the appointment is to be made. The chaplain so appointed must be a regularly ordained minister of some Christian denomination and will receive the pay and allowances of captain of cavalry.[9]

---

9. *War of the Rebellion*, 154.

Sunday Mass for 69th New York Infantry Regiment. (Public domain image from the Library of Congress, LC-BB13-3713-A.) Photograph showing Father Thomas Mooney, Chaplain of the New York State Militia and Irish-American soldiers at Fort Corcoran, Arlington Heights, VA, June 22, 1862.

Confederate Chaplain
John William Jones,
Company D, 13th and 25th Virginia Regiments.
Photo by C. R. Reese & Company, Richmond. (Public domain image from the Library of Congress, #Lot 15158–1, no. 941.)

Faced with having to establish itself with a working government, form an army, and fight for survival—all simultaneously—the new Confederate government did not view establishing a chaplaincy as a priority. Jefferson Davis himself questioned whether there were enough qualified individuals in the South to serve in the capacity. There was also a reluctance to have government-appointed and paid chaplains because it conflicted with the concept of "separation of Church and State." Still, because of the strong support from military leaders and clergy for chaplains in the field, the Confederate Congress on May 3rd of 1861 approved a bill authorizing them.[10]

> There shall be appointed by the President such number of chaplains, to serve with the armies of the Confederate States during the existing war, as he may deem expedient; and the President shall assign them to such regiments, brigades or posts as he may deem necessary; and the appointments made as aforesaid shall expire whenever the existing war shall terminate.[11]

While the need for chaplains was recognized in both armies at the outset of hostilities and appointments began to be made, it was not a carefully thought out process. Prior to 1863, there was no real job description for chaplains. The *job*, as it were, had to be defined by the chaplain himself based on his experience and the soldiers' needs. Finally, in 1863 an *Army Chaplain's Manual* was published for the Union Army. It was not a compendium of regulations but rather a detailed overview of ministry conditions and what priorities should be for chaplains in the field. Appended to the manual were readings from the Psalter and New Testament, prayers for worship, an extended section of devotional readings to be used with the sick and dying, prayers for private devotion, and texts for fifty-two well-known hymns.[12]

From the first, military officials in both the North and South recognized the essential role of music both as a communal activity and in worship. It fell to the chaplain to plan and incorporate singing both in formal worship, informal prayer gatherings, and often around the campfire. An excellent example was Charles A. Humphreys (1838–1921), a Unitarian minister who served as chaplain with the Massachusetts Cavalry Volunteers from 1863 to 1865. As he recalled it in his memoirs, Humphreys's only official duties were "to hold worship on the Sabbath when convenient and bury the dead."[13] He supplemented his duties, however, by:

---

10. Dickens Jr., "Standardization of the Military Chaplaincy," 96.
11. Pitts, *Chaplains in Gray*, 39.
12. Hammond, *Army Chaplain's Manual* (1863).
13. Humphreys, *Field, Camp, Hospital, and Prison*, 26. Humphreys's two years of

- keeping and utilizing a variety of religious materials as needed for a truly nonsectarian, inclusive ministry: both Catholic and Episcopal prayer books, Methodist songsters, and New Testaments in English, Italian, French, and German.
- visiting and encouraging the men in their tents.
- bringing with him a large library of over two hundred volumes—a gift from Henry Wilder Foote of Boston—which he made available to lend.
- arranging with local women to make cavalry mittens for use in holding a horse's reins for long periods and in cold weather. He also collected knit caps for the men and food items for the sick.
- keeping a record of known needs of the servicemen and making them known in the surrounding community.
- collecting money from the men to be sent home to their families and mailing it.
- acting as postmaster for the regiment and providing writing materials to its men
- serving as a sounding board for inexperienced recruits, not accustomed to military discipline, as well as a father confessor for others.
- making regular visits to base and field hospitals, bringing special food items and pillows to relieve or prevent bed sores. He also brought games and puzzles. By this point in the war, patients commonly included both Union and Confederate patients, and Humphreys, like many chaplains, was committed to treating all equally, regardless of allegiance.

Humphreys went on to outline his responsibilities on a typical Sabbath. There was the usual morning worship service for the regiment (more about that later). This was followed by three services at the base hospital—three because of the impracticality of moving patients from one ward to another. On Sunday afternoon there was the regimental dress parade with its own worship moment, and there were the funerals—one or more every weekend.[14]

---

service encompassed some of the bloodiest years of the war. As a chaplain in the Army of the Potomac, he was actively involved in the Wilderness Campaign and became a prisoner of war, ministering to fellow prisoners in Lynchburg and Richmond, Virginia, under horrific conditions. His very detailed and literate descriptions of these experiences have made his memoirs a valuable resource for historians of the war.

14. Humphreys, *Field, Camp, Hospital, and Prison*, 40.

Delegates, Missionaries, and Colporteurs

While Charles Humphreys set a high standard for himself, one can see that, for a chaplain truly committed to serving a regiment of up to eight hundred men and their officers, the demands were beyond the ability of a single individual. The myriad tasks facing Civil War chaplains—which included planning for and incorporating music into worship—could be daunting. Others—noncommissioned civilians—were needed to play a critical role in supporting the chaplaincy. Churches of different denominations sent representatives to lend a hand. First, there were the itinerant lay preachers—a tradition hearkening back to the early nineteenth century and the first camp meetings. Itinerant preachers would follow troops in their movements, offering to preach for meager sums or donations. Then there were the so-called missionaries. These were generally local clergy sent by a denomination or a nearby church and compensated by them to either supplement preaching by the chaplain, or in some cases to provide short-term aid in regiments where there was no chaplain. But none of this was sufficient to deal with the scale of need that existed.

When the United States entered into World War II in 1941, a cooperative relationship was set up between the American Red Cross and the USO (or United Service Organizations) to promote good morale among the troops, oversee medical care, and even provide avenues of entertainment. None of this existed in the 1860s, but both the Union and Confederate governments recognized a need. On the Union side, two large organizations were formed independent of the government. The United States Sanitary Commission was principally concerned with medical and hospital care issues, while the United States Christian Commission, affiliated with the YMCA, was intended to aid the chaplaincy.

The United States Christian Commission

The work of the United States Christian Commission or USCC was primarily focused on bringing a spiritual witness to the troops, but along with doing that, it was tasked with providing a degree of comfort to the lives of Union soldiers. The USCC grew directly out of the activities of the New York City chapter of the Young Men's Christian Association, the YMCA.[15]

The USCC's early efforts were well-intentioned but flawed by disorganization. This would improve, however, with time. Volunteers, referred to

---

15. Cannon, "United States Christian Commission," 63, 66. The role of the YMCA as a force for evangelistic witness would continue long after the Civil War through Dwight L. Moody's close ties to the organization.

as "delegates" and receiving no compensation other than reimbursement of expenses, were sent south to follow the various Union armies. Often a delegate's obligations included many of the tasks the army chaplains had been doing on their own: distributing hundreds of evangelical tracts, pocket New Testaments, and hymnal songsters. They also organized Bible studies and prayer meetings, taught classes in basic literacy, picked up and delivered mail, and even preached when needed. Delegates were also expected to be present at brigade hospitals, working with chaplains to provide comfort and assurance to the critically ill and dying. This typically included prayer, reading of Scripture, and singing.[16]

The Confederacy had no national organizations to parallel the USCC; however Confederate chaplains and religious leaders were well aware of the important work it did. By 1863, several Christian associations modeled after the USCC had been organized within the Army of Northern Virginia:

- Soldiers' Christian Association of the Tenth Regiment, Virginia Volunteers
- North Carolina Christian Association
- Georgia Soldiers' Christian Association
- Young Men's Christian Association of Kemper's Brigade
- Christian Association of the Stonewall Brigade[17]

---

16. Cannon, "United States Christian Commission," 66.
17. Daniel, "Christian Association."

Tracts, Hymnals, and Songsters

> **HYMNS,**
>
> RELIGIOUS AND PATRIOTIC,
>
> FOR
>
> THE SOLDIER AND THE SAILOR.
>
> PUBLISHED BY THE
> AMERICAN TRACT SOCIETY,
> 28 CORNHILL, BOSTON.

Cover page, *Hymns, Religious and Patriotic for the Soldier and the Sailor.* (Boston: American Tract Society, 1861). (https://www.google.com/books/edition/Hymns_Religious_and_Patriotic/vDRGAA AAYAAJ?hl=en&gbpv=1&dq=Hymns,+Religious+and+Patriotic&printsec=frontco ver)

Also, commonly present among both Northern and Southern armies were colporteurs or peddlers of religious books and tracts. The term colporteur was derived from the French, *colporteur,* meaning "to bear." The concept of colportage arose during the Protestant Reformation when publishers and book merchants hired itinerant peddlers to sell inexpensive editions of reading material in rural areas remote from booksellers' shops. The colporteur differed from the chaplain, USCC delegate, and missionary in that he was a salaried employee of a publisher.

In the United States before and during the Civil War, most colporteurs were employed by the American Tract Society or ATS.[18] In 1859 the ATS reported 780 colporteurs working throughout the continental United States, of whom 174 were part-time college or seminary students. About half were active in the Confederacy.[19] In its Annual Report for 1863, reprinted in the *New York Times*, the ATS indicated that it had produced an amazing 8,182,562 separate publications, including several hymnal songsters like the one pictured on the previous page.

Worship and Revivalism during the Civil War

Christian ministry impacted Civil War soldiers, North and South, in many ways. Weekly regimental worship services were held on the Sabbath except under extraordinary circumstances. While attendance was not generally required, large numbers of recruits attended. In addition, prayer meetings during the week were common, often led by USCC delegates, visiting missionaries, or colporteurs.

A significant group of works, from memoirs of actual participants and observers to recent historical studies, has dealt with revivals during the Civil War, in which large numbers of soldiers experienced conversion to Christianity. While the large numbers of converted cited in some period sources must be suspect, there can be no doubt that large numbers of combatants found comfort through revivalistic experiences.[20, 21]

Being able to worship on the Christian Sabbath or have it as a "day of rest" was important to the Civil War soldier. In fact, for much of America in the nineteenth and twentieth centuries, civil laws were enforced forbidding most commercial business on Sunday. The fact that the Battle of Shiloh, April 6–7, 1862, was initiated on a Sunday morning was cited by many Southern soldiers and generals as the reason for their army's defeat. Several

---

18. The American Tract Society had been founded in 1825 with the purpose of supplementing the work of the American Bible Society by producing religious tracts of a nondenominational nature.

19. "Colportage as Conducted by the American Tract Society," 3.

20. Two of the most useful and often referenced sources on revivalism in the Confederate Army must be used with care. They are J. William Jones's *Christ in the Camp* and William W. Bennett's *Narrative of the Great Revival*. In both cases, the authors write from the perspective of the Lost Cause, implying that though defeated, the Confederate struggle was a holy one to preserve a way of life, and that somehow the Confederate soldiers and generals, as a group, were more devout than their Union antagonists.

21. See Steven E. Woodworth's *While God Is Marching On* for an in-depth survey of revivalistic activities in both Northern and Southern armies.

other major battles were initiated on the Sabbath, and the losing side was frequently apt to blame their defeat on God's scorn.

In November of 1862, President Lincoln issued a proclamation regarding Sabbath observance in the military:

> The President, Commander-in-Chief of the Army and Navy, desires and enjoins the orderly observance of the Sabbath by the officers and men in the military and naval service. The importance for men and beast of the prescribed weekly rest, the sacred rights of Christian soldiers and sailors, a becoming deference to the best sentiment of a Christian people, and a due regard for the divine will demand that Sunday labor in the Army and Navy be reduced to the measure of strict necessity.
>
> The discipline and character of the national forces should not suffer nor the cause they defend be imperiled by the profanation of the day or name of the Most High. "At this time of public distress," adopting the words of Washington in 1776, "men may find enough to do in the service of God and their country without abandoning themselves to vice and immorality." The first general order issued by the Father of his Country after the Declaration of Independence indicates the spirit in which our institutions were founded and should ever be defended: "The General hopes and trusts that every officer and man will endeavor to live and act as becomes a Christian soldier defending the dearest rights and liberties of his country."[22]

Lincoln's was not a lone voice. In September of 1861 General George McClellan, commander of the Army of the Potomac, issued the following order:

> Unless in the case of an attack of by enemy, or some other extreme military necessity, it is commended to all commanding officers that all work shall be suspended on the Sabbath; that no unnecessary movements shall be made on that day; that the men shall, as far as possible, be permitted to rest from their labors; that they shall attend divine service after the customary morning inspections; and that officers and men alike use their influence to insure the utmost decorum and quiet on that day.[23]

Robert E. Lee issued a similar directive to his Army of Northern Virginia in 1864:

---

22. Lincoln, "General Order Respecting the Observance of the Sabbath," 170.
23. "News of the Day," 4.

General Orders No. 15.
Hdqrs. Army of Northern Virginia,
February 7, 1864.

I. The attention of the army has already been called to the obligation of a proper observance of the Sabbath, but a sense of its importance, not only as a moral and religious duty, but as contributing to the personal health and well-being of the troops, induces the commanding general to repeat the orders on that subject. He has learned with great pleasure that in many brigades, convenient houses of worship have been erected, and earnestly desires that every facility consistent with the requirements of discipline shall be afforded the men to assemble themselves together for the purpose of devotion.

II. To this end he directs that none but duties strictly necessary shall be required to be performed on Sunday, and that all labor, both of men and animals, which it is practicable to anticipate or postpone, or the immediate performance of which is not essential to the safety, health, or comfort of the army, shall be suspended on that day.

III. Commanding officers will require the usual inspections on Sunday to be held at such time as not to interfere with the attendance of the men on divine service at the customary hour in the morning. They also will give their attention to the maintenance of order and quiet around the places of worship and prohibit anything that may tend to disturb or interrupt religious exercises.

R. E. Lee, General.[24]

The civil and military leadership recognized positive benefits to be derived from Sabbath observance. Regiments in both the North and the South, when not on the move, had services—attendance optional—on Sunday mornings after inspections were complete.[25] The format for these services was uncomplicated: Scripture readings, hymn singing, and a sermon or homily. Union chaplains were expected to follow a prescribed worship format on Sundays in the field. Regimental worship was limited to twenty or thirty minutes and usually began with a hymn. This was followed by a Scripture reading, a short homily based on it, and the singing of another hymn appropriate to the theme of the day. A prayer for home and family typically

---

24. Jones, *Christ in the Camp*, 50.
25. *Revised United States Army Regulations of 1861*, 46.

came next, followed by the singing of a familiar hymn stanza. The chaplain would then deliver a short exhortation equating the following of Christ, "the captain of our salvation," to service in the military. This was followed by the singing of a hymn and the benediction. To close the service recruits stood to sing the doxology, "Praise God from Whom All Blessings Flow." There could be no clearer indicator of the importance of or the participation in congregational singing among enlisted men than this: five hymns sung in a service lasting less than thirty minutes, and, no doubt, mostly sung from memory!

Regimental worship had to be scheduled so as not to conflict with other soldierly duties and the question was often where to have it. Throughout the war when weather was temperate, and particularly when troops were on the move, worship out-of-doors was the logical choice. Union chaplain Frederic Denison remembered that for much of 1861 and 1862, services were held in groves or open fields. As the fighting became more frequent and intense in 1863 and after, he recalled having worship in open air forts and entrenchments.[26]

Chaplain Humphreys recalled that when he was assigned to the chaplaincy of the Massachusetts Cavalry Volunteers the regiment was bivouacked for the winter near Vienna, Virginia. "Once I took my colored servant and my little hatchet, and went out at nine o'clock Sunday morning, cleared away the underbrush from a small amphitheater in a neighboring wood, and at ten o'clock the chief bugler sounded the church call at the camp and then again at the place of meeting. Somehow it did not seem strange, but the most natural place in which to worship. The groves were God's first temples."[27]

A similar description was provided by Lieutenant John H. Worsham (1839–1920), Company F of the Twenty-first Virginia Infantry. He recalled an evening revival service of the Army of Northern Virginia shortly after its defeat and retreat south after the Battle of Gettysburg. The Southerners encamped for the winter at Montpelier, Virginia, on the banks of the Rapidan River.

> The place selected for preaching in our camp was on a hillside, in a large wood, the road running on one side of the place, and a small branch on the other. The ground was slightly inclined; trees were cut from the adjoining woods, rolled to this spot, and arranged for seating at least two thousand people. At the lower end, a platform was raised with logs, rough boards were placed on them, and a bench was made at the far side for the seating

---

26. Miller, "In God's Presence," 114.
27. Humphreys, *Field, Camp, Hospital, and Prison*, 12.

of the preachers. In front was a pulpit or desk, made of a box. Around this platform and around the seats, stakes or poles were driven in the ground about ten or fifteen feet apart, on top of which were baskets made of iron wire, iron hoops, etc. In these baskets chunks of lightwood were placed, and at night they were lighted, throwing a red glare far beyond the confines of the place of worship. The gathering, each night, of the bronzed and grizzly warriors, devoutly worshiping, was a wonderful picture in the army; and when some old familiar hymn was given out, those thousands of warriors would make hill and dell ring.[28]

The horror and carnage experienced at Gettysburg, of course, affected combatants on both sides of the conflict. The bodies stacked one over the other at the stone wall following Pickett's ruinous charge left many Union defenders as shaken as their Confederate adversaries. For many a soldier, continuing to face death with any sort of peace and confidence required a faith undergirded by prayer and spiritual counsel. Worship helped to provide this. Immediately after the charge, soldiers in the 64th New York Regiment prevailed upon Chaplain John Stuckenberg of the 145th Pennsylvania Regiment to hold a worship service:

> The men were behind their breastworks. I stood in front of them. Brisk skirmishing was going on all the time, rebels and our men . . . could be seen running and firing. A rebel flag was also seen at the edge of the woods. Worship at such a place, at such a time, with fearful scenes just enacted and being enacted, was very solemn. I thanked God that we had been spared, prayed for the many wounded and remembered the relatives and friends of the killed. The soldiers felt deeply, and many were moved to tears.[29]

Having a formal service in a carefully planned and created wilderness area was often neither possible nor necessary. Henry Trumbull, a Union Army chaplain with Grant's Army of the Potomac in 1864, explained that open air meetings were often the only practical alternative since there simply was not time to fabricate a covered worship space. "The only way to gather men for worship," he wrote, "was on the open field where we bivouacked by the roadside as we halted on a march, or in a shady ravine within reach, if we had a few hours rest in a wooded region."[30]

---

28. Worsham, *One of Jackson's Foot Cavalry*, 181–82.
29. Stuckenberg, *I'm Surrounded by Methodists*, 83.
30. Trumbull, *War Memories of an Army Chaplain*, 33–34.

J. M. Jones, who served the Confederacy during the "Valley Campaign," late in the war, provided a vivid description of more spontaneous wartime worship among the Southern armies:

> And there upon some green sward [i.e., a grassy surface of land] on the banks of the Shenandoah, . . .we lay us down to rest. Oh, so sweet after a hard day's march. But before the bivouac is quiet for the night there assembles a little group at some convenient spot hard by, who strike up some dear old hymn . . . From all parts of the bivouac, men hasten to the spot; the song grows clearer and louder, and in a few moments a very large congregation has assembled . . . the chaplain reads some appropriate Scripture, leads in fervent prayer, and speaks words of earnest counsel, faithful admonition or solemn warning . . . On that whole campaign, I never found the men too weary to assemble promptly for the evening service. Indeed, we accustomed ourselves to make sermons on the march [and to] preach when we should go into bivouac in the evening, and while in some respects it was sermonizing under difficulties, I doubt if we ever made better sermons than under the . . . consciousness that we were preparing to deliver the last message of salvation which many of those brave fellows would ever hear.[31]

When an army was stationary and bivouacked for the winter, outdoor worship could be impractical. Efforts began in the fall of the war's first year to provide covered shelter for regimental worship gatherings. To address this need, rough-hewn log buildings and later more elaborate structures were devised, both with heat from a wood fire. Commanding General George McClellan sought authorization from the War Department to appropriate lumber to construct temporary chapels. Secretary of War Edmund Stanton replied succinctly and memorably, "The Lord's will be done."[32] Another option for shelter were so-called "tabernacle tents." Humphreys remembered borrowing walled hospital tents for services until they were needed elsewhere, and then holding services in an abandoned barn, with cattle present and occasionally participating.[33] Other regiments met in abandoned churches, theaters, and warehouses.

Soldiers of the Army of the Potomac when in occupied territory would often have worship in abandoned churches and chapels along the way. In 1862, Chaplain Trumbull was stationed with his regiment in Florida at the

---

31. Jones, *Christ in the Camp*, 251.
32. Norton, *Struggling for Recognition*, 97.
33. Humphreys, *Field, Camp, Hospital, and Prison*, 39.

old Castillo de San Marcos on the ocean front at St. Augustine, which had been renamed "Fort Marion." The fortress chapel became a worship space for the regiment that Trumbull remembered as a "quaint and solemn place for a religious service." It was, he wrote, "in the central casemate, directly opposite the sally-port. It had an elaborate entrance or portico, a niche for a holy water receptacle, and an altar fixed against the opposite wall.... Our Catholic soldiers valued its hallowed associations, and our Protestant soldiers were glad to be there."[34]

When there was no chaplain on hand in a regiment, not an uncommon situation, soldiers often journeyed to local churches to worship with local citizens. It was not always a positive experience. Colonel Elisha Hunt Rhodes, stationed near Winchester, Virginia, wrote this in his diary:

> Sunday, October 16, 1864—Attended church this morning, but I can hardly say "worship" for at the only church (an Episcopal one) the minister is a regular old Rebel. I hope we shall have another one opened soon.[35]

Even when armies were on the move there could be times of respite. Beginning in 1863, the USCC managed a program to provide construction plans and waterproof canvas roofing for portable tent/chapels which could be carried with regiments and erected quickly when there was a need. Confederate troops devised similar structures. As the war progressed, the extended siege, lasting weeks or months, became a common battle tactic. With opposing armies entrenched for an extended siege, the need for reassurance, prayer, and worship among the troops could be pressing. At Petersburg, the longest and most grueling of all the sieges, hundreds of worship spaces appeared, from large tents to elaborate, church-like structures.

---

34. Trumbull, *War Memories of an Army Chaplain*, 32.
35. Rhodes, *All for the Union*, 183.

Built by 50th New York Regiment and used during the Battle of Petersburg, ca. 1865. T. O. Sullivan, photographer (Library of Congress call # E468.7 .G2, v. 2, no. 74 (Case Y) [P&P]). (https://www.loc.gov/pictures/item/2007685812)

Hymn Singing in the Camp

Prior to the Civil War, congregational singing in small towns and rural areas, North and South, had generally been limited to psalms and a few well-known, lined out hymns. Nevertheless, certain hymns—some learned in Sunday school, others sung around the home fire or recreationally—were known to many. More often than not, the Civil War soldier hailed from such small towns and rural areas. The war would open his eyes to new and memorable experiences in hymn singing.

During the Civil War era, many Christian hymns became well known and popular beyond the confines of worship. Hymns like "Rock of Ages," "All Hail the Power of Jesus' Name," "My Faith Looks Up to Thee," and "Sweet Hour of Prayer" were universally enjoyed and sung alongside secular tunes on both sides of the Mason–Dixon line. Chaplains and the soldiers themselves would gravitate toward these popular and well-known hymn choices. "The fact that soldiers, from the indifferent to the most ardent believer, sang hymns while marching, or back-to-back with minstrel songs, helps explain the place and presence of hymns in American culture. And it was this natural practice of hymn singing that prompted Christian organizations to publish small collections of hymns for soldiers."[36]

Professor Mark D. Rhoads, who has done significant research regarding hymn singing during the Civil War and published a hymnal for historically informed Civil War reenactments, suggests that a common core of hymns appeared in both Northern and Southern songsters. Rhoads's observations are borne out in a comparison of *The Hymnbook for the Army and Navy*, published for Union troops by the American Tract Society, and the *Soldiers' Hymnbook for Camp Worship*, published by the Soldier's Tract Society, an organ of the Methodist Episcopal Church South, for use by the Confederate Army. The actual repertoire of hymns known to have been commonly sung during the conflict was quite broad and impressive.

A Charge to Keep	My Faith Looks Up to Thee
All Hail the Power of Jesus' Name	Nearer My God to Thee
Am I a Soldier of the Cross?	O, for a Thousand Tongues to Sing
Amazing Grace	O, For a Closer Walk with God
Blow Ye the Trumpet, Blow	O Happy Day that Fixed My Choice
Come Thou Fount of Every Blessing	O Sing to Me of Heaven
Come, We (or Ye) that Love the Lord	Praise God from Whom All Blessings Flow (Old Hundredth)
Gently Lord, O Gently Lead Us	
Guide Me, O Thou Great Jehovah	Rock of Ages
How Firm a Foundation	Say, Brothers, Will You Meet Us?
I Will Not Live Always	Soldiers of Christ, Arise
Jerusalem, My Happy Home	Sweet Hour of Prayer
I'm a Pilgrim and I'm a Stranger	There Is a Fountain Filled with Blood
Jesus, Lover of My Soul	There Is a Happy Land
Jesus Shall Reign	There Is a Land of Pure Delight
Just as I am Without One Plea	When I Can Read My Title Clear
Mid Scenes of Confusion	When I Survey the Wond'rous Cross
My Days Are Gliding Swiftly By	

Hymns containing militaristic imagery were drawn on for wartime worship. Union troops sang "Soldiers of Christ, Arise," "Guide Me, O Thou Great Jehovah," and "Marching Along," which, as the title suggests, was sung by troops on the march.

> The soldiers are gath'ring from near and from far,
> The trumpet is sounding the call for the war,
> The conflict is raging, 'twill be fearful and long;
> We'll gird on our armor and be marching along.

---

36. Rhoads, "Hymns in the Lives of American Soldiers," online blog. Mark Rhoads is a professor of music at Bethel University in St. Paul, Minnesota.

CHORUS.
Marching along, we are marching along;
Gird on the armor, and be marching along;
The conflict is raging, 'twill be fearful and long;
Then gird on the armor and be marching along.[37]

While on the march, Confederates were known to sing, "O When Shall I See Jesus," possibly to the famous *Southern Harmony* tune, "The Morning Trumpet." The second stanza:

But now I am a soldier. My Captain's gone before.
He's given me my orders and tells me not to fear.
And if I hold out faithful, A crown of life he'll give,
And all his valiant soldiers, Eternal life shall have.[38]

The hymn "Stand Up, Stand Up for Jesus" (text, George Duffield; tune, George James Webb), written in 1858, was a favorite of both Northern and Southern armies.

Two other standard hymns that were sung frequently by both armies were "How Firm a Foundation" and "There Is a Fountain Filled with Blood." The words of assurance in "How Firm a Foundation" made it particularly resonate with soldiers facing battle and it was one of the most common hymn choices to call troops to worship and for funerals in the field.

When through the deep waters I call thee to go
The rivers of sorrow shall not overflow
For I will be with thee, thy troubles to bless
And sanctify to thee thy deepest distress

When through fiery trials thy pathways shall lie
My grace all sufficient shall be thy supply.[39]

"How Firm a Foundation" was so popular among the Southern armies that W. W. Bennett referred to it as the "official hymn" of the Confederacy.[40]

While the unintentionally gruesome imagery of the first line of "There Is a Fountain" has caused it to be eliminated from many modern hymnals, it was one of the most often sung hymns of the Civil War era.[41] One can

---

37. "Marching Along," words by Mrs. M. A. Kidder; music by W. B. Bradbury. (New York: Firth, Pond, & Co., 1862.)

38. "O When Shall I See Jesus?," no. 122 in *Southern Harmony and Musical Companion*, 1854 ed.

39. "How Firm a Foundation, ye saints of the Lord". Text by "K" in John Rippon, *A Selection of Hymns* (1787).

40. Bennett, *Narrative of the Great Revival*, 206.

41. The words were written by the eighteenth-century evangelical William Cowper

imagine, from the perspective of soldiers on both sides, the equation of blood with sacrifice for the redemption of sin would powerfully resonate. This, they believed, was a holy war for a sacred cause, one for which a blood sacrifice was to be expected.

Singing among African American Troops

"Go Down, Moses" or "Let My People Go," which had been sung by the slaves at Fortress Monroe, had a deep spiritual resonance for Blacks throughout the war years. Gradually, as the conflict continued, however, the singing of traditional plantation spirituals disappeared or went underground. In their place came improvised songs inspired by new surroundings and the struggle for freedom. The First US Colored Infantry expressed a newfound militance in their adopted marching song:

> We are the gallant First,
> Who slightly have been tried,
> Who order to a battle,
> Take Jesus as our guide.[42]

The siege of Vicksburg, Mississippi in July of 1863 ended in victory for the Union Army, and, along with the Battle of Gettysburg, was pivotal in determining the war's outcome. Vicksburg also represented a turning point for the United States Colored Troops. It was the first major engagement involving Black infantry, and they played a major role in both the siege and its aftermath. Over seven thousand Black troops are buried in the military cemetery at Vicksburg.[43] Mary Ann Loughborough, a Mississippi woman, had the misfortune of arriving in Vicksburg to visit friends only to find herself trapped in a city under siege. She wrote a memoir of her experience in which she remembered:

> I heard, one night, a soldier down the ravine singing one of the weird, melodious hymns that negroes often sing; and, amid the firing and crashing of projectiles, it floated up to me in soft, musical undertones that were fascinating in the extreme: the wailing of the earthly unrest—the longing for the glorious home that

---

(1731–1800) and inspired by a passage in the Old Testament Book of Zechariah: "On that day a fountain shall be opened for the house of David and the inhabitants of Jerusalem, to cleanse them from sin and impurity" (Zech 13:1).

Cowper used the imagery of blood as a metaphor for life and the shedding of Jesus's blood, symbolic of God's sacrifice to redeem the sins of humankind.

42. *Christian Recorder*, April 16, 1864.
43. McBride, "Battle of Vicksburg Being Fought Again."

the warm imagery pictures to be glorious in golden lights and silvery radiance—a song and brilliant happiness! The voice was full and triumphant. Then the rapid change, in low and mournful cadence, to the earth, the clay, the mire—to dearth[sic.], to suffering, to sin: "I wonder, Lord, will I ever get to heaven—to the new Jerusalem?" came with the ending of every verse. I bowed my face in my hands. Yes! Heaven was so far off.[44]

Throughout the war, remnants of a distinctly African American approach to singing could be observed. The subject matter of the soldiers' songs, however, had become more imbued with pride rather than the underlying melancholy of many antebellum spirituals. Call-and-response singing, where bits of melody were delivered and improvised upon by a song leader and then picked up and further amplified by a chorus, remained the standard. Colonel George Goddard Thomas observed this communal approach to music creation among Black troops at Petersburg in the hours before the ill-fated explosion and Battle of the Crater.

> The night we learned that we were to lead the charge the news filled them too full for ordinary utterance. The joyous negro guffaw always breaking out about the campfire ceased. They formed circles in their company streets and were sitting on the ground intently and solemnly "studying." At last, a heavy voice began to sing,
> "We-e looks li-ike me-en a-a-marchin' on,
> We looks li-ike men-er-war."
> Over and over again he sang it, making slight changes in the melody. The rest listened to him intently; no sign of approval or disapproval escaped their lips or appeared on their faces. All at once, when his refrain had struck the right response in their hearts, his group took it up, and shortly half a thousand voices were upraised extemporizing a half dissonant middle part and bass. It was a picturesque scene—these dark men, with their White eyes and teeth and full red lips, crouching over a smoldering camp-fire, in dusky shadow, with only the feeble rays of the lanterns of the first sergeants and the lights of the candles dimly showing through the tents.[45]

---

44. Loughborough, *My Cave Life in Vicksburg*, 46.

45. Thomas, "Colored Troops at Petersburg," 563–67. Note: There is also a sad, even tragic aspect to this song. The Battle of the Crater was one of the classic examples of mismanagement in American military history. Black troops had repeatedly been denied the opportunity to fight, and, when Colonel Thomas observed them singing, they had just been told they would be leading the charge into and around the Crater, something they had been training for weeks. At the last moment, however, a decision was

We Are Marchin'

"We Are Marchin'," melody and harmony as transcribed by Col. George C. Thomas following the Battle of the Crater (1864). As with all transcriptions by whites from this era, it must be viewed as only an approximation of the actual song as it was performed.

The Power of Sacred Song

Hymn singing was a common occurrence enjoyed by large numbers of Civil War soldiers, whether it occurred in a formal worship setting, a revivalist event, an evening prayer meeting, or recreational music making around a campfire. The singing of hymns served to prepare troops for battle, provide a momentary respite in the heat of conflict, or as a salve in aftermath of fighting. Group singing of sacred hymns and secular songs was a favorite communal activity of Civil War soldiers. Dozens of additional eyewitness incidences beyond those above could be cited. Among them:

- Elias Nash of the 4th Michigan Infantry recalled troops joining to sing the "Hail Columbia," "The Star-Spangled Banner," and finally "Old Hundredth" in the hours just prior to the Battle of Bull Run in July of 1861.[46] Following the battle, which was a disastrous Union defeat, exhausted and dispirited troops were heard intoning "There Is a Fountain Filled with Blood."[47]

---

made to have the charge led by a white unit, inexperienced recruits who had received virtually no training. The Black regiment followed, ending up trapped. Over 40 percent of the regiment was to die.

46. Meacham and McGraw, eds., *Songs of America*, 86–87.
47. Moss, *Annals of the United States Christian Commission*, 92–93.

- The April 30, 1862, issue of the *National Intelligencer* reported the nighttime singing of "Old Hundredth" by what sounded to the writer like a "thousand" Union voices at the Siege of Yorktown, Virginia.[48]
- At the end of the first day of the Battle of Shiloh (also in 1862 in southwestern Tennessee), when a Confederate victory seemed assured, Captain Alfred Fiedler recalled leading his regiment in worship and singing the hymn "God of My Life Whose Gracious Power."[49]
- On the second day at Shiloh, the tide of battle turned to favor the Union, but both armies suffered grievous losses in numbers unheard of to that time. One of the more touching accounts of the power of hymn singing at the battlefront came from an anonymous Union veteran who recalled the wounded soldiers littering the battlefield singing "When I Can Read My Title Clear." [50]
- After the crushing Union defeat at Fredericksburg (December 1862, Virginia), the 11th Division of the Georgia Militia, commanded by General George T. ("Tige") Anderson was left behind to defend the city. On Sunday, December 21, the regimental worship was led by a Reverend Potter, who recited the words of a John Newton hymn:

    Safely through another week, God has brought us on our way.
    Let us now a blessing seek, waiting in His courts today.
    Day of all the week the best, emblem of eternal rest.[51]

- The Reverend William Barrow wistfully recalled the singing of the 22nd Massachusetts Regiment in April 1863 at Stoneman's Station (near Fredericksburg). The service began with the singing of Lowell Mason's "Nearer My God to Thee," the third stanza of which reads:

    There let me see the sight, An open heaven;
    All that Thou sendest me, In mercy given.
    Angels to beckon me Nearer, my God, to Thee,
    Nearer, my God, to Thee, Nearer to Thee.[52]

There are numerous references to worship before, during, and after the Battle of Gettysburg. Perhaps the most memorable use of a hymn during the three days of fighting occurred after Pickett's infamous and unsuccessful

---

48. "April 30, 1862."
49. Dollar, "'Soldiers of the Cross,'" 99.
50. "When I Can Read My Title Clear," text by Isaac Watts (1707); often sung to the traditional hymn tune "Pisgah."
51. Woodworth, *While God Is Marching On*, 78.
52. Smith, *Incidents of the Christian Commission*, 44–47.

charge, when numerous witnesses heard a Confederate band playing "Nearer My God to Thee" as those Southern troops surviving trudged back to safety.[53]

At this point, let us diverge for a moment from the subjects of ministry and hymn singing on the battlefield. One of the most written-about events in American history, one that ever after has helped to shape the American identity, occurred in November of 1863. On Thursday the eighteenth, President Abraham Lincoln had arrived by train in Gettysburg, Pennsylvania. He was scheduled to speak the next day at the dedication of a new national cemetery on Gettysburg battlefield.

That evening, Lincoln was serenaded by the National Union Musical Association, a choral group directed by Wilson G. Horner (1834–1864). Among other tunes, they sang the popular song with Old Testament overtones "We Are Coming Father Abraham," the words being a response to Lincoln's 1862 call to draft 300,000 additional volunteers.

> We are coming, Father Abraham, three hundred thousand more,
> From Mississippi's winding stream and from New England's shore.
> We leave our plows and workshops, our wives and children dear,
> With hearts too full for utterance, with but a silent tear.
> We dare not look behind us but steadfastly before.
> We are coming, Father Abraham, three hundred thousand more![54]

The dedication was planned as a memorial service for the over 23,000 Union lives lost in the battle, and, while seldom emphasized, sacred music had an important part. The event opened with a prayer and the crowd—numbering about fifteen thousand—joined in reciting the Lord's Prayer. The Marine Band's playing of "Old Hundredth" followed, once again underlining the familiarity of that venerable psalm tune.[55] After a speech by the famed orator Edward Everett, the Baltimore Glee Club rose to sing a "National Consecration Chant," written especially to commemorate the occasion, with words by Major Benjamin Brown French (1800–1870), and music by Horner. French had been a familiar figure in government circles for years and was chief marshal for Lincoln's inaugural parade in 1861. He

---

53. The three combined Confederate divisions of Generals George Pickett, J. Johnston Pettigrew, and Isaac Trimble, which participated in what is known as "Pickett's Charge," numbered about 12,500 men. The assault, lasting less than an hour, resulted in 50 percent casualties including over a thousand killed and around five thousand wounded or captured.

54. "We Are Coming, Father Abraham, 300,000 Strong" (1862), words by James S. Gibbons. Several musical settings of the text were published, including one by Stephen Foster that was quite popular.

55. Horner, "Sergeant Hugh Paxton Bigham."

oversaw funeral arrangements for Lincoln's son Willie in 1862 and would do the same for President Lincoln's funeral in 1865.[56]

The "Consecration Chant" was a short, strophic piece in five stanzas, written in the style of an Anglican chant.[57] It was intended to add to the solemnity of the occasion. French's text began by honoring the sacrifice of the Union dead and their families and then transitioning to prayer, that God might lead the army to final victory, protecting the freedoms Americans held dear.

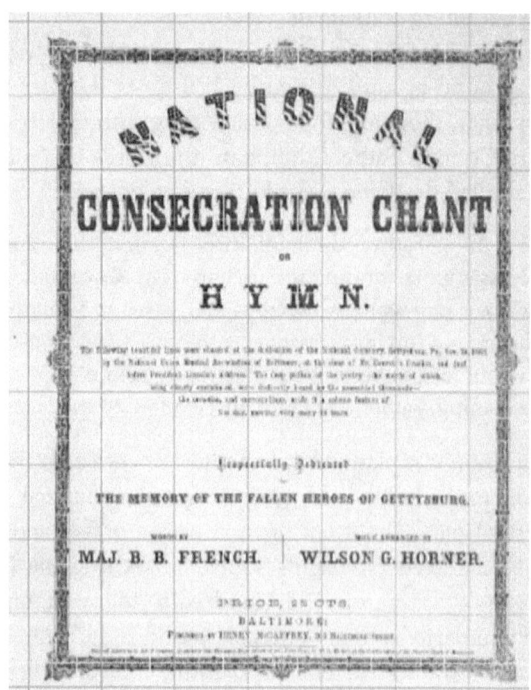

---

56. Spangler, "Benjamin Brown French."

57. The use of the Anglican style of chant in worship (to be discussed in more detail in chapter 9) had been growing in popularity since the 1840s, both among Episcopalians and other Protestant sects. The fact that a composition in chant form was used for a commemoration as significant as that at Gettysburg shows that this form of worship music, once abhorred, was now gaining general acceptance.

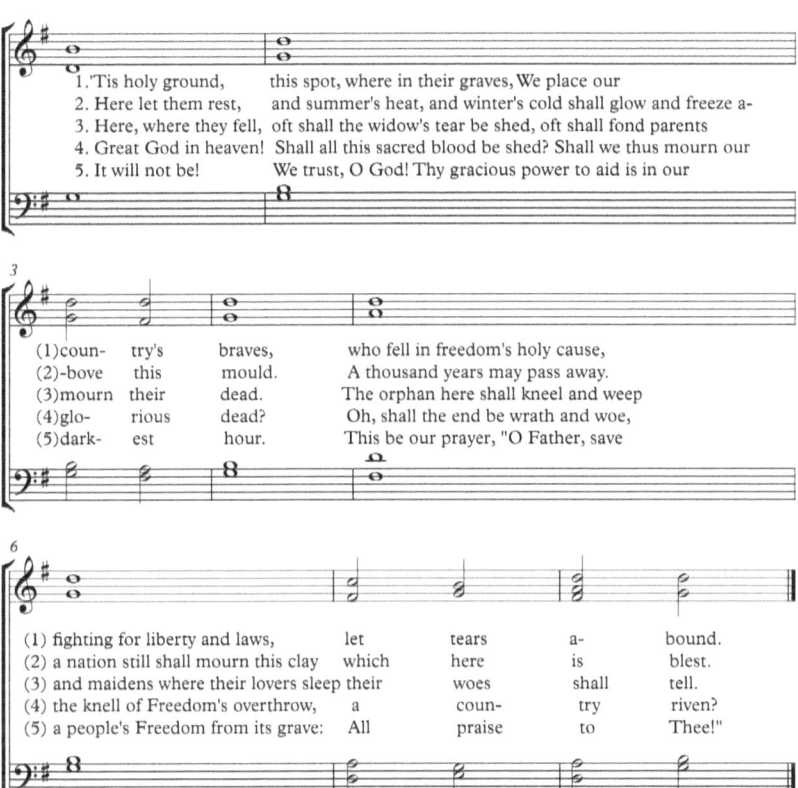

"National Consecration Chant or Hymn."
(Baltimore, MD: Henry McCaffrey, 1863.)

The final year of the war, spring of 1864 to spring of 1865, brought the conflict to a peak of carnage and destruction. One of the most gruesome contests was the Battle of Spotsylvania Courthouse (March 1864, Virginia). Union Major Abner Small wrote of Union troops singing "Old Hundredth" in the battle's aftermath.[58] Meanwhile a Confederate band struck up "Nearer My God to Thee" from their embattled earthworks.[59]

---

58. Small, *Road to Richmond*, 145.
59. Pawtak, "Music on the Spotsylvania Earthworks."

Wartime Advancement of Music in the United States

Historians frequently catalog the many advances made during the Civil War in terms of weapons development and battlefield tactics. But other advancements are important to remember as well:

- Advancements in printing made possible the production of thousands of songsters and devotional materials as well as a highly lucrative business in publishing patriotic and sentimental songs and piano pieces, again in both North and South.

- Printing advancements also had permitted the publication of the first modern hymnals with music and text on the same page. In the years after the war, this would end the necessity of publishing hymnbooks and tunebooks separately.

- Industrial advances allowed for the production of high-quality band instruments in the United States rather than having to import them.

- The proliferation of military bands brought numerous professional musicians into the military service and exposed many recruits to a quality and variety of music they had not previously experienced. Many of those professional musicians would take leadership roles in church music during the post-war decades.

Soldiers in the Civil War played a variety of musical instruments and, when relaxing in camp, in worship services, and in prayer meetings, it was common for singing to be accompanied instrumentally.

> In some tents vocal or instrumental music was a feature of the evening. There was probably not a regiment in the service that did not boast at least one violinist, one banjoist, and a bone player in its ranks—not to mention other instruments generally associated with these—and one or all of them could be heard in operation, either inside or in a company street, most any pleasant evening.[60]

Some of the most memorable accompaniments for hymn singing were by the regimental bands. Bands played from collections of tunes containing marches (quicksteps), dance tunes, operatic excerpts, popular melodies, and usually a few familiar hymns. Union Chaplain Charles A. Humphreys recalled that he always tried to "have the help of a good brass band in the

---

60. Billings, *Hardtack and Coffee*, 35.

service, and oftentimes the exercises have an unwonted solemnity with that help. I believe music may be made the handmaid of religion."[61]

In past chapters, we have surveyed the gradual but often reluctant acceptance of choirs in American churches. Ubiquitous group singing and the organization of regimental choirs during the Civil War would have a major impact on ameliorating negative attitudes. *The Army Chaplain's Manual* of 1863 made organization of choirs a priority for chaplains.

> Music will be found a great auxiliary in rendering the chaplain's religious services attractive. Singing has always been regarded as an important feature of worship. It is one of God's best gifts to man and should be freely used in setting forth His praise and glory. It is also a part of the worship in which many can take an active part, and it often penetrates to the lowest depths of the heart, when spoken words fail to make even an impression.
>
> It will be well, therefore, for every chaplain to give some time to the formation of a choir. If he understands music, he can superintend the work in person. If he does not, the best plan will be to select one who is competent to lead, and delegate to him the power to take such steps as may be necessary. The choir, when formed, should be requested to hold regular meetings for practice and improvement. And these should be punctually attended by the chaplain, whether he understands music or not: for, at any rate, his presence will prove the importance which he attaches to the undertaking, and will animate and encourage to perseverance, those who have interested themselves in the work. Good singing will always give life, and add an interest to worship, which, otherwise, would prove tedious and unattractive to the heart of the natural man.[62]

Captain Ira Blanchard, serving in the 20th Illinois Regiment, recalled singing in a Union-appropriated church during the Vicksburg campaign.

> There were several fine churches in town, but I always attend the Methodist Episcopal Church, which was sometimes presided over by our Army Chaplain, and sometimes by their regular pastor, a southern man. We formed a choir, composed of several soldiers, Miss Jennie Hammett, and two Miss Longs of Vicksburg. Our leader was a young doctor who had lately been discharged from the Confederate Army where he served as an

---

61. Humphreys, *Field, Camp, Hospital, and Prison*, 17.
62. Hammond, *Army Chaplain's Manual*, 107–8.

> Ensign. We had bulley times as we would meet in some high-toned houses for rehearsal, and bulley music we made.[63]

The 11th Illinois Regiment at the opening of the war had a choir of about twenty-five men practicing regularly in the mess hall.[64] Choirs also existed in the Confederate Army. A military service held at a Presbyterian Church in Rome, Georgia had two thousand soldiers in attendance and featured a choir singing the benediction.[65]

Charles Wellington Reed, recipient of the Medal of Honor for heroism at Gettysburg and a bugler for the 9th Massachusetts Battery, wrote home that he hoped to organize a male quartet.

> The next thing I most desire . . . a college song book . . . I am about forming as quartet to enjoy our evenings with. It is very pleasant to have a quiet little sing now and then, and, as that book has four parts in it, it will be easy to learn from.[66]

In the Confederate Army conscripted singing masters were known to organize singing schools to encourage singing among the troops. W. J. Moseley, a major in the 10th Georgia Infantry, attended one and enthusiastically wrote his mother about the influence the school was having:

> There are some boys here that start playing cards and gambling as soon as they draw their money, and in two days they haven't got a cent . . . I have been in the war two years, and I don't know one card from another, but I do know my notes, and we have some of the finest singing around the campfire I have ever heard since Troupe Evans and E. T. Pound . . . teach singing school.[67]

African American troops were particularly attracted to group singing and enthusiastically became involved in choral ensemble singing. Slaves frequently had been enjoined to form singing groups to entertain their masters and guests. Members of the United States Colored Troops, now freedmen, sought opportunities to sing publicly and demonstrate "the merits of their culture."[68] One of the more famous Black choral groups was the Shaw Glee Club of the 54th Massachusetts Infantry, named in honor of

---

63. Blanchard, *I Marched with Sherman*, 107.
64. Woodworth, *While God Is Marching On*, 153.
65. Woodworth, *While God Is Marching On*, 117.
66. Kelley and Snell, eds., *Bugle Resounding*, 210. Reed was a talented artist and made over seven hundred sketches of soldier life during the Civil War. After the war, he became an illustrator for the *Boston Globe*.
67. Steele and Hulan, *Makers of the Sacred Harp*, 18.
68. Wilson, *Campfires of Freedom*, 165.

their commander, Colonel Robert Gould Shaw, who died in the assault on Fort Wagner, South Carolina.

The Importance of Sacred Music during the Civil War and Its Future Impact

Clearly, sacred music was an intrinsic part of formal military worship on both sides during the American Civil War. It was also integral to informal worship on the battlefield and around the campfire. Bands, choirs, instrumental and vocal soloists, not to mention the common soldier himself seeking solace in hymns of faith and praise, were a part of daily life in the Civil War military.

When the Civil War ended, thousands of young men returned to their homes. Many of them had witnessed death firsthand either on the battlefield or in a field hospital. As noted previously, the vast majority of common soldiers came from a rural background. Few among them could afford to pay a conscript to serve in their place. Evangelical religion and singing had been their comfort during their most harrowing experiences. They were returning to a nation drastically changed and would bring with them an evangelical mindset. No longer could populist music of the masses be regarded as simply a regional aberration. *The Civil War changed all of that.* As American society transitioned from largely rural to industrial, farm boys, immigrants, and freed African Americans converged on the major cities with an unquenchable need for employment. Worship styles, once easily dismissed or ignored, were now cropping up "just two blocks over." Mammoth "tabernacles"—often cheaply fabricated and intended only for temporary use—sprang up in major cities where thousands gathered in an explosion of evangelistic fervor. A new day had dawned, and battle lines were drawn. The division between the cultivated and populist in American church music had hardened so as to be impenetrable.

Chapter 8

THE CULTIVATED CHURCH AND ITS MUSIC IN POST-CIVIL WAR AMERICA, 1865–1885

THE FIRST TWO DECADES following the American Civil War were a critical time of transition for music and ministry in the American church. When Johnny did come marching home, the world he found had changed pointedly. The sheer scope of technological advances in the latter part of the nineteenth century in America is astounding:

- *Transportation*: Significant improvements in steam engines and locomotives; completion of the transcontinental railroad. In 1865 there were 35,000 miles of railroad track in the United States. By 1900, that number had increased to 200,000.
- *Communication*: Telegraph, telephone, trans-Atlantic cable, typewriter, and rotary printing press (linotype).
- *Agriculture*: Development and manufacture of barbed wire; deep-well drilling.
- *Domestic life*: electric lighting, sewing machine, phonograph.

The list goes on, but the most significant change was that, for the majority of Americans, labor was in the service of others and not linked to one's own property or ownership.

The country, once largely agrarian, was rapidly becoming an industrial monolith. While antebellum businesses had been mostly locally based, now developments in transportation and communication made the way for nationalized marketing and distribution of products. Vast populations once tending farms and livestock now sought factory work in cities. Because of the growth in factory-based labor, millions of Americans now worked on an hourly basis. The colloquialisms "be on time!" and "by the clock" originated in the 1880s because of rigid train schedules and clock-based employee sign-ins at factories.

In 1860, one American in six lived in a city with a population exceeding eight thousand. By 1900, it was one in three. The populations of Pittsburgh, Cincinnati, Cleveland, Detroit, and Chicago would all more than double between 1865 and 1900. Also, thanks to rapidly expanding railroad access, St. Paul, Minneapolis, St. Louis, Denver, Seattle, and San Francisco would each grow exponentially. All of those population centers would have their worker and management classes, immigrant enclaves, and clear-cut divisions between the poor and the privileged.

Still, some things had *not* changed. "Old stock Northeastern elites had kept an extraordinarily tenacious hold on wealth and power since the Civil War." Though the sectional conflict had often been promoted as a struggle for "equal rights," the post-war period "was not marked by democratization and elite decline, but by the reinforcement of elite power in new corporate and bureaucratic forms."[1]

The transition was wide ranging and included changing perceptions of the role of music in worship as well as what was acceptable in the devotional life of communities now defined by social strata.

The Gilded Age[2]

The existing mainline denominations experienced a tremendous surge in growth after the Civil War. This meant more churches, a greater variety of theological perspectives, and an even greater diversity in the kinds of music used.

> Churchgoing was a normal, mannerly and even fashionable activity. Signs of the popularity of the churches abounded. The churches were well attended. Costly and imposing edifices were built to match the increasing prosperity of their clientele, and congregations vied with each other to possess the tallest steeple as a symbol of wealth and prestige. The acquisition of large pipe organs and paid quartets, the adoption of high-priced music

---

1. Lears, *No Place for Grace*, xi.

2. The term "Gilded Age" generally refers to the period from the end of the Civil War in 1865 to the "Panic of 1893," which began in February of that year.

budgets, and the hiring of preachers highly skilled as orators, were all signs of this competitive drive.[3]

Winthrop Hudson, of course, was here referring only to America's most elite parishes. Musical culture in the United States was still divided between cultivated and vernacular traditions. Those on the cultivated side viewed European art music as the apogee of what Americans should aspire to. Music that did not fit into this perspective was viewed as tasteless and inappropriate or worse. Prior to the war the cultivated tradition was most firmly rooted in older and wealthier congregations along the Eastern Seaboard. The Civil War, however, brought with it vast growth and wealth to the Midwest and a new class of nouveau riche seeking cultivation and respect. Conversely, a large vernacular contingent valued homemade, often sentimental art beyond any import. For them, the focus on high art was elitist and out of touch with the mass of Americans.

New Realities and Shifting Theological Currents

Many theological trends were afoot in Victorian America, and adjectives commonly used to describe and define those trends can be confusing and misleading. "Conservative," "liberal," "evangelical"—all have been stretched by religious historians so far beyond their antebellum connotations that they are ripe for misinterpretation.

In studying American religion in the first half of the nineteenth century, the use of these terms is fairly straightforward. "Conservative" and "evangelical" were terms used to differentiate between two broad branches of Protestantism. "Conservatives" were generally bedrock Calvinists and those whose theology reflected Calvinistic influence.[4] Evangelicals, on the other hand, were willing to set aside or moderate Calvinist views on predestination and preach promised salvation to all who believe. The span of views falling under the evangelical umbrella was wide—from mildly liberal preacher/theologians like Lyman Beecher and C. G. Finney to bedrock fundamentalists of the camp meeting variety.

The clear lines between conservatism and evangelicalism would be challenged to the breaking point in the 1850s with the rise of liberal theology. The chasm between the nation's wealthy elite and middle and

---

3. Hudson, *Religion in America*, 294.

4. The words "conservative" and "evangelical" are themselves a source of confusion because of the contradictory ways in which they have been used. In the twentieth century, the two words are often used together. Christian fundamentalists, for example, are often referred to as "conservative evangelicals."

lower classes was ever widening, forcing a loosening of old Puritan views on excess and extravagant living. The publication of Charles Darwin's *On the Origin of Species* in 1859 caused a virtual firestorm of divergent views on how Scripture was to be understood and interpreted. There were also the overarching issues of slavery, secession, and impending war that cast a shadow over everything. The abolitionist cause had forced an intense debate pitting biblical inerrancy versus interpretation based on historical and social precedent.

The period from 1858 through the First World War has been referred to by William G. McLoughlin of Brown University as the Third Great Awakening in American history. During this period, liberal theologians and clergy sought to make sense of the changes they were experiencing and to adapt to them theologically. McLoughlin lists five theological trends which together would become known as the "New Theology" of the nineteenth century:

1. Progressive orthodoxy: Perhaps the most influential proponent was the Congregationalist Horace Bushnell (1802–1876) who in his preaching and in his seminal treatise, *Christian Nurture* (1847), questioned the validity of immediate conversion. For Bushnell, the conversion process was a gradual, lifelong experience, beginning with the nurture and teaching of children. A second influential and highly controversial work came in 1851, *Christ in Theology*, in which Bushnell declared that literal and dogmatic interpretation of Scripture was apt to miss its deeper spiritual intent.

2. Theistic evolution: Theology for the new age must adapt to new understandings of science and the origins of life.

3. Higher criticism: Biblical higher criticism, originating in Europe, sought to investigate and interpret biblical documents like any other document of antiquity. Higher critics were interested not only in the Bible's primary literary sources but also in the operative and undisclosed assumptions of biblical writers themselves.

4. Historicism: Related to higher criticism was the notion that biblical knowledge must be tempered by ongoing development of society and acquisition of knowledge since biblical times—in other words, history. One of the arguments against slavery, for example, was that while a type of slavery was condoned in the Bible, civilization had since condemned the practice.

5. The "Social Gospel": While the term did not come into use until after 1900, social gospel adherents were responding to the unique problems arising from urban growth and the marginalization of industrial

workers, immigrants, and people of color. To address them, they advocated societal reforms based on Jesus's teachings.[5]

Progressive Christians in the late nineteenth century all adhered to aspects of the New Theology to varying degrees. They sincerely believed that progress through science and a new understanding of Scripture would lead to a new millennium.

Premillennialism and Postmillennialism

Eschatology, or the study of the ultimate destiny of human history based in part on the book of Revelation, figures prominently in American religious life from the Civil War through the early twentieth century. Theologians divide millennialists into two competing camps. Proponents of the New Theology, and in fact most religious leaders of earlier generations, were *postmillennialists*. They believed the Christ's second coming would follow a thousand-year golden age when Christian ethics would flourish. Clergy, chaplains, abolitionists, and apologists for slavery all declared the war to represent a cleansing, a necessary step toward the promised new Jerusalem. The 1858 revival and almost continuous outbreaks of revivalistic enthusiasm in both armies during the conflict supported this view. Following the war, all thought the surge of industrial growth and progress of science and concepts of social Darwinism were signs of millennial progress.

Millennial thinking had its shadow side—premillennialism. Premillennialism, based on an interpretation of the book of Revelation, suggested that society was in an inexorable state of decline which would climax in the *great tribulation*, or time of war, disaster, and famine, to be followed by a thousand-year reign of Christ. God would protect true believers from the calamitous tribulation by taking them unto himself through the rapture.

Opponents to the New Theology saw Darwinism, higher criticism, urban decay, and rampant immorality in politics as signs of societal disintegration and decline. Dwight Moody, the great revivalist of the time, famously said "I look upon this world as a wrecked vessel. God has given me a lifeboat and said to me, 'Moody, save all that you can.'"[6]

---

5. McLoughlin Jr., *Modern Revivalism*, 10.
6. McLoughlin Jr., *Revivals, Awakenings, and Reform*, 144.

The Church "Evolves"

Charles Darwin's theory of evolution shook the theological foundations of American Protestantism. Many prominent ministers and theologians, already influenced by perfectionist tendencies of decades prior, aligned themselves sympathetically with Darwin and the scientific and intellectual climate of the time. Henry Ward Beecher, Phillips Brooks, and Horace Bushnell have all been referred to as Christocentric liberals, for their changing views on biblical interpretation. By 1870, Beecher had rejected hell and all concepts of future accountability.[7] One important theme in Brooks's sermons was "an insuperable optimism concerning the goodness of man." "He would lapse into a kind of agnosticism concerning the more abstract theological issues," according to Linda Jane Clark.[8] All of this reflected the characteristic optimism of the post-war generation and the conviction that exposing congregations to only the best art, the most inspiring preaching, the most tasteful church décor was appropriate in a society "evolving" toward the new millennium.

Reading sermons and articles from the period, the word "optimism" was often inextricably tied to another—"progress." Progress from developments in industrial technology was universally celebrated by businessmen, politicians, ministers, journalists, even labor leaders and socialists.[9] The British sociologist Herbert Spencer (1820–1903) combined all of these concepts into a theory of evolutionary positivism.[10] In November 1882, Spencer was honored with a banquet in New York City attended by such luminaries as Andrew Carnegie and Henry Ward Beecher. Guest speaker Secretary of State William W. Ewert praised Spencer for treating "evil, not as eternal, but as evanescent" and society as evolving to "what is sought through faith in the millennium—that condition of affairs in which there is the highest morality and the greatest happiness."[11]

Americans of the Victorian era were confident in their millennial progress and an alliance between society and heaven. But while their theology

---

7. Carter, *Spiritual Crisis of the Gilded Age*, 123.

8. Clark, "Music in Trinity Church, Boston," 67–68.

9. Lears, *No Place for Grace*, 7–8.

10. The concept of "positivism" holds that the only valid knowledge is scientific or based on direct experience of natural phenomena. It rejects all metaphysical knowledge, a core component of theological teachings. August Comte originated the concept of positivism in his six-volume *Course on Positive Philosophy* (1830–1842). Comte divided human history into three stages: the theological, the metaphysical, and the positive, with the last representing the triumph of science and rationalism.

11. Lears, *No Place for Grace*, 22.

was imbued with often voiced thoughts on love and charity, it "failed to address the daunting social problems of a competitive market economy."[12]

Total acceptance of the Darwinian view conflicted with the reality of exploding urban populations and conflicting needs related to class and national origin—problems still being addressed in the twenty-first century. The threat of chaos traumatized both middle and upper classes in the post-war years. The industrializing, urbanizing nation was absorbing millions of immigrants from other cultures. It was experiencing an almost incomprehensible degree of structural change and spatial mobility. A huge population shift from the countryside and small town to the city seemed to be imperiling the very basis of the traditional order.[13]

Postmillennial optimism could only carry one so far. As cities grew, the flaws in what had been intended as urban Edens became apparent. Wealthy patrons of large downtown churches, confronted by the din of factories and poverty on street corners, moved to quiet, tree-lined suburbs. Their churches usually moved with them, further isolating both church and home from the real world of urban life. The Victorian era church designer George Bowler theorized that churches that chose to remain in the city were temples of Mammon and church location from henceforth should be determined by where it was most convenient for the true (i.e., cultivated) worshipper. "Bowler felt the church should cast its lot with those true worshipers whose homes were defined in opposition to life in the city. The domestic sphere with its 'hallowed associations' was perceived to be in opposition, both physically and morally, to the public life of the city."[14]

Sacralization

While the seeds were there earlier, in the post-war years we see genteel sensibilities and elitist sentimentality leading to a "sacralization" of church music. A word of explanation is in order. After all, what is sacred music if not sacred? Sacralization, as I am using it here, refers to an effort made by many nineteenth-century clergy and musicians to assign sacred and divine qualities to certain music (much of it of European origin). Conversely it was suggested that music lacking those supposed divine qualities was inappropriate—or worse—for use in the church. Gradually over time sacralization became the gauntlet thrown down by the traditional church to block every effort to develop a more inclusive, eclectic approach to church music

---

12. Orr, *Dudley Buck*, 11.
13. Levine, *High Brow, Low Brow*, 176.
14. Kilde, *When Church Became Theatre*, 86.

that ministered to congregations across boundaries of class, education, race, and national origin. Magazine articles and popular books about music attributed holy imagery to well-known European masterworks, some from dubious sources and apocryphal tales, others wholly made up.

Sacralization could be applied not only to music but also to certain highly esteemed musicians performing it. A 1905 tribute to the conductor Theodore Thomas (1835–1905) provides an excellent example. *Dwight's Journal* hailed him as a "true missionary of art."[15] An article in the *Boston Herald* regarding Thomas's funeral in 1905 was even more to the point:

> The comments of the clergymen of Chicago on Theodore Thomas' service to humanity are very suggestive. They frankly recognize that he was both priest and prophet, and not only a great spiritual force by reason of his gifts as a conductor and the effects he produced on men's higher being by his orchestra's rendering of great masterpieces, but also a great spiritual force . . . We have said good-by to a priest and prophet. It makes no difference that Theodore Thomas never acknowledged his divine call to a high noble ministry. Music is the soul's expression of that irrepressible desire for harmony and aspiration after concord which is the heart of true religion.[16]

Was certain music, by its artistic merit alone, divinely inspired while other music was not? And to what degree should musical taste be a factor in the choice of music for worship? Ralph Locke writes that during the post-Civil War years, elite and educated pillars of the church began "carving out institutions that . . . promoted an ideology of art as transcendent or sacred. In many cases, the art experience was now carefully stratified and 'framed' in ways that intimidated or even effectively excluded members of the poor and working classes."[17] Edward Baxter Perry's description of the elevated status of serious classical artists, written in 1892, underlines this exclusive and stratified point of view. The artist's work, he wrote, "is, or should be, a religion." When he steps upon the stage "in his capacity as high priest in the temple of the beautiful, his devout fervor should lift his audience above the trivial, petty phases of mere sensuous pleasure or superficial enjoyment, to a higher . . . plane of spiritual aesthetic gratification."[18]

---

15. Thomas, *Memoirs of Theodore Thomas*, 20–21.
16. Thomas, *Memoirs of Theodore Thomas*, 562–63.
17. Locke, "Music Lovers, Patrons, and the 'Sacralization' of Culture," 151.
18. Levine, *High Brow, Low Brow*, 134–35.

The Reverend Henry Ward Beecher, Plymouth Church, Its Choir, and Congregational Singing

Despite efforts going all the way back to Thomas Symmes's *Reasonableness of Regular Singing* in the 1720s, the general state of congregational singing was woeful in the United States for much of the nineteenth century. By the 1840s, many of the leading churches in the Northeast had dispensed with congregational singing entirely, paying a hired group of singers to sing hymns in place of the congregants. Where congregational singing did exist, it was often limited to a repertoire of hymns learned by rote.

The church with the greatest tradition of congregational singing in late nineteenth-century America was Henry Ward Beecher's Plymouth Church in Brooklyn. Beecher himself was a tireless and influential promoter of general participation in singing. The fact that he was also America's greatest and most popular preacher—one on whom the press had bestowed near divine status prior to his stunning fall from grace in the 1870s[19]—placed him in a unique position to bring about change. People listened to "what Mr. Beecher said."

> Within the past few years, a large number of respectable and not unintelligent people have acquired a new criterion by which to gauge the integrity of belief. The fresh standard appears to answer the purpose admirably. His pulpit is a sort of Procrustean bed on which worshippers voluntarily stretch themselves. "Mr. Beecher says so," is the knife that trims them into spiritual symmetry, and they obviously enjoy the metaphysical mutilation. We are not blaming Mr. Beecher—far less seeking to cast a slur on him. . . . For Mr. Beecher, we have little but admiration and esteem . . . it is not his fault that his sermons are more constantly reported and quoted than those of any other clergyman in the United States. There is always a great demand to hear what he says, or editors, who spend their lives in studying the public taste, would not perpetually yield him the space they do. There are thousands of souls who place more reliance upon what this virile and florid divine says than they do on the Bible, which they profess to make their only standard of religious faith and practice. They make Mr. Beecher their text quite as much as he makes the Scriptures his. . . . Plymouth Church is with them

---

19. News of a scandalous affair between Henry Ward Beecher and Elizabeth Tilton dominated press headlines for a full three years, from 1872 to 1875. Throughout, Beecher proclaimed his innocence, kept his pulpit, and continued to preach.

the keystone of sound doctrine, and "Mr. Beecher said so," the sesame of salvation.[20]

As the late nineteenth century's apostle of congregational singing, Beecher used his power and influence to forcefully promote it nationally and was recognized for his success in developing it in his own church. Beecher's sermons were laced with references to hymns, and he was outspoken in his insistence that his congregation sing and sing well. A Plymouth member recalled:

> I have often seen him jump up from his chair right in the middle of a hymn and hold up his hand for silence. "You are not singing this hymn right," he would say. "Sing it with more spirit and let everybody sing." The effect upon the congregation would be electric, and after that the church would fairly tremble with the volume.[21]

Beecher further clarified his thoughts on the importance of congregational singing in a sermon from the 1870s, "The Religious Uses of Music":

> We owe something, I think, of this reviving of music to the humble Methodists—to what were called "wild revivalists." Those who conducted revivals followed the impulse of men closely, they studied human nature; and these revivals were the truest schools of preaching, and also of singing. Although we were accustomed, formerly, to speak slightingly of Methodist hymns and tunes, and to ridicule revival melodies, yet the poorest tune or hymn that ever was sung is better than no tune and no hymn . . .
>
> The hymnbook is the system of theology which has been most in vogue among the common people. If you compare, point by point, the teaching of hymns or creeds or catechisms, I think you will join with me in saying that it is a pity that there has not been more singing. I do not say but that the catechisms may have a place; but the instruction which is given by hymns is more like the instruction which is given by the Word of God than is the catechism. The Word of God seldom analyzes; it seldom runs into abstractions; it seldom presents truth in a philosophic view; it almost invariably appeals through the imagination to the feelings, and through the feelings to the reason. The form of presenting truth by hymns is the highest form of presenting it—truth as it is in the heart, and not truth as it is in the head . . .

---

20. "Mr. Beecher Says So," 5.
21. Griswold, *Sixty Years with Plymouth Church*, 54.

It is on this account that I think hymns and psalms will be among the great influences which will bring together the church of the future, and make substantial harmony between those who never could be reconciled by their confessions and by their catechism. It is remarkable to see how men will quarrel over a dogma, and then sit down and rejoice over a hymn which expresses precisely the same sentiments about which they have differed. A man will dispute with you in regard to the absolute divinity of Jesus Christ, but he will sing Coronation with you because he carries out his own idea as he goes along.

As a preparation, then, for religious meetings, sing. As a preparation for the sanctuary and its privileges, sing. As a preparation for self-examination, or as a means of pushing in the worldly stops, and drawing out the religious stops of the organ, sing. And let the children sing.

Let us, then, pray for the days of song. Sing, man; sing, woman. Or, if you cannot sing, make a joyful noise to the Lord. Sing in your house. Sing by the wayside. Sing upon the sea. Sing in the wilderness. Sing always and everywhere. Pray by singing. Recite truths by chanting songs. Sing more in the sanctuary. All of you sing. Sing from city to city, from state to state, and from nation to nation. Let your songs be like deep answering to deep, until that day shall come when the heaven and the earth shall join together, and the grand and final chorus shall roll through the universe; when "the kingdoms of this world are become the kingdoms of our Lord and his Christ, and he shall reign forever and ever."[22]

Just as hymn singing was abundant in a service of worship at Plymouth, Beecher also felt sacred song needed to become an important part of everyday life. So frequently did he draw allusions between the beauties of nature and the musical art that the line separating them becomes indistinct.

> You can never have congregational singing, if that is all you have. Unless you have singing in the family and singing in the house, singing in the shop and singing in the street, singing everywhere until it becomes a habit, you can never have congregational singing. It will be like the cold drops, half water, half ice, which drip in March from some cleft of rock, one drop here and another there; whereas it should be like the August shower, which comes ten million drops at once, and roars on the roof . . . It is with the singing of the congregation as with the sighing of the wind in

---

22. Beecher, "Religious Uses of Music," 288, 293–94, 294–95, 297–98, 301.

the forest, where the notes of the million rustling leaves, and the boughs striking upon each other, altogether make a harmony, no matter what be the individual discords.[23]

The universality of hymns and their path to the emotions is a subject taken up by Cheryl C. Boots in her thought-provoking dissertation "Earthly Strains." In it she refers to a concept of egalitarian resonance, which is similar to the idea promoted by Beecher. "Egalitarian resonance," she writes, is the concept "that individuals who sing together or who listen to singing sympathetically . . . share equality with each other."[24]

Dwight's Journal commented on the excellence of singing at Plymouth Church during the early years of Beecher's ministry. The writer said Plymouth Church, Brooklyn, was "one living, active, tangible example of what all will agree to be genuine church music." Singing at Beecher's church, the article pointed out, was "as much a part of the worship as the prayer or sermon." As for congregational singing, the writer could point to no other place "where this has been so satisfactorily accomplished as in the Society of the Rev. Henry Ward Beecher, Plymouth Church."[25]

> If anyone doubts the efficiency or practicability of Congregational singing, let them attend Mr. Beecher's church one day, and their doubts will vanish. I have repeatedly heard persons not particularly susceptible to musical impressions, express themselves greatly pleased, and in some cases they would be deeply moved while listening to the singing at Plymouth Church. It is emphatically *Congregational singing.* You can hear voices from every part of the house.[26]

Plymouth's large volunteer choir was the focal point of its music program. The choir was not placed in either of the two galleries, but in a loft of its own directly behind the minister's platform. At Plymouth "the chorus choir [was] preferred [not] merely for its own singing, but because it served best the congregation."[27] The choir had a massive sound that, coupled with the church's resonant acoustics, did much to encourage people to sing. There was never any doubt as to the choir's function, and most of its rehearsal time was devoted to hymns in *The Plymouth Collection.* These were sung robustly and with enthusiasm.

---

23. Proctor, *Life Thoughts,* 129.
24. Boots, "Earthly Strains," 5.
25. "Description of Music at Plymouth Church."
26. "Description of Music at Plymouth Church."
27. The "chorus choir" concept will be discussed later in this chapter.

The Plymouth Collection and Its Influence

It was not until the 1850s that Henry Ward Beecher introduced the first modern American hymnal to his congregation in Brooklyn. Almost immediately after arriving at Plymouth Church in 1847 Beecher began the process of developing a hymnal for his congregation. The first attempt, *Temple Melodies*, published in 1851, contained some two hundred hymns printed in three staves with the archaic practice of the tenor line on top.

The anonymous Preface to *Temple Melodies* provides a clear summary of Beecher's rationale in publishing the volume. The act of congregational singing is described as "That very part of our religious service which is the nearest akin to heaven, and which is capable of elevating us to the most delightful and divine emotions . . ."[28] In light of that, it was inexcusable to Beecher that worshippers in too many churches sat in silence.

> If we seek for cause of these abuses, we shall find it, in no small measure, in the habitual silence of those who comprise our congregations during the exercise of singing. This places those who should be worshipers, in the attitude of mere listeners. If the music happens to strike their fancy, they express admiration; if it displeases them, they find fault. The praise of God is thus placed on a level and is constantly compared with the exhibitions of the concert room. If the choir sing exquisitely, they are praised; if only tolerably, they are blamed . . . *The mass are not partakers, but mere auditors . . .*
>
> The only sure remedy for these abuses is to enlist *the people*—the people generally—in the performance of this part of worship.[29]

While the concept for *Temple Melodies* was Beecher's alone, he enlisted the help of his choirmaster, Darius Jones. His publisher, Mason & Law, however, refused to put Beecher's name on the title page because of his outspoken support for abolition.

For Beecher *Temple Melodies* was just an initial thrust toward a much more ambitious goal. Working with Plymouth organist John Zundel, he collected over 1,300 hymns and tunes into a massive new collection. *The Plymouth Collection*, published in 1855, had many innovative features calculated to improve and make more varied a church's singing. It was the first major hymnal to have complete hymn texts printed on the same page with the tunes to which they were to be sung. *The Plymouth Collection* was also notable for the diversity of its sources. All denominational traditions were

---

28. Jones, *Temple Melodies*, i–vi.
29. Jones, *Temple Melodies*, i–vi.

represented. The use of so-called "Catholic hymns" such as "Far, Far O'er Hill and Dell," set to Benjamin Carr's tune, "Spanish Hymn," caused a storm of protest.[30]

The Plymouth Collection of Hymns and Tunes for the Use of Christian Congregations.
(New York: A.S. Barnes & Co., 1855), p. 367.

Presbyterians and Methodists issued hymnals modeled after *The Plymouth Collection* in the 1870s. The Protestant Episcopal Church in the United States would not authorize its first modern hymnal, with music and text on the same page, until 1916.[31]

Many churches in the 1860s and '70s continued to use words-only collections. The reading of hymns as devotional poetry was common. Pocket

---

30. The writer of the hymn text was anonymous, and Benjamin Carr was Episcopalian. Carr's well known work in Philadelphia's Roman Catholic churches, however, was sufficient reason for critics to label the hymn as "Catholic."

31. There were, however, musical companions to various editions of the Protestant Episcopal Hymnal published independently. Among them, *The Hymnal with Tunes New and Old, to the words-only hymnal* (1872), edited by John Ireland Tucker, and *The Church Hymnal Revised and Enlarged,* which was compiled and edited by Horatio W. Parker.

songsters functioned not only as hymnbooks, but also as treasured repositories of devotional poetry. The hymnwriter/poet's versified interpretation of spiritual truths could provide a comforting alternative to cold, hard Scripture or sermonizing. These text-only compilations were small, easy to carry in pocket or purse, and inexpensive. One reason that hymnals with hymn and tune on the same page were slow in coming was opposition from clergy and congregants who found the insertion of staves and notes interfered with their reading. The poet Emily Dickinson (1830–1886) was thoroughly familiar with the hymns of Isaac Watts and grew up in a family tradition of hymn reading.[32]

Birth of a Choral Tradition

When researching American church music during the first half of the nineteenth century, it is risky to assume what was meant when the terms "choir" and "church choir" were used. The role of the choir was often thought of as an "office" of the church rather than a specific type of ensemble. Professional singers, most often in paid quartets or octets, were hired to lead and, in many cases, took the place of the congregation in singing. Their music tended to be soloistic rather than choral, but quartets were often called "choirs" because of the office they held.

True choral music, of course, did not disappear entirely. When the old singing schools departed, many of them left behind "Singing Societies" made up of former students who wished to continue singing together. The oldest of these still in existence, the Stoughton (Massachusetts) Singing Society, was founded in 1786. As time went on, these groups frequently became independent of the churches and started a flourishing tradition of secular choral music

---

32. Phillips, "Emily Dickinson's Hymnody of Privacy." The fact that nineteenth-century Christians commonly read hymns as poetry for meditative and devotional purposes should be thought-provoking for twenty-first-century church musicians. To the modern mind, most hymns are inextricably tied to a particular hymn tune, and, in fact, one rarely thinks about textual content without a melody running in the background. This is unfortunate because many hymns have profound meaning that deserves focused reflection. That a Civil War soldier facing battle or an Emily Dickinson found solace in reading hymns as poetry should give us pause. It has been said that aside from Scripture itself, hymnody can be the most powerful source of theological truth. Unfortunately, too often and unintentionally we create roadblocks to this powerful resource with music. Twenty-first-century congregations never rehearse. Hymn sings and other opportunities to learn hymnody in a relaxed, nonthreatening atmosphere are rare. Instead, we expect worshippers—most of whom have minimal or no music reading skills—to sing unfamiliar words to complicated tunes, and therein for worship to occur. The other alternative, too frequently resorted to, is to abandon hymns entirely for brief and often shallow snippets of text. The richness of devotional poetry is lost and with it, an important part of corporate worship itself.

across New England. The Boston Handel and Haydn Society, an example of this, was founded in 1815 and was directed by Lowell Mason himself from 1827 to 1838. At its founding, the society consisted of a hundred singers—ninety men and ten women drawn from singing schools throughout the area.

The proliferation of singing societies and oratorio choruses skyrocketed after the Civil War. Some of the most prominent were the Arion Society (Brooklyn, 1865), the Mendelssohn Club (New York City, 1866), the Chicago Oratorio Society (Chicago, 1868), the Apollo Club (Boston, 1871), the Orpheus Club (Philadelphia, 1872), and the Brooklyn Apollo Club (founded by Dudley Buck in 1877).[33] When Patrick Gilmore recruited his mammoth chorus for the National Peace Jubilee in 1869, he was able to draw singers from 102 choral societies from Massachusetts, New Hampshire, Vermont, Maine, New York State, and even Cleveland, Ohio .

Another important influence going back many years came out of German immigrant communities. *Liedertafeln* or *Männerchor*, male choruses devoted to the singing of German secular and folk music, had been a significant part of Teutonic musical life since the founding of the first such group in Berlin in 1805. Like the American singing societies, they were known to join together to form large leagues or *sängerbund* and hold festivals (*sängerfeste*).

The National Peace Jubilee

All of this musical activity and the prominent role played by music in the Civil War set the stage for a virtual explosion of interest in choral singing in the 1870s—both sacred and secular, in the church as well as outside. No single event was more responsible for kindling this passion for vocal harmony than Patrick S. Gilmore's National Peace Jubilee in Boston in 1869. The Irish-born Gilmore, the Civil War's most famous bandmaster, wrote of a vision he had in 1867 for a mammoth celebration/musical extravaganza.

> A vast structure rose up before me, filled with the loyal of the land, through whose lofty arches a chorus of ten thousand voices and the harmony of a thousand instruments rolled their sea of sound, accompanied by the chiming of bells and the booming of cannon,—all pouring forth their praise and gratulation[34] in loud hosannas with all the majesty and grandeur of which music seemed capable.[35]

---

33. Orr, *Dudley Buck*, 12.
34. Gratulation (def.): feelings of happiness and joy.
35. Gilmore, *History of the National Peace Jubilee*, 2.

Gilmore tapped Dr. Eben Tourjée, the most esteemed choral conductor in America at the time and a founder of the New England Conservatory, to recruit and organize a ten thousand-voice mixed chorus. It was to be drawn from singing societies across New York and New England, and as far west as Ohio. Nothing of this size and scope had ever been attempted in the United States, and Tourjèe's organizational structure, revolutionary at the time, would become a template for American choral festivals in the future.

The National Peace Jubilee would extend over five days with concerts featuring orchestra and chorus on all but one of them. The festival opened with a chorus and orchestra rendering "Ein Feste Burg," text translated "God is a castle and defense." The final concert featuring the massed chorus ended, appropriately, with Handel's "Hallelujah Chorus" from *Messiah*. In between was a feast of sacred music from massive renditions of German chorales to oratorio excerpts. Handel was well represented. The chorus sang "Glory to God" and "And the Glory of the Lord," also from *Messiah*, as well as "See the Conquering Hero Comes" from *Judas Maccabeus*. In addition, the repertoire included choruses from Mendelssohn's *Elijah* and *St. Paul*, the *"Inflammatus"* from Rossini's *Stabat Mater*, the "Gloria" from *Mass No. 12*, spuriously attributed to Mozart, and three major choruses from Haydn's *Creation*.

The Jubilee was not a perfect creation. It was intended to appeal to a variety of tastes from cultivated to the least refined. Some showmanship aspects actually bordered on vulgarity and ostentation, including:

- Verdi's "Anvil Chorus," from *Il trovatore*, accentuated percussively by a hundred firemen striking anvils and cannons fired remotely from the conductor's podium.
- Newspaper ads and handbills inviting people to see the "world's largest bass drum."[36]

Still, the National Peace Jubilee was a pivotal experience for singers, and they took home with them an invigorated passion for choral music, which ultimately would be acted out in innumerable church choirs across the land.

Choral Performance Becomes an Accepted Component of Protestant Worship

As late as 1850, many churches—perhaps the majority—allowed their choirs to sing special music only on occasions such as Thanksgiving Day

---

36. Darlington, *Irish Orpheus*, 50.

and Christmas. John W. Moore's *Encyclopedia of Music*, published in Boston in 1854, reveals the low status of the anthem as worship music in his scanty definition of the term. He closes with the following statement: "But as anthems are not often introduced in the service of our churches, and as it is presumed they will only be attempted when there is an able and well-instructed choir, under the direction of an experienced leader, further observations are not required in this place."[37]

The work done at Beecher's Plymouth Church was instrumental in building interest in large volunteer choirs with a professional nucleus. What was new after the Civil War was the growing mass of potential amateur choir singers available to churches. As noted earlier, choral festivals and societies had been gaining in popularity across New England and New York throughout the first half of the century. By the 1880s, every major city had more than one society competing for singers. For soldiers returning from the Civil War, group singing—often by hundreds of men—was a common experience that inspired a passion for choral and congregational singing. Gilmore's National Peace Jubilee in 1869 and his even larger World Peace Jubilee in 1872 exposed thousands to choral singing and skilled leadership. As a result, the generation reaching adulthood in the early 1870s was far more interested in choral singing and far more sophisticated musically than earlier ones.

The concept of a chorus choir, an ensemble made up of a large group of volunteer singers with a professional quartet or octet as the nucleus, was not new. It predated the choirs at Plymouth by a decade or more. W. B. Bradbury wrote anthems for choirs with a quartet nucleus which he may well have used at the Broadway Tabernacle. New York's Calvary Episcopal Church had had a well-publicized chorus choir since 1847.

There were challenges to establishing a large and effective choral group, one of which was the sheer cost of sheet music. A cheaper means of publishing individual anthems was needed for chorus choirs. The octavo[38] anthem, an English rather than American innovation, was the answer. *The Musical Times*, a British periodical published by Alfred Novello since 1844, included sample anthems printed in a cheap octavo format with each issue. In 1852, Oliver Ditson Company of Boston became Novello's American representative, but it was not until later that the first octavo anthems from the English publisher were shipped to the US to be sold in music stores. The first American company to imitate *The Musical Times* format in an American publication was Boston's White, Smith and Company, established in 1867.

---

37. Moore, "Anthem Singing," 54.

38. "Octavo size" refers to music printed on 7" x 10¾" pages.

The company's journal, *The Folio,* which began publication two years later, proudly included sixteen pages in each monthly issue.

Edward Morris Bowman

Two of the more powerful voices advocating choral music in worship in the years immediately following the Civil War were Dudley Buck and Edward Morris Bowman. Buck's significant contribution to sacred choral and organ music in America will be discussed later.

Edward Morris Bowman (1843–1913) was born in Bernard, Vermont but spent many of his early years in the Midwest. He learned to read music in Moses Cheney's singing school[39] and began to study piano at the age of ten. In 1867 Bowman moved to St. Louis, where he began to build a reputation as one of the nation's leading church musicians. During the period 1872 to 1874 he went to Europe to study organ with August Haupt and Rohde in Berlin. A second European sojourn in the 1880s took Bowman to England and Paris. In England, he studied with J. Frederick Bridges at Westminster Abby and the eminent composer/organist George A. McFarren, while in Paris he studied under Guilmant. Bowman was among the first Americans to pass the exam of the Royal College of Organists.

Edward Morris Bowman. Image courtesy of Archives and Special Collections, Vassar College Library, E. M. Bowman Collection, P. F. 6.21.

---

39. Moses Cheney's work as a singing school master is referenced in chapter 1.

Bowman worked for three churches during the twenty years he was employed in St. Louis (1867–1887). The three-hundred-voice Sanctuary Choir at Second Baptist Church, under Bowman's direction, became the most famous choir in the city. When the minister at Second Baptist moved to Peddie Memorial Church in Newark, New Jersey, Bowman followed. The all-volunteer Caecilian Choir at Peddie Memorial Church in Newark was organized by Bowman in 1887, his first year there.

Bowman was one of the few musicians of his generation to take the potential of volunteer choirs seriously. During his career he devoted his time exclusively to the development of such choirs. Bowman was confident that amateur singers could be trained in the aspects of musicianship needed to become good choristers. In large choirs of amateurs, the size of the ensemble reduced the need for individual singers with expensively trained voices. Bowman saw the training of volunteer choirs as a task that any able and personable leader could accomplish. He was convinced that volunteers could be motivated to sing well and be responsible choir members without the promise of monetary gain. With that in mind he set about devising an organizational structure that would encourage the fidelity and dependability of the members.

Bowman's three prerequisites for the permanent success of a volunteer choir program were: (1) regular and punctual attendance; (2) a self-governing organizational structure that promoted good fellowship among the singers; and (3) a respected leadership.[40]

The Caecilian Choir was well known not only for its musical excellence but also for its organization. Bowman conceived the eighty-voice ensemble as one that could be divided into four complete choirs of twenty voices each called the first, second, third, and fourth "divisions." Each division got one Sunday off out of every four consecutive weekends. Thus the actual singing choir, except for special occasions, was a balanced ensemble of sixty voices. The Caecilian Choir's division system proved to be an effective answer to the problem of irregular attendance among volunteers and was copied by choirs throughout the country.[41]

Between 1891 and 1895, Bowman, in addition to his work at Peddie Memorial, served as professor of music at Vassar College. In 1895, he resigned from both positions to become organist/director of music at the prestigious Baptist Temple in Brooklyn. With the two-hundred-voice Temple Choir, Bowman further refined his ideas about choral organization and developed a sophisticated system of choir officers and social activities.

---

40. "Temple Choir."
41. "Temple Choir."

From 1906–1913, Bowman worked at Calvary Baptist in New York City, organizing a large choir along the same lines as the one at Baptist Temple.[42]

Edward Morris Bowman, like his older contemporary, Dudley Buck, worked diligently to improve standards for church music and choral music in general in the United States. In 1872 he was elected president of the Music Teachers National Association (MTNA), and with Buck, spearheaded a drive to establish an American College of Musicians (ACM), which would serve to set standards for certification of professional musicians.

It was through the chorus choir and the vision of musicians like Edward M. Bowman that the transition was first being made from a mostly soloistic church music to one that was more oriented toward choral music. Volunteers, working side by side with professionals, increased their skills dramatically, and, as the skills of choirs increased, there was less need to hire soloists at all. Bowman's work with volunteer singers, especially in the decades following the Civil War, however, was the exception rather than the rule. The last quarter of the nineteenth century would also be the peak of involvement for professional musicians—singers, organists, and others—in American church music.

---

42. "Temple Choir."

Chapter 9

THE LITURGICAL CHURCH, PART 2

Ritualism and Liturgical Renewal in the Nineteenth Century

The second half of the nineteenth century was characterized by an almost mind-bending confluence of trends in the American church and American church music history. This chapter will focus on the late-nineteenth-century Protestant Episcopal, Lutheran, and Roman Catholic denominations. Subject areas will include the rise of ritualism, pioneers in the integration of the arts into priestly ministries, the boy choir movement, and the role of women.

Ritualism, the Legacy of the Oxford Movement in America

"It is clear to me that the Tract writers missed one great principle, namely that of Aesthetics, and it is unworthy of them to blind themselves to it." [John Mason Neale, 1844][1]

The reformers of the Oxford Movement and the Tractarians, with their focus on a return to historic pre-Reformation liturgical practice, spawned a heightened interest in ritualism. In a 1993 *Choral Journal* article, David A. Moore enumerated the many aspects of ritualistic worship that began

---

1. De Hart, "Influence of John Mason Neale," 2.

to appear in nineteenth-century American churches.² Among other things, the movement encouraged:

- The observance of the church year with special attention to festival days.
- The restoration of historic, pre-Reformation Catholic liturgies.
- The music of worship to be chosen for its scriptural and liturgical appropriateness, not popularity either in style or content in secular society.
- The wearing of vestments, both by clergy and choirs (all male, of course) with stoles and paraments appropriate to the liturgical season.
- The use of liturgical art.
- The use of symbolism in church architecture and in the form of crosses, crucifixes, and a variety of other items.
- A renewed interest in plainchant and chant-like free rhythm in compositional styles for church music.

In summation, the movement aspired to make the liturgical church a place set apart, imbued with a sense of the holy, the awesome, the *mysterium*.

The campaign to restore ritualism in the Church of England, while not exactly a part of the Oxford and Tractarian movements, was certainly related and ran parallel to it. It was centered not at Oxford but at Cambridge, when a small group of priests began to study Christian symbolism in church architecture. As membership in the group grew and the focus broadened to an array of subjects, it was formally instituted in 1839 as the Cambridge Camden Society. In 1841 the society began publication of a magazine entitled *The Ecclesiologist*, and in 1846 it changed its name to the Ecclesiological Society. The Anglican priest John Mason Neale (1818–1866) was involved from the very beginning.

In an introductory essay to Bishop William Durandus's *The Symbolism of Churches and Church Ornaments,* Neale and Benjamin Webb—both on the faculty of Trinity College, Cambridge—provided a detailed exposition on the spiritual power of symbolism in worship. "The higher principle behind symbolism Neale described as *Sacramentality*. Symbolism and ritual were established according to the providence of God for the purpose of elevating ordinary objects or human actions beyond their common use and thereby enabling them to serve a higher purpose. The Old Testament idea

---

2. Moore, "Victorian Anthems of the Oxford Movement," 9–10.

of consecration, which takes the profane and elevates it to a new and higher design, is closely tied to Neale's definition of sacramentality."[3]

Thanks to the Oxford Movement and the Tractarians, the post-Civil War years would also become a watershed in the development of ritualism in America. As a result, there would be a growing fascination with a liturgical and priestly role for choirs, particularly choirs of men and boys with vestments. Congregational singing of hymns, processionals, the routine singing of anthems, Anglican chant, plainchant, and liturgical art—all of these would be clothed in new respectability as indispensable components of historic and traditional liturgy.

Lest there be any doubt, *Tracts for the Times* and ritualism faced a virtual torrent of protest from evangelical, low church Episcopalians in the United States. George DeMille wrote that any Episcopal priest in 1800 seen to be wearing a surplice was branded, pejoratively, as a ritualist. Churches found to be celebrating communion on a weekly basis were accused of being secretly papist. The Rt. Rev. Manton Eastburn, Bishop of Massachusetts from 1843 to 1872, was an arch foe of Tractarian reform and ritualism. When the Church of the Advent, Boston, was founded in 1844 on Tractarian principles—free and open seating rather than rented pews, weekly communion, and restoration of historic liturgical practices of Anglicanism—Bishop Eastburn refused to set foot within its doors. The blessing of confirmands had to be moved to other churches before the bishop would agree to participate.

A chief spokesman for the evangelical wing of the Protestant Episcopal Church was the Rt. Rev. Charles Petit McIlvaine, Bishop of Ohio from 1832 to 1873. A bitter and vocal opponent of Tractarianism, he wrote, "It is a systematic abandonment of the vital and distinguishing principles of the Protestant faith, and a systematic adoption of that very root and heart of Romanism."[4] He railed against those who would worship by the "mere contemplation . . . of the sacred 'Catholic Symbols,' . . . the Triangle, the Fish, the Anchor, the Pelican, added to the manipulations and genuflexions of the Priest, his diverse bowings and incensings, accompanied with the aid of rich altar-cloths, symbolic candlesticks, splendid sacerdotal vestments, and enchanting choral music."[5]

Another pungent critique came from Lydia Maria Child, the prominent nineteenth-century feminist, abolitionist, and novelist:

> Another class of minds rise to a higher plane of reverence; this passion for the past becomes mingled with earnest aspiration

---

3. De Hart, "Influence of John Mason Neale," 3.
4. McIlvaine, *Oxford Divinity*, 14.
5. McIlvaine, *Oxford Divinity*, 283.

for the holy. Such spirits walk in a gold fog of mysticism, which leads them far, only to bring them back in a circling path to the faith of childhood, and the established laws of the realm . . . To such, Puseyism[6] comes forward, like a fine old cathedral made visible by a gush of moonlight. It appeals to the ancient, the venerable, and the moss-grown. It promises permanent repose in the midst of agitation. The young, the poetic, the mystical are charmed with "the dim religious light" from its painted oriels; they enter its gothic aisles, resounding with the echoes of the past, and the solemn glory fills them with worship . . .[7]

The advocates of Anglo-Catholicism, Tractarianism, and ritualism would persevere over their critics.

The Choir's "Priestly" Role

One important aspect of the new emphasis on historic liturgical tradition was the restoration of the priestly function of choirs. Ritualists believed that it was the proper office of the choir to sing certain service music, while it was the duty of the people to participate in the singing of hymns, psalms, and canticles. This, it was noted, was in the tradition of Old Testament times when priests and Levites performed the musical offices of the temple. The new focus was a considerable shift from earlier concepts of the church choir and its station. Choirs had customarily been treated by an unwritten policy of *disassociation*. The eighteenth-century gallery choir was viewed as an outside guild of amateur musicians, welcome guests perhaps, but with no liturgical function. They were neither congregation nor clergy. This attitude of disassociation between church members and church musicians needed to be ended in order to legitimize the choir's role in the church's ministry.

---

6. "Puseyism" was named for Edward Bouverie Pusey (1800–1882), the English theologian who, along with John Henry Newman, was at the very center of the Oxford Movement in England. Pusey contributed a tract on "Fasting" to Newman's "Tracts for the Times," and devoted his life to the cultivation of the spiritual life through devotion to the sacraments and rigid discipline. When Newman seceded from the Anglican Church and became a Roman Catholic in 1845, Pusey became the leader of the movement. "Puseyism," as a pejorative, was commonly used in reference to the Oxford Movement by those opposed to ritualistic reform in the United States.

7. Child, *Letters from New York*, 241.

The Choral Service

The Anglo-Catholic musical traditions that the ritualists hoped to restore fell under what, somewhat confusingly, is referred to as the "Choral Service." One must remember that after the American Revolution and for decades into the nineteenth century, orders of worship in Episcopal parishes were mostly spoken. The Psalter, if sung at all, followed the Puritan/Calvinist practice of metrical psalm settings with a precentor to lead.[8] Proponents of ritualism sought to enrich the worship experience by moving to a *pointed* Psalter. While four-part harmonizations of the chants might suggest choral performance, this was always thought to be optional. The concept was embodied in a statement appearing in the Protestant Episcopal Church's own manual for clergy on the subject: "The Choral Service being essentially melodic in character, any accompaniment by the organ or harmonization for the choir must be regarded as extraneous."[9] In other words, while portions of the service could be sung by a choir, this was essentially *congregational* music, and it was perfectly appropriate for it to be sung in unison. The term "Choral Service" was very flexible. It could refer just to the singing of parts of the Service of Morning Prayer and Sermon or, as was more the case, applied to the celebration of the Eucharist and Evensong.

Heretofore, most psalm singing in American churches of all denominations had required the use of metrical Psalters, collections of poetic paraphrases of the Psalms. It was a tradition going back to colonial times. The pointed Psalters of the nineteenth century for the first time allowed the Psalms to be sung in their familiar King James English rather than in a paraphrase. The concept of pointing had the congregation singing most of the text of each verse of the psalm on a single psalm tone with a clearly prepared harmonic cadence for the final syllables.

Episcopal ritualism was, of course, about more than singing psalms. There was a whole package of architectural, ornamental, liturgical, and artistic aspects of Anglo-Catholic heritage which the reformers sought to restore to America's churches. Latin terminology[10] was co-opted from the

---

8. The use of the term "precentor" here is not to be confused with its use in the colonial period where it was the lector who led the congregation in the singing of metrical psalms. The word "precentor" is thought to be a clumsy derivation of the Latin *primus cantor*, or first singer.

9. *Choral Service*, ix.

10. Latin terminology from the Roman liturgy was co-opted by the ritualists to designate chants and service music even though they were actually sung in English translation. Common examples from the Choral Service: *Kyrie eleison*, the *Gloria Patri* and *Gloria in excelsis*, the *Venite exultemus*, the *Te Deum*, the *Benedicite, omnia opera Domini*, and so on. This is a tradition that still applies in hymnals and service books of

Roman service book. Essential to the concept of the Choral Service, if done in its traditional form, was the divided chancel with two semi-choirs seated in stalls to the right and left of the altar. With the altar traditionally on the east end of the edifice, choir stalls on the left or north side were the *cantoris*, the stalls to the right or south, the *decani*. The precentor or first singer now became the choir leader. The divided chancel concept was important because where a choir was present, the chants were to be sung antiphonally. On shorter responses, the priest or precentor would intone the first phrase of a text—the *incipit*—with the choir and/or congregation responding.

The example below from John Ireland Tucker's pioneer collection, *The Service Book*, indicates how the first phrases of the *Te Deum*, as set in Anglican chant form by Edward Hodges, might be sung. *(Note: Full means "full choir"; "Dec." means semi-choir on right side of chancel or decani; "Can." refers to cantoris, the singers on the left.)*

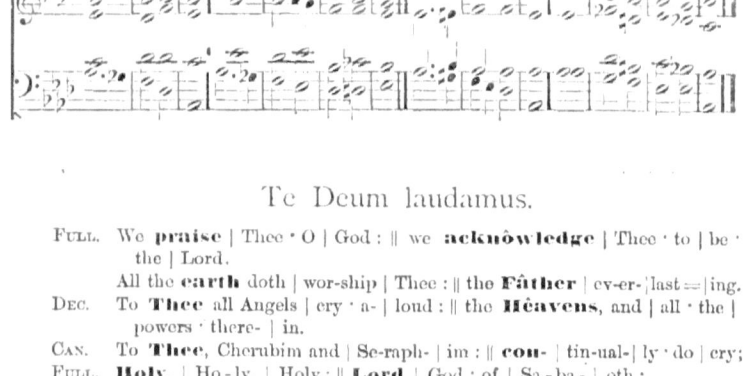

Edward Hodges, Double Chant in A Flat, with "Te Deum" text in John Ireland Tucker's *The Service Book, A Manual of Anglican Chants and Gregorian Tones adapted to the Canticles* (New York: F. J. Huntington and Co., 1873), p. 7

---

the Episcopal Church.

Musical Reform at "Mother Church," Trinity Parish, New York City

Chapter 4's discussion of musical activity in the Protestant Episcopal Church concluded with the tenure of Edward Hodges at Trinity Church in New York City, "mother church" to the denomination. Unfortunately, Hodges suffered what was likely a stroke in September of 1855, and was granted a three-month leave of absence from the parish to recover. In November, he wrote to the Trinity vestry, saying,

> I think that my general health has continued to improve . . . My infirmities, however, have not been totally removed. A finger and thumb still remain in a kind of non-natural condition, and now and then there are other indications that all is not right yet . . . Without proposing to relinquish the general superintendence of the work, or even thinking of withdrawal from active participation in it, I shall need (not a substitute but) an assistant; and I would wish to know how the idea strikes you. With such help (which would at the same time put a young man into good training for future usefulness), when I resume duty, I may possibly be enabled to hold on for a few years longer; without it, I have every reason to believe I should very soon break down again.[11]

The Trinity vestry did not approve Hodges's request for an assistant, and one of his students served at the organ until he was able to resume his duties in January of 1856. A year later, in January of 1857, a Boston organist Henry Stephen Cutler, probably at Hodges's urging, applied to be an assistant organist for Trinity Parish. He was not hired. Hodges, determined to soldier on, continued to preside at the organ. On September 1 of 1858, he played for a celebration, held at Trinity, commemorating the "successful laying of the Atlantic telegraph cable." His popular *New York Service* was performed.[12] It would be Hodges's last appearance at the parish. Following the celebration, the Trinity organ was taken out of service for repair, and on September 26, Hodges suffered yet another and more debilitating stroke. The Trinity Vestry immediately contacted Henry Cutler in Boston.

Henry Stephen Cutler

Henry Stephen Cutler (1825–1902), a student of pioneer Boston organist A. W. Hayter, had continued his studies, traveling to Germany in 1844 and then to England. There he visited many English cathedrals to familiarize

---

11. Ogasapian, *English Cathedral Music*, 192–93.
12. McClenachan, *Detailed Report*, 59.

himself with their musical practices. When he returned to Boston in 1846, Cutler first became organist at Grace Church. There he aspired to establish a choir of men and boys in the English cathedral tradition, but the church's wardens and vestry "saw revolution in the idea . . . The Tractarian movement of the Church of England, and the term, 'Puseyite', left an unwholesome taste in the mouth of well-intentioned churchmen. Nothing seemed to emphasize the principles of that movement so much as [boy choir] singing."[13] Critics found all aspects of the movement distasteful, from the pageantry of processional hymns to the introduction of anthems into the service proper. No item seemed to offend them more, however, than the use of choir vestments. Whenever this radical step was proposed, hostility was vented, and vociferous debate became the order of the day.

Thoroughly frustrated, in 1852 Cutler left Grace Church to become organist/choirmaster at Boston's Church of the Advent. There he did succeed in establishing a choir of men and boys which received national recognition for being the first surpliced[14] choir in America. It was that recognition which drew the attention of the ailing Edward Hodges. Cutler received the call to become organist at Trinity Church, New York City, in late 1858.

Henry Stephen Cutler.
Public domain image. (https://hymnary.org/person/Cutler_HS)

---

13. Berge, "Vested Choirs," 34, 36.

14. Liturgical vestments referred to in this chapter include the "surplice" and the "cassock." The surplice is a white, generally knee-length, overgarment. Most American churches, in their initial gravitation toward ritualism, outfitted choirs with the surplice only. Only later did it become common to wear it over a cassock. The cassock is a close-fitting, ankle-length garment traditionally worn by clergy and lay liturgists in the Roman Catholic and Eastern Orthodox traditions.

The Liturgical Church, Part 2

Upon his arrival, Henry Cutler made significant changes in the music program. Up to that time Trinity Parish had remained rather conservative in its approach to music in worship. The large, historic Erben Organ, dedicated in 1846, had been installed in the church's gallery (or rear balcony). A mixed chorus with professional quartet nucleus was stationed there and remained there through the Hodges years. By March of 1859 Cutler had dismissed the few women still singing in the church's choir, revitalized training for choir boys, and moved the singers to the Chancel. The change—separating the singers a great distance from the gallery organ—led to problems:

> The music gave proof of the progress made under Mr. Cutler's direction, though still leaving much to be desired. The boys and men choristers are rightly placed in the chancel, as they have been for some time past . . . The organ too is at a distance which renders it almost impossible for voices and instruments to keep well together . . .[15]

As Cutler had experienced at Grace Church in Boston, there was also resistance at Trinity to the wearing of vestments. Morgan Dix, who had arrived at Trinity as an assistant rector to the Reverend William Berrian in 1859, recalled the appearance of Cutler's singers around the time of his arrival:

> The men and boys had been transferred, some years before, from the organ gallery at the east end to the chancel, where they occupied benches, and presented a motley array of secular costume, in frockcoats, jackets, and garments of diverse colors and patterns, with variegated neckties. A full set of vestments, presented by a generous layman, had been carefully put away in the sacristy, objection being made by certain influential members of the Parish to their use.[16]

The lack of an organ in the chancel was a daunting and ongoing problem for Cutler. Trinity's choir was often noticeably singing flat or trailing behind the gallery organ accompaniment.

> The choir, accompanied by the organ at the other end of the church, could not, and did not, keep up to pitch; the complaints of flat singing were continuous.[17]

Cutler repeatedly sought approval from Trinity's leadership to purchase a pipe organ for the chancel, but his entreaties were ignored. The matter came

---

15. Rasmussen, *Musical Taste*, 379.
16. Dix, *History of the Parish, Part 5*, 471.
17. Messiter, *History of the Choir*, 96.

to a head in late 1860. With unemployment rising and the nation spiraling toward civil war, President James Buchanan proclaimed a National Day of Fasting for January 4, 1861. For a worship service on the appointed day, as a stopgap measure, Trinity purchased a French-made Alexandre harmonium (or reed organ), but another problem soon became apparent. The harmonium was pitched lower than the Erben in the gallery, and the two instruments could not be used together.[18] Finally, in January of 1863, a committee was formed to study the need for a chancel pipe organ. In December of that year a two-manual, fifteen-stop Hall and Labagh organ, intended specifically for accompaniment of the choir, was dedicated.

The vestments controversy, thankfully, was resolved by the visit to New York of Albert Edward, Prince of Wales and eldest son of Queen Victoria, and the future King Edward VII of England. Dix recalled going with a member of the vestry to Rev. Berrian and imploring him "to allow the choir to be 'decently habited' on that occasion, lest the Prince and his companions should be provoked to derisive laughter at the sight of the motley crowd of singers, and scandal thereby brought upon the Parish."[19] In anticipation of the prince's attendance in worship on October 14, 1860, the Trinity vestry agreed to having a service of festive elegance in the British cathedral tradition. It would be a fully Choral Service. A Litany would be intoned by the liturgist, and the *Gloria in excelsis* sung by all in attendance. The Nicene Creed would be sung to Gregorian "Tone 8," and an anthem by Marcello would be sung. The choir would be vested. Because of the prince's attendance, all segments of New York society were in attendance and the press marveled at the ceremonial splendor. It would be a turning point for acceptance of ritualism and liturgical art in American Protestant worship. Henry S. Cutler continued to serve at Trinity until May of 1865. Of Cutler, Arthur Messiter would later write:

> The permanent results of Dr. Cutler's administration, vested choir and Choral Service, constitute no small achievements. For these, now generally accepted as the normal and proper material and method for conducting divine service, due credit should be given to the man who sustained the struggle and persistent effort necessary for their introduction. The foundation was well and truly laid by Dr. Hodges. His successor built up the edifice in a substantial and finished style to the first story.[20]

---

18. The harmonium's pitch was eventually adjusted to resolve the issue.
19. Dix, *History of the Parish, Part 5*, 472.
20. Messiter, *History of the Choir*, 110.

Arthur H. Messiter

Arthur H. Messiter (1834–1916), a British organist, would become the organist/choirmaster for Trinity Church in 1866. His long and illustrious tenure would extend to 1897. When Messiter arrived at Trinity in 1866 there was still much to be done to achieve the reform of the liturgy advocated by the Tractarians. Fortunately, he had a strong and enthusiastic ally in the Rev. Morgan Dix, who had become rector two years earlier. At a celebration in 1891 recognizing his twenty-five years of music ministry, Messiter gave the following tribute to Dix:

> The writer ... here puts on record his gratitude ... to the Rector, the Reverend Morgan Dix, not only for ... the kind consideration and cordial encouragement extended to the writer for a quarter century; on the part of the chief authority of the Parish, everything has been done to make the way smooth for the organist and great indulgence has been shown for shortcomings.[21]

Indeed, the Dix-Messiter collaboration would be one of the longest and most productive in the history of American church music.

Arthur H. Messiter.
Public domain image. (https://hymnary.org/person/Messiter_Arthur)

---

21. Messiter, *History of the Choir*, 256.

From the previous regime, Arthur Messiter inherited a twenty-one-voice choir vested in "loose surplices" without cassocks. There were no choral processionals, and Holy Communion still was celebrated only once a month. Though Cutler had published a pioneering musical Psalter for use at Trinity, it had proven hard to use and metrical psalms were still the norm. Despite a century and a half of music making, there was still no music library at the New York landmark. Each individual organist had brought his own scores and left with them. A notation in Messiter's diary for June of 1866 lamented "Psalms poor; Te Deum bad; Litany bad; Kyrie bad with no anthem."[22]

He began to address these issues immediately. In the spring of 1869, the church adopted as its hymnal *Hymns, Ancient and Modern*, the historic British hymnal of the Oxford Movement.[23] Messiter also went to work creating a musical Psalter better suited to the needs of the parish and congregational singing. Liturgical renewal had brought with it a desire "to return to the wording of the Psalms as found in the King James and the Prayer Book Versions."[24] The *Trinity Parish Psalter*, created by Messiter in 1869 and later revised, was first used in worship on the second Sunday after Easter in 1870. It was the first "pointed" Psalter to be embraced for long-term use in the parish.

Priest-Musicians in the Protestant Episcopal Church

By tracing the work of Hodges, Cutler, and Messiter, we can see a gradual transition taking place at Trinity from a somewhat conservative low church perspective to high church ritualism. That trajectory, however, was not made possible by musicians alone. It was a collaboration between musician and pastoral leadership. Church music historians, however, have sometimes passed over the role of clergy or given it short shrift. This is particularly unfortunate when dealing with the liturgical renewal and ritualism of the late nineteenth century, *which was largely clergy driven.*

A special class of priest-musicians would have a major influence that would have obvious implications for worship in the Protestant Episcopal Church. In a broader sense, their work served as a model for the role non-ordained musicians might play in the life of the church, whether liturgical or not. If ordained priests were making musical leadership an important

---

22. Messiter, *History of the Choir*, 115–16.

23. The first complete edition had been published in London in 1861.

24. Dix, *History of the Parish, Part 5*, 90. In modern parlance, Dix is referring to "prosody," a term for the patterns of syllabic stress in a language.

part of their ministries, a message was sent that the role of church musician could be viewed as a "called ministry" in any denomination.

The New York Ecclesiastical Society and the Church Choral Society

The work of John Mason Neale and that of the British Ecclesiological Society were followed closely by seminarians from the General Theological Seminary in New York City. A New York Ecclesiastical Society was founded in 1848 and continued through the late 1850s. Its membership included W. A. Muhlenberg, John Henry Hobart, Milo Mahan, Morgan Dix, and John Henry Hopkins Jr. Influenced by John Mason Neale, the Reverend William McVickar, society president, said this of sacred symbolism:

> That Presence is indeed in it, and he everywhere beholds it, sanctifying the Beautiful, consecrating even the very dust of the Temple, inscribing upon its portals "Holiness unto the Lord," . . . the Church's Apostolic Faith in speaking symbols, and its penitent love in memorial windows, all going to make good the prophetic picture of what a Christian temple should be, "its walls salvation and its gates praise." This may be termed the Ecclesiology of the heart.[25]

The primary concern of New York Ecclesiological Society was church architecture, furnishings, and liturgical art. It did, however, set a goal of acquiring a library of music suitable for liturgical worship. The Reverend Edwin M. Pecke, a graduate of Trinity College in Hartford, addressed the need for clerical training in music in a speech to the Society in 1851.

> Some provision should be made for the musical education of the clergy. We may establish choral societies, train up choirs of boys, and find good musicians among the members of the church who can ably sustain their part, but *unless there be some provisions made for the musical education of the clergy*, it will be of no avail.[26]

Another organization, the Church Choral Society, spearheaded by the same GTS alumni, would take a first step in meeting Pecke's challenge.

Edward Hodges, while still working at Trinity, also taught at the General Theological Seminary. There, he championed the formation in 1851 of the Church Choral Society. The society, with Hodges as its driving force,

---

25. *Third Annual Report*, 10.
26. Pecke, "Choral Services of the Church," 142.

was made up of clergy and seminarians, many of whom were from GTS. Hodges formed it to study English cathedral music, learn correct techniques for performing both Anglican and Gregorian chant and present public demonstrations of ritualistic music. Years later in a letter to Hodges's daughter Morgan Dix recalled fondly the society's work:

> Dr. Hodges was our drill master, *Choragus* and *Coryphaeus*,[27] and the Rev. John Henry Hopkins the enthusiastic secretary. When the society felt strong enough to appear in public, they decided to sing a Choral Service . . . in Trinity Church . . . After that, it was only a question of time how long it would be until the fullness of our triumph [would win] over the fears and dislikes of the crude and untaught people. To your father belongs a large share of the honors . . .[28]

The Church Choral Society presented nine Choral Service demonstrations during the two years of its existence (1852–1854). It helped greatly to assuage the concerns of ritualism's critics and was a harbinger of the massive liturgical renewal that occurred later in the century.[29] Several priest-musicians who would be leaders in the movement for liturgical reform in the Protestant Episcopal Church in the late nineteenth century were among the participants in the society. In addition to Dix, there were J. S. B. Hodges (son of Edward), John Ireland Tucker, and John Henry Hopkins Jr. The contributions of these pioneer clergyman-musicians will be examined in the following pages.

The Reverend John Ireland Tucker

John Ireland Tucker (1819–1895) was the child of "Major" Fanning C. Tucker, a prominent Brooklyn politician, and Anna Sands, a member of one of the founding families of St. Ann's, Brooklyn's oldest church.

In 1832, John Ireland Tucker, or "Jack" as he was known to his friends, was enrolled at the Flushing Institute. There he would come under the tutelage of W. A. Muhlenberg, whose persona and influence would be major factors in shaping Tucker's career.[30]

---

27. "Choragus" and "Coryphaeus" were terms for chorus director in ancient Greek drama.
28. Rasmussen, *Musical Taste*, 385.
29. Rasmussen, *Musical Taste*, 379–86.
30. Muhlenberg's long career is discussed in more detail in chapter 4.

The wise headmaster lived out the Church Year after a fashion unknown in the experiences of the new land. He marked days and seasons, upon occasion by sunrise services, by emblems and lighted candles, by evergreens and flowers, but, in particular, with hymns and carols and by appropriate chanting.[31]

After Flushing, Tucker entered Columbia College in Brooklyn, graduating in 1837 and later enrolled at the General Theological Seminary with the intention of going into the ministry. After graduation in 1844 he served briefly as organist for St. Thomas Church in New York City, and in July he was ordained a deacon in the Protestant Episcopal Church.

John Ireland Tucker.
Public domain image, from Christopher Knauff, *Doctor Tucker, Priest-Musician* (New York: A. D. F. Randolph, 1897).

Meanwhile, a development that would have important implications for John Ireland Tucker's life was playing out north of New York City in the town of Troy. St. Paul's Episcopal Church had been founded in 1804, with construction funded in part by a grant from Trinity parish in New York City. In the 1840s St. Paul's had disbanded its choir in favor of a professional quartet. A group within the congregation, favoring more ritualistic worship

---

31. Knauff, *Doctor Tucker, Priest-Musician*, 17–18.

and use of the Choral Service, saw a need to establish another Episcopal church in the community. The Church of the Holy Cross was completed in the fall of 1844, and a young deacon whom the vestry had been told showed great promise was called to serve there. The first services at the Church of the Holy Cross were held on Christmas Eve, 1844, with the Rev. John Ireland Tucker officiating.[32]

Tucker almost immediately began expanding and enhancing the liturgy along Tractarian lines. He organized a mixed treble choir and taught them the Gregorian tones and Anglican chants for the Psalter. We can hear his frustration in a diary notation from 1846 where he was laboring to present a full Choral Service for the coming consecration service:

> I intoned the service. My object in intoning is to prevent the inconsistency of reading half a verse [as in the versicles] and singing the other half; another reason is to get rid of the organ accompaniment in the versicles and amens. They cannot "keep the key" unless I intone, and thus [I] keep it for them. I am now convinced that the whole must stand or fall together. The singing of the versicles or responses merely, is an imperfect, a halfway sort of thing, defective in a musical as well as ecclesiastical point of view. If the Choral Service is to be maintained, it must be the whole service and not in part.[33]

Nevertheless, Tucker was determined and noted in his diary for April 14, 1848: "I *chanted* the morning prayer, the choir responding as it is given in the Tallis service."[34]

Tucker was ordained and the Church of the Holy Cross consecrated in December of 1848. The sophisticated music used was indicative of his high church liturgical aspirations.

Venite & Psalms	Lord Mornington in E[35]
Te Deum & Jubilate in A	Felix Mendelssohn
Anthem: 122nd Psalm	Johann Naumann
Communion Service (*with a Kyrie written for the occasion.*)	Edward Hodges[36]

---

32. Because Tucker had not been ordained to the priesthood, the church could not yet be consecrated by the bishop.

33. Knauff, *Doctor Tucker, Priest-Musician*, 140.

34. Knauff, *Doctor Tucker, Priest-Musician*, 147.

35. Garrett Wellesley (1735–1781), Lord Mornington, was a composer and professor of music at Trinity College, Dublin.

36. Ellinwood, *History of American Church Music*, 92.

Throughout his tenure, Tucker was intimately involved in the church's music. He initiated a more intensive singing curriculum incorporating *solfeggio* and Concone vocal exercises and also sought to improve congregational singing across the Episcopal denomination by editing a musical companion, *The Hymnal with Tunes New and Old*, to the words-only hymnal of 1872. Later, Tucker co-edited a musical edition for *The Hymnal, Revised and Enlarged, as adopted by the General Convention of the Protestant Episcopal Church* (1892).

John Ireland Tucker remained at the Church of the Holy Cross until his death in 1895, a remarkable tenure of fifty-one years. Of his work there, Knauff wrote:

> The little ecclesiastical structure upon the hill of Mount Ida has been called a "Church of First Things," for the reason that many of our customs—reverent methods and fitting ornaments of service now firmly established—made their first start, and had their American introduction, at the Church of the Holy Cross in Troy. Here was settled the due observance of the Holy days of our Lord and Saints' days. Here was started, for all America, the preaching in the surplice; the introduction of flowers as an adornment for the sanctuary; the turning toward the East in Gloria and Creed, and the use of colored stoles ... Among other features of restoration, distinctly traceable to the work at Troy, was the use of the Choral Service.[37]

An August 1895 issue of the *Brooklyn Life* magazine had the following tribute by the periodical's editor:

> I note the death, which occurred a week ago this Saturday, of the Rev. John Ireland Tucker, rector of the Church of the Holy Cross of Troy, N.Y. ... His chief distinction in the church was attained through his musical talents, which were of a very high order. He was a composer and authority in hymnody, as well as a teacher of music, and the present authorized hymn book of the Episcopal Church, which is remarkably well selected and arranged, is the result of his efforts. It is a remarkable fact that Dr. Tucker refused numerous calls to rich parishes in large cities, among them being the rectorship of Grace Church on the Heights ... The church of the Holy Cross in Troy, to which he went in 1844, was his first and only charge ...[38]

---

37. Knauff, *Doctor Tucker, Priest-Musician*, 144, 146.
38. Obituary, *Brooklyn Life*, August 24, 1895, 9.

The Reverend John Henry Hopkins Jr.

John Henry Hopkins Jr. was born in Pittsburgh in 1820. His mother, Melusina Hopkins, was said to have a voice of "rare richness, sweetness, and power ... with perfect truth of intonation combined with quality of tone."[39] His father, John Henry Hopkins Sr. (1792–1868) was a true Renaissance man and would become one of the most powerful voices in the Protestant Episcopal Church during the first half of the nineteenth century. Hopkins Sr. was an artist and watercolorist, an ironmaster, a violinist and cellist, an organist, a composer, a lawyer, a theologian, and an authority on Gothic architecture.[40] While not embracing the Oxford Movement and much of Tractarianism, Hopkins made himself knowledgeable regarding the historic liturgies of the church and favored use of hymnody and chant as well as other means to enrich the Episcopal liturgy. In 1832, Hopkins Sr. was elected bishop of Vermont and the family moved to Burlington. There he began teaching seminary classes out of the church rectory. It was the beginning of what would become the Vermont Episcopal Institute.

Though only a teenager, John Jr. was already following in his father's footsteps with precocity in art, languages, and music. (To avoid confusion, he would often sign personal letters as "Henry," and that was how family and friends addressed him.) In Burlington, he tutored the young seminarians in Latin and French, taught drawing, played flute and bugle in the school orchestra, and sang in a local church choir.[41] John Jr. composed "Oh Dear" as a humorous round for the students he was tutoring at the institute.

---

39. Sweet, *Champion of the Cross*, 4.

40. *Essay on Gothic Architecture in Various Plans and Drawings for Churches*, by John Henry Hopkins Sr., was the first authoritative book on Gothic architecture to be published in the United States.

41. Sweet, *Champion of the Cross*, 11.

Oh Dear, What Shall I Do! (canon)

John Henry Hopkins Jr. (1843)

[Musical notation with lyrics:] Oh, dear! What shall I do? The les-son's so hard and it's all new too! Stu-dy, stu-dy, stu-dy hard, and you'll get through!

J. H. Hopkins, Jr., "Oh Dear, What Shall I Do!" (Canon),
as appearing in Charles F. Sweet, *A Champion of the Cross, being the Life of John Henry Hopkins, S.T.D. including selections from his Writings* (New York: James Pott & Company, 1894), p. 26.

Hopkins graduated from the University of Vermont in 1845 with bachelor's and master's of fine arts degrees, but the thought of some sort of work in the church had already been in the back of his mind. In a May 1843 letter to his father, he wrote about meeting with Edward Hodges at Trinity Church:

> I called on Dr. Hodges and introduced myself. I had a good deal of pleasant chat with him and sang in St. John's [Chapel] choir in the afternoon of Sunday. He asked me to play on the organ after church, but I was really afraid to try the huge thing. I was longing to be at it when nobody was by but myself. I told him I would practice hard the next year and play for him when I came back. I asked him about my being his assistant when the new Trinity is finished, and he seemed to like the idea well. I have little doubt that I could make it go, if I chose.[42]

In 1847, John Henry Hopkins Jr. enrolled in the General Theological Seminary in New York.

> It was a very different institution from what it is now. The buildings were shabby and mean, even at their best, and quite insufficient for the needs of the school. The library had very inadequate quarters, and in consequence could not be arranged so that full use might be made of the collection of books, which was a very good one. The chapel was a wretched, mean room, and celebrations of the Eucharist were not held except once or

---

42. Sweet, *Champion of the Cross,* 24–25.

twice a year . . .There was no ritualism in those days, but there was the soul of it . . .[43]

Henry saw the faculty at GTS divided into two camps regarding the use of chant in Episcopal worship. There were the "Gregorians," led by preacher/theologian Milo Mahan (1819–1870), and the "Anglicans," who were headed by Samuel H. Turner, professor of Hebrew. Mahan had been a classmate of John Ireland Tucker at the Flushing Institute, where they both were mentored by W. A. Muhlenberg. He advocated the embracing of Gregorian chant in Episcopal worship. Turner, on the other hand, favored the use of Anglican chant and pointed Psalters.

John Henry Hopkins Jr. (1820–1891).
Public domain image. (https://www.findagrave.com/memorial/46557057/john-henry-hopkins)

Contemporaries of John Henry Hopkins Jr. remembered him as masterful at accompanying Anglican chant as well as being quite flexible in adapting to other needs of churches, both low and high. He was an ardent believer in the need for restoration of historic ritual in worship and saw it as essential if the Episcopal Church was to thrive in the coming years. As he saw it, it was not so much a conflict between low church and high church as a struggle to combat unthinking rigidity throughout the denomination. But, first and last, his great battle was against the party of stiffened Anglicanism, with its balancing, its unintelligent horror of Rome, its isolation from

---

43. Sweet, *Champion of the Cross*, 45.

both the great currents of Catholic life and from the zeal of Methodism, its dread of offending the world, and its ostentatious avoidance of any form of spiritual life that spoke of the need for conversion.[44]

"What, after all, was ritualism?" Hopkins was asked by a parishioner in the 1860s. He answered,

> In an "Independent" Bethel, if the minister begins to wear a black silk gown instead of a dress coat, it is "Ritualism." In a Presbyterian congregation, the introduction of chanting is "Ritualism." Among the Dutch Reformed, the observance of Lent is a "Ritualistic abomination." Among the German Reformed, the new Liturgy which is framed upon the altar idea rather than the pulpit idea, is loudly denounced by its opponents as "Ritualistic." In one of our own parishes, which heretofore has had the three-decker arrangement, it is "Ritualism" to build out a distinct and properly arranged chancel . . . In some parishes it is "Ritualism" to have candlesticks on the Altar, even if the candles are not lighted. In others it is not "Ritualism" to have them, but it is "Ritualism" to light them, unless it be too dark to see to read without them.
>
> In some parishes it is "Ritualistic" to sing the Amens; in others, even the full Choral Service is not "Ritualism." Thus, we might go on, almost *ad infinitum*. But one short summary covers the whole—Anything, in any particular parish, no matter how slight, that indicates any movement toward an increase of Churchliness that is to say, an increase in the beauty, dignity, edification, or attractiveness, of public worship, especially if it tend to show increasing honor to our Blessed Lord or the Sacrament of His precious Body and Blood—is Ritualistic.[45]

Given Hopkins's passion for the restoration of ritual and ritualistic music in the church, it is no surprise that he quickly sought out and was active in both the Church Choral Society, in which he served as an officer, and in the Ecclesiological Society. He became an authority on the medieval modes, the German chorale repertoire, and Renaissance polyphony.

He returned to the General Theological Seminary and served as its first professor of music from 1855 to 1857. While at GTS, Hopkins composed the words and music for the beloved Christmas carol "We Three Kings of Orient Are." Over the course of his life, he composed a broad range of music for liturgical use: canticle settings, chants, anthems, and hymns.

---

44. Sweet, *Champion of the Cross*, 78.
45. Sweet, *Champion of the Cross*, 121–22.

His *Carols, Hymns, and Songs* (1883) was widely used. His Pentecost hymn, "Blow on, Thou Mighty Wind" (1858), shows the influence of plainsong and free meter:

J. H. Hopkins, Jr. "Blow On, Thou Mighty Wind"
as appearing in Charles F. Sweet, *A Champion of the Cross, being the Life of John Henry Hopkins, S.T.D. including selections from his Writings* (New York: James Pott & Company, 1894), p. 65. [Note: Notation changed to 4/2 from 4/1 for easier reading.]

Hopkins was a strong advocate for the congregational singing of hymns and offered this advice on the subject: "The only way to test a hymn is, not merely to read it silently, or even aloud, but to sing it, over and over again, to its own tune . . . The reason why we have so much unsatisfactory material thrust upon the Church, is that, for the most part, the writers of the words have known little about music, and the writers of music have had little taste or power in the poetic field, and therefore there was no felt organic connection betwixt the two."[46]

John Henry Hopkins Jr. also made a far-reaching contribution to the nineteenth-century church as a religious journalist. In an April 1872 article entitled "The Decline and Fall of the Low Church Party," he stated his position on the need for clergy trained in music. While he was specifically

---

46. Sweet, *Champion of the Cross*, 68–69.

directing his comments to the priesthood of the Church of England, they applied equally to the American church.

> Although all the Cathedral clergy are bound to sing their part in the Choral Service, men are not infrequently appointed who cannot tell one note of music from another, or who perhaps never even tried whether they could hum a tune or not until after they received their appointment. It became customary therefore to get a set of second-class clergy to do the singing, while the first-class dignitaries took the fat incomes, the Minor Canons being kept on starvation salaries, I suppose, because empty vessels are best for sound. With Dean and Chapter thus appointed and thus exercising the duties of their office, it is no wonder that great decay and demoralization have attended these magnificent foundations . . .
>
> We *have* inherited not a few of the evil results of the English system, and these are they which produce the visible and undeniable practical anomalies of which we complain.[47]

The Reverend Morgan Dix

When the Rev. Morgan Dix was called to serve as assistant rector at New York's Trinity Parish in 1855, the church's longtime rector, William Berrian (1787–1862),[48] was in ill health and in the final years of his life and ministry. Berrian, who followed John Henry Hobart as Trinity's rector, was a Hobart disciple. He supported Tractarian positions on the restoration of sacraments such as infant baptism and weekly observance of Holy Communion but was conservative regarding ritualism. The arrival of Dix and his partnering with Arthur C. Messiter ensured changes were in store.

---

47. "Decline and fall," cited in Sweet, *Champion of the Cross*, 363.
48. Berrian was Trinity's rector from 1830 to 1862.

Morgan Dix.
Public domain image licensed by Creative Commons.org. (http://anglicanhistory.
org/usa/mdix/index.html)

Morgan Dix (1827–1908) was the son of Major General John A. Dix. His father, as a teenager, served in the War of 1812, had a successful career as a politician serving a term in the United States Senate, and was called out of retirement to serve in the Union Army during the Civil War.[49] A scholar of Latin and classical languages, John Dix was also fluent in French and German, and founded a magazine focused on literature and science. It was from his father that Morgan Dix received his first musical instruction and became proficient in both keyboard and voice.

Dix's formative years were those in which *Tracts for the Times* had taken hold in America's high church environs. In later years he would recall the time and conflicts that arose:

> The airs that blew . . . from England were warm and reviving, having at once an effect of life-giving energy, and results followed swiftly. The young men studying in the seminaries took fire quickly, and some of them, as is always the case, were carried by the current to extremes which, in turn, provoked again the ire of opponents. Before the movement crystallized around

---

49. Because of his advanced age at the time of the Civil War, Major General John Dix primarily served as an administrator. He is chiefly remembered for his role in quelling the New York draft riots in 1863 and maintaining order afterward.

loyal Churchmen, some of the students fell away and went over to Rome. So great was the alarm over this drift that, in 1844, a committee of the House of Bishops was formed to investigate the teachings of the General Theological Seminary. A letter presented before the House of Bishops in 1844 condemn(ed) in round terms "the blasphemous doctrine of Transubstantiation, and the abominable idolatries of the Mass."[50]

The strong influence of Calvinism on English parish worship had been exported to the American colonies, where it became rooted in the Anglican chapels. It survived the exodus of the Methodists and the War for Independence and became ensconced in the low church wing of the newly formed Protestant Episcopal Church. Dix blamed the dissension regarding liturgical renewal on a long-simmering debate over the church's true identity.

> Within our own communion the influence of the Puritans was largely responsible for the party often broadly referred to as Evangelicals. Almost from the beginning of the Reformation, evangelical thought had a large following in the Church of England. It crossed the ocean to America in the early days. Differences between Catholic and Evangelical thought dates back, therefore, to the earliest days of the colonies.[51]

For Dix, that which divided evangelicals from high church Episcopalians was a disagreement over the very nature of the church and its purpose. The evangelicals "laid great stress on piety and prayer, on the need for [a] personal spiritual experience. Religion, they felt, was a highly individual experience, clouded, rather than helped, by adherence to ancient forms." The so-called "high churchman," Dix believed, held to a near opposite track. He preached that a Christian's faith could not be reduced to individual experience only. "Our Lord very definitely commissioned the Apostles, and he therefore held fast to the tradition of His Church and to the authority of sacraments."[52] Dix's assessment was telling. The division of American Christianity into two opposing camps, one focused on the individual's personal faith and the other viewing sacramental worship as primary, would fuel discord across all denominational lines for the rest of the century and beyond.

Morgan Dix entered the General Theological Seminary in 1849 and graduated in 1852. It was precisely the time when enthusiasm for liturgical renewal and ritualism was at its height.

---

50. Dix, *History of the Parish*, Part 5, 41.
51. Dix, *History of the Parish*, Part 5, 52.
52. Dix, *History of the Parish*, Part 5, 33.

He was ordained a deacon in the Episcopal Church the following September and accepted a call to St. Mark's Episcopal in Philadelphia, where he was ordained to the priesthood in May of 1853. Dix received the call from Trinity Church in New York to be its assistant rector and began his service there in September of 1855. With Cutler's arrival in November of 1858, efforts began to make changes that would bring the practice of music in the English cathedral tradition closer to fruition. In 1866, with Arthur Messiter now overseeing the music, regular use of processionals began. The weekly singing of psalms in the style of Anglican chant form came in 1870. Plainsong also became a regular component in Trinity's worship starting in the 1880s.

While Henry Ward Beecher and other prominent religious leaders of his generation focused on social and evangelical issues, Morgan Dix focused all of his energies on teaching about, restoring, and implementing the historic liturgies as living worship. This included observance of the major feast days of the Christian year and, above all, the "supreme importance of the two great sacraments, Baptism and Holy Communion."[53]

Dix himself was actively involved musically at Trinity. Throughout his tenure he worked with the parish school for girls at St. Paul's Chapel, organizing, directing, and accompanying a treble chorus there. He also regularly visited mission schools sponsored by the parish, reaching out through music. In an 1863 diary entry he wrote: "Played and sang for about an hour and a half, sometimes piano, sometimes organ; . . . filling my pockets with packs of powder crackers to bestow upon destitute children, who thankfully, . . . and with surprise accepted them, blessing my name."[54]

In an 1867 sermon, Morgan Dix spoke of his vision for Trinity and Episcopal church life that encapsulated much of the principles of Tractarianism:

> This church of ours, which we so dearly love . . . is a branch of the Holy Catholic Church. Her sympathies are with the great body whose organic life she shares . . . The hand of Almighty God has been with us from the first, through all the work of restoration. For these are not innovations; they are reconstructions. What belongs to us, we have been recovering; that is the whole story . . .[55]

---

53. Dix, *History of the Parish, Part 5*, 108. It was Morgan Dix who insisted that the chancel of Trinity Church (Episcopal), New York City, be reconfigured, bringing the Communion table forward so the celebrant could face the congregation when consecrating the elements. It was also during Dix's tenure, in 1870, that John Jacob Astor agreed to pay for the magnificent *reredos* that towers over Trinity's chancel, replete with symbolic carving.

54. Dix, *History of the Parish, Part 5*, 107.

55. Dix, "Sermon for the Times," 16.

Twenty years later, he expanded on that theme:

> Now mark this well. The Oxford Movement was a spiritual revival. It was such as no politician or worldly-wise man dreams of. It was a movement to save the church, and strangely enough, the idea was to save her, not by compromise, nor by giving in, nor by pleading for pity . . . , but by asserting the spiritual character of the church, announcing her Catholic claims, exerting her apostolic hierarchy, and rallying men to her defense as God's own creation . . .[56]

> The *Tracts for the Times* went straight against the whole course of the Church of England for the last three centuries. The Church had generally given up fasting, daily common prayer, Saint's days and Holy days, the observance of Ember days, the study of the primitive Fathers, . . . [and] the necessity of the sacraments.[57]

In 1908, a committee of New York clergy issued an "Obituary Minute" to be read at Morgan Dix's funeral. In it, they spoke of his leadership in music ministry:

> For the improvement of Church Music, and the program among us of the Choral Service, he did more than will ever be known, for into this, in his unobtrusive way, he threw the whole influence and the resources of his parish; and, somehow, many clergy men and laymen, who would not have liked such music or such methods for themselves, seemed to feel that it was well and proper for Trinity Parish to show what might be done in that line if anybody had the means and a mind to.[58]

John Sebastian Bach Hodges

The Rev. J. S. B. Hodges (1830–1915), son of Edward Hodges, was born in Bristol, England, in January of 1830. He was the fifth of seven children, many of whom had been christened with musical or biblical names—George (George Frederick Handel Hodges, 1822–1842), Jubal, Asaph, Miriam, Deborah, Celia (for St. Cecilia, patron saint of music), and Faustina. He entered the General Theological Seminary in 1854 and was ordained an

---

56. Dix, "Oxford Movement," 8.
57. Dix, "Oxford Movement," 9, footnote.
58. Manning, "Morgan Dix, Priest and Doctor."

Episcopal priest in 1854 and set out to serve parishes in Chicago and Grace Episcopal Church in Newark, New Jersey.[59]

In June of 1864, the Reverend Doctor William E. Wyatt died after fifty-one years as the rector of St. Paul's Parish, Baltimore.[60] Milo Mahan, in addition to his work at the General Theological Seminary, had become a nationally known preacher. "It was under those circumstances that, in the summer of 1864, Dr. Mahan accepted, after long deliberation, and with great reluctance, the call to the rectorship of St. Paul's Church, Baltimore, then vacant from the decease of the venerable Dr. Wyatt."[61]

> There was, withal, such a traditional attachment to the memories of the past century, that to make essential improvements was painfully difficult, and to make them rapidly was simply impossible. In his usual quiet method, little was said, and there was nothing in the way of complaint, or fuss, or the appearance of any great thing to be done. There was no shock, no jolt, no revolution, no newspaper chronicle of improvement. But quietly and silently one dropped stitch after another was taken up; one want after another was supplied. To the Daily Service was soon added the weekly Celebration, besides that on Saints Days; and an early service during Lent which was afterwards continued all year around. The Alb and the chasuble (of white linen)[62] were introduced. The one Altar-cloth was supplemented by another of white, and then others of other colors.[63]

Mahan sought to invigorate worship at St. Paul's and advocated return to historic liturgical and ritualistic practices. He also formed altar guilds and introduced the wearing of clerical vestments as well as the use of candles.

---

59. J. S. B. Hodges composed a number of hymn tunes. He is perhaps best remembered today as composer of "Euchasistic Hymn" ("Bread of the World in Mercy Broken").

60. St. Paul's parish had a long history of progressive and cultivated music. Its first pipe organ, imported from England, was installed in 1753. In 1804 that instrument, which had a history of breakdowns, was replaced with an organ from the British builder George Pike. In 1820, Christopher Meineke became the organist at St. Paul's and would remain there until 1855. (See Beirne, *St. Paul's Parish, Baltimore*.) The son of the German composer Karl Meineke, he was living in Vienna between 1817 and 1819 and was acquainted with Beethoven.

61. Hopkins Jr., "Memoir of the Rev. Milo Mahan," 8.

62. The alb is a plain, ankle-length tunic with long sleeves. It is more loose fitting than the cassock and is usually worn with a rope cincture around the waist. The chasuble, when worn, is the outermost vestment worn by a priest/celebrant in worship. It is an ornate circular garment with a hole in the center for the wearer's head.

63. Hopkins Jr., "Memoir of the Rev. Milo Mahan," 8.

The monastic tradition of daily worship was introduced. Unfortunately, Mahan was suffering from heart disease and died in the St. Paul's rectory on September 3, 1870. St. Paul's called a promising young clergyman to succeed him—GTS graduate and Mahan disciple John Sebastian Bach Hodges. He would serve there for thirty-five years and build one of most famous boy choir programs in the United States.

John, being the son of the famous Edward Hodges and an alumnus of GTS, was steeped in the English cathedral tradition and the influence of the Tractarians. One can discern Hodges's high church leanings from an early sermon he preached in Pittsburgh in 1856. In it he evoked the centrality to religious faith of the church as an institution, rather than an individual's conversion experience. He viewed the prayers and praise of God's people in the acting out of the church's liturgy as an essential expression of that faith.

> The service is not the worship of individuals, nor of an association of individuals who have severally been received into GOD's favor, but it is the worship of a body which, as a body, has had a new principle of divine life imparted to it, and it is designed to sustain and strengthen that life, first, in the body at large, and through it in every several member; to present that life as an offering to GOD; and to celebrate continually the marriage of the Church with her heavenly bridegroom. Thus considered, and thus realized, the public service of the Church becomes the highest, the noblest, and the most solemn act in which a mortal can be engaged.
>
> The prayers which ascend are the prayers of a community sanctified by GOD's truth—called out and separated from the world—seeking, not its own glory, but the glory of GOD—hallowed by the indwelling of the Holy Spirit—and interceding for the guilty world.[64]

A first order of business for Hodges as rector was to revitalize the church's music. When he arrived in 1870, St. Paul's still had a mixed chorus choir with quartet nucleus stationed in the gallery. They sang in street clothes and were screened from view of the congregation. He immediately began preparations for establishment of a choir of men and boys. While there was some dissention within the church—one prominent family left in protest—his emphasis on ritualism was more easily accepted because of the work done by Mahan before him.

St. Paul's, Baltimore—unlike most churches of the period—already had a ready source of choir boys when J. S. B. Hodges arrived there in 1864.

---

64. Hodges, "Nature of Worship."

The St. Paul's Boy's School, incorporated in 1853, was established to serve indigent boys in the neighborhood and already provided instruction in a variety of subjects, including music. The student body had both day and live-in students. Once installed as pastor, Hodges took over administration of the school, configuring it after an English choir school model. According to John Ogasapian, the St. Paul's Boy's School would be the first boy choir school in United States history.[65]

The great American poet Sydney Lanier was also a flautist and played in an orchestra for a festival Christmas Day service at St. Paul's in 1873. He wrote a colorful description of worship and ritualism as it was evolving under Hodges's leadership:

> The service was nearly three hours long, and music, music all the time . . . This is a wonderfully ritualistic church. A shrine is in front center, flanked by two enormous lighted candles, and arched over by a number of smaller ones. Three clergymen and a number of acolytes, boys, etc. assisted in the service. The Rector marched in stately fashion down from the dais, the other clergymen, the acolytes, and the choir, filed two and two behind him; all marched down into the body of the church, singing a fine chant . . . The chant was kept up long after they had disappeared, and the door was shut, and as the voices receded and receded, until nothing but the clear treble of the boys could be heard, 'twas dramatically very beautiful.[66]

The Boy Choir Movement in the United States

The boy choir movement in America is usually dated to the establishment of a boy choir at Flushing Institute in Long Island in 1828 by W. A. Muhlenberg. His work with the boys at the institute soon inspired the Reverend Francis L. Hawkes at St. Thomas Hall, also in Flushing, to organize a similar program. Boys matriculating out of Muhlenberg's choirs soon began singing in New York area churches and in 1846, Muhlenberg established a permanent choir of men and boys at the Church of the Holy Communion.

The emphasis on liturgical renewal during the 1870s and '80s led to a surge in interest in establishing choirs of men and boys. Leading churches including St. Thomas's, Grace, and St. Bartholomew's in New York, and Trinity and Emmanuel in Boston, abandoned their well-known mixed choirs and quartets to adopt such ensembles. Parishes in every corner of

---

65. Ogasapian, *Church Music in America*, 215.
66. Beirne, *St. Paul's Parish, Baltimore*, 79, 129.

New England followed in their wake. Two churches were the undisputed standard bearers of the movement: Trinity Church in New York and the Church of the Advent in Boston.

Boy choir music in Boston was dominated by two men, Samuel Brenton Whitney (1842–1914) and Warren A. Locke (1847–1920). Both were New Englanders and were closely associated with music at Appleton Chapel on the Harvard University campus. Whitney, who served as choirmaster and organist at the Church of the Advent from 1871 to 1909, was known for his interpretations of Bach organ literature[67] and for his outstanding boy altos. He was known to choose certain boys specifically for their low range and "trained them to sing alto from the start."[68] In doing this, he set aside the common wisdom of the time that all boys should be started out as sopranos and moved down as their voices matured.

Though he was probably the most knowledgeable American-born boy choir trainer in the late nineteenth century, Whitney's work and that of other nineteenth-century choirmasters suffered from the absence of opportunities for specialized training. Father William J. Finn, founder of the Paulist Choristers and a student of Whitney, admired his knowledge of English cathedral music. Nevertheless, he noted that neither Whitney nor any other choirmaster of the time had a real understanding of the potential of boys' voices.[69]

The change from a mixed chorus gallery choir to a choir of men and boys stationed in the chancel could be expensive. While a typical chorus choir could be made up entirely of volunteers or have a nucleus of paid singer/soloists, boys had to be trained, and those able to manage the challenges of the cathedral repertoire typically had to be paid. A typical stipend for a boy soloist in New York or Boston was $800 per year, and twenty or more boys were usually needed for an ensemble. In addition, sanctuaries often needed to be modified architecturally, organs moved or replaced, and so on. The following letter, written around 1880 and pertaining to music at St. Paul's Episcopal in Boston, highlights many of the concerns of church music committees and members of vestries:

> My Dear Mr. Vowden:
> I have given much thought to your letter regarding music for the coming year but have not as yet arrived at as definite a conclusion as to figures & wish to do before making a formal proposition to the music committee of St. Paul's Parish.

---

67. Finn, *Sharps and Flats*, 12.
68. Rockwood, "Our Early Church Choirs."
69. Finn, *Sharps and Flats*, 12–13.

Aside from my own personal feelings, I can't help thinking that the one simple solution of the whole matter is a choir of men and boys, but that, almost at the outset, seems to involve placing them at the front of the church, adding an expense. With the proposed appropriation of $2000, I am certain from talks I have had at the request of the Rector with various managers of boy choirs in the city at different times, that far better work can be done than with women—by this I mean financially, & as to the musical effect, I can hardly feel that part can be questioned.

So far as I remember, I should say it might be possible to keep the men as at present and make the number of paid men and boys twenty on that appropriation, and to add to that number, as at present, people who may come in for the practice and for an interest in the church services. If the music must be kept where it is now, I have been thinking that it might be wise even to reduce the number to eight of a better class of voices than we have at present, making the music at least more finished and artistic and less unwieldy than it is now, with the very limited space at our disposal.

I write to you, knowing that the question of the music will have a part in the proceedings at the meeting of the Vestry today, and as I know that considerable[work] has been done since the last meeting. If you wish, I have no objection to having the contents of this letter made known to the Vestry.

Very faithfully yours,
Wm. B. Pistin[70]

Some urged the establishment of choir schools in the English tradition, but this was also an expensive undertaking that most churches could not afford to consider. Only two such schools were established before the beginning of the twentieth century: at St. Paul's in Baltimore in 1873, and at Grace Church, New York City, in 1894.[71]

St. Paul's, Boston, did eventually get its boy choir, but it took several years to build the program. Warren A. Locke became organist/choirmaster at the Boston church in 1888, and in September of that year a choir of men and boys made its first appearance. Locke was a graduate of Harvard, where he studied organ with John Knowles Paine. During his thirty-one years at St. Paul's Church, his choir became well known for its excellence. He also

---

70. Letter, Wm. B. Pistin to Mr. Vowden, n.d. (ca. 1880) in Archives, the Episcopal Diocese of Massachusetts.

71. The aforementioned school at Trinity, New York City, was not a choir school, but classes in singing were taught.

organized a vested choir that for many years provided music at Appleton Chapel on the Harvard campus.

The installation of boy choirs brought with it certain perennial difficulties that were an aggravation even to the movement's most loyal supporters. Directors with training were hard to find, and many aspiring directors could offer no better credentials than a diploma from one of several choir schools attached to large churches. Peter C. Lutkin characterized the typical aspiring boy choir director as "some enterprising person whose entire preparation for the exacting task consists in the fact that he, at one time, as a boy or man, sang in a vested choir."[72] Many boy choir directors lacked even a basic understanding of vocal training techniques.

Boy choirs were still considered to be an exotic area of music-making, and the techniques required for leading them were learned mainly by observation. A director's ability to recruit boys and maintain good discipline in the rehearsal room was often considered far more important than his musical training. This, Lutkin said, was unfortunate, for the finer points of singing were often ignored.

> To take a boy off the streets and to change his natural inclination to yell in his chest tones to habits of really good and correct tone production, is a task so difficult that it borders on the miraculous. In addition to the necessary technical knowledge, it requires infinite patience, tact, and unfailing good humor. It is the lack of this knowledge of how to produce good and agreeable tones that lies at the root of the general unsatisfactoriness of our so-called "boy choirs." As a rule, our boys don't sing—they shout or yell.[73]

There was much disagreement concerning whether chest or head tones should be encouraged in training of choirboys. While many choirmasters saw the development of a head register of primary importance, there were still those who preferred the carrying power of the pure chest voice. It was said by some that development of the head tones was simply an effort to change the "natural, robust quality" of the voice "to one that is false and effeminate."[74]

---

72. Lutkin, *Music in the Church*, 177.

73. Lutkin, *Music in the Church*, 175–76.

74. Messiter's recollections suggest that both Edward Hodges's and Henry Cutler's choirs had limited high ranges and compromised intonation. This likely was the result of overemphasis on the chest voice, which Messiter also subscribed to. The various directors in Trinity Parish were not of one voice on this subject. William Bond Gilbert (1829–1910), the Oxford-trained organist at Trinity Chapel, had a strong preference for head tones. He had a favorite maxim painted on the blackboard of his choir room;

The most commonly used American training manuals were not published until after the turn of the century: *The Essentials of Choir Boy Training*, by Walter Henry Hall (1906), and A. M. Richardson's *The Choirtrainer's Art* (1914). George Edward Stubbs, professor of sacred music at the General Theological Seminary, and organist at St. Agnes Chapel in New York City, published two helpful books somewhat earlier, *How to Sing the Choral Service, A Manual of Intoning for Clergymen* (1899) and *Practical Hints on the Training of Choir Boys* (1888, rev. 1897).

Despite these challenges, boy choirs had become fashionable. As early as 1871, there were boy choirs organized in sixteen of the dioceses of the Protestant Episcopal Church.[75] In 1895, Nickerson's *Illustrated Musical and Church Choir Directory* listed forty-one New York-area Episcopal churches out of which twenty-six had adopted choirs of men and boys, either exclusively or in combination with a quartet or chorus choir.[76] A more thorough study of New York Episcopal churches in the *Church Almanac* for 1890 listed seventy-four churches of which thirty-three had adopted vested choirs of men and boys.[77]

As boy choirs became ever more numerous in the 1880s, it became more and more difficult to find good boys' voices. Arthur Messiter found it necessary to continually recruit from throughout the New York metropolitan area and Brooklyn to find sufficient boys' voices for his choir. Clarence Dickinson, writing in 1910, recommended choirmasters regularly visit the public schools, listen to the singing, and befriend the teachers to find suitable candidates. He also gave choir members finder's fees for each singer

---

"Shouting is *not* singing!." (See Dix, *History of the Parish of Trinity Church*, Part 5, 245.) George Fitz Curwood Le Jeune (1841–1904), at St. John's Chapel led one of the most famous boy choir programs in America. H. E. Krehbiel observed that Le Jeune's method consisted of restricting all singing to the head register. "This is not because he believes that the chest tones . . . cannot be used effectively, but because he holds that it is impossible to bridge over the break between the registers in the three or four hours study a week." (See Krehbiel, ed., *Review of the New York Musical Season, 1886–1889*, 27.) The concept of a "complete" voice, wherein emphasis was placed on smoothing over register breaks and melding chest, mid-range, and head tones into one continuous vocal compass was little known before 1900. One early adherent of this idea was Arthur E. Cooke at Calvary Church, New York. According to Krehbiel, Cooke "split up the voice into more than two registers, believing also in cultivating the medium tones, on the ground that . . . sweetness and purity of tone are gained by developing the head tones downward."

75. West, "History and Development."
76. *Nickerson's Illustrated Church Musical and School Directory*, Part 2, 186–223.
77. "Choirs of New York."

they brought with them to choir practice—twenty-five cents for each soprano, a half-dollar for altos.[78]

"Every church, down to the smallest and poorest," Lutkin wrote, "must enjoy the picturesque spectacle of a surpliced choir whether or not the conditions warrant it. We have a subconscious feeling that doctrinal, utilitarian, or sentimental reasons exist which justify the use of boy choirs, no matter how much they offend our ears or violate our artistic senses."[79] The Reverend P. Landon-Humphrey was speaking of English parish churches in his book *The Evolution of Church Music*, but his criticisms applied equally well to American congregations:

> The popular idea seems to be that all that is needed to obtain a boy choir is to gather a mob of street urchins, give them books and a few rehearsals, put vestments on them and turn them into the stalls. They may sing flat and sing sharp, they may murder the service and drag through the hymns, they may shout and scream with voices that would scratch glass, they may rattle the windows with *Nunc dimittis*—but the parish has a boy choir and the Rector is happy, even though the longsuffering congregation be literally sung out the doors.[80]

The Exclusion of Women from Ritual Leadership: Theologically Defending the Indefensible

Putting a choir in vestments, moving it to the chancel, and giving it a prominent role in the liturgy was not simply a musical problem. It raised the whole issue of women making inroads into the patriarchal, male-dominated world of Christian ministry. In his Introduction to Stubbs's *Practical Hints on Boy Choir Training*, J. S. B. Hodges outlined the traditional rationale behind the changes taking place:

> It is only a short time since . . . the choirs of our churches, in England and in this country, were composed of men and women singers, placed aloft in a gallery, generally at the western end of the church, entirely separated from the congregation, and shut in by curtains which excluded them from all observation . . .[81]

---

78. Dickinson, "Choral Music and Choir Direction," 345.
79. Lutkin, *Music in the Church*, 177.
80. Norden, "Boy Choir Fad," 197.
81. Stubbs, *Practical Hints*, 13.

> We have been coming back to a recognition of what the Church, nearer to apostolic times, recognized, that the singers in the church have an important and holy office—that they constitute one of the lower ministries, almost an order. And, following out this line of thought, and to bring home to them the sacredness of their office, . . . they are given a distinctive dress, a white garment, which is never to be dishonored by improper act or manner. They are placed in full sight of the congregation and given a position in a very holy part of the church, in the Chancel, and near the altar of God.[82]

The scriptural justification most often cited for the exclusion of women seems to have been the passage in First Corinthians where Paul prescribes proper behavior for those attending church.

> Let your women keep silence in the churches: for it is not permitted unto them to speak; but they are commanded to be under obedience, as also saith the law. And if they will learn anything, let them ask their husbands at home: for it is a shame for women to speak in the church. (1 Cor 14:34–35, KJV)[83]

If a choir was to be a holy order and a ministry, and if it was to be stationed appropriately in the chancel, the accepted view of Episcopalians and Roman Catholics was that women must be excluded from singing.

The Reverend Phillips Brooks,[84] one of the nation's most famous preachers and later the Episcopal bishop of Massachusetts, was no conservative evangelical. He was passionately committed to the ritualistic ideals of the Tractarianism and an outspoken opponent of slavery. That being said,

---

82. Stubbs, *Practical Hints,* 14–15.

83. To exclude women on the basis of this scriptural passage was a classic example of biblical misinterpretation. F. C. Eiselen, in the *Abingdon Bible Commentary*, questioned whether Paul even wrote the directive. He noted that it appears out of the general context of the chapter, and contradicts statements made earlier by Paul in chapters 1 and 2 of 1 Timothy. At any rate, the passage in 2 Corinthians has nothing to do with singing.

84. The Rev. Phillips Brooks (1835–1893) served Trinity Church, Boston, from 1869 to 1891, at which time he was elected bishop of Massachusetts, a post he held until his death fifteen months later. Like Morgan Dix, Brooks was deeply committed to restoring the historic ritualistic and liturgical practices promoted by the Oxford and Tractarian Movements. The original church having been destroyed in the Great Boston Fire of 1872, it fell to him to oversee the rebuilding at its present location. A collaboration with architect Henry Hobson Richardson, muralist John LaFarge, and stained glass artists William Morris and Edward Burne-Jones resulted in an architectural masterpiece. Among many notable features was the first freestanding liturgical altar in the United States.

while Brooks was traveling abroad in 1890, he wrote the following to his assistant rector at Trinity Church, Boston, the Reverend Reuben Kidner:

> Not a surpliced female choir, my dear friend! Almost anything but that! But let us set ourselves against that most fantastic and frivolous affectation which has turned up in these days, when surely the church is young-ladyish enough without putting young-ladyism, decorated for a spectacle, in the seat of prominence and honor. Surely it is amazing how much attention clothes enlist in all the operations of our great Communion. Let us keep our simplicity, and so, no vested female choirs! Almost anything but that![85]

Brooks, the hymn writer of "O Little Town of Bethlehem," was responding to a trend that had been brewing in Episcopal churches for some time. John Ireland Tucker had set an example for the use of girls singing the liturgy from the chancel as early as the 1840s. He drew his Church of the Holy Cross choirs from the Mary Warren Free School. While not attired in surplices and cottas, they were uniformly dressed with "a straw-colored bonnet with pink lining, and a lilac calico dress, with white cape."[86] The Reverend Charles R. Hodge, while vicar of Grace Episcopal in New Lenox near Chicago, wrote the manual, *Clergy and Choir*, in which he advocated "adjunct choirs" of girls and women.

> But most clergymen and choirmasters, following churchly tradition and usage, are decided in their objection to a female element in the vested choir . . . But that leaves out all this rich and plentiful mass of musical talent in our parishes unless we can organize a girls' choir . . .[87]

It is unfortunate but true that sexist views were as prominent in the life of the church during the late nineteenth century as in the rest of American society. However valid the historical precedent for moving from mixed choirs to those of men and boys in the ritualistic churches, prejudice motivated the change in many cases.

For the most part the church was *not* a place where women needed to strive for acceptance—society bestowed on women the responsibility for tending to the cultural and religious upbringing of the family. "Women not only controlled education and religion, but largely dictated the standards of literature and art and clothed culture so ostentatiously in feminine garb that

---

85. Allen, *Life and Letters of Phillips Brooks*, 755.
86. Knauff, *Doctor Tucker, Priest-Musician*, 136.
87. Hodge, *Clergy and Choir*, 18.

the term culture itself came to have connotations of effeminacy."[88] Women carried much of the burden for keeping the churches going in the nineteenth century. They taught Sunday school, chaired committees, did much of the church's missionary work, and banded together to evangelize the communities in which they lived.

> One of the most refreshing and entertaining lights in which woman presents herself to the eye of the critic is that in which she is seen when she is engrossed in the performance of duties or of what she takes to be duties connected with church. She worships her pastor with a lesser kind of adoration and this regard is visible in all she does. Deferential as is the submission with which she bears the advice or suggestion of father or husband, it sinks into insignificance beside the profound reverence with which she listens to the counsel of her spiritual head.[89]

As in other areas of church life, women made significant inroads in church music during the nineteenth century. In many churches women had been singing in volunteer choirs for decades. The professional soprano soloist was perhaps the most important member of a quartet, for the melody in the four-part homophonic quartet style was usually given to the top treble voice. No male singers could hope to command the price of female singers like Emma Thursby, Antoinette Sterling, or Corrine Rider-Keisey. In an area of such opportunity, was there really discrimination?

The answer was yes. Though there had been little effort to exclude them in the past, as concepts of the priestly function of the choir began to be discussed the propriety of women's participation as singers came into question. If music was truly to become a priestly office, some clergy argued that women had no place in it. Sophie Drinker outlined the rationale in her 1948 book *Music and Women*. Drinker pointed out that "a distinction was . . . drawn between liturgical singing and other religious choruses." As long as the music had the flavor of "a kind of sacred concert," Drinker noted, women were quite free to sing, "but where music is a liturgy and the members of the liturgical choir are thought of as attendants of the priest at the altar, women are excluded."[90]

> Women may entertain an audience, even in church, and attract people into the service by their voices, but they may not be official representatives of worship. This prohibition applies

---

88. Commager, *American Mind*, 23.
89. "Women at Church," 5.
90. Drinker, *Music and Women*, 249–50.

wherever there is liturgy in its ancient and traditional sense in the church service—whether the church be Catholic, Greek Orthodox, Jewish or Protestant.[91]

Edward G. Stubbs, speaking as an Episcopalian, noted historical and doctrinal precedents for the exclusion of women in a 1917 article in *Musical Quarterly*. Praise and adoration of the Almighty, he said, were the chief characteristics of Temple worship revealed in the Old Testament. Singing was the logical vehicle for praise. "The intoning of the officiating priests and the responses of the choristers," Stubbs said, "formed a choral unity and were inseparable." Because of this, it followed that choristers were part of the ministerial body and had to be male. The exclusion of women, he added, was adhered to "both in theory and in practice by the Primitive Church."[92]

Nineteenth-century fiction had treated women as having ministerial qualities. In deference to the women in their congregations, ministers themselves were more apt to use feminine analogies for God, Christ, godliness, and Christian living. Bushnell equated God's love to a mother's. Henry Ward Beecher preached that a mother's love is "a revelation of the love of God."[93] Feminine metaphors aside, however, as one can intuit from Phillips Brooks's letter above, women's inroads into worship ministries in churches were too often viewed as a threat by clergy rather than as an opportunity for collaboration. A classic case was that of the Congregational Church in Medway, Massachusetts, where the male leadership of the church objected to the establishment of such a school on the basis that "these women will be in the pulpit next!"[94]

With regard to choirs, many churches were faced with a dilemma. It was felt that admitting women to the chancel was a betrayal of church doctrine and that women had no business interfering with the priestly role of the choir. What to do? In many cases, if women were not allowed to sing, the church's music program faced ruin. Churches found themselves in a frightful quandary. The majority of churches could not muster enough singers to staff a full mixed-voice gallery choir plus a vested choir of men and boys, and newer churches were being built with no gallery anyway.

When Everitt Titcomb arrived at Boston's Church of St. John the Evangelist in 1910, he found it necessary to recruit women to, as he said, "help the boys who certainly needed help."[95] This was true even though his choir's

---

91. Drinker, *Music and Women*, 250.
92. Stubbs, "Why We Have Male Choirs," 423.
93. Douglas, *Feminization of American Culture*, 130–31.
94. Douglas, *Feminization of American Culture*, 133.
95. Titcomb, "Twenty-Five Years," 63.

singing was restricted to service music, hymns, and the Psalter. They sang no anthems or motets. Titcomb tried placing the female singers behind the organ console and also behind a vanity screen so they would not be visible to the congregation. St. Michael's Church in New York City, which had two choirs of equal size, one of boys and one of girls, took a similar approach. The girls, "not vested, sat behind the boys in a screened part of the chancel and supported them."[96] This curious and contradictory practice of concealing singers was used at other churches in the New York area, according to *The American Church Review* in 1889. The editor noted, however, that no churches, to his knowledge, had approved the vesting of women "and truly we should not care to see them."[97]

The exclusion of women applied not only to chancel choir singers and choirmasters. Organists were also affected. Female organists found the prejudicial views of their male peers presented a formidable obstacle to their finding work. Even with the finest college training and credentials, some churches would not even consider a woman for an organist position if men were also applying. Reba Broughton Maltby told of applying for forty-seven positions in the New York area around 1900, but not one church music committee would hear her play. When the chairman of the music committee at New York Avenue Methodist in Brooklyn told Maltby bluntly, "We don't want a woman organist," she responded irately, "You don't want an organist—what you want is a pair of pants!" Her saucy persistence caused the committee to rethink its position and she was hired.[98]

A few vested choirs of men and boys would survive and thrive into the twentieth century and help preserve a great tradition of English cathedral music in the United States. Many more, however, would not. The challenges were too great, and the motivation questionable.

Lutheran Worship in the Nineteenth Century

In colonial America the earliest Lutherans settled along the Eastern Seaboard. In the nineteenth century, however, Lutheran immigrants followed the same routes of westward migration as other groups—westward through New York State into Pennsylvania, then either south into Virginia and North Carolina or moving farther west into Ohio and beyond. Lutheran immigration spiked during the nineteenth century. A first wave of Lutheran immigration, between 1840 and 1880, was largely from Germany. A second wave,

---

96. Peters, *Annals of St. Michael's*, 85.
97. "Music of the Church: Women in Choirs."
98. Maltby, "How Woman Organist Overcame," 6.

largely from Scandinavia, peaked around 1882 and continued through the outbreak of the First World War. The growing Lutheran population caused an acceleration in the building of schools, colleges, and seminaries, as well as hospitals, nursing homes, orphanages, and institutions providing immigration services.[99]

The nineteenth century was a fractious time for Lutherans in America. According to historian Mark Granquist, "One of the primary struggles for Lutherans in America was how to be both Lutheran and American."[100] Cultural and theological differences and differences in worship practices resulted in numerous divisions and schisms with key points of divergence revolving around language. Very few Lutherans immigrating from Europe in the mid- to late nineteenth century were English speaking. While some basic English literacy was necessary for them to function in American society, speaking the native tongue with family and friends and in church was seen as "a means whereby immigrants, a minority in a strange land, could maintain their ethnic separation from the dominant culture, a sense of ethnic solidarity, and the deep sense of the community in which they belonged, were understood, and could express their faith."[101] Depending on point of origin and level of assimilation into American ways, nineteenth-century Lutherans might worship in English, German, Swedish, Norwegian, or Danish.

Many of the oldest Lutheran communities on the coast and as far west as Philadelphia had become increasingly Anglicized, and this became a point of contention between them and the newer arrivals. In the first half of the nineteenth century, when most Lutheran prayer books were in German, a few congregations adopted the Episcopal *Book of Common Prayer*, an act which was seen by sister churches as scandalous. By 1850, however, attitudes had begun to ameliorate. By then, over half of all English-speaking Lutherans in the United States had begun using *Hymns Selected and Original*, first published in 1828 by the General Synod of the Lutheran Church in the United States, with hymns in English translation. Still, many among the incoming flood of Lutheran immigrants brought with them prayer books and hymnals from the Old Country in their native languages. In 1862, the German Lutheran Synod published the *Evangelisches Gesangbuch*, a hymnal in the German Reformed tradition.[102]

---

99. Granquist, *Lutherans in America*, 172–82.
100. Granquist, *Lutherans in America*, 162.
101. Granquist, *Lutherans in America*, 126.
102. Westermeyer and Music, *Church Music in the United States*, 238.

Among the second wave of Lutherans arriving in the post-Civil War years were an impressive number of Norwegians. It has been estimated that by 1880, 25 percent of Norway's total population had immigrated to the United States. Many in that group were family units that chose to settle in Minnesota, Wisconsin, and North Dakota in order to farm in rural areas. There churches were small, struggling, and separated by miles of prairie and farmland. Congregational singing was in Norwegian and the *Landstads kirkesalmebog* or "Lanstad Hymnal," the official hymnal of the Church of Norway, was commonly used.[103]

The level of denominational unity and coalescence around basically two fundamentally different approaches to worship that existed among Episcopalians[104] was not a realistic possibility for American Lutherans. The Oxford Movement had had little impact on them, and even the great tradition of Lutheran chorales was slow to find acceptance. Some communities eagerly assimilated popular gospel songs into their liturgies while others looked on in horror. While Lutheran congregations on the prairie often had small choirs (they seldom had quartets), these were almost exclusively to support congregational singing.

The Church and Opera: Roman Catholic Worship Music in Nineteenth-Century America

As late as 1840 there was no singing at all in two-thirds of the Roman Catholic churches in the United States.[105] The total number of Catholic choristers in Boston in 1836 was only twenty.[106] Catholicism was a minority faith seeking to find acceptance amid the rampant anti-Catholicism in America. It did not help that Roman Catholic church music was at a low point in its history.

The Church at Rome had shown little interest in controlling the worship practices of its churches in the Western hemisphere. Working in a vacuum, so to speak, Catholics in both North and South America embraced quartet choirs and flashy operatic singing to attract approbation from the public. Churches also were drawn to popular choral/orchestral settings of the mass in the Neapolitan style by Rossini, Donizetti, and Mercadante, as well as nonliturgical masses and other sacred music of Haydn, Mozart, and Beethoven. Any sense of liturgical integrity was missing.[107]

---

103. Bergmann, *Music Master of the Middle West*, 63.
104. I.e., ritualistic versus non-ritualistic.
105. Page, "Musical Organizations in Boston," 105.
106. Page, "Musical Organizations in Boston," 106.
107. Fellerer and Brunner, *History of Catholic Church Music*, 171–72.

The epitome of operatic church music was achieved in the singing of the Roman Catholic mass in some New York churches. Millard's *Popular Mass in G* (1866), which was sung regularly at St. Stephen's, St. Ann's, St. Columbia's, the Church of St. Francis Xavier, and the Church of St. Charles Boromeo in Brooklyn is a good example.[108] E. de Lussan, soprano soloist at St. Stephen's, provided a testimonial letter to the publisher regarding the mass's usefulness. "The work is easy," she said, "and my solos, without being elaborate, are agreeable to sing, particularly the *'Qui Tollis,'* in[to] which any good singer can throw a deep heartfelt expression."[109] Easily sung, with effective solo writing—these were the ingredients which made for successful quartet masses. An examination of Millard's work reveals much about the prevailing style. The *Popular Mass in G* was written almost as a miniature cantata mass. That is, while the work was short enough to be practical for liturgical use, the Credo and Gloria were broken up into short movements that gave more opportunities for solo voices. The *tutti* sections, such as the Kyrie, were written with choral performance as an option, but the work was usually sung simply with the four soloists in ensemble. Unison was used effectively to provide contrast to harmonized sections, and though suggestions were made for organ registration, the accompaniments were quite pianistic.[110]

Two Catholic parishes in New York City exemplified the operatic trend. The Church of St. Stephen the Martyr made a practice of contracting singers from touring opera companies. Adelina Patti and the great nineteenth-century basso, Carl Formes, both sang there.[111]

The Church of St. Francis Xavier, also in New York City, was particularly noted for the operatic orientation of its music. This reputation was achieved while the eminent "Professor" William Berge was organist there. Berge, who had German university training, served from the consecration of the church in 1847 until it was torn down to make way for a new edifice in 1880. Although he was said to have belonged "to the most pronounced style of French organists,"[112] Berge was well aware that Italian Catholics made up

---

108. Examples of operatic stylistic elements in mid-nineteenth century sacred music appear in the next chapter.

109. Quoted in Millard, *Millard's Popular Mass in G*, 2.

110. Millard's accompaniments resemble orchestral reductions, and it may be that he intended orchestral accompaniment for many of his large works. At any rate, this was the case for the *Popular Mass in G*. A complete set of parts is housed at the Library of Congress. Nevertheless, there can be no question that the composer intended his sacred music for practical church use.

111. "Church Music in New York," 404.

112. "Organs, Organists, and Church Music," 110–11.

a sizable portion of the congregation. Therefore, "the music of his regime consisted mostly of solo singing by Italian operatic artists."[113] Among the artists who sang regularly at the Church of St. Francis Xavier were Madame Bertucca Maretzek, who sang (and played the harp) for the Abbey Opera Company. At the peak of its popularity in 1873, the choir consisted of a double quartet plus a chorus of sixteen. The sanctuary was "always crowded and a very large proportion of the congregation in the body of the church attend[ed] solely for the purpose of enjoying 'a musical treat.'"[114] *Dwight's Journal* noted that the singers at St. Francis Xavier were "capable of executing the most difficult compositions extant."[115] The Italian composer Saverio Mercadante so respected Berge's work that each month he sent a new mass in manuscript for the choir to sing.[116] One reviewer noted hearing "a mass by Luzzani, the organist to the Emperor of Brazil, of which Dr. Berge' possesses the only copy in this country and that was sent to him by the composer."[117] It was also noted that the performance was especially admirable given the fact that the singers "frequently sang difficult music with hardly one good rehearsal."[118] Berge was referred to as "an autocrat of the choir [who sat] upon his organ bench with as imperious an air as if it were a throne."[119]

Early Efforts toward the Reform of Catholic Church Music

Despite the patently secular leanings of Roman Catholic worship and music in the nineteenth century, there was a growing interest in some circles in restoring the worship music practices of the pre-Reformation faith. For example, the Boston Gregorian Society was organized specifically to improve choral singing in the Roman Catholic churches in the Boston area. Also, in the 1840s the American Sodality, a fraternal order, had published a first collection of Catholic hymns.

Meanwhile in Rome, the founding of Academy of St. Cecilia would have a significant impact on Catholic music in the United States. The fact that this development was contemporaneous with the emerging Oxford Movement in England and the founding of Solesmes Abbey in France—all three squarely focused on aspects of liturgical renewal—is striking. In 1830,

---

113. "Organs, Organists, and Church Music," 110–11.
114. "Church Music—Church of St. Francis Xavier," 2.
115. "Church Music in New York," 404.
116. "Church Music in New York," 404.
117. "Church Music—Church of St. Francis Xavier," 2.
118. "Church Music—Church of St. Francis Xavier," 2.
119. "Church Music—Church of St. Francis Xavier," 2.

Pope Pius VIII declared the organization a "pontifical academy," the Italian Society of St. Cecilia. Membership requirements were added including qualifications needed to teach music, to be a choirmaster, to be an organist or a singer in the papal choir.[120]

Concurrently a movement arose in Germany that would have an even greater impact for American Catholics. In the late eighteenth century and early nineteenth, the Protestant composer E. T. A. Hoffman, among others, had sought to revive interest in the music of Palestrina and other composers of the late Renaissance Roman school. The Catholic Church enthusiastically supported the effort, for while Hoffman viewed the music as choral chamber music, the church viewed chant-based polyphony as the ideal in liturgical worship music.

In Munich, early efforts to draw attention to unaccompanied polyphonic sacred music began with Kaspar Ett's performance of the Allegri *Miserere* in 1816.[121] The efforts came to full flower at the Munich Conservatory with the work of composer and music theorist, Josef Rheinberger (1839–1901)[122] and the establishment of a "choir singing school" directed by the German conductor and teacher Franz Wüllner.[123]

An even more aggressive move toward change was occurring to the north in Regensburg. The German Catholic priest Karl Proske (1794–1861), who had been made canon and kapellmeister of the Regensburg Cathedral in 1830, began a lifelong effort to transcribe and have performed choral works of the Renaissance masters. This led to the publication of his multi-volume *Musica Divina* between 1852 and 1863. Proske's work made Regensberg the unofficial capital for early music studies in Germany.

With the way paved before him by Proske, Franz Xavier Witt (1834–1888) established the *Allgemeiner Cäcilien-Verband für Deutschland* or the German St. Cecilia Society in Bamberg in 1868. On January 1 of that year, he published a paper, "Legendre Blatter für Kirchenmusik," directed to teachers, organists, and choirmasters, in which he declared the objective of the society would be "to make war upon existing conditions in church music."[124]

---

120. Keith F. Pecklers, "Evolution of Liturgical Music," 151.

121. Liebergen, "Cecilian Movement," 13.

122. Rheinberger was a major exponent of Bach's harmonic style as a basis for the teaching of theory. Richard Wagner, who had hoped the Munich Conservatory would develop into a school of the "new music," viewed Rheinberger as an enemy, teaching "against" his style rather than preparing students to comprehend it.

123. Irmen, *Gabriel Josef Rheinberger*, 48.

124. Otten, "Franz Xavier Witt," 654.

With his vigorous pen and spoken word he urged upon church musicians, priests, and laymen the moral obligation of obeying the laws of the Church, and a return to the Gregorian chant as the basis and informing principle of all music for liturgical use.[125]

The "Cæcilian Movement" in America[126]

Meanwhile, during the same period, signs of change were occurring in the United States, not in New York or New England but in the Midwest. John Martin Henni (1805–1881), a Swiss theology student, immigrated to the United States in 1829 and enrolled at the Catholic seminary in Bardstown, Kentucky. After ordination, Fr. Henni served German Catholic parishes in Cincinnati and Canton, Ohio. He became pastor of Holy Trinity Church in Cincinnati in 1834 and vicar general of the diocese. In 1844, Henni established the first American chapter of the American Cæcilian Society to promote the reform of Catholic worship practice. That same year, however, he was consecrated to the episcopacy and made archbishop of Milwaukee. Acting in that capacity, Bishop Henni established the St. Francis Seminary[127] out of his home in St. Francis, Wisconsin. He also founded the Catholic Normal School of the Holy Family to train instructors—including music teachers—for the area parochial schools. Knowing they shared a fervor for liturgical reform, Fr. Henni contacted Franz Xaver Witt in Bamberg, Germany, to see if one of his Cæcilian disciples might come to Wisconsin to teach music.

As a result, one Johann Baptist Singenberger (1848–1924), a.k.a. "John" B. Singenberger, arrived in the Milwaukee area in 1873. He immediately established a chapter of the American Cæcilian Society and, a year later, began publication of the society's journal, *Cæcilia*. In its inaugural issue Singenberger stated the society's objectives. They included banishing "from our churches all music of a profane and worldly character and to substitute the sublime compositions of such authors as Palestrina." To be banished, he wrote, were "soft sentimental duets, solos, and opera melodies" as well as mass settings of Haydn, Mozart, and Beethoven.[128] A stated

---

125. Otten, "Franz Xavier Witt," 654.

126. "Cæcilian" is German for Cecilia, the patron saint of music. The American Cæcilian Society, in deference to its origin, retained the Germanic spelling.

127. Now known as the "Saint Francis de Sales Seminary," it is the oldest continually operating Catholic seminary in the United States.

128. Ogasapian, *Church Music in America*, 221.

objective also reinforced church directives that women not be allowed as singers or organists except in convents.[129]

John B. Singenberger.
Public domain image. (https://www.facebook.com/bohemianaccents/posts/johann-baptist-singenberger-john-singenberger-25-may-1848–9-sept-1924-swiss-comp/395257354413638/)

Cæcilia, along with its founder, Singenberger, soon gained a national following. The Third Plenary Council of the Roman Catholic Church in Baltimore in 1884 would be considered the high point of the Cæcilian movement in the United States and featured presentations by a choir of men and boys. Unfortunately, Cæcilianism was a movement ahead of its time and did not achieve the churchwide changes it aspired to. Those would have to wait for the *Motu proprio* of 1903.

The Broader Implications of Ritualism across Denominations

Leonard Ellinwood, in his 1953 *The History of American Church Music*, suggested that ritualism was important only among American Episcopalians.[130] In fact, however, the Oxford and Cæcilian Movements had a significant impact beyond their respective denominations in the years from 1860 to 1930. One sees in it an increased interest in ordered worship, in the teaching of

---

129. Ogasapian, *Church Music in America*, 221.
130. Ellinwood, *History of American Church Music*, 76–77.

the mechanics of worship in seminaries, in the use of art and pageantry, and often in the observance of the seasons of the church year. We have already seen how the Cæcilian Movement was working to bring plainchant and polyphony back into Roman Catholic worship. As church leaders in so-called nonliturgical denominations —Presbyterians, Baptists, and Methodists, for example—came to see the power of traditional ceremonial practices, the boundaries between liturgical and nonliturgical worship became blurred. As Waldo Selden Pratt wrote in 1901, "All methods of conducting public worship in any of its parts, with whatever historic traditions and doctrinal prepossessions, constitute what may be called 'liturgical.' Consequently, even those churches that are popularly called 'non-liturgical' necessarily have liturgical responsibilities."[131] One of those responsibilities, he declared, was to make appropriate use of the arts.

> The church has also been constantly expressing itself artistically in its practices of public worship ... and has thus unconsciously displayed its inner nature in a way both vivid and monumental. Common thought recognizes this.[132]

The ritualistic movement, with its focus on historic Christian practices, and the Cæcilians with their determination to restore polyphonic music and chant to worship, were both evidence that the leadership of music in the life of the worshipping community was coming to be viewed as a sacred calling. Ministry, with its dual emphases of integrity of leadership and sacrificial servanthood, essentially modeled Christ's earthly ministry. Thus, we see the beginning of the concept of "music ministry": serving God and the community of believers through the art of music.

---

131. Pratt, "Liturgical Responsibilities of Non-Liturgical Churches," 642.
132. Pratt, "Liturgical Responsibilities of Non-Liturgical Churches," 644.

Chapter 10

THE RISE OF PROFESSIONAL CHOIRMASTERS, ORGANISTS, AND SINGERS AS CHURCH MUSICIANS

By the mid-nineteenth century, for many church leaders and clergy, the improvement of congregational singing seemed to be a hopeless cause. Why flail away at it, when professional singers could be hired? Many viewed music as simply another commodity like pew cushions, carpet, and communion ware. While to modern eyes such crassly materialistic attitudes may seem wholly out of place, there was at the base of it a recognition of a real need. Professional leadership *would* ultimately be needed to solve the church's problems regarding music in worship. No, soloists could never replace the power and spiritual depth of an entire assembly in song, but what was missing—and what would come to fruition only gradually—was an understanding of *corporate* worship as opposed to *spectator* worship and all that entails. In the cultivated urban churches of the late nineteenth century, achieving the high levels of sacred musical art they aspired to required professional leadership—conductors, singers, and organists.

The transition to paid musical leadership in New York and New England churches was very gradual. By 1800 a few churches were supplementing the income of local singing school masters to lead their gallery choirs on Sunday mornings. Other churches began paying organists around the same time. The amount was generally small and was only intended to supplement the organist's or singing master's other income. Musicians might earn a livelihood from private teaching, the singing school, the sale of tunebooks, or an outside profession. "Socially and economically the church musician seem[ed] perpetually to suffer from inadequate income and the inconveniences attendant upon subordination to clergy who [were] not always notable either for musical knowledge or for personal understanding..."[1]

Realistically the minister or pastor of a large congregation could not effectively lead all aspects of worship without help. Concerns about the need for professional help had been expressed from the 1830s onward, and a few prominent churches had hired full-time professional leadership in response. Edward Hodges at Trinity Church, New York, and John Zundel at Plymouth Church in Brooklyn are examples.

An examination of the salaries of choirmasters and organists at churches in Boston and New York sheds some light on the status of church musicians. Grace Church and St. Bartholomew's in New York City, Boston's First Congregational Church, and others like them were America's wealthiest churches. They were the trendsetters. Their large, well-heeled congregations could afford to hire the best available musicians, and did. While the figures below will not support a generalization as to what ordinary church organists and choirmasters were paid, such statistics do give an idea of the premium salaries of the time. A premium salary for a church organist might have been $200 a year during the 1830s, a bit over $6,000 in 2021 dollars. A tutor at Princeton University during the same time period commonly received the equivalent of $400 a year, including board, fuel, and maid service. A typical fee for a manservant in New York City was $132 a year.[2] The average pay for a common laborer on the Erie Canal was about $234 a year, while team drivers made around $546.[3] A common laborer in Philadelphia made about $312 per year, and New England farm laborers generally averaged $139.[4]

After studying salary figures for church musicians in the New York area between 1800 and 1850, Anton Paul Allwardt stated that "no one could devote his life exclusively to the music of the church and hope to have even a subsistence.... The unfortunate musician, assuming he was interested in Church Music, had to resort to whatever source of additional income that might be available to him, whether in the theater and other places of amusement, in the construction and sale of instruments, in the editing and selling of music, in teaching, or in business quite unrelated to musical pursuits."[5]

---

1. Allwardt, "Sacred Music in New York City," 128.

2. See Allwardt, "Sacred Music in New York City"; Chorley, *Centennial of St. Bartholomew's Church*; Pierce, ed., *Records of First Church, Boston, 1630–1868*; Page, "Musical Organizations in Boston," 161.

3. *Historical Statistics of the United States*, 164.

4. *Historical Statistics of the United States*, 163.

5. Allwardt, "Sacred Music in New York City," 161.

Even a figure as highly respected in New York as Thomas Hastings was able to command a salary of only $400 a year at St. George's Church in 1842. The English organist Henry Wellington Greatorex, whose name was synonymous with the best quartet singing in America, also worked at St. Georges in 1848, but received only $300 for his services.[6]

The following letter to the editor of *Century Illustrated* in 1884 summarized the post-Civil War employment situation for organists:

> [T]he reform in church music has begun, and indeed made good progress, and the question would seem to be, what can be done to aid in the good work, and to carry the same on toward completion?
>
> Money will be a potent factor in this, as in all good works, so I will first take up the question of salaries; and, in behalf of my brother organists and choir-masters, I claim that the salaries generally offered are totally inadequate to pay for the services expected and demanded. I know I shall be met here, and at once, with the statement that "the pay is fully as good as the services rendered"; and my retort will be that "the services are fully as good as the pay." And both statements will, in the great majority of cases, be very near to the truth . . . I know of a city claiming to have over one hundred thousand inhabitants, and also claiming a great amount of musical culture, where, as I am informed by good authority, the highest salary paid to any organist is the munificent sum of four hundred dollars. One church in said city, and one of the largest and most prosperous, paying its minister a salary of five thousand dollars, had an organist who served them well and faithfully for many years. Him they discharged a year ago, because—why, because another organist could be secured for fifty dollars less . . .
>
> There are very many churches in America abundantly able, and which ought to be willing, to pay to their organist and choirmaster "a living salary"—a salary sufficient for all his needs—so that he would not be forced to gain a livelihood by other means, but would be able to devote his entire time and work to the service of the church . . .[7]

A shift in clergy attitudes regarding compensation was taking place. The Reverend Duncan Kennedy's 1865 *Sermon on Sacred Music* reflected this:

---

6. Anstice, *History of St. George's Church*, 178.

7. Witherspoon, "Church Music," 475.

> Some have cherished the impression that the spiritual prosperity of the people needs only the most ordinary style of sacred praise, and that any advance beyond this tends to beget a spirit of pride and worldliness. . . . Cherishing such views, they have always been backward in making appropriate pecuniary expenditures in this direction . . . It is a melancholy fact, that the theater, as a general rule, has been more generously furnished with musical talent than the sanctuary of the Most High. Satan has thus been permitted to wield the power of music with appalling success.[8]

The Professional Church Singer

The role of the professional singer in American church music was a controversial one in the nineteenth century. The whole question of volunteerism among singers was hotly debated. The same critics who decried the singing of untrained members of the congregation when hymns were sung questioned the propriety of half-trained amateurs singing in the choir.

> A volunteer choir, with any ambition to sing creditably, assumes a great burden. They assume first the burden of always being at church, whether they be sick or well. They assume the expenditure of a great deal of time for rehearsals. They assume a thousand vexations. They expose themselves to the criticism of those who will not touch their burden with one of their fingers. Who blames free men and free women for refusing to become slaves of others? We have known those who voluntarily carried the burden of the music of the church for many years as a Christian duty, and we give them all honor; but we have no right to ask it of them—no more right, really, than to ask a minister to give us his time for nothing . . . It is very pretty for a congregation to gather and hear good singing, and not have it cost them anything; but the fact is, all good singing—all singing worthy of the House of God—costs somebody a great deal. Why should a choir bear the whole of this cost, and the congregation none of it?
>
> Those who devote their lives to music are those best calculated to perform acceptably the music of the sanctuary. We should add to this class all who by the expenditure of abundant time and money have become excellent in this accomplishment. To the first of these, music is the instrument by which they win their livelihood; to the last, it has been a costly thing, and they

---

8. Kennedy, *Sermon on Sacred Music*, 35–36.

The Rise of Professional Choirmasters, Organist, and Singers 317

deserve return. It is just as reasonable, and just as legitimate, for a man to sing God's praises for a living, as it is to preach God's truth or lead in any other department of Christian worship for a living; and a church or a parish which shrinks from assuming its part of the burden of church music, can only justify itself by the plea of poverty or constitutional meanness.[9]

The rise of the professional church soloist had its origin in wealthier, urban New York and New England churches. The preference for trained singers performing tasteful music paralleled the increasing popularity of opera in secular society. The opera singer represented to many cultivated Americans the highest peak of vocal achievement during the 1820s and '30s. Much of this was probably due to the influence of touring opera companies. Both foreign and American companies gave Eastern audiences their first taste of serious musical theater during the second decade of the nineteenth century. The first foreign-language opera productions were those brought to New York by the Spaniard Manuel del Populo Vicente Garcia, in 1825.[10] Garcia premiered a repertory of eleven operas: *Il Barbiere di Siviglia, Cenerentola, Semiramide, Tancredi*, and *Il Turco in Italy*, all by Rossini; Mozart's *Don Giovanni*, and lesser-known works by Zingarelli and Garcia himself. The opening production, *The Barber of Seville*, featured Garcia's daughter, Maria Félicita, as Rosina, who later became world famous under her married name, Maria Malibran.[11] Opera did not end with Garcia's return to Europe. The New Orleans Opera Theater, made up of French émigrés, visited New York, Boston, Philadelphia, and Baltimore, bringing with them a repertory of French and Italian operas. Other touring companies introduced works of Bellini and Donizetti.[12]

This interest in opera spilled over into church music. Maria Malibran (1808–1836), who had married a wealthy New York merchant Francois Eugene Malibran in 1826, remained in the city for two years before returning to Paris. During this time, her weekly appearances in the gallery of Grace Church, where she had been hired by Pastor Jonathan Wainright

---

9. "Church Music," 74.

10. Ewen, *Music Comes to America*, 49.

11. The names Manuel Garcia and Maria Malibran are legendary in the history of opera. Rossini created the role of Count Almaviva in *Il Barbieri di Siviglia* for Garcia, a sought-after tenor as well as impresario. Malibran's voice was described by contemporaries as remarkably brilliant and incredibly agile with an always warm vibrant tone quality. Her vocal range—E flat below middle C to C6—was unusually wide, permitting her to effectively perform both contralto and high soprano roles. She died tragically at twenty-eight from injuries received when thrown by a horse.

12. Hitchcock, *Music in the United States*, 93.

(1792–1854),[13] were nearly as well-known as her exploits on the stage. Malibran's performance of the aria "Angels, Ever Bright and Fair," from Handel's *Theodora*, was typical. When she performed it for a concert of the New York Sacred Music Society at Zion Church on February 28, 1827, one reviewer wrote:

> During the performance of the song, so silent was the audience, that not even a whisper was heard. She performed it beautifully, as a matter of course, although the admirers of the simplicity of Handel had to regret the introduction of so much ornament. She was clad in robes of virgin white, and at the words, "Take, O Take Me to Thy Care," she raised her hands and eyes in an imploring attitude to heaven in so dramatic and touching a manner as to electrify the audience, and to call down a universal outburst of approbation, a very unusual occurrence in a church in this country.[14]

Many prominent singers of the nineteenth century received recognition as church singers. The great American sculptor Thomas Ball (1819–1911) sang professionally in quartets at Boston's St. Paul's Church and at King's Chapel between 1836 and 1865. He was also one of the most popular soloists appearing with the Handel and Haydn Society.[15]

The opera singer Henry Clay Barnabee (1833–1917) sang for nearly twenty-three years in the quartet at Boston's Church of the Unity, in addition to his regular appearances with the Boston Ideal Opera Company.[16] Even Lowell Mason, who disdained the use of paid singers over volunteers, found it necessary to make exceptions to this due to the scarcity of solo voices. He so much appreciated the rich soprano of Miss Anne Folsom of

---

13. Stewart, *Grace Church*, 266.

14. Hubbard, ed., *American History and Encyclopedia of Music: American Music*, 218.

15. Ball's greatest work, a statue of George Washington, was completed in 1864. Two other well-known works were his Emancipation (1875), which depicted Lincoln with a kneeling slave, and his statue of Daniel Webster, which was placed in New York's Central Park in 1876. During the 1830s and '40s, Ball often sang the bass arias of Haydn's *Creation* with the Handel and Haydn Society. He also essayed bass solo parts in Rossini's *Moses in Egypt*, Handel's *Messiah*, and Neukomm's *David*. Charles E. Horn, director of the society in 1848, assigned Ball the title role in the Boston premiere of Mendelssohn's *Elijah*. During the 1848–49 season, Ball sang twelve performances of the work and was given so many accolades that, in 1851, he was "permanently assigned" the role by the society's governing board. During his years of singing, Ball often sang opposite the famous American soprano Anna Stone.

16. Barnabee, *Reminiscences*, 119.

Exeter that he invited her to live at his Boston home in order that she might sing in his Bowdoin Street choir.

Church singers who had achieved celebrity status could command higher salaries. Anna Stone, the operatic soprano, received a salary of $700 in 1853 to sing in St. George's Church in New York City. This was raised to $1,000 the following year.[17] Emma Thursby (1845–1931), the famous concert singer, kept careful records of her earnings during her church singing career, and these provide valuable documentation as to what some of the finer singers were paid. During her years at Plymouth Church, under Henry Ward Beecher, Thursby was paid $900 a year. She noted in her diary that she usually accumulated an additional $900 from concerts and private teaching for a total income of $1,800 a year between 1869 and 1871.[18] Thursby sang at the Reformed Dutch Church in Brooklyn for three years, from 1871 to 1874. Her total earnings during her last year there were $2,753.[19] The highest annual salary Thursby ever received for singing in churches was $1,800, or about $50 for each of thirty-six Sundays in the contract year. In addition, she usually was given the proceeds of at least one church concert or recital per year.

Appearances of renowned singers in American churches peaked in the 1850s. Jenny Lind sang from the gallery of Calvary Church in New York in 1850 shortly after her arrival on American soil. Later, an elderly Calvary member would recall that "Nobody had ever heard anything like it. She was the sweetest singer we had ever heard."[20] Henriette Sontag (1806–1854) presented a benefit concert at Plymouth Church in Brooklyn in 1852. The concert was given to raise funds for the church's organist, John Zundel, and featured a first singing of his well-known hymn tune, Beecher ("Love Divine, All Loves Excelling"). A contemporary description of the concert is so colorful as to warrant quotation:

> We soon discovered the important fact—that is necessary *to learn how* to attend a concert . . . In the first place, there was a vast deal of anxiety manifested as to the identity of the "stars" of the evening. "There she is!"—"Who?"—"Sontag!"—"Where?"—"There!"—"You don't say so!"—"No, that ain't her!"[21]

---

17. Anstice, *History of St. George's*, 178.
18. Gipson, *Life of Emma Thursby*, 74.
19. This would be equivalent to about $67,000 in 2021 dollars.
20. Shoemaker, *Calvary Church*, 96–97.
21. "Madame Sontag in Brooklyn," 162–63.

Emma Eames (1865–1952), an operatic soprano from Maine, like many others, got her start as a church singer in the Boston area around 1883:

> Oh, how I remember those days, crossing the unpaved Common —a primitive Boston before all these modern improvements— in rubber boots to get to the Boston and Albany Railroad station to take a train to Newton. Twice on Sundays I made this journey and once on Friday, when I rehearsed and read for the first time the music that I was to interpret the following Sunday. In snow, in slush, in sleet, in rain! A good hardening process![22]

Kathleen Howard (1884–1956), another successful American operatic soprano, recalled that singing in churches was often essential if young singers were to survive the years of study in New York.

> I don't know what I should have done if a friend had not advised me to try for a "church position," that invaluable means of adding to the resources of a student, which is possible only in America. Besides offering a splendid chance of financial assistance, the church position system is an infallible test of the money value of one's voice.[23]

According to Howard and other singers, the professional church position provided pocket cash and served to improve sight-reading and musicianship, even if a singer could not make a living at it. The experience in ensemble singing was invaluable and hard to gain anywhere else. Such experience made singers acutely aware of intonation and blend. Most important, the church position was often a singer's first opportunity to regularly sing before an audience.[24]

This was indeed a strange period—an almost schizophrenic period— in American church music. Operatic bonbons had found favor among many congregations. Their pastors, knowing this, sought out performers to provide them. But the trend could also be a liability. It grated harshly against a deep-seated American prejudice against theatricality. Some of America's most prominent clergy preached untiringly against the evils of the theater and opera. T. DeWitt Talmadge[25] called theater a "destructive sport," echo-

---

22. Eames, *Some Memories and Reflections*, 29–30.
23. Howard, *Confessions of an Opera Singer*, 21.
24. Howard, *Confessions of an Opera Singer*, 22.
25. Thomas De Witt Talmadge (1832-1902) was minister at the Brooklyn Presbyterian Tabernacle beginning in 1869. He had a magnetic, sensational style, and at the height of his career his sermons were printed in 3,500 American newspapers each week.

ing the corruption in ancient Greece and the licentiousness of Nero's Rome. English miracle plays, he said, were blasphemous productions in which intoxicated actors tried to represent God in costume on a stage.[26]

> How many of you would like to have your sons and daughters grow up and launch out in the association of play-actors? . . . The most prominent actors in the country have not suffered or lost their popularity by the discovery of their licentiousness. The crimes which wither other men seem to excite no astonishment when performed by these so-called "educators of public taste." . . . Why is it when you speak of a woman's attachment to the stage, you speak of it in a whisper, saying, "She is an actress?" . . . Show me one person connected with the theater regularly, and for a long time, who goes about performing Christian offices, and serving God and serving his Church; show me one such person, and I will show you a hundred who have been ruined for time and eternity through the influence of the American theater . . .[27]

The lack of piety and questionable behavior of church musicians frequently inspired local gossip and remonstrances from the pulpit. The *New York Musical Pioneer* noted that it was customary in that city's Episcopal churches for singers "to sneak out, one after the other, as soon as the [sermon] text was given out."

> The soprano will first gather up her skirts, perhaps bend her head a little so as to avoid the notice of the congregation, and step gingerly out of the organ loft, not infrequently, however, sweeping down a few books, or upsetting a chair, in spite of all her care. The basso, having no skirts to impede his progress, darts out a few minutes after, and makes no noise 'til he gets to the stairs, where, unless he takes the trouble to slide down on the balusters, his heavy boots are heard trampling down like the rumbling of distant thunder. The alto and tenor follow, unless indeed, they prefer to remain and have a quiet little flirtation together during the sermon time. The organist, having to play the concluding voluntary, groans inwardly because he is thus debarred from the privilege of flight, but consoles himself and supports the tedium of "the preached word" by stealing out to a neighboring bar-room—there are plenty of those accessible on a Sunday, by back doors, to the initiated—where he can snatch

---

26. Talmadge, *Sports That Kill*, 9–11.
27. Talmadge, *Sports That Kill*, 16–18.

a sherry cobbler or a glass of lager, and be back in time to play the congregation out.[28]

Henry Ward Beecher referred to the theater as "the door to all kinds of iniquity," and added that one need only go there "to be injected with each vice in the catalogue of depravity."[29] Beecher recognized the secular origins of certain religious music (German chorales, for example), but felt there needed to be a strong difference between the music of the sanctuary and that identified with secular society. He felt the church had to maintain its otherworldly cloak. "We have a right to say," Beecher proclaimed, "we did not come to church for the sake of having our memories of the theater or the opera revived."[30] He condemned the florid singing of some quartet choirs.

> There is a great deal of gymnastics of music that is proper in some places, which would not be proper in a church; as there is a great deal in calisthenics that would be proper in a hall devoted to physical training, which would not be proper here on this platform. That place has one object, while this place has another. And I affirm that any use of music, in regard to sacred things, which makes it merely a physical accomplishment and which addresses it to wonder and curiosity and admiration, is a desecration of the Sabbath of the sanctuary, and of sacred music itself.[31]

As a result of these prejudices, a new breed of singer began appearing in American galleries during the 1860s and '70s. This was the singer without operatic pretensions who wished to make a career as a performer of sacred and concert music. Two prominent examples were Emma Thursby, discussed previously, and Myron W. Whitney (1836–1910). Whitney, a bass with a range of three octaves, was one of the most well-known American vocal students of Luigi Vannucini in Florence. He also studied oratorio literature with Alberto Randegger in London. While in England in 1873 Whitney sang the title role in a Birmingham Festival performance of Mendelssohn's *Elijah*, and this immediately earned him international acclaim. He also sang the role of Polyphemus in a production of Handel's *Acis and Galatea* at Oxford University. Whitney remained active as a church and oratorio singer throughout his life.[32]

---

28. Liemohn, *Organ and Choir in Protestant Worship*, 123–24.
29. Beecher, "Religious Uses of Music," 290.
30. Beecher, "Religious Uses of Music," 290.
31. Beecher, "Religious Uses of Music," 292.
32. Matthews, ed., *Hundred Years of Music*, 214.

Female singers were under particular pressure to avoid the questionable morality of the theater and opera. Operatic performances were popular, and audiences who attended them were respectable. "Yet she who essayed the operatic stage [needed to] prepare herself for estrangement from most of her friends, as one who had practically renounced the Saviour for the Devil."[33] Clara Louise Kellogg (1842–1916), the South Carolina girl whose "Margherita" in Gounod's *Faust* was a sensation in Europe and America, found the decision to sing opera a most difficult one. She often recalled having "the painful task of calling her friends together to tell them that she would understand if they no longer chose to bow or speak to her."[34]

Emma Thursby (1845–1931) chose church singing and the concert stage to avoid this dilemma. Her biographer, Richard M. Gipson, noted that:

> As absurd as some of the moral notions of that day may appear to us, to one living within their influence they were very real and compelling. Escape from them could be made only at great cost. To Emma Thursby, indeed, escape would have meant the breaking down not only of some abstract principle, but also the moral fiber of herself, developed in a noble tradition, even though in the prejudice of the day.[35]

Thursby was most famous for her solo work, between 1868 and 1871, at Henry Ward Beecher's Plymouth Church in Brooklyn. The music program at Plymouth Church consisted of a quartet plus a choir of seventy-five voices under the leadership of John Zundel. Beecher's and Thursby's friendship lasted long after her employment there. She was also a featured soloist with Patrick Gilmore's famous Twenty-Second Regimental Band, touring with them throughout the United States in the 1870s.

Because of its enormous popularity, quartet singing in churches had become institutionalized by the second half of the nineteenth century. Spring was traditionally hiring season, and shortly after Christmas each year singers would begin to look for new, more promising employment. In New York City, contracts were usually dated from May 1, and the bulk of the auditioning for jobs was done between January 15 and April 1.[36] Large cities such as New York, Boston, Hartford, and Portland generally had several talent agencies devoted exclusively to the placement of church singers. *Dwight's Journal* listed Wardell's as New York's top agency in the 1860s.[37] In

---

33. Gipson, *Life of Emma Thursby*, 68.
34. Gipson, *Life of Emma Thursby*, 68.
35. Gipson, *Life of Emma Thursby*, 81.
36. Saenger, "How to Succeed as a Public Singer," 311.
37. "Church Choirs in America," 338.

1899, the *New York Times* noted that Addison P. Andrews's office on East Twenty-Second Street was the most popular.[38] Agents would require an audition from the prospective singer and a fee to take on a new account. In return, the agent agreed to put the singer in touch with churches looking for vocalists. The client usually also agreed to give the agent a percentage of his or her first year's salary.

Jobs in quartets being at a premium, it was not unusual for committees and agents to treat singers unfairly. "Choir candidating" was a common practice. Candidates would usually be invited to sing without charge one Sunday so the congregation could hear them. Often the church would pay only the singer's trolley fare. "This process is repeated with success in some cases which have recently become known, until, for several months, the vacant position has been filled by aspirants, the Committee meanwhile congratulating themselves upon their economical administration of the church's finances."[39] The practice was used on occasion to fill more than one position, and during February and March, it was not unusual in some churches to find all members of the quartet and the organist performing *gratis*.[40] Some churches attempted to avoid the committee process by paying an agent to choose a soloist or quartet for them. The agent would be given a sum of money from which he was to extract his fee plus a negotiated amount to pay each singer. Unfortunately, less reputable agents could usually find enough gullible young singers who were willing to work for the experience alone, that they could pocket the entire amount.[41]

The contract system had grave shortcomings for church musicians. First, it encouraged committees to be governed by the whimsy and minor bickering of the congregation and pastor. Second, it encouraged church musicians to think of their work as being only a job, a transitory one at that, and something not to be taken seriously. Church singing was often viewed as something to be done either between stints of more lucrative employment or to supplement one's income. Third, the contract system was devastating to musical goals and aspirations. The quartet often had only a bit over three months to achieve its optimum performance. Shortly after Christmas, singers began looking for better positions. With the personnel always in so

---

38. "Changes in Church Choirs", 17.
39. "Choir Candidating," 88.
40. "Choir Candidating," 88.
41. "Choir Candidating," 88. According to Allwardt, the competition between agents was often quite fierce. Offering to provide singers at a lower salary than the one being offered to guarantee placement was a common tactic. (Allwardt, "Sacred Music in New York City," 128.)

tenuous a state, there was little incentive to develop a polished ensemble or a challenging repertoire.

At the ninth annual meeting of the Music Teachers' National Association in 1885, one H. P. Stark—a veteran quartet singer himself—enunciated the standard applied by many music committees. "Church music committees usually select the best talent their means will afford, without reference to the theological bias of the parties employed, for most church members prefer to hear beautiful music rendered artistically even by an unbeliever than otherwise by the most devout worshipper."[42] Stark was unintentionally raising the questions facing the church of his time if music was to one day be a ministry: Should sacred music performed in the church be any different than if performed in a concert hall? Can there be a "spiritual dimension" to music in the church, both in content and performance, that witnesses to a congregation? And, if so, does that affect the spirituality of the performer? Is that even important?

Archibald Davison, in his *Protestant Church Music in America*, which was written at the end of the era, was critical of the music committee approach to hiring but also touched on the deeper, more systemic issue: the role of music as a ministry in the church. "If there is to be a music committee, then why not a preaching committee to regulate the tone of the minister's voice?"[43] The reason, according to Davison, was that the minister had an unspoken authority over his domain that had not been extended to the church musician. "The layman," he said, "expects the minister to teach him, but considers it the function of the choirmaster [and singer] to give him what he wants."[44]

> He says that the choir is paid too much and sings too little; or, if the music displeases him, he concludes that the entire organization ought to be dismissed, and this he forthwith sets about accomplishing. He feels in view of the high salaries paid to the quartet, that the soprano ought to have been able to produce more power on that high note in the morning's anthem and that the bass ought to be made to understand that the creation of an artificial double-chin supported by a blood-thirsty expression such as Captain Kidd might have worn, does not really take the place of the low note he tried to make everybody think he was singing.[45]

---

42. Cornell, "What Is Church Music?," 103.
43. Davison, *Protestant Church Music in America*, 67.
44. Davison, *Protestant Church Music in America*, 67.
45. Davison, *Protestant Church Music in America*, 67.

The Boston music critic Philip Hale wrote sympathetically about the of church singers in a 1904 article in *Choir and Choral Magazine*. Members of quartets, he noted, seldom sang for enjoyment or educational opportunity, but simply because they needed the money. Many church musicians were career singers, living alone and struggling to survive. They were expected to be in good shape vocally regardless of the weather or time of day. Reliability in terms of attendance, punctuality, and infallible sight-reading were requirements of the job. A typical singer's week, according to Hale, would include two services on Sunday, one rehearsal, and "outside calls" at various church functions for which the singer was expected to sing for nothing. The singer had to be tolerant of congregations that were highly capricious in their criticism and had to ignore hiring practices that were often unfair to them professionally. In addition, Hale said, vocalists were expected always to "support the organist in his belief that he is always right," and never to complain about the literature being sung even if it was totally unsuited to their voices.[46]

> There is something pathetic in this annual uneasiness of choir singers. The salary means so much to many of them! And clergymen, music committees, and congregations speak so lightly, so capriciously of these changes. Think for the moment of the life of a young soprano. She is often far from home and obliged to live by herself in one room, of which she wearies as though it were a prison cell. She supports herself by her voice. She earns with it the money for board and lodging, lessons and dress. She must be most economical, sometimes at the expense of health as well as reasonable comfort. Sickness, even a cold, means to her a loss of income. She has her church position; she sings, now and then, in towns about Boston for small sums, from $10 to $25, and she exposes herself to storm and risk of throat trouble. Her life is full of petty annoyances and disappointments. Living alone, she is exposed, if she be personally attractive, to contemptible gossip. She sees singers of unbounded assurance and little art do unworthy things to gain a hearing. One coaches with a person of authority and pays a large sum, not for helpful instruction, but for the sake of an engagement which is in the power of this man to give. Another, wholly unfit, plays the parasite and works through social graft. Yet, undisturbed, indomitable of purpose, the singer keeps on her way, sustained by sublime confidence in her voice, in her musical intelligence, in her dramatic instinct. She at last triumphs, but in a foreign town; her name blazes on the operatic firmament; and the city in which she was merely the

---

46. Hale, "Psychology of the Church Soprano, Part 2," 8.

plaything of music committees or petty managers, plumes itself on the fact that she was once a sojourner within its gates. Or she dies, worn out with the struggle, prematurely old, with the bitterness of the thought that she too, might have been famous, if her path had been made only a little smoother, if her genius had been recognized by those whose duty it was to recognize and help.[47]

Finding adequate rehearsal time was frequently a problem. Even when all four vocalists approximated each other in matters of volume and tone, there often was little opportunity to achieve a finely wrought ensemble sound. Low pay and a condescending attitude toward the singers by some church members did little to motivate quartets to rehearse. According to Clarence Dickinson, it was most difficult to get young professionals to rehearse sufficiently. "They sometimes labor under the impression that their acknowledged musicianship and professional standing enables them to sing the Sunday service with a short rehearsal Saturday or immediately before the service, when they see the music for the first time."[48] Dickinson was not implying that professional singers were an unconscientious lot. He was merely recognizing that out of necessity, church musicians had to stay quite busy to earn a living. It was not unusual for organists and singers to be employed at two or even three religious institutions on the weekend. Herbert Stavely Sammond, who was both an organist and concert singer, recalled one such schedule of activities:

There was a time when I was playing in a Presbyterian Church Sundays, playing Requiem Masses in a Roman Catholic Church on weekdays (having previously held a position in a Catholic church to which I had gone from a Congregational church), a Hebrew temple on Friday and Saturday, and occasionally a Y. M. C. A. Sunday afternoons or Evangelistic shop meetings at noon of a weekday. This varied experience, if it did nothing more, made me a firm believer in the brotherhood of man.[49]

The Quartet in Nineteenth-Century Worship

In the popular mind no institution better personifies American church music in the nineteenth century than the notorious "quartet choir." The quartet was not a choir at all, but simply four professional singers who *functioned* as

---

47. Hale, "Psychology of the Church Soprano, Part 2," 8.
48. Dickinson, "Choral Music and Choir Direction," 353.
49. Sammond, "How Can a Young Organist?"

a choir. Historians have not been kind to quartet choirs. By the first decades of the twentieth century quartets had come to symbolize all that was artificial in sacred song. The caustic generalizations of twentieth-century critics prevented any objective appraisal of the quartet's contribution to American church music. The virtues of quartet singing, the reasons quartets came to exist, and the other manifestations of professionalism in church music were virtually ignored by twentieth-century critics. As a result, a distorted, wholly negative view of the quartet choir has come to be accepted. Modern research has done little to correct that distortion.

Stevenson devotes but two pages to quartets,[50] identifying them only with the music of Dudley Buck. He fails to mention that Buck's music came rather late in the quartet's development, and that much of it was intended to be sung by a choir of volunteers with a quartet as the nucleus, not by a quartet alone. Ellinwood, on the other hand, devotes a brief chapter to "The Quartet Choir," but his examination of the subject is superficial, treating it only as a parenthetical aberration during the rise of the Oxford Movement in America.[51] Quartets were still providing all of the music sung in some prominent New York and New England churches as late as 1930.

It is not possible to date precisely when quartets of professional singers first became fashionable or, for that matter, precisely to date the progress of their demise. It is known that Grace Church in New York City hired its first quartet of singers in 1825.[52] Many of the more prominent New York and Boston churches were quick to follow suit. Alice Morse Earle recalled attending a church service in the 1860s in Worcester, Massachusetts, when a particularly touching example of clerical protest took place:

> An old clergyman, the venerable "Father Allen" of Shrewsbury, then too aged and feeble to preach, was seated in the front pew of the church. When a quartette of singers began to render a rather operatic arrangement of a sacred song, he rose, erect and stately, to his full gaunt height, turned slowly around and glanced reproachfully over the frivolous, backsliding congregation, wrapped around his spare, lean figure, his full cloak of gilded black silk, took his shovel hat and his cane, and stalked indignantly and sadly the whole length of the broad center aisle, out of the church, thus making a last but futile protest against modern innovations in church music.[53]

---

50. Stevenson, *Protestant Church Music*, 113–14.
51. Ellinwood, *History of American Church Music*, 72–75.
52. Allwardt, "Sacred Music in New York City," 64.
53. Earle, *Sabbath in Puritan New England*, 228–29.

The Rise of Professional Choirmasters, Organist, and Singers 329

By 1900, there were four hundred churches in Boston and the surrounding communities that had quartets of paid professional singers.[54]

The *Boston Choir Directory*, a twice-yearly publication used to keep agents abreast of personnel changes, listed fifty churches in the Boston area in its 1876–77 issue. Of these, thirty-one had quartets, three others had quartets as the nucleus of a chorus choir, while six had chorus choirs with paid section leaders who did not perform as soloists.[55] The *New York Times* in 1899 listed personnel changes in the quartets of thirteen Brooklyn churches and fifteen leading churches of various denominations in the New York area.[56] *Nickerson's Illustrated Musical and Church Choir Directory of the City of New York* (1895) offered the most comprehensive overview, however, of the extent to which quartets were used. Sixty Baptist churches were listed, of which fifty maintained paid quartets and double quartets. Literally every Congregational church and Reformed Jewish synagogue appeared to have had a quartet,[57] and some of the city's most prominent Presbyterian congregations had hired them. First Presbyterian had a quartet plus a chorus of fifty, while the Church of the Puritans, Rutgers Riverside, West Church, and Scotch Presbyterian, each had turned their music over to solo singers exclusively. Only the Lutherans, with their predominantly German congregations, maintained a large percentage of volunteer choirs. Methodist churches were about equally divided between chorus choirs and quartets. On the other hand, by the 1890s, many Episcopal churches had abandoned the quartet for vested choirs of men and boys.

Quartets in American churches sang a broad variety of music. Repertoires might include everything from English cathedral music to operatic-sounding Latin masses imported from Italy. In addition to music borrowed from other traditions, a great deal of music was written specifically for quartets after 1840. Congregational singing was often severely curtailed in

---

54. Fisher, "Growing Importance of Music," 55.

55. *Boston Choir Directory* (June 1876). Only one all-volunteer choir was listed. Ten churches, however, had abandoned all ensemble singing and had begun to devote their attention entirely to congregational singing.

56. "Changes in Church Choirs," 17.

57. The Jewish reform movement was organized in South Carolina in 1824 and was aimed at "cultivating the manners and practices of Protestant churches as a step towards assimilation into the American culture." According to Arthur C. Edwards and Thomas Marocco in *Music in the United States*, "reformed congregations abbreviated Hebrew texts, introduced prayers and hymns in English, installed organs and engaged professional [quartet] choirs." Saturday worship services in the synagogue provided a convenient way by which singers and organists could earn additional income. Both Nathan Hale Allen (1848-1925) and Arthur Foote (1853-1937) wrote music for synagogue choirs in addition to substantial amounts of choral music for Protestant churches.

churches with quartets. In place of hymn tunes intended for congregational singing, hymn texts were often coupled with familiar operatic melodies. Since many church soloists in New York and Boston were active as opera singers and recitalists, this would have been familiar territory. For example, the Charlotte Elliott hymn, "Just as I Am Without One Plea" was sung to the theme from the famous quartet in Act 3 of in Verdi's *Rigoletto*:

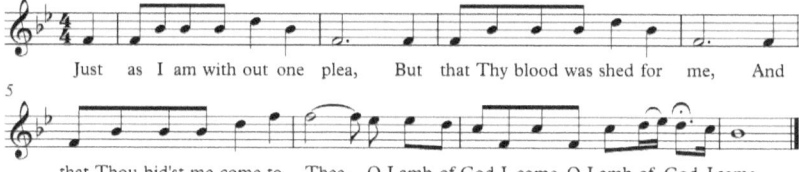

"Just as I Am Without One Plea."
Text: Charlotte Elliott (1836). Music: Giuseppe Verdi, "*Bella figlia dell'amore,*" (Quartet) from the opera, *Rigoletto* (1851).

Vocal lines tended to be soloistic rather than conducive to group singing.

Closing cadenza from Harrison Millard, "Ave Maria" (New York: G Schirmer, 1865).[58]

---

58. Harrison Millard (1830–1895) was a popular concert tenor, composer, and director of quartet choirs. He studied voice in Italy and toured Europe as a recitalist and oratorio soloist between 1851 and 1854. He created a sensation by singing his "Viva l'America" at a social gathering in Washington. Lincoln, on hearing of the incident, sent for him and commissioned him as a lieutenant of the 19th U.S. Regiment. .

The Rise of Professional Choirmasters, Organist, and Singers 331

Operatic arrangements, like the one below based on a Donizetti melody and arranged by William Kipp Bassford,[59] often provided the basis for church quartet music.

---

59. Note: A concert pianist, William Kipp Bassford (1839–1902) toured the United States before settling down in New York, his home. There, he taught, composed, and served as organist at several prominent local churches. These included, most notably, Madison Avenue Presbyterian Church and St. Bartholomew's. As a choirmaster, Bassford probably worked exclusively with quartets. His compositions, very soloistic in nature, include a *Mass in E Flat* which was dedicated to William Berge at the Church of St. Francis Xavier.

"Come Weary Souls." Text: Anne Steele (eighteenth century); music: arrangement from Donizetti Opera by W. K. Bassford, in *Madison Square Church Collection of Sacred Music* (n.d., ca. 1870).

Operatic indulgences aside, there was a certain universality to much quartet writing in the latter part of the century. The style could be described as sentimental, rather chromatic, and yet unobtrusive, routine, and even "ordinary" in the overall impression it left. A lyric style of part writing was often present, and the quality of craftsmanship frequently betrayed the European training of the compilers. As a rule, quartet composers used more sophisticated techniques and seemed to have a better understanding of the lyric potential of the voice than did, for example, Mason and Hastings.

During the last decades of the nineteenth century, some quartet composers began to move away from sentimental and operatic excess toward a more ecclesiastical simplicity. The following response was written by James

Cutler Dunn Parker (1828–1916) for the quartet at Trinity Church, Boston. Parker was organist there from 1864 to 1891, serving there with Phillips Brooks. He would be succeeded by a more famous organist with the same surname, Horatio Parker. The response, "I Will Lay Me Down in Peace," by J. C. D. Parker, is a good example of the composer's style. While written for quartet, it could easily have been sung chorally and likely was.

James Cutler Dunn Parker, "I Will Lay Me Down in Peace (Sentence)." Individual voice parts in manuscript in the Spaulding Library of the New England Conservatory of Music.

The next generation of quartet composers after J. C. D. Parker continued this trend toward a more liturgically appropriate style of writing. The music of Arthur Foote (1853–1937) represented the high-water mark of quartet writing in the late nineteenth century. Foote wrote sacred music for choir as well as solo voices, but his best material was in the quartet idiom. The harmonic and melodic idioms Foote used were fresh and original. His style was dignified and expressive. Foote's setting of the Christina Rossetti text, "Does the Road Wind Uphill All the Way?," is an example.

The Rise of Professional Choirmasters, Organist, and Singers

**Arthur Foote, "Does the Road Wind Uphill All the Way?"
(Boston: Arthur P. Schmidt Co., 1903.)**

The long reign of the quartet choir can be attributed to several factors. First, their music was consistent with the cultivated parlor, concert, and operatic music of the time. Second, the demand for singing professionals was in keeping with the concept of perfectionism. It was felt that the musical taste of congregations could only be reformed by exposing them to the very best music available.[60] Third, the quartet provided an intensely personal style of music that was well suited to the sentimental theology and preaching of the day. Economic factors also played a role: the quartet was often seen as a financial necessity in mid-nineteenth-century churches. In an era when conductors, trained to work with amateur choirs, were practically

---

60. There were of course huge inconsistencies here. Even when performed by highly trained professional singers—and the average quartet outside of major metropolitan areas did not have access to such musicians—much of the music sung by quartets could hardly be called "the best music available."

nonexistent and the additional rehearsing required was expensive, paying a professional quartet could be seen as cost-effective.

Organ Manufacture in America

The pipe organ made its first appearances in the American colonies at the beginning of the eighteenth century, and its use in worship followed a similar trajectory to other aspects of colonial church music. With the end of the War for Independence, there was a growing aspiration to model American worship music on European standards and a weakening of Puritan rigidity regarding what was musically appropriate. One result of this was a growing interest in organ music, both for the church and in the home, throughout the first half of the nineteenth century. The most important organ builder in colonial America was the Moravian, David Tannenberg (1728–1804). The majority of organs, however, were in Anglican chapels and were imported from Great Britain.[61] At first, most viewed organs as strictly aids to congregational singing.[62]

During the first half of the nineteenth century, there was growing interest in organ music, both for the church and in the home. By the late 1860s, it was common for smaller churches, revivalist tents and tabernacles, chapels and even private homes to have reed organs, melodeons, or harmoniums (all designed to be pumped manually by the feet). Large pipe organs were gaining acceptance in the larger and wealthier urban parishes. Organ recitals would become a popular attraction in the last decades of the nineteenth century. The European-trained organist/composer Dudley Buck built a national reputation and set an example for a generation of Victorian-era American organ recitalists.

---

61. English organs, in general, were small. None had more than two manuals until after the Restoration in 1660. Pedal divisions on Continental organs dated back at least to the fifteenth century but were rare in Britain before 1790. (Freeman, "English Organ-Cases.")

62. Anglican (later Protestant Episcopal) organists and church organ positions were by far the most numerous in the eighteenth century. Since nearly all had to be brought over from England, organists were in chronically short supply. This was not the case in the Lutheran and Moravian communities of Pennsylvania and North Carolina. According to Orpha Ochse (*History of the Organ in the United States*, 46), the Moravians had an ample supply of organists. In Bethlehem, Pennsylvania, with a population of around five hundred, there were typically at least six well-trained organists, each required to know four hundred hymn tunes and able to play them in any key. Organists served as volunteers, playing in worship once every six weeks.

Pump Organs, Reed Organs, Harmoniums, and Melodions

When discussing the rise of the organ-building industry in the United States, frequently glazed over, or ignored entirely, are portable, self-contained reed or pump organs. This is unfortunate because these instruments would become a mainstay in Victorian parlors and the organ of choice for the many smaller and rural churches. They were far less expensive than pipe organs, and there were smaller lap and spinet models that were portable. The larger parlor and sanctuary models, like any piece of furniture, were easily movable and required no modification of the room where they were used.

The defining characteristic for these instruments was the use of "free reeds," the type of pitch producer or aerophone common in harmonicas and pitch pipes and accordions. With a pipe organ or a wind instrument of the orchestra, the character or timbre of sound is greatly affected by the shape of the tube from which the sound emits. Free reeds, however, produce their sound purely from the vibration of a metal tongue or reed. European and American reed organs were differentiated by how wind pressure was used to activate the metal reed. Harmoniums—manufactured in England and Europe but not in America—functioned much like a whistle, fife, or flute with air blown past the reed and outward, causing the reed to vibrate and resulting in a bright, accordion-like sound. Conversely, the American reed organ, beginning in the 1830s, used the bellows to suck air into the instrument and past the reeds rather than pushing it out. The resulting sound tended to be mellower and more organ-like.

Successful marketing powered the huge demand for both reed and pipe organs in the late nineteenth century. Newspapers and magazines included a profusion of advertising by reed organ shops. Large pipe organ installations were touted in newspapers, feeding a public fascination in the exotic, thundering instruments. Organs—reed or pipe—were promoted as *the* historically appropriate instrument for worship in the church. For the church that could not afford a pipe organ, reed organs were marketed as the ideal substitute—a wholesome, cultivated instrument for church or home. They would gradually replace the bass viol as the preferred accompaniment instrument for church choirs, singing schools, and congregational singing and Sunday schools in smaller churches. Prior to the Civil War, many itinerant Baptist and Methodist preachers carried portable melodeons to accompany hymn singing. When a new church was established ministers commonly entered into reciprocal agreements with reed organ manufacturers. In return for encouraging congregants to purchase instruments for their homes, the church got an instrument for their parish at a steep discount.[63]

---

63. Waring, *Manufacturing the Muse*, 25.

The terms "melodeon," "reed organ," and "pump organ" were used indiscriminately. The reed organ most commonly used in churches was a moderately large instrument with substantial pedals for the bellows at its base. It was often configured to look like a pipe organ console.

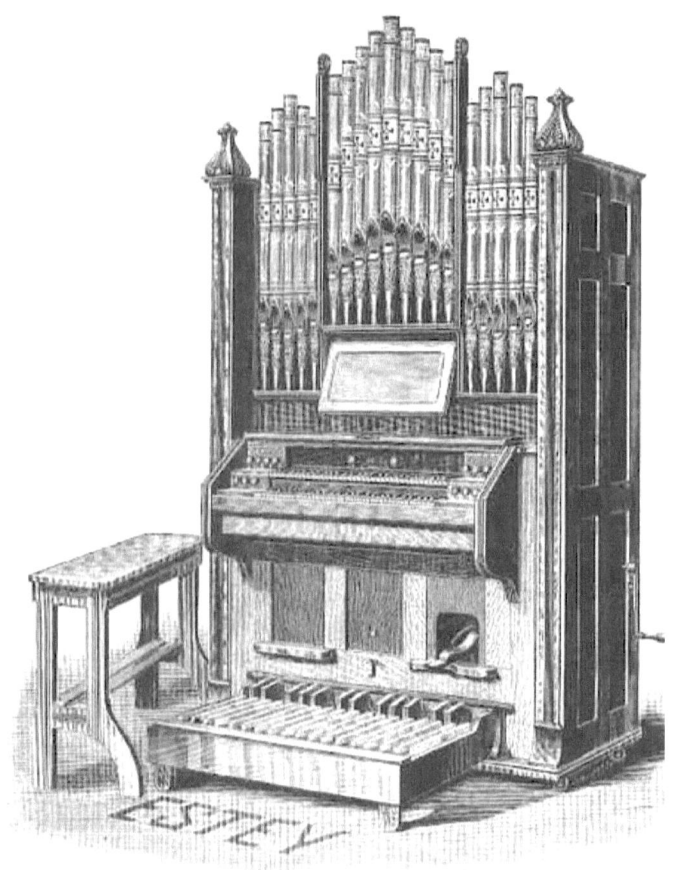

Reed organ for church use with bank of faux pipes.
Public domain image from nineteenth-century Estey Organ Company catalogue,
courtesy of Wikimedia Commons.

Parlor instruments utilized a more refined design with an appearance similar to the "square grand" pianos of the Victorian era.

The Rise of Professional Choirmasters, Organist, and Singers

Portable Melodeon, ca. 1867. Public domain image courtesy of Creative Commons.

The zenith of reed organ manufacture and marketing occurred between 1870 and 1900. In 1855, Mason & Hamlin produced its first models of "flat top" or cabinet organs. Many models included a bank of non-working pipes to further mimic the look of an actual pipe organ.

Following the Civil War, the Estey Organ Company, the Story & Clark Organ Company, and Kimball Organs joined Mason & Hamlin as giants in the reed organ business, but there were dozens of smaller shops producing melodeons and reed organs throughout the country. Even the catalog merchants, Sears Roebuck and Montgomery Ward, sold organs under their brand names.

Church music historians have typically disparaged the reed organ and its place in American church music, ignored it entirely, or relegated it exclusively to the revival tent. In truth, for the majority of Americans in the nineteenth century, organ music was defined by the sound of reed instruments. This is yet another example of the aesthetic polarization festering in the American church related to music. To be sure, reed instruments were *not* pipe organs despite the overly aggressive marketing of some manufacturers. Comparing the two serves no purpose. On the other hand, the instruments provided a starting point for many a musician hoping to graduate eventually to a pipe organ. Without a doubt, reed instruments were responsible for keeping interest in the King of Instruments alive in remote and rural communities across the nation. They were also the source of endless hours of pleasurable music making in American parlors, and reed organs and melodeons *were* the instrument of choice for revival singers such as Ira Sankey and Philip Bliss. As such, they became much loved by common Americans. Their denigration by cultivated musicians and critics simply served to widen the gulf between cultivated and populist sensibilities. When the era of reed organ finally came to an end in the 1930s, taking its place would be electronic instruments, the Hammond B-3, the Wurlizer, and ultimately digital keyboards, all of central importance to popular, gospel, and pop-sacred stylings, and all equally dismissed by cultivated church musicians.

Melodeons and pump organ used by Philip P. Bliss as a singing school instructor and singing evangelist with both Dwight L. Moody and Daniel Webster Whittle. Photos courtesy of the Philip P. Bliss Songwriters Museum, Rome, Pennsylvania.

The Rise of the Professional Organist and John Zundel

There were capable organists active on the Eastern Seaboard during the first three decades of the nineteenth century. George K. Jackson, Lowell Mason, and W. B. Bradbury were all active as organists, though their careers were directed toward composing, compiling tunebooks, and conducting. Nevertheless, the organ was still a novelty and most organists were self-taught amateur players. Nathan Gould provided a delightful description of the era in his *Church Music in America* (1853).

> At the commencement of the present century, there were but few organs in the country. These were among the wonders of the age. The sound of this instrument, to an unaccustomed ear, was calculated to surprise, astonish and delight all who had souls for music. And whenever a person from the country visited Boston, when he returned, one of the first questions asked him was, "Did you go hear the organ?" And if his answer was in the negative, he was considered wanting in taste and having neglected to examine one of the principal curiosities of the city . . .[64]

---

64. Gould, *Church Music in America*, 178.

The Rise of Professional Choirmasters, Organist, and Singers 341

While production had increased and public interest with it, American organ building was in a developmental stage and was deficient in some areas. W. S. B. Matthews, a respected organist himself, wrote this of the pre-Civil War years:

> With the organ in vogue in the churches of America a generation ago, it would have been impossible to do much with legitimate playing. The swell organ was what is called short, the most of the stops in it stopping at tenor C; the pedal keyboard was only an octave and a half in compass, and the stops allotted to it no more than one or two in number. The effect of the full organ was rather shrill and screamy, due to the scarcity of eight-foot stops (on which the solidity of tone in the ensemble depends) and the preponderance of improperly voiced mixtures . . . Naturally the standard of playing followed that of the instruments.[65]

While the first documented use in America of an organ in worship occurred at Philadelphia's Gloria Dei Lutheran (Old Swede's) Church in 1703, the names of most early nineteenth-century organists are lost to us. In keeping with the lowly place of organ music in most worship services, the vast number of church organists had meager training, and little was expected of them. The concept of a career ministry for a church organist did not exist in America prior to the 1840s.

John Zundel.
Public domain image, pre-1882,
Wikimedia Commons. (https://commons.wikimedia.org/w/index.php?search=John+Zundel&title=Special:MediaSearch&go=Go&type=image)

---

65. Matthews, *Hundred Years of Music*, 237.

John Zundel (1815–1882) is generally remembered today for only two things: his close relationship with Henry Ward Beecher at Plymouth Church in Brooklyn and the composition of the hymn tune "Beecher." Zundel was one of America's first concert organists. He was a composer of hymns and was instrumental in the production of the first church hymnal of modern design. In addition, he was one of the most highly respected teachers of organ during the Civil War era, and his *The Modern School for the Organ* (1860) was the first comprehensive teaching method published for American organists. He also published a *Treatise on Harmony and Modulation*, a text designed for students wishing to learn about those subjects on their own. Most important for this study, Zundel was a full-time, career church musician at a time when such careers were a rarity.

Zundel was born in Hochdorf, Germany, and studied music at the Royal Academy in Esslingen. There he studied organ with Heinrich Rinck (1770–1846). In 1840, Zundel traveled to St. Petersburg in Russia, where he became organist at the Lutheran Church of St. Peter and St. Paul. He left Russia in 1847, arriving in Brooklyn, New York, near the end of that year and would remain there for thirty-one years. Zundel's pedal technique won him great renown and made him in high demand as a recitalist at churches throughout Brooklyn and Manhattan. The following review of a June 2, 1848 Zundel recital reflects the enthusiastic response elicited by his playing:

> Mr. Zundel, from St. Petersburgh, succeeded Mr. Greatorex. We had heard much of the great powers of this gentleman, and we were therefore fully prepared for a performance of great excellence. We were not disappointed; indeed, the reality far exceeded our expectations.
>
> He performed an introduction and variations upon a Russian theme. The composition was strictly adapted to the Organ and was in every respect admirable. A chaste and subdued feeling pervaded it, and although the fancy stops and various combinations were allowed sufficient scope, still it lost nothing of its classical tone, for there was no frivolity apparent, nor was there any striving after startling effects which the character of the Organ will not permit without desecration.
>
> Mr. John Zundel possesses an admirable organ touch and a thorough grasp of the powers and capabilities of the instrument. His pedal playing excels all that we have heard in this country. The lamented young Alpers was an admirable pedalist; Dr. Hodges is also no mean performer, but Mr. Zundel is essentially a great pedal player, and stands alone in that department of his art. Altogether his performance was admirable, and we cordially

welcome Mr. Zundel among us, for he is an ornament to the profession.[66]

In 1848, Zundel became organist at the Church of the Savior in Brooklyn. The church had installed a two-manual, twenty-four-stop, E. and G. Hook organ with a one and one-half-octave pedal division in 1844. Zundel, hired in 1848, was the church's first full-time organist/choirmaster. "Four to six paid singers, supplemented with a volunteer choir, regularly sang at each service. During especially wealthy years, an entire chorus was hired; in leaner years, congregational singing supplanted the choir. Its success was deemed minimal, however, and the church eventually abandoned congregational singing altogether."[67] The church made efforts to compensate Zundel generously, but in 1850 he accepted the position of organist at Plymouth Church on the invitation of Henry Ward Beecher.

While most of Zundel's career would be at Plymouth, his tenure was not continuous. From 1853 to October of 1854, he served as organist at St. George's Episcopal Church, Manhattan, which was just completing installation of a three-manual Henry Erben organ with a two-and-one-half-octave pedal compass. Again, the church's singing was led by a paid quartet choir. After his resignation from St. George's, Zundel returned briefly to the Church of the Savior before coming back to Plymouth.

One cannot escape the suspicion that part of Plymouth Church's attraction for John Zundel was Henry Ward Beecher's commitment to robust congregational singing. "Zundel found in Henry Ward Beecher a staunch supporter of church music and musicians, and the two men worked together closely and effectively."[68] Zundel also would be serving Plymouth strictly as its organist while the choir was directed by Henry Camp. In 1858, following a trip back to Germany, Zundel decided to found a school for organists in Brooklyn, based on the rigorous curriculum he had experienced under Rinck. Students had to enroll for at least one month with daily lessons that included playing technique, thoroughbass, tuning, and organ maintenance. Zundel had an organ studio in his home and many students boarded there during their studies.

Zundel's reputation as a teacher had spread widely. In the 1860s he was a sought-after instructor in organ, theory, and piano at the Geneseo, New York Normal Academy of Music. Zundel resigned his position at Plymouth in 1865 to tour the American West as a concert organist. However, during that same year the church purchased and had installed a four-manual E. &

---

66. "Opening of a New Organ," 28.
67. Rigler, "John Zundel as Pedagogue," 17.
68. Rigler, "John Zundel as Pedagogue," 24.

G. Hook organ with fifty-two stops and sixty-four ranks,[69] one of the largest organs in the country at the time. As a result, Zundel quickly returned to resume his work there. A weekly series of Saturday organ recitals was initiated, of which there would be two hundred in all. With both he and his wife in ill health, John Zundel resigned from Plymouth Church a final time in 1878. He returned to Germany to live near Stuttgart, and died there in 1882.[70]

A Perennial Problem: The Need for a Higher Standard of Training for Musicians

Higher education for musicians had been nonexistent prior to the Civil War, with Oberlin—the first American conservatory of music—established in 1865. In 1862, John Knowles Paine, who had just returned from study in Europe, was hired as chapel organist at Harvard. Paine was given the status of full professor of music in 1875 and tasked with establishing the first music department in an American university.[71] The state of education for musicians at the time was abysmal. Opportunities to study beyond singing schools were limited. Colleges, universities, and other institutions commonly conferred doctor of music *honoris causa* degrees to prominent musicians—among the more outstanding examples were Lowell Mason and Thomas Hastings.

Edward Morris Bowman (1841–1913) and Dudley Buck (1813–1905) spearheaded a drive to establish the American College of Musicians (the ACM), which would serve to set standards for certification of professional musicians in the 1870s. Its goal was to set strict standards of training and skill before a musician could be granted a degree title. The ACM offered its own levels of certification: Member ACM, Fellow ACM, and Master of Musical Arts. MusDoc degrees were not considered legitimate titles and debased the profession.

Normal Schools of Music

In discussing the cultivated tradition in New England and New York, I have frequently cited three principal figures: Lowell Mason, Thomas Hastings,

---

69. Organ Historical Society Database, 2012.
70. Rigler, "John Zundel as Pedagogue," 39.
71. The first college curriculums specifically focused on sacred music would not appear until the twentieth century.

and W. B. Bradbury. A fourth important name to add to that group is George Frederick Root (1820–1895).

George Frederick Root, ca. 1895.
Public domain image,
Library of Congress
Digital ID cph 3a02045. (http://hdl.loc.gov/loc.pnp/cph.3a02045)

Like Mason, Root excelled in many areas of music. He taught with Mason in the Boston Public Schools, was a highly regarded choral conductor and church musicians, and was composer of some of the most famous songs to come out of the American Civil War.[72] After the war, Root became a partner in one of the largest music publishing concerns in American history, the Root and Cady Publishing House of Chicago.

In his autobiography, Root described the birth of the normal school of music concept:

> With every Teacher's Class and Convention that I attended with Mr. Mason and Mr. Webb I became more interested in the improvement of the teachers who came to be instructed. I saw how inadequate the time was for much improvement, not only in my department (the voice), but in the art of teaching and in harmony and general musical culture. Early in 1852 I conceived the idea of having a three months' session for this work. It must be in the summer, because then the teachers had more leisure.

---

72. Root's song "The First Gun Is Fired" was published on April 14, 1861, just two days after the firing on Fort Sumpter. "The Battle Cry of Freedom," probably the most famous song actually sung by the troops, was published in 1862. Two other very popular Root songs were "Just Before the Battle, Mother" (1863) and "Tramp! Tramp! Tramp! The Boys Are Marching" (1864).

It must be in the city of New York, for I must be there where my work was. I knew the expenses of advertising and place of meeting would be large, but I believed that from all the States and Canada enough teachers, and those who wished to become such, would come, to save the enterprise from pecuniary loss.

I went immediately to Boston, where Mr. Mason still lived, and told him my plan. It did not strike him at first as feasible. He did not believe any considerable number of persons could be induced to come, especially from a distance, on account of the great expense of traveling and of such a stay in New York City, in addition to the cost of instruction. I said, "Well, I am going to have such a class. You are the proper person to appear at the head of it, and to be the real head when it comes to the teaching, but I do not expect you to do any of the work of getting it up; I'll see to that. It will be a better opportunity than you have ever had to make your ideas of notation, teaching, and church music really known, for you will have time enough thoroughly to indoctrinate people with them, and that you know you never have had in Teachers' Classes and Conventions . . . I knew this would move him if anything would. No word of money or remuneration for his services passed between us . . . Mr. Mason finally agreed to be at the head of the enterprise, which I decided to call "The Normal Musical Institute" . . .

In the summer of 1853, the first Normal Musical Institute was held. Its sessions were in Dodworth's Hall, Broadway, New York, and continued three months. The principal teachers were Lowell Mason, Thomas Hastings, Wm. B. Bradbury and myself; assistant teachers, John Zundel, J. C. Woodman, and some others, for private lessons, whose names I do not now recall. The terms were $25 for the normal course; $50 if private lessons were added. There were upwards of a hundred from abroad, and enough singers from the city to make a good chorus. I think we met but one evening a week for chorus practice; certainly not more than two. Working as we did all through the day in the hot city, we did not think it safe to add much evening work. We gave no concerts. It was years before the "Normal" thought of deriving any revenue in that way. In fact, it was not exactly business to any of us (excepting to those who gave private lessons). Each had his regular occupation in other ways. As the years went on, modifications in many things were made, and improvements in some of the studies introduced, but the main objects of the institution and the program of daily work have remained in this

The Rise of Professional Choirmasters, Organist, and Singers

and have been adopted in the other institutes that have sprung up since, essentially as in that first memorable session.[73]

Root contacted the publisher Mason & Law, operated by Mason's sons, Lowell Jr. and Daniel Gregory Mason, to underwrite the normal school project. The daily schedule, as he envisioned it, would include lectures on the art of teaching by the elder Mason, lessons in harmony and composition led by Richard Storrs Willis, voice classes taught by Root, and part-singing led by Bradbury. A requirement for enrollment was that students have some musical experience and sight-reading skill.[74] Those attending were required to sign a statement at the conclusion of the gathering "commend[ing] the Institute to all who may wish to acquire a practical knowledge of music . . . and especially . . . to all those who wish to become qualified as teachers for the masterly development and elucidation of the true principles of teaching, as well as an exhibition of the proper method by which those methods are reduced to practice."[75]

Root's normal institutes of music continued annually through 1885. During that time, the curriculum was enlarged to four eleven-week sessions per annum. Root hoped, with the expanded schedule, to offer a comprehensive course of study for "those who wish to become accomplished performers, and especially those who intend on making music their profession . . ." They were offered at such disparate locations as North Reading, Massachusetts; Chicago, Illinois; Geneseo, New York; Wooster, Ohio; Winona, Minnesota; and Janesville, Wisconsin.[76]

Choirmasters in the Late Nineteenth Century

Working with volunteer singers required both an understanding of the human voice and a knowledge of the rudiments of conducting. In each of these areas, mid-nineteenth-century organists were often lacking. In Leipzig, organ students devoted practically all of their energy to becoming concert performers. Moritz Hauptmann (1792–1868) of the Leipzig Conservatory, who had taught W. B. Bradbury, felt very incompetent working with voices despite his work with the choir at the *Thomaskirche*. Hauptmann himself could not sing and confessed to a friend that voice students at the conservatory probably came away worse off than when they started. He further pointed out that the mechanics of the voice were little understood by the

---

73. Root, *Story of a Musical Life*, 82–88.
74. Hash, "George F. Root's Normal Musical Institute," 271.
75. Hash, "George F. Root's Normal Musical Institute," 271.
76. Hash, "George F. Root's Normal Musical Institute," 271.

conservatory faculty.[77] Leonard Phillips, in his dissertation *The Leipzig Conservatory* (1979), found that some of this may have been due to a German "inferiority complex" with regard to vocal techniques and choral work. Knowledgeable instructors were hard to find outside of Italy.[78]

In America, an aspiring organist/choirmaster had few avenues of instruction to pursue. As late as 1914, choirmasters still learned their techniques mostly by personal observation.[79] A knowledge of vocal technique could be gotten from the study of singing with a good studio teacher. Choral techniques, however, could only be learned by joining a choir and observing its leader.[80] Class study either in choral conducting, or in church music generally, was unheard of and the first choral method books did not become available until after 1900.[81]

This deplorable lack of interest in training methods for choirs was discussed by a writer in *Etude Magazine*.

> But if choristers appear to loaf and sulk, a certain amount of excuse can be found for them. They are, as it were, orphans among musicians. An enormous amount of highly specialized aid is nowadays thrust upon all types and grades of music students, but scant attention is given toilers in the important field of choral music. A careful search through musical literature discloses the fact that these are largely left to grope their way about as best they may. There are hosts of books devoted to the orchestra and the opera; but those which discuss choral music are few and brief. The vital part played by choristers in their own field is usually taken for granted; whether they are deemed to be above or beneath criticism doth not yet appear. Throughout his entire career, the student of piano is swamped with guides, axioms and suggestions; the budding violinist similarly nurtured and admonished, while the prospective solo singer is the object of

---

77. Hauptmann, *Letters of a Leipzig Cantor*, 367.
78. Phillips Jr., "Leipzig Conservatory" 160.
79. Sammond, "How Can a Young Organist?," 380–82.
80. Sammond, "How Can a Young Organist?," 380–82.
81. The most popular methods were F. W. Wodell's *Choir and Chorus Conducting* (1900); and *Choral Techniques and Interpretation* (ca. 1912) by the English festival conductor Henry Coward. Despite the rise in popularity of vested choirs of men and boys after the Civil War, methods, even in this unfamiliar area, were learned mainly by observation. The first available training manuals were *The Essentials of Choir Boy Training*, by Walter Henry Hall (1906), and A. M. Richardson's *The Choirtrainer's Art* (1914). In addition, George Edward Stubbs, organist at St. Agnes Chapel in New York City, published two helpful pamphlets on the subject, "How to Sing the Choral Service" (1899) and "Practical Hints on the Training of Choir Boys" (1897).

a tremulous and prayerful solicitude. Words of inspiration and encouragement, however, rarely reach the chorister.[82]

Choirmasters with even a modicum of training and practical experience were few in number. S. Archer Gibson (1875–1952), organist of New York's Brick Church, observed that "comparatively few churches can afford to pay for the services of a choirmaster competent to organize and control a chorus choir of merit, while four soloists can pull through on very little rehearsal if lazily inclined." His preference for quartets was shared by many. Arthur Foote (1853–1937) continued working with quartet choirs throughout his thirty-two years at First Unitarian Church, Boston (1878–1910).

Dudley Buck, Organist, Church Musician, and Composer

Dudley Buck.
Public domain image. (http://ctoldhouse.com/Dudley-Buck.html)

We turn now to one of the most important and influential voices in American church music during the post-Civil War decades, Dudley Buck (1839–1905). Buck's musical career was multifaceted. He was one of the country's first native-born virtuosos of the pipe organ and a nationally known touring artist. He was a sought-after teacher who trained many of America's most prominent organists of the late nineteenth and early twentieth centuries. He was also a composer of works in a variety of mediums from organ music to symphonic works, oratorio, and choral music.

Finally, unlike other concert artists of his time, he *chose* to be a church musician. Even when he was actively concertizing, he was also working as a church organist. Most of his published writings were intended for church

---

82. Burroughs, "Amateur Chorister," 603.

musicians, to build techniques and to deal with common problems. Finally, after stepping away from recitals and touring, Buck served for twenty-five years as one of the finest, most respected organist/choirmasters in the East.

Dudley Buck was born on March 10, 1839, in Hartford, Connecticut, the son of a wealthy shipping magnate. While the family was not particularly musical, Hartford had been a center of musical activity for much of the century. Hartford's Choral Society, established in 1827, had performed excerpts from the staple oratorio repertoire of Handel, Beethoven, and Haydn. Exposure to organ music would have been an important childhood experience for Dudley Buck. The Buck family's church, Christ Church Episcopal of Hartford, installed one of the first pipe organs in the state, a Catlin, in 1801. When the church was rebuilt in 1827, it installed an organ by the famous builder Henry Erben. It was the first three-manual instrument in the state of Connecticut.[83]

Like most young people with a musical bent, Buck's first formal instruction in music was through a nearby singing school. While Dudley's parents remained dubious of any value to be achieved from the study of music, they purchased both a flute and a melodeon for him when he was twelve years old. They were shocked, however, to find him already able to make music at the keyboard when the new instrument arrived. William K. Gallo was able to interview Buck's daughter-in-law, Helen Buck, who remembered that early on, Buck had made a "mock instrument of his own construction" on which to practice.[84] A 1906 letter to Buck from one of his childhood friends, Charles Parsons, also made reference to this:

> I struck another old friend of yours . . . It was Allan Bourne of Hartford. He says that he used to be your playmate and well remembers a fake organ that you rigged up at your house before you had ever tackled the melodeon.[85]

His father initially looked askance at the young Buck's musical interests, but upon recognizing his budding talent, relented and arranged for organ study with respected local organists, including the European-trained Henry Wilson. By 1856 Buck, then seventeen years old and a freshman at Hartford's Trinity College, had served as Wilson's supply organist at Christ Church and served briefly as organist at St. John's Episcopal. His musical gifts were obvious and his family, in order that he might have the best instruction available, agreed to his study at the Leipzig Conservatory

---

83. Orr, *Dudley Buck*, 3.
84. Gallo, "Life and Church Music of Dudley Buck," 5–6.
85. Gallo, "Life and Church Music of Dudley Buck," 6.

in Germany. Between 1858 and 1861, he studied composition and theory at the conservatory, where his classmates included Edvard Grieg and Arthur Sullivan. He became fluent in Italian, French, and German. In 1862, he moved to Dresden, where he studied organ briefly with J. G. Schneider before returning to the United States.[86]

Upon his return, Buck became organist/choirmaster at the North Congregational Church in Hartford, with its famous pastor/preacher Horace Bushnell. It was during the years 1862 to 1871 that Buck established himself, not only as an organist, but also as a composer of church choir music—anthems specifically designed for performance by chorus choirs. Buck scholar N. Lee Orr has written that Buck's two collections of church choral music, published in 1864 and 1871, are "arguably the two most important events in the development of the American anthem during the last half of the nineteenth century."[87] The eminent critic and organist W. S. B. Mathews wrote the following regarding Buck's first *Motette Collection* in his *One Hundred Years of Music in America* (1889):

> This book of Buck's was notable because it was the first collection published in America in which modern styles of German musical composition were freely used, with unlimited freedom of modulation and the addition of an independent organ accompaniment, after the best traditions of the German school. In the latter respect the book had a vast influence. For many organists it was the first authentic information they had received concerning the proper manner of using the organ effectively for accompanying and heightening the effect of the choir singing.[88]

---

86. Gallo, "Life and Church Music of Dudley Buck," 4–6, 10.
87. Orr, *Dudley Buck*, xi.
88. Matthews, *Hundred Years of Music*, 680.

Dudley Buck, "But the Lord Shall Arise" from Buck's Second Motette Collection (1871).

Dudley Buck, in addition to being a composer, was one of the leading choir trainers of his day. Buck's son, who sang in his choir for many years, referred to his father as "a born conductor, magnetic, insistent upon balance, clearness, and tone quality." He was said to be "at heart, a very religious man" who "enthused the singers to exceptional effort and stimulated their imagination."[89] An 1897 article in the *Brooklyn Eagle* revealed Buck to be concerned with many facets of good choral singing. He sought clarity of attack and insisted his singers *think* their pitches before singing. Crisp rhythm, careful diction, and perfect choral discipline were all stressed in

---

89. Boyd, "Choir Development Since 1876," 72.

rehearsals of Buck's choir at Holy Trinity Episcopal in Brooklyn.[90] What follows is a detailed account of choir rehearsal under Buck.

> On the following Saturday, we had the pleasure of being present for the rehearsal of the choir of Holy Trinity, when the unanimity of phrasing and expression was fully disclosed. Not one whit of it was the result of genius, except it be the genius of painstaking work. The librarian having passed out copies of a setting of the *Te Deum*, Mr. Buck, seated at a grand piano in the lecture room with his choir seated around him exactly as in church, said, "Are you ready?" A few chords and soon the choir are in full cry. The tenors at one point overblow their reeds, and Mr. Buck says, "Too raspy!" in a voice not over free from raspiness itself, and with a look at the offenders of a very commanding kind, not to be misunderstood. Again the piano stops, and Mr. Buck says, "Oh no, no, no !" The failure this time is more general and is in the matter of rhythm, which is not crisp enough to please his exact ear. The words are, "Thou art the only begotten son."
> "Say it like this"—Mr. Buck plays the passage with the most clear-cut rhythm. He never permits himself to illustrate any musical effect with his voice. Here is another of his directions: "Whisper that passage with staccato tones." Nor will he be satisfied with less than perfect obedience. Mr. Buck did not speak of intervals nor of pitch names during the whole time of the rehearsals. But he did say to the sopranos, "See you bring out well that sol-la-sol on the words, 'be confounded.'" At the words, "For He hath visited and redeemed his people," he said, "Now, it is not an accident that the composer wrote that in just that way; it was his purpose that every note should do its own work." Again, it was the true rhythm he was after.
>
> In one of the anthems, the altos had a flat seventh over which they fumbled. To them he said, "Now, you ought to read ahead and see what is coming and get ready for it, and not jump at it at the last minute." At one passage a slight tendency to shout was manifest and he said, "Don't try to sing loud, but I want it forte just the same." The result showed that the choir perfectly understood what he meant by the distinction between trying to sing loud and a true forte.

---

90. Buck became organist at Holy Trinity Episcopal, Brooklyn, in 1878, and remained there through 1903.

Between the pieces, whilst the librarian is distributing the next piece, the members may talk if so inclined, but woe betide the luckless member who tries to say a word during a rest in the music. The choir were about to take up a practically unaccompanied piece of some difficulty. As he was about to play the prelude, Mr. Buck said, "I do not want to play this over more than once nor need I if everyone will watch." An injunction which did not need to be repeated. Once Mr. Buck suddenly stopped the piano and said, referring to the word, "multitude," "that word is made up of all the letters put together; see you don't leave any of them out." Again, "That passage is not to be staccato, only distinct." A good effect was produced in one of the pieces by having the choir hum a kind of echo of the preceding phrase during a short rest in the music. Mr. Buck will not tolerate a balky start, and it was worth a good deal to hear that choir declaiming an intricate fugue and notice how deftly Mr. Buck accompanied them while so doing. A satisfied, "Ach!" from Mr. Buck announced that the rehearsal was over and the choir dispersed, certainly all the more fit for tomorrow's work after their hour of earnest rehearsal.[91]

Dudley Buck instinctively understood the potential power of choral music to Protestant worship. Through his compositions and through the choirs he conducted, he was able to demonstrate that choirs made up largely of amateur singers could sing well and serve the church admirably through a ministry of music. While he didn't silence all his critics, choral music including anthems sung by chorus choirs rather than quartets alone would become an increasingly common and expected part of worship in American churches in the late nineteenth and early twentieth centuries.

Buck's importance to organ music in America can hardly be overstated. The 1929 edition of the *Dictionary of American Biography* declared:

> Buck was one of the first . . . to possess musicianship of genuine solidity, with respect to technical equipment and creative ability. American organ-music practically begins with him. A concert-organist of imposing ability, his extensive tours during the first fifteen years of his public life helped greatly to uplift standards of organ-playing and organ-music, both of which were in dire need of improvement.[92]

During his time in Leipzig, Dudley Buck studied harmony, composition, piano, and orchestration, though he was disappointed to find no

---

91. Cited in Gallo, "Life and Church Music of Dudley Buck," 96.
92. Cole, "Dudley Buck," 222–23.

The Rise of Professional Choirmasters, Organist, and Singers 355

satisfactory instructor in organ. When his orchestration professor, Julius Reitz, left the conservatory in 1860 to accept the post of music director for the city of Dresden, Buck followed him. It was there that he came under the tutelage of the organist Johann Gottlob Schneider. "He was one of the first organists since the Baroque era to develop the technical ability needed to play the difficult pedal parts in Bach's organ music."[93] Schneider's skills on the pedals clearly influenced Buck, since throughout his years as a concert artist critics would comment on his impressive pedaling.

When Buck returned from Europe in 1862, he immediately began performing as an organ recitalist. In February of 1867, Buck was commissioned to perform the dedicatory recital for the new three-manual W. A. Johnson organ at Chicago's First Baptist Church, the largest organ in the city. It was a major musical event with a standing-room-only audience. Buck's playing was lionized in the press, and soon he was enticed to move to Chicago to become organist at St. James Episcopal Church. He moved to Chicago in May of 1869 and set about building a lavish new home with attached studio, recital hall, and space for storage of his extensive music library. His collection included one-of-a-kind original manuscripts of his own works and scores of other composers imported from Europe.

Chicago in the post-Civil War years was the greatest railroad hub in the United States and the ideal launch site for Buck as a traveling concert artist. Over the next two years he was able to perform recitals throughout the eastern half of the United States. Works of J. S. Bach and his own compositions were a part of every program. He also played works written for organ by other nineteenth-century composers, with the Mendelssohn sonatas being a frequent recital staple. Buck's recitals also invariably included transcriptions of popular overtures, movements from Beethoven symphonies, arrangements of popular melodies, and so on. The transcriptions, expertly played and demonstrative of Buck's virtuosity, were audience favorites but also the subject of criticism.[94]

Herein was a dilemma. Was he to embrace American society, still a bit rough around the edges, bringing with him a repertoire balanced between meaty classics and the readily accessible to the less sophisticated in his audience? Or was he to follow the example of John Knowles Paine and others who, according to N. Lee Orr, "found themselves unable to bridge the gap between their professional artistic tastes and the generally undeveloped musical culture in this country. Feeling isolated from the popular culture of

---

93. Orr, "Dudley Buck, Leader of a Forgotten Tradition," 11.
94. Gallo, "Life and Church Music of Dudley Buck," 22.

their own country, they often withdrew into the university or the conservatory..."⁹⁵

Critics who disliked the inclusion of theatrically showy transcriptions in the recital repertoire, as was common in recitals of the day, distinguished between "legitimate organ music"—that which was originally conceived for the instrument—and "illegitimate organ music," anything that was not. Buck made his position clear on the subject in an article for Chicago's *The Musical Independent* in 1869:

> [T]he playing of light overtures may find a certain justification in this land, where so much musical missionary work has yet to be done, anything which will give them a taste for the mere tones of so noble an instrument is not to be utterly rejected.
>
> This is the great debatable ground of the strict Legitimists, they who would have nothing played except that originally composed for the organ. Without giving a dogmatic opinion, . . .
>
> It is certain that from a true art standpoint, an organist should throw his influence towards works originally composed for his instrument. Yet this matter of overture playing not unfrequently serves as a stepping stone to better things.⁹⁶

Buck further elaborated on this train of thought in his lecture, "The Influence of the Organ in History" (1882):

> There are those, however (and their opinions are entitled to respect), who claim that such free treatment of the organ is improper. These persons would, with little or no exception, limit the repertoire to such works as have been originally written for the organ; and when they got outside fugue or canon, would still remain carefully within the limits of purely contrapuntal orthodoxy. Any other treatment is styled "illegitimate." I had hoped to avoid this terrible word,—the great bugbear among conscientious students of the organ,—nor do I propose to enter into any analysis of what the "legitimate" may or may not consist in. . . .
>
> I am by no means arguing that the organist should avoid these stricter forms on this account; quite the contrary; but simply that the judicious liberalism above referred to should provide as great a variety of musical food as will suit and satisfy the musical appetite within the means of the instrument as it now exists. Nor should the "milk for babes" be despised. The workings of

---

95. Orr, *Dudley Buck*, 85.
96. Buck, "On Recital Repertoire," 146–47.

this principle will surely attract rather than repel, and maturer musical strength will instinctively call for heartier food. *We have to deal with men as we find them, and tastes vary....* Real musical hunger can only be satisfied with solids; but if we first quiet the deeper cravings with roast beef, I know of no moral obligation why we should not finish with ice-cream ...[97]

There is little doubt that Dudley Buck planned to make Chicago his home for the foreseeable future, but disaster would upset those plans. The Great Chicago Fire on the evening of October 8, 1871, leveled about 3.3 square miles of the city, leaving six hundred dead, and more than 100,000 homeless. Buck was in Albany, New York, for a recital when he received the devastating news. St. James Church and Buck's home, which he used most of his inheritance to build,[98] were destroyed in the Chicago fire. Thankfully, his wife and family were spared, along with a few possessions they were able to carry on their persons. Shaken and saddened by all that had been lost, Buck immediately left Chicago and returned to the East Coast. St. James Church would rise again from the ashes, and the music program established by Dudley Buck and leaders to follow him would include three major figures in the development of American church music: Peter Christian Lutkin, Clarence Dickinson, and Leo Sowerby.

The move east was immediate, and there was no looking back. Just a month after the fire destroyed his Chicago home, Buck accepted the position of organist at St. Paul's Episcopal Church, Boston, and his name appeared on the faculty roll at the New England Conservatory. The following April, he was tapped to become organist at the Boston Musical Hall, performing three one-hour recitals per week during concert season. Buck's days as a touring organist, however, were over. The Boston Music Hall recitals would be his last.

Buck's writings reveal a passion to educate. This was also exemplified in his 1871 "Hints for Young Organists":

> In America, the first musical interest of which the majority of persons are conscious is apt to be awakened by church music and the practice of it. This interest has received a powerful impetus during the last few years by the introduction of pipe organs into many small churches ... The expression "pipe" organ is here employed because it has come into use in contradiction to the "Melodeon in disguise," entitled by its manufacturers "Cabinet"

---

97. Buck, "Influence of the Organ in History," 63–64.

98. Note: Buck's parents had died a few months apart in 1863, willing the bulk of their assets to him.

organ. These have been greatly improved of late years, it is true, and are susceptible of many good, and a few charming effects, these latter however, only when used in combination with other instruments. The best use to which Providence has called these instruments—their moral affect so to speak—seems to be in this fact, that as far as their employment in church is concerned, they soon create a sort of musical hunger for something better . . .

And first then, let us note the fallacy often expressed thus, "I have never taken any regular organ lessons, but I know the touch because I have a Cabinet organ at home."

Piano practice is worth ten-fold more . . . because the modern organ, with its present quick speech and improved mechanism, requires the same high and accurate lifting of the fingers, the same thorough fall of the key struck as does the piano—whereas the touch of the Cabinet organ is, to say the least, *sui generis*, only like itself[99]. . . The technique of all three instruments mentioned is the same as to scales, arpeggios, etc., and is far more easily and thoroughly learned in the first place on the piano . . .[100]

In 1875 Buck moved to New York, ultimately settling in Brooklyn. He was still only thirty-six years old. He served as organist/choirmaster at St. Ann's Episcopal Church for the 1876–1877 church year and then moved over to Holy Trinity Episcopal, where he remained until his retirement in 1902. During his time at Holy Trinity, Buck established a Sunday afternoon vespers series featuring choral and organ music. In the 1890s, he shepherded the church through a transition from quartet choirs to chorus choirs made up of volunteers with a professional core. Over the course of Dudley Buck's tenure, Holy Trinity became recognized as having one of the outstanding music programs in the Northeast.

Throughout his career Dudley Buck was also a selfless advocate for advancement of educational opportunities for professional training of musicians in the United States. As early as 1868, he attended the National Music Teachers Convention in Boston, where the American Musical Congress—an organization formed specifically to address this need—was founded. He was active in the organization until its demise in 1870. In the 1880s, he was a founding member of the American College of Musicians (ACM) and served on its administrative board for ten years.

---

99. The melodeon's mechanical action rendered its touch stiffer than that of the piano or mid-century organs with their pneumatic action.

100. Buck, "Hints for Young Organists," 9–10.

In 1884 Yale University—though it had no course of study in music or degree program—awarded Buck the honorary degree of MusDoc. Buck refused to accept it and made his refusal in a public statement. He felt that to have done so privately would imply he saw such degrees as valid. Nonetheless, his decision was controversial, and he suffered much criticism for having made it. "No one could appreciate better than myself the high honor of such a compliment, coming from such an institution as old 'Yale,'" Buck wrote, "but I must say I have a distaste amounting to unconquerable repugnance to all titles of this kind in my profession."[101] While some critics were vocal, others applauded him for his courage to take a stand. As evidence of the high respect in which Dudley Buck was held, he was named honorary president of the American Guild of Organists for the years 1896 to 1899.

Buck's teaching, in both organ and composition, had a major impact on the next generation of organists and church musicians. His students included Frederick Grant Gleason (1848–1903), Harry Rowe Shelley (1858–1947), William H. Neidlinger (1863–1924), Raymond Huntington Woodman (1861–1943), and John Hyatt Brewer (1856–1931). Shelley would become one of the most prominent and popular composers of anthems and church music prior to World War I.[102]

Dudley Buck's most famous student and arguably the most important organist of the late nineteenth century was Clarence Eddy (1851–1937). The young Eddy studied with Buck during the Hartford years and, following Buck's example, studied in Europe from 1871 to 1874. He would go on to become America's first international touring artist of the organ, playing to massive audiences in Paris, first in 1888 and again in 1895.[103]

In sum, Dudley Buck's influence as an organist, composer, teacher, choirmaster, and advocate was manifold. His passion for and unflagging commitment, not simply to perform but to raise the standard of music for an entire nation, must not be ignored.

An Impediment to Progress

The polarization that existed in the nineteenth century between advocates of the cultivated tradition in church music and those supporting a broad outreach to all classes of worshippers, stood in the way of developing any overarching approach to music as a ministry in America's churches. That

---

101. Orr, *Dudley Buck*, 82–83.
102. Gallo, "Life and Church Music of Dudley Buck," 89.
103. Osborne, *Clarence Eddy*, 9–89.

polarization was reflected in a confrontation between the Boston composer George Whitefield Chadwick (1854–1931) and George Frederick Root.

On December 27, 1876, a distinguished organization with a long and storied history was born, the Music Teachers' National Association (or MTNA). The objective of the MTNA was to raise professional standards for teachers of music nationally. Dr. Eben Tourjée of the New England Conservatory had been elected president of the new association, and its first meeting was held in Delaware, Ohio, just north of Columbus.

The keynote speaker for the meeting was George Frederick Root, the pioneer music teacher and one of the country's most popular composers. Also scheduled to speak was a young George Whitefield Chadwick, destined to become one of America's preeminent composers. Chadwick, then just twenty-two years old, was a New Englander and the precocious student of some of the most respected teachers in the East. Just one year later he would undertake the required three-year sojourn to Europe to study at the Leipzig Conservatory, giving him the ultimate stamp of approval in cultivated musical circles.

The topic of Chadwick's address was "The Popular Music of the Day Wherein Reform Is Necessary," and in it he condemned much of the music which had been a staple in America's parlors for the past twenty years as well as on the war's battlefields. He charged that popular ballads of the era were shallow, lacked originality, and were wholly commercial in their appeal. He cited the typical eight-bar phrases and very basic harmonic structure, tonic—dominant—subdominant, as indicative of a complete lack of creativity. "Why does all this weakness, this trash, this dishonest, miserable stuff—why does this flood our homes and choir galleries, and fill the whole land with its senselessness?" Chadwick demanded. "Those who furnish the popular music have not paid," he declared, "either in money or in mental discipline, the price of true and first-class musicians. Therefore, they furnish to the people their wares, manufactured from the slender stock of knowledge they have acquired, at so cheap a rate that it floods the market to the exclusion of true music."[104]

Sitting in the audience was George Frederick Root, the indefatigable proponent of music education for decades prior. He had been the principal advocate for normal schools of music, had studied voice in Paris, and was the composer of some of the country's most beloved popular songs from the war years including "The Battle Cry of Freedom." Root, now fifty-six years old and twenty years Chadwick's senior, addressed Chadwick's complaints with simplicity, humility, and directness. He stated that he knew full well

---

104. Faucett, *George Whitefield Chadwick*, 41.

The Rise of Professional Choirmasters, Organist, and Singers

that his songs did not rise to the standard of high European art, but "that 'simple' music played a vital part in the lives of the masses of Americans, and in the development of their musical taste."[105]

Herein, in a disagreement between two musicians, is a perfect example of division that would plague American church music and indeed American society in the late nineteenth century. The choice had to be made between music and ministry to a select, elite, cultivated few, or to the teeming masses flooding America's cities. Root, a disciple of Lowell Mason, would certainly have agreed with Chadwick that artistic music was to be aspired to, but for there to be any progress, he also saw a need for music that resonated with the general public where they were. For Chadwick, it was necessary to choose sides.[106]

Following the Civil War, a new class of professional musical leadership—choirmasters and organists—began to make their voices heard regarding what music was appropriate for worship. Like Chadwick, their views were heavily weighted toward the use Eurocentric organ, quartet, and choral music in worship. There were, however, those masses of Americans referred to by Root whose musical taste was limited to the simple and tuneful. A movement, now known as the social gospel movement, was in progress that sought to reach some of those not being reached by wealthy and elite churches of the Victorian era.

---

105. Carder, "George Frederick Root, Pioneer Music Educator," 37.

106. Later in life, Chadwick looked back at the exchange with Root and admitted that "I was perhaps rather too much in earnest." Root, he said, "made a very courteous but effective reply, which I confess, modified my opinions to a certain extent. He was one of the finest gentlemen I have ever met, and a real folk-song composer." (Faucett, *George Whitefield Chadwick*, 42.)

Chapter 11

UNFULFILLED ASPIRATIONS
Reconstruction and the Social Gospel Movement

The late nineteenth century in America was a period of great hopefulness, and many were convinced a new millennium of peace and prosperity was at hand. For some the optimism was fueled by astounding technological progress being made in industry. They celebrated the growth of industrial monoliths along with the urban centers surrounding them, and rejoiced in the building of great churches within those centers—Gothic temples to human progress as well as to divine aspiration. All things considered, it was a stark contrast from the hopelessness and sacrifice of wartime.

For many wealthy and cultivated churches in major cities, the music and worship of working-class citizens, the poor, immigrants, and people of color was a subject for embarrassment or outright denigration. As a result, the "wall" separating the cultivated and vernacular traditions in church music became even more impregnable during the latter half of the century. A common view of cultivated Christians in Victorian America toward the less fortunate was "benign neglect." Lyman H. Atwater, a leading Presbyterian editor of the time, quoting the Gospel of Matthew, opined that poverty and the unequal distribution of wealth was perfectly defensible in Scripture.

> Now it is in accordance with the immutable law of God . . . that "he that worketh not, neither shall he eat." . . . Now the cause [of labor unrest] we have found to be mainly, the effort of such vast numbers to eat the bread of idleness; to live upon the labors and earnings of others, in whole or in part . . . Let all be prudent, live within, rather than beyond, their means, and lay up something

"in store against the time to come." Let all who have done their best, be thankful and content with such things as they have . . . Whatever any lay up on earth, let them first of all lay up treasures in heaven, which they shall have at the resurrection of the just. . . . Let them learn the divine wisdom, "in whatsoever state they are, therewith to be content," since, at the worst, "these light afflictions shall work out for them a far more exceeding and eternal weight of glory . . ." So, even if poor of this world, shall they be rich as heirs of God.[1]

Such a stance, of course, ran counter to traditional Christian teachings regarding charity and Jesus's teachings regarding ministry to the poor.

For another group of post-Civil War Americans, however, there was determination to confront society's evils and bring change. The focus of some would be on bringing formerly enslaved African Americans to full citizenship and equality through education and social reform—federal Reconstruction. Other reform-minded individuals and groups mounted idealistic crusades to address a broad range of issues:

- Working conditions for the common laborer including union organizing.
- A five-day workweek.
- An end to child labor.
- Education and opportunity within the inner city and minority ghettos.
- Reconstruction of the conquered South.

These reformative efforts would represent the first stirrings of what would become known as the "social gospel movement." Powered by idealism as they were, many of these reform efforts had only marginal success initially. Others were hampered by the deep-seated Anglo-Saxon nativism among some of the reformers themselves and a failure to confront the systemic racism that was endemic. Nevertheless, they offered a new vision of what a moral and truly inclusive America might look like.

The reform activity between 1870 to 1900 was represented in its sacred music. A product of Reconstruction, the concept of the "concert spiritual," was viewed as a way to familiarize whites with African American song. The social gospel movement brought to the fore a whole repertoire of Protestant hymnody focused on societal reform issues.

Previous chapters have dealt with musical and religious developments in some of America's large, elite churches in the Northeast and Midwest in the years after the Civil War. Thousands of practicing Christians, perhaps

---

1. Atwater, "Our Industrial and Financial Situation," 517, 527–28.

even a majority, were *not* members of those churches. Many were immigrants, minorities, or poor with neither the interest in nor the possibility of fitting into communities of wealth and privilege in the suburbs of major cities. Many also were poorly paid industrial and office workers, often with a limited education, living in less desirable areas. For them the magnificent Gothic churches, appearing not unlike medieval castles or fortresses, would have seemed intimidating. There were also the veterans. A great many of those returning from the war had experienced the evangelistic fervor of preachers and chaplains at the front and were not receptive to the stiff, undemonstrative ways of cultivated worship.

Despite a war fought largely to ensure racial equality across the land, there were still racial barriers. Even in the strongholds of abolitionism like northern Ohio and Indiana, African Americans were often unwelcome in all-white sanctuaries. While systemic racism had hardly been quelled by the war, a hopeful sign was the courageous work done by student singers from Freedman's Bureau-established colleges in the South. Inspired by the successful northern tours of the Fisk University's Jubilee Singers, choral groups from the Hampton Institute in Virginia, and other schools brought a new understanding and appreciation for the African American spiritual. Perhaps even more important, the Jubilee Singers[2] definitively established for white audiences that Black Americans were capable of artistic excellence.

Finally, there were *the lost*—a vast hoard of humanity finding itself in a new and completely foreign environment—they who had left the relationships and comfort of rural communities to encounter the anonymity, coldness, and cramped conditions of life as lower- or middle-class workers in the city. For them, social gospel proponents such as the Rev. Washington Gladden and Jane Addams labored mightily, often at odds with clergy contemporaries, to advocate for Christian ministries in the inner city, unions, and social programs to ease the plight of the disenfranchised.

Washington Gladden and Social Awareness in the Nineteenth-Century Church

The Reverend Washington Gladden (1836–1918), a Congregationalist minister often called the "Father of the social gospel movement," writing in 1909, recalled what it was like to leave a small New England town and encounter urban living for the first time:

---

2. The success of the Fisk Jubilee Singers was such that the word "jubilee" itself came to represent a style of singing and a generic term for types of ensembles singing unaccompanied, arranged spirituals in the Jubilee Singers' style.

The city, from the first day, was a thing stupendous and overpowering, a mighty monster, with portentous energies. To one who had nursed his fancies for the greater part of his life in the solitude of a back-country farm, and who had breasted no currents of life stronger than those which meander through the streets of a quiet village, the contact with the strenuous life of the great city was a revelation. One was standing in the center of a galvanic field, with lines of force crossing each other in every direction. Everything was alive, yet there was a vivid sense of the impersonality and brutality of the whole movement, of the lack of coordinating intelligence.[3]

Washington Gladden, ca. 1905.
Public domain image,
Library of Congress.
(https://www.loc.gov/pictures/item/2017656304/)

Shifting views regarding theology in post-Civil War America helped to make condemnation of the vanquished peculiar institution more palatable. The emerging New Theology represented a shift from biblical literalism to so-called "historicism." Proponents declared that God, working through all of history, had authored the only acceptable moral code, one overriding Scripture, and one in which slavery was repugnant.[4] Washington Gladden wrote:

And when Christ appeared, declaring that the law and the prophets were all summed up in the rule which bids us do to

---

3. Gladden, *Recollections*, 90.
4. Oshatz, *Slavery and Sin*, 99.

others as we would have others do to us, the doom of the system was sealed. There is no express legislation against it in the New Testament; but there is no great need of express legislation against wearing fur overcoats in July. What Christianity did was to create a moral atmosphere in which slavery could not exist.

Men have always been quoting the Bible on the side of slavery; but while pettifogging theologians have been searching its pages for texts with which to prop their system, the spirit of the book has been steadily undermining the system. There are those who still choose to represent Christianity as the ally of despotism . . . In contradiction to this . . . , we may quote the whole of history. Go back to the dark ages, to the period when the Church was most corrupt and faithless, and you will find that even then it always was the champion of the oppressed.[5]

The term "social gospel" was apparently coined by the Reverend Charles Oliver Brown in his 1886 book *Talks on the Labor Troubles*, a discussion of issues raised by Henry George's seminal work on social justice, *Progress and Poverty* (1879). Prior to 1900, however, Protestant reform activities were generically referred as "social Christianity" or "evangelical liberalism."[6] The term "social gospel" did not come into general use until the second decade of the twentieth century through the influence of the theologian Walter Rauschenbusch.

Social Reform Hymnody Prior to the Civil War[7]

Just as the origins of the Christian reform era can be traced back to abolitionism and other activist causes well before the Civil War, so too can

---

5. Gladden, *Working People and Their Employers*, 31–32. While recognizing the evils of human bondage and passionately committed to reform in the workplace, neither Gladden nor most other pioneers of post-war social reform were particularly enlightened regarding the need for racial equality. He was ambivalent regarding Reconstruction and opposed negro suffrage as "the disfranchisement of the people of intelligence and character, and the enthronement of the illiterate and degraded." (Quoted in Oshatz, *Slavery and Sin*, 150.) That being said, Gladden strongly supported the work of Booker T. Washington and was deeply touched by W. E. B. Du Bois's *Souls of Black Folks*.

6. White and Hopkins, *Social Gospel*, 246–47.

7. The words "hymn" and "song" (or "gospel song") are used so interchangeably that a word of explanation is needed. In this study, the word "hymn" is used in its classical sense, that is, a form of poetry intended to be sung. The melodies associated with hymns are referred to as the "hymn tunes." Most hymns are metrical poetry allowing for use with a variety of hymn tunes having the same metrical phrasing. "Songs"—whether sacred songs, spiritual songs, or gospel songs—imply an organic link between text, tune, and often accompaniment. When it comes to songs, the composer of the

reform hymnody. In 1844 the American poet, critic, and editor James Russell Lowell (1819–1891) wrote a ninety-line poem entitled "The Present Crisis." Lowell was fervently committed to the abolition of slavery. He presciently saw that a war with Mexico would open up new territories into which the peculiar institution might be expanded. The poem combined a warning with a challenge, beginning:

> When a deed is done for Freedom, through the broad earth's aching breast
> Runs a thrill of joy prophetic, trembling on from east to west,
> And the slave, where'er he cowers, feels the soul within him climb
> To the awful verge of manhood, as the energy sublime
> Of a century bursts full-blossomed on the thorny stem of Time.[8]

The British dissenter, social activist, and poet W. Garrett Horder revisited Lowell's poem in 1894, extracting and—in some cases—adapting lines to create one of the great hymns of social consciousness:

> Once to ev'ry man and nation
> Comes the moment to decide,
> In the strife of truth and falsehood,
> For the good or evil side;
> Some great cause, some great decision,
> Off'ring each the bloom or blight,
> And the choice goes by forever
> 'Twixt that darkness and that light.[9]

Other reform focused hymns appeared before the Civil War. The American Unitarian minister from Massachusetts, Edmund Hamilton Sears (1810–1876), showed awareness of the plight of the poor in the third stanza of his well-known carol, "It Came Upon a Midnight Clear," written in 1849.

> And ye, beneath life's crushing load,
> whose forms are bending low,
> who toil along the climbing way

---

tune and lyricist are often the same person. The lyric and tune, at least originally, were intended to be sung together exclusively.

8. Lowell, "Present Crisis," 96.

9. The hymn "Once to Every Man and Nation", commonly sung to the Welsh tune "Ton-Y-Botal" or "Ebenezer," is, I believe, one of the truly great American hymns of commitment and moral resolve. It uses the male pronoun to mean all of humanity, a practically universal practice among male and female writers in the nineteenth century. That this was representative of the patriarchal society of the Victorian era cannot be denied. Nonetheless, it is a truly great text, and its omission from the repertoire is unfortunate. The great import of Lowell's text, I feel, far outweighs in importance any suggestion of exclusiveness.

with painful steps and slow,
look now! for glad and golden hours
come swiftly on the wing.
O rest beside the weary road,
and hear the angels sing!

Another example of social awareness was expressed in Theodore Parker's "O Thou Great Friend" written in 1846:

O Thou great Friend to all the sons of men,
Who once appeared in humblest guise below,
Sin to rebuke, to break the captive's chain,
And call Thy brethren forth from want and woe.

Thee would I sing: Thy truth is still the light
Which guides the nations groping on their way,
Stumbling and falling in disastrous night,
Yet hoping ever for the perfect day.

The Quaker poet John Greenleaf Whittier (1807–1892) wrote numerous hymns, including "O, Sometimes Gleams Upon Our Sight." Written in 1850, the hymn expressed the fraught nature of a perilous time as well as millennial optimism:

O sometimes gleams upon our sight
Through present wrong the eternal right,
And step by step, since time began,
We see the steady gain of man,

That all of good the past hath had
Remains to make our own time glad,
Our common, daily life divine,
And every land a Palestine.

Notice that all the foregoing hymns share certain characteristics in common. Each is an appeal addressed to all of humanity. There are no references to doctrinal beliefs of individual sects. Each reference social rather than purely spiritual or religious concerns. For Lowell, it is the eternal struggle between good and evil. For Sears, it is recognition of the struggle of the poor. For Parker, it is a call to the nation to seek the light of truth, while Whittier seeks hope in a time of divisiveness and discontent.

The Social Christianity Movement

Principal leaders of the social Christianity movement included Washington Gladden (1836–1918), Lyman Abbott (1835–1922), Josiah Strong

(1847–1916), Jane Addams (1860–1935), and Frank Mason North (1850–1935). Gladden, Abbott, and Strong were prominent Congregationalist preachers, public figures, and influential writers on the subject of social reform. All three shared a deep concern for what they saw as deterioration of family life among urban factory workers and the poor. Josiah Strong summed up the issue in his *Challenges of the Cities*, writing that workers rarely owned their own homes or land because it was unaffordable. Instead, they commonly lived in crowded tenements, and, where a family was involved, both parents too often had to work just to survive.[10] Addams saw hope in social engineering through the settlement houses she encountered in England. Gladden and Abbott traced much of the problem to inequities in the workplace, while Strong felt change would only come through curbing immigration and recognizing the superiority of white Anglo-Saxon culture and values. From this group of reformers, two names stand out for contributions to sacred music, Frank Mason North and Washington Gladden.

Frank Mason North

The Reverend Dr. Frank Mason North, a prominent Methodist, was active primarily in New York City. He was an advocate for societal reform throughout his ministerial career. A graduate of Wesleyan University in 1872, he served churches in New York and Connecticut before being called to serve on the national level leading mission programs.

Frank Mason North.
Public domain image, *Federal Council Bulletin: A Journal of Religious Cooperation and Inter-church Activities* (public domain ed.), New York City, vol. 1. (https://books.google.com/books?id=lEVQAQAAMAAJ)

---

10. Curtis, *Consuming Faith*, 72.

In 1891, North wrote a series of articles on what he visualized as "Christianized socialism." In 1893 in the Boston periodical *Zion's Herald*, he observed that the "problem of poverty lies very close to the problem of sin."[11] He was instrumental in the establishment of the Open and Institutional Church League (1894), the founding of the Methodist Federation for Social Service (1907), and the creation of the Federal Council of Churches in 1908. Perhaps his greatest achievement was leading his denomination in 1908 to adopt its "The Social Creed of the Methodist Episcopal Church." It was a revolutionary document declaring a church-wide commitment to "equal rights and complete justice for all." It also declared support for industrial reform and labor unions, the abolition of child labor, a reduction in the hours employees could be mandated to work, and better wages. [12]

North's perspective on the social gospel movement is of interest. He was a strong proponent of social justice but saw much of it as the church's institutional responsibility, *not* to be farmed out to private or governmental agencies. The Church of All Nations in New York's Bowery, during North's pastorate, was the embodiment of these ideas, providing food, shelter, and religious support to [the] destitute and [the] outcast. The church was a significant example of what came to be known as an "Institutional Church."[13]

Five Classic Examples of Social Gospel Hymnody

1. *Washington Gladden, "O Master, Let Me Walk with Thee" (1877)*

No hymn is more closely identified with social reform in the late nineteenth century than this one. It originally appeared as a five-stanza poem entitled "Walking with God," which was published in 1879 in *Sunday Afternoon*, a magazine Gladden edited. A friend, Charles H. Richards, saw Gladden's poem and published four of the six stanzas in the hymn form we now know. The four stanzas focus on Christian service as a ministry requiring a servant's heart, concern for the lost, patience, and a firm belief in a hope-filled future because of God's love.

> O Master, let me walk with Thee
> in lowly paths of service free;   SERVANTHOOD
> tell me Thy secret; help me bear
> the strain of toil, the fret of care.

---

11. Lacy, *Frank Mason North*, 83.
12. Richey, Rowe, and Schmidt, *Methodist Experience in America*.
13. Vignone, "Long History of Community Service."

Help me the slow of heart to move	
by some clear, winning word of love;	LOVE, COMFORT,
teach me the wayward feet to stay,	AND CONCERN FOR
and guide them in the homeward way.	THE LOST
Teach me Thy patience, still with Thee	
in closer, dearer company,	PATIENCE
in work that keeps faith sweet and strong,	
in trust that triumphs over wrong.	
In hope that sends a shining ray	
far down the future's broad'ning way;	HOPE FOR FUTURE
in peace that only Thou canst give,	
with Thee, O Master, let me live.	

Two stanzas, which Richards apparently convinced Gladden were "not suitable for the worship services of a church", say much about the trials and criticism Gladden likely faced as prophetic voice for reform. He had been a visible and vocal advocate for working Americans, supporting unionization of industry, and writing *Working People and Their Employers* in 1876. The verses below evoked the courage needed to weather challenges he no doubt faced.

O Master, let me walk with thee	The sore distrust of souls sincere,
Before the taunting Pharisee;	Who cannot read thy judgements clear,
Help me to bear the sting of spite,	The dullness of the multitude
The hate of men who hide thy light,	Who dimly guess that thou art good.

2. Washington Gladden, "Behold a Sower! From Afar" (1904)

This hymn appeared in the 1916 Disciples of Christ hymnal, *Hymns of the United Church,* under the heading "Social Aspiration and Progress" and sung to the tune "Ellacombe." In this hymn, Gladden paraphrases the parable of the sower (Mark 4:3—8) as a reflection of humanity's progress toward the promised millennium:

> Behold a Sower! from afar, He goeth forth with might;
> The rolling years His furrows are, His seed, the growing light;
> For all the just His Word is sown, It springeth up alway;
> The tender blade is hope's young dawn, the harvest, love's new day.
>
> Light up Thy Word; the fettered page from killing bondage free;
> Light up our way; lead forth this age in love's large liberty.
> O Light of light! within us dwell, through us Thy radiance pour,

That word and life Thy truths may tell, and praise Thee evermore.

The text perfectly embodies the essential characteristics of social reform hymnody: optimism and a plea for unity transcending denominations.

3. *Frederick Hosmer, "Thy Kingdom Come, O Lord" (1904)*

Frederick Hosmer (1840–1929) wrote this hymn incorporating a plea for Christian unity with a metaphorical representation of "the kingdom of God." While the term "kingdom of God" appears only in the New Testament, the concept of God as ruler over his kingdom is common in both the Old and the New Testaments. The concept of a New Testament kingdom of God is central to the theology of Walter Rauschenbusch and therefore is key to understanding the theology of the social gospel movement of the early twentieth century. For Rauschenbusch, the kingdom of God would be one in which all Christians, unbound by denominational differences, would unite to create a society and a world modeled after Christ's example. In his *A Theology for the Social Gospel* (1917), Rauscehnbusch wrote:

> IF theology is to offer an adequate doctrinal basis for the social gospel, it must not only make room for the doctrine of the Kingdom of God, but give it a central place and revise all other doctrines so that they will articulate organically with it.
>
> This doctrine is itself the social gospel. Without, the idea of redeeming the social order will be but an annex to the orthodox conception of the scheme of salvation . . . To those whose minds live in the social gospel, the Kingdom of God is a dear truth. . . . It was dear to Jesus. He too lived in it, and from it looked out on the world and the work he had to do.
>
> Jesus always spoke of the Kingdom of God. Only two of his reported sayings contain the word "Church," and both passages are of questionable authenticity. It is safe to say that he never thought of founding the kind of institution which afterward claimed to be acting for him.[14]

Hosmer's hymn has appeared in over seventy denominational hymnals since its writing, including the 1982 hymnal of the Protestant Episcopal Church. It is usually sung to the hymn tune "St. Cecilia," by Leighton G. Hayne.

> Thy Kingdom come, O Lord, Wide-circling as the sun;
> Fulfill of old Thy word, And make the nations one,
> One in the bond of peace, The service glad and free
> Of truth and righteousness, Of love and equity.

---

14. Rauschenbusch, *Theology for the Social Gospel*, 131–32.

> Speed, speed the longed-for time Foretold by raptured seers,
> The prophecy sublime, The hope of all the years,
> Till rise at last, to span Its firm foundations broad,
> The commonwealth of man, The city of our God.

4. *Henry Van Dyke, "Joyful, Joyful, We Adore Thee" (1907)*

It will no doubt be surprising to some that this extremely popular hymn, sung to Beethoven's immortal "Ode to Joy," comes from the social gospel tradition. Henry Van Dyke (1852–1933) was an ordained Presbyterian minister who was a professor of English literature at Princeton from 1899 to 1923. He also served briefly as US ambassador to the Netherlands. Theologically, he embraced the New Theology as a Christian evolutionist, and this was reflected in his preaching. For Van Dyke the heart of the evolutionary message was not survival of the fittest, but rather the inexorable progress of humanity through science. In "Joy and Power," a sermon preached to the Presbyterian General Assembly in Los Angeles in 1903, he summarized these views:

> But there is a new and more wonderful proof of God's presence in the world,—the argument from moral ends in evolution. Every real advance of science makes the intelligent order of the universe more sublimely clear. Every century of human experience confirms the Divine claims and adds to the Divine triumphs of Jesus Christ. Social progress has followed to a hair's breadth the lines of His gospel; and He lays His hand today with heavenly wisdom on the social wants that still trouble us . . .[15]

Reading the familiar words of "Joyful, Joyful" once more while attuned to Van Dyke's theology brings additional color and clarity to the hymn's meaning:

> Joyful, joyful, we adore You, God of glory, Lord of love;
> Hearts unfold like flow'rs before You, Op'ning to the sun above.
> Melt the clouds of sin and sadness; Drive the dark of doubt away;
> Giver of immortal gladness, Fill us with the light of day!
>
> Mortals, join the mighty chorus, Which the morning stars began;
> God's own love is reigning o'er us, Joining people hand in hand.
> Ever singing, march we onward, Victors in the midst of strife;
> Joyful music leads us sunward In the triumph song of life.

---

15. Van Dyke, *Joy and Power*, 22–23.

5. *Frank Mason North, "Where Cross the Crowded Ways of Life" (1905)*

Here, along with Gladden's "O Master, Let Me Walk with Thee," we have one of the most well-known hymns of the social gospel era. North, whose career and accomplishments are discussed briefly above, was a leading figure in missions for the Methodist Episcopal Church during the first decades of the twentieth century. Like all the social reformers of his own time and before him—Gladden, Abbott, Strong, Addams, and Rauschenbusch—he was troubled by brutality, poverty, and injustice he saw in the inner city.

How North came to write this great hymn is illustrative of the passion and idealism imbuing the social gospel movement from its birth. While in New York City in 1905, North was called to preach and chose as his text Matthew 22, the parable of the wedding banquet.

> And Jesus answered and spake unto them again by parables, and said, "The kingdom of heaven is like unto a certain king, which made a marriage for his son, and sent forth his servants to call them that were bidden to the wedding: and they would not come . . . Then saith he to his servants, "The wedding is ready, but they which were bidden were not worthy. Go ye therefore into the highways, and as many as ye shall find, bid to the marriage." So those servants went out into the highways, and gathered together all as many as they found, both bad and good: and the wedding was furnished with guests . . .[16]

Shortly thereafter, while at Methodist headquarters, North was asked to write a hymn text on a missionary theme. Instead of opting for the imperialistic tone of many missionary hymns of his time, North looked to the scenes where much of his own ministry had taken place—the city—and the Matthew text still ringing in his ear, "Go ye therefore into the highways . . ."

> Where cross the crowded ways of life,
> where sound the cries of race and clan,
> above the noise of selfish strife,
> we hear your voice, O Son of Man.

The hymnologist Albert E. Bailey provided a thoughtful perspective on the scriptural basis for North's text. Of the opening stanza, he wrote, "The essence of this stanza lies in the final line: We hear the voice above the city's clamor and strife. And what does that voice say? We may well guess, 'Come unto me, all ye who are weary and heavy laden, and I will give you rest.'"

---

16. Matthew 22:1–3, 8–10 (KJV).

> In haunts of wretchedness and need,
> on shadowed thresholds fraught with fears,
> from paths where hide the lures of greed,
> we catch the vision of your tears.

Bailey continues his exegesis, "Now comes the enumeration of details implicit in stanza 1: the squalid tenements of the slums, the dumbbell-shaped apartments where the only light and air for inner rooms is a narrow shaft into which tenants throw their rubbish . . . , the one hall toilet serving half a dozen families . . . We middle-class respectables *have no conception* of the way people in our great cities have to live . . ."

> Till all the world shall learn your love,
> and follow where your feet have trod;
> till glorious from your heaven above
> shall come the city of our God.

North's third and final stanza, according to Bailey, effectively unites his passion for ministry to the contemporary city with the city of God: "The driving power behind sacrificial service is love and love someday will build the city of God where now is our wretched city of slums."[17]

Rauschenbusch and the Social Gospel

The essential purpose of Christianity was to transform human society into the kingdom of God by regenerating all human relations and reconstituting them in accordance with the will of God. [Walter Rauschenbusch, 1907][18]

---

17. Bailey, *Gospel in Hymns*, 570–71.
18. Rauschenbusch, *Christianity and the Social Crisis*, 15.

Walter Rauschenbusch.
Public media image courtesy of Creative Commons. (http://spider.
georgetowncollege.edu/htallant/courses/his338/students/kpotter/walter.jpg)

Christianity and the Social Crisis, a book published in 1907, sold over fifty thousand copies and went through thirteen printings, exceeding all expectations of its publisher. The book was by Walter Rauschenbusch (1861–1918), a theologian and Baptist minister who taught at the Rochester Theological Seminary in New York. His "kingdom of God" theology was discussed earlier. Harry Emerson Fosdick, one of the greatest preachers of the twentieth century, said Rauschenbusch's work and writings did much to shape his early ministry. He wrote of Rauschenbusch:

> [T]o understand his passion for the Christian social gospel, one must go back to that decade, beginning in 1886, when he was pastor of a little church in "Hell's Kitchen" in New York City. There in the overcrowded, health-destroying, crime-breeding, slums was lighted his burning conviction that a merely individualistic gospel, taking no responsibility for the social conditions that condemn multitudes to physical and moral ruin, was both practically futile and profoundly un-Christian. His social outlook came, as he said, "through personal contact with poverty, and when I saw how men toiled all their life long, hard. toilsome lives, and at the end had almost nothing to show for it; how strong men begged for work and could not get it in hard times; how little children died."[19]

---

19. Fosdick, *Living of These Days*, 109.

Christianity and the Social Crisis, for the first time, drew broad support from clergy and seminarians. It was through Rauschenbusch's writing that what had been many disparate voices coalesced into an actual movement.

Social Hymns of Brotherhood and Aspiration

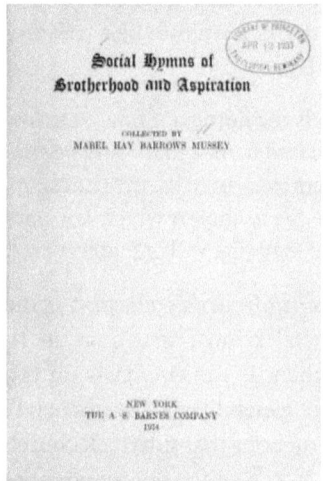

Title Page,
Social Hymns of Brotherhood and Aspiration (1914).
Mabel Mussey, editor.
(https://babel.hathitrust.org/cgi/pt?id=osu.32435017197518&view=1up&seq=5&skin=2021)

One aspect of Walter Rauschenbusch's legacy seldom mentioned was his desire to organize an accessible body of hymns focused on social justice for use in Christian worship. In 1909, he wrote, "[The] Church has developed hymns, prayers and sacraments connected with private redemption, . . .[but] very little about social redemption. . . . We need these social expressions of emotion and purpose. If [we] cannot find them, [we] must create them."[20] Rauschenbusch himself followed through on this concern by contacting the Methodist Episcopal Department of Temperance and Reform the following year and offering to put together a large collection of such hymns if they would publish it. They wouldn't.

A Rauschenbusch hymnal was never completed, but the need had become known, and a number of volumes were produced to fill the void.

---

20. Spencer, "Hymns of the Social Awakening," 85.

Among them were Henry Sloan Coffin's and Ambrose W. Vernon's *Hymns of the Kingdom of God* (1911) and *Social Hymns of Brotherhood and Aspiration* (1914), compiled and edited by Mabel Mussey (1873–1931).

Social Hymns of Brotherhood and Aspiration contained only 111 hymns, but all had a social gospel focus. The seven subject headings around which the hymns are organized reflect this: Aspiration and Faith, Liberty and Justice, Peace, Labor and Conflict, Brotherhood, and Patriotism. Mussey did not intend *Social Hymns* to be a traditional worship hymnal. In the preface, she explained:

> Social aspiration is the dominant note in this book. The editor's first object was to find hymns that could be sung by all people in all places,—in churches, in halls, in schools, in the open. Many hymns, therefore, were chosen which Jew and Gentile, Protestant and Catholic may sing with equal fervor.[21]

Unifying all the hymns in Mussey's collection is the progressive optimism so characteristic of social reform yearnings in the post-Civil War era. A second unifying element is the emphasis on brotherhood. Creeds and dogmatic doctrines were generally viewed by social gospelers as "time- and energy-consuming distractions that sidetrack churches from their true mission of following Jesus in caring for the marginalized, feeding the hungry, and assisting the poor."[22]

Contained in *Social Hymns* is an impressive grouping of hymns by many of the most prominent proponents of the liberal New Theology and social gospelers: Washington Gladden, Theodore Parker, Frank Mason North, Henry Van Dyke, Frederick Hosmer, Samuel Longfellow, John Greenleaf Whittier, Oliver Wendell Holmes, Edwin H. Sears, and James Russell Lowell.

The Legacy of the Social Gospel Movement for the Church and Its Music

For the social gospelers—activists, missionaries, and theologians—the "kingdom of God" was achievable through human endeavor. Settlement houses, achieving justice in the workplace, unions, institutional churches, educational programs, and employment centers—all were a means to this end. Unfortunately, the movement was short-lived. World events and social

---

21. Mussey, ed., *Social Hymns of Brotherhood*, ii.

22. Bjorlin, "Songs of the Kingdom," 20.

unrest inevitably brought into question the bold millennial optimism underpinning the movement.

Reformers of any age are nearly always limited in their vision by cultural norms of the environment in which they are active. Josiah Strong's outspoken view that white, Anglo-Saxon male values and culture were the standard upon which all social progress must be measured was shared by most American Christians, including the reformers.[23] As a result, while much attention was placed on poverty and overcrowding in the inner city, little was said about ethnic prejudice. How was it possible, during the time of the near extermination of the plains Indians, that we find no outcry from an Abbott or a Gladden? How was it possible during an era of such rank injustice that Jane Addams—as great a proponent of social justice as there ever was—could excuse lynching as unfortunate but justifiable when Blacks and whites had to live in close proximity?[24] For that matter, one must question how a movement that was born out of the abolitionist struggle could countenance the rank evil of Jim Crow. Too often, the implied message of reform hymnody was paternalistic: that the reformed and aggrieved should

---

23. In Strong's classic *Our Country* (159–161), he wrote: "The Anglo-Saxon is the representative of two great ideas, which are closely related. One of them is that of civil liberty. Nearly all of the civil liberty in the world is enjoyed by Anglo-Saxons: the English, the British colonists, and the people of the United States . . . In modern times, the peoples whose love of liberty has won it, and whose genius for self-government has preserved it, have been Anglo-Saxons . . . It was left for the Anglo-Saxon branch fully to recognize the right of the individual to himself, and formally to declare it the foundation stone of government. The other great idea of which the Anglo-Saxon is the exponent is that of a pure spiritual Christianity. It was no accident that the great reformation of the sixteenth century originated among a Teutonic, rather than a Latin people . . . Most of the spiritual Christianity in the world is found among Anglo-Saxons and their converts; for this is the great missionary race."

24. In an article entitled "Respect for the Law," written for Boston's *The Independent*, January 3, 1901, Addams wrote, "We are obliged to remember this . . . when we speak of the problems which face the present generation of Southern men: Added to all the difficulties of Reconstruction and restoration of a country devastated by war, they must deal with that most intricate of all problems—the presence of two alien races . . . Let us then assume that the Southern citizens who take part in and abet the lynching of negros honestly believe that that is the only successful method of dealing with a certain class of crimes; that they have become convinced that the southern negro in his present undeveloped state must be frightened and subdued by terror . . . We would send this message to our fellow citizens of the South who are once more trying to suppress vice by violence: That the bestial in man, that which leads him to pillage and rape, can never be controlled by public cruelty . . . Brutality begets brutality." While Addams says lynching and other forms of violence are ineffective to achieve social reform, at no point does she say it is murder. She also seemed to suggest that crimes such as looting and rape actually occurred leading to lynching when, in fact, such infractions were rarely proven in a court of law.

have the same worldview as the mostly white, male, and Anglo-Saxon reformers. An example from Algeron C. Swinburne's "We Mix from Many Lands" (1909):

> O sorrowing hearts of slaves,
> We heard you beat from afar!
> We bring the light that saves;
> We bring the morning star;
> Freedom's good things we bring to you
> Whence all things are.
>
> These have we, these are ours,
> That no priests give nor kings;
> The honey of all these flowers,
> The heart of all these springs;
> Ours, where freedom lives not,
> There live no good things.

Nevertheless, there *was* a developing realization that music had a power akin to the spoken word to inspire, to draw the worshipper to a higher plane of spirituality, and to motivate to action. The hymnody of social reform did much to drive that home. It proved that congregational music could be challenging as well as consoling, prophetic as well as pleasant. It also provided a repertoire of hymns that addressed universally recognized social problems that could be sung universally, regardless of denominational preference. Because it succeeded in doing these things, some social gospel hymnody of the nineteenth and early twentieth centuries has endured to the present day. Inspired by the activist theology of Rauschenbusch and others, socially conscious hymns continue to be written:

> Georgia Harkness, "Hope of the World" (1954)
>
> Fred Pratt Green, "The Church of Christ, in Every Age" (1969)
>
> Dan Schutte, "Here I Am, Lord" (1981)
>
> Martin Leckebusch, "In an Age of Twisted Values" (1995)

The Black Church

Following the Civil War, most former slaves remained in the South. Though aspiring always to self-sufficiency, they were forced into sharecropping as a necessary intermediate step. In that system the landowner owns the land, provides the tools, and rents the tenant farmer living space. In return, the tenant farms the land. When the produce is sold, the tenant receives an agreed upon percentage of the profit, minus his rent, cost of seed, and other miscellaneous expenses. While no longer slaves, southern Blacks found themselves far from self-sufficient and caught in a morass from which they could not easily escape.

The sharecropping system also continued the isolation Blacks had experienced before emancipation. Now freed, the emancipated faced chaos without an anchor for their society. Having churches of their own provided the sense of community they so desperately needed. "An organized religious life," according to E. Franklin Frazier, "became the chief means by which a structured or organized social life came into existence among the negro masses."[25] The Black church and the Black preacher/pastor became the central focus of their communities. Consequently, between 1865 and 1900 the African Methodist Episcopal, African Methodist Episcopal Zion, and other Black denominations surged in growth. Also, several new denominations came into being, such as the Colored Methodist Episcopal Church (1870),[26] the Reformed Zion Union Apostolic Church (1869), and the National Baptist Convention (1880).

A Younger Generation Turns Away from the Songs of Slavery

With Emancipation and war's end in the former Confederacy, traditional spirituals—sung, danced, and shouted as they always had been—still could be heard in isolated communities of older freedmen. But the communal singing of spirituals, and an understanding of how they were sung in the praise houses of slavery, was disappearing.

The reminiscences of some of the original Fisk University Jubilee Singers are indicative of the prevailing attitude of young people regarding the slave songs in the years immediately after the Civil War. Soprano Georgia Gordon Taylor (1855–1913) remembered that an AME church was adjacent to the Fisk campus and that the singing of the old songs could regularly be heard wafting in the air, but that was the music of her parents' generation.[27] Maggie Porter (1853–1942), the group's leading soprano and a frequent soloist, expressed what likely was the common attitude of her peers when the idea of singing spirituals was first broached to the group:

> It was not common for us to spend much time singing slave songs—the tendencies of the freedmen being to leave them behind in the grave of slavery—indeed some seemed almost to regard them as signs of their former disgrace to shun them as one would the prison clothes of the days of his incarceration . . .[28]

---

25. Frazier, *Negro Church in America*, 36.
26. It was renamed the Christian Methodist Episcopal Church (CME) in 1954.
27. Graham, *Spirituals and the Birth*, 30–31.
28. Anderson, *"Tell Them We Are Singing for Jesus,"* 39.

Accompanist Ella Sheppard (1851–1915) provided more detail on the choir's initial exposure:

> The slave songs were never used by us then in public. They were associated with slavery and the dark past and represented things to be forgotten. Then too, they were sacred to our parents who used them in their religious worship and shouted over them . . .[29]

Many Blacks living in the North had an even more visceral dislike of spirituals and sorrow songs. John Wesley Work II (1871–1925), a professor of history and eventual director of the Jubilee Singers, said this of them:

> They have come nearer experiencing civic and political freedom than their brothers in the South and have had their racial bonds greatly weakened. They simply hate the thought of slavery, despise any reference to it, and turn away from anything that reminds them of it. They naturally care nothing for the songs born in slavery. They see no beauty in them, nothing commendable, nothing worthwhile. They do not study them, because obviously they are not fit subjects for serious thought.[30]

Seeking a Musical Bridge between Race and Class —The Spiritual

Between 1865 and 1900, a curious transformation took place. The singing of spirituals, a staple of worship among the slaves in their antebellum invisible churches, would gradually disappear from many Black sanctuaries. They were viewed by many Blacks as unprogressive, old-fashioned, and reminder of a dark time in the African American experience. Some of the old songs had even become common currency in minstrel shows, a denigration of the form and of African American heritage. At the same time, however, the singing of *arrangements* of spirituals, reimagined in full harmonizations often with keyboard accompaniment, would gradually become a performance art in concert halls and even win accolades in Europe. This would earn African Americans the grudging respect of many in bastions of artistic culture. This change was largely brought about by the singing of the Fisk Jubilee Singers, George White, their director, and his accompanist/assistant, Ella Sheppard.[31]

---

29. Graham, *Spirituals and the Birth*, 31.
30. Work II, *Folk Song of the American Negro*, 118.
31. Ella Sheppard Moore (1851–1914)—she married George Washington Moore in

George Leonard White.
Public domain image from *The Story of the Jubilee Singers with Their Songs,* 1880. (https://archive.org/stream/storyofjubileesio2mars/storyofjubileesio2mars#page/n24/mode/1up)

In June of 1866 the name of one George Leonard White (1838–1895) appeared for the first time on the faculty roll of the Fisk Free Colored School. White was born in Cadiz, Cattaraugus County, New York, the son of a devout Baptist blacksmith who played in the town band. At the age of twenty George set out on his own to be a teacher in the town of Chillicothe in southern Ohio. White soon became aware of the town's sizable population of free Blacks. Assisted by friends, he organized a sabbath school in a wooded grove nearby and proceeded to teach basic literacy. Classes were held out-of-doors, using logs and rails for seating.[32]

Though having no formal musical training, White shared his father's love of music. He played the violin, and while he "made no pretensions as a vocalist, his schools [in Chillicothe] were famous for the good singing

---

1882—was central to the story of the Fisk Jubilee Singers. She was born a slave in Nashville. At age five, racial tensions in the city caused her family to flee north to Cincinnati, where she received her musical training. Ella Sheppard was not a student at Fisk University, but rather a member of the teaching staff. She had returned to Nashville after the Civil War to teach piano privately and was recruited to teach music at Fisk. While credit for founding the Fisk Jubilee Singers must go to George White, Ella Sheppard is known to have arranged most of the spirituals the singers sang in common-practice, four-part harmony. She also served as a vocal coach and administrator for the ensemble when it was on tour.

32. Clayton, *History of Davidson County,* 442.

which he had the knack of getting out of his pupils."[33] He had an excellent ear and strong leadership skills, which made him ideally suited for the work of a choirmaster. Those skills would be critical in the years ahead.[34]

White's association with the Fisk Free Colored School, and later, Fisk University,[35] came at the invitation of John Ogden, the school's first principal, in June of 1866. Ogden was overwhelmed with Fisk's meteoric growth and needed administrative help. Before his discharge from the army, White had served briefly as a clerk to Union General "Fighting Joe" Hooker, and this caught Ogden's attention. Initially George White's work at Fisk was purely voluntary. While working at the Freedmen's Bureau, he occasionally helped in Ogden's office and began teaching night classes in music and penmanship.

White also began inviting students to gather in his apartment for evenings of informal singing, and the popularity of the gatherings resulted in increased enrollment in his singing classes. "The progress made by his large singing classes was a surprise and delight to him. With a presentiment, seemingly, of what was coming, he began to pick out the most promising voices and give them that special training for which his own remarkable range of voice, instinct for musical effect, and magnetism as a drillmaster so well fitted him."[36]

Once he had singled out a balanced ensemble of the better singers, White initiated rehearsals for a concert, "A Grand Entertainment," to be presented at the Masonic Hall in Nashville in late May of 1867. The program included a costumed "Harvest Festival Tableau" and selections from the Lowell Mason tunebook *The Song Garden*. Included also was an arrangement of the abolitionist hymn, "No Slave Beneath the Starry Flag," a courageous choice given the simmering racial antagonism in the South at the time. The concert was an impressive achievement, given the slim resources available to White, and raised $400 for the school.

---

33. Marsh, *Story of the Jubilee Singers*, 12.

34. White's Jubilee Singers were almost universally lauded for their transparent blending of voices, a characteristic rather extraordinary for a nineteenth-century choral group. White's leadership, rehearsal discipline, and auditory prowess were largely responsible.

35. In August of 1867, the Tennessee General Assembly authorized the Fisk Free Colored School to be incorporated as "Fisk University."

36. Marsh, *Story of the Jubilee Singers*, 13.

Ella Sheppard (Ella Sheppard Moore), ca. 1870. Public domain line engraving, courtesy of the New York Public Library.

Fisk University and the Spiritual

It was after the arrival in September of 1870 of Adam Spence (1831–1900),[37] Fisk's new president, that we first hear of an interest being expressed in the singing of slave spirituals—the music that would make the Fisk Jubilee Singers famous. Exactly where and when it all started is a mystery. George White, like the missionaries at Port Royal some years before, was intrigued by the music some called "plantation songs" and "sorrow songs." He no doubt encountered them in the contraband camps during the war and heard

---

37. Adam K. Spence was born in Aberdeen, Scotland, in 1831. His family immigrated to Michigan shortly after his birth. He studied at both Oberlin College and the University of Michigan, where he later taught Greek, French, and Latin. Spence organized the first YMCA on the University of Michigan campus, which brought him to the attention of the American Missionary Association and its field secretary, Erastus Milo Cravath. It was Cravath who brought Spence to Nashville as principal of the Fisk Free School and to oversee the transition to a university. (See *Guide to the Spence Family Collection, 1812–1961.*)

them floating on the air from churches near the Fisk campus. He jotted them down when possible. Students also shared songs they remembered. A tradition at Fisk holds that White's choral students informally gathered after regular rehearsals to sing the songs recreationally. Ella Sheppard,[38] White's longtime accompanist, brought several pieces to his attention, including "Swing Low, Sweet Chariot," which her mother had taught her. Also, students arriving at Fisk from different locales would share with each other tunes they had heard their parents sing. Soon hundreds of melodies and melodic fragments had been collected, and Ella began transcribing the melodies onto manuscript paper.

It is likely both she and White took part in harmonizing them, but White—himself a skilled singer—devised a formula for arranging them in straightforward, common-practice four-part harmony. He envisioned hymnlike pieces based on the plaintive spiritual melodies he loved, a bit exotic perhaps but crafted for polished performance. The more rough and improvisatory elements of authentic spiritual singing were mostly replaced by the more refined, cultivated sounds of Bradbury and Mason. Indeed White, and very likely his students, were simply reflecting the musical taste and aspirations of their time.

> What is quite likely is that a more authentic performance would have had difficulty finding an audience in 1871. The irregular rhythms, rhapsodic singing, rasping voices, and bodily movement would have seemed at that time an irreligious blending of the minstrel show and a church service, too offensive to be tolerated. Those southern listeners who observed "praise meetings" were usually horrified by what they heard.[39]

At any rate, Spence recalled, "In the summer of 1871, . . . one day there came into my room a few students with some air of mystery. The door was shut and locked, the window curtains were drawn, and, as if a thing they were ashamed of, they sang some of the old-time religious slave songs now long since known as Jubilee songs."[40] Spence's heart was warmed, and he became an enthusiastic advocate for the singing of the inspiring melodies. Even when the Jubilees were away on tour, Spence insisted that spirituals were regularly sung at college chapel services. This was true even when students were less than enthusiastic about participating. The pioneer African American choral conductor John Wesley Work II, who directed the Fisk Jubilee Singers from 1899 to 1903, said Adam Spence was largely responsible

---

38. Ella Sheppard Moore (1851–1914).
39. Epstein, "Black Spirituals," 63.
40. Ward, *Dark Midnight When I Rise*, 110.

for making the spirituals an essential part of campus life at Fisk and encouraging White to make them the focus of the Singers' repertoire. Work also fondly remembered the effect Spence's love for the spiritual had on him personally.

> When Professor Spence would rise in chapel services and "start" one of these songs, requesting the students to "join in," they would "join in" with a chorus of cold silence. They knew enough to comprehend slavery dialect and bad grammar, and they would have none of either. But Professor Spence would analyze and explain individual songs and show their beauty. This he did day in and day out, illustrating with his own sweet voice and sweeter soul the virtues expressed by the music, until he finally led them to an understanding; and now, at all religious services, these songs are sung in melody abundant and divine. So important a place has this music assumed in the worship and in the life of Fisk that both teachers and students feel that something is lacking, and that there is a distinct loss, if these songs are not sung.[41]

In the spring of 1870, George White planned his most ambitious presentation to date, a fully costumed performance of W. B. Bradbury's *Esther, the Beautiful Queen*. It is not surprising that he was drawn to Bradbury's music. William Batchelder Bradbury (1816–1868) was one of the most successful American composer/educators of the 1840s and '50s. Ticket sales for the concert brought in $300.

The decision was made in June of 1870 to perform Bradbury's cantata at the Greenlaw Opera House in Memphis. Federal Reconstruction was well underway. African Americans for the first time were holding elected office in Tennessee, and angry white Democrats had already begun an effort to unseat them. White's *Esther* cast, on their way back to the Memphis train station, found themselves confronted by a mob of disaffected locals. George White courageously stepped forward, positioning himself between his terrified singers and the disgruntled crowd. He did not flinch when epithets were hurled at him, accusing him of being a damn "Yankee nigger schoolteacher." Instead, he turned to his student singers and asked them to sing a hymn. It was not a spiritual. The text had been written in 1857 by the great Scottish hymn writer Horatius Bonar. It had just recently been set to a tune by Bradbury, which is likely the one White had taught his singers.

---

41. Work II, *Folk Song of the American Negro*, 114–16.

"Beyond the Smiling and the Weeping."
Text: H. Bonar; music: W. B. Bradbury. No. 126 In *The New Golden Shower* (New York: W. B. Bradburty, 1866).

As the music drifted over the belligerent crowd, Ella Sheppard would recall, they became quiet and slowly drifted away. Left standing there alone was their ringleader who, dissolved into tears, begged the students to sing the hymn once more.[42] This experience, along with the reception the singers had received at the National Teachers' Convention two years before, likely

---

42. Ward, *Dark Midnight When I Rise*, 118–19.

helped inspire White to a more radical and unheard-of plan for outreach and fundraising—a national tour.

By early spring of 1871, George White was convinced that a small, highly select, well-trained ensemble of student singers, touring the northern states could be an effective way to raise funds while, at the same time, enhancing the school's reputation as an institution of higher education. But first, there was the question of how Caucasian audiences would respond to an African American group singing in concert. In no way did the association want to sponsor performances that might be confused with the blackface minstrel shows then pervasive. Those tended to be vulgar, patronizing to Blacks, offensive to churchgoers, and identified with the theater against which there was deep-seated Victorian prejudice. Second, it needed to be asked: Was this scheme providential or was it simply the product of overreaching ambition and hubris? Finally, there was the most burning concern of all—financial viability.[43]

When September of 1871 arrived, White found himself at his Rubicon. The singers had rehearsed throughout the hot summer months on faith that the hoped-for tour would materialize. In desperation, he told his father-in-law, Erastus Cravath,[44] "It will kill them . . . if they don't go." The prospects for success were dismal. The band of singers had no appropriate performance attire. Not one owned an overcoat to face the colder northern winter.[45]

The Tour

On October 6, 1871, a party of twelve musical missionaries from Fisk University arrived at the Nashville train station and prepared to board a train for Cincinnati. They included George White, the director, nine singers, Ella Sheppard, their accompanist, and Mary Wells, who was assigned by the AMA to chaperone. "Taking every cent he had, all the school treasury could spare, and all he could borrow, and leaving his invalid wife and two small children in the care of a faithful colored nurse," Ella wrote years later, "Mr. White started, in God's strength . . ."[46] Their long-awaited tour of the northeastern United States had begun. Adam Spence came with them to the station and offered this prayer:

---

43. Anderson, *"Tell Them We Are Singing,"* 31–32.

44. Erastus Milo Cravath (1833–1900) was a field secretary of the America Missionary Association who had been actively involved in the founding of Fisk University as well other Black colleges in Georgia and Tennessee. George White married his daughter Laura.

45. Anderson, *"Tell Them We Are Singing,"* 35.

46. Sheppard Moore, "Historical Sketch," 46.

Oh Lord, if this thought comes from Thee, prosper the going out of these young people. Care for and protect them and bring them back to us bearing their sheaves with them, and we shall give Thee the glory.[47]

George White had planned the first leg of the tour following the path of the Underground Railroad northward through Ohio. Early on they would make appearances in Cincinnati and Chillicothe, places White knew well, then north to Columbus, Oberlin, and Cleveland with numerous stops between. The typical plan was to sing in worship at one or more large white churches, using those appearances to promote an upcoming concert where admission would be charged. When singing in small-town churches they would seek a freewill offering. A typical concert would open with White, one of the students, or a representative of the American Missionary Association delivering a message about the mission to the freedmen in the South, a historical sketch of Fisk, and a plea for donations. White did not conduct the singers in concert. Rather he stood "like a coach at the sidelines," while responsibility for cuing the singers and giving pitches was left to Ella Sheppard at the keyboard.

At this point repertoire for the tour consisted of a variety of solos and choral selections that White hoped would be pleasing to audiences in the North. Stephen Foster's "Old Folks at Home" was a concert staple as was the shape-note white spiritual "Washed in the Blood of the Lamb." Each program would also include several slave songs, but they were not the focus of the repertoire in early tour concerts. "Go Down Moses" was generally featured prominently. "Steal Away," soon to become a "signature song" for the Fisk singers, also appeared frequently. A few other spirituals, often not listed in printed programs, were inserted as entr'actes or encores.

Racial discrimination dogged White and his singers throughout their nine months on the road. It began at the very start as the group boarded a train in Nashville headed north. White had purchased first-class tickets but because of their color the singers were crowded into the caboose, a conveyance characterized by them as a "chicken box."[48] After spending their first night away in a Black boarding house, the Fisk students visited the fine arts building of the Cincinnati Industrial Exposition then in progress. There, White asked Ella Sheppard to play and his ensemble to sing. Pike's description of white northerners, so unaccustomed to artistry by African Americans, would characterize most audiences the group would encounter in the weeks and months to come.

---

47. Ward, *Dark Midnight When I Rise*, 126.
48. Pike, *Singing Campaign*, 75.

> On reaching the musical department, Professor White requested Miss Sheppard to play Annie Laurie, with variations upon the piano. Almost at once a crowd gathered, and exclamations were heard on all sides, "Only see! She's a nigger." "Do you see that?" "Do you hear that? Why, she's a nigger."
>
> On being invited to sing, the troupe gave [the] "Star-Spangled Banner" . . . and other favorites, every note seeming to increase the crowd, till it became so great one could scarcely tell where it commenced. Wherever the Singers moved the crowd followed, with an admiration entirely new to these people, who, for many years, had no rights a White man was bound to respect.[49]

On November 15, 1871, the near-exhausted Fisk band arrived in Oberlin, Ohio, for the founding convention the following day of the National Council of Congregational Churches. The following afternoon, White and his ensemble gathered in the gallery of Oberlin's First Congregational Church while the council meeting droned on below. The agenda was tight, they had been told, and the only option was to sing during a recess to the afternoon session. At the appointed time, delegates rose from their seats to stretch and mill about the hall. Over the clamor, the chairman stood and asked if those present would listen to "the colored youngsters of Fisk University." Wolcott added a few brief remarks, but few were listening.[50]

The students stood to sing. Because of the narrow time slot, a decision was made that the ensemble would sing only spirituals. It would have been reasonable to stun the crowd into silence with something loud and brash, but, instead, the singers began pianissimo with a rendition of "Steal Away." The gathered delegates quickly became silent and gave the music their rapt attention. Ella Sheppard recalled that those attending were "deeply impressed and endorsed our cause."[51] The Fisk performance earned sustained applause, and a spontaneous collection raised $131 for the group. One connection made at Oberlin would have far-reaching implications for the tour: Among the delegates was the Reverend Thomas K. Beecher, pastor of the Independent Congregational Church in Elmira, New York, and the brother of Henry Ward Beecher. Beecher invited White and his singers to perform in Elmira.

After the Oberlin performance, George White knew that, no matter how polished their singing, they could not continue as "the colored choir from Nashville." They needed an identity—a name which encapsulated who

---

49. Pike, *Singing Campaign*, 76.
50. Ward, *Dark Midnight When I Rise*, 135.
51. Sheppard Moore, "Historical Sketch," 46.

they were and what their purpose was. He found himself drawn to the word "Jubilee." Leviticus 25 spoke of the "Year of Jubilee," when trumpets would sound, slaves freed, and all debts forgiven. In addition, and likely based on that same scripture, January 1 had been celebrated as Jubilee Day since the signing of the Emancipation Proclamation in 1863. The next morning White greeted his singers with the news. From henceforward they would be known as the Jubilee Singers.

After a brutal two-month performance schedule White and his singers finally left the state of Ohio, traveling due east to Meadville, Pennsylvania, and on to New York State. Upon arriving at Elmira, New York for the highly anticipated concerts at the Reverend Thomas K. Beecher's First Presbyterian Church, the old problem of lodging raised its head again. Arriving after midnight, White tried unsuccessfully to board the singers at three different hotels, all of which refused. It was after midnight when lodging was found and the nine exhausted singers and their accompanist stumbled to their rooms for a few hours of sleep.

On Sunday, December 10, in Elmira, the singers were featured at a praise meeting at Beecher's church, which was followed later in the week by an admission-required concert at the Elmira Opera House. The opera house concert would be the best attended and most successful financially of all the performances so far. Perhaps the most important takeaway from Elmira, however, was that the Rev. Beecher wrote his brother, Henry Ward Beecher, strongly recommending that the Jubilee Singers be allowed to sing at Plymouth Church in Brooklyn.

After midnight on December 14, 1871, the Fisk University Jubilee Singers checked into New York City's Cosmopolitan Hotel. At first it appeared their luck had finally run out. They had no problem getting rooms, but in the morning they were informed that persons of color could not be seated in the hotel dining room. They would have to take meals in their rooms and would be charged twice the usual rate. White complained. After he explained the group's mission to hotel management, the dining room restriction was lifted, and they were offered a discounted room rate. Even with the discount, however, White realized that he and his singers would be completely destitute if they stayed at the Cosmopolitan more than a day or two. Fortunately, the national headquarters of the American Missionary Association and Erastus Cravath's office were in New York City. Cravath and two other officers of the association opened their Brooklyn homes for the next six weeks to White and his troupe.[52]

---

52. Marsh, *Story of the Jubilee Singers*, 28.

Unfulfilled Aspirations

Unbeknownst to White and the Jubilees, George Whipple from the AMA had met with Beecher and got an invitation for the ensemble to sing a few selections at the close of the church's Friday evening prayer meeting on December 22.[53] Having already gotten an enthusiastic letter from his brother, Thomas, Henry Ward promptly agreed. Friday evening prayer meetings at Plymouth were no insignificant affairs. Because of Beecher's standing as a pulpiteer, they were commonly attended by seven to eight hundred people, a broad cross-section of Brooklynites and New Yorkers. Beecher prayer meetings tended to be informal affairs where the famous preacher, sitting on a platform in a comfortable, upholstered, throne-like easy chair would receive questions ranging from theology to social issues, literature, and the arts. The Brooklyn and New York papers eagerly covered the meetings and detailed Beecher's every thought on a weekly basis.[54]

The singers had stationed themselves behind Beecher's rostrum, concealed by a curtain. George White—all 6'5" of him—crawling on hands and knees gave pitches for the opening song.[55] Pike's narrative provides a feeling for the Jubilees' presentation:

> The first hymn they sang was, " O, how I love Jesus!," and I shall never forget the rich tones of the young men as they mingled their voices in a melody so beautiful and touching, I scarcely knew whether I was "in the body or out of the body." So abiding was the impression it made upon my mind. I could not be satisfied for a long time to have them appear in public without giving the people the benefit of this hymn. Slave songs followed, occupying about twenty minutes, when Mr. White motioned to the Singers to retire.[56]

---

53. Marsh, *Story of the Jubilee Singers*, 29.

54. Ward, *Dark Midnight When I Rise*, 153.

55. There is disagreement about which song opened the Jubilee's program. Gustavus Pike, who was present, remembered it being the gospel song "Oh How I Love Jesus," while Maggie Porter remembered it being the spiritual "Steal Away." I believe the gospel song is the more likely. The text was relatively new at the time, first published in 1855, while the traditional melody with its verse/chorus format first appeared as an early nineteenth century campmeeting song. According to Ellen Jane Lorenz "Oh How I Love Jesus" was well known to the plantation slaves. "Steal Away," which was becoming the Jubilee's signature song, makes perfect sense to have been White's choice for the closing—a perfect "sending forth."

56. Pike, *Jubilee Singers*, 109.

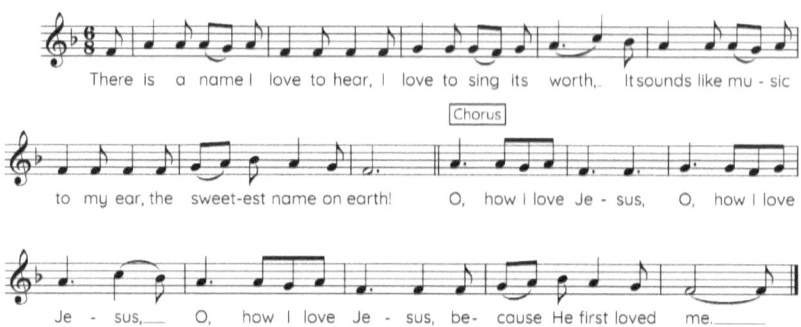

"O How I Love Jesus."
Verse text: Frederick Whitfield, 1829–1904; melody and chorus, traditional African American.

"I often feel my heart quicken," Maggie Porter, principal soprano soloist for the group, wrote, "when I recall myself for the first time standing before the vast audience . . . and again hear my voice tremble as I attempted to lead, 'Steal Away to Jesus.'"[57] The following account of a later Jubilee performance in London in 1873 captures the effect "Steal Away" had on listeners:

> They stand with head erect and somewhat thrown back, and looking upwards, or with eyes nearly closed. It is evident the audience is nothing to them, they are going to make music and listen to one another. Their first song was, "Steal away to Jesus." It was sung slowly; the first chords came floating on our senses like gentle fairy music, and they were followed by the unison of phrase, "Steal away—to Jesus," delivered with exquisite precision of time and accent; then came the soft chords, and bold unison again, followed by the touching, throbbing cadence, "I hain't got long to stay here"; next follows the loud, lofty trumpet call in unison, " My Lord calls me, the trumpet sounds it in my soul; I hain't got long to stay here." But it seems as though the angels also were speaking to the sufferer, for we hear again those beautiful chords delivered with double *pianissimo*, whispering to the soul, "Steal away to Jesus."[58]

The Jubilee presentation lasted about twenty minutes throughout which the audience was transfixed. Beecher himself was brought to tears at points and wrote later, "It was as still as death. They sang two pieces. Tears were trickling from a great many eyes. They sang three pieces, and

---

57. Ward, *Dark Midnight When I Rise*, 153.
58. Pike, *Singing Campaign for Ten Thousand Pounds,* 33–34.

[the audience] burst out into a perfect enthusiasm of applause; and when they had sung four and five pieces, my people rose up in mass . . ."[59]

Porter recalled that the prayer meeting offering brought in about $250, but White and his troupe had a sense that the ground had indeed shifted. With Henry Ward Beecher's enthusiastic endorsement, the ensemble was inundated with invitations to sing. The tour would continue through March of 1872—eight months on the road. By mid-February, they were often performing every evening with occasional school appearances during the day. A highlight came on Tuesday, March 5, 1872, when the Jubilee Singers were invited to the White House to sing for President Grant. Appropriately, given the song's identification with the emancipation of the slaves, they sang "Go Down Moses."

When the Fisk University Jubilee Singers returned to the Nashville campus in March, they had not only raised sufficient funds to erase the indebtedness incurred from their travels, but also brought with them the necessary $20,000 to purchase the Fort Gillem site for the new campus. Just two months later White and many of the same singers would depart on a second, triumphal, ten-month tour of New England highlighted by a featured slot at Patrick Gilmore's World Peace Jubilee in July. Just one month after their return to Nashville from that foray, the Jubilees embarked on twelve-month tour of the British Isles. Additional American and European tours followed. The Fisk Jubilee Singers would, in total, raise over $150,000 for the fledgling school, which included the cost to construct Jubilee Hall, the first classroom building on the Fort Gillem campus. It is still in use and a national historic landmark.[60]

---

59. Graham, *Spirituals and the Birth*, 43.

60. The complete history of the Fisk Jubilee Singers has been told and retold. The most complete and authoritative modern studies include Ward's *Dark Midnight When I Rise* and Toni Anderson's *"Tell Them We Are Singing for Jesus."* For the most detailed period account, see Gustavus Pike's *Jubilee Singers and Their Campaign for Twenty Thousand Dollars*.

Jubilee Hall, Fisk University. Public domain image, Library of Congress, Call number HABS TENN,19-NASH,7A—9.

Henry Ward Beecher never forgot the Fisk University Jubilee Singers or his role in bringing them to the attention of the American public. He reflected on that experience in a speech given to the Freedmen's Aid Society in London in 1886, just six months before he died.

> I think there never was such a phenomenon as the building of Fisk University. We talk about castles in the air. That is the only castle that ever I knew built by singing from foundation to top . . . They sang through our country, and it is one of the things that I cherish with pride that they took their start from Plymouth Church Lecture Room . . . From that, they went on conquering to conquer. They sang up and down our own country; they sang here; they sang in the presence of the Royal Family; they sang before the Emperor William; and when they came back, they had earned one hundred and fifty thousand dollars for the building of Fisk University.[61]

---

61. "Henry Ward Beecher and the Fisk Jubilee Singers," 3. The success of the Fisk Jubilee Singers spawned a host of imitators. By 1900 there were at least eighty-five ensembles active in the United States, Europe, South Africa, Australia, New Zealand, and India identifying themselves as "jubilee" ensembles. Some were minstrel entertainments trading in nothing more than racial stereotypes and the basest humor. Post-war

Aftermath

THEY THAT WALKED IN DARKNESS sang songs in the olden days—Sorrow Songs—for they were weary at heart . . . Ever since I was a child these songs have stirred me strangely. They came out of the South unknown to me, one by one, and yet at once I knew them as of me and of mine. Then in after years when I came to Nashville I saw the great temple builded [*sic.*] of these songs towering over the pale city. To me Jubilee Hall seemed ever made of the songs themselves, and its bricks were red with the blood and dust of toil. Out of them rose for me morning, noon, and night, burst of wonderful melody, full of the voices of my brothers and sisters, full of the voices of the past.

Little of beauty has America given the world save the rude grandeur God himself stamped on her bosom, the human spirit in this new world has expressed itself in vigor and ingenuity rather than in beauty. And so by fateful chance the Negro folk song—the rhythmic cry of the slave—stands today not simply as the sole American music, but as the most beautiful expression of human experience born this side of the seas. It has been neglected, it has been, and is, half despised, and above all it has been persistently mistaken and misunderstood, but notwithstanding, it still remains as the singular spiritual heritage of the nation and the greatest gift of the Negro people. —W. E. B. Du Bois, 1903[62]

What George White and Ella Sheppard did was develop and make popular arrangements of traditional spiritual melodies, recast using European harmonic principles. The Jubilee Singers made it no secret that what they were offering was cultivated and artistic. Black folk spirituals as sung

---

Black colleges, however, saw in the Fisk musicians an example to be emulated. Among the more prominent were the Hampton Institute Singers from Virginia and the Tennesseans from Fisk's sister school in Nashville, Central Tennessee College. There were also the Shaw Jubilee Singers of Raleigh, North Carolina, the New Orleans Jubilee Singers, and Sheppard's Colored Jubilee Singers, who performed mostly in Connecticut and Vermont. Of these, the Hampton Singers and the Tennesseans are most noteworthy. While inspired by the success of the Jubilees, they chose to build their repertoire around singing spirituals in the more free-wheeling style of slave cabin worship. The Tennesseans carried the idea a step further by presenting Slave Cabin Concerts which were fully costumed and colorfully staged. In essence, these groups were drawing a distinction between what ethnomusicologist Sandra Jean Graham calls the "concert spiritual" as innovated by the Jubilee Singers and the "folk" or traditional spiritual of the plantation.

62. Du Bois, *Souls of Black Folk*, 250–51.

on antebellum plantations were participatory, requiring clapping, dancing, and a variety of sounds beyond singing. Words and melody could be endlessly variable, because there was no one correct set of lyrics or tunes. The participants were their own audience. Improvisation was a key element and was linked directly to the emotion of the individual singer. In contrast, the spirituals as sung by the Jubilees were conceived to be performed for an audience with perfectly understandable diction and a flawless transparent blending of voices. They stood still while performing, allowing the emotional fervor of the music to be conveyed by voices and facial expression only.

The Jubilee Singers narrative has important implications for the development of African American music in America. Their unaccompanied singing of concert spirituals was the beginning of a tradition which would extend through generations to the present day. From Hall Johnson, Harry Burleigh, John W. Work, William Dawson, and Jester Hairston, to Wendell Whalum, Andre Thomas, Moses Hogan, and Rollo Dilworth—all the master arrangers of the choral spiritual must trace their lineage back to George White, Ella Sheppard, and the Jubilee Singers.

Reconstruction and Reform in the Late Nineteenth Century

The period 1865 to 1900 was both momentous and heartbreaking with regard to African American history. Systemic racism, somewhat overshadowed by the abolition debate in the North, resurfaced everywhere after the Civil War and gained traction as African Americans moved north in search of employment and places where they hoped to enjoy their newly acquired freedoms. Federal Reconstruction, though a noble experiment, met stiff resistance in the South aided greatly by the perpetrations of the Ku Klux Klan. When the federal government officially ended the program in 1877, white supremacy—with Blacks relegated to second-class citizenship—became the norm. Racial segregation, already ubiquitous in the South, became federally endorsed on the national level when its constitutionality was upheld by the United States Supreme Court in *Plessy vs. Ferguson* (1896).

Meanwhile to the North, the Protestant-led social gospel movement focused largely on issues related to urban decay, unemployment, and abuses in the industrial sector. "African Americans were cast as members of a separate, far less developed race and thus were set outside the bounds of 'civilized' society."[63] They found themselves usually excluded from employment on the factory line and forced into lower paying and less desirable

---

63. Jackson, *Singing in My Soul*, 10.

occupations. The social gospelers largely ignored what was referred to as the "negro issue" or minimized its significance.

Jane Addams's biographer, Robin Benson, noted that the first great influx of African Americans came to Chicago after *Plessy v. Ferguson* in the mid-1890s, and that during the establishment of Hull House Addams had little contact with them. She, Benson wrote, was also a pragmatist. "She knew she needed to keep her pool of wealthy White donors, many of whom, despite their liberality in other areas, still operated under profound racist assumptions."[64] Washington Gladden, though he preached in later life in support of the writings of W. E. B. Du Bois, declared that extending voting rights to African Americans would lead to "the disenfranchisement of people of intelligence and character and the enthronement of the illiterate and degraded." Lyman Abbott, who chaired the Mohonk "Conference on the Negro Question,"[65] defended the exclusion of Blacks from attending while "White southern gentlemen" would be welcomed. In the *Christian Union*, he wrote: "A patient is not invited to the consultation of doctors on his case."[66] It was paternalism in full view.

---

64. Benson, *Jane Addams*, 48.

65. When Federal Reconstruction ended in 1877 with the withdrawal of troops from the last two southern states, it was felt by many to be a relief. Violence, lynching, and concern about Jim Crow intolerance were gnawing concerns, however. This led to two conferences "On the Negro Question" at Lake Mohonk, New York, in 1890 and 1891. The conferences were significant historically because they represented a first effort to bring northern and southern leaders together to discuss the issue of race. Unfortunately, no African Americans were invited to participate, and opinions expressed at the conferences were shaped by the white racial bias of the time.

66. Abbott, "Lake Mohonk Conference," 830.

Booker T. Washington

Booker T. Washington.
Photographic portrait by Francis Benjamin Johnston, ca. 1895. Creative Commons. (https://commons.wikimedia.org/wiki/File:Booker_T._Washington_by_Francis_Benjamin_Johnston,_c._1895.jpg)

Booker T. Washington (1856–1915) was a leading voice for racial justice in the years after the war who recognized the power of sacred music and in particular the power of singing. A former slave himself, Washington believed that equality would come when Blacks achieved economic independence. He fervently supported educational programs focused on workplace and agricultural skills, which he believed would boost the value of Black workers and create a demand for products of their own creation. Washington considered going into the ministry and pursuing a seminary degree.

> In 1878 I went to Wayland Seminary in Washington and spent a year in study there . . . The deep religious spirit which pervaded the atmosphere at Wayland made an impression upon me which I trust will always remain.[67]

Washington spoke publicly on many occasions about the critical role the church played in the African American community. In essence, he viewed religious faith for its usefulness as a bulwark against disappointments, pain, and injustice. In a lecture to students at Tuskegee, he said:

> I have spoken of these as some of the things that we do not want to have you do at school. What are some of the things that we do want you to learn to do? We want to have you learn to

---

67. Washington, *Story of My Life*, 45.

see and appreciate the practical value of the religion of Christ. We hope to help you to see that religion, that Christianity, is not something that is far off, something in the air, that it is not something to be enjoyed only after the breath has left the body. We want to have you see that the religion of Christ is a real and helpful thing; that it is something which you can take with you into your classrooms, into your shops, on to the farm, into your very sleeping rooms, and that you do not have to wait until tomorrow before you can find out about the power and helpfulness of Christ's religion.[68]

In his autobiography *Up from Slavery*, he recalled that as a nine-year-old boy he had witnessed the scene among the slaves when the Civil War ended. Freedom for all was at long last a reality, and the singing made an indelible impression on him:

As the great day drew nearer, there was more singing in the slave quarters than usual. It was bolder, had more ring, and lasted later into the night. Most of the verses of the plantation songs had some reference to freedom. True, they had sung those same verses before, but they had been careful to explain that the "freedom" in these songs referred to the next world and had no connection with life in this world. Now they gradually threw off the mask and were not afraid to let it be known that the "freedom" in their songs meant freedom of the body in this world.[69]

Later in life he expanded on his love of the music he had grown up with, in a lecture to students at Tuskegee:

There is no part of our chapel exercises that gives me more pleasure than the beautiful Negro melodies which you sing. I believe there is no part of the service more truly spiritual, more elevating. Wherever you go, after you leave this school, I hope that you will never give up the singing of these songs. If you go out to have schools of your own, have your pupils sing them as you have sung them here, and teach them to see the beauty that dwells in those songs . . .

What is the most original product with which the Negro race stands accredited? . . . Without hesitation I answer: . . . Those beautiful, weird, quaint, sweet melodies which were the simple, child-like expression of the anguish, the joy, the hopes, the

---

68. Washington, *Character Building*, 228.
69. Washington, *Up from Slavery*, 19–20.

burdens, the faith, the trials of our forefathers who wore the yoke of slavery.[70]

Booker T. Washington's legacy was not, however, without blemish. In *Up from Slavery*, he wrote that, for the majority of slaves, relationships with masters and overseers were practically congenial. This naively positive view did not reflect the reality of slavery for many. It played directly into the lost cause myth which empowered white supremacy and Jim Crow. Washington's very success caused him to be criticized as a Black elitist, out of touch with society—especially urban society.

W. E. B. Du Bois

W. E. B. Du Bois.
Photographic portrait by C. M. Battey, ca. 1919.
Creative Commons. (https://commons.wikimedia.org/wiki/File:W.E.B._William_Edward_Burghardt)_Du_Bois,_1868-1963_LCCN2003681451.jpg)

A leading voice for a *new* generation of African Americans was William Edward Burghardt Du Bois (1868–1963). Unlike Washington, W. E. B. Du Bois was a member of the post-slavery generation. He grew up in Great Barrington, Massachusetts, and was not a descendant of slaves. He was active in the First Congregational Church of Great Barrington, and the congregation took up a collection to cover his tuition when he went off to college at Fisk University in Nashville. After Fisk University, Du Bois went on to Harvard to earn a second bachelor's degree in history and did graduate work

---

70. Washington, *Character Building*, 251, 253.

in philosophy in Berlin. Returning to the United States in 1895, Du Bois became the first African American to earn a PhD from Harvard University. He taught briefly at Wilberforce University in Ohio, and the University of Pennsylvania, before beginning a long tenure at Atlanta University. He also served as director of publications for the NAACP in New York. Over the course of his long career, Du Bois never hesitated to champion racial equality with a prophetic zeal to the discomfort of his peers.

In 1897, he presented a paper to the American Negro Academy in which he directly challenged Frederick Douglass's premise that Black Americans needed to be integrated into white society. For Du Bois there was a tormenting duality to existence for African Americans. "One ever feels his two-ness," he wrote, "an American, a negro; two souls, two thoughts, two unreconciled strivings; two warring ideals in one dark body, whose dogged strength alone keeps it from being torn asunder."[71]

Over time, Du Bois also came to differ sharply with Booker T. Washington. The idea that southern Blacks were being asked to be patient and submit to continued discrimination, segregation, disenfranchisement, and employment abuse in return for northern investment in Black businesses and education as well as a few crumbs from the southern establishment was abhorrent to him.

> Today, two classes of Negroes, confronted by a united opposition, are standing at a parting of the ways. The one counsels patient submission ... The other class believes that it should not submit to being humiliated, degraded and remanded to an inferior place ... It believes the Negro should assert his full title to American manhood and maintain every right guaranteed him by the Constitution of the United States.[72]

Du Bois spoke often and without reservation about the importance of sacred song to the cultural identity and faith of African Americans. References to spirituals are ubiquitous throughout *The Souls of Black Folk* each chapter being introduced with a quotation from one of them. Though writing three decades after the Civil War, W. E. B Du Bois still viewed the African American spirituals not simply as quaint and curious relics, but as a key component in Black spirituality.

> Even so is the hope that sang in the songs of my father's well sung. If somewhere in this whirl and chaos of things there dwells Eternal Good, pitiful yet masterful, then anon in His

---

71. Du Bois, "Strivings of the Negro People," 194.
72. Du Bois, "Strivings of the Negro People," 194.

good time America shall rend the Veil and the prisoned shall go free. Free, free as the sunshine trickling down the morning into these high windows of mine, free as yonder fresh young voices welling up to me from the caverns of brick and mortar below—swelling with song, instinct with life, tremulous treble and darkening bass.[73]

Such a range of disparate subjects in a single chapter! But there are commonalities and lessons among them all regarding ministry. The reform movements of the post-Civil War years may have been flawed; their reformers unsuccessful in achieving all they aspired to. Yet the hymns and songs of both the social Christianity/social gospel movement and the Fisk Jubilee Singers were incontrovertible evidence of music's power for prophetic witness.

---

73. Du Bois, *Souls of Black Folk*, 263.

Chapter 12

"THE GREAT URBAN REVIVAL" OF MOODY AND SANKEY

To this point, we have surveyed four significant strains of church music activity during the post-Civil War period. Elite, mainline churches brought new levels of professionalism to music leadership: choral directors and organist/choirmaster combinations, rehearsing chorus choirs, and professional quartets. New and more impressive pipe organs became commonplace. A second strain, the fledgling social gospel movement, was particularly prominent among Congregationalists and Unitarians. Both the cultivated mainliners and the social gospelers were driven in part by the liberal New Theology and Christian Darwinism. Meanwhile, a third strain consisting of missionaries and reformers from the Freedmen's Bureau chose an independent path focused on the plight of newly emancipated African Americans. A fourth strain descended directly from the United States Christian Commission of the Civil War and the YMCA. It spoke largely for white evangelicals who rejected Darwinism and social gospel thinking and were determined to bring about a new age of revival to America's rapidly growing cities.

Personifying that fourth strain were the revivals of Dwight Lyman Moody and his musician/collaborator, Ira David Sankey. They provided a theological and musical counterweight to the social and theological trends within mainline Protestantism. The intended target of Moody's witness, the white middle and lower classes, set him apart. An avowed premillennialist, Moody also stood apart in rejecting the optimism of many Victorian Christians regarding social progress. The hot-button issues—social justice for the poor, unemployment, worker's rights, unions, suffrage, and racial equality—concerned him little. The driving force behind Moody's witness, which he inherited from generations of conservative evangelicals before him, was the immediate and imperative need for *conversion*. The influence of his revivals was vast. So successful was the Moody/Sankey juggernaut that revivalists to the present-day model their efforts at least in part on it.

In January of 1866 the *Chicago Tribune* devoted a large column to a growing revival at the Clark Street Methodist Episcopal Church. Ordinarily such events would warrant a short paragraph in the paper's "Religious Intelligence" section. In this case, however, over twelve column inches were allotted in the prized "City News" section. Something was afoot. The *Tribune* took note:

> Yesterday was the second day of the week of concerted prayer, held in all parts of the world by all classes of Christians on land and sea, at all missionary stations . . . And even before the week has been entered upon, it is noticeable that from all parts of the country are being brought tidings of a work already begun widely throughout the land.[1]

Each day of the week, sermons and testimonies were featured on designated topics: duties of Christians to each other; confession; the Christian church; the Christian nation; the family; missions; and promised blessings to faithful believers.

On Tuesday, January 9, the topic for the day was "The Christian Church."

> At the stroke of nine, the main audience room of the Clark Street M. E. Church presented a large audience, to which additions were constantly made during the first thirty minutes of the hour to which the session is confined, there being arrivals even later. Nine o'clock comes early on a mid-winter morning. Among those present were many of our city pastors, and many of those present had come directly from church prayer meetings of an even earlier hour . . .[2]

Midway through the service, a young man (Dwight Moody) rose to speak. His observations were brief and to the point. "Too few Christians in Chicago", he said, "knew what God was doing in our midst." He went on to cite the impressive number of conversions that German-language churches on Chicago's north side were receiving and wondered aloud why mainline churches were falling behind. Dwight Moody, then twenty-eight years old,

---

1. "Week of Prayer," 2.
2. "Week of Prayer," 2.

was well known to Chicagoans. Before the war he had been a successful entrepreneur selling shoes, an impetuous recruiter of inner-city youth to enroll in Sunday schools, and an enthusiastic promoter of the Young Men's Christian Association (YMCA). Later in 1866 he would be appointed vice president of the Chicago Sunday School Union.

Massachusetts-born Dwight Lyman (D. L.) Moody (1837–1899) had arrived in Chicago just ten years earlier. He was born on a small hardscrabble farm in East Northfield, Massachusetts, to Edwin J. and Betsy Holton Moody. In 1854, against the wishes of his mother, D. L. left home and traveled to Boston in search of opportunity beyond the confines of East Northfield. Moody was only in Boston for two years, 1854 to 1856, but they were formative years for all that he would become. First, he was able to prove himself as a shoe salesman. Such was his prowess in sales that, less than two years later, he would be considered to manage a shoe store himself when it opened. Second, Moody began what would become a lifelong connection with the YMCA.[3] Third and most important, he found Christ through the teaching and witness of a Boston Sunday school teacher, one Edward Kimball. Prior to his arrival in Boston, one might say D. L. was only nominally "religious." Though their connection was brief, Kimball's influence on Moody's life was momentous. It was Kimball to whom Moody credited his conversion.

Shoe Salesman Turned Evangelist—Moody in Chicago

Bret Harte, the American short story writer and poet, called Chicago "the Queen of the West."[4] Chicago in the 1850s was a capitalist's dream. It was built on the entrepreneurial spirit, the desire to make money and lots of it. Historian Donald Miller describes it as "a scene of boiling economic activity and technological ingenuity, American industrialism's supreme urban creation."[5] During the decades after the Civil War, it would become a city of mind-boggling contrasts. "City of millionaires, Chicago had some of the

---

3. The YMCA was established as a nondenominational evangelical organization in London in 1844. In the United States, it would be a driving force behind the 1857–1858 "Businessman's Revival." It would also play an important supporting role in the activities of the United States Christian Commission (USCC) during the Civil War and the Great Urban Revivals of Moody and Sankey in the post-war years. Beginning in the 1880s and gaining traction after 1900, the association would transition to a more secular organization focused on physical fitness and recreation. (Zald and Denton, "From Evangelism to General Service.")

4. Cited in Sheahan and Upton, *Great Conflagration*, 184.

5. Miller, *City of the Century*, 17.

worst slums in the civilized world."[6] While often referred to as the "most American of cities," "over three-quarters of its residents were of foreign parentage in 1893."[7] A center for America's temperance movement, it nevertheless had a saloon for every two hundred inhabitants and its next-to-largest industry was distilling liquor. It was both a stronghold of anti-labor forces and a home base for trade unions.[8] The wide-open promise of Chicago appealed to Dwight Moody's need for adventure. Its pioneer spirit, as compared to New England's stuffiness, also drew him west. On September 15, 1856, D. L. boarded a train for the thousand-mile journey to Chicago. After arrival, he quickly established an outstanding reputation as a shoe salesman.

> "He would never sit down in the store," writes one of his fellows, "to chat or read the paper, as the other clerks did when there were no customers, but as soon as he had served one buyer, he was on the lookout for another. If none appeared, he would start off to the hotels or depots, or walk the streets in search of one. He would sometimes stand on the sidewalk in front of his place of business, looking eagerly up and down for a man who had the appearance of a merchant from the country, and some of his fellow-clerks were accustomed laughingly to say, 'There is the spider again, watching for a fly.'"[9]

By 1860, according to his son, William, Dwight had accumulated between seven and twelve thousand dollars in savings (equivalent to $350,000 in 2021 dollars). [10]

The combination of magnetic charisma, dogged determination to succeed, and aggressive salesmanship—qualities honed in Boston and perfected in Chicago—served Dwight Moody well. It was his gift, and he soon realized it could be utilized in his spiritual life as well. When he arrived in the Windy City, fresh from his spiritual conversion a year earlier, Dwight set about finding a church home. He brought with him a letter of introduction from the Reverend Kirk at Mount Vernon Church in Boston and found a warm welcome at Chicago's Plymouth Congregational Church.

Moody immediately began putting his entrepreneurial skills to work in the service of the church. Plymouth, like most churches of the era in England and America, required church members to rent pews, its principal

---

6. Miller, *City of the Century*, 191.
7. Miller, *City of the Century*, 191.
8. Miller, *City of the Century*, 191.
9. McDowell et al., *What D. L. Moody Means*, 59.
10. Moody, *Life of Dwight L. Moody*, 63.

source of income.[11] Moody saw this as a recruitment challenge. He rented a pew initially and went out into the streets.

> Remembering, it may be, his success in childhood as a recruiting agent for the Sunday School at Northfield, he conceived the idea that he had a special talent for this work, and at once hired a pew, which he undertook to fill every Sunday. He would hail young men on the street corners, or visit their boardinghouses, or even call them out of saloons to share his pews. Whether the novelty of the invitation or the irresistible earnestness and cordiality of the young man induced a large number to attend, the object was at any rate attained, and before long he was renting four pews, which he filled every Sunday with his strangely assorted guests.[12]

Between 1857 and 1861, Dwight Moody made his mark on Christian education to the poor and dispossessed in Chicago. Working with likeminded friends, he established the North Market Street Mission School in the very heart of Chicago's underbelly, the notorious Levee District, known as "Little Hell." Moody's friend from the Chicago YMCA, William Reynolds, looked in on a class and recalled:

> The first meeting I ever saw him in was in a little old shanty that had been abandoned by a saloonkeeper. Mr. Moody had got the place to hold a meeting in at night. I went there a little late; and the first thing I saw was a man standing up, with a few tallow candles around him, holding a negro boy, and trying to read him the story of the Prodigal Son; and a great many words he could not make out, and had to skip. I thought, "If the Lord can ever use such an instrument as that for His honor and glory, it will astonish me." After that meeting was over, Mr. Moody said to me, "Reynolds, I have got only one talent; I have

---

11. By the early nineteenth century, even New England's Reformed churches could no longer receive funding from state taxes. The era of "disestablishment" had begun. One of the most popular ways to generate funds was the "pew rental system." It was based on the idea that in a typical church only a fraction of the total member population attended regularly and provided the bulk of financial support. Those members, therefore, were offered their choice of seating with the cost of rental determined by the location of the pew. There would be a few "free" pews available, but they were usually in less desirable locations, and there was commonly a stigma associated with them as they tended to be occupied only by visitors and "charity cases." (See Olds, "Privatizing the Church," 292–93.)

12. Moody, *Life of Dwight L. Moody*, 47.

no education, but I love the Lord Jesus Christ, and I want to do something for Him . . ."[13]

The North Market Street Mission School well reflected Moody's personality and priorities. It was completely nonsectarian with an evangelistic focus. From the start he recognized that the street children, many from broken homes with little education and most undisciplined and hardened by day-to-day survival, could not be taught in a conventional manner. He saw in them the same challenges he had faced at their age and fervently hoped to reach them on their level. Moody himself still struggled with reading, comprehension, and grammar. To address the need, he brought in assistants to instruct while he focused on recruiting and building a personal connection with the students. The meetings were at first more fellowship gatherings than formal classes. They were typically held on Sunday afternoons and lasted about two hours. A lesson was followed by a free time activity, often recreational, and then singing.

By 1861, weekly attendance had ballooned to over a thousand children a week divided into over seventy classes. The number in attendance was so astounding that visitors from all over the city and far away came to observe. Dwight's extraordinary success as an organizer and recruiter was gaining him national attention. En route to Washington DC for his inauguration, President-elect Abraham Lincoln stopped to look in on Moody's North Market Street Mission School and to marvel at Moody's work. A Mrs. N. M. Simonds recalled:

> It was after Mr. Lincoln had been elected President the first time and before his inauguration. At that time, I was a teacher in the North Market Street Mission, of which the late John V. Farwell was superintendent, and the late Dwight L. Moody was the evangelistic worker. My class was known as the Bridewell class, because it had so many rough boys out of the Bridewell.
>
> I suppose it was through Mr. Farwell that Mr. Lincoln came to attend the Sunday school one time. Of course, it was very exciting for the boys to have the coming President visit them. Mr. Lincoln took much interest in the lesson and the method of instructing the boys, and he admired the enthusiasm with which they sang.[14]

---

13. Daniels, *D. L. Moody and His Work*, 36.
14. Simonds, "At the Sunday School," 87.

John Farwell himself recounted Lincoln's words.

> As he was about to leave, Mr. Moody remarked . . . "If Mr. Lincoln desires to say a word, as he goes out, of course all ears will be open."
>
> As he reached the center of the hall—evidently to go without saying a word—he suddenly stopped, and made a most appropriate Sunday School address, in which he referred to his own humble origin, and closed by saying, "With close attention to your teachers, and hard work to put into practice what you learn from them, some one of you may also become president of the United States in due time like myself, as you have had better opportunities than I had."[15]

In his mission school work Dwight Lyman Moody was instinctively, if not consciously, reaching out to a segment of society the established churches had left behind:

> Fine architecture, fresco and gilding; inlaid pulpits and upholstered pews; three-bank organs; quartette choirs, whose music costs a dollar a stave; chimes of bells; elaborate vestments; rhetoric, poetry, and all manner of literary and social attractions, as used in the higher circles of society—are so many arguments in favor of [Moody's] missionary sugar, which better than any of the aforementioned persuasions, was adapted to coax these young barbarians to attend the means of grace . . . By its help, it is said that Moody made the acquaintance of every child within reach of his Mission; and, through the children, he was known by almost every man and woman . . .[16]

Concurrent with his mission work, Dwight Moody took a key role in the founding of Chicago's chapter of the YMCA in 1858.

By 1860, Dwight had reached spiritual crossroads. Despite his success in business, his evangelical work had become his true passion. He decided to follow his faith. "The greatest struggle I ever had in my life was when I gave up business," Moody often said in later life.[17]

---

15. Farwell, *Early Recollections*, 9.
16. Daniels, *D. L. Moody and His Work*, 38–39.
17. Daniels, *D. L. Moody and His Work*, 38–39.

Evangelist in Wartime

During the Civil War, Dwight Moody chose to serve, not in the military, but as a delegate for US Christian Commission and a missionary representing the Chicago YMCA. Over the four years of wartime, Moody took an active role in raising volunteers for the 72nd Illinois Volunteer Regiment and building a ministry to the troops stationed at Camp Douglas, near Chicago.[18] His superb organizational and management skills were ideally suited for this. Within a short time, Moody had gotten 3,500 hymnals printed for distribution to the troops.[19] He either led or oversaw eight to ten prayer meetings every twenty-four hours at the camp and arranged for a "Christian Association Tent" erected for each regiment.

The United States Christian Commission would send out five thousand delegates over the course of the Civil War. Among the first wave of those delegates was Dwight Moody, dispatched south to Kentucky in October of 1861.[20] Having heard of his work at Camp Douglas, the chaplain of an Illinois regiment stationed near Elizabethtown requested Moody minister at their encampment. In all, Dwight Moody went to the front lines of the Civil War nine times.

The war years were a blur of hyperactivity for Moody. "Back and forth, between Chicago and the various camps and battlefields, with tireless vigor and jubilant faith, Mr. Moody toiled and traveled, during the four terrible years of the war; which by the work of the Christian Commission, were transformed from four great harvests of death into four great harvests of souls . . ."[21] In the first days of 1863, Moody actually found himself in the field of fire while tending to the wounded at the Second Battle of Murfreesboro (also known as the Battle of Stones River). Moody would also be present for Second Battle of Chattanooga in August of 1863, the famous Hampton Roads Peace Conference at City Point, Virginia, and the liberation of Richmond in 1865.

---

18. Construction of Camp Douglas had begun shortly after the surrender of Fort Sumter in the spring of 1861. It was named for Senator Stephen A. Douglas, who donated some of the land for the site. It was used exclusively as a regimental training camp from November of 1861 through February of 1862, after which it was made a prisoner of war camp. Because of its lack of drainage, inadequate latrines, no medical facilities, and moist conditions from Lake Michigan, about 17 percent of all prisoners housed there died of pneumonia and other diseases. Because of that, Camp Douglas has often been referred to by historians as "the northern Andersonville."

19. Probably the first edition of *The Soldier's Hymn Book* published by the Chicago YMCA in 1862.

20. Dorsett, *Passion for Souls*, 91.

21. Daniels, *D. L. Moody and His Work*, 96.

The Civil War can be seen as a pivotal experience in Dwight Moody's life. He went into the war, confident in his faith but insecure as a public speaker. His success ministering among the troops was life-changing. He came out of the war ready to pursue a career as an itinerant evangelist. From thence forward, he would commit himself to national and international revivalism. This would include the "Great English Campaign" of 1873 to 1875, which would bring him international fame, his triumphal return to the United States, and a series of mammoth revivals in Philadelphia, New York City, Chicago, and Boston between 1875 and 1877.

Re-envisioning Revival for the Late Nineteenth Century

Dwight L. Moody.
Public domain engraving. Library of Congress. (http://hdl.loc.gov/loc.pnp/cph.3b08344)

Aspects of the Great Urban Revival as envisioned by Dwight Moody were obviously rooted in the revivals of Charles Grandison Finney a half century before. Principal among them was the focus on "second birth" regeneration or conversion over all else. Doctrinal differences, denominational identity, and social concerns—all were of secondary importance to being "born again."

Conversely, there were important differences. Unlike Finney, Lyman Beecher, George Whitefield, and other famous revivalists of the past, Moody was not ordained and did not desire to be. His revivals were almost entirely lay driven. While he labored valiantly to garner support and cooperation from the various denominations, he saw most doctrinal differences as a stumbling block to successful evangelism. While preaching in Edinburgh, Scotland, Moody was quoted in the press asking, "If we're going to live in heaven together, why shouldn't we be united here?" Moreover, he declared, "It did little good to work for a denomination, if one wasn't working first for

Christ."[22] Late in life, Moody went on to say, "Too frequently when Christians get together, they seek points upon which they differ, and then go at it ... The Christian denominations too often present a spectacle of a political party, split into factions and unable to make an effective fight."[23]

Another striking change from earlier revival efforts was Moody's use of "marketing" and his open dependence on the moneyed classes for funding. Again, given Dwight's unqualified success as a salesman and connections in the business community, it was natural that as an evangelist he would utilize the tools and methods he earlier had honed. "Some ministers think it undignified to advertise their services," Moody wrote. "It's a good deal more undignified to preach to empty pews, I think." [24] All of this was expensive, and, beginning with J. V. Farwell back in Chicago, Dwight Moody depended on the support of America's titans of business to mount his witness. His list of elite supporters also included mining magnate William E. Dodge, Cyrus McCormick, and John Wanamaker.[25]

A Standardized Formula

Dr. James C. Downey (1931–2010), late professor of music and humanities at William Carey University, described a typical pre-Civil War revival meeting as follows:

> A revival meeting may be described as a mass-assembly of people of various ages who gather to hear forceful preaching of an evangelist who denounces them for reprehensible social practices—called "sin" by the revivalist. The people are encouraged to seek an intense emotional experience called "conversion" which absolves them of their wrong-doing and assures them of "salvation," or a blissful life after death through the objective atonement of Christ on the Cross.[26]

---

22. Evensen, *God's Man for the Gilded Age*, 29.

23. "Quotable Moody."

24. Bell, *Crusade in the City*, 216–17.

25. John V. Farwell (1825–1908) founded the John V. Farwell Company, a highly successful dry goods business in Chicago. He was also a founder of the Chicago YMCA. William E. Dodge (1805–1883) co-founded Phelps, Dodge & Company which would become one of America's largest mining concerns. He also served in the US House of Representatives representing the state of New York. Cyrus McCormick (1809–1884), also based in Chicago, was an inventor and founder of the McCormick Harvesting Machine Company. John Wanamaker (1838–1922) founded Wanamaker's Department Store in Philadelphia and served as US Postmaster General during the administration of Benjamin Harrison.

26. Downey, "Revivalism, the Gospel Songs," 115–16.

Dwight Moody held to that definition in the post-Civil War years but softened it. The hyper-emotion and violent conversions of the camp meeting era were replaced with warm, personalized invitation. Instead of focusing on a wrathful, judgmental God, the image of Jesus as "protector, friend, and brother" was evoked.[27]

The entire dramatic progression of the revival meeting was directed toward conversion. The great American revivals—Brooklyn, October to mid-November 1875; Philadelphia, mid-November 1875 to January 1876; New York City, February through April 1876; Chicago, the fall of 1876; and Boston, January of 1877—all had three services most days (morning, afternoon, and evening). Each meeting began with an extended period of congregational singing supported by large choirs intermingled with solos usually performed by Ira D. Sankey. It was followed by a time of prayer. The message, delivered by Moody himself or another member of the evangelistic team, was generally thirty to forty minutes in length. Moody avoided theological intricacies, focusing instead on a specific theme—love, spiritual peace, or forgiveness, for example—and then providing a biblical basis using a broad range of Scripture. Well known stories from both Old and New Testament and the parables of Jesus were a favorite resource, combined often with personal anecdotes from his life. A plea for converts and more music closed the service as converts were directed to the "Inquiry Room" (on a lower floor or a nearby but separate space).[28]

Moody and the Music of Revival

Singing held prominent place in Moody's work in Chicago from his earliest Sabbath school efforts on.

> The scholars were bubbling over with mischief and exuberance of vitality and sorely tried the patience of the teachers; but the singing was a vent for their spirits, and such singing I never heard before. The boys who sold papers in the street had an indescribable lung power, and the rest seemed not far behind.[29]

Singing, of course, had been an important part of the early nineteenth-century camp meeting experience. But it was *ad hoc* and informal—individual preachers and exhorters moving about the grounds, encouraged singing,

---

27. Downey, "Revivalism, the Gospel Songs," 118.

28. The "anxious seat" or "mourners' bench" of the Finney era was replaced by Moody with the more personalized (and less intimidating) post-meeting "inquiry room."

29. Moody, *Life of Dwight L. Moody*, 56.

usually improvised, as the spirit led them. At a Moody revival, at least one half of every meeting was devoted to song. This was something new, and Moody was not a passive observer. He would even at times even take on the role of conductor with the congregation as his choir.

> "You sing over there!," he would call out. "Now you sing. Now you sing down there. And now, everybody sing!" When asked why he did this, Dwight replied earnestly, "They will forget what I say, but if they learn 'Jesus, Lover of My Soul,' and will sing it to themselves, they will get it in their mouths at least, and they will get the Gospel along with it!"[30]

One of Moody's biographers, J. W. Chapman, painted an indelible eyewitness portrait of the evangelist as a champion of singing in corporate worship:

> When he was sitting during the first part of the service, . . . you would scarcely think he was noticing what was going on, and suddenly he would be on his feet announcing a hymn, and while he could not sing himself, yet he was superb in his power to make other people sing. "Isn't that magnificent," he would say, as voice after voice would take up the great chorus. "Now the gallery, sing—that is my choir up in the gallery! Now show the people what you can do; now the men, now the women, now altogether," until it would seem as if greater singing one had never heard in all his life.[31]

One can speculate about how Dwight Moody came to place such a priority on congregational singing and devotional solo work as he envisioned a newer approach to revivalism. Both Jerome Stillson and John Farwell, who worked side by side with him as he built the North Market Street Mission School program, wrote of the calming effect singing had on normally rambunctious youth and how Moody used it to reorient their attention back to the more serious subject matter of the day. Moody himself repeatedly observed that lengthy sermonizing was ineffective, and music was essential to keep audiences engaged.

Moody's Civil War experiences almost certainly influenced his prioritizing of music in worship. Accounts of Christian Commission delegates suggest that many a dying combatant's last wishes were to hear a hymn sung. Dwight Moody knew this and recognized the spiritual power of song.

---

30. Harvey, *D. L. Moody*, 88–89.
31. Chapman, *Life and Work*, 20.

Moreover, most veterans returned home with a fondness for the singing they experienced during the war, and Moody instinctively tapped into this.

As for outside influences prioritizing music in worship in the post-war years, two immediately come to mind: the work of Philip Phillips, the "Singing Pilgrim," and the "Praise Meetings" of Eben Tourjée.

Philip Phillips, the "Singing Pilgrim"

Philip Phillips,
The Singing Pilgrim. Public domain engraved image taken from *Biography of Gospel Song and Hymn Writers* (1914). (https://commons.wikimedia.org/wiki/File:Biography_of_Gospel_song_and_hymn_writers.djvu)

Philip Phillips (1834–1895) received his early instruction in music from a singing school and had an outstanding and expressive tenor voice. He started his own singing school at the age of nineteen and went into business selling pianos and melodeons. He built a singing career, initially singing temperance songs while accompanying himself at the keyboard. Around 1857 he was engaged as director of music at the First Baptist Church in Fredonia, New York. It was there that he refined his skills in programming sacred vocal selections to carefully match scriptural texts being read.

> After the minister had ended his discourse, Philip, imbued with the spirit of the subject, would deliver the same subject in song. Many a conscience which could not be aroused by the sound reasoning or the fervent appeals of the sermon, was suddenly stirred under one of these sweet songs which followed. The solo was sung just before the invitation to penitents was given, and it, no doubt, had much to do with the increasing numbers that pressed forward from evening to evening for prayers. After the meeting, Philip would frequently invite unconverted young

men to his room and there pray with them and urge them to become Christians . . . In this distinctive feature of evangelical service, Philip Phillips evidently is the pioneer.[32]

Word of Phillips's work in Fredonia spread, and he was soon leading musical conventions and selling melodeons throughout western New York State and Pennsylvania. He also began compiling and publishing tunebook collections of his own songs and those of others. Like Dwight Moody, Phillips chose not to enlist when war came, but to become active with the US Christian Commission. His second collection, *Musical Leaves* (1863), was distributed widely among the troops; and Phillips regularly visited US Army field hospitals to sing, always with his melodeon in tow.

Phillips's travels with the USCC culminated in the invitation to sing for the commission's fourth anniversary commemoration before the US House of Representatives on January 29, 1865, with President Lincoln in attendance. Phillips sang his own musical setting of a poem by Ellen B. Gates, "Your Mission."

> If you cannot on the ocean
> Sail among the swiftest fleet,
> Rocking on the highest billows,
> Laughing at the storms you meet,
> You can stand among the sailors,
> Anchored yet within the bay.
> You can lend a hand to help them
> As they launch their boat away.
>
> If you cannot in the conflict
> Prove yourself a soldier true—
> If where fire and smoke are thickest,
> There's no work for you to do;
> When the battlefield is silent,
> You can go with careful tread.
> You can bear away the wounded;
> You can cover up the dead.
>
> O not, then, stand idly waiting
> For some greater work to do;
> Fortune is a lazy goddess—
> She will never come to you.
> Go and toil in any vineyard,
> Do no fear to do or dare;
> If you want a field of labor,
> You can find it anywhere.

Lincoln was clearly moved and passed a note to his Secretary of State, William Seward, who was chairing the meeting:

> Near the close, let us have "Your Mission" repeated by Mr. Phillips. Don't say that I called for it. A. Lincoln.[33]

Lincoln's approbation was picked up in the national news and was pivotal for Phillips's career. As a result, he decided to focus his career on a

---

32. Phillips and Clark, *Philip Phillips*, 18.
33. Phillips, *Singing Pilgrim*, 99.

singing ministry. Drawing from his repertoire of sacred vocal music, which included many songs in popular gospel/Sunday school style, he devised what he called a Song Service. Later, he expanded on the concept, introducing what he referred to as "sermons in song." His concerts lasted about ninety minutes with Bible readings interspersed with solo rendering of songs.[34] Phillips ultimately made four highly successful tours of the British Isles, the first in 1868, and paved the way for the historic two-year Moody/Sankey tour that began in 1873.

By 1870 Philip Phillips's singing artistry was well known in Chicago, and he was at the height of his fame. He had sung there many times, including at Farwell Hall, where he and Dwight Moody became acquainted. In the spring of 1871 Moody was invited to speak at the California Sunday School Convention and decided to expand the trip, preaching in San Jose, San Francisco, Salt Lake City, and Denver. Philip Phillips came along to provide musical leadership.

The similarities between Phillips's and Moody's juxtaposing of Scripture and sermon with appropriate music are telling. Dwight Moody knew that the spiritual thrust of his ministry required music. "He had long realized the importance of song in gospel meetings. Although he himself . . . was not a singer, he could be powerfully impressed by a hymn. He saw that singing created a mood of worship and response . . ."[35]

Eben Tourjée and the "Praise Meeting"

Eben Tourjée.
Public domain image from January–June 1913 issue of *Etude* magazine. Courtesy of Wikimedia Commons. (https://commons.wikimedia.org/wiki/File:Eben_Tourjee_001.jpg)

---

34. Phillips's gospel songs were strophic, but without the popular chorus/refrains for audience participation that would be characteristic of many Moody/Sankey gospel hymns.

35. Harvey, *D. L. Moody*, 88.

Another important development in the mid-nineteenth century in the area of congregational singing was the work of Eben Tourjée (1834–1891). Tourjée, a Rhode Islander of Huguenot ancestry, became editor of the *Massachusetts Musical Journal* and built an estimable reputation as a teacher and leader of musical conventions while still in his teens.[36]

Musical credentials aside, Eben Tourjée was an evangelistically oriented Methodist. Like Dwight Moody, he was closely associated with the YMCA, serving as president of the Boston Chapter from 1871 to 1872, and enthusiastically supporting Moody's revival work. For the 1877 Boston Revival, Moody selected Tourjée to organize and direct a two thousand-member chorus, divisible into four separate ensembles that would alternate between services for the four months of the campaign.

Tourjée had a lifelong commitment to congregational singing. Beginning in 1851, he hosted informal evening Meetings of Praise or Sings in his home and later at churches. So was born Tourjée's concept of a "praise meeting." As attendance grew, he made these gatherings church-wide activities. In the pre-Civil War years, choirs were often independent groups drawn from an area singing school. Sunday schools were also lay run and seen as independent from the basic church program. Tourjée managed to bring together choir, Sabbath school, and a large contingent from the congregation into a single activity intended to encourage congregational singing—the praise meeting.

The praise meeting concept engendered great interest because it went beyond harangues from the pulpit and heavily marketed tunebooks and songsters and was focused instead on getting people singing—all kinds of people, musically literate or not. The concept was straightforward: a worship service comprised almost entirely of music. Tourjée built each service around a general spiritual theme and alternated Scripture readings with appropriate hymns. Hymns were either well known or easily taught.[37] The

---

36. Early on Tourjée recognized the need for academic and professional training for musicians. In 1854 he opened a music school in Fall River, Massachusetts, "based on the conservatory or class system of instruction, perhaps the first of its type in the United States." From 1855 through 1860 he worked as an organist and private music teacher in Newport and then, in 1861, became music director of the East Greenwich Seminary. He traveled to Berlin In 1863 to explore continental church music practices, returning to take up residence in Boston, and, in 1867, co-founded the New England Conservatory of Music. In both 1869 and 1872, Tourjée was selected by Patrick Gilmore to organize and direct mammoth choruses for his Peace Jubilees. At that point, he was arguably America's most well-known choral conductor and one of its most highly esteemed teachers of music. (See Eskew, "Eben Tourjée.")

37. Nason and Beale, *Lives and Labor*, 297.

similarity between Tourjée's praise meetings and Philip Phillips's Song Services and Sermons in Song is plain to see.

> An exercise so arranged may teach many truths impressively and be carried on with far more life and spirit than an ordinary prayer meeting. It tends also to call forth the inert musical ability of the people and to promote congregational singing in the churches.[38]

From the late 1860s forward, Tourjée tirelessly toured, lectured, and led praise meeting demonstrations, all for the cause of better, more spirit-filled congregational singing. It was no accident that in the Great Urban Revivals of Moody and Sankey, the opening section of singing followed Tourjée's model closely and was sometimes referred to as the "praise meeting."

The Preacher and Pitch

Dwight Moody himself did not sing and considered himself unable to. Virtually all of Dwight Moody's contemporary biographers refer to him as having difficulty with pitch differentiation. With minimal schooling and constantly doing odd jobs to help his struggling family survive, it is quite possible he had little exposure to music of any kind before his late teens and that may have accounted for it.

Moody's challenges with pitch were legendary and well known to all who worked with and for him. George Stebbins recalled being introduced to Dwight in Northfield in 1876, who then invited him to accompany a praise and prayer meeting that evening. While playing the church's cabinet organ he was disconcerted by discordant sounds and stopped playing to determine if the instrument was malfunctioning.

> I was not long in doubt, however, for I soon heard the voice of Mr. Moody, singing away as heartily as you please, with no more idea of tune or time than a child. I then learned for the first time that he was one of the unfortunates who have no sense of pitch or harmony, and hence are unable to recognize one tune from another or to sing in unison or harmony with others.[39]

Moody, though not himself a singer, knew that if group singing was to be a critical part of his ministry, he needed competent musicians to lead it. Therefore, from his first forays into Sunday school work he always had at least one singer/song leader at his side. At the North Market Street

---

38. Nason and Beale, *Lives and Labors*, 298.
39. Stebbins, *Reminiscences*, 64–65.

School, Jerome Stillson and one T. B. Carter—both of whom could sing—filled that role.

It is noteworthy that the first musician Moody contacted to assist him in his "Great English Campaign" of 1873 to 1875 was Philip Phillips. Phillips, having prior commitments, was unavailable, so Moody approached Philip Bliss (to be discussed below). Bliss was also committed with church and revival responsibilities and was reluctant to leave his young family for an extended period of time, and so Dwight turned to Ira D. Sankey. So began one of the great collaborations in the history of American sacred music.

The most prominent of Dwight Moody's musical associates were George Coles Stebbins (1846–1945), Philip Paul Bliss (1838–1876), James McGranahan (1840–1907), Daniel Brink Towner (1850–1919), and Ira David Sankey (1840–1908), all of whom gravitated to Chicago from the East in the post-war years.

Ira David Sankey

Ira Sankey was born on August 28, 1840 and raised on the far western end of Pennsylvania in the unincorporated community of Edinburg. Sankey had his introduction to music joining in the singing of hymns with his mother and father during cold winter evenings. In 1857, the family moved four miles east to the town of New Castle. The seventeen-year-old Sankey, already showing promise as a singer, was hired as choir director at the Jefferson Street Methodist Episcopal Church.

Ira D. Sankey.
Public domain image (Library of Congress No. xmp.did:E347439585F0E111803D8 4EEA038F15F).

With the coming of war in 1861, Sankey enlisted in the 22nd Pennsylvania Regiment and was stationed at Fort McHenry in Baltimore.[40] While enlisted, Sankey organized a male chorus and assisted the regimental chaplain with worship services. "I soon found several other young men who could render the same service," Sankey wrote. "And we were frequently invited out by families who heard of the singing of the 'boys in blue.'"[41]

Sankey's fateful connection with Dwight L. Moody came through the YMCA. In 1867, a chapter of the association was opened in New Castle, and Ira Sankey became its secretary and later, its president. In that role, he attended the International Convention of the Young Men's Christian Association in Indianapolis, in 1870. Sankey and friends from New Castle were in the audience for a prayer meeting at which Dwight Moody was preaching.

> It was announced that Moody of Chicago would lead a six o'clock morning prayer-meeting in the Baptist Church. I was rather late, and therefore sat down near the door with a Presbyterian minister, the Rev. Robert McMillan, a delegate from my own county, who said to me, "Mr. Sankey, the singing here has been abominable; I wish you would start up something when that man stops praying."[42]

Sankey wisely chose that most well-known hymn of the post-Civil War years, "There Is a Fountain Filled with Blood," text by William Cowper and tune by Lowell Mason. The singing was predictably robust and caught Moody's attention. When Sankey and he were introduced, Dwight impulsively told him he should immediately give up his work in New Castle and join his evangelistic efforts.

---

40. There is much conflicting information regarding the length of Ira Sankey's military service. Sankey himself in his biography, *My Life and the Story of Gospel Hymns and Sacred Songs and Solos,* says only "[a]t the expiration of my term" (17). Mel Wilhoit, in an October 1992 *Cross Rhythms Magazine* article, wrote that Sankey "served two short terms in the Union Army." (Numerous biographers state or at least imply he served through 1863 (Wikipedia, for example), while others suggest he served throughout the war (Wilder, "Shelter in the Time of Storm"). Charles Ludwig, in *Sankey Still Sings*, implies that Sankey remained in military service through 1863 and was discharged with the rank of sergeant. Some of the confusion arises from Sankey himself. He often told a tale of encountering a former Confederate sharpshooter who remembered an incident in 1862. The man said he had Sankey in his sights, but hearing him singing "Saviour, like a shepherd, lead us," he was unable to pull the trigger. A good story, but evidence suggests Sankey had mustered out of the military by that time. I would like to thank Corie Zylstra, archivist with Crowell Library of the Moody Bible Institute, for locating Sankey's official record in the National Park Service Civil War Database, which says Sankey served for three months in 1861 and was discharged with the rank of private.

41. Sankey, *My Life,* 16.

42. Sankey, *My Life,* 18.

As Sankey prepared to return home to New Castle, Moody approached him again. Nonplussed, Sankey boarded his train east, but soon decided indeed he would cast his lot with Moody. He returned to Chicago in early 1871, leaving his wife, Fanny, for the time being in New Castle, and began a busy schedule of music ministry with Dwight Moody and his evangelistic circle.

On October 8, of 1871, when the Great Chicago Fire struck, Moody and Sankey were together leading an evening prayer meeting at Farwell Hall. Sankey, like Moody, had painful memories of the conflagration.

> At the close of his address, Mr. Moody asked me to sing a solo, and standing by the great organ at the rear of the platform I began the old, familiar hymn, "Today the Saviour Calls." By the time I had reached the third verse, "Today the Saviour calls: For refuge fly. The storm of justice falls, And death is nigh," my voice was drowned by the loud noise of the fire engines rushing past the hall, and the tolling of bells, among which we could hear, ever and anon, the deep, sullen tones of the great city bell, in the steeple of the old court-house close at hand, ringing out a general alarm.
>
> Tremendous confusion was heard in the streets, and Mr. Moody decided to close the meeting at once, for the audience was becoming restless and alarmed. As the people dispersed, I went with Mr. Moody down the small back stairway leading into the old Arcade Court, and from our position there we watched the reflection of the fire, half a mile away, on the west side of the city, as it cast its ominous glare against the sky.[43]

Since coming to Chicago, Sankey had taken up temporary lodging in an apartment at Farwell Hall. It was in the direct path of the fire and would be destroyed. He managed to gather up his essential belongings and spent several anxious hours in a small boat offshore in Lake Michigan as he watched the city reduced to ashes. As soon as he was able he boarded an eastbound train for Pennsylvania. "It seemed as though this might end my work in Chicago," Sankey recalled, "but two months later Mr. Moody telegraphed me to return and help him in the new temporary 'Tabernacle,' which had by that time been erected."[44]

---

43. Sankey, *My Life*, 27.
44. Sankey, *My Life*, 15.

A Moody-Sankey Partnership Is Born

The year 1873 brought Moody's history-making two-year tour of England, Scotland, and Ireland with Sankey as his soloist and songleader. In June of 1873, Sankey and Fanny sailed across the Atlantic to Liverpool. While this was Dwight Moody's third trip to the British Isles, he was relatively unknown. Nevertheless, through his YMCA contacts he had many friends and was able to secure several churches for a sequence of revival meetings in York.[45] The meetings were a success and enthusiasm for Moody's message only increased in the months to come. A spring 1875 revival, held at London's "Agricultural Hall" seating between fifteen and twenty thousand people, was invariably standing-room-only with many having to be turned away. In August of that year, Dwight Moody and Ira David Sankey returned to America as international celebrities.

George Stebbins, a singer himself who worked directly with Ira Sankey throughout the revival years, wrote of him: "His voice was a high baritone of exceptional volume, purity, and sympathy . . . Seated at a low-top organ with which he always accompanied himself, he, without ostentation, sang his messages into the hearts and consciences of people in a way that justly made him famous."[46] J. Wilbur Chapman, one of Moody's best biographers among his contemporaries, said of Ira Sankey:

> It was not alone the novelty of his method that aroused interest in Mr. Sankey's songs to such a high degree. He possessed a voice of unusual purity and strength, and even when facing a great congregation of seventeen or eighteen thousand people, could make every word which he uttered so distinct that it was heard on the very outskirts of the throng. His vocal method has been criticized, undoubtedly with justice, but it can be said that, whether his method was correct or incorrect artistically, it was at least effective.[47]

Similarly, W. H. Daniels, another Moody contemporary wrote:

> No singing master or conservatory of music ever placed a professional stamp on him. His style was acquired in the Sunday School, in the regular services of the house of God . . . He was accustomed to pray over his singing as a minister prays over his sermon, and thus receiving the baptism of the Holy Ghost, he was able to go forth in the name of the Lord, . . . making melody

---

45. Moody, *Life of Dwight L. Moody*, 162.
46. Stebbins, *Reminiscences*, 211.
47. Chapman, *Life and Work*, 131.

in his heart unto God, and thereby leading thousands of others to understand and join in, the service of praise as they had never done before. From first to last, he was never a professional musician . . .[48]

In each of these comments the observers pointedly reference Sankey's lack of formal vocal training and lack of professional aspirations. What are we to make of this? First, it is indicative of the times. Even in cultivated circles, anything suggestive of the theater or secular musical performance for compensation was suspect. Professional singers, even those singing in churches for a living, were constantly faced with questions regarding the sincerity of their faith. This resonated even more within the general population who disdained the airs put on by the concert- and opera-going public. To say Sankey had no professional or performance aspirations was to say he was *one of them*. Dwight Moody, when questioned about Sankey's vocal technique said, in essence, that he didn't know whether Sankey sang correctly or not, but he believed deeply in *what* he was singing, was able to communicate that to audiences, and thus led them to belief as well.

Philip Paul Bliss

Philip P. Bliss.
1838 public domain image from ca. 1870, Carte de visite. Courtesy of Wikimedia Commons.

Philip Paul Bliss grew up in northeastern Pennsylvania. His father, Isaac, was a poor but devout Methodist who loved to sing. Philip inherited a love of music from him and learned to sing, vocalizing with his father on the porch of their farmhouse in Clearfield County, Pennsylvania. Like

---

48. Daniels, *D. L. Moody and His Work*, 234–35.

Sankey, he followed this up by attending a musical convention led by W. B. Bradbury in the 1850s.[49] Bliss's remarkable baritone voice, passion for music, and natural bent for teaching led him to find employment as a music instructor at the Rome Academy in Rome, Pennsylvania in 1858.

Bliss was drafted into the Union Army at the age of twenty-seven in 1865, but with the war almost over he was discharged after only two weeks. Hoping to quickly start a singing career, either as a soloist or ensemble singer, Bliss and his spouse, Lucy, headed for Chicago in 1865. Once there he was hired by the Root and Cady Music Company, which paid him $100 a year to be among its stable of song composers. He also received a sizable income leading a steady stream of musical conventions—up to thirteen per year—with each lasting three to four weeks. [50]

According to Bliss, his connection with Dwight Moody began with a Sunday stroll in 1869. He and Lucy were sauntering down Clark Street in Chicago when they came upon what he described as an open-air meeting outside of Colonel Wood's Museum.[51] As was his custom, Moody was calling attention to the prayer meeting he would be leading that evening. Intrigued, Philip and Lucy decided to attend. Bliss later recalled:

> That night, Mr. Moody was without his usual leader for the singing, and the music was rather weak. From the audience, I helped what I could on the hymns, and [this] attracted Mr. Moody's attention . . . He had my name and history in about two minutes and a promise that, when I was in Chicago Sunday evenings, I would come and help in the singing at theater meetings.[52]

Bliss soon took a leadership role in Moody's Chicago evangelistic work and, through that, connected with Daniel Webster Whittle (1840–1901). Whittle quickly recognized Bliss's musical skills and enlisted him to assist him in his own preaching endeavors. He also arranged for Bliss to become the director of music at Chicago's First Congregational Church. Bliss had shifted his composing interests from humorous and sentimental parlor songs to music for Sunday school use. He published his first collection, *The Prize*, in 1869 and followed it with three additional collections by 1874. His

---

49. Whittle, ed., *Memoirs of Philip P. Bliss*, 19.

50. Whittle, ed., *Memoirs of Philip P. Bliss*, 39.

51. "Wood's Museum" was the Chicago version of P. T. Barnum's "American Museum" in New York City, offering educational exhibits as well as the sensational, weird, and exotic. Moody staged prayer meetings in a variety of popular Chicago venues including Wood's while Farwell Hall was being reconstructed.

52. Whittle, ed., *Memoirs of Philip P. Bliss*, 41.

Gospel Songs for Gospel Meetings and Sunday Schools (1874) is generally considered to be the first use in print of the term "gospel song."

Unfortunately, Philip Bliss, along with his wife, Lucy, died tragically in the Ashtabula Train Disaster on December 29, 1876. He was only thirty-eight years old.[53] Dwight Moody said of him, "In my estimate, he was the most highly honored of God, of any man of his time, as a writer and singer of Gospel songs, and with all his gifts, he was the most humble man I ever knew. I loved him as a brother, and shall cherish his memory, giving praise to God for the grace manifested in him . . ."[54] Bliss's friend and fellow hymn writer George Stebbins wrote that, "As to Mr. Bliss' place among the writers of gospel hymns, . . . he occupied a preeminence that still stands unrivaled, and to my mind it is a just estimate. There has been no writer of verse since his time who has shown such a grasp of the fundamental truths of the Gospel, or such a gift for putting them into poetic and singable form as he."[55]

A similar judgement on Bliss's hymn output has been made by author and music educator Stanley Heard Brobston:

> Bliss should receive more credit than he is generally given for the beginnings of the gospel hymn movement. . . . It is certain that an analysis of Bliss' contributions, compared with those of Sankey, would confirm this. Such a comparison . . . should make a strong case for Bliss . . . to be considered the "Father of the Gospel Song." Bliss' untimely death and Sankey's association

---

53. Philip, Lucy, and their two children had spent Christmas at the family homestead in Rome, Pennsylvania. Bliss received a telegram urgently asking him to return to Chicago to help head a service at Farwell Hall on Sunday, the 31st. Leaving the children in Rome, the couple boarded a train of the Lake Shore and Michigan Railway, bound for Chicago. While crossing a bridge traversing the deep Ashtabula River gorge in northeastern Ohio, the bridge failed, plunging all but the lead locomotive into the gorge below. Ninety-two of the approximately two hundred passengers and crew were killed either in the wreck itself or the fire that followed. Many of the dead, the Blisses included, were burned beyond recognition. Upon receiving news of the accident, D. W. Whittle, Philip's friend and colleague, rushed to the crash site and spent three days attempting to identify remains or any possession that could be linked to Philip or Lucy. Bliss and his beloved wife, along with the other unidentified, were buried in a mass grave in Ashtabula's Chestnut Grove Cemetery. Major memorial services for the Blisses were held in Pennsylvania and Chicago with Dwight Moody preaching. Sunday schools in Chicago and elsewhere mounted a "penny collection" to provide support for the two Bliss children, and nearly $10,000 was raised. Proceeds from publication of the Bliss memoirs were dedicated to erecting a monument near Rome and providing support to other members of the extended family.

54. Whittle, ed., *Memoirs of Philip P. Bliss*, 7.

55. Stebbins, *Reminiscences*, 193.

with the widely known evangelist, Dwight L. Moody, account for a great deal of the credit accorded the latter musician.[56]

Stebbins, McGranahan, and Towner

Tenor George C. Stebbins was born in New York State. He received early training in music from singing schools and studied voice with prominent studio voice teachers. Stebbins moved to Chicago in 1869 and went to work for the Lyon & Healy music store, which was the Midwest representative for Oliver Ditson. He also became director of music for the First Baptist Church on Chicago's South Side. While at FBC he arranged selected hymns for male quartet and chorus. They were so well received that he was contracted by Root & Cady to publish four collections for male voices. It was around this time that Stebbins came in contact with Philip Bliss and the two became close friends. It was to George Stebbins that Bliss brought the initial draft of his most famous song, "It Is Well with My Soul" ("When peace like a river attendeth my way").[57]

James McGranahan, also a powerful tenor, received early training in a singing school in Adamsville, Pennsylvania, and played bass viol to accompany the local church choir. He went on to become a singing master at the age of nineteen, and even considered an operatic career. Of those in the Moody circle, McGranahan was perhaps the most adept ensemble trainer and choral conductor. He studied conducting at the Normal School Academy of Music at Geneseo, New York, with Carl Zerrahn, eminent director of the Boston Philharmonic and the Handel and Haydn Society. His work with glee clubs and choruses earned him national recognition, and he served for three years as head of the National Board of Normal Institutes of Music. McGranahan made his mark as a composer setting hymn texts of others to music. He collaborated with a dozen of the nineteenth century's most prominent hymn writers, with musical settings numbering about 150. It was through the evangelistic work of D. W. Whittle and Philip Bliss that James McGranahan became associated with Dwight Moody. After Bliss's tragic death in 1876, McGranahan would step in to collaborate with Ira Sankey on *Gospel Hymns*, volumes 2 through 6.

D. B. Towner was perhaps the most highly trained of all of Dwight Moody's musical associates. He studied voice and composition with a

---

56. Brobston, *Daddy Sang Lead,* 72n68.

57. Stebbins was probably the last in the Moody circle to see Philip Bliss alive. They spoke as Bliss was boarding a train for the fateful trip east from Chicago to Pennsylvania for the Christmas holiday.

number of prominent teachers, including George Frederick Root, and completed a course of study at the Cincinnati Conservatory. He had a remarkable bass-baritone voice, toured widely as a soloist, and was a sought-after leader of musical conventions. Towner was a prolific composer of gospel hymns, with over two thousand in print during his lifetime and many more left unpublished. He joined the Moody circle in the 1880s and eventually became director of music at the Moody Bible Institute in Chicago.

Late Nineteenth Century White Gospel Hymnody

In 1873, as Dwight Moody and Ira Sankey prepared to sail for the British Isles, the terms "gospel song" and "gospel hymn" were not in use. Philip Bliss's *Gospel Songs for Gospel Meetings and Sunday Schools*, the first known use of the term "gospel song," would not be published for another year. The term "gospel hymn" would have to wait for the Sankey-Bliss-McGranahan collaborations which resulted in *Gospel Hymns, 1–6*.

To understand the genesis of gospel songs and hymns, one must look first to the Sunday school hymns and songs of the early nineteenth century. As soon as the 1820s, collections of music for Sunday School singing were being published. Two of William B. Bradbury's collections were widely used during the 1860s, *Bright Jewels for the Sunday School* (1860) and *Bradbury's Golden Shower of S. S. Melodies, a New Collection of Hymns and Tunes for the Sabbath School* (1862).[58] Bradbury, as we have seen, was an incredibly successful New York composer in the tradition of Lowell Mason and Thomas Hastings. His songs and hymns tend to be simple, strophic, with no rhythmic complexities and following standard-practice European rules for harmonization. Texts were geared toward mainstream church use. They lack the focus on the urgency of conversion reflected in the Moody/Sankey hymns and were intended for use in a cross-section of mainstream churches. That being said, there is notable preference for the skipping 3/4 and 6/8 meters, which would characterize much Civil War band music and the gospel hymns that would come later. Notable also is the inclusion of a "chorus" or "refrain", a standard feature of the Moody/Sankey songs to come.

In the following Bradbury chorus, "Above the Clouds," another characteristic is evident. The text is not scriptural, but rather a simple lyric of encouragement: "the toils and suffering on earth will pass; focus instead on your heavenly reward." The song is not a traditional worship hymn. There is

---

58. Bradbury's well-known children's hymn, "Jesus Loves Me," first appeared in this collection.

no doctrinal complexity, and the message is one which would be uplifting to large groups of people from a variety of backgrounds. Textually, its antecedent is not hymns of Wesley and Watts but rather the camp meeting spirituals of the Second Great Awakening. It is revival music!

"Above the Clouds." Text: Mary Ann Pepper Kidder (1820–1905); music: W. B. Bradbury in *Bright Jewels for the Sunday School* (New York: Biglow & Main, 1869), p. 15.

While Bradbury's work was a key influence in the development of gospel hymnody, the popularity of Philip Phillips must also again be considered. Phillips had revised his popular 1863 collection *Musical Leaves* in 1868, for his first tour of Europe and the British Isles. The songs had a simple, folklike quality. In No. 9, "O What Are You Going to Do, Brother," there's the pervasive 6/8 time. The word "brother" employs a delightful Scotch snap,[59] and a marchlike flavor prevails throughout. Again, Phillips employs a chorus, but this time the repetition of "Then what are you going to do, brother? Say, what are you going to do?," lends itself to audience participation.

"What Are You Going to Do, Brother?"(excerpt), Words & Music by Philip Phillips in *Musical Leaves* (Cincinnati, OH: P. Phillips/Hitchcock & Walden, 1867), p. 9.

---

59. The Scotch snap is a melodic/rhythmic figure, generally a sixteenth note followed by a dotted eighth with the stress falling on the sixteenth. It usually appears stepwise in the melodic line. It was commonly used in classic art music of the eighteenth century. Because it appears frequently in Scottish and Gaelic folk music, British and American musicians refer to it as the "scotch snap", however it is common to music of other cultures.

Gospel Songs, 1–6

The sale of printed songbooks became a standard component of the Moody/Sankey revivals, resulting in a historic multivolume collection, *Gospel Hymns No. 1–6*. As an indication of how successful marketing was for the hymnal, the Root & Cady publishing house in Chicago sold over eighty million copies of *Gospel Songs, 1–6*, before 1890—more than any other book published in America except the Bible.[60] In fact, the money coming from songbook sales became the chief way revival organizers were able to meet expenses and eventually made Dwight Moody and Ira Sankey relatively wealthy men.

The gospel hymns of the Moody/Sankey era were evolved from the camp meeting songs, shape note spirituals, and Sunday school hymnody of an earlier era, but they were also unique in form and purpose. They were conceived for a specific purpose—revival use, not traditional worship. While often focused on the immediate need for conversion, they also touched on temperance, sexual activity before marriage, gambling, and other vices. Indeed, many were intended for a specific revival meeting audience and to be paired with a specific theme. Like the hymns of the social gospelers, also active at the same time, they were consciously nonsectarian and avoided divisive doctrinal issues like the Trinity. More significantly, Jesus was portrayed as being fully present, and the chief joy of life was to have a personal relationship with him. Ethnomusicologist James C. Downey characterized this as a direct attempt to reassure persons who no longer controlled their existence (factory and office workers and the poor, for example) and who felt lost in an impersonal urban society—that indeed there was someone who cared for them deeply on a personal level: Jesus.[61]

In perusing the gospel hymn repertoire, we see a shift from the colonial and early nineteenth-century depictions of sinful humanity as "worms" to "poor sinners" in the post-Civil War era. Victorian evangelists, in contrast, attempting to minister to the urban poor, "were unable to ignore the ways in which social conditions made it virtually impossible for many individuals not to fall into sinful patterns."[62] Though Moody and his circle saw the end times as near and inevitable, they focused their witness positively on a promise of a life with Christ as a result of conversion rather than the sinfulness of fallen humanity.

---

60. *Gospel Hymns, Volumes 1 through 6*, was always a collaborative effort. Sankey partnered with Philip Bliss to produce Volume 1. Following Bliss's untimely death, Sankey partnered with James McGranahan to produce succeeding volumes.

61. Downey, "Revivalism, the Gospel Songs," 117.

62. Mouw and Noll, *Wonderful Words of Life*, 243.

Sandra Sizer, in *Gospel Hymns and Social Religion*, divides all hymnody into three broad categories:

- *Descriptive, no audience specified*: This includes hymns that are personal pleas and affirmations ("More Love to Thee, O Christ," "My Faith Looks Up to Thee"); and also hymns that tell a story (Sankey's "There Were Ninety and Nine" is a classic example, but there are hundreds of others).
- *Exhortations to a human audience*: These are hymns that function as a plea to mortals to turn from sin or go forward in the faith. (Examples: "Turn Back, O Man," Bliss's "Rescue the Perishing").
- *Direct address to the Deity*. ("God of Our Fathers," "How Great Thou Art").[63]

While the third category, "Direct Address to the Deity", is by far the most widely used in classical hymnody, the first two, "Descriptive" and "Exhortation," predominate in late nineteenth-century gospel hymnody. As with the preaching, the hymns tended to be topical and highly personalized. Some common themes of songs in *Gospel Hymn, 1–6* include:

(Theme) Inevitability of Death and Urgency of Conversion:

No. 140, "Saved by the Blood" (W. H. Doane)

No. 569, "Almost Persuaded" (Bliss)

No. 585, "Pass Me Not, O Gentle Saviour" (W. H. Doane)

No. 656, "Why Not Tonight?" (Sankey)

(Theme) Trusting the "Old Story" (return to a faith based in traditional roots):

No. 28, "Tell Me the Old, Old Story" (W. H. Doane)

No. 30, "I Love to Tell the Story" (W. G. Fischer)

(Theme) Rest for the Weary:

No. 473, "O Wondrous Land of Pure Delight" (Sankey)

No. 673, "Rest for the Weary" (McDonald)

(Theme) Repentance, Conversion, and Salvation:

No. 46, "Wishing, Hoping, Knowing" (Bliss)

---

63. Sizer, *Gospel Hymns and Social Religion*, 169.

(Theme) Exhortation:

No. 47, "Precious Name" (Baxter/Doane)

(Text: "Take the name of Jesus with you")

(Theme) Assurance:

No. 573, "It Is Well with My Soul" (Spafford/Bliss)

Common also were metaphors pertaining to the Christian life as perceived from the evangelical viewpoint:

The quenching of thirst:

No. 178, "Ho, Every One that Thirsteth" (Bliss)

No. 274, "Come to the Fountain" (Stebbins)

No. 560, "As Pants the Hart" (McGranahan)

No. 273, "Behold a Fountain Deep and Wide" (Sankey)

Darkness to light:

No. 51, "Pull for the Shore" (Bliss)

(Text: "Light in the darkness, sailor; day is at hand!")

No. 103, "Arise and Shine" (Lathbury/Bliss)

(Chorus: "Arise and shine in youth immortal, Thy light is come!")

No. 113, "There's a Light in the Valley" (Bliss)

The world and earthly life as a storm:

No. 119, "When the Storms of Life Are Raging" (McGranahan)

No. 115, "Out of the Ark" (Harrington/Bliss)

No. 139, "I'll Stand by You" (McGranahan)

(Text: "Fierce and wild, the storm is raging")

No. 366, "Jesus, Saviour, Pilot Me" (Hopper/Gould)

Nautical metaphors:

No. 45, "Let the Lower Lights Be Burning" (Bliss)

No. 592, "Rescue the Perishing" (Crosby/Doane)

No. 270, "In the Hollow of His Hand" (Stebbins)

(Text: "O soul, tossed on the billows, afar from friendly land")[64]

---

64. Examples are all from Sankey, Bliss, McGranahan, and Stebbins, *Gospel Songs, No's 1 to 6 Complete*.

Dwight Moody was a "topical" preacher. He drew topics from Scripture, the news, and his own life experience to undergird the points he was making in preaching. The rigorous analysis and biblical criticism of Scripture—exegesis—was of little interest. The thematic and topical nature of gospel hymns made them particularly useful to him. Over five hundred of the 739 gospel hymns in *Gospel Hymns 1–6* include Scripture references next to their titles, not a common feature in nineteenth-century hymn collections. This is indicative of how the collection editors hoped to facilitate the coupling of appropriate music with Moody's messages.

Moody frequently drew sermon topics from Bible stories and parables. As noted earlier, among his very first requests of Ira Sankey was that he sing W. H. Doane's "The Prodigal Child" before he preached on the parable of the prodigal son (Luke 15:11–32). Sankey's most famous solo, "The Ninety and Nine," was meant to be coupled with a sermon on the parable of the lost sheep (Luke 15:3–7).

Being a premillennialist, Moody often described the world as a "battleground." He admonished any individual who answered Christ's call to be on the defensive against worldly values. It was spiritual warfare. Therefore, militaristic imagery in hymn texts and melodic settings reminiscent of the army "quickstep" were particularly appropriate and resonated with the many veterans in his audiences. The George Duffield hymn "Stand Up for Jesus," with its reference to "Ye soldiers of the cross" was a perennial favorite of veterans. Numerous other hymns from past generations elicited wartime memories among revival attendees, and were sung regularly at Moody and Sankey revivals. In the decades after the Civil War, a conflict that touched nearly every one of his generation, Moody regularly related anecdotes from his own experience as a Christian Commission delegate in his sermons. He also referenced familiar battles and the experiences of others where they served to illustrate a point. Philip Bliss's "Hold the Fort," inspired by a Civil War battle, was probably his most famous song during his lifetime. The song was based on an incident during the 1864 Battle of Altoona Pass in Georgia during Sherman's famous march to the sea. Confederate General John Bell Hood elected to attack the Union supply depot at Altoona Pass, Georgia, with a force far outnumbering the Union troops defending the depot under the command of General Samuel G. French. Union General John M. Corse, recognizing the eminent threat, used signal flags to alert Sherman, who signaled back, "Hold Altoona, and I will assist you." Bliss, applying a bit of poetic license, made the message "Hold the Fort for I Am Coming." Dwight Moody used the onslaught at Altoona Pass as a metaphor for the Christians holding fast against sin.

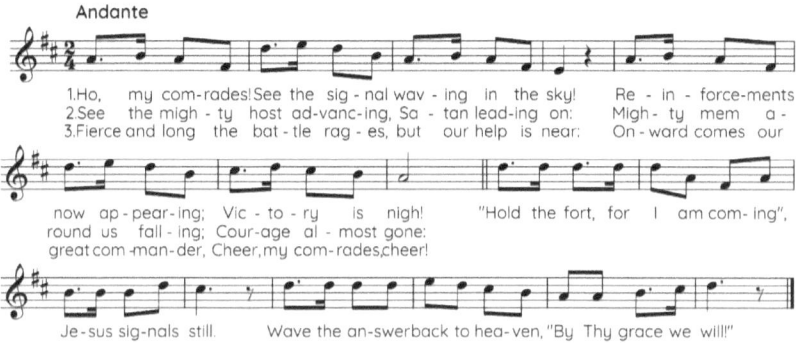

Phillip P. Bliss, "Hold the Fort," no. 79 in *Gospel Songs* (Cincinnati, OH: John Church, 1874).

One of the most descriptive gospel hymns, also by Philip Bliss, predated *Gospel Hymns*. Bliss wrote the text and music for "Roll on, O Billow of Fire!," inspired by living through the Great Chicago Fire and dedicated it to Dwight Moody. It appeared in his pioneering collection *Gospel Songs: A Choice Collection of Hymns and Tunes, New and Old* (1874). His colorful use of the conflagration to deliver the evangelical message is stunningly effective.

1. Hark! The alarm, the clang of the bells!
Signal of danger, it rises and swells;
Flashes like lightning illumine the sky,
See the red glare as the flames mount on high!

2. On, like a fiend in its towering wrath,
On, and destruction alone points the path;
"Mercy, O heaven!" the sufferers wail,
Feeble humanity, naught can avail.

3. Thousands are homeless and quick to their cry,
Heaven-born charity yields a supply,
Upward we glance in our terrible grief,
"Give us this day", brings the promised relief.

4. Treasures have vanished, and riches have flown,
Hopes for the earth-life are blasted and gone.
Courage, O brother, yield not to despair,
"God is our refuge", His kingdom we share.

Chorus
Roll on, roll on, O billow of fire!
Dash, with thy fury-waves, higher and higher!
Ours is a mansion, abiding and sure,
Ours is a kingdom, eternal, secure. [65]

Regarding the harmonic settings of late nineteenth-century gospel hymns, unlike Bach chorales for example, the harmonic rhythm is slow and easily adaptable to improvised or ornamented keyboard accompaniments. Song settings are primarily limited to the three primary chords, tonic, dominant, and subdominant. Standard four-part SATB scoring was used with occasional cues for a keyboard. However, it should be understood that the

---

65. Philip P. Bliss, "Roll On, Billow of Fire," no. 104 in Bliss, *Gospel Songs*.

hymns would typically be sung in unison with keyboard accompaniment, the vocal harmonization only used when a chorus was present.

The Moody/Sankey gospel songs often were written in a verse/refrain format. Texts were decidedly evangelical, "setting in sharp contrast this world and its problems with heaven and its bliss."[66] All of Dwight Moody's song leaders were soloists with keyboard proficiency. Following the model of Bliss and Sankey, they often led and sang from the keyboard—typically a low-boy pump organ or melodeon.[67] How a particular hymn was sung at a particular service could vary. The soloist/song leader might deliver the entire piece as a solo or invite the audience to join in on the chorus/refrain. More familiar songs might be sung throughout by the entire assembly. *Gospel Hymns 1–6* gives us hints of how solo voices were used. "The Ninety and Nine" (no. 570), Ira Sankey's signature song, is pointedly labeled "to be only sung as a solo." McGranahan's "Hallelujah for the Cross" (no. 400) seems likely intended for vocal quartet with solo soprano or tenor. George Stebbins's rollicking "Throw Out the Lifeline" (no. 441) carries the notation, "May be sung as solo or chorus." Philip Bliss's "Ah My Heart" (no. 25) is scored for two responding solo voices and a simple four-part refrain. It is likely this was one of many songs Bliss and his wife, Lucy, sang on the revival circuit.

Many of the songs have a stirring rhythmic base—6/8 being a favored meter. More militant selections often seemed to be inspired in part by band music of the war years. The more lyric songs showed a strong kinship with sentimental parlor ballads of post-Civil War period. Repetitive choruses were designed to be quickly learned and sung full-throatedly by revivalist crowds.

Reassessing the Gospel Hymn Repertoire

The popularity of the Moody/Sankey gospel songs naturally elicited a visceral response from the many preachers and musicians on the cultivated side. For example, the music critic of *The Nation*, in what was intended to be a tribute to Ira Sankey at the time of his death, could not resist the following diatribe:

> The distinctive feature of Mr. Sankey's book [*i.e., Gospel Hymns 1–6*] is those lively, rattling pieces like "Hold the Fort" and "Pull

---

66. Blumhofer, "Fanny Crosby and Protestant Hymnody," 226.

67. With Sankey and Bliss, the preferred accompaniment instruments were small, low-boy reed organs and melodeons. For a traveling evangelist, these were transportable, making them an essential accouterment. In addition, they were commonly used in middle-class homes and small, often rural churches and, as such, were regarded as instruments of the common people. In this sense, the instruments fit quite naturally into the middle class, populist focus of late-nineteenth-century revivalism.

to the Shore" and the crudely sentimental hymns of Fanny J. Crosby, P. P. Bliss, and their imitators. The music, from the point of view of a severe critic, is as contemptuous as that of a music-hall ditty; but it has some of the same popular qualities. The air is simple, strongly marked, easy to sing, easy to remember, "catching"—just the thing for children and for adults who in their musical taste are still children . . . The people who sing [these songs] with such zest would not appreciate the delicacy and refinement, in thought and expression, of the great hymns. For these honest folk, the triviality of the music, the cheapness of the style, the shallowness of conception, and the cloying sentimentality are exactly what lend charm to *Gospel Hymns*.[68]

Many church musicians of the twenty-first century find it easy to dismiss gospel hymnody because of the style in which it is written rather than do due diligence to evaluate individual hymns musically, textually, and especially in terms of their effectiveness in worship. Too often, evangelical zeal is unfairly equated with theological shallowness. Gospel hymns were never intended to be concert music, nor were many intended for use in a formal worship service. Many served their purpose in their time and should justly be forgotten. As a genre, however, the gospel hymn was a very important step in the development of American church music. Today's evangelical and "contemporary Christian" music has roots in the gospel hymns of the Moody/Sankey era. But the importance of the gospel hymn repertoire is even broader than that. To experience the mass singing of classics like "It is Well with My Soul" and "Blessed Assurance"[69] is to grasp something of what revivalism felt like in the 1870s, and therefore, a bit of our heritage as Americans.

---

68. "Gospel Hymns, 80,000,000 sold," 156.

69. The gospel hymn "Blessed Assurance," music by Phoebe P. Knapp (1839–1908) and words by Fanny Jane Crosby (1820–1915), remains one of the most-often sung gospel hymns of the nineteenth century. Crosby is said to have written lyrics to over eight thousand hymns and songs. Ira Sankey attributed much of the success *of Gospel Hymns, 1–6*, to the many Crosby hymns in the collection.

CHAPTER 13

BARBERSHOPS, BALLYHOO, AND BLUE NOTES
Black and White Gospel Music in the Late Nineteenth and Early Twentieth Centuries

SLAVERY HAD BEEN ABOLISHED in New York State in 1827. By 1900, the African American population of New York City numbered about 60,500 people, most of them laborers and domestics. The Black population increased exponentially with the Great Migration that began in the 1890s.[1] The migrants gravitated to Harlem, which, during the 1920s, became the first "exclusively Black ghetto" in the state.[2] The Abyssinian Baptist Church of Harlem, with roots going back to 1808 and a huge membership, was an anchor church for the community.[3] The same exponential growth of African American communities was occurring in all major population centers in the North and West during the late nineteenth and first quarter of the twentieth centuries.

---

1. The "Great Migration" is a term commonly applied to the movement of some six million African Americans from rural areas of the South to urban areas in the North. Scholars differ about when it started, but racism, segregation, lynching, and lack of economic opportunity in the South were certainly factors motivating it. It occurred in two distinct time periods, starting with *Plessy vs. Ferguson* in 1896 through 1930, and resuming from 1941 through 1970.

2. Allen, *Singing in the Spirit*, 21.

3. Later in the century Abyssinian Baptist would play a key role in the development of African American gospel music. During the pastorate of Edward Martin Waller, his son Thomas (a.k.a. "Fats") played the organ. Among many other important events, the church was the scene of Nat King Cole's wedding and the funeral of "the Father of Blues," W. C. Handy, in 1958.

Chicago and Bronzeville

In Chicago the primary residential and commercial district for African Americans was in an area of south Chicago known as Bronzeville. Between 1910 and 1920, the Black population there increased from 44,000 to 109,500. By 1920, more than 80 percent of Bronzeville's population was born outside of the state of Illinois. Many male migrants were employed in the city's sprawling steel mills and slaughterhouses. When possible, they resumed the kinds of work they had done in the South—janitorial services, waiting tables, elevator operators, and so on. Women sought employment as maids and laundresses. Those who could afford it trained as beauticians and teachers. Provident Hospital, staffed by and catering to African Americans, offered training for future nurses.[4]

When Black migrants arrived in Chicago they found long-established or "old-line" African American churches. Long time Black Chicagoans commonly attended historic churches such as Quinn Chapel African Methodist Episcopal Church, established in 1847; Olivet Baptist, founded in 1850; and Bethel AME, founded in 1862. In addition, there were conveniently located smaller traditional African American churches, but the onslaught of new residents presented challenges. Chicago's Methodist churches, for example, claimed only two hundred Black members in 1903. By 1918, they listed over five thousand, spread out over four congregations. To meet the need, established churches added additional services and staff, but it was hard to keep up. The Wiley College sociologist V. E. Daniel categorized four types of Black churches on Chicago's South Side:

- liturgical churches (Roman Catholic and Lutheran).
- "deliberative or sermon-centered" churches (Baptist, Methodist Episcopal, African Methodist Episcopal, and Christian Methodist Episcopal).
- "semi-demonstrative" churches (individual mainline churches that allowed some degree of emotive worship. According to Daniel, they might allow "a shout or two").
- Ecstatic Cults (Church of God in Christ, Church of the Living God).[5]

By the 1920s Philadelphia's Black community had become centered on the west side of the city with a total of twenty-nine major African American churches. In addition to thirteen African Methodist Episcopal and African Methodist Episcopal-Zion churches, there were six Baptist, two mainline

---

4. Marovich, *City Called Heaven*, 13.
5. Marovich, *City Called Heaven*, 17.

Methodist Episcopal, two Presbyterian, three Episcopal, and one Black Roman Catholic parish. Black Methodists tended to work in the building trades or as servants to elite white families. Black Episcopalians and Presbyterians were often independent entrepreneurs such as caterers, barbers, and proprietors of local businesses.

Earlier, we touched briefly on the contrasting views of two of the principal role models for African Americans at the dawn of the twentieth century—Booker T. Washington and W. E. B. Du Bois. It may be overly simplistic to say that older, established, and traditional Black churches in the North embraced Washington's worldview, but the desire to adapt and appropriate white values was certainly present. Nowhere is this more evident than with regard to worship style and musical preferences of the older congregations and their members. The traditional improvisatory and physically demonstrative singing of the plantation was replaced with carefully rehearsed and dignified choral presentations as well as hymns such as those of Watts and Charles Wesley.

Churches like Quinn Chapel in Chicago had large choirs and proudly promoted presentations of classic oratorios with orchestra. During the early years of the century Jubilee singing groups—some independent, some from Black colleges, but all modeled after the famous Fisk ensemble—were lionized by older African Americans as examples of Booker T. Washington's *Up from Slavery* ethos. Their arrangements of spirituals "offered a felicitous convergence of African American heritage with the politics of uplift."[6] The Jubilee style of unaccompanied, precise, and carefully blended singing "demonstrated an African American mastery of Western classical forms."[7] Beginning in the 1920s, and following in the footsteps of the Jubilee Singers and groups emulating them, were touring professional Black choruses such as the Hall Johnson Choir and the Eva Jessye Choir. The latter group, based in Baltimore, was initially called the Original Dixie Jubilee Singers.[8] Like many Caucasian churches of the time, congregational singing in the old, established Black churches tended to be anemic or had disappeared almost entirely. In its place, services focused largely on preaching and elaborate choral music. This type of worship left many newly arrived migrants perplexed. "Rural southern Blacks had been reared on what Woodson called 'manifestation of the Spirit.'"[9]

---

6. Jackson, *Singing in My Soul*, 13.

7. Jackson, *Singing in My Soul*, 13.

8. Allen, *Singing in the Spirit*, 23

9. Marovich, *City Called Heaven*, 20. Reference is to Carter G. Woodson (1875–1950), one of the most prominent African American historians of the twentieth century.

Du Bois famously spoke of the duality of the Black experience—an eternal struggle between the need for acceptance and the need to shoulder and value one's uniquely Black identity. Where Washington prioritized assimilation, Du Bois focused on independence and identity. The Du Bois stance can be seen in the thousands of Black migrants who could not find solace in tradition-bound larger churches, but instead struck out on their own. They were "accustomed to small, intimate churches that stressed fundamentalism, and a more emotional demonstrative [style of] worship."[10] James Baldwin evoked the spirit of this type of worship in his novel *Go Tell It on the Mountain* (1952):

> The Sunday morning service began when Brother Elisha sat down at the piano and raised a song . . . The song might be: "*Down at the cross where my Saviour died.*" . . . They sang with all the strength that was in them and clapped their hands for joy. There had never been a time when John had not sat watching the saints rejoice with terror in his heart, and wonder. Their singing caused him to believe in the presence of the Lord; indeed, it was no longer a question of belief, because they made that presence real . . . Something happened to their faces and their voices, the rhythm of their bodies, to the air they breathed; it was as though wherever they might be became the upper room, and the Holy Ghost was riding in the air.[11]

Much of *Go Tell It on the Mountain* was inspired by Baldwin's own life experiences. He was born in Harlem. The church Baldwin described was one of the many storefront churches that dotted the Harlem landscape. It was in such churches and barbershops that a new era of African American sacred music was born.

Urban Blacks Find Their Voice

Just when white America was first really becoming aware of the folk spirituals of enslaved African Americans, most freedmen were eager to distance themselves from that part of their history and its music. While Jubilee choirs and the dissemination of traditional songs from the antebellum plantations would turn out to be an important early step in the improvement of race relations in the northern states, urban Blacks—especially those escaping the Jim Crow South—sought forms of musical expression better suited to their

---

10. Allen, *Singing in the Spirit*, 22.
11. Baldwin, *Go Tell It on the Mountain*, 6–7.

needs. They sought a music growing out of and integral to their culture yet new and forward-looking, a music rising out of the urban experience.

For many Black migrants arriving in the North in the late nineteenth century, gospel songs in the Moody-Sankey tradition seemed fresh and appealing. From the early days of slavery, Blacks had displayed a remarkable ability to assimilate music from the dominant white culture and, through their innate improvisatory skills, make it their own. At any rate, the gospel hymnody of the Great Urban Revival was eagerly embraced by urban African Americans. According to Melva Costin, the Black assimilation of white revival hymns was "simply a reminder of the African American gift for improvising, contextualizing, and, more specifically, 'blackening' music from other traditions and claiming it [for use in worship]."[12] Many of those songs remain in the repertoire of beloved hymnody of the Black church. Among them are "I Need Thee Every Hour" (Hawks/Lowry, 1872); "The Solid Rock" (Mote/Bradbury, 1863); "Jesus, Keep Me Near the Cross" (Crosby/Doane, 1869); "Sweet Hour of Prayer" (Walford/Bradbury, 1861); "Blessed Assurance" (Crosby/Knapp, 1873); "To God Be the Glory" (Crosby/Doane, 1875); and "Leaning on the Everlasting Arms" (Hoffman/Showalter, 1885).[13] The great utility of the tunes was due to their effectiveness and flexible performance requirements. Their catchy rhythmic melodies, with improvised accompaniments built around basic harmonic schemes, made them perfectly suited to be assimilated into African American worship. Keyboard accompaniments, often reinforced with drums and other instruments, added another key element—*rhythm*.

"Blackening" the music generally involved several elements. Since the melody was dominant, the songs lent themselves to solo performance and the freedom of each individual singer to add their own expressive ornaments. A typical four-square, eight-bar phrase in the original song could be shortened or extended at will, thus making room for ornamentation. The verse with repeating chorus format of many popular gospel tunes made them ideal for group singing with a song leader/congregation interchange.

Ronald Radano has written extensively on the uniquely African American incorporation of rhythm into urban worship music. Radano makes it clear that one cannot separate African American sacred song from developments in secular music going on at the same time. Between 1880 and 1900, professional Black singers and instrumentalists were ubiquitous in certain areas of popular music: medicine shows, circuses, minstrel troops, and

---

12. Costen, *In Spirit and in Truth*, 81.

13. Costen, *In Spirit and in Truth*, 81. The only hymns *not* included in *Gospel Hymns, 1–6* are "To God Be the Glory" and "Leaning on the Everlasting Arms."

vaudeville. Their success required innovation. "The shift in public perception that reinvented Black music as rhythm music occurred over a twenty-year period, during the last two decades of the nineteenth century."[14]

Rhythmic innovation in Black sacred song grew in part because that was what was expected by white audiences wanting to hear Negro music. It was also, however, rooted in African tradition where rhythmic expression, singing, and physical movement were integral to daily living. Whether at work or play, music and singing were acts of worship. Ultimately, what is perceived as a "Black rhythmic nature" became inextricably embedded in the very nature of African American sacred song.[15]

C. Eric Lincoln has divided the development of African American gospel music into three distinct periods:

- The transitional or pre-gospel period, beginning around 1900 with the music and ministry of Charles A. Tindley.
- The traditional period or Golden Age of Gospel between 1930 and 1960, highlighted by the work of Thomas A. Dorsey and careers of Black recording artists.
- The contemporary gospel period of the 1960s and '70s.[16]

Sherwood's Hymnal

In 1893, the Black Virginian evangelist William Hall Sherwood (1854–1911) published *Harp of Zion*. The hymnal contained a variety of standard hymnody from Lowell Mason and some white gospel songs from the Moody/Sankey era, all with melody and harmonization notated. Sherwood's collection also contained twenty-one worship songs of his own composition, making it the first hymnal to include hymnody not only by an African American but also one specifically intended for African American worship. The melodies, harmonies, and, to an extent, the rhythm, all foreshadowed later trends in Black worship music.[17] The rhythmic and melodic character of Sherwood's hymns would be embraced and further refined by Charles A. Tindley.

---

14. Radano, *Lying Up a Nation*, 272.
15. Radano, *Lying Up a Nation*, 272.
16. Lincoln and Mamiya, "Performed Word," 53, 55.
17. Boyer, *Golden Age of Gospel*, 26–27.

Tindley, the Progenitor

Charles A. Tindley.
Public domain image courtesy of Wikimedia Commons. (https://en.wikipedia.org/wiki/Charles_Albert_Tindley)

No one in the African American tradition better represents the convergence of music with ministry than Charles Albert Tindley (1856–1933). William Herbert Brewster, an important preacher and gospel hymn composer of the 1930s and '40s, said of Tindley, "To my mind he was one of the greatest, if not *the* greatest, songwriter I ever knew." Thomas A. Dorsey, often referred to as the "Father of Gospel Music," said that Tindley "originated [the gospel] style of music, and what I wanted to do was to further what Tindley started."[18] Tindley's rise from servitude and poverty to leadership of the largest Methodist Episcopal congregation in the United States, as well as his work as a composer, make for one of the great stories in American church music history.

Charles Tindley was born in Berlin, Maryland, in 1856. His father was a slave. Though his mother and he were legally free, life was challenging. Unable to go to school, he learned to read on his own and with the help of others who tutored him. After the war, like so many other Blacks, Charles migrated north to Philadelphia. There he went to work as a laborer, carrying bricks for a bricklayer. He married his wife, Daisy, in 1873, and the two attended St. John's Methodist Church, where he donated his time as church sexton. Meanwhile he was eager to learn. He sought help to study Hebrew at a nearby synagogue and took a correspondence course to learn Greek. In 1885, though having no degree in theology, he took and passed the certification examination to enter the Methodist ministry. He was ordained a Methodist deacon in 1887 and an elder in 1889. As was customary, Tindley

---

18. Boyer, "Charles Albert Tindley," 103.

was initially assigned to an itinerancy serving churches in Maryland, New Jersey, and Delaware, and in 1900 he was appointed presiding elder for the Wilmington, Delaware district of the Methodist Episcopal Church.[19]

Tindley's life came full circle when he was assigned the pastorate at Bainbridge Methodist Church in Philadelphia in 1902. At the time of his arrival, the church had a membership of 130, but within a year it had grown by leaps and bounds, requiring a move to a larger facility and a new name, "East Calvary Methodist Episcopal Church." [20] Kenneth Goodwin, who was baptized by Tindley, recalled that an emphasis on prayer bands and small group worship at Tindley's churches was also a tradition in tidewater Maryland.

> The Eastern Shore had weekend groups that exalted the Lord by singing and praying. They were held, as the slaves used to do, when for fear of being punished they had to steal away into the woods to hold prayer meetings. The women were in White dresses. The men were in White shirts with collars built in, singing and praying all night.[21]

Tindley was a gifted and riveting preacher. His preaching style and the style of worship at his churches, however, was not typical of other Black Methodist Episcopalians. According to a former pastor and Tindley associate, the style of worship could easily be confused with that of a Baptist or Pentecostal congregation. It was not, he recalled, the "staid, quiet, reserved, dignified" style one might expect of Philadelphia's Methodist Episcopalians.[22]

By 1920 East Calvary under Tindley's pastorate had a membership of over ten thousand, and plans were underway for a new and much larger building. In Tindley's honor the church was later renamed Tindley Temple and is now a national historic landmark. Tindley was a respected member of the community, a friend of John Wanamaker, and a social activist. He participated in protests against the Black stereotyping in the 1912 *Cakewalk and Ball* and in the *Soap Box Minstrel Show* at the Philadelphia Academy of Music. Tindley also joined other civic leaders to protest the showing of D. W. Griffith's movie *The Birth of a Nation*, in September 1915. Over a

---

19. Boyer, "Charles Albert Tindley," 104.

20. St. John's would later be renamed Bainbridge Street Methodist Episcopal Church. In 1906, the Bainbridge congregation purchased a new and larger facility that had housed the former Westminster Presbyterian Church. It was renamed yet again, becoming East Calvary Methodist Episcopal Church.

21. Reagon, ed., *We'll Understand It Better*, 39.

22. Reagon, ed., *We'll Understand It Better*, 38.

thousand African Americans rioted in front of the Forrest Theater and, in the confrontation, Tindley suffered minor injuries.

Charles Tindley saw his churches as an anchor for the community he served. His churches took a leadership role in providing food, housing, and clothing as well as spiritual guidance to members and nonmembers alike. Spiritual guidance and emotional support for church members were central to Tindley's ministry. "Members were counseled on ways to survive in an urban setting."[23]

Tindley's sermons were peppered with stories and illustrations, biblical yet born out of his hardscrabble life in the South. One listener remembered a particularly impactful Tindley message from his childhood.

> I remember, I couldn't have been more than ten years old, he was preaching about a tree. "Has anyone ever seen a fruit tree partake of its own fruit?" The congregation said, "No." [Tindley continues:] "You've never seen a peach tree eat its own peaches. You've never seen an apple tree eat its own apples. But you have seen a tree so laden with fruit that its branches reach the ground so a toddler can pick and partake. Our lives should be like that tree. Not what we maintain for ourselves but give to others, as God gave his son."
>
> He didn't teach us how to die and about the hereafter. He taught us how to live. How to love each other. How to emulate Christian principles. That was the great thing about him.[24]

A recurring theme in Tindley's preaching and his hymns was that "true change or release from worldly bondage can be attained only through struggle." One of his most famous sermons, "The Furnace of Afflictions," is a powerful example.

> I welcome this morning, all the persecutions, unkindnesses, hard sayings and whatever God allows to come upon me. I welcome the hottest fire of trials if it is needed for my purification. Oh the things we have in our lives that can never go in heaven are more numerous than we are apt to think. They must all be taken out before we leave this world. God's way to get them out may be the way of the furnace.[25]

Another favorite Tindley metaphor equated life with going through a storm. The images of storm and struggle would appear in two of his most famous

---

23. Reagon, ed., *We'll Understand It Better*, 41.
24. Reagon, ed., *We'll Understand It Better*, 43.
25. Reagon, ed., *We'll Understand It Better*, 45.

hymns. His "When the Storms of Life Are Raging, Stand by Me" and "We'll Understand it Better By and By" are known and loved across the spectrum of American Protestant Christianity.

His "I'll Overcome Someday" is thought to be the inspiration for the text of "We Shall Overcome," the anthem of the Civil Rights era.[26]

I'll Overcome Some Day

"I'll Overcome Some Day." Words & music by C. Albert Tindley, in *Soul Echoes: A Collection for Religious Meetings*, no. 2 (Philadelphia: Soul Echoes Publishing Company, 1909), p. 42.

Composed around 1900, the hymn has a solid, straightforward harmonization. It displays none of the parlor piano sweetness of many white revival songs of the period. Also, the text is personalized. The sixth stanza, not printed here, casts facing life's tribulations as a pilgrim journey to become more like Jesus. Horace Boyer wrote that Tindley's hymn lyrics dealt "forthrightly with such subjects as the joys, trials, and tribulations of living a Christian life in the twentieth century."[27] "I'll Overcome Someday," however,

---

26. As noted, Tindley's text is thought to have been an inspiration for "We Shall Overcome." The melody, however, was derived from the classic spiritual, "No More Auction Block for Me."

27. Boyer, "Charles Albert Tindley," 104.

does not reflect other style characteristics that make Tindley hymns unique for their time. For the most part this was not music which looked back to the antebellum spiritual. Rather, Tindley borrowed liberally from the dotted and syncopated rhythms of the popular 2/4-time cakewalk or African American walk-around.

No. 2 in *Soul Echoes* (Philadelphia: Soul Echoes Publishing Company, 1909).

Note the syncopation in Tindley's "Stand by Me." Note also how the last note of each phrase is held, making room for improvised responses or ornamentation, and the use of a pentatonic or gapped scale. The latter was characteristic of folk music, but not the white gospel hymns of the Moody/Sankey type.

A "nautical" or "storm" motif is prominent in two of Tindley's most famous hymns, "By and By" and "Stand by Me." This directly parallels themes borrowed from nature in the Moody/Sankey repertoire, for example Fanny Crosby's "Rescue the Perishing" and P. P. Bliss's "Let the Lower Lights Be Burning." But where the white revivalist hymns tend to threaten damnation to all but the converted, Tindley's are characterized by irrepressible hope.

We'll Understand It Better By and By

Tindley C. A. Tindley (ca. 1906)

[musical score]

We are tossed about and driven on the restless sea of time, Somber skies and howling winds oft succeed a bright sunshine. In that land of perfect day, when the mists have rolled away, We will understand it better by and by.

Chorus: By and by, when the morning comes, All the saints of God are gathered home. We'll tell the story how we've overcome, For we'll understand it better by and by.

No. 30 in *Soul Echoes*
(Philadelphia: Soul Echoes Publishing Company, 1909).

Tindley wove a new song for the new century. The poetry of his lyrics came straight out of the personal and collective testimonies of the people he ministered to from his pulpit and in the streets and in the soup kitchens he organized.[28]

The Holy Spirit Sings! Sanctification, Holiness, and Pentecostalism

The work of C. A. Tindley suggests that a new era in African American sacred song was being born. But the development of Black gospel singing as a unique performance style, standing midway between the jazz club and the church, required more than the work of a single composer. It required throwing off the rigidly conventional practices of older urban Black congregations and completely re-envisioning worship as an expression of free, unbounded joy. Migrants from the South, whose faith was oriented toward

---

28. Reagon, Liner notes for *African American Gospel* (1994 recording).

"sanctified" or "holiness" ministries focused on the workings of the Holy Spirit, did much to power the transition.

The Pentecostal movement was founded on the book of Acts, chapter 2, and the biblical description of the day of Pentecost: the wind, the flame, the speaking in tongues, and the indwelling of the Holy Spirit. The passage has been interpreted in myriad ways through history, but of one thing we can be sure: the Acts of the Apostles provide a window into the beliefs and customs of early Christians that included a real and tangible interrelationship between the Spirit and believers.

It is far too simplistic to attribute the emergence of charismatic, Holy Spirit-oriented worship among African Americans in the early twentieth century to a single event, time, or place. John Wesley and his followers in America believed passionately in sanctification.[29] The sanctified life, Wesley preached, was imbued with the spirit of Christ. Once sanctified, the believer became a new creation. Stories of Wesley's ministry are replete with emotional outpourings and physical manifestations of the Holy Spirit at work. He was often criticized by fellow clergy in the Church of England for the "enthusiasm" of his followers. The concept of sanctification was undoubtedly encountered by southern Blacks in the late eighteenth century in the preaching of Methodist circuit riders and lay preachers. During the nineteenth century, they came to embrace it. [30]

Two landmark events occurring on the cusp of the twentieth century would have a significant impact on the future of Black gospel music. First was the founding in 1897 of the Church of God in Christ. Charles Harrison Mason (1864–1961) and Black Baptist preacher Charles Price Jones (1865–1949) organized a study group that led them to conclude that "the ecstatic worship that had been a mainstay of religion among African Americans during slavery had also been a vital component of early Christianity."[31] In June of 1896 Mason and Jones, having been expelled from the local Baptist Association in Little Rock, Arkansas, for preaching holiness and

---

29. Because similar sounding words—sanctify, sanctification, sacred, and sacralization—are used throughout this study, a word of explanation is called for: the term "sanctified church" comes directly from the founding of the Church of God in Christ by Charles Mason and Charles Price Jones. COGIC and various groups that splintered off of it saw their members as "set apart"—instantly cleansed of sin through the blood of Christ and the workings of the Holy Spirit. The term is used most often in reference to African American worshipping communities. Most but not all sanctified churches are Pentecostal. The style of worship tends to be both free and exuberant. By the second decade of the twentieth century, the word "sanctified," as used in the African American church, is a general term for the state of being anointed by the Holy Spirit.

30. Cusik, *Saved by Song*, 120–21.

31. Jackson, *Singing in My Soul*, 15.

sanctification, organized a new fellowship of churches, The Church of God in Christ.

A second crucial development occurred on April 9, 1906, with the beginning of the years-long Azusa Street Revival in Los Angeles. The evangelist Charles F. Parham had founded Bethel Bible School in Topeka, Kansas, in 1900, and in 1905 opened a second campus in Houston, Texas. The African American preacher William J. Seymour was one of his Houston students. Parham charged all his students to develop an Acts 2-based approach to worship, utilizing the gifts of the Holy Spirit, and Seymour wholeheartedly pursued this. In 1906 Seymour was called to pastor a holiness mission in Los Angeles, but the pastorate was not to be. Seymour, nevertheless, organized study groups meeting in homes focused on Acts 2 and incorporated a ten-day fast. When word was received that group members had begun speaking in tongues—including Seymour himself—the fledgling class quickly became a revival and a movement. It soon became necessary for Seymour and his followers to move into an abandoned AME church at 312 Azusa Street, which they renamed the Azusa Street Mission.

The revival at the Azusa Street Mission experienced phenomenal growth. For nearly three years, services ran continually from midmorning until midnight, seven days a week. At its height as many as 1,500 people crowded into the tiny worship space for worship. The music was a complete departure from the a cappella choral music of the Jubilee choirs, tending instead toward freewheeling individual expression. An attendee would stand to testify, often alternately speaking and quasi-singing. In call-and-response style, congregants would respond. "Much of the singing featured guttural sounds and shrieks."[32] There were no restrictions in terms of physicality or use of musical instruments. Foot stomping, handclapping, complex rhythms supported by drums, cymbals, brass, and other instruments—all were common.[33, 34]

---

32. Jackson, *Singing in My Soul*, 23.

33. Cusik, *Saved by Song*, 121.

34. The Azusa Street Revival was a completely interracial, egalitarian gathering, and it was clearly Seymour's intention that the holiness movement it sparked be inclusive as well. Due to commonly held racist views of the time, however, that was not to be. Whites separated to form their own denominations, most notably Assemblies of God.

Black Gospel Music and the Storefront Church

There is little doubt that Black gospel music and its style came from the Pentecostal churches, particularly the work of Charles Harrison Mason (1866–1961), founder of the Church of God in Christ.[35]

The Reverend R. C. Lawson, who founded Harlem's Church of Christ Apostolic Faith in 1919, understood what many of the disaffected migrants were seeking. He spoke out against the rigidity and impersonal nature of the old, established African American churches. They were, he said, copying the white man's style. His church, in contrast, offered recent migrants a touch of fire and brimstone and personal Christianity characteristic of religion in the rural South.

Gilbert Osofsky, professor of Black history at the University of Illinois, wrote of the emerging new Black worship style in his *Harlem: The Making of a Ghetto* (1963):

> Only about a third—fifty-four—of Harlem's churches were housed in regular church buildings—and these included some of the most magnificent and costly church edifices in New York City. The rest held services in stores and homes and appealed to Harlem's least educated people. "Jack-leg preachers," "cotton-field preachers," as their critics called them, hung out their poorly printed signboards and "preached Jesus" to all who wanted to listen. One self-appointed pastor held meetings in the front room of his home and rented chairs from the local undertaker to seat his small congregation . . .
>
> Services were fervent, loud and boisterous as members felt the spirit of the Lord and shouted and begged for His forgiveness. Tambourines sometimes kept up a rhythmic beat in the background and heightened the emotionalism to a state of frenzy. Neighbors of one storefront church sued the congregation for "conducting a public nuisance." The "weird sounds" which emanated from the building, they complained, seemed like a jazz orchestra![36]

When Black newcomers failed to find a church home in which they were comfortable, a common recourse was to organize prayer groups of like-minded folk to meet in homes. These were known as "prayer bands," and hundreds of them sprung up in Harlem, Bronzeville, and other metropolitan areas during the early years of the Great Migration. Anthropologist Diedre H. Crumbley writes that "the founding saints did not see themselves

---

35. Boyer, "Charles Albert Tindley," 108.
36. Osofsky, *Harlem, the Making of a Ghetto*, 144–45.

as a part of a vast evangelizing movement changing the religious topography of the earth, but rather as a 'select and chosen few' waiting for the millennial reunion of the saved found on the periphery of institutional Christianity."[37] As a prayer band's membership increased, and it outgrew the living room or parlor in which it had been meeting, members would pool financial resources and rent a larger space—very often a derelict storefront.

Sociologist Robert Austin Warne provided a colorful but condescending description of what he had seen upon entering typical storefront churches in New Haven, Connecticut in the 1920s.

> Poverty, lack of ability, the caste line, and ignorance provide the isolation from general cultural influences and the milieu which naturally encourage the continuance of backward customs . . . The essential fittings consisted of a pulpit; a Bible; some folding chairs, secondhand pews, or benches; musical instruments such as a triangle, tambourine, a pair of cymbals, or a battered piano; framed mottoes and a religious picture or two; and a dingy curtain shutting off a portion of the room behind the platform.[38]

By definition, storefront churches were highly individualistic both in how they defined their faith and how they expressed it. Some were closely bound to a mainline denomination and held to its theology and worship practices. In others, migrants sought to reconstitute their home churches in the South. Storefront churches generally had two common characteristics. First, they tended to be small enough that members and pastor could know each other. Second, they provided a faith haven for newly arrived laborers and domestics, poorest of the poor, the lowest social caste within urban Black society. Storefront faith communities espoused a wide variety of individualistic approaches to faith, but most were conservative and evangelical and encouraged their membership to express that faith in a way true to African American culture.[39] Those which embraced the holiness theology of Seymour and others were known as "sanctified" churches. The Methodist historian William Warren Sweet wrote of the storefront churches:

> Their appeal, however, . . . [was] to people belonging to about the same cultural and economic level. Perhaps it is not out of place to class all of these bodies as Churches of the disinherited, or Churches of the underprivileged. Among them the old type

---

37. Crumbley, *Saved and Sanctified*, 3.
38. Warner, *New Haven Negroes*, 214.
39. Cusik, *Saved by Song*, 121–22.

of revivalism succeeds and they reach large numbers of people who do not feel at home in the larger evangelical Churches.[40]

E. Franklin Frazier, in his seminal text *The Negro Church in America*, noted that in the twelve major northern cities he studied, out of 2,014 Black churches, 777 were storefronts.[41]

The Storefront Church in Chicago

Storefront churches first began appearing on Chicago's South Side in 1904. By 1929, there were 113 meeting regularly.[42] Chicago's first sanctified church, the Holy Nazarene Tabernacle Apostolic Church, was established by the female evangelist Mattie L. Thornton in 1908. By 1919, there were twenty sanctified churches in the Windy City. Many sanctified storefronts nationally were affiliated with the Church of God in Christ, including the United House of Prayer in Charlotte, North Carolina; Chicago's Church of the Living God; and the Church of Christ, Apostolic Faith in Chicago.

Into this mix of cultures in Chicago at the turn of the century came Pentecostalism and the Church of God in Christ (COGIC). Charles H. Mason was quite musical and firmly believed that music would need to be an essential component in spirit-filled worship. He aggressively encouraged singing in the churches he served and composed two hymns that remain standards to the present day in Pentecostal worship, "I'm a Soldier in the Army of the Lord" and "Yes, Lord" (commonly referred to as the COGIC chant). It was Mason who originated the practice of having each church member at least once lead the congregation in song. This usually occurred when a new communicant had accepted Christ as savior and, for the first time, professed to be empowered by the Holy Spirit. The frequent alternating between song and testimony as a core part of worship practically guaranteed strong congregational singing with leading voices spread throughout the membership.

In Chicago, Bishop William Matthew Roberts (1878–1954) birthed Roberts Temple Church of God in Christ in 1916, on State Street. The music was "spontaneous in every sense of the word. No pianist, organist, or choir director interferes with the freedom . . . A spiritual may be started at any time in the service and by anyone who feels the urge to sing."[43] Roberts Temple and Chicago's storefront churches were emblematic of a new and

---

40. Sweet, *Revivalism in America*, 63.
41. Frazier, *Negro Church in America*, 58.
42. Marovich, *City Called Heaven*, 23.
43. Marovich, *City Called Heaven*, 31.

White Urban Revivalism after Dwight Moody: The Preachers and Their Musician Associates

> The man "born down to Babitt's Corners" may find a deep appeal in the simple but acute Gospel hymns of the New England "camp meetin'" of a generation or so ago. He finds in them—some of them—a vigor, a depth of feeling, a natural-soil rhythm, a sincerity—emphatic but inartistic—which, in spite of a vociferous sentimentality, carries him nearer the "Christ of the people" than does the *Te Deum* of the greatest cathedral. These tunes have, for him, a truer ring than many of those groove-made, even-measured, monotonous, non-rhythmed, indoor-smelling, priest-taught, academic, English or neo-English hymns (and anthems)—well-written, well-harmonized things, well-voice-led, well-counterpointed, well connected, and well O.K'd, by well corrected Mus. Bac. R.F.O.G.'s[44]—personified sounds, correct and inevitable to sight and hearing; in a word, those proper forms of stained-glass beauty which our over-drilled mechanisms—boy choirs—are limited to.
>
> But if the Yankee can reflect the fervency of "Aunt Sarah," who scrubbed her life away for her brother's ten orphans, the fervency with which this woman, after a fourteen-hour work day on the farm, would hitch up and drive five miles through the mud and rain to "prayer meetin'," her one articulate outlet for the fullness of her unselfish soul—if he can reflect the fervency of such a spirit, he may find there a local color that will do all the world good. If his music can but catch that spirit by being a part with itself, it will come somewhere near his ideal—and it will be American, too . . . (Charles Ives, ca. 1915)[45]

The evangelist Dwight Lyman Moody changed the face of white American revivalism, and his influence is still felt today. Keep in mind, however, that Moody never operated in a vacuum. From the very beginning of his inner-city evangelistic activities, Moody had help—preachers,

---

44. Ives is deploying a humorous mash-up of the acronyms for Fellow of the Royal College of Organists (F.R.C.O.) and Fellow of the American Guild of Organists (F.A.G.O.).

45. Ives, "Epilogue," 80–81.

mission schoolteachers, administrators, and musician song leaders. After he returned from his triumphal tour of the British Isles in 1875 and inaugurated his Great Urban Revival in America, Moody increased his staff, adding, for example, secretarial help and advance men to coordinate revival preparations in various cities. He also brought together a host of preachers and musicians, all trained in his methods, and all committed to moving revivalism forward.

Several preacher/musician teams with Moody connections went on to lead successful revival tours themselves. Among the earliest was Major Daniel Webster Whittle (1840–1901), who partnered with the singer/songwriter Philip P. Bliss to mount evangelistic crusades from 1873 until Bliss's death in 1876. The Rev. Reuben Archer Torrey (1856–1928) came to Chicago in 1889 to serve as superintendent of what is now the Moody Bible Institute. He would go on to found the Bible Institute of Los Angeles (now Biola University). Torrey teamed up with the singer and choral conductor Charles M. Alexander (1867–1920), a graduate of the Moody Bible Institute, for evangelistic tours to virtually every corner of the globe between 1902 and 1907.

Alexander conducting mass children's choir in Ottawa, Canada, in 1905.
From Helen C. (Dixon) Alexander and J. Kennedy Maclean, *Charles M. Alexander: A Romance of Song and Soul-Winning* (London: Marshall Brothers, Ltd, 1920), p. 113.

In 1907 Alexander joined forces with another Moody associate, the Presbyterian evangelist and Moody biographer, John Wilbur Chapman (1859–1918), for mammoth revivals in Pennsylvania and North Carolina in 1908, and another world tour during 1910. The Chapman-Alexander partnership continued until Chapman's death in 1918.

According to Donald Hustad, Alexander's expertise in organizing and conducting mass choirs and congregations in a revival setting "brought the [white] 'gospel choir' to its zenith."[46]

> A striking feature of the London Mission was the great attention paid to it by the secular press, and the interest aroused by the music among secular musicians. H. Hamilton Fyfe, the eminent critic, in describing the opening meeting at Royal Albert Hall, wrote in the Daily Mirror of February 6, 1905: "The voice belongs to the most remarkable conductor I have ever seen. I have watched the methods and the triumphs of the most famous baton-wielders of the time—Colonne, Nikisch, Mottl, Weingartner, and Henry J. Wood. Never have I been so much impressed as I was by this bright-faced, energetic young evangelist. As the leader of a choir, he has an amazing and almost magical influence, not only over the trained choir; he simply makes everybody sing, and sing as he wants them to. "Watch my hand!," he calls, and the men's unaccompanied voices rise and fall in crooning cadences with an effect any conductor might be proud of. Watch his hands? Why we are watching every part of him; we cannot take our eyes off of him; we are fascinated, hypnotized, bewitched. Never for a moment is he still. Now we see him "fine down" [sic.] a passage from *fortissimo* to *piano*. All done with the turn of the wrist! That marvelous magic hand of his thrills with the feeling he wants to put into the music. "Sing it as if you mean it!," he cries to the choir. But they *do* mean it. This is no pretense, no artistic make-believe. That is why the singing is unlike anything I have ever heard before. That—and the wonderful conducting of this young man.[47]

Edwin Othello Excell (1851–1921) served outside the Moody circle but wrote in the same sentimental style. Commonly referred to as "E. O." Excell, he served as chorister and vocal soloist for the evangelist Samuel Porter Jones from 1888 to 1899, after which he performed as a vocal soloist with the Winona Lake Bible Conference and the touring British evangelist Gypsy Smith. Excell and Jones shared a bond of mutual respect. Representative songs of Towner and Excell employed some dotted rhythms but, to contrast them with the Tindley example above, syncopation or any suggestion of dance rhythms are avoided.

---

46. Hustad, *Jubilate*, 247.
47. Alexander and Maclean, *Charles M. Alexander*, 106–7.

E. O. Excell ca. 1890.
Public domain image courtesy of Wikimedia Commons,
https://en.wikipedia.org/wiki/E._O._Excell.

Samuel Porter Jones (1847–1906) captured national attention after his three-week revival in Nashville, Tennessee, in May of 1885. Jones led four services a day beginning at 6 AM, with attendance averaging six thousand per service. One can see a definite progression toward the spectacular in Jones's revival meetings. Rather than the simple reed organ of Ira Sankey, he insisted on two grand pianos and, where possible, a brass band.

As with all the late nineteenth-century revivalists, influence of Dwight Moody is evident in the evangelistic crusades of Jones. Jones's use of promotion in the press, his organization of volunteers, his enlisting of local churches and clergy to assure the revival's success—all were based on Moody's template. Jones's decision to employ soloist/song leaders was modeled after Moody's partnership with Ira Sankey. In other ways, however, the path taken by Jones diverged.

Jones's theological emphases and priorities differed significantly from Moody's, and his changed priorities may be seen as a turning point in American revivalism. Unlike Moody, Jones's stance was decidedly anti-intellectual. He frequently dismissed "formal theology as the unintelligible chattering of A. B.'s, PhD's, L.L.D.'s, and A.S.S.'s."[48] He was critical of Moody for preaching the dogma of conversion while saying nothing about the life of obedience that should follow it.[49] In keeping with this perspective, Jones's preaching often centered on the behavioral issues of right living. Backsliders needing conversion included anyone who condoned dancing, card playing,

---

48. Grem, "Sam Jones, Sam Hose," 38.
49. Grem, "Sam Jones, Sam Hose," 38.

gambling, circuses, swearing, theatergoing, billiards, baseball, low-cut dresses or any sort of immodest apparel, society balls, novel reading, social climbing, prostitution, or drinking.[50] For Jones, unlike Moody, conversion meant simply agreeing to reform one's behavior.

Jones's emphasis on the social mores of his time rather than conversion removed much of the religiosity that had been characteristic of Moody's revivals. While Moody had prided himself on the decorum of his audiences, Jones relished boisterous interchanges with attendees. His incorporation of huge choruses and often band instruments lent an atmosphere ranging from celebratory to carnival-like. His approach would be honed to perfection by the first great revivalist of the twentieth century, Billy Sunday, and his popular song leader, Homer Rodeheaver.

Billy Sunday

Billy Sunday.
Public domain image, Library of Congress. (http://hdl.loc.gov/loc.pnp/cph.3b05466)

Robert F. Martin, in explaining the rise in popularity of Billy Sunday's revivalism, wrote, "Ultimately, what enabled the revivalist to reach millions of Americans was the congruence between his life and work and the hopes and fears of people struggling to cope with the myriad of uncertainties inherent in the transition from a rural, agricultural nation to an urban, industrial one. . . . Sunday was a hero for millions who were struggling to reconcile the present with the past."[51]

---

50. McLoughlin Jr., *Modern Revivalism*, 282.
51. Martin, *Hero of the Heartland*, xiv.

William Ashley Sunday (1862–1935) was born near Ames, Iowa, the son of William Sunday (born 1828) and Jennie Cory. By 1880, the eighteen-year-old Sunday was gaining a reputation as an athlete and swift base runner. This led to his recruitment onto the Marshalltown Fire Company baseball team. When the team won a state championship, Sunday came to the attention of Adrian Anson, manager of the professional Chicago White Stockings, who signed him onto the team in 1883. Sunday was, according to Anson, "as good a boy as ever lived, being conscientious in a marked degree, hardworking, good-natured and obliging."[52]

> He was, in my opinion, the fastest man afterwards on his feet in the profession, and one who could run the bases like a scared deer. The first thirteen times that he went to bat after he began playing with the Chicago's he was struck out, but I was confident that he would yet make a ball player and hung onto him, cheering him up as best I could whenever he became discouraged. As a baserunner his judgement at times was faulty and he was altogether too daring, taking extreme chances because of the tremendous turn of speed that he possessed. He was a good fielder and a strong and accurate thrower, his weak point lying in his batting.[53]

Billy Sunday, ball player, ca. 1890.
Public domain image. (http://thisdayinbaseball.com/famed-evcangelist-billy-sunday-dies-at-the-age-of-72)

Over the next eight years, Sunday would be known primarily for his speed. Fans were thrilled by his seemingly impossible dives and catches, but he also committed many errors and frequently struck out at bat.

---

52. Anson, *Ball Player's Career*, 133.
53. Anson, *Ball Player's Career*, 133.

In 1886, Sunday and a group of ballplayer friends encountered a "gospel wagon" at the corner of State and Van Buren streets in Chicago. A motley group of singers accompanied by a brass ensemble was parked on the street and Sunday was entranced and moved to tears by their singing.[54] Sunday, inspired by that encounter, attended worship that evening at the Pacific Garden Mission on South Clark Street. "I went to the mission that evening," Sunday recalled, "and liked what I heard. I went back again and again, and one night I went forward and publicly accepted Christ as my Savior."[55]

In March of 1891, while he was playing for the Philadelphia Phillies, Sunday asked to be released from his contract, gave up professional baseball, and went to work for the Chicago YMCA. While in Chicago, he heard Moody preach and, by his example, began visiting the sick, praying and counseling the troubled, and became a familiar presence in local bars inviting patrons to visit evangelistic meetings. In 1893, Sunday became J. Wilbur Chapman's full-time assistant on his revival tours.[56] He acted as Chapman's "advance man," learning every aspect of tour management. Chapman also mentored Sunday on qualities of effective preaching.

In 1896, Sunday set out on his own, preaching at small-town tent revivals in Iowa and Illinois. He called it the "kerosene circuit" because electric lighting had not yet arrived there.[57] Sunday's reputation as an evangelist had grown sufficiently by 1910 that he was leading revivals at mid-sized cities throughout the Midwest, including Youngstown, Ohio, and Wilkes-Barre, Pennsylvania.[58] Five years later, he had remade his revivals into a sustainable, profitable enterprise. He demanded a high level of commitment from local churches. They were required to cancel all activities during the weeks he would be in town and instruct their congregations to worship at the specially built Sunday Tabernacle.

> Wherever he goes Sunday erects a special tabernacle for his meetings. There are many reasons for this. The very building of a tabernacle dedicated to this one special use helps create an interest in the campaign as something new come to town. But primarily, the evangelist's purposes are practical. In the first place,

---

54. Martin, *Hero of the Heartland*, 33.

55. Sunday, *Sawdust Trail*, 50.

56. Chapman, as noted previously, was a longtime friend, associate, and biographer of Dwight Moody.

57. Beginning in 1906 and by Moody's example, Sunday began requiring communities to construct wood-frame tabernacles.

58. Martin, *Hero of the Heartland*, 21.

everything has to be on the ground floor. Converts cannot come forward from a gallery. In addition, existing big buildings rarely have proper acoustics. Most of all Sunday, who has a dread of panics or accidents happening in connection with his meetings, stresses the point that in his tabernacle people have their feet on the ground . . . every aisle, lengthwise and crosswise, ends in [an exit] door.[59]

A January 1915 revival led by Sunday was the largest and most spectacular in Philadelphia history.[60] Under Sunday's leadership revivals had become "unabashedly dramatic performances where audiences laughed at, cried over, cheered and applauded the histrionics of a master showman who personified the ideals [for the time] of American Christianity."[61] William Firstenberger colorfully described a classic Sunday oration:

During the sermon, Sunday spoke from behind the pulpit, in front of the pulpit, and his favorite place, on top of the pulpit. His original sermon notes in loose-leaf binders show the oversize typeface and all-caps printing style that he used for his handwritten notes so that he could easily view the text as he sprinted past the pulpit. He smashed his fists on the top and sides of the pulpit, attempting to break off a small piece, if he was lucky, for dramatic effect. He leaped from pulpit to piano, ran up and down the aisles, slid on the stage as if he were sliding into home plate, and often smashed an ordinary chair to bits. He performed these physical feats to drive home his points of theological fundamentalism and simultaneously kept his audience spellbound.[62]

Like Sam Jones, Billy Sunday was an unapologetic anti-intellectual. He liked to say, "I am a rube of the rubes. I am a hayseed of the hayseeds, and the malodors of the barnyard are with me yet . . . I have greased my hair with goose grease and blacked my boots with stove Blacking. I have wiped my old proboscis with a gunny-sack towel; I have drunk coffee out of my saucer, and I have eaten with my knife. I have 'done it' when I should have said 'did it,' and I have 'saw' when I should have 'seen,' and I expect to go to heaven just the same. I have crept and crawled out from the university of poverty and hard knocks and have taken postgraduate courses."[63] When

---

59. Ellis, *Billy Sunday*, 31.
60. Ellis, *Billy Sunday*, 85.
61. McLoughlin Jr., *Modern Revivalism*, 400.
62. Yeo, "Homer Rodeheaver," 6.
63. Ellis, *Billy Sunday*, 11–12.

critics assailed his vulgar language, he retorted, "I want to preach the gospel so plainly that men can come from the factories and not have to bring along a dictionary."⁶⁴

Homer Rodeheaver

Homer Rodeheaver (1880–1955).
Public domain image ca. 1915,
Library of Congress Control Number 2014703816.

Music and singing were not strengths Billy Sunday possessed. As for reading music, he had famously quipped that he could not tell the difference between "a note and a horsefly."⁶⁵ In 1910, Sunday hired as his soloist and song leader Homer Rodeheaver, the person whose name would be forever linked with his. "Rody," as he was known, more so than any of his predecessors, was the ultimate master of ceremonies. Where Ira Sankey, especially later in life, could seem aloof and self-involved, Rody excelled as a suave and congenial host. His was a complete contrast to the rough, country boy façade cultivated by Sunday. He was a capable singer and humorist, and his expertise as a trombonist was a highlight of every appearance. Rodeheaver's importance to Sunday's revivals was well described in a *New York Times* review from 1917:

> Most prominent outside the Sunday family is undoubtedly Homer A. Rodeheaver. "Rody" is usually one of the most popular members of the party. Schoolboys like him tremendously;

---

64. Ellis, *Billy Sunday*, 34.
65. Martin, *Hero of the Heartland*, 51.

> so do grown men; nor are the ladies backward. Rodeheaver is musical director. He leads the singing, "lining out" the hymns, getting the left half of the house to sing the first line of a stanza, the right half the second line, the choir the third and the whole congregation the fourth. He can sing himself, in an oily resonant voice—a good voice, as gospel singers go. And he plays the trombone to lead the choruses with devastating effect. Rodeheaver is a man of immense value. Whatever he gets for his services, he is worth it. A man with his mixing ability and his capacity for molding a crowd into just the right state of mind in preparation for Sunday's arrival would be worth a fortune to a political leader.[66]

Rody had a unique ability to engage "in friendly banter with the audience," direct choirs of up to two thousand singers, and even do magic tricks for the entertainment of the children.[67]

Following the Moody example, a Sunday revival opened with thirty minutes of singing and special music. Like Sam Jones, Sunday was drawn to brass music and often engaged brass ensembles to play, which is no doubt one of the things which drew him to Homer Rodeheaver.

> The chief lieutenant was Homer Rodeheaver. Tall, cherubic, his dark hair set against a White suit, the musical director would twitch the smallest finger of his left hand and ignite a huge choir. In city after city, Rody warmed up the tabernacle crowds, preparing the way for the evangelist. In his soft Tennessee accent, the good-natured former coal miner could put almost anyone at ease and the glorious Rodeheaver trombone was a weapon of the Lord, marshalling the troops in song . . . Starting a Billy Sunday revival without Rody, one observer once quipped, would be like starting a minstrel show without a brass band. Rody lugs the trombone around the stages as if it were glued to him; he points it, twirls it, tucks it under his arm, and, at last, plays it . . .[68]

Rodeheaver and Sunday shared a preference for optimistic, upbeat songs. B. D. Ackley's "If Your Heart Keeps Right," a Rodeheaver favorite and a staple of Sunday rallies, is an excellent example.

---

66. "Sunday's 19 Aids Draw Trail-hitters", 6.
67. Martin, *Hero of the Heartland*, 52–53.
68. Bruns, *Preacher: Billy Sunday*, 103–104.

If Your Heart Keeps Right

L. Darmond
B. D. Ackley

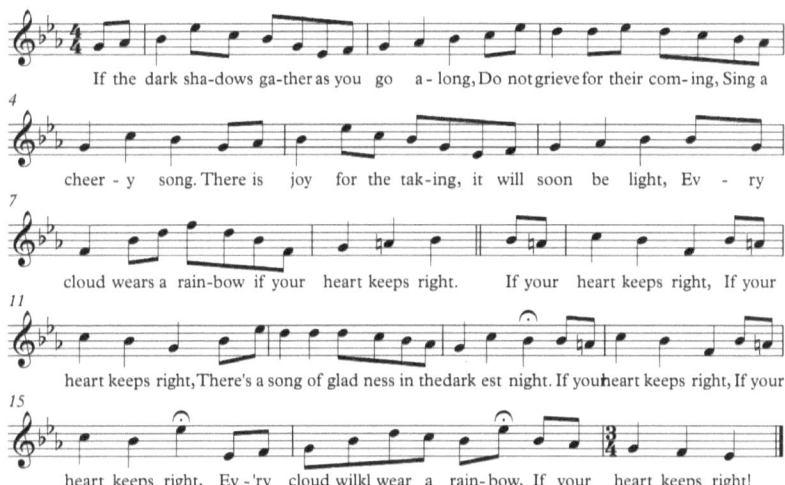

Copyright © 1912, Homer A. Rodeheaver

"If Your Heart Keeps Right," B. D. Ackley. (Copyright 1912, Homer Rodeheaver.)

Other songs were mildly rhythmic and akin to the tin pan alley tunes of pre-World War I. Among the most popular of all was Charles H. Gabriel's "Brighten the Corner Where You Are."

Servanthood of Song

"Brighten the Corner Where You Are." Music by C. H. Gabriel in *Great Revival Hymns, No. 2.*, Homer Rodeheaver/B. D. Ackley eds (Chicago: Rodeheaver Company, 1913), p. 40.

Rodeheaver himself provided a vivid description of why "Brighten the Corner" was appreciated and how it was used.

> "Brighten the Corner" was a general favorite as a congregational song because of the stunts it made possible. When the tabernacle was filled, we would have one section on one side sing the first phrase of the chorus, then, jumping across the tabernacle, the section on the opposite side sings the second phrase, and then we would pick out the ten back rows of the tabernacle, often nearly a short city block away, to sing the last "Brighten the Corner." We used this antiphonal idea effectively with many other songs, but none were as universally popular as "Brighten the Corner Where You Are."
>
> It was not written for a devotional song, and we were criticized for introducing a song of this kind into a religious service; but those who criticized never knew the real purpose back of it. It was never intended for a Sunday morning service, nor a devotional meeting—its purpose was to bridge the gap between the popular song of the day and the great hymns and gospel songs, and to give men a simple, easy lilting melody which they could learn the first time they heard it, and which they could whistle and sing wherever they might be.[69]

Both of the above songs reflect a prime characteristic of what made Billy Sunday successful. The lyrics are full of positivity and optimism and bereft of theological depth. Missing completely are adoration of a higher power, recognition of social miasma and despair, or a Moody-esque urgent plea for conversion. While Sunday espoused a conservative, fundamentalist biblical understanding, he avoided being confrontational. Moreover, Rodeheaver's words betray a realization that Sunday's revivals were to be viewed at least partially as secular entertainment.

The spectacular success of the Sunday/Rodeheaver partnership was not to last. Post-World War I giddiness and the 1918–1919 flu pandemic were significant distractions, while the manifold greed and materialism of the Roaring Twenties further decimated Sunday's audience. In addition, Sunday's penchant for reserving donations received on the final day of a revival as a love offering for himself was receiving widespread criticism by 1920. Though he had contributed generously to philanthropic causes throughout his ministry, his evangelical work had made him a millionaire, and he was proud of it.

---

69. Rodeheaver, *20 Years with Billy Sunday*, 78.

Traditional Evangelism and the Rise of Fundamentalism

At the dawn of the twentieth century many evangelical Christians and leading revivalists were filled with optimism. Attendance at the great revival meetings of the era was front-page news, and there had been great progress in world missions. Many believed that this would be Christianity's great century. Each of the mainline Protestant denominations had its conservative, evangelical wing, and therefore there was a spirit of cross-denominational cooperation to realize the Great Commission of the New Testament. "For Evangelicals, the church was the body of true believers, united by a common experience of grace and devotion to Christ as Savior, wherever they were to be found."[70]

The great tradition of American evangelism had been interdenominational. Moody and his contemporaries sought common ground with mainline faiths—focusing on sharing the "good news" and encouraging worshippers to attend the church of their choice. Moody's revivalist theology was reduced to the simplest, most basic components, "soul-saving and practical Christianity."[71] By the dawning of the twentieth century, however, some revivalists were taking a much more regimented view on what was and was not *correct* belief. In an 1899 survey the question was asked, "What was the teaching of Christ regarding his disciples' attitude toward error and toward those who held erroneous doctrines." The second generation Moody disciple Reuben A. Torrey (1856–1928) responded:

> Christ and His immediate disciples immediately attacked, exposed, and denounced error. We are constantly told in our day that we ought not to attack error but simply teach the truth. This is the method of the coward . . . it was not the method of Christ.[72]

Torrey's confrontational view, which was shared by others, bespoke trouble on the horizon, which would lead to the erosion of much of the good will fostered by Moody. Lyman Stewart (1840–1923), millionaire founder of Union Oil and Biola University, was a conservative evangelical who was troubled by what he saw as a retreat from basic foundational precepts of the Christian faith. Between 1910 and 1915, Stewart personally funded the publication of *The Fundamentals, a Testimony to Truth,* a series of ninety essays delineating and defending foundational beliefs of evangelical Christianity. Many of the leading evangelical voices of his time from each of the major

---

70. Treloar, *Disruption of Evangelicalism,* 2–3.
71. Marsden, *Fundamentalism,* 44.
72. Marsden, *Fundamentalism,* 43.

Protestant denominations contributed essays. Lyman Stewart's effort was published in twelve volumes between 1910 and 1915. Included were spirited defenses of a variety of orthodox and foundational beliefs, among them:

- the deity of Christ,
- the virgin birth,
- the incarnation,
- the deity of the Holy Spirit,
- the nature of regeneration (conversion),
- the acceptance of miracles as the supernatural workings of God, including Paul's conversion on the Damascus Road and Jesus's resurrection,
- and the second coming of Christ.

The Fundamentals gave the movement we call fundamentalism its name. Much of it, however, simply reinforced commonly held beliefs. The Presbyterian General Assembly of 1910, for example, adopted a statement declaring five essential doctrines of the Christian faith: the inerrancy of Scripture, the virgin birth, Christ's atonement, his resurrection, and "the authority of miracles."[73]

The issue that would threaten to drive a wedge between evangelicals, however, was not stressed in Stewart's anthology. Moody had been influenced to adopt premillennial theology, which embraced concepts of an inevitable apocalypse followed by the second coming of Christ. Premillennialists generally dismissed the common optimism of the Victorian era, and instead focused on the urgency of conversion in order to be selected for the promised rapture. Moody himself, however, chose not to make premillennial belief a definitive test of orthodoxy. He "did not want to close off any potential alliances with churchly conservatives or other anti-modernists who might have somewhat different views."[74] The revivalists who succeeded him, on the other hand, took an increasingly firmer stand.

With the growing acceptance of Darwinism, the use of textual criticism, and the approach of a world war, the first two decades of the twentieth century were fertile ground for premillennial belief. Some adherents saw the war as Germany's just punishment since liberal theology had its roots there. Reuben Torrey declared that the poison gas Germans used in trench warfare "is not nearly so dangerous and damnable as the poison gas that German university professors have been belching into the universities and

---

73. Marsden, *Fundamentalism*, 117.
74. Sutton, *American Apocalypse*, 86.

theological seminaries in America."[75] In 1917, when Woodrow Wilson depicted America's entrance into the First World War as a crusade to make the world safe for democracy, many premillennialists refused to enlist, saying the conflict was apocalyptic and any possibility of future peace was doomed to failure.

Rigid fundamentalism as a major factor in American religious thought waned in the 1920s. The war, the Scopes Monkey Trial of the 1920s, and a general ebbing of interest in revivalism were factors causing it to become a subculture. It would reemerge, stronger and more vibrant, after World War II.

The Dilemma: Confronting Divisions of Class and Caste

An undercurrent throughout the previous chapters has been the widening gulf between working classes and elites, cultivated versus populist religion, between liberal and evangelical theological outlooks. The word "evangelism" is derived from the Greek *euangelion* and the Middle English *evaungel,* meaning "good news." One of the best biblical examples of the commissioning of evangelists occurs in Acts, chapter 6:

> Now during those days, when the disciples were increasing in number, the Hellenists complained against the Hebrews because their widows were being neglected in the daily distribution of food. And the twelve called together the whole community of the disciples and said, "It is not right that we should neglect the word of God in order to wait on tables. Therefore, friends, select from among yourselves seven men of good standing, full of the Spirit and of wisdom, whom we may appoint to this task, while we, for our part, will devote ourselves to prayer and to serving the word." (Acts 6:1-4, NRSV)

Notice the stress Scripture places here on ministry to the less fortunate. While Moody and those following him genuinely wanted to reach out to poor and unchurched in the inner city, the audiences they drew were largely from middle-class churchgoers. However pure their motivations, Moody, Jones, Torrey, Sunday, and the other sawdust evangelists[76] all were infected

---

75. Sutton, *American Apocalypse,* 91.

76. "Sawdust" and "sawdust trail" were common descriptors pertaining to the ministries of tent revivalists. The ground on which the revival tent was erected was typically covered in sawdust to dampen the sound of shuffling feet and absorb ground moisture. When an "altar call" was made, attendees filed forward therefore over the "sawdust trail."

with the prevailing white, middle-class myopia and racism. In many cases the disenfranchised simply rejected evangelistic faith entirely. An example of this rejection, clearly directed to revivalist preaching and the Salvation Army, can be seen in the Joe Hill's 1911 song "The Preacher and the Slave." It was regularly sung to the tune of "In the Sweet Bye and Bye" at union meetings of the International Workers of the World (the IWW):

	Chorus:
Long-haired preachers come out every night;	You will eat, by and bye,
Try to tell you what's wrong and what's right.	In that glorious land above the sky;
But when asked, "How 'bout something to eat?"	Work and pray, live on hay,
They will answer in voices sweet:	You'll get pie in the sky when you die![1]

The many divisions between evangelicals, progressives, reformers, and the ordinary folk they strived to minister to were difficult to surmount. The nearly century-old conflict between proponents of the New Theology versus conservatives raged on. The unbending theological views of fundamentalists added to the dissension. Musically, the old barriers between the vernacular/populist and cultivated traditions were firmly in place and would remain so for years to come. Out of that polarization, nonetheless, came two distinct strains of American sacred song in the late nineteenth and early twentieth centuries—one white and one Black.

---

1. The lyrics for "The Preacher and the Slave" were written by the labor activist Joe Hill (1879–1915).

Chapter 14

A NEW CENTURY FOR MUSIC AND WORSHIP IN THE CULTIVATED CHURCH

THE TWENTIETH CENTURY OFFICIALLY began on January 1, 1901, but not surprisingly preachers and pundits began heralding the new century a year before that. The December 31, 1899 issue of the *New York Times* devoted a full four columns to the impressive list of innovations of the previous decades—the steam engine, railroads, the telegraph and the telephone, ocean liners, the cash register, electric lighting, and the daguerreotype.[1]

> We step upon the threshold of 1900, which leads to the new century, facing a still brighter dawn of human civilization. Through agitation and conflict European nations are working toward an ultimate harmony of interests and purposes and bringing awakened Asia into the sweeping current of progress. Light has been let into the "Dark Continent" beyond the ancient borders and is rapidly spreading. America is facing westward and beginning to take its part in carrying the regenerating forces of popular government to the uttermost parts of the earth.[2]

A Time for Optimism

Preaching to the congregation of the First Presbyterian Church of New Orleans on January 1, 1901, the Reverend Benjamin M. Palmer struck a

---

1. Daguerreotypes were the first commonly used form of photography. The process was developed in France by Louis Daguerre (1787–1851).
2. "Nineteenth Century," 20.

similarly optimistic note. "I suppose there is no intelligent person, old or young, male or female, that has not entertained the majesty of this moment in their conception. We stood yesterday upon the edge of the past and bade it farewell. This morning, clouded as it is, shutting out the face of the sun, opens to us another hundred years—not another twelve months but another century."[3] Palmer went on to cite the conflicts between the Christian nations of the west with the "heathen hordes" of China and Africa. These, he believed, foretold an ultimate victory for the cause of Christ. Noting the increased immigration of Chinese to the Pacific coast, he questioned, "Shall the strong destroy the weaker and reign supreme, or shall they be strangely united and through the amalgamation bring out a third civilization, having the best qualities of each?"[4] He closed his message by evoking the book of Revelation and a coming day when "God shall be honored by the whole universe for his matchless justice, upholding government, providing salvation for the lost, and building up for Himself a kingdom which shall never be moved."[5]

In like fashion, the Reverend Newell Dwight Hillis held forth at Brooklyn's Plymouth Church, having recently been installed at the church made famous by Henry Ward Beecher. "Laws are becoming more just," Hillis declared, "rulers more humane, music is becoming sweeter and books wiser; homes are happier, and the individual heart is becoming at once more just and more gentle."[6] During the following year Hillis published a collection of fifteen lectures he had delivered at various colleges and universities. In them he predicted the coming century would be a new creative era. "Plainly," he said, "there is a new spirit in letters, art, in philosophy, and in religion."[7] For Hillis the moral imperative of the church was to embrace a progressive theology shaped by progress in scientific knowledge, and to raise American culture through the arts. On the provocative issue of evolution, he said:

> Herbert Spencer has given no student higher praise than Romanes.[8] But it was evolution that led Romanes, the agnostic, to those "altar stairs that slope through darkness up to God," and

---

3. Palmer, "On the first day of the new year," 11.

4. Palmer, "On the first day of the new year," 13.

5. Palmer, "On the first day of the new year," 17. Palmer was the first moderator of the Presbyterian Church of the Confederacy and a fervent supporter of secession.

6. Lord, *Good Years*, 2.

7. Hillis, *Influence of Christ*, x.

8. George John Romanes (1848–1894) was a biologist, physiologist, and disciple of Charles Darwin. He laid the foundation of what he called comparative psychology, postulating a similarity of cognitive processes and mechanisms between humans and other animals.

made him in his last book say, "Science is moving with all the force of a tidal wave toward faith in Jesus Christ as the world's Savior."[9]

Hillis continued, "The physicist, the biologist, the students of force and life alike, in reverent voice have spoken to God and said, 'O Father, where art Thou?' And out of the rock and wave, out of the herb and flower, has come a voice answering, 'God is here!'"[10] Hillis's various addresses are replete with references to music and song, not for their ability to evangelize but for their connection to nature and therefore to the very essence of humanity.

The optimism described by Palmer and Hillis was by no means universal among Americans at the dawn of the twentieth century. The Harvard psychologist and philosopher William James described two very clear and contrasting streams of religious thought operating at the time, the *institutional* and the *personal*.

> At the outset we are struck by one great partition which divides the religious field. On the one side of it lies institutional, on the other personal religion. As M. P. Sabatier[11] says, one branch of religion keeps the divinity, another keeps man most in view. Worship and sacrifice, procedures for working on the dispositions of the deity, theology and ceremony and ecclesiastical organization, are the essentials of religion in the institutional branch . . . In the more personal branch of religion, it is on the contrary the inner dispositions of man himself which form the center of interest, his conscience, his deserts, his helplessness, his incompleteness.[12]

The *personal* mindset, as exemplified among the evangelical revivalists, has been characterized as "heart to heart" and "soul to soul." The *institutional* Christian, to use James's verbiage, was committed to a more intellectually

---

9. Hillis, *Influence of Christ*, 207.

10. Hillis, *Influence of Christ*, 207.

11. William James (1842–1910) was the brother of novelist Henry James and a prominent teacher of philosophy. In this quote, he is referring to Charles Paul Marie Sabatier (1858–1928), a French Calvinist pastor and historian who was nominated for the Nobel Prize multiple times for his writings. Sabatier's *The Life of St. Francis of Assisi* was the first modern study of the saint's life and is still considered a classic. In Sabatier's collection of lectures, *Modernism* (1908), he distinguishes between the austere institutional approach to religion of the Roman Catholic church of his time and what he saw as the more modern "personal" (evangelical?) theology of young incoming clergy. See Sabatier, *Modernism*, 253–54.

12. James, *Varieties of Religious Experience*, 30.

and culturally based understanding of religion. Their optimism was based on a sincere belief in America's manifest destiny.[13]

The rise of fundamentalism ultimately laid bare the rift between religious conservatives and progressives. It was a contest, still with us in the twenty-first century: modernists versus fundamentalists, evolutionists versus creationists, biblical literalists versus theological progressives.

Sacred Music and Mainline Protestantism: Hymnody and Hymnals

> There will always be congregations who will want to give expression to their faith with the emotional coloring that music gives to our utterances. They will want hymns and other congregational music in which they can participate—simple music, tuneful music, perhaps music that approaches some of the characteristics of folk music.
>
> CLARENCE DICKINSON, 1962[14]

Certainly, one place where the yawning gulf between progressive and evangelical existed was in the matter of church music. Talmage W. Dean, late director of graduate studies in church music at Southwestern Baptist Theological Seminary and later, dean of the Hardin-Simmons University School of Music, observed that musicians joined with theologians in the early twentieth century to keep the gospel hymn repertoire out of mainline Protestant hymnals. The rationale for doing this was based on literary values, theological content, and musical style content.[15]

> The gospel song was derided by many as being no more than doggerel verse, written by amateurs with little poetic skill. The texts were also attacked as being sentimental, egocentric, having

---

13. Dean, *Survey of Twentieth Century Protestant Church Music,* 12–13.

14. Dickinson, "Music in the Churches," 8.

15. For the church music historian the musical style argument presents an interesting conundrum. The progenitors of the cultivated tradition were Lowell Mason and Thomas Hastings with Hastings's *Dissertation on Musical Taste* regarded almost as holy writ. W. B. Bradbury and George F. Root, disciples of Mason, with their successful songs, hymns, and marketing skills, were the musicians upon whom Bliss, Sankey, and many others saw as mentors. Whatever quibbling there might be about style, the songs followed standard common-practice harmonic rules.

crude poetic imagery, and having little foundation in Biblical theology.[16]

The need for a highly personal commitment, so integral to evangelistic religion, was completely lost on progressives. The critics argued that gospel hymns that focused on the human need for conversion or interpersonal testimony were too subjective and therefore unfit for corporate worship. James Bissett Pratt (1875–1944), professor of philosophy at Williams College, argued that the *only* true worship was objective and impersonal.

> But we must go deeper than this and ask ourselves the question whether we really believe that worship is any longer possible in the modern world at all . . . The question, therefore, narrows to this: Is any kind of objective worship possible for the man of our age? . . . There is a kind of worship that is perfectly objective and sincere and that is quite as possible for the intelligent man of today as it was for the ancient:—namely that union of awe and gratitude which is reverence, combined perhaps with consecration and a suggestion of communion, which most thoughtful men must feel in the presence of the Cosmic forces and in reflecting upon them.[17]

James Pratt viewed liturgical worship, and its traditions going back to the medieval era, as the ideal that the church of his time needed to emulate. It is also hard to miss the elitist slant of his writing, which seems to suggest that true worship could only be appreciated by intelligent men.

The enmity that cultivated musicians felt regarding the popular gospel hymn repertoire was palpable. The organist Henry M. Dunham, who was a professor of organ at the New England Conservatory well into the twentieth century and one of the nation's premier concert organists, was asked to resign from a church because he refused to play improvisations on Ira Sankey hymn tunes. Perhaps the most visceral condemnation came from the famous New England composer Horatio Parker, in an address to the American Guild of Organists in May of 1900. He railed:

> So is evil music as harmful to our sense of beauty, to our aesthetic sensitiveness. . . . People ask for bread and we give them sponge cake; for fish, and they are lucky if they get eels—sometimes real snakes, loathsome, wriggling, slimy, moody and snakey snakes—vulgar with the vulgarity of the streets and the music

---

16. Dean, *Survey of Twentieth Century Protestant Church Music*, 91.

17. Pratt, *Religious Consciousness*, 308. James Bissett Pratt should not to be confused with Waldo Selden Pratt, whose important writings on church music will be discussed later.

hall. [Great applause.] If sentimentality is evil,—and I think no one here will care to deny it—what shall we say of vulgarity? ... Let the stuff be confined to the mission, where it may do good. Among people of any appreciable degree of refinement and culture, [it] do[es] harm.[18]

Those advocating for evangelistic hymnody were not about to take vitriol like that of Parker and others sitting down. They retorted that if the church was to be fishers of people it had to interact with them on a personal level. Pietism and Arminianism, foundation blocks for much of America's denominational Christianity, were in essence *subjective*. Many of the Psalms were intentionally subjective in their use of personal pronouns, and indeed that may account for their usefulness as an aid to devotion:

> The Lord is *my* shepherd, *I* shall not want. He makes *me* lie down in green pastures; he leads *me* beside still waters; he restores *my* soul. He leads *me* in right paths for his name's sake.
> Even though *I* walk through the darkest valley, *I* fear no evil; for you are with *me*; your rod and your staff—they comfort *me*.
> You prepare a table before *me* in the presence of *my* enemies; you anoint *my* head with oil; *my* cup overflows. Surely goodness and mercy shall follow *me* all the days of *my* life, and *I* shall dwell in the house of the Lord *my* whole life long.
> (Psalm 23, NRSV)

As for the criticism that gospel songs lacked the musical integrity of traditional hymns, advocates pointed to the cloying chromaticism of much quartet music and the harmonic and rhythmic complexity of many hymns. They noted these were impediments to congregational singing. Gospel hymns, on the other hand, had gotten thousands singing and prepared them to receive the Word. Their success was irrefutable.

At any rate, the divide between gospel hymn proponents and those favoring traditional, classic hymnody was tangible. Talmage Dean concluded wistfully that "the majority of the denominational hymnals retained their European traditions and, in many cases, were ignoring a large body of excellent literary hymnody already being written in America."[19]

It is worth considering that Harry Emerson Fosdick, known by many of his generation as a divisive influence for his controversial sermon, "Shall the Fundamentalists Win?," is now remembered for a hymn intended to bring people together, "God of Grace and God of Glory." It was written as a

---

18. McDaniel, "Church Song and the Cultivated Tradition," 478–79.
19. Dean, *Survey of Twentieth Century Protestant Church Music*, 91.

processional for the opening of Riverside Church on October 1930 and was used again when the church was dedicated in 1932. Composer and hymnologist Carlton R. Young has noted that it is not coincidental that Fosdick's hymn was written at the very beginning of the Great Depression. The text of the second stanza seems to anticipate Franklin Roosevelt's stirring words, "the only thing we have to fear is . . . fear itself . . ."[20]

> Lo! The hosts of evil round us scorn thy Christ, assail His ways.
> From the fears that long have bound us, free our hearts to faith and praise.
> Grant us wisdom, grant us courage for the living of these days.

By the mid-1890s, the use of words-only songsters was finally falling out of favor in the mainline denominations. The period from 1895 to 1930 saw a profusion of modern, text-with-music denominational hymnals published. The trend to have music and text on the same page and to put such hymnals in the hands of every worshipper was nearing universal acceptance. Among the more notable examples were the *Hymnal of the Methodist Episcopal Church* (1878); *The Hymnal* (Presbyterian) of 1895, Louis Benson, editor;[21] the Congregationalist *Pilgrim Hymnal* of 1912; and *The Hymnal* (Protestant Episcopal) 1916. In addition, by 1900, publishers had collected plates for virtually all the standard hymns then in use. This made it financially feasible for many larger urban parishes to publish their own custom collections.

The influence of the Oxford/Ritualistic Movement and the British *Hymns, Ancient and Modern* (1861) is obvious in all these hymnals. All prioritized literary quality in the texts chosen. Victorian English composers such as Henry Smart, Arthur Sullivan, S. S. Wesley, Joseph Barnby, and John B. Dykes were well represented. There was also a cross-denominational interest in Reformation chorales, owing in part to the growing influx of immigrants from Germany and Nordic countries.

Reed and Pipe Organs in Turn-of-the-Century America

The first quarter of the twentieth century represented a turning point in America for the development of both reed organs and pipe organs. Where

---

20. Roosevelt, "Inaugural Address," March 4, 1933.

21. Louis Fitzgerald Benson (1855–1930) had a profound influence on American church music through his work as an author and hymnologist. Born in Philadelphia, he studied law at the University of Pennsylvania and was admitted to the bar in 1877. In 1888, he was ordained a Presbyterian minister and was editor of *The Hymnal* (1895) and several other hymn collections. He was a prolific writer on hymnologic subjects. His two-volume *Studies of Familiar Hymns* (1903, 1926) and *The English Hymn: Its Development and Use in Worship* (1903) are still important as scholarly resources.

once simple hymns and gospel songs had reigned in Victorian parlors, now the popular appetite was for the catchy rhythms of ragtime and the cakewalk—not at all in the reed organ's comfort zone. Furthermore, the invention of the gramophone or disc record player in 1894 by Emile Berliner, a significant improvement over Edison's cylinder phonograph, allowed music to be heard in the home in a closer approximation to what had been recorded—an argument for dispensing entirely with home music-making. Reed organ manufacturers struggled on, and in fact, the portability of the instruments made them popular with military chaplains during World War 1. However, the invention by Laurens Hammond of Chicago of the "Hammond Organ" in 1935 was the death knell of the reed organ. Like them, the electrically powered Hammonds were small enough to be movable yet had a much broader tonal palate and were more effective for playing popular music.

At the turn of the twentieth century the pipe organ was at the very pinnacle of its popularity. In 1915 at the Panama Pacific Exposition in San Francisco, over three hundred thousand people purchased tickets to hear concerts of organ music.[22] The pipe organ had come into its own and could be found not only in churches, but also in department stores and municipal halls, college and university chapels and, by the 1920s, in movie theaters. Programs of organ music were a daily feature on the radio. Many of America's wealthiest families had concert instruments installed in their homes. Harry Rowe Shelly, the organist at Park Avenue Baptist Church in New York (before it moved and became Riverside Church), served as the organist in the summer home of John D. Rockefeller in Pocatalico Hills, New York. The Rockefeller house organ was designed with multiple manuals and pipe chests so it could be played from any floor of the house. To facilitate keeping it in tune, the home had an innovative system for temperature control. Walter C. Gale (1872–1938), in addition to being the organist at the Broadway Tabernacle from 1905 to 1932, was organist at the palatial home of Andrew Carnegie, 5th Avenue at 91st Street.[23]

The number of pipe organs built for churches during the same period is impressive. Everett Truette's journal, *The Organ*, listed over one hundred organ installations representing all corners of the United States just in the year 1892. Of those, twenty-eight were impressive enough that a full description of manuals and stops was included.[24] *Diapason Magazine* in 1918 published an even more impressive list of new organs and said that the average size of instruments had increased. "An instrument of four manuals and

---

22. Fitts, "Aspects of American Musical Life," 155.
23. Hummel, "Music on Demand."
24. *The Organ, A Monthly Journal*. E. Truette, ed. Vol. 1 (1892).

fifty to sixty stops is no longer unusual and is being 'lost in the shuffle' when we are finding an instrument of 120, 126, 138, 163, 168, 232 . . ."[25]

A person who contributed greatly to this American organ renaissance was William C. Carl (1865–1936). Carl served as organist at the First Presbyterian Church in New York City from 1882 to 1935, over fifty years.

William C. Carl.
Public domain image. (https://hymnary.org/person/Carl_William)

After he studied with Alexander Guilmant in Paris the two became lifelong friends. Shortly after coming to First Presbyterian, Carl began a series of recitals at the church that gained national attention. "The church was filled to capacity at most concerts and police had to control the crowds on Fifth Avenue."[26] Another activity that was heavily covered in the press was Carl's presentation of a concert version of Wagner's opera *Parsifal,* which, at the time, could only be performed fully staged at Bayreuth.

In 1898, while Guilmant was in America on tour, teacher and student met and agreed to open a school for organ instruction based on Guilmant's methods of teaching. The Guilmant Organ School became one of the premier institutions for the study of organ and church music in the United States. Clarence Dickinson, whose contributions will be discussed later, served as examiner for the school for a number of years.[27]

---

25. Fry, "From the Brattle Organ to ———?," 19.

26. Entriken, "Guilmant Organ School."

27. The Guilmant Organ School remained based at New York's First Presbyterian Church until 1963, and its new president Dr. George Markey hoped to expand its course offerings to make it competitive with sacred music programs at Union Seminary and Westminster Choir College. Unfortunately, after leaving First Presbyterian Church, the school was unable to find a permanent home and closed in the early 1970s.

The pipe organ boom of the early twentieth century would not last. The advent of radio and the phonograph as well as the Great Depression caused recital attendance to decline. Lack of funds temporarily retarded church installations as well. Nevertheless, the capability of pipe organs with skilled organists to not only accompany but to actually *lead* a worshipping assembly had been well established.

The Second New England School of Composers

Much of the musical activity discussed in recent chapters occurred in America's Midwest and South. This represented a remarkable change from the almost exclusively New England-centered focus of the cultivated tradition in the early nineteenth century, and certainly is indicative of America's growth as a nation after the Civil War. All the same, progress in sacred music was hardly stagnant in the Northeast.

A coterie of New England composer/musicians living in or associated with the Boston area was active from the 1890s through the 1920s (and, in the case of Amy Beach, well into the 1930s). The musicologist H. Wiley Hitchcock referred to them as the "Second New England School" to differentiate them from Billings and the other tunesmiths of the colonial era.[28] This group has been given many names: Gilbert Chase called them the "Boston Classicists";[29] Rupert Hughes, acerbic author of *Contemporary American Composers* (1900), labeled them the "Boston Academics,"[30] while John Tasker Howard simply referred to them as "the Boston Group."[31] Most general histories discuss the work of these musicians as a final chapter in the history of American music in the nineteenth century. However, their lives and influence extended well into the twentieth century, especially regarding church music, which explains why they appear in this chapter instead of earlier.

The five composers generally identified with the Second New England School, who were either active church musicians or composed music for church use, were Arthur Foote (1853–1937), George Chadwick (1854–1931), Arthur B. Whiting (1861–1936), Horatio Parker (1863–1919), and Amy Marcy Cheney Beach (1867–1944).

---

28. Hitchcock, *Music in the United States*, 143.
29. Chase, *America's Music*, 365.
30. Hughes, *Contemporary American Composers*, 145.
31. Howard, *Our American Music*, 306.

Arthur B. Whiting and Arthur Foote

Arthur Batelle Whiting.
Public domain image. (https://en.m.wikipedia.org/wiki/File:Arthur_B._Whiting_1904.jpg)

Arthur Batelle Whiting and Arthur Foote both served as church organists but were better known as concert pianists and composers of secular concert music. Whiting's service to churches was brief. After a short tenure during the 1870s at a church in Boston, he became organist at All Saints Episcopal Church in Worcester, Massachusetts. In 1881, Whiting was promoted to organist/choirmaster, leading the church's choir of men and boys. He continued in that capacity through 1884 and then resigned to devote himself full time to performing, composing, and lecturing.[32] Whiting was best known as a concert pianist, a pioneer harpsichordist, and a passionate advocate for early music, but also had a gift for choral writing and published ten church anthems.

---

32. *All Saints Church, Worcester, Massachusetts*, 43.

Arthur Foote, ca. 1904.
Public domain photograph. From Louis C. Elson, *The History of American Music* (New York: The Macmillan Company, 1904), p. 212.

Arthur Foote was a native of Salem, Massachusetts. He showed an early interest in the organ and studied with Benjamin Johnson Lang in Boston. Foote recalled Gilmore's "Peace Jubilee" in 1869 as his "great awakening" to the power of music.[33] In 1878, Foote began a thirty-two-year tenure as the organist at the First Unitarian Church of Boston. He would become one of the founders of the American Guild of Organists.

First Unitarian Church had been in existence for 150 years when Arthur Foote joined its staff. It was a Congregational meetinghouse in colonial times but joined the Unitarian movement in the mid-nineteenth century. The liturgy at First Church was typical of elite Boston churches, with a quartet choir leading the service musically. Foote established a custom of mini-recitals featuring a mix of organ music and congregational singing on Thursday afternoons.[34] He was exceptional among members of the Second New England School for preferring to work with quartet choirs. He wrote around thirty-five sacred choral works for mixed voice quartet, including a "Te Deum" and a setting of the Harriet Beecher Stowe text, "Still, Still with Thee," which remained popular long after his death.[35]

---

33. Foote, "Bostonian Remembers," 38.
34. Blanchard, "Life and Works of Arthur Foote," 11.
35. Blanchard, "Life and Works of Arthur Foote," 14.

Amy Marcy Cheney (Mrs. H. H. A.) Beach

Amy (Mrs. H. H. A.) Beach.
Public domain image,
Library of Congress Digital ID cph 3b04622. (hdl.loc.gov/loc.pnp/cph.3b04622)

Amy Marcy Cheney Beach (1867–1944), who was known for most of her professional life as Mrs. H. H. A. Beach, has only in recent years been recognized for her amazing legacy as a pioneer among women in music. She was born in New Hampshire to a musical family. Her mother Clara Cheney, a singer and pianist, began teaching her piano at the age of four. At age seven she was performing as a pianist in public, often programming pieces she had written. In 1883, at just sixteen years of age, Amy Marcy Cheney made her concert debut playing the *Piano Concerto in G minor*, Opus 60, of Ignaz Moscheles. A year later she appeared with the Boston Symphony as soloist in the *F minor Concerto* of Chopin and in one of the Mendelssohn concertos with Theodore Thomas and his orchestra.

Early on, Beach showed a special interest in sacred choral music. Her *Mass in E flat,* Opus 5 gained national attention when it was premiered in February of 1892 by the Boston Handel and Haydn Society and Boston Symphony Orchestra conducted by Carl Zerrahn. Another large work for chorus and orchestra was the *Festival Jubilate,* Opus 17, written for the 1893 Columbian Exposition in Chicago. For Beach, the setting of sacred texts to music was spiritual. Near the end of her life, she wrote that "there can be no greater experience than the act of entering into the great religious texts with the intimacy that we must feel in order to put such words into adequate music."[36]

Amy Beach had a close affiliation with the Protestant Episcopal denomination throughout her life. After coming to Boston in 1875 her family attended Trinity Church on Copley Square, where the future bishop of

---

36. Block, *Amy Beach, Passionate Victorian,* 161.

Massachusetts, Phillips Brooks, was pastor. Brooks was a close family friend and officiated at her marriage to Dr. Henry Beach.[37] While Beach attended the Church of the Advent with Henry during her married years, she had never joined. After Henry's death, however, she elected to be baptized and joined Emmanuel Episcopal Church in Boston. When settled in New York, she moved to St. Bartholomew's and there, with the strong support of organist/choirmaster David McK. Williams, she wrote some of her most substantial sacred choral music.

Over the course of her career as a composer, Amy Beach wrote thirty-five sacred choral works. Five were major works for soloists, chorus, and orchestra: the *Mass in E flat* (1890), the *Graduale*, a movement added to the Mass in 1892, the *Festival Jubilate* (1891), the *Canticle of the Sun* (1928), and *Christ in the Universe* (1931). Another composition of major work proportions was her *Service in A* (1905/1906) for soloists, chorus, and organ. The remaining twenty or so shorter pieces were anthems and responses for use in worship. In 1932, Beach was quoted in the press as saying, "I think my church music appeals to me more than anything I have done. I have written the anthems and oratorios and a whole Episcopal service with great joy, and they have become a part of me more than anything I have done, I am sure."[38] Most of these were scored for soloists, chorus, and organ, but not with soloists functioning as an independent quartet. Beach produced two anthems for unaccompanied chorus with no soloists at all. "Help Us, O God," Opus 50 (1903) is a challenging work with a text apparently adapted by Beach from the Psalms. There is divisi in all voices, and, at twenty-three pages in length, it was probably intended as a concert piece or selection for a Lenten vespers.

As more and more of Amy Marcy Cheney Beach's compositional legacy is finally being revealed through live and recorded performances, one cannot help being struck by the unique creative spark that inhabited her writing. This is true of her church music, from simple anthems to the complex five-voice choral fugue in "Help Us, O God." Her contribution to

---

37. Reigles, "Choral Music of Amy Beach," 9. Dr. Henry Harris Aubrey Beach (1843–1910) was a noted Boston surgeon and professor of anatomy at Harvard. It was a second marriage for Dr. Beach, whose first wife had died in 1880. As a field surgeon during the Civil War, Dr. Beach was noted for being the first to apply an antiseptic during a surgical procedure. The doctor was musical, having grown up singing in the boy choir at Boston's Church of the Advent and having studied both organ and piano. In adulthood he had been a longtime singer with the Handel and Haydn Society. During their marriage which lasted until Henry's death in 1910, Amy refrained from recital playing, but did make occasional appearances with the Boston Symphony, most notably in a performance of the Third Concerto of Beethoven in 1888.

38. E. McCann, 1932, Clipping file in Music Division, New York Public Library at Lincoln Center.

American church music was sizable and only now in the twenty-first century is being recognized.

George Whitefield Chadwick

George Whitefield Chadwick.
Public domain image, Library of Congress Digital ID cph 3c19834. (hdl.loc.gov/loc.pnp/cph.3c19834)

A fourth member of the Second New England School was George Whitefield Chadwick (1854–1931). Chadwick was a native of Lowell, Massachusetts. As a child he sang alto in the Lawrence Street Church choir. When his voice began to change the church organist, one Sam Ellis, selected George to be his blower boy. He delighted in mischievous activities such as stopping pumping just before Ellis was to play the final note of a piece.[39] One thing led to another, and soon young Chadwick was taking organ lessons. He followed Ellis as the church's organist.[40]

In the spring of 1872, as Gilmore's second stupendous offering, the "World Peace Jubilee," approached, Chadwick assisted Sam Ellis in preparing the Lowell church choir for the event. His father and brother had sung in the 1869 event. He would sing bass in the 1872 Jubilee chorus. That same year, Chadwick enrolled in the New England Conservatory, where he studied piano and music theory. While in Boston, he also studied organ with both George Elbridge Whiting, Eugene Thayer, and Dudley Buck.[41] In September of 1877, Chadwick departed for Europe for three years of study, first at Leipzig and later in Berlin. Returning to Boston in 1880, he served as organist for

---

39. Geary, "Chadwick and the Nineteenth-Century American Te Deum," 5.
40. Faucett, *George Whitefield Chadwick*, 17.
41. Geary, "Chadwick and the Nineteenth-Century American Te Deum," 8.

varying lengths of time at five Boston churches between 1881 and 1893. In 1897, Chadwick was appointed director of the New England Conservatory.

While he served regularly as an organist, Chadwick's fame rested chiefly on his work as an instrumental composer of three symphonies, several overtures, string quartets, secular songs, and works for the stage. Even so, Chadwick understood the importance of choral music to church life. In an address to the National Institute of Arts and Letters in 1913, he recalled that once in New England "every village had its church and every church its choir, and in that church and choir the social as well as the religious interests of the place were largely concentrated." He went on to bemoan the invasion of quartets into Protestant worship:

> And how is it now? In the country, beyond the reach of the trolley, a musical desert, a barren waste broken only by the occasional squeak of a wheezy cabinet organ drooling out a ragtime gospel hymn, or a vulgar scrap of vaudeville music issuing from the strident horn of a talking-machine. The village Blacksmith no longer rejoices to hear his daughter's voice singing in the choir. He listens to a paid—and usually overpaid—quartet choir simpering and snickering behind their curtain and to an organist who regales the congregation with selections from the operas, or thinly disguised imitations of them.[42]

Horatio Parker

Horatio Parker, ca. 1916.
Public domain image, Library of Congress.
Digital ID cph 3b04623.

---

42. Chadwick, "Plea for Choral Singing," 95–96.

The fifth and most prominent member of the Second New England School as a church musician was Horatio William Parker (1863–1919). At the turn of the twentieth century, Parker was America's most famous composer and music educator. Of the members of the Boston clique, he was the most active as a church musician and devoted the most effort to the composition of music for worship.

Horatio Parker was born in Auburndale, Massachusetts, in 1863. His father, Charles Edward Parker, was a well-known architect. The family was devoutly Episcopalian, and Horatio would be closely associated with the Protestant Episcopal Church throughout his life. In 1879, Parker became organist at St. Paul's Episcopal Church in Dedham, Massachusetts. He walked to the church and back home twice weekly—a distance of ten miles—all for a salary of $300 per annum. At the age of nineteen, Parker set out for Boston, where he studied organ briefly with George Chadwick as well as various teachers at the Conservatory. He also served briefly as organist at St. John's Episcopal Church in Roxbury. Chadwick saw Parker's musical potential and encouraged his parents to consider European study for him. On July 1 of 1882, Parker set sail for Europe and Munich, where he would be taught by Josef Rheinberger. The Munich experience and the music he heard at St. Michael's Cathedral there left Horatio Parker with a lifelong passion for choral music. One of his fellow students at the *Hochschule* said of Parker, "He was confessedly far the best pupil in the school—that no one could compete with him in organ playing, in conducting, or in composition."[43]

In April of 1891, Horatio Parker began composition of the work which would help to define his career moving forward and would secure for him a place of honor in the history of American music. The oratorio *Hora novissima* was Parker's setting of the majestic twelfth-century Latin hymn "The Rhythm, of Bernard de Morlaix, Monk of Cluny, on the Celestial Country."[44] He set the eleven-movement work in Bernard's original Latin with an alternate English text by his mother, Isabella G. Parker, which exactly mirrored the prosody of the Latin.

Hora novissima was completed in April of 1892, exactly a year after it was begun. Parker dedicated the work to his father, who had passed away in October of 1890. Even before he finished it, word had spread that *Hora* was destined to be the first great American oratorio. It was published by Novello early in 1893 and had its premier with the Church Choral Society of New York conducted by Richard Henry Warren, in May. Performances

---

43. Kearns, *Horatio Parker, 1863–1919*, 8.

44. Bernard's "Rhythm on the Celestial Country" was an excerpt from his much longer sardonic poem, *Contemptu Mundi*.

soon followed by the Handel and Haydn Society and Cincinnati May Festival Chorus conducted by Theodore Thomas. The performance of *Hora novissimna* at the Three Choirs Festival in Worcester England in September of 1899 with Parker himself conducting was a crowning achievement of his life. Over two thousand were in the audience.

Soon after *Hora's* premier in New York City, Horatio received a call from Trinity Church on Copley Square in Boston to become its organist/choirmaster. The position paid $650 a month, "the largest income ever granted to a Boston church musician."[45] Trinity Church, Boston, had a large, well-established chorus choir. Parker eagerly accepted the position, and he and his wife Anna moved back to Boston in the fall of 1893. Just a year later in 1895 Horatio Parker was offered and accepted the Battell Professorship of Music at Yale University.

Parker's Boston period, 1893 to 1903, was when he made his greatest contributions to American church music. It was during this time that he wrote most of his church anthems. He also labored to produce a new musical edition to the *Hymnal Revised and Enlarged* of the Protestant Episcopal church, which would be published in 1903.[46] Parker included thirty of his own hymn tunes to the *Hymnal Revised*. Of these, several continued to appear in denominational hymnals, including the Episcopal Hymnal 1940.

While acceptance of the teaching position at Yale made it necessary for him and Anna to move to New Haven, Parker did not relinquish his post at Trinity Church. Instead, he commuted once or twice weekly between Connecticut and Boston. (When commitments at the university made that impossible, George Chadwick frequently substituted for him at the organ.) To add to an already busy schedule, Parker became director of the New Haven Symphony in 1894 and organized the New Haven Oratorio Society in 1903.

The hectic schedule was eventually to take its toll. In addition, with New Haven becoming more and more the focus of his energies, old bonds with friends and colleagues in Boston had weakened. Around 1903 Parker began casting about for a suitable church position in the New York area and in February of 1904, he accepted the call to be organist/choirmaster at the Collegiate Church of St. Nicholas, a wealthy Dutch-Reformed congregation at 5th Avenue and 48th Street. It would be his last church engagement.

Over the course of his career, Horatio Parker wrote twenty-two church anthems. The most popular of them—"Bow Down Thine Ear," "Christ Our

---

45. Kearns, *Horatio Parker, 1863–1919*, 21.

46. Parker's was one of several musical editions that were published. So esteemed was Parker in the Episcopal denomination, however, that he would be asked to consult on the 1916 edition of the *Hymnal*, the first denomination-wide hymnal in the modern format with music and text on the same page.

Passover," "The Lord Is My Light," "Give unto the Lord," and "I Will Set His Dominion in the Sea"—were all published between 1890 and 1891. In a 1924 survey by Harold W. Thompson over half of the 104 prominent American choirmasters found Parker's music useful in their work. Leonard Ellinwood did a similar survey in the 1950s and found Parker's music still being performed regularly in many churches.[47] Dwight Steele in his 1955 index of anthem literature, *Music for the Protestant Church Choir*, still listed four Parker anthems as "Standard Repertoire" for churches. Among them were "Brightest and Best" from 1904 and "To Whom Then Will Ye Liken God" (1909).[48]

Writing in 1930, David Stanley Smith, one of his students at Yale, said of Parker's anthems:

> No choirmaster can fail to be grateful for these compositions. They combine in a curious way respect for tradition (Parker was always a faithful communicant of the Episcopal Church) with an escape from the dullness that is the distinguishing mark of much of the older church music of this type. It is English, but with an ingratiating admixture of New World buoyancy. A loss of sternness is compensated for by original touches of harmony and pleasantness of melody. Parker, even in these simple compositions, . . . is unmistakably Parker. He wrote always with a chorus in mind and disapproved of the church quartet (the expression "quartet choir" was always an anathema to him, and he regarded it as a contradiction in terms).[49]

Parker was indeed critical of much of the church music of his time and earlier. He spoke glowingly of the music of Palestrina, alluding to it as the ideal toward which all church musicians sand composers of sacred choral music should aspire. "Nothing," he wrote, "exists of earlier or later date which may be compared with it. It is ideal church music, ideal religious music; the greatest and purest ever made; and it can never be surpassed."[50] Nevertheless, when considering his own music for church choir and its marketability, Parker was a realist. While his anthems are scored for chorus choir, soloists and quartet are approached as separate entities, rarely intertwined within the choral texture. In this sense, they follow much the same pattern as Buck's anthems of three decades earlier.

---

47. Ellinwood, *History of American Church Music*, 134, 139.
48. Steere, *Music for the Protestant Church Choir*, 18, 48.
49. Smith and Strunk, "Study of Horatio Parker," 155–56.
50. Parker, "Contemporary Music."

A New Century for Music and Worship in the Cultivated Church 493

The organists, choral conductors, and composers of the Second New England School were among that last class of American musicians for whom study in Europe was essentially mandatory for them to have any sort of credibility.[51] As such, they believed, as Lowell Mason did long before, that European art music—its style and compositional processes—were that to which American composers should aspire.

Dvořák Inspires a Dialogue on the Need for Music Uniquely "American"

In 1895, the Czech composer Antonin Dvořák was at the end of his historic, three-year sojourn to the United States.[52] During that time he was director of the National Conservatory of Music in New York City. In an article published in *Harper's New Monthly Magazine,* he wrote that the "inspiration for a truly national [i.e., American] music might be derived from the Negro melodies or Indian chants."[53]

> It is a proper question to ask, what songs, then, belong to the American and appeal more strongly to him than any others! What melody could stop him on the street if he were in a strange land and make the home feeling well up within him, no matter how hardened he might be or how wretchedly the tune were played? ... The most potent as well as the most beautiful among them, according to my estimation, are certain of the so-called plantation melodies and slave songs.[54]

Dvořák's embrace of the African American musical tradition was by no means an empty verbal gesture. Upon accepting the directorship of the conservatory, he and the institution's principal benefactor, Jeanette M. Thurber (1850–1946), made the radical decision to make an offer of free admission available to musically gifted African Americans. An official announcement appeared in newspapers nationally in late May of 1893:

> The National Conservatory of Music of America proposes to enlarge its sphere of usefulness by adding to its departments a branch for instruction in music of colored pupils of talent, largely with the view of forming colored professors of merit. The

---

51. Amy Beach was the lone exception, but she studied with Ernst Perabo in New York. Perabo was trained under Reinecke at the Leipzig Conservatory.

52. Dvořák arrived in America in September of 1892 and returned to Czechoslovakia in April of 1895.

53. Dvořák, "Music in America," 432.

54. Dvořák, "Music in America," 432.

aptitude of the colored race for music, vocal and instrumental, has long been recognized, but no definite steps have hitherto been taken to develop it.[55]

Dvořák chose as his assistant at the conservatory a then-unknown African American singer, Henry Thacker ("Harry") Burleigh (1866–1949).[56] Burleigh included the following statement regarding the nature and substance of the Black spiritual in his collection, *Negro Spirituals*, published in 1917.

> The plantation songs known as "spirituals" are the spontaneous outbursts of intense religious fervor, and had their origins chiefly in camp meetings, revivals, and other religious exercises. They were never "composed," but sprang into life, ready-made, from the white heat of religious fervor during some protracted meeting in camp or church, as the simple ecstatic utterance of wholly untutored minds, and are practically the only music in America which meets the scientific definition of Folk Song. Success in singing these Folk Songs is primarily dependent upon deep spiritual feeling. The voice is not nearly so important as the spirit; and then rhythm, for the Negro's soul is linked with rhythm, and it is an essential characteristic of most all the Folk Songs.[57]

In response to Dvořák's challenge, a number of younger American composers—Henry Gilbert (1868–1928), Arthur Farwell (1872–1952), John Alden Carpenter (1876–1951), Charles Wakefield Cadmon (1881–1946), and John Powell (1882–1963)—had already begun to produce music based on Black and Native American folk traditions. Henry Gilbert, perhaps the most outspoken of them, threw down a gauntlet, saying, "Let me say at once that music written by American composers in conformity to European models is not American music. It is imitation European music, and frequently a pretty poor imitation ... There is almost no real American music at present in existence."[58]

Dvořák's ideas, however, were guaranteed to elicit a visceral reaction from the German-trained composers of the Second New England School. Amy Beach, while not rejecting the theory out of hand, had misgivings:

---

55. "Musical Matters."

56. Burleigh is remembered today chiefly for inspiring the plaintive melody Dvořák used in the slow movement of his *New World Symphony*, however, any influence Burleigh may have had cannot be documented. Of far more consequence were Burleigh's many masterful arrangements of traditional spirituals for concert use.

57. Burleigh, *Celebrated Negro Spirituals*, 1.

58. Gilbert, "Composer Gilbert on America's Music."

> Without the slightest desire to question the beauty of the negro melodies of which [Dvořák] speaks so highly, or to disparage them on account of their source, I cannot help feeling justified in the belief that they are not fully typical of our country. The African population of the United States is far too small for its songs to be considered "American."[59] It represents only one factor in the composition of our nation. Moreover, it is not native American. Were we to consult the native folk songs of the continent, it would have to be those of the Indians and Esquimaux, several of whose curious songs are given in the publications of the Smithsonian Institute. The Africans are no more native than the Italian, Swedes or Russians.[60]

Commenting on Dvořák's use of spiritual-inspired melodies in his *New World Symphony,* Beach said, "It seems to me light in calibre, however, and to represent only the peaceful, sunny side of the Negro character and life. Not for a moment does it suggest their suffering, heartbreaks, slavery."[61]

Chadwick, according to biographer Bill Faucett, "simply did not subscribe to an American style—he did not think a single type of such music was possible; he did not believe that his definition of American was the same as anyone else's."[62] In a lecture given at the Peabody Institute in Baltimore in 1897, Horatio Parker declared that "there is no 'indigenous' American music."[63]

Arthur Whiting was perhaps the most prescient of the Boston coterie. Writing in *The Outlook* in 1915, Whiting stated, "The Negro influence has been one of propinquity. The African slave is a singer whose life of suffering and hardship has brought to the surface all his powers of expression."[64] He acknowledged that white composers, even if not realizing it, had been influenced by music of their Black brethren. "A humble member of the national family from the beginning, his songs of pathos and glorification have made a deep impression on every music-loving child, who, on becoming later a

---

59. Beach's statement was, of course, inaccurate regarding the sizable Black population of the United States, but it exemplifies the provincial views of a New England aristocracy that tended to view all non-Anglo Saxons as part of insignificant minorities.

60. Reigles, "Choral Music of Amy Beach," 55.

61. Block, *Amy Beach, Passionate Victorian*, 88. While Beach was specifically referring to the plaintive theme of the second movement of Dvořák's *New World Symphony*, it suggests an unfamiliarity of the vast body of spirituals that do reflect the suffering of the enslaved African American people.

62. Faucett, *George Whitefield Chadwick*, 194.

63. Kearns, *Horatio Parker*, 40.

64. Whiting, "American Composer," 401–2.

trained musician, finds his own speech somewhat akin to that of his old friend." As for the existence of an American musical style that was truly indigenous, he urged patience since efforts at serious musical composition in the United States had only begun a half century earlier. "The most homogeneous people have produced the most characteristic [national] art. The music of Germany is pure German; the music of Italy is the very essence of Italian minds."[65]

> Johann Sebastian Bach, the supreme music product of the world, was the result of a thousand influences, operating for centuries. The work of thousands of minor composers before him had to die and rot and be ground into compost before the soil would be rich enough to grow the glory of German art.[66]

Choral Music Becomes a "Cultivated Commodity"

A mantra heard throughout the centuries and especially after the birth of the Oxford/Ritualistic Movement is that the church and the world are, or should be, separate spheres—*in the world but not of the world*. Nevertheless, the surge in interest in sacred choral and organ music was in large part due to worldly influences. Touring choruses and organists like Eddy mounted highly anticipated concerts in every corner of the country. The concomitant promotions and eager coverage in the press helped to fuel interest, and by the 1920s, radio and recordings were playing a role.

The well-promoted tours of professional and professional-sounding choirs were hugely influential. Their directors became recognized as authorities on the choral art and wrote prolifically about it. Also, by the 1920s the nation's elite choruses were regularly featured in radio broadcasts and were among the first to make commercial recordings.

The St. Olaf Lutheran Choir

Among the first of these highly influential ensembles was the St. Olaf Lutheran Choir with its famous director F. Melius Christiansen. Norwegian Lutheran congregations, many of which settled in Minnesota and Wisconsin in the mid- to late-nineteenth century, had never embraced the quartet choir. Most had small choirs directed by minimally trained individuals who may have taken a music class or two at a normal school.

---

65. Whiting, "American Composer," 401–2.
66. Whiting, "American Composer," 402, 404.

A New Century for Music and Worship in the Cultivated Church

F. Melius Christiansen, ca. 1926.
Photographer: J. A. Glander.
Public domain image, Minnesota Historical Society. (https://en.wikipedia.org/wiki/F._Melius_Christiansen)

Fredrik Melius Christiansen (1871–1955) was a Norwegian violinist who immigrated to the United States in 1888 and enrolled at the Northwestern Conservatory of Music in Minneapolis in 1890.[67] After completing courses with honors in music theory and counterpoint, he spent two years in Leipzig studying with Gustav Schreck, choirmaster of the famous *Thomaskirche*, and director of *Thomasschule*. In 1901 Christiansen was hired by John Kildahl, the president of St. Olaf College in Northfield, Minnesota, to head the music faculty there. The college needed an instructor capable of directing the college band, the Choral Union, and the choir at St. John's Lutheran Church. Melius with his varied skills and training seemed an ideal choice for the position.

The roots of the St. Olaf Lutheran Choir were in the church choir of St. John's Lutheran Church in Northfield. When Christiansen began his tenure at the college, St. John's Lutheran was essentially the campus chapel. It was the church attended by most of the college's students, and college president

---

67. The Northwestern Conservatory of Music was established in 1885 by the New England organist and composer Charles Henry Morse, who had been on the faculty at Wellesley College. The school offered courses of study in organ, voice, piano, music theory, and related areas. Upon completion of required studies, students received a diploma or performance certificate. The Northwestern Conservatory of Music in Minneapolis is not to be confused with the Northwestern University Conservatory of Music in Evanston, Illinois, which, under the directorship of Peter C. Lutkin, also occupies a prominent place later in this narrative.

Kildahl was also the church's pastor. Services were conducted entirely in Norwegian.

In 1906, St. Olaf College dedicated its first on-campus worship space, the Hoyme Chapel, capable of seating one thousand. A year later, the Annual Conference of the Norwegian Lutheran Church of America was scheduled for the campus's new chapel. For the occasion Christiansen and Kildahl collaborated on an innovative concept, a "song service" or *sang-gudstjeneste*. The service was well received, and a news release colorfully described the presentation:

> Professor Christiansen had picked a chorus of forty voices composed of students and faculty members, and a program of church hymns, [some] contrapuntally arranged especially for singing, was prepared. After each hymn, Dr. J. N. Kildahl spoke briefly, touching upon the text just sung and introducing the theme of the next.[68]

Song services would be presented regularly on the St. Olaf campus for the next nine years. These were not unlike the praise services innovated by Eben Tourjée decades earlier. They combined Scripture readings and short devotionals with appropriate traditional Lutheran chorales. These were either sung by the congregation in Norwegian from the church's hymnal, the *Landstads kirkesalmebog*, or sung by the choir in expanded or developed chorale settings composed by Christiansen.[69] "Fixed more firmly in Christiansen's mind [was] the belief that, difficult though the task might be, the people could be educated to appreciate and use the best in Lutheran church music."[70] The song service format, which combined elements of a worship service with a concert, would be reflected in all St. Olaf Choir concert appearances during Christiansen's directorship.

Each year the St. John's Choir progressed musically, and in 1912 a decision was made that it should represent the campus on a tour of Wisconsin and Illinois. To do that effectively the ensemble required a name change, and so the St. John's Church Choir became the St. Olaf Lutheran Choir. In 1913 the choir made the first of many tours of Norway. Over Christiansen's forty-three years as director of the choir it performed in virtually all the capitals of Europe and America's most prestigious concert halls. It also recorded prolifically and for many Americans personified the peak of musical accomplishment in choral art.

---

68. Robinson Jr., "Genesis of Cultivated Choral Tone," 302.

69. Many of Christiansen's "developed" chorales and hymns have become staples of American sacred choral literature.

70. Bergmann, *Music Master of the Middle West*, 115.

P. C. Lutkin called Melius the "Prince of Choirmasters" and a pioneer of *a cappella* singing in America.[71] Anton Armstrong, current conductor of the St. Olaf Lutheran Choir, has written:

> One of Christiansen's greatest contributions to the choral art was his programming of sacred choral music for the concert hall. Previously, much of the repertoire of collegiate choral ensembles consisted of second-rate, glee club songs. Christiansen's programming of nineteenth-century unaccompanied choral works of the German and Russian schools as well as motets of J. S. Bach was an important addition to the choral concert repertoire of the day. This rebirth of sacred choral literature not only served as a catalyst for the development of accompanied school and college ensembles but also fostered the growth of volunteer church choirs in the middle decades of the century.[72]

---

71. Bergmann, *Music Master of the Middle West*, 170.

72. Armstrong, "Musical Legacy of F. Melius Christiansen," 11. Note: The pioneer work of F. Melius Christiansen spawned what is commonly referred to as the "Lutheran Choral Tradition." Christiansen retired in 1943 and was succeeded at St. Olaf College by his son, Olaf (1901–1984). His son Paul (1914–1997) directed the Concordia College Choir from 1937 to 1986. Students of F. Melius Christiansen included Edwin Liemohn, who founded the Wartburg College Choir in 1937 and remained its director through 1968, and Joseph Edwards, who founded the "Choir of the West" at Pacific Lutheran University in 1926. These choirs as well as nationally known ensembles at Luther College, Gustavus Adolphus College, and Augustana continue to tour extensively and serve as outstanding examples of a cappella singing in the tradition of F. Melius Christiansen and the St. Olaf Choir.

John Finley Williamson and the Westminster Choir

John Finley Williamson. Public domain image, German Federal Archives. (https://commons.wikimedia.org/wiki/File:Bundesarchiv_Bild_102-07656,_Berlin,_Gastspiel_des_Dayton-Westminster-Chors-John_Finley_Williamson.jpg)

Another giant among early twentieth century choral conductor/church musicians was John Finley Williamson (1887–1964). The son of a United Brethren minister, Williamson was born in Canton, Ohio. In 1908, he enrolled in the Davis Conservatory of Music at Otterbein University, Westerville, Ohio. After graduation in 1911 he had hoped to pursue an operatic career. Williamson moved to Dayton, Ohio, and opened a voice studio. Unfortunately, his singing aspirations were quashed due to a botched tonsillitis surgery that left his vocal cords damaged irreparably. [73]

Needing to use his training, Williamson became director of music at the First United Brethren Church in Dayton. Meanwhile, however, the congregations of two Presbyterian Churches—the First Presbyterian Church and Third Presbyterian Church situated just blocks apart—had decided to come together. The churches had split over theological issues in the 1830s. A new church, Westminster Presbyterian, was founded in 1919, and John Finley Williamson was called to be its first director of music. It was an exciting time. The merged congregation, now 1,100 members strong, soon announced plans to build a magnificent new neo-Gothic facility.

While Williamson's training as a conductor was meager, the quality of his church choir from the very beginning was stunning. His wife, Rhea, later wrote that, "The only thing he knew was to teach voice . . ." But, she went on,

---

73. Robinson Jr., "Genesis of Cultivated Choral Tone," 409.

"Somehow Jack had an inner ear for music and quickly developed a church choir to such a degree of excellence that a New York manager contracted to take it on tour—this at a time when [most] churches were served by quartets not choirs."[74]

Just five years after Williamson's arrival, the Westminster Presbyterian Choir was known throughout the region for its excellence. A 1924 tour was limited to Michigan and Chicago, but the following year the choir made appearances throughout the midwestern and northeastern states. A major break for Williamson and his choir came in 1928, when they were invited to perform with the Cincinnati Symphony under the baton of internationally known conductor Fritz Reiner. The concert was broadcast "coast to coast" on Cincinnati radio station WLW. Beginning in 1937, the choir was featured nationally in weekly "Bach Concerts" on radio station WABC. Their stature was such that in 1939, President Franklin Roosevelt asked them to perform in Russia as musical ambassadors. That same year, the Westminster Choir began weekly broadcasts of Sunday afternoon concerts with the New York Philharmonic.[75] The choir had been making commercially marketed recordings since the 1920s. Through its touring, radio presence, and prolific recording, it is fair to say that Williamson's Westminster Choir did more than any other ensemble to bring choral music into the American consciousness. John Finley Williamson's outsize influence, however, went far beyond his work as a master choral conductor. His work as an educator and advocate for music as a ministry in American churches will be discussed later.

"The Great War" and the End of an Era

On July 28, 1914, Austria-Hungary declared war on Serbia, plunging Europe into the First World War. In many ways the war would be a turning point. Nothing that followed would be the same. By 1920, large organ installations had declined, and the day of famous touring concert organists was on the wane as well. The war was a particularly painful reality for members of the Second New England School. All of Boston was shocked by the arrest and imprisonment of Karl Muck (1859–1940), the German-born conductor of the Boston Symphony and a well-loved member of the Boston musical community. Muck's arrest was especially troubling for Amy Beach, who counted him among her closest friends. Chadwick's two sons Theodore and Noel

---

74. Williamson, "My Career," 90.

75. As of 2014, the Westminster Choir of Westminster Choir College had appeared as featured artists with the New York Philharmonic over three hundred times. See Beck, *America's Choral Ambassador*, 7–8.

had both enlisted, and the welling up of anti-German sentiment caused Chadwick himself to choose a British subject for his 1915 symphonic tone poem *Tam O'Shanter*.

Horatio Parker was the most visibly shaken among all the Boston group during this period. Parker had suffered from gout for years, had a delicate temperament, and was prone to anxiety. After the spring of 1916, he had to severely reduce his travels and performances. Two of his sons-in-law had enlisted and one was destined to serve at the front. In addition, his wife Anna's family in Germany was a matter of deep concern. According to Parker biographer, William K. Kearns, he "must have felt the profound disillusionment of his generation, which had been thoroughly rooted in nineteenth century optimism."[76]

In the spring of 1919, the last year of his life, Yale University commissioned Horatio Parker to set to music a poem by Brian Hooker. It was to be presented "in memory of the Two Hundred and Twenty-one Yale Men Who Gave their Lives in the World War and in Recognition of the Service Rendered to the Allies by the Eight Thousand Yale Men Who Responded to the Call to Arms."[77] Hooker's text, quoted in part here, was both stirring and poignant.

What of the many others,
Forever overseas,
Lovers and sons and brothers,
Like these, yet not like these?
For two shall have toiled and striven,
Equal in worst and best,
And to one shall be glory given,
And to another, rest.
For two shall have trod one measure,
And of one cup drunk deep,
And one shall have sweet pleasure,
And one shall have sweet sleep.

For our fathers gone before us,
That they have not toiled in vain,
For the mother hearts that bore us
And shall not waste their pain;
For the childhood games and laughter
And the sorrows that turn their tears
to a song in the heart hereafter
Unto the end of years.
For these, and what else unspoken
Live when a soldier dies:
You are the body broken,
You are the Sacrifice.

Parker himself conducted the premier performance of *A.D. 1919* at the Yale commencement on June 1, of 1919. It would be his last public appearance. He died on December 18 of that year. George Chadwick said *A.D. 1919* was "a heroic tribute to heroic men, some of whom were his students," and that, in it, "Parker had written his own requiem."[78] Indeed, *A.D. 1919*

---

76. Kearns, *Horatio Parker, 1863–1919*, 72.

77. Quoted from Dedication, piano/vocal score, *A. D. 1919* (New Haven: Yale University Press, 1919).

78. Chadwick, *Horatio Parker, 1863–1919*, 19.

could also be seen as a requiem for an era coming to an end. Chadwick, who was organist for Parker's funeral, wrote an "Elegy" and dedicated it to his dear friend.

George Whitefield Chadwick, "Elegy" for Organ,
published in *American Organ Monthly* 1:10 (Feb. 1921), p. 29.

Chapter 15

THE *MOTU PROPRIO* OF 1903 AND ITS AFTERMATH

Throughout the generations, regardless of denomination, regardless of worship style, and regardless of the focus being regenerative or sacramental, there has always been a deep aspiration for vital and engaged corporate worship. The Roman Catholic Church in America in the late nineteenth century had reached a tipping point. By the post-Civil War period, its worship had descended into malaise. Father William Finn described most colorfully what he experienced at the beginning of his career in 1890s Boston and Chicago.

> Unwittingly, the clergy had permitted the sung portions of the Liturgy to become a travesty. The *Kyrie, Gloria, Credo, Sanctus,* and *Agnus Dei* were as five acts of a garish musical drama. Frequently the Masses sung suggested the emotional developments unfolded in a mid-nineteenth century opera. In the *Kyrie,* the female soprano soloist would reveal her animosity towards the contralto. The *Gloria,* act two, would hint of the baritone's jealousy of the tenor (the latter having the inside track with the soprano) while the bass began nefarious plottings. And so on. Choruses would trip gayly through lively movements while the text was imploring the forgiveness of God for the sins of mankind, including those of the choir and the congregation. Often a flourishing cadenza gave the leading lady a showy opportunity for a finale with chorus. The *Benedictus* not infrequently resounded through churches, after the solemn moment of the *Consecration,* as a mocking serenade by Mephistopheles. There

were anguished love laments, seductive *Ave Maria's,* soldiers' chorus *Tantum Ergo's.* The priest at the Altar would often be obliged to delay the progress of the Holy Sacrifice while the music intimated that the contralto and baritone were arranging a rendezvous in the moonlight. The music was not only unchurchly, unspiritual, unbecoming; it was grotesque. *Tosca* and *Manon* in the west-end choir loft, Carmens "habanera-ing" to the pews, and Elsa duetting with Lohengrin while a corpse was being conducted up the aisle for a Solemn Requiem Mass.[1]

By the late nineteenth century, there was a widespread belief among the Catholic hierarchy that something needed to be done and a realization that change would not come easily. As early as the 1840s the Boston Gregorian Society had sought to incorporate plainchant into Catholic worship in "Beantown." Singenberger, his American Cæcilian Society, and its journal *Cæcilian* aggressively took up the cause in the 1870s and had some moderate success attracting disciples.

On August 4, 1903, following the death of Pope Leo XIII, Giuseppe Melchiorre Sarto was elected to the papacy as Pope Pius X. His reign, which lasted eleven years, transformed Roman Catholic church music for generations to come. His groundbreaking *Motu Proprio* or papal edict was entitled *"Tra le Sollecitudini"* (tr. "among the concerns") and was issued just three months after Sarto's ascendancy.

While the *Motu Proprio* included a focus on music in worship, Pope Pius X's reign, in a broader sense, was focused on achieving order in a time when the Church seemed to have lost its moorings. Organist, conductor, and historian Edward Schaefer outlined the many factors accumulating for over a century that culminated in the pope's actions:

- The consequences of secularism, which began with the Enlightenment.
- Increasing knowledge of science, psychology, psychiatry, and an emphasis on education that seemed to challenge reliance on religious faith.
- Advances in technology and industry.
- Forces of nationalism, imperialism, militarism, and economic rivalries—all drawing the major world powers toward war.
- The liberal call for the church to moderate its views on marriage and regarding religious and economic freedom.

---

1. Finn, *Sharps and Flats for Five Decades,* 60.

- A challenge to the centuries-old position of Thomas Aquinas on "objective supernatural revealed order," seeking to have it replaced with order dictated by the "subjective needs of humanity."
- The prevailing interest at the time in historicism, biblical criticism, and Christian Darwinism.[2]

Tra le Sollecitudini has the distinction of being the longest, most comprehensive papal statement on music in the history of the Catholic faith. Issued on November 22, 1903, it was a multipage document beginning with an extended introduction followed by a twenty-nine-part *"Instruzione sulla musica sacra"* or "Instruction on Sacred Music." The purpose of the edict, Pius X explained in the introduction, was to emphasize the responsibility of every parish to maintain and promote "the decorum of the House of God in which the august mysteries of religion are celebrated . . . Nothing should have place, therefore, in the temple calculated to disturb or even merely to diminish the piety and devotion of the faithful; nothing that may give reasonable cause for disgust or scandal; nothing, above all, which directly offends the decorum and sanctity of the sacred functions and is thus unworthy of the House of Prayer and of the Majesty of God."

Principle tenets of the *Tra le Sollecitudini* included:

1. That Gregorian Chant must be the preeminent music for liturgical use.
2. That Renaissance polyphony, and especially the music of Palestrina, represents the ideal for sacred choral music, the standard by which all later compositions must be judged, and the model for liturgical music of the future.
3. That the use of secular music and music influenced by the secular is expressly prohibited for liturgical use.
4. That the liturgy must conform to prescribed Latin texts.
5. That the organ be the only generally authorized instrumental music in worship. Pianos and "noisy or frivolous instruments such as drums, cymbals, bells, and the like" are forbidden without exception. "In some special cases, within due limits and with proper safeguards, other instruments may be allowed, but never without the special permission of the Ordinary (i.e., local bishop) . . ."
6. That in keeping with priestly tradition, "it follows that singers in church have a real liturgical office, and that, therefore women, being incapable of exercising such an office, cannot be admitted to form part

---

2. Schaefer, *Catholic Music Through the Ages*, 121.

of the choir. Whenever, then, it is desired to employ the acute voices of sopranos and contraltos, these parts must be taken by boys, according to the most ancient usage of the church."

7. That congregational singing of chant (*participatio actuosa*) be encouraged.
8. That "in general it must be considered a very grave abuse when the liturgy in ecclesiastical functions is made to appear secondary to and in a manner at the service of the music, for the music is merely a part of the liturgy and its humble handmaid."[3]

Since the singing of chant was to be mandated, a first question had to be "how shall it be sung?" The sticking point had always been rhythm. Chant notation contains no indications of note values. In 1900 some were advocating a "free" rhythmic approach determined entirely by accentuation of the text. The monks at Solesmes, however, favored an approach determined largely by the rise and fall of the melodic line. The Cæcilians at Regensburg were conservative and promoted retention of the old *Editio medecea* chant book, in which some chants had been truncated to correspond with the needs of Renaissance choral composers. Pope Pius X, in collaboration with Solesmes-trained Lorenzo Perosi, embraced the Solesmes approach and it became the standard approach to chant singing from that time forward.

Fr. Robert A. Skeris (born 1935), an authority on the use of Gregorian chant in the twentieth-century Church and formerly on the faculty of Pontifical Institute of Sacred Music in Rome, described the root motivation for the *Motu Proprio* as a profound understanding of the spiritual and ministerial role music should play in worship. To Pope Pius X sacred music was "not merely a means to beautify, or to 'carry out,' or to 'shape' and 'form' the worship service. *Musica sacra* is itself worship, and it is related to worship like color is to sunset, like thought to mind. Sacred music is not *like* prayer, it IS prayer. Sacred music raises the *mind* (hence intelligent listening as well as intelligent singing) and raises the *heart* (hence artistic music will call up a valid emotional response) to *God* (and not only to neighbor, for worship is directed to God)."[4]

Two areas of consequence addressed in the papal decree that need to be highlighted dealt with congregational singing and what Pius X referred to as "modern music." First, the decree stated that "special efforts are to be made to restore the use of Gregorian Chant *by the people,* so that the faithful may again take a more active part in the ecclesiastical offices, as was the case in

---

3. Pius X, *Tra le Sollecitudini*.
4. Skeris, "Sarto, the 'Conservative Reformer,'" 7.

ancient times." In such a long and cumbersome document, the pope's words might easily be overlooked, but they were *earthshaking* for a faith in which the people for too long had worshipped in silence. Edward Schaefer has noted that *Tra le Sollecitudini* was the first time the subject had been broached in centuries.[5] Father William Finn, who will be discussed later, wrote:

> And Pope Pius X wishes the Catholics of this century to sing; he wishes them to join ... in chanting those beautiful hymns and prayers in which the liturgy of the Church abounds ... They must unite in the *Gloria* of Christmas, the *Miserere* of Lent, the *Alleluias* of Easter. They must no longer be passive spectators at a religious ceremony or auditors of a sacred concert; they must participate personally and actively in the solemnities of public worship.[6]

When Pius X referred to modern music he was, of course, differentiating between music of the eighteenth and nineteenth centuries as opposed to chant and the classic polyphony of the Renaissance. Advocates of the cultivated tradition in America deified European art music and proclaimed it the epitome of church music. The pope's restrictions were head-turning and provoked consternation in some circles. Finn addressed the issue firmly yet positively:

> First of all, we must understand that modern music as such, and apart from the question of its adaptability to liturgical use, is not disparaged in the least ... [Its] inherent beauty and artistic merit is not to be impugned. We Catholics need offer no apology for the profound and solemn emotions they have awakened in us in the past, nor for the sentiment which, by reason of long and pleasant association with them, moves us to defend them from the contumely of those who would presume to challenge their musical excellence.[7]

Rather, Finn went on to explain that the music of the liturgy operated on a different plane. It needed to project not human emotion and sentimentality but the *mysterium* of God's presence.

The *Motu Proprio* of 1903 had explosive ramifications for Roman Catholic church music in the United States. Generally speaking, activities of the American Church had not been a priority concern for Rome in the past. Local parishes were accustomed to a certain level of impunity regarding

---

5. Schaefer, *Catholic Music Through the Ages*, 130.
6. Finn, Wells, and O'Brien, *Manual of Church Music*, 115.
7. Finn, Wells, and O'Brien, *Manual of Church Music*, 102–3.

their music. There was also the issue of American religious pluralism. Roman Catholicism was not a state religion in the United States, nor could it be perceived as one. Though as a denomination Catholicism had experienced significant growth in the late nineteenth century, it was still one denomination among many, and Catholics were divided culturally. Immigrant French, German, Hispanic, and Irish Catholics all had their own musical traditions that were closely tied to their cultural identity. While Church leaders were mostly united in their determination to make Pope Pius X's vision a reality, the challenges were staggering.

The *Motu Proprio*, however, was a papal *edict* and not a mere suggestion. As noted earlier, reform had been sought years earlier by Singenberger and the American Cæcilian Society, but in many circles the society's goals were viewed as overly aggressive or elitist. Now that reform had been mandated by the Holy See, resistance in the United States was inevitable. Letters to the editor of the *New Music and Church Music Review* gave a laundry list of opinions why Catholics should protest the pope's edict:

- Some insisted the modern music, *circa* 1900, was no less sacred than plainsong.
- Others warned that there were few who would recognize chant as "beautiful" and that "an entire service of plainsong is tiresome."
- The New York organist Channing Lefebvre observed that some of Palestrina's own contemporaries felt his music was inappropriate for use in the liturgy because he had abandoned the ancient church modes.
- It was also pointed out that Palestrina was "dismissed from the Vatican for bad behavior." (In actuality, he was dismissed because he was married, and celibacy was a requirement for employment. He was dismissed regretfully and awarded a generous pension. Later, he was brought back to St. Peter's as principal composer for the Papal Choir. There was never an accusation of "bad behavior.")
- Another critic complained of "sloppy chanting with no musicality or devotion in evidence."[8]

In America the first pressing issue was language. Latin, as the *Motu Proprio* stated, was the language of the Church and had been since antiquity. Be that as it may, the last decades of the nineteenth century up until World War I were a peak time for immigration from non-English-speaking countries. A very large percentage of those immigrants were Roman Catholic. Having all or part of worship in the vernacular of their culture was an

---

8. Fitts, "Aspects of American Musical Life," 87–88.

important need for survival in what often seemed an alien environment.[9] Thus a mix of Latin and the vernacular was common in immigrant worship, and when lingual rigidity was applied to liturgy, conflicts were inevitable. Finally, because America was a multicultural society, fluency in English—whether openly stated or not—was viewed as a requirement to be fully American. The very use of Latin in the Roman liturgy tended to feed long-held prejudices among Protestants and especially evangelicals.

A second priority for Pius X was to prohibit the use of inappropriate, un-worshipful music in worship, replacing it with traditional chant and polyphony. The ethnomusicologist Ann L. Silverberg has observed that the restrictive reforms of *Tra le Sollecitudini* and the idealization of chant and polyphony were nothing new. Johann Josef Fux had explored the techniques of Renaissance counterpoint in his *Gradus ad Parnassum* of 1725. It was written as a dialogue between teacher and student in which the teacher is thought to represent Palestrina himself. The work of the Benedictine monks at the Abbey Saint-Pierre Solesmes and the Cæcilians at Regensburg had been advocating for plainchant for over a half century. Also, throughout the nineteenth century there had been a growing romanticized view of things medieval.[10] Even Johannes Brahms had organized a choir to plumb the polyphonic choral repertoire.

American clergy and church musicians strove valiantly to realize change. One of the most active in responding to the pope's call for widespread training in the singing of plainchant was Justine Bayard Ward (1879–1975). She was an accomplished musician and Catholic convert who was inspired by the *Motu Proprio*'s promise of reform. Ward made a number of trips to the Isle of Wight to study with the Solesmes monks. She joined the faculty of Catholic University in 1910 and developed the "Ward Method," a widely used training technique for teaching chant to primary school children. Ward's curriculum was published in two volumes in 1915. It has been estimated that within a decade over thirteen thousand church musicians had adopted her program either through use of her training materials or attendance at summer chant workshops. She was also instrumental in founding liturgical music programs at Catholic University and the Pius X School of Liturgical Music at Manhattanville College.[11]

Following in the wake of Ward's pioneering work, other institutions and organizations arose to support revitalization of chanting in local parishes. The St. Cloud Music Institute was founded in 1928. In 1935 the diocese

---

9. Ebaugh and Chavitz, "Dilemmas of Language."
10. Silverberg, "American Catholic Liturgical Music," 48.
11. Pecklers, "Evolution of Liturgical Music," 163–64.

of St. Paul established a program of summer workshops required for diocesan church musicians to be certified in liturgical arts. The trend continued with the founding of the Gregorian Institute of America in the 1940s. John Singenberger, the Association of St. Cæcilia, and its journal continued for decades to promote the use of polyphony and chant in worship. Various organizations were set up to aid Catholic church musicians in choosing appropriate mass settings and choral music for worship as dictated by the *Motu Proprio*. Singenberger published a *Guide to Catholic Church Music* in 1905 with a supplement issued in 1911. The 270-page guide enumerated over a thousand "acceptable" masses, motets, offertories, and organ pieces for liturgical use.[12] The St. Gregory Society of America was founded in 1913, a year before Pius X's death, and had as its *raison d'être* facilitating adherence to the tenets of the *Motu Proprio*. The society was active until Vatican II, merging with the Society of St. Cecilia in 1964, to form the Church Music Association of America. Throughout its existence the St. Gregory Society continued the practice of issuing "white lists" of music approved for use and also "black lists" for that which was forbidden.

Inappropriate liturgical music was only one of the problems rampant among American Catholic parishes. In Section Two of the *Motu Proprio*, Pius X ordered that "special efforts are to be made to restore the use of Gregorian Chant *by the people*, so that the faithful may again take a more active part in the ecclesiastical offices, as was the case in ancient times."[13] This, of course, was yet another plea for more active involvement in congregational singing. But would a papal edict get to the bottom of the problem? It was true that many chant melodies were brief, limited in range, and could be easily taught. But for many the unfamiliar musical style coupled with ecclesiastical Latin, another source of discomfort, was felt to be cold, impersonal, and not a little intimidating.

Harold Becket Gibbs,[14] a respected American organist/choirmaster and authority on plainchant, was a firm advocate for the reforms dictated in the *Motu Proprio*, including full congregational participation in the sung liturgy. Yet achieving that, he had come to realize, was problematic.

---

12. Pecklers, "Evolution of Liturgical Music," 162.

13. Pius X, *Tra le Sollecitudini*, no. 3

14. Gibbs (1868–1955) was born in Sussex, England. He was a life member of the English Plainsong and Mediaeval Society. In 1893 he traveled to Solesmes, the first of many visits there during which he became a lifelong friend of Dom Mocquereau. He immigrated to the United States at the request of Pope Pius X following the issuance of the 1903 *Motu Proprio*, serving at St. Mary's Cathedral Basilica of the Assumption in Covington, Kentucky, and founding a Gregorian Society there. He then relocated to the Cathedral Basilica of St. Peter in Chains in Cincinnati, where he also took courses in church music at the Cincinnati Conservatory.

> First of all, I submit that the lack of a proper system of instruction for the people was the main cause of failure. I have frequently heard the congregation invited to sing in such and such parts of the service, but the invitation is left unclothed. They are evidently expected to "pick it up." Does it occur to the authorities that, if the regular singers require two or three practices a week to enable them to "get through" their duties in spite of their acknowledged ability, how much more should the congregation (who are supposed to be less "musical") require a proper course of training? To expect them to "pick it up" is an inconsistency, nay, an absurdity quite out of place in God's House. And to make matters worse, I have noticed that in every congregation there are just a few who have the courage to make an attempt to "pick it up" and persevere, in the face of the most hideous difficulties for a while. Their disastrous failure, which was a foregone conclusion, not only silences them but serves as a warning to others not to make a similar attempt and so bring ridicule on themselves. In such a church the rule of golden silence prevails . . .[15]

Additionally, for some Catholic immigrant communities the very act of congregational singing was foreign to their culture. Only the Germans had a long-standing tradition of singing hymns in worship. Many Irish Catholics, for example, were not accustomed to singing in worship and viewed it with distaste as a Protestant innovation.[16]

Hymns in the vernacular had been making an incursion into Catholic Church life in the United States. Hispanic communities, for example, commonly incorporated the singing of religious folk songs in their worship practice, but they were neither liturgical nor in Latin. As early as 1811, *Recueil de Contique*—a collection of hymns in French—had been published for immigrants to Baltimore. German Catholics had adopted the *Katholisches Gesang und Gebetbuch*, published in New York in 1858.[17] All of these presented challenges to the restrictions put in place by the pope.

By the late nineteenth century many English-speaking Catholics—like their Protestant neighbors—had become accustomed to singing hymns in English at nonliturgical functions such as the *novenas* or days of prayer leading up to major feast days. Songs such as "In a Monastery Garden" (1915), "Mother Dear, O Pray for Me" (1880), and "Bring Flowers to the Fairest" (1871) tended toward the maudlin and sentimental. In them was an unmistakable kinship to Victorian parlor songs. Paul Hume, reflecting

---

15. Gibbs, "Congregational Singing," 26.
16. Pecklers, "Evolution of Liturgical Music," 162.
17. Schaefer, *Catholic Music Through the Ages*, 128.

back on the first half of the twentieth century, wrote that most hymns sung in Catholic churches were "execrably bad music and therefore entirely unfit for use in the church."[18] There was a prevailing attitude that "It's okay to sing anything in church, just so long as you don't sing it during mass."[19] Hymn singing served for masses of American Catholics as a cherished means of personal devotion that they were reluctant to part with. The problem was basically ignored or overlooked by the church until the 1940s.

Another inflammatory issue arising out of the *Motu Proprio* had to do with the recommended use of choirs of men and boys and the resulting exclusion of women from singing. It was not the intent of the *Motu Proprio* to exclude women entirely from singing in worship, but to remove them from liturgical choirs. Nevertheless, it was painful. In the larger urban churches with quartets, women had often been the most celebrated singers. In small parishes struggling to have any choir at all, women had been mainstays to keep programs going. Two of the most successful teachers of Gregorian chant in the United States were women. Justine Bayard Ward and Mother Georgia Stevens taught thousands of schoolchildren, teachers, and male church musicians during the fifty years prior to Vatican II. "It seems that both women successfully sidestepped (or ignored) the inherent paradox involved in learning, teaching, and singing music that Pius X had intended to keep from women."[20] Ward even received special dispensation to teach chant at the Pius X School of Liturgical Music in New York, a further contradiction to the spirit of the pope's edict.

The organization of all-male choirs predictably faced the same challenges facing Protestant Episcopal churches during the same era, with one important exception: they were not optional! Finding the needed number of musically trainable boys was a test even for large, wealthy, urban churches. Not only did such choirs have to be organized, but they needed to be trained in liturgical chant. A universal stumbling block to realizing any sort of reform was the lack of a sufficient number of trained church musicians to implement change. Msgr. Richard J. Schuler—priest, church musician, and music historian—wrote that "If there was one single difficulty that surfaced . . . in fully implementing the orders of the Church, it would be the lack of professional training of those who were trying to fulfill the decree."[21] The Reverend H. T. Henry of the St. Charles Borromeo Seminary in Overbrook,

---

18. Hume, *Catholic Church Music*, 65.
19. Hume, *Catholic Church Music*, 71.
20. Silverberg, "American Catholic Liturgical Music," 56.
21. Schuler, "Chronicle of Reform," 356.

Pennsylvania, made the same observation just two years after the *Motu Proprio* was issued.

> With respect to the introduction of Gregorian chant, we face the fact that organists, choirmasters, teachers of music know next to nothing of its notation, its rhythm, its spirit . . . intimate knowledge which alone can rescue plain chant from a ludicrous misinterpretation of its real function as a mere drapery thrown about the text . . .[22]

Father Finn

Father William J. Finn.
Image courtesy of the Archives of the Missionary Society of St. Paul the Apostle.

No one did more to promote the acceptance of boy choirs and all-male choirs in America's Roman Catholic churches than Father William Joseph Finn (1881–1961). He was born in Boston and had an extensive education in music. In his teens, he studied organ and boy-choir methods with Samuel Brenton Whitney at the Church of the Advent. From there, he went on to study at Catholic University and the Pontifical Institute of Sacred Music in Rome where he was declared *Magister Cantorum* in 1912.

In 1906, Finn was ordained a priest and assigned to Old St. Mary's Church in Chicago, where he founded the Paulist Choristers.[23] The ensemble became nationally famous due to a six-month tour in 1918 to raise

---

22. Henry, "How Shall the Reform in Church Music be Effected?," 3.

23. St. Mary's Cathedral in Chicago had been destroyed in the Great Chicago Fire of 1871. The congregation relocated to the former Plymouth Congregational and renamed it St. Mary's Catholic Church, where it was under the auspices of the Paulist Fathers order.

funds for the restoration of churches in France damaged during the First World War.

Father Finn published two books of inestimable importance for the post-*Motu Proprio* Catholic Church in America, the *Manual of Church Music* (1905) and *The Art of the Choral Conductor* (1939). The *Manual of Church Music* was commissioned by the church specifically to address concerns related to the 1903 papal decree. In the preface, the Reverend Herman J. Heuser, founder of the *American Ecclesiastical Review*, wrote disapprovingly of the callous disregard he was seeing to the reforms Pius X was seeking:

> What would one be led to think of some pastors who have not as yet made a single move toward the desired reform; who even forget their sacred mission to such an extent as to permit, in open disregard of every Church discipline, the printing of pompous programmes of objectionable music with the names of soloists, etc., as is practiced in theaters and concert halls, and the distribution of same during the celebration of our august Mysteries? A parish priest who permits such abominations in the House of God, or who has not the power or courage to put a stop to such sacrilegious abuses, is unworthy of his high and sacred office.[24]

Throughout the *Manual*, Father Finn came across as both positive and hopeful. In Part One he surveyed the challenges facing Catholic organists and choirmasters. He observed that too often church music staffs consisted of an organist and a paid quartet. The church's music library commonly consisted of a single collection of so-called "standard masses." Singing of polyphonic repertoire was rare, and many sanctuaries were designed without a chancel, making the placing of a liturgical choir there an impossibility. This sad state of affairs "so long prevailed among us," Finn wrote, "that it was only with difficulty that some were brought to see the purpose and advantages of this radical reform."[25]

Next Finn devoted a long section to practical issues regarding the organization of choirs of men and boys, how to audition for them, the ideal balance between boys and men, and maintenance of choir discipline. Finn made a strong appeal for the teaching of music theory, sight singing, and chant in the parochial schools. He cited a ruling from the Archdiocese of New York "that systematic teaching of music be required in all Catholic schools . . . to comprise a) sight reading; b) voice training; and c) the of the

---

24. Finn, Wells, and O'Brien, *Manual of Church Music*, vii.
25. Finn, Wells, and O'Brien, *Manual of Church Music*, 2.

various chants of High Mass, Vespers, and Benediction."[26] He also noted, as the Episcopalians already knew, that for a boy choir program to succeed, boys would need to be compensated.[27] Chapters also were devoted to placement of choirs within parish chancels, choir placement when there was no chancel, and Finn's views on the role of choirmasters.

Finn's words on the ministerial role of the organist/choirmaster are both profound and prescient. After enumerating the professional qualifications needed, he wrote:

> There is, of course, more than a professional side to a choir master's relation to a church. His obligations to a parish are not satisfied when he has fulfilled the requirements of a contract made out upon a business basis. He has the exalted vocation of assisting the people to pray, and of preaching to their hearts of God and the holy things of religion by the subtle eloquence of the musical art. What greater vocation is there than to help men to come near to God? Does he not share this privilege with the priests? Says Dr. Haberl, "No matter how great his musical talents otherwise may be, the choirmaster who cannot identify his way of thinking with that of the Church as expressed in her liturgy, and who fancies that he adequately discharges his duty by merely making music whilst a religious function is being gone through, is deficient in one of the most important qualifications for his position."[28]

Throughout his life, Father Finn remained a firm advocate for choral music in worship. In 1934 he spoke of a delicate balance needed for music to play its proper role in worship—musical excellence both technically and aesthetically, but in the service of vital and engaging worship.

> The service of an ecclesiastical choir is two-fold, first, of course, to religion and then to the art of music itself. These twin services must be accomplished with understanding and care. There was no confusion as to the purposes of Church music in the early or mediaeval Church. During the last few generations, however, there has been so much confusion as to cause serious deterioration in Church music generally.
>
> Some ecclesiastics feel that music must only worship, and that it matters little how aesthetically it worships, provided it sings

---

26. Finn, Wells, and O'Brien, *Manual of Church Music*, 31.
27. Finn, Wells, and O'Brien, *Manual of Church Music*, 31.
28. Finn, Wells, and O'Brien, *Manual of Church Music*, 44. The reference to "Dr. Haberl" is to Franz Xavier Haberl of the Cæcilian community at Regensburg.

> with somber strains, avoiding the manifestation of personal emotion and adhering to the elusive criteria of tradition. This point of view keeps Church music cold, depressing and hopelessly ineffective.
>
> On the other hand, there have been musicians, especially in the latter half of the Nineteenth Century who have adverted to the religious vocation of Church music only casually. Their chancels and choir lofts were Sunday concert halls. There was much gaiety, drama, melodrama and operatic bombast in their offerings. The liturgy served as a libretto which gave singers rich opportunity for self-exploitation and little opportunity for the congregation to be moved by the spiritual appeal of the ritual.[29]

Finn, through his work with the Paulist Choristers and his teaching, strove to show that musical excellence in a church setting was not only possible for Catholic parishes, but also an essential aspiration.

The Aftermath of the Motu Proprio

History and centuries of Christian experience leave no doubt as to the efficacy of plainchant and high Renaissance polyphony as worship music. Nevertheless, it was becoming clear by the 1930s that the restrictions posed by the 1903 *Motu Proprio* were meeting a great deal of resistance within the American church. Despite the good work of John Singenberger, Justine Bayard Ward, Beckett Gibbs, Father Finn, and a legion of others, there was simply not enough trained leadership to bring its reforms to reality. The edict seemed to ignore the diversity of ethnic and cultural traditions within the Church. The singular focus on Gregorian chant seemed to be inhibiting congregational singing rather than encouraging it. Restrictions on hymn singing and the use of the vernacular in celebration of the solemn liturgy was making Catholic worship appear coldly impersonal for many.

Msgr. George V. Predmore, pastor of Holy Apostles Roman Catholic Church in Rochester, New York, a respected composer and writer on sacred music, wrote in 1924:

> Much of the apathy and adverse criticism [of the chant] comes from people who are unable to appreciate the real art of music. What they do not understand they condemn as worthless; what they do not like, they are prejudiced against. Their standards of judging the true worth of a musical composition are not the standards of a musician. Those who are ready to condemn the

---

29. Finn, "Father Finn's Views," 301.

chant by saying that they cannot see any charm or beauty in it are those who, never having heard it rendered properly, have little or no conception of its true character, rhythm, phrasing, and expression.[30]

Rome was not oblivious to these issues. A number of papal pronouncements over the next sixty years attempted to address specific needs. In observance of the twenty-fifth anniversary of the *Motu Proprio* in 1928, Pope Pius XI issued *Divini cultus sanctitatem* or "The Holiness of Divine Worship." In it he reaffirmed the basic substance of the 1903 edict while ordering that any individual aspiring to the priesthood must be taught Gregorian chant and receive adequate vocal instruction to be able to sing it in Latin. In addition, *Divini cultus* encouraged the establishment of choir schools ("Scholas") in every diocese. Instead of outright prohibition of the orchestral accompaniments, Pius XI stated, "We hereby declare that singing with orchestra accompaniment is not regarded by the Church as a more perfect form of music [i.e., than singing] or as more suitable for sacred purposes."[31]

In 1931, Pius XI issued *Deus scientiarum Dominus est* (tr. "God is the Lord of Science"), which was directed at religious studies in universities and seminaries. It required uniform standards for priestly training including, once again, curricula focused on liturgy and chant.

With *Mediator Dei* of 1947, another pope, Pope Pius XII, provided a profound and detailed statement on the liturgy of the Catholic faith and its critical importance to every communicant. The edict also reaffirmed the *Motu Proprio*'s commitment to full corporate participation in that liturgy.

> It is therefore the keen desire of the Church that all of the faithful kneel at the feet of the Redeemer to tell Him how much they venerate and love Him. She wants them present in crowds—like the children whose joyous cries accompanied His entry into Jerusalem—to sing their hymns and chant their song of praise and thanksgiving to Him who is King of Kings and Source of every blessing. She would have them move their lips in prayer, sometimes in petition, sometimes in joy and gratitude, and in this way experience His merciful aid and power . . .[32]

This was followed in 1955 by the groundbreaking papal encyclical on sacred music, *Musicae sacrae disciplina*, in which Pius XII opened the door to hymn singing in the vernacular.

---

30. Hume, *Catholic Church Music*, 46.
31. Pius XI, *Divini cultus sanctitatem*.
32. Pius XII, *Mediator Dei*, papal encyclical.

We must also hold in honor that music which is not primarily a part of the sacred liturgy, but which by its power and purpose greatly aids religion. This music is therefore rightly called religious music. The Church has possessed such music from the beginning, and it has developed happily under the Church's auspices. As experience shows, it can exercise great and salutary force and power on the souls of the faithful, both when it is used in churches during non-liturgical services and ceremonies, or when it is used outside churches at various solemnities and celebrations. The tunes of these hymns, which are often sung in the language of the people, are memorized with almost no effort or labor. The mind grasps the words and the music. They are frequently repeated and completely understood. Hence even boys and girls, learning these sacred hymns at a tender age, are greatly helped by them to know, appreciate and memorize the truths of the faith. Therefore, they also serve as a sort of catechism. These religious hymns bring pure and chaste joy to young people and adults during times of recreation. They give a kind of religious grandeur to their more solemn assemblies and gatherings. They bring pious joy, sweet consolation and spiritual progress to Christian families themselves. Hence these popular religious hymns are of great help to the Catholic apostolate and should be carefully cultivated and promoted.[33]

Nevertheless, it was too little, too late. Even a casual survey of these actions by the Vatican during the first half of the twentieth century indicates that a primary goal of the *Motu Proprio*, full participation in the family of faith, had still not been achieved at the century's midpoint. In June of 1963, after the death of Pope John XXIII, Giovanni Montini ascended to the papacy as Pope Paul VI. With his ascendancy, he inherited leadership of the Second Vatican Council, organized in the previous year. One of council's objectives was to address the long-standing problem of congregational participation in worship.

In December of 1963 the council, more familiarly known as Vatican II, issued one of the most wide-reaching and revolutionary mandates in the history of Roman Catholicism, *Sacrosanctum Concilium*. It would replace use of the traditional Latin Liturgy with worship in the vernacular. Earlier dictums requiring the use of Gregorian chant and polyphonic music were abrogated in favor of contemporary stylings more accessible to congregants.[34]

---

33. Pius XII, *Musicae sacrae disciplina.*

34. The actions of the Second Vatican Council, their aftermath, and societal

CHAPTER 16

SACRED MUSIC EDUCATION AND THE FLOWERING OF MUSIC AS A MINISTRY IN THE UNITED STATES

Two individuals, Waldo Selden Pratt and Archibald Thompson Davison, both highly regarded professors in New England schools, exerted a great deal of influence on perceptions of sacred music in the early decades of the twentieth century.

Waldo Selden Pratt

**Waldo Selden Pratt, ca. 1902.
Public domain image.**

(https://www.geni.com/people/Waldo-Pratt/6000000052024530961)

---

undercurrents pervading the decade of the 1960s are discussed in chapter 20.

Born in Philadelphia, Waldo Selden Pratt (1857–1939)[1] became professor of music history and hymnology at Hartford Theological Seminary in 1882 and continued to teach there until the time of his death. He was also a frequent lecturer in music history at both Smith College and Mt. Holyoke College, a president of the Music Teachers' National Association, and an honorary vice president of the American Guild of Organists. Pratt edited the 1931 edition of *The New Encyclopedia of Music and Musicians* and co-edited various American editions of *Grove's Dictionary of Music and Musicians*. His *The History of Music: A Handbook and Guide for Students* (1907) was a standard text for college students for much of the first half of the twentieth century. *The Music of the Pilgrims: A Description of the Psalm-book brought to Plymouth in 1620* (1921)—a study by Pratt of the *Ainsworth Psalter* of 1612—was a significant pioneering contribution to American church music history studies.

Pratt was an organist, a skilled choral conductor, and a passionate advocate for church music. He wrote articles for many popular American periodicals demanding better training for church musicians, including college curricula designed especially for them. He was a tireless promoter of the concept of music ministry and did much to make church music a viable profession for musicians. Pratt distilled many of his beliefs into a landmark book, *Musical Ministries in the Church: Studies in the History, Theory and Administration of Sacred Music*, which was published in 1902. Pratt's book was based on a series of lectures presented at McCormick [Presbyterian] Theological Seminary in Chicago in 1900. Since the lectures were directed toward divinity students, not musicians, they were "intended to treat principles of thought and action rather than musical technicalities."[2] For church musicians laboring in the twenty-first century, Pratt's *Music Ministries in the Church* is compelling reading. This is especially true for musicians working outside the Protestant Episcopal/Roman Catholic realm. While some topics are dated (the chapter on quartet choirs, for example), his thoughts on music as an essential component of worship as well as a ministry are timeless.

In the first chapter Pratt expounds on the historical relationship of music and religion, the key role religion played in the development of

---

1. While forgotten today, Pratt deserves a special place in the history of American church for his vision and influence. As noted, he was gifted writer and musicologist, respected organist, a president of the Music Teacher's National Association, and an honorary vice president of the American Guild of Organists. His *History of Music* (1907) was the standard college music history text in the early years of the twentieth century. See W. L. Hubbard, ed., *American History and Encyclopedia of Music, Musical Biographies, Volume 2*, 174.

2. Pratt, *Musical Ministries in the Church*, 5.

music, and the importance of music as a means of illuminating a text or evoking a religious experience. He writes that "Music is to a striking degree the creation or child of the Church. Many of its most ordinary techniques, ways, and resources were discovered or invented primarily because the Church needed them."[3] Writers on church music in this era were preoccupied either with the cultivation of taste in church music or, conversely, proclaiming the merits of anti-elitist, mass evangelistic song. One finds very little middle ground between the two. Pratt was an exception. "The fitness of any example of musical production for use in public worship," he wrote with unusual perceptiveness for the time, "does not depend wholly upon its merely formal excellence. Some very poor music has proved itself liturgically useful; some very perfect music has proved itself liturgically pernicious."[4]

In chapter 2, "Hymns and Hymn Singing," Pratt wrote eloquently on the need for corporate participation in singing to be taken seriously. On the issue of gospel songs, so incendiary in the early twentieth century, Pratt's stance was reasoned and conciliatory:

> We are all familiar with the tedious debate about the value of the whole class of hymns and tunes known as "gospel hymns." Much of the criticism of these "hymns" is reckless, both because it fails to note the fact that different grades of artistic beauty in poetry and music have always been required among Christians of differing degrees of culture, and also because it assails indiscriminately a class of hymns and tunes that is not homogeneous enough to be either approved or condemned in bulk . . . The assailants of the system have sometimes weakened their case by basing it too exclusively on the reasons of taste, without showing how vulgarity is dangerous . . . The defenders of this popular hymnody have a right to urge that hymnody must adapt itself to actual conditions, that the immature and uncultivated cannot be driven by force into a full appreciation of the most high, poetic hymns or the most highly musical tunes . . .
>
> For myself, I am disposed to believe that the original impulse toward the so-called "gospel hymns" was emphatically good, that much of their use has been worthy, and that some of them are likely to continue useful in many conditions . . . Yet I cannot help deploring certain other results . . . From the standpoint of general culture, it is clear that the exclusive use of ephemeral hymns and tunes is harmful because it has prevented the knowledge

---

3. Pratt, *Musical Ministries in the Church*, 14.
4. Pratt, *Musical Ministries in the Church*, 42.

of others that are too precious inheritances from the past to be discarded.[5]

Here Pratt is addressing an issue central to this entire study: the unfortunate, dualistic, archetypal, patently American thinking that says, "We will tolerate only music which, by our standards of taste, seems appropriate, and disparage, condemn, or simply ignore all music which falls outside that parameter." By taking this position, Pratt was advocating for a holistic approach to church music that encompassed the needs of diverse congregations.

Three remaining chapters in *Musical Ministries* were titled, "The Choir," "The Organ and Organist," and "The Minister's Responsibility." His most important observations pertaining to this study related to the education of church musicians and pastors. They needed at minimum a basic grounding in music history and an overview of sacred music literature.

> It may draw forth a smile if we venture to urge that a musical leader needs to know something about music. Yet there are leaders who can play or sing very fairly who are yet not even fair musicians. I mean, of course, that they know little of music as a general art, little of its literature or its history or its theory or its diversified styles and their applications, particularly as all these have to do with church music.[6]

Speaking from his own experience as a church organist, he wrote, "The musical leader is an assistant pastor. All of his functions are parts of the general pastoral function. They are all features of the administration of public worship as a church exercise."[7] He believed that to be an effective church musician training was needed well beyond applied music study.[8] It needed to include *specialized instruction in church music as a pastoral function.*

A Congregationalist, he was especially attuned to the needs of mainline nonliturgical or semi-liturgical churches. The worship of most denominations by the opening of the twentieth century, he observed, had become at least to some extent liturgically influenced.

> In as much as public worship in some form is an institution peculiar to the church, necessary to its existence, expressive of

---

5. Pratt, *Musical Ministries in the Church,* 59–61.
6. Pratt, *Musical Ministries in the Church,* 137.
7. Pratt, *Musical Ministries in the Church,* 135.
8. The use of the word, "applied," here and in connection with all types of musical instruction ("applied organ," "applied voice," and so on) refers to instruction in performance technique as opposed to academic courses in music history, church music, hymnology, and the like.

its character, and definitive of it as a social fact, all churches are really "liturgical," in spite of their doctrinal theory and outward ceremony.[9]

He noted that historically, dissenting churches commonly bolted in protest from the mother denomination over issues related to liturgy and proceeded to establish liturgical practices of their own, different though no less binding.

Because of the diverse varieties of liturgies being practiced it was even more critical that clergy and musicians be well-trained in liturgics of the churches in which they would be working. Whether a church followed a traditional worship outline or not, clergy still had to plan week-to-week services. Pratt believed that an understanding grounded in liturgical practice through the ages would greatly aid this process.[10]

Education in church music was only rarely available at seminaries and the subject was usually taught in a haphazard fashion. Pratt pointed out that for music to be a ministry, church music needed first to be accepted as a profession and musicians trained specifically to work in it. Courses in church music history, hymnology, conducting, sight singing, choral methods, and harmony and analysis needed to be offered, all from the perspective of Christian ministry.

> Something should be done in the matter. We have seminaries for training pastors, schools for training lay teachers and helpers of various kinds, and numerous temporary classes and assemblies for studying all sorts of Christian work. But what about this uniquely effective arm of [the] parish organization—the music? There is a noble opening for a school exclusively devoted to training church musicians. The conditions of admission should be simply genuine Christian enthusiasm, a declared intention to serve the musical needs of the churches, and reasonable musical aptitude. Courses should be provided for both organists and singers, but all should have . . . discipline as leaders and teachers.[11]

Pratt felt that one objective of improving education for church musicians was to change the image people had of them. "Does [the church musician] belong in the same category as sexton," Pratt asked, "or is he in a class with ministerial officers?" Pratt did not agree that just because music was known primarily as a secular calling, secular musicians should be hired to provide it for the church. "Musical directors," he said, "should be selected

---

9. Pratt, "Liturgical Responsibilities of Non-Liturgical Churches," 642.
10. Pratt, "Liturgical Responsibilities of Non-Liturgical Churches," 650.
11. Pratt, "Wanted, Specialists in Church Music," 317.

primarily because of spiritual qualifications."[12] The role of choirmaster or organist/choirmaster, he repeated once again, was to be as an assistant pastor to the congregation. Such persons would be elected by the "full body of the church," and the work of the church's pastor and his assistant would be a joint enterprise.[13] Pratt summarized the ministerial function of the choir in the following way:

> If now, we carry out the analogy between the duties of the minister and those of the choir, we note that the choir should be (1) a leader and guide in all congregational music, (2) a substitute for the congregation in such musical utterances as the people would offer if they could, and (3) a stimulus to the people to devoutness in worship. Furthermore, as the minister is also herald or teacher, so the choir should also strive to convey spiritual instruction through the medium of song.[14]

In a lecture delivered to the Royal Musical Association in London in 1895, Pratt spoke on the challenge facing secular musicians attempting careers in the church. It was a poignant statement embodying perennial conflicts:

> For himself, the church musician may claim that there is such a thing as worship in and through music, as vital and soaring as ever rose to heaven in the flame of sacrifice, the smoke of incense, or the rhapsody of liturgic prayer. He may urge that when prayer takes to itself the pinions of music and becomes praise, the blended unity of words and tones is more complete and true as an expression of the human soul in the presence of God than any material or merely verbal symbol can be. Yet, as he watches those whom he is trying through song to lift into the highest levels of worship, how rarely does he feel the popular heart responding in evident sympathy with his heart! He mounts up as on wings of eagles, but too often cleaves the upper air alone.
>
> Or the church musician may content himself with believing that music, like every artistic influence, may at least work as an indefinite emotional quickener, unlocking the gates of the inmost heart, and ministering through the avenue of aesthetic delight and zest to a somewhat intangible growth in the warmth of soul-life, so that other influences may then seize upon the spirit and put it in touch with divine realities. He may simply seek to

---

12. Pratt, "Status of Church Musicians," 208.
13. Pratt, "Status of Church Musicians," 208.
14. Pratt, "Choir," 450.

make an emotional atmosphere in which religious experience may bud and blossom without really knowing why or how or to what end. And yet here, too, how much of his most loving labor is wasted, misunderstood, misapplied! He has appealed to the love of beauty that its sisters, the love of truth and the love of righteousness, may spontaneously awake. But how sadly he finds that in the popular mind there is either a dull insensibility to beauty or a wide chasm between aesthetic and other mental activities, so that at the best he has ministered merely to a selfish and worldly craving for excitement.

These disappointments, or something like them, are the inevitable lot of most church musicians who labor with a deep philosophic sense of the mission of their art. I imagine that they befall artists of every kind. Sometimes they so crowd upon the thought as to give rise to the despairing belief that in this practical age, with its feverish material ambitions and its exaggerated estimate of merely scientific attainment, there is no room for art and the empire of feeling to which it belongs. What wonder that the church musician, like many another artist, comes to feel that he dwells apart, in a different world from the generality of men, isolated and alone![15]

What Pratt was so profoundly describing was *the very sacrificial nature of ministry itself*. Music by itself, he believed, could not minister. To become a ministry, it needed to be *set apart* from the commonalities of the concert hall. It needed to become a melding of faith-based leadership, sacrifice, and humility, working collegially with the pastoral and preaching ministries of the church to facilitate active and engaged worship among the people. Though replete with frustrations and sometimes retarded by human frailties, a ministry of music could be punctuated with flashes of joy, transformation, and transcendence.

---

15. Pratt, "Isolation of Music," 157–58.

Archibald T. Davison

Archibald T. Davison.
Public domain image courtesy of Creative Commons. (https://www.discogs.com/artist/3014101-Archibald-T-Davison/images)

Archibald Thompson Davison (1883–1961) was born and raised in the Boston area. His father, Archibald Davison Sr., immigrated from Nova Scotia in 1868 to study medicine at Harvard. He received his medical degree in 1871 and became a specialist in respiratory diseases, particularly tuberculosis. The Davisons were a devout Baptist family and lived in the Dorchester neighborhood of Boston.[16] While young Archie[17] clearly was a precocious musical talent, there is no record of early training in piano or organ. However, in 1901 he became organist at the Highlands Methodist Episcopal Church in Holyoke, Massachusetts, ninety miles west of Boston. A year later he is known to have appeared in recital with an ambitious program of works by Bach, Du Bois, Dvořák, and Lemmens.[18]

In the fall of 1902 Archie Davison enrolled at Harvard University. During his years of undergraduate and graduate study at Harvard, Davison established himself as a musician of stature and developed philosophies of music education and church music that he would adhere to for the rest of his life.

---

16. Tovey, "Archibald T. Davison," 3–4.

17. While Archie was the nickname by which childhood friends and teachers seem to have known him, in his family he answered to "Tom" to avoid confusion, since his father was also named Archibald. During his many years as a professor at Harvard, he was simply known as "Doc."

18. Tovey, "Archibald T. Davison," 3–4. During his professional career, Davison was recognized as being among the outstanding concert organists of his generation. He, along with Clarence Eddy, Camille Saint-Saens, and others, was a featured performer at the Panama-Pacific International Exposition in San Francisco in 1915. See Tovey, "Archibald T. Davison," 204.

Davison also became organist/choirmaster at All Saints Episcopal Church in the Boston suburb of Ashmont. It was his first and only experience working in high Episcopal worship. He had a thirty-voice choir of men and boys. Following graduation, Davison was awarded a fellowship for a year's study in Europe. He arrived in Paris in the summer of 1908 to study organ with Charles-Marie Widor. He sang Bach in a choral ensemble under Widor's direction, with Albert Schweitzer as continuo accompanist. There Davison also had his first exposure to *solfeggio* as a teaching technique and probably his first instruction in voice. [19]

Nearing the end of his sojourn in France, Davison received a communication from back home that would have profound implications for his life going forward. Walter R. Spalding, professor of harmony at Harvard, wrote to say that an additional music theory instructor was needed and hoped that Davison would be interested. Davison accepted the offer and began a forty-five-year career teaching at Harvard University in 1909. He became an assistant professor of music in 1917, associate professor in 1920, and full professor of music in 1929.[20]

Davison was made organist/choirmaster at Harvard's Appleton Chapel in 1910, the position once occupied by John Knowles Paine. Davison's first task was to reorganize the chapel's music around a thirty-voice all-male chorus.[21] On his insistence singers had to audition and those chosen received a small stipend for each semester of participation. Years later, Walter Spalding recalled the transition:

> After an interregnum of five months ... Dr. Archibald T. Davison was appointed organist and choirmaster and the boy choir was abandoned in favor of a men's chorus formed from the students themselves ... The works of Italian, German, and English composers of the fifteenth, sixteenth, and seventeenth centuries, for their note of spiritual contemplation and exaltation, have always been considered by expert musicians to represent the Golden Age of church music. Dr. Davison, therefore, has trained his choir to sing the best examples, so far as they can be arranged for men's voices, of Palestrina, Victoria, Allegri, Byrd, Bach, and Handel. The anthems are sung a cappella, the organ only being used in the prelude and the postlude and to lead the singing of the congregation.[22]

---

19. Tovey, "Archibald T. Davison," 34–36.
20. Tovey, "Archibald T. Davison," 37.
21. Harvard University did not become a coeducational institution until 1946. When Davison needed female singers, he drew them from Radcliffe College.
22. Spalding, *Music at Harvard*, 118.

Spalding went on to say that Davison's innovations were a refreshing change. Chapel worship seemed to have a "more religious tone" and the unaccompanied singing of the choir lent a "spiritual purity" that had been absent before. As Spalding noted, Davison changed not only the voicing of the chapel choir but also its repertoire. He used the opportunity to also revamp the choir's repertoire from stodgy Victorian anthems and hymnody to music of the Renaissance and Baroque eras, which he skillfully transcribed for unaccompanied male voices. Davison's transcriptions for the Appleton Chapel were the first in a long list of arrangements and transcriptions he would produce for men's, women's, and mixed choral ensembles that would be core repertoire for American church choirs throughout the twentieth century. In 1912, Davison's success with the Appleton Chapel Choir led to an invitation to coach the Harvard Glee Club, and eventually he became its director.

During this same period Davison's name was added to the faculty roster of the Harvard Divinity School. Between 1911 and 1929 he taught courses there in *Appreciation of Church Music, The Conduct of Church Music, The History and Development of Church Music,* and *Hymnology.* These were all one-semester, elective courses consisting of a single two-hour class per week. Unfortunately, none of them were required within the curriculum of the Divinity School. Davison also collaborated in 1926 with Edward C. Moore to publish a new *Harvard University Hymnbook.* The influence is evident of Ralph Vaughan Williams's groundbreaking *The English Hymnal* of 1906.[23] In 1933 Davison published his *Protestant Church Music in America,* one of the more controversial volumes in the history of American church music.

Though Archibald Davison was born a generation later than Pratt, the two shared similar backgrounds: both were well-known organists and respected educators who lectured and wrote voluminously on church music. Discussing the two in juxtaposition makes for interesting comparisons since they were polar opposites in much of their thinking regarding music for worship. Pratt was ever the pragmatist, willing even to acknowledge some benefit to be derived from the popular gospel hymnody. For him, musical styles and repertoire were secondary to the spirit in which worship was conducted. He spoke at length on the need for music ministry as a career vocation requiring specialized training and deserving of respect. Davidson, on the other hand, was rigidly dogmatic regarding worship. Overly idealistic and even elitist though he may have been, he possessed a deep understanding of music as a vehicle for spirituality and warned prophetically of what would be lost amid the encroachment of secularism in the church. Implicit

---

23. Tovey, "Archibald T. Davison," 206, 209.

in the writings of both men was a profound belief in the importance of music and the need for well-trained leadership. It was a conviction shared by the founders of the American Guild of Organists.

The American Guild of Organists

A sign of changing attitudes with regard to the role of music and musicians in worship was the establishment of the American Guild of Organists 1896. The AGO of the twenty-first century has changed considerably from what it was when originally conceived. Most of its founders were actively involved in church music and its founding principles were clearly directed toward church work as a profession. The purpose of the organization was clearly indicated by the *New York Times* headline announcing the guild's founding: "THE GUILD OF ORGANISTS TO BRING MUSICIANS AND CLERGYMEN TOGETHER. A New and Influential Organization Which Will Improve the Quality and Appropriateness of Church Music."[24]

Gerrit Smith (1859–1912), organist and choirmaster at South (Dutch Reformed) Church and later to be on the faculty at Union Theological Seminary, provided the initial leadership that made the organization possible. The idea of an organization of church musicians specifically geared to the promotion of better church music resulted from a trip Smith made to England in 1894. After studying the certification program of the Royal College of Organists in London, he became convinced that an organization was needed in America that would set standards of musicianship for the country's church musicians.

The cause was a worthy one and interest in it crossed all denominational bounds. The organizational meeting of the New England Chapter was held in Everett Truette's[25] Boston studio in December of 1905. One hundred forty-five of the leading church musicians of turn-of-the-century America were gathered. Among them were many figuring prominently in this study:

Dudley Buck (Holy Trinity Church, Brooklyn)

Edgar Morris Bowman (Baptist Temple, Brooklyn)

George Chadwick (New England Conservatory)

Clarence Dickinson (Brick Church, New York City)

---

24. "Guild of Organists," 5.

25. Everett Truette (1861–1933) was one of the premier organists of his generation. In addition to serving churches in the Boston area, he performed over four hundred recitals across New England and New York State and was a featured performer at both the St. Louis World's Fair (1904) and the Pan-American Exhibition in Buffalo (1901).

Henry M. Dunham (New England Conservatory)

H. Clarence Eddy (Tompkins Avenue Congregational, Brooklyn)

Arthur Foote (First Unitarian, Boston)

Walter C. Gale (Broadway Tabernacle, New York)

Benjamin Johnson Lang (King's Chapel, Boston)

Warren A. Locke (Appleton Chapel, Harvard, St. Paul's Cathedral)

Peter Christian Lutkin (Cathedral of St. Peter and St. Paul, Chicago)

John Knowles Paine (Harvard University)

Horatio Parker (Yale University)

Harry Rowe Shelley (Park Avenue Baptist, New York City)

George C. Stebbins (Northfield, Massachusetts)

George Edward Stubbs (St. Agnes Chapel, New York City)

George Elbridge Whiting (New England Conservatory, Church of the Immaculate Conception, Boston)

Samuel Prowse Warren (Grace Church, New York City)

Samuel Brenton Whitney (Church of the Advent, Boston)

Though some were strong supporters of chorus choirs (e.g., Parker and Chadwick), others favored boy choirs (Stubbs and Whitney), and still others preferred retention of the traditional quartet. All, however, were united in their desire to see progress in sacred music among the nation's churches.

The relationship between the original American Guild of Organists and the church was an intimate one. From the outset Gerrit Smith was in close consultation with Charles C. Hall, then president of Union Seminary. Smith desired that the new organization be directed especially toward the church musician and asked Hall to be the guild's first chaplain. Serving in that capacity, Hall wrote the guild's "Declaration of Religious Principles." Embodied in the declaration was the concept of music ministry:

> We believe that they who are set aside as Choirmasters and Organists in the House of God ought themselves to be persons of devout conduct, teaching the way of earnestness to the choirs committed to their charge. We believe that the unity of purpose and fellowship of life, between ministers and choirs should be everywhere established and maintained.[26]

---

26. As quoted in the mission statement of the American Guild of Organists, Harrisburg, Pennsylvania chapter. https://www.harrisburgago.org/mission-1. While some

The original purposes and goals stated for the guild were consistent with Hall's Declaration:

1. to advance the cause of church music.
2. to elevate the status of church organists.
3. to increase their appreciation of their responsibilities, duties, and opportunities as conductors of worship.
4. to obtain acknowledgment of their position from the authorities of the church; and
5. to provide musical exams and set standards of efficiency and grant certificates of Fellowship, Associateship, and Choir-mastership to members of the Guild who pass such examinations.[27]

In a time when educational opportunities for church musicians were limited, the American Guild of Organists filled an important need with its certification process. When the organization was chartered by the New York Board of Regents in 1896, it was granted authority to administer a comprehensive series of examinations for professional certification in "organ playing, choral techniques, conducting, and the theory and general knowledge of music, and to grant certificates to those who pass such examinations at specified levels of attainment."[28]

Music Ministry Education

AGO certification helped to underscore certain professional qualifications to be expected of church musicians, but where was comprehensive training in church music to come from? At the dawn of the twentieth century, there were many hopeful signs with regard to college-level musical training in the United States. Oberlin Conservatory in Ohio had been awarding bachelor's degrees in music since 1865. John Knowles Paine's pioneering work at Harvard had already begun, and Hugh Archibald Clark's at the University of Pennsylvania came soon after.[29] Curricula leading to bachelor of arts

---

AGO chapters still include the reading of the Declaration in their annual installations of officers, its use is optional. Eric Birk, executive assistant at AGO, national headquarters, provided this explanation: "This [the *Declaration of Religious Principles*] was part of the original Guild service. Its use was always optional. The reason for its decline in use is that the AGO is a secular organization." (Letter to the author, August 24, 2021.)

27. Baldwin, "American Guild of Organists," 289–95.

28. From the American Guild of Organists website: https://www.agohq.org/about-the-ago/history-purpose/.

29. In 1875, the prominent organist/composer John Knowles Paine had been given

degrees in music were introduced at the University of Michigan in 1880, at Yale in 1894, and Columbia University in 1896. Dozens of smaller conservatories and schools of music focused primarily on applied instruction and offered diplomas or performance certificates. While some seminaries offered electives in music and courses in liturgics, programs leading to a professional degree in sacred music were nonexistent.

Edmund S. Lorenz in his *Practical Church Music* (1909) felt that the seminaries needed to do more. He complained that the training future ministers were receiving seemed only focused on abstract scholarship and not the practical needs of churches that included music.

> A theological student at Yale can secure the best possible instruction in Sanskrit, Syriac, Arabic, philosophy, sociology, physiological psychology . . . but in spite of the magnificent Lowell Mason Music Library, which until very recently lay . . . unused and unexploited, and practically uncared for, he can get no musical instruction that will have any practical bearing on his management of a church and its services.
>
> Yes, the University has Horatio W. Parker, a strong composer in advanced modern style, at the head of its music, but Mr. Parker is an idealist who must have the largest possible resources at his command, both vocally and instrumentally, if he is to achieve results, and would be as helpless as a school girl in three out of five churches that are to be supplied by the students of the divinity school.[30]

As for Union Theological Seminary at the turn of the century, Lorenz is no less flattering.

> It has a large hymnological and musical library, rich in materials for the study of this important phase of church work, but there is no effort made to interest the students in its treasures. There is an endowment fund of $20,000, the income of which goes to sustain a professorship filled by Dr. Gerrit Smith, the president

---

a full professorship in music at Harvard University. While Paine is often credited with being the first to hold such a position, he was not. The French composer and teacher Frédéric Louis Ritter began his professorship at Vassar a year earlier. A Canadian, Hugh Archibald Clarke, began his professorship in music at the University of Pennsylvania the same year as Paine.

30. Lorenz, *Practical Church Music*, 131. It is important to note Lorenz's diatribe refers to Yale University quite early in the century. The Yale partnership with the School of Music of Union Theological Seminary and the more recent establishment of the Yale Institute of Sacred Music were important developments in the history of American church music.

of the American Guild of Organists. He gives a few lectures at the opening of the year on the history of music and teaches the rudiments of music to a small class of students who voluntarily attend.[31]

Lorenz listed areas he felt the seminaries needed to address to improve the state of church music.

1. Every seminary graduate must be able to read music.
2. Required to graduate: completion of a comprehensive course in the history of sacred music.
3. Required to graduate: Course in hymnology.
4. Provide instruction in how to encourage and lead congregational singing.
5. Provide instruction in choir organization and administration.
6. Provide general knowledge of keyboard instruments.

Seminaries unfortunately were focused on training candidates for the ordained pulpit ministry and *not church musicians*. Moreover, the avenue of a seminary education was one completely closed to women even though beyond the Eastern Seaboard, the majority of church organists were female.[32]

Leonard Ellinwood, writing in the 1950s, observed, "Music education has always been one of the most neglected aspects of church work in this country."[33] There were colleges, conservatories, and universities offering courses including hymnology, liturgical subjects, and music history usually to be taken along with applied organ lessons. Some of those curricula led to diplomas or performance certificates while others led to a generic bachelor of arts in music. There were, however, no standardized curricula, the quality of instruction depended largely on the limited number of experienced teachers available, and professional degrees in sacred music were unheard of.

Professor William Benton Chamberlain established the School of Sacred Music at the Chicago Theological Seminary in 1902. It was a four- to six-day extension program designed to bring musicians and seminarians together and offered courses in elementary singing, hymnology, and history of church music. A student choir was also organized, but Chamberlain's program offered no degree or diploma.

---

31. Lorenz, *Practical Church Music*, 132.
32. McDaniel, "Church Song and the Cultivated Tradition," 648.
33. Ellinwood, *History of American Church Music*, 145.

The Trinity School of Church Music may have been the first formally organized school offering a comprehensive sacred music curriculum. It was founded in 1913 by Felix Lamond (1862–1940). Lamond, an Englishman, had been organist at Trinity Chapel of Trinity Parish, New York, since 1897 and taught organ and music-related subjects at Columbia University Teachers College. The advertisement below appeared in the October 12 issue of the *New-York Tribune*.

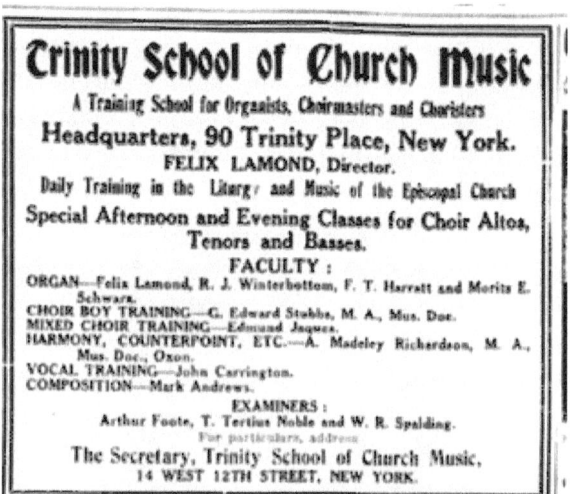

The *New York Times* trumpeted enthusiastically the exaggerated claim "First School Here for Church Music . . . Demand for organists can't be supplied— None being trained in this country!" The *Times* went on to describe the program:

> The new school, which opens this Fall, will have a course of thirteen weeks for three years. The tuition has been fixed at $250 a year, and it is expected the students will be attracted from every part of the country. Lectures will be given daily, and practice will be afforded in all of the nine chapels of Trinity besides Trinity Church itself; and the Cathedral of St. John the Divine, Grace Church, and St. Thomas's Church have expressed interest and willingness to cooperate. . . . The new school will be devoted exclusively to the training of organists and choirmasters for the Episcopal church service, but in some departments will take students in other services.[34]

---

34. "First School Here for Church Music," 6.

The Trinity School of Church Music unfortunately existed for only five years.[35]

Offering a parallel curriculum to the Trinity School, but for Roman Catholics, was the Pius X School of Liturgical Music, founded by Georgia Stevens and Justine Ward in 1918 in New York City.

The decade of the 1920s was an important one for sacred music education in the United States. The School of Gospel Music, which had been established at Southwestern Baptist Theological Seminary in 1915, was renamed the School of Church Music in 1921. Peter Christian Lutkin (1858–1931), best known today for his anthem setting of "The Lord Bless You and Keep You," was a pioneer of the a cappella choir movement and in 1896 became founding director of the Northwestern University School of Music.

Peter Christian Lutkin.
Public domain image, Library of Congress. (http://hdl.loc.gov/loc.pnp/ggbain.06444)

It was Lutkin who in 1926 oversaw the establishing of a department of choral and church music at Northwestern, the first of its kind at a major university. Two other institutions with even broader influence would be birthed before

---

35. With the advent of World War I, Felix Lamond enlisted as a major in the American Red Cross and played a pivotal role in supervising aid to thousands of wounded veterans returning from overseas. After the war, he became director of the American Academy in Rome, the music division of which had been conceived to provide encouragement and fellowships to talented composers in the United States. The American Academy in Rome would produce some of the twentieth century's most famous composers of choral music, including Leo Sowerby, Howard Hanson, Randall Thompson, and Samuel Barber. Lamond continued in his post with the AAR until his death in 1940.

Sacred Music Education and the Flowering of Music Ministry

the end of the decade: The Westminster Choir College (1926) and the Union Theological Seminary School of Sacred Music (1928).

The Founding of Westminster Choir College

The Westminster Church Choir, ca. 1925, in Dayton, Ohio.
Public domain image, courtesy of Rider College Archives.
(https://www.rider.edu/academics/colleges-schools/westminster-college-arts/wcc/about/historic-westminster)

John Finley Williamson's enormous contributions to American choral singing through his work with the Westminster Choir were chronicled previously, but his most lasting legacy was in sacred music education. Williamson, from the very early days of his work at Westminster Presbyterian Church in Dayton, Ohio, had been committed to the idea that local churches should be centers for music for the surrounding neighborhood. "The church," he declared, "must go hand in hand with the public schools in the musical development and musical education of the community."[36] He was among the first advocates for graded choir programs that would be nearly universal in churches, small and large, by mid-century. Williamson was a firm believer in the all-volunteer choir. He felt that choir directors and organists should be prepared to educate and motivate singers and members of the congregation in every aspect of worship participation, including congregational singing. When Williamson arrived at Dayton's Westminster Presbyterian Church in 1918, he immediately established a level of musical

---

36. Williamson, "Choir Organization and Training," 5–6.

discipline seldom matched since. Every choir member received individual choir training [i.e., voice lessons] from Williamson, and his teaching was not limited either to choir members or to vocal instruction.[37] He was intimately involved in all aspects of church life. Encouraging congregational involvement in hymn singing was a particular interest he would carry with him throughout his career. "We are attempting," he would say later, "to recreate an interest in the art of hymnology, the very source from which our old reformers—Hus, Knox, Calvin, Luther, Wesley and the rest—received their inspiration . . . We should never lose sight of the fact that the one and only purpose of church music is worship. Music in itself is not religious, but if it is to serve its purpose in the church it must arouse emotions that are religious. In most churches today music occupies [a large percentage of the] service yet often it has little to do with it."[38]

Because of his commitment to church music education, John Finley Williamson—assisted by his wife, Rhea—founded the Westminster Choir School in Dayton in 1926. It had an initial enrollment of sixty and a faculty of ten. The school was nonsectarian, with a three-year program culminating with a diploma upon successful completion. By 1929, the Westminster Choir School had outgrown the rooms available to it at Westminster Presbyterian and moved to the campus of the Ithaca Conservatory of Music[39] in Ithaca, New York. It also expanded to a four-year program designed specifically for students in the field of sacred music and became the Westminster Choir College. The school awarded its first bachelor's degrees in sacred music in 1930. In 1932, the school moved once again, to Princeton, New Jersey, where classes were held initially at the First Presbyterian Church and on the campus of Princeton Seminary.

---

37. Schmoyer, "Contribution of the Westminster Choir Movement," 13.
38. Williamson, "Williamson Defends Purpose of Church Music," 2.
39. Now Ithaca College.

Sacred Music Education and the Flowering of Music Ministry

Clarence Dickinson

Clarence Dickinson.
Image courtesy of Yale Institute of Sacred Music Archives.

Clarence Dickinson (1873–1969) was the son of the Reverend William C. Dickinson, a Presbyterian minister. His grandfather, Baxter Dickinson, had served on the staff of Lane Seminary in Cincinnati under Lyman Beecher. He enrolled at Northwestern University in 1890 planning to major in Greek, but his skill as an organist soon became the talk of Chicago. A student of Clarence Eddy, he was hired as organist at the Church of the Messiah (Unitarian) in 1892. Barely in his twenties, Dickinson was developing a national reputation as a concert performer. He was a featured performer at the Chicago World's Fair and drew crowds to his weekly Tuesday evening recitals at the Church of the Messiah. From 1897 to 1898, Clarence Dickinson was organist at St. James Protestant Episcopal Church (now St. James Cathedral).[40] He also served regularly as accompanist to Peter C. Lutkin's choirs at Northwestern University.

In the fall of 1898, Dickinson left America to take an obligatory two-year musical study tour of Europe. He studied organ with Heinrich Reimann at the *Kaiser Wilhelm Kirche* and theory with Otto Singer in Berlin. Later, Clarence relocated to Paris to study organ with Alexandre Guilmant. While there he also studied composition with Gabriel Pierné, accompaniment of plainsong with Louis Vierne, and served briefly as organist at the American Church.[41] Dickinson returned to Chicago in 1901 and his old job at St. James Episcopal. There he was able to build experience working with the Episcopal liturgy and a sixty-voice choir of men and boys. St. James was

---

40. Weadon, "Clarence Dickinson," 19–30.
41. Weadon, "Clarence Dickinson," 23.

also his first exposure to other Anglican/Episcopal traditions. He was able to put his French training in plainchant to use and weekly Sunday afternoon musical vespers provided yet another vehicle for him to shine as a master organist. In addition to his work at St. James, Dickinson's hectic schedule included teaching organ, and conducting commitments:

> My weekly schedule soon meant catching a 5:30 train for the hour ride to Aurora, and getting dinner on the train. The train was a deluxe express—first stop Aurora—and the thru passengers were allowed to come into the diner . . . So, I always had my dinner and arrived at the hall in time to rehearse the orchestra for an hour, and the chorus for an hour and a half. Catching a ten o'clock train back to Chicago, I then crossed to another station and caught the sleeper to Dubuque, Iowa, where I taught for four hours the next day, then had rehearsals for the Bach Society of Dubuque, following the same routine of rehearsing the orchestra first and the chorus last. I then caught the sleeper back to Chicago, where I taught at the Cosmopolitan School, of which I was the director, until the middle of the afternoon, and then rehearsed the boys at St. James. I took the evening off! On Thursday, I was back at school for classes in the morning, rehearsal for the Musical Art Society at 2:30, a rehearsal of the English Opera company at 4:00, and, at 6:30, the chorus of the Sunday Evening Club rehearsal. Friday morning was given up to organ lessons at the church . . . Friday evening was given over to rehearsing the men and boys of St. James for the Sunday service. Saturday morning was the service at *Temple Kehilath Anshe Mayriv*. In the afternoon, I practiced for various services. Sunday morning and afternoon was spent at St. James Episcopal Church. Once a month, in the afternoon, there was a large important festival service with a short organ recital following. Then came the Sunday Evening Club, a service held at Orchestra Hall, for which we had distinguished preachers from all over the country, a large chorus, and a fine quartet of soloists. I played a half-hour program of organ music, and then, putting another organist on the bench, conducted the chorus . . .[42]

In September of 1909, Dickinson became organist at Brick Presbyterian Church on Park Avenue at 91st Street in New York City. His first year there was a tumultuous one. The pastor, Dr. William C. Richards, died suddenly in January and the eminent clergyman, Princeton professor of English, author, and former ambassador to the Netherlands, Henry Van Dyke,

---

42. Weadon, "Clarence Dickinson," 24.

was brought in as interim. On April 9, all of New York society gathered at Brick Church for the funeral of Samuel Longhorn Clemens (Mark Twain) for which Dickinson was the organist. Finally, in May of 1911 the Reverend Dr. William Pierson Merrill (1867–1954) of Chicago was called to be Brick Church's new pastor.

Merrill, now regarded as one of the preeminent liberal theologians of the early twentieth century, was a staunch advocate for modernist thought. It was Merrill who rose in defense of Harry Emerson Fosdick and his sermon "Shall the Fundamentalists Win?" He was also a progressive in his views of the aesthetics and music of worship. In a speech before the New Jersey Council of the National Association of Organists, he urged a collegial relationship between pastor and church musician, striving for a unified worship experience thematically through coordinated music and sermon planning. A hymnwriter himself,[43] Merrill placed special emphasis on hymn selection. He noted that many pastors "form a little circle of favorite hymns and trot around inside it Sunday after Sunday." Merrill encouraged the church musicians in his audience to work with such pastors to expand their hymnological horizons.[44]

Merrill closed his address with comments touching on the sensitive issues of art, musical taste, and worship.

> View your work as primarily worship and secondarily art. While mindful of your art, never forget God, and that you are serving Him through your art. Take pains to become a part of the church you serve. Be something more than an organist. Get into the work and life and fellowship of the church, for your own sake, and for your work's sake. Show that you are genuinely and sacrificially interested in the purposes and aims of the church, and are not a mere ornamental and aesthetic adjunct . . . The relation between organist and minister can never be right until it is based on a clear recognition of the close kinship of music and religion . . . There is nothing in all the vast realm of man's interests so closely akin to his religion as music.[45]

Merrill's views regarding the role of music in worship and the ministry of church musicians were truly progressive for his era. He would be a major

---

43. Merrill wrote a number of published hymn texts and at least seven tunes. Of them, the one most well-known—one suspects to Merrill's dismay—is "Rise Up, O Men of God." A far greater text, "Not Alone for Mighty Empire," still appears in numerous denominational collections.

44. Merrill, "A Noted Divine's Advice."

45. Merrill, "A Noted Divine's Advice."

influence in shaping Clarence Dickinson's own approach to church work, his teaching, and his copious writings on sacred music.

Brick Church had a reputation for its fine music program before 1909, "but the tenure of Clarence Dickinson put the music of the church amongst the greatest in New York and indeed the country."[46] His responsibilities included morning, afternoon, and evening services on Sundays plus the attendant rehearsals.

Upon Dickinson's arrival at Brick Church, changes were instituted. Unusually for a Presbyterian church, he insisted his choirs be vested because it provided uniformity of appearance. He saw choir leadership in worship as a ministerial role and vestments appropriately symbolized this. In 1910, Dickinson initiated a series of Oratorio Services beginning with Part One of Handel's *Messiah* and Stainer's *Crucifixion*, performances of which continue to the present day. Volunteer singers were dismissed in 1913, and the Brick Church Chancel Choir became a twenty-one-voice all professional ensemble. In 1920, to celebrate the dedication of the new Aeolian Skinner organ, he inaugurated "Friday Noon Hours of Music," a concert series which included choral major works with orchestra and recitals of prominent soloists, including Dickinson himself at the organ.

With William P. Merrill's installation in 1911, Dickinson and he began a collaboration to achieve a unified worship experience for the Brick Church congregation. The unified service would become an integral part of Dickinson's philosophy of church music for the rest of his career. Based on this concept, pastor and musician would carefully plan the sermon-centered services so that every element of the service order—hymns, prayers, sermon, anthems, organ music—followed a central theme. Dickinson set as his goal that "All the music before the sermon should create the spirit or the atmosphere in the service which will prepare the way for the sermon."[47] Texts to all vocal music were to be printed in the service bulletin.[48] Sermon-focused worship, as opposed to liturgically focused, was well within Dickinson's Presbyterian comfort zone. Later he would collaborate with his wife, Helen, and the Reverend Paul Austin Wolfe[49] to write *The Choir Loft and the Pulpit: Fifty-Two Complete Services of Worship*,[50] which was intended to flesh out the unifying principle.

---

46. Quoted from "Music at the Brick Church," 1963 pamphlet published by Brick Church, in Weadon, "Clarence Dickinson," 60.
47. Weadon, "Clarence Dickinson," 91.
48. Garner, *Clarence Dickinson*, 65.
49. Wolfe became pastor at Brick Church in 1932.
50. Dickinson, Dickinson, and Wolfe, *Choir Loft and the Pulpit*.

In an undated lecture, "Music and Worship," Dickinson wrote, "The music must reinforce the message of the sermon, must imbue it with appeal and with an emotional quality which will win the heart when the mind does not follow."[51] As for the choice of choral and organ repertoire, Dickinson espoused a rather open-ended approach he called his "theology of beauty."

> There are three great avenues of life and thought as I feel it— three doors that make up the triune gateway to heaven: Truth, Goodness, and Beauty. The scientists concern themselves with truth, and the scholars and the literalists. The chief interest of the church's ministry since Puritan days in this country has been goodness or morality.
>
> But there is a third door, and many who become as children and enter the Kingdom of Heaven, enter through the gate of pure beauty. And this is largely what we are called upon to do as musicians in the church. The beauty of music is not an ornament to the building we call worship, it is a portal. It awakens man's sensitivity to the highest and loveliest things . . .[52]

Good and beautiful music for worship need not be unattainably difficult, Dickinson wrote.

> We must keep ever in mind the power of music to lift the individual person out of his self-centered existence. When he joins in singing as hymn or listens to an anthem, he ceases to be wholly individual; the congregation becomes one, and he a part of it. Personal differences of creed, questionings, doubt, disbelief are forgotten as hearts and voices unite in gratitude, joy, and aspiration . . . A large element in salvation or redemption is just this release from the tyranny of self and its demands, its smallness and its limitations.[53]

Dickinson's "theology of beauty" addressed the mystical power of music to draw worshippers into the spiritual realm. But to achieve this across the spectrum of American religious preferences would demand flexibility and openness from church musicians as style preferences and tastes changed. Near the end of his life, he wrote a forward-looking and perceptive article for the *Choral Journal,* in which he said:

> First of all, I believe the church is here to stay, and it will always have good news to proclaim to the people who desperately need

---

51. Dickinson, "Music and Worship," 1.
52. Dickinson, "Music and Worship," 4.
53. Dickinson, "Music and Worship," 6.

it. Theological leaders will adapt this good news to the needs of the day, but the thread will be unbroken ...

Second, there will always be congregations who will want to give expression for their faith with the emotional coloring that music gives to our utterances. They will want hymns and other congregational music in which they can participate—simple music, tuneful music, perhaps music that approaches some of the characteristics of folk music.[54]

Union Theological Seminary

Union Theological Seminary (UTS) in Morningside Heights, New York City, is the nation's oldest nondenominational Protestant seminary. It was founded in 1836, just eighteen years after the Episcopalian General Theological Seminary. While founded by Presbyterians, it was always intended to be nonsectarian and enjoyed a level of independence from the doctrinal disagreements that had roiled relationships between Christian denominations in America from the beginning. Because of that independence, by the late nineteenth century UTS had become a stronghold of liberal thought. It broke with the Presbyterian Church in 1893 to become a fully independent institution.

The need for classes in sacred music was recognized from the outset at UTS. Both Thomas Hastings and George F. Root taught at Union during the 1840s, and Lowell Mason taught there during the 1854/55 academic year. Classes were taught in music reading, congregational and choral singing, but usually with the rather superficial approach taken at Mason's Musical Conventions. Students usually met in the basement of the Mercer Street Presbyterian Church. After Mason's retirement in 1855, the school did not have another music instructor for twenty years.[55]

By the 1880s a need was widely felt for a more substantial regimen of study. In 1886, a faculty committee recommended that a curriculum for instruction in sacred music be formulated to go into effect the next year. Further, the committee urged the swift appointment of a standing committee on music, which was to look into the matter of hiring a full-time instructor. Nevertheless, instruction in church music continued to be limited to applied music. Reinhold L. Herman, a recently immigrated German who had taught at the Stern Conservatory in Berlin, was hired to teach general music at the seminary. Herman succeeded in making class attendance compulsory

---

54. Dickinson, "Music in the Churches," 8.
55. McDaniel, "Church Song and the Cultivated Tradition," 650–51.

though students only met for "one hour of an evening each week."[56] In addition, a choir was organized for those divinity students with special musical talent. In 1890, Herman returned to Germany and was replaced at Union by Gerrit Smith. Smith was named "Harkness Instructor in Sacred Music." He taught beginning and advanced music theory, a class in *The Elements of Singing*, and directed the chapel choir. His public lectures on the history of sacred music at Union were well respected, and his course *The History of Sacred Music* would remain in the seminary curriculum from then on. Smith, however, was extremely active in the New York area as a concert organist, a choral conductor, and one of the founders of the American Guild of Organists. Teaching at UTS was not the primary focus of his career. On July 21, 1912, while vacationing at his summer cottage in Darien, Connecticut, Gerrit Smith died suddenly and unexpectedly of pneumonia. Just three weeks later a telegram was sent to the organist/conductor Clarence Dickinson, asking him to take Smith's place.

Dickinson by that time was well known in New York as well as on the Union campus. He had performed in recital all over the city including at the seminary. He and Gerrit Smith had been close friends.[57] William P. Merrill, an 1890 graduate of the seminary, provided another influential endorsement for adding Clarence to the faculty roster. Dickinson would continue as organist at Brick Church until 1960, but with his work at Union Theological Seminary he would make his most important contributions to American church music.

The duties of the new professor included playing organ at the seminary chapel services, Monday through Friday, directing the seminary choir, and teaching classes in composition and music history. Almost immediately, Dickinson replaced the music history class with one more focused on the music of the church, including units on the history of the organ, oratorios, carols, and sacred folk music. In 1914 he gave the first of his Historical Organ Lecture-Recitals. Held on Tuesday afternoons in February, "they were designed to educate both the students and the public about the organ, music, and its relationship to the church and life in general."[58]

In 1926 another kindred spirit entered Clarence Dickinson's professional life when the Rev. Henry Sloane Coffin became president of Union Theological Seminary. Coffin had a transcendent vision of the role church musicians should be playing in church life. "As a minister, Dr. Coffin had deplored the wide-spread practice of bringing the professional musician

---

56. McDaniel, "Church Song and the Cultivated Tradition," 651.
57. Garner, *Clarence Dickinson*, 84–85.
58. Garner, *Clarence Dickinson*, 86.

into the church without any preparation for his part in the life of the church. Twenty-five years in the pastoral ministry had taught him the importance of good church music and the need for sensitive church musicians."[59] This was a vision Dickinson shared. He spoke of it in a speech at Coffin's retirement celebration in 1945.

> I had been tremendously interested in the idea of such a school for perhaps three main reasons: The first (and least important) was the idea of putting the ministry of music in the church on as high a plane professionally as possible—the minister has his general undergraduate course, usually in Arts, then this theological school. It would be interesting to have the Ministers of Music carry out something like the same idea . . .
>
> The second idea was the providing of a theological background, as it were, for the Minister of Music. Would that we could insist on the same degree of musical background for the minister in the pulpit! . . . I have long felt that we would have a different attitude toward our profession and our church music would be pervaded by a different spirit if her musicians had a knowledge of the Church and her history; of the historic liturgies and worship, of the Bible and of Christ, and we have felt here that it would be an enormous advantage for ministers and ministers of music to associate in classes and in daily fellowship.
>
> And thirdly we have hoped through such a School to further the development of a realization of how high a calling is ours. Of what it can mean to the Church's worship in lending it emotional appeal—and that faith in the unseen and eternal—something beyond the sphere of reason, which music is able to impart; and . . . the Service of the worship of God with that beauty which surely God must love, as it [is] so richly present in His created world.[60]

The UTS School of Sacred Music

In 1928, Clarence Dickinson with the support of UTS president Henry Sloane Coffin established the School of Sacred Music at Union Theological Seminary. It would be the first nondenominational institution offering masters-level training for church musicians in the United States. It cannot be emphasized enough that the establishment of the UTS School of Sacred

---

59. Skinner, *Sacred Music at Union Theological Seminary*, 27.
60. Weadon, "Clarence Dickinson," 170.

Music was a collaborative effort shared by Dickinson and Coffin. It was Coffin who had to go to the New York University Board of Regents to advocate for the concept and have a charter drawn up by the state. Years later, Coffin summarized the original vision of the school as being "to supply the church with competent musicians thoroughly conversant with the thought, worship and work of the church . . . musicians who can be genuine partners of ministers in the pastoral office."[61] The equally important goal, Coffin noted, was a mixed-discipline approach that exposed seminarians to some sacred music education and church musicians with training in basic theology, church history, and liturgics. An important outgrowth of this would be a collegial relationship between musicians, seminarians, and clergy. "In such an atmosphere, the church musician, the religious educator, and the minister meet and train together in much the same way as they will work together in actual parish situations."[62] Unfortunately and to the detriment of American church music in the future, Coffin's vision of a reciprocal interaction between ministry and music students never materialized.

Funded at first for a conditional three years, the School of Sacred Music was a graduate school intended for students who had already completed their baccalaureate training in music elsewhere. Required for graduation from the program were completion of sixty semester hours, a thesis, two compositions—one choral and one instrumental—and a conducting assignment. The first School of Sacred Music class, consisting of two men and five women, received their master of arts in sacred music in the spring of 1930. A doctoral program, added for the 1941/1942 academic year, was the first such program in the United States.[63]

"Minister of Music," a Title and a Concept

In the December 1891 issue of the *Hartford Seminary Record,* Waldo Selden Pratt posed a provocative question. "Might not the great problem [of church music] be permanently cleared up," Pratt asked, "if our churches would insist that all who are called to undertake the management of the musical arm of public worship be formally set apart or ordained to their office, so they may truly be pastoral assistants?"[64] He was motivated to ask this by the ordination in 1891 of the Rev. Henry D. Sleeper as a Congregational minister

---

61. Skinner, *Sacred Music at Union Theological Seminary,* 28.
62. Skinner, *Sacred Music at Union Theological Seminary,* 29.
63. Weadon, "Clarence Dickinson," 204.
64. Pratt, "Recent Ordination," 42.

specializing in sacred music—the nation's first formally degreed minister of music.

Henry Dike Sleeper.
Public domain image courtesy of Smith College Archives.
(https://www.smith.edu/news/saq-womens-suffrage-camp-marbury)

Before coming to the Hartford Seminary, Henry Dike Sleeper (1865–1948) had studied music theory and composition at Harvard, under John Knowles Paine. During his Harvard years, Sleeper collected and edited an edition of *Songs of Harvard* (1890).[65] While in the Boston area, he also studied organ with Clarence Eddy. At the seminary, Sleeper studied under Pratt, receiving a thorough grounding in the history of sacred music.

Recognizing the historic significance of Sleeper's ordination, the *Hartford Seminary Record* devoted a full paragraph to it.

> Still another ordination in the same class was that of H. D. Sleeper at Worcester, Mass., on November 24. The occasion had particular interest because it was the first at which the Hartford idea that the oversight of church music is properly a specialized function of the ministry was fully recognized. Mr. Sleeper goes in January next to Beloit, Wisconsin, where he will have charge of the new music department of Beloit College and be choirmaster and organist in the First Congregational Church. He sought ordination primarily as a church musician and council agreed to its advisability.[66]

---

65. Sleeper, ed., *Songs of Harvard*.
66. "Untitled Description of Henry D. Sleeper's Graduation," 71.

After Sleeper arrived in Beloit and began his work at church and college, the *Hartford Seminary Record* proudly reported on his progress.

> Henry D. Sleeper, '91, is filling his position as instructor of music in Beloit College with marked acceptance, and is also gaining for himself a large place in the community. From a local report of a Song and Organ Recital, recently given in the College Chapel by Mr. Sleeper and Mr. W. H. Rieger, the following excerpt is made: "Mr. Sleeper seems to possess the instrument, the music and the audience. His playing is always refined. His sympathetic touch and true musical feeling make his playing delightful, and the community is greatly indebted to him for so rare a program." It will be remembered that Mr. Sleeper is probably our only Congregational minister who was ordained with the express understanding that he was to make music his profession.[67]

Henry Sleeper recognized the unusual status that had been granted him as a minister of music and bemoaned the lack of training common to church musicians of his generation. In an 1909 essay, "Church Music," clearly influenced by Pratt's teaching, he expanded on this. After providing a brief review of the American church music history from colonial times, he turned to status of music in the church at the turn of the twentieth century. Much advancement, he noted, had been made in organ construction, and he cited progress in the publication of church hymnals. The ongoing popularity of Moody/Sankey gospel songs, however, was troubling. "These books," he wrote, "have been gotten out to meet the ravenous demand of an untutored public; they have greatly aided the efforts of evangelists, but it is to be regretted that they have become, even temporarily, the standards of taste in so many churches."[68] The problem was not just one of lack of taste, Sleeper believed, but lack of knowledgeable and committed leadership.

> It must be candidly admitted that the state of music today in the non-liturgical churches of America leaves much to be desired. The pastors and the churches which exercise an intelligent and effective supervision over their music are all too few. The prevailing custom is to leave, not only the manner of performance, but the selection of all music, except perhaps the hymns, entirely to the organist or choirmaster. When this officer is well-trained or has shown evident fitness for such responsibility this may result in no serious evil. But when we consider that organists, if trained at all, are as a rule trained simply as players and not

---

67. "Untitled Alumni Report on Activities of H. D. Sleeper," 155.
68. Sleeper, "Church Music," 388.

as *church* organists, and that choirmasters, as a rule, are trained only as to their voices and not at all as to their judgement or taste in the special field of church music, we must not be surprised to find Wagner's "Evening Star" as the organ prelude to the morning service, or the overture to *'Stradella* as the postlude, or a harvest anthem sung in March, or *Gallia* given at an Easter Sunday praise service.[69]

While Sleeper was degreed as a minister of music, the focus of his career was teaching. Pratt's dream of musicians specially trained and committed to careers in full-time ministry through music was yet to be realized.

The common use of the professional title "minister of music" likely originated with John Finley Williamson. Because of Williamson's aggressive work at Westminster Church in Dayton to build an all-encompassing church music ministry, the church formally bestowed upon him the title "minister of music." Williamson was proud of the designation and years later would claim he coined the term. He insisted that all graduates of the Westminster Choir College be known as "ministers of music" and thousands of future WCC graduates would claim it as their professional title. It would also be very appropriately used by graduates of the UTS School of Sacred Music.[70]

---

69. Sleeper, "Church Music," 388.

70. *A personal note*: How important really is a title? While many church musicians—particularly in the nonliturgical denominations—are employed as ministers of music, the validity of the designation is sometimes questioned. Those who object generally feel that only ordained clergy can be referred to as "ministers." The salient factor for this writer has never been what the church musician calls him or herself or what it says on an employment contract. What *is* important is what he or she does. Leaders in American church music for two hundred years—from Thomas Hastings to Pratt, Dickinson, and Williamson—had wanted musicians in the church to be recognized educators, liturgists, praise leaders, and witnesses to the faith, not hired hands to sing, play the organ, or direct a choir—in short, leaders in ministry. Titles help to define that ministry but are of little significance for the musician who has a true calling to this work.

Chapter 17

GOSPEL METAMORPHOSIS

Bridging the Gap between Sacred and Secular in Black and White Gospel Music

From the beginning American Christianity's simultaneous disdain for and embrace of secularism and commercialism is head-scratching. Bedrock Calvinists railed against using musical instruments—associated with dancing and who knows what other immoral activities—yet found ways to justify their use. First pitch pipes and tuning forks, then a cello here and there, the list goes on . . .

Critics were quick to decry commercialism in sacred music yet singing school masters North and South—nearly always regarded by churches as outside agents—survived on tunebook sales. The competition for sales was fierce. It was commercialism of the first order, and their customers were the churches and singers within them. One would be hard pressed to find purveyors more adept at selling tunebooks than the circle of musicians around Lowell Mason. In the late nineteenth century, Dwight Moody's use of profits from *Gospel Songs, 1–6* was a frequent target of detractors, yet the collection ranked with the Bible as one of the best-selling volumes of the era.

And then there was the bugaboo of professionalism. Thousands of sermons were preached against the licentiousness of the theater, yet Boston's flagship Baptist Church—the Tremont Temple—functioned as a theater and concert hall during the week. Operatic extravagance was roundly condemned, yet many of the nation's most elite churches hired quartets of opera singers to display their musical prowess on Sunday morning. In short, there was a bewildering inconsistency between what the church *said* about secularism, greed, and commercialism and what it actually *did*.

There *was* an ecclesiastical sphere and a secular one, but the boundary between them was frequently breached. A melding of religious music and popular culture—the blending of sacred and secular—was taking place long before 1900. Much of that was made possible by the development of print media. As music printing became more economically feasible in the late nineteenth century, the mass marketing of hymnals and inexpensive octavo music for church choirs became possible. It also made possible a huge market for revivalist songs and hymnbooks—the contents of which, while sacred in orientation, were promoted for use outside of traditional worship. That caveat opened the door to utilization of parlor ballad sentimentality and rhythms more associated with ragtime than classic hymnody. A raft of temperance songs, sentimental ditties such as "The Church in the Wildwood," and shallow positivity like "Brighten the Corner Where You Are" became the stuff of populist religion. The sale of religious songbooks was lucrative. From Moody to Billy Sunday, it was a major source of funding for revivalism.

The boundary between sacred and secular would be further obscured in the twentieth century by the marketing of religious (and *religious sounding*) music in recordings, broadcast media, and television. By the waning years of the twentieth century, proponents of contemporary Christian worship would openly acknowledge and welcome the integration of pop styles, artists, and glitz in worship spaces. The "seeds of commercialization" were sowed, among other things, by Black and white gospel quartets that were becoming a popular and common presence on radio and in the 1930s. Black gospel performers like Sister Rosetta Tharpe, singing their music in non-religious settings such as nightclubs and concert halls, not only generated notoriety but also a large following outside the church. Following World War II, white southern gospel quartets followed a similar trend. Long held relationships with churches and tunebook publishers were severed and ensembles like the Statesmen Quartet became top-selling recording artists in their own right. Secular western and country artists assimilated gospel music into their repertoires. From jazz singer Ethel Waters singing "His Eye is on the Sparrow," to Elvis and his rendition of "Peace in the Valley," to Dolly Parton and "Precious Memories," the trend was clear. It can legitimately be defended for making the gospel message widely available or cursed for making sacred music little more than a commercial commodity.

Blessing or curse, the drift of gospel music into the secular arena would provide as-yet-unseen challenges to defining the role music could or should have in worship. To understand this relentless drift, one must explore what was to become a new genre and style of sacred music.

Gospel Music in the Twentieth Century

Stephen Sheeron and Harry Eskew defined gospel music as "A large body of Christian songs and hymns of predominantly American origin with strophic texts and often refrains that reflect aspects of the personal religious experiences of evangelical Protestants. In addition to drawing on sacred sources, gospel music typically incorporates elements of popular music styles."[1] A definition so broad, of course, limits its usefulness. While the terms "gospel songs" and "gospel hymns" came out of the Moody/Sankey era, they are often applied to some pre-Civil War hymns and Sunday school songs of W. B. Bradbury. Also pre-dating Moody and Sankey were songs used for evangelical witness by Philip Phillips in his "sermons in song" and Eben Tourjée in his "praise meetings." To be clear then, when discussing gospel music in the context of the twentieth century, we are referring to more than a song type but a *stylistic genre* that over time assimilated qualities of popular secular music.

Eskew and Shearon identified four distinct periods in the development of American gospel music up to around 1980.[2] I have expanded upon them as follows:

1. Northern Urban Gospel: *The era of the Great Urban Revival of Moody, Sam Jones, and Billy Sunday, among others.*

2. Southern Gospel: *The era of seven-shape tunebooks, rural singing schools, singing conventions, and white male and family quartets.*

3. Black Gospel and Gospel Blues: *The era of gospel singing by Blacks following the Great Migration to urban centers of the North.*

4. Country, Bluegrass, and Western Gospel: *The assimilation of southern gospel styling into the repertoire of individual recording artists—the Nashville Sound.*[3]

---

1. Eskew and Shearon, "Gospel Music."
2. Eskew and Shearon, "Gospel Music."
3. Note: The term "gospel music" has been used as a generic term to describe all of the music types above. The term "Southern gospel," however, is properly applied only to vocal ensemble music, not that which is sung by a single vocalist. Piano accompaniment is assumed whether indicated or not. The term came into use in the 1970s. The term "Black Gospel Blues" was used by Thomas A. Dorsey to describe his style of songwriting in the 1930s and continues to be used by some historians.

In 1862 Joseph Funk—the successful Mennonite singing school master, tunebook compiler, and publisher in Singer's Glen, Virginia—had died. Funk left his publishing enterprise, Joseph Funk and Sons, to his grandson, Aldine Kieffer, and his granddaughter's husband, Ephraim Ruebush. In 1878 the company moved to Dayton, Virginia, and in 1890 it was renamed the Ruebush-Kieffer Company. Building on Joseph Funk's legacy, Ruebush-Kieffer established the Virginia Normal School of Music in 1874 in New Market, Virginia, to train aspiring singing masters. When the company moved to Dayton its classes were taught on the campus of the Shenandoah Seminary.[4] The normal school utilized the seven-shape notational system exclusively in its teaching method and became the principal training ground for singing school masters in the early twentieth century. The Ruebush-Kieffer Company continued to be a major publisher of gospel and singing school music through 1942, and the three most recognized leaders of the next generation all had strong Ruebush-Kieffer connections.

James Vaughan and the Southern Gospel Tradition

A direct beneficiary of the Funk-Ruebush-Kieffer legacy was James David Vaughan (1864–1941). A highly successful songwriter, publisher, and promoter, he is frequently referred to as the "founder" of the Southern Gospel tradition.

---

4. Shenandoah Seminary had been chartered as a United Brethren institution in 1876. In 1884, the seminary was re-chartered as "Shenandoah Institute" and experienced rapid growth over the next two decades. No doubt in part due to the normal school's presence, a strong musical focus was present, and this was amplified with the hiring of James H. Ruebush, the son of Ephraim Ruebush, to head its music department in the 1880. In 1902, the Shenandoah Institute was renamed "Shenandoah Collegiate Institute and School of Music," and from 1909 to 1922 Ruebush was its president. In 1944, the institute was again renamed, becoming the Shenandoah Conservatory of Music. The Conservatory was relocated to its present location in Winchester, Virginia, in 1960. The author is a proud alumnus. See *Shenandoah University Historic Timeline*. Special thanks also to Dr. Jonathan A. Noyalas, director of the McCormick Civil War Institute at Shenandoah University, and his unpublished paper, "Backbone, Reflections on the Life of James H. Ruebush."

James D. Vaughan.
Public domain image. (http://www.hymntime.com/tch/bio/v/a/u/g/vaughan_jd.htm)

James David Vaughan was raised in Giles County, Tennessee, on the border between Tennessee and Alabama. His father was a Confederate veteran. To this day, Giles County is a center for the Appalachian folk music traditions, which likely helped shape the young Vaughan's interest in music. He grew up in the Southern Methodist Church but later joined the Church of the Nazarene.

Vaughan composed and self-published his first collection of gospel songs, *Gospel Chimes*, in 1900. In 1902, he established his own company, the James D. Vaughan Publishing Company, and began a longtime practice of publishing at least one collection of songs per year. The company's focus was on providing training materials for singing schools and, in particular, the rural singing conventions that occurred annually. Each collection included a few old favorites such as "When I Can Read My Title Clear," to the folk hymn tune "Pisgah."

Pisgah, no. 75 in *Perfect Praise*, edited by James D. Vaughan. Lawrenceburg, Tennessee, 1905.

Each collection also included songs by Vaughan himself and by other popular composer/singing masters of his generation. "He Keeps Me Happy," by South Carolina composer McDuffie Weams (1876–1943), is an example.

Note the echo of the refrain, the use of shape notes, the absence of accidentals, and the jazzy scotch snap which appears in each phrase. The cheerful, rhythmic style of such songs, influenced clearly by the ragtime epoch then in progress, was immediately popular. On average, Vaughan sold sixty thousand copies of his collections each year through his death in 1941.

McDuffie Weams, "He Keeps Me Happy." No. 10 in *Carol Crown for Sunday Schools, Revivals, Singing schools, Conventions* (Lawrenceburg, TN: James D. Vaughan, 1915).

The Vaughan and Stamps-Baxter Normal Schools

In 1911 James Vaughan founded the Vaughan Normal School of Music in Lawrenceburg, Tennessee. It was conceived after the example of the Ruebush-Kieffer Virginia Normal School. Vaughan had a deep appreciation of rural life in the South. His vision was to continue the rural shape-note singing school tradition by providing a "constant stream of singing school-teachers" trained at the Vaughan school (and, ever the salesman, more likely to use Vaughan materials in their teaching). Since rural church music was his focus, Vaughan also saw the importance of a spiritual component. In the 1920s, therefore, he added daily Bible classes that he often taught himself and renamed his school the Vaughan Conservatory of Music and Bible Institute.[5]

Virgil Stamps founded the V. O. Stamps School of Music in Jacksonville, Texas, in 1924. When he partnered with J. R. Baxter in 1926, it was renamed the Stamps-Baxter Normal School of Music. It was so well received that an eastern campus was added in Chattanooga, Tennessee in 1926. A third school in Dallas was opened in 1929.[6]

Unlike formal colleges and conservatories, the Vaughan and Stamps-Baxter concept of a normal school was to provide continuing education. Students signed up for three- to six-week sessions and would typically return multiple times to sharpen skills. The schools were originally conceived to offer a six-week course of study leading to a certificate of completion. The curriculum was reduced to three weeks during the 1930s and to two weeks in the 1950s. According to Dr. Jeanette Fresne, professor of music education at Lamar University, "They were both set up to teach music using shaped note notation in the gospel music tradition."[7] Normal school training was intended to equip students to become singing school teachers. The three-week curriculum included one hundred hours of classroom instruction, or about six hours per day. Classes were held Monday through Friday, days and evenings. Courses offered included the rudiments of music, sight reading, ear training, directing, and harmony. Perhaps the most influential courses the Vaughan and Stamps-Baxter schools offered in the long term involved the training of male quartets.

---

5. Goff, *Close Harmony*, 71–72.
6. Fresne, "History of the Stamps-Baxter Singing Schools," 28.
7. Fresne, "History of the Stamps-Baxter Singing Schools," 30.

The Publisher/Church Connection: A Formula for Success

A major reason for Vaughan's success and later that of his chief rival, the Stamps-Baxter Publishing Company, was the aligning of publishers directly with the churches to which they sold functioning as a one-stop resource providing everything needed to encourage congregational singing in the shape-note tradition. This relationship differed significantly from that of tunebook compilers in the previous century. In the halcyon days of the 1830s and '40s, southern singing schools existed mostly on the periphery of church life.

Vaughan and Stamps-Baxter led the way in changing this. If a church wanted a "Sing In"—usually a one-day affair with lunch on the grounds—the church would contact the publisher to recommend a teacher in the area. Once an agreement was reached, the teacher would arrive at the appointed time with textbooks, music dictionaries and ruled blackboards, all provided at a cost, and songbooks provided at a bulk discount.[8]

The vision impelling James Vaughan forward was not one of radical change. The white Pentecostal/Holiness mindset that permeated singing schools—like that of the burgeoning fundamentalist movement—feared modernity and championed the retention of cherished traditions of past generations. It sought fervently to return to an earlier time and cherished memories of camp meetings, community revivals, and annual church home-comings. Though James Vaughan continued to publish new songs to the time of his death, the prevailing style never differed from that of Charles H. Gabriel ("Brighten the Corner Where You Are") and Homer Rodeheaver.[9]

---

8. Fresne, "History of the Stamps-Baxter Singing Schools," 27.

9. Rodeheaver was, in fact, a significant force in the ongoing development of both white and Black gospel music. He had established his own music publishing company in 1910 which produced a popular monthly journal, *The Gospel Choir*. The Vaughan-Kieffer Quartet stayed in Rodeheaver's home while touring Indiana in 1921. See Goff, *Close Harmony*, 76.

Virgil O. Stamps and the Stamps-Baxter Music Company

V. O. Stamps.
Public domain image. (https://www.findagrave.com/memorial/28806103/virgil-oliver-stamps)

Virgil Oliver Stamps (1892–1940) was born and raised in Upshur County, Texas, where his father, William Stamps, operated a sawmill. The Stamps were a Methodist family. Virgil developed an early interest in shape-note singing, purchasing every singing book he could obtain. Stamps self-published his first song in 1914, a secular ditty entitled "The Man Behind the Plow," selling copies for ten cents a sheet. Shortly thereafter he traveled to Lawrenceburg, Tennessee, where he enrolled in the Vaughan Normal School of Music. He excelled in his studies, and James Vaughan hired him as traveling representative of the Vaughan Company. Stamps, "V. O." as he was known at the time, quickly became a most successful and aggressive salesman. In 1915, James Vaughan himself noted in the *Musical Visitor* that "Virgil is a sure enough hustler. We are mighty glad to have him as a member of the Vaughan bunch."[10]

Having reached this peak of success, however, Virgil Stamps elected to leave the Vaughan company and start his own publishing enterprise, the V. O. Stamps Music Company. Based in Jacksonville, Texas, the fledgling company struggled at first, and in 1926 Stamps partnered with Jesse Randall Baxter Jr. (known professionally as "J. R.") to form the Stamps-Baxter Music and Printing Company. Baxter, a well-known composer/song leader himself, had been mentored by Anthony Showalter[11] at his Southern Normal In-

---

10. Goff, *Close Harmony*, 84.

11. Anthony Johnson Showalter (1858–1924), like James Vaughan, was a successful gospel music composer and publisher who received his formal training at the

stitute. Stamps-Baxter was organized around the same model as Vaughan's company, with a nearly identical corporate structure and goals.

Singing Conventions and Commerce

Historian Brooks Blevins has defined the component activities from which southern gospel music originated as a "three-legged stool." Working in tandem were (1) the promotional activities of the publishers, (2) the singing schools that purchased their wares, and (3) the annual singing conventions that drew thousands of singing masters and shape-note singers.[12]

Conventions were many things. For inveterate shape-noters there was the chance to test their sight-reading skills on music hot off the press. For the sales representatives of the publishers, conventions were not-to-be-missed opportunities to meet or surpass sales quotas. For song leaders and singing masters, they provided invaluable opportunities to drum up teaching opportunities at church as well as make contact with seldom seen colleagues. There was, of course, a spiritual element. The seven-shape-note conventions usually had a revivalist flavor. Prayer and Bible study classes were frequently offered.

The commercial viability of shape-note conventions depended upon several things. Rural churches needed to continue to prefer the so-called "old-fashioned" gospel harmony. They, in turn, needed to sponsor singing schools in sufficient numbers so that singing masters could make a living and inspire in their students an insatiable thirst for new music to sight read from shaped notation. Conventions in the 1920s and early '30s were a successful mix of singing, fellowship, and skill-building with wholesome religious overtones. There was also a competitive aspect with the best singers eager to show off their sight-reading skills. It was "a point of pride for gospel singers to have the ability to pick up an unfamiliar piece of music and sight read it perfectly."[13] The following description, while of a shape-note singing school in 2011 Arkansas, could be applied to the earlier conventions as well:

> The silver-haired song leader peers over tiny spectacles, chops the air with her right arm, swings it to the left, to the right and

---

Ruebush-Kieffer Virginia Normal School of Music. He established the Showalter Music Company in Dalton, Georgia, in 1884. It would become a principal publishing rival to both the Vaughan Company and Stamps-Baxter. Showalter is commonly remembered as the composer of the song "Leaning on the Everlasting Arms," although the music and text were likely a collaboration with his nephew, Samuel Duncan, and Elisha A. Hoffman. He also founded the Southern Normal Institute of Music.

12. Blevins, "Upbeat Down South," 137.
13. Blevins, "Upbeat Down South," 140–41.

back up to its starting point, and we are off. Six-year-old sopranos, eighty-year-old tenors, teenage wanna-be basses hold their paperback songbooks as instructed—out from the body in one hand (the other is for "leading")—and follow their respective parts. The tenors lead: "*mi, mi do, mi.*" Half a beat into the second measure, everyone else joins in ... Shape notes the first time through followed by three verses of a newly minted song called "A Godly Man." It will likely never appear in another songbook; once the new books arrive for next year's school, it may never be heard or sung again.[14]

Gospel publishers like Vaughan, Stamps-Baxter, and Showalter profited from producing new songbooks each year for convention use, always trumpeting the "new" content within. While they did produce some memorable songs, those stood out within a dense forest of less worthy pieces serving only as fodder for convention songfests.

Male Quartets and White Southern Gospel Music

Historians almost universally cite James David Vaughan as a progenitor of southern gospel music, yet curiously it is not because of the music he composed or published. It is because of a novel approach he innovated to promote his company's publications.

Vaughan Quartet, ca. 1915.
Public domain image.

---

14. Blevins, "Upbeat Down South," 136.

Vaughan since his teen years had been attracted to male quartet singing, and at some point in the early days of his publishing, he came to see a well-trained quartet as an ideal means to promote his publications. The quartet, as he envisioned it, would be an integral part of convention experience. They would sing with convention-goers through all the reading sessions, plug Vaughan's music whenever possible, and, as a special treat, perform a bit on their own as a break between sessions of group singing. James Vaughan personally trained the first Vaughan Quartet and in 1910 sent them out as guest performers at singing conventions and revivals.[15] Sales for Vaughan songbooks had totaled thirty thousand in 1909. With the introduction of the quartet professionally singing selections from the 1910 collection, sales doubled, and by 1912 were totaling eighty-five thousand copies a year. Soon, Vaughan made quartet training an important class offering at his normal school and by the late 1920s he had over fifteen quartets on the road promoting Vaughan products. Vaughan quartets sang with lightly embellished piano accompaniment, much as one would expect the music to be performed in rural churches.

Once Vaughan's successful integration of quartet singing into promotion became obvious, his publishing competitors rushed to emulate. Rival publisher Anthony Showalter sent out his "Big Quartet" in 1918. From the first, Virgil Stamps's V. O. Stamps School of Music offered courses in quartet training and in 1924, the first Frank Stamps Quartet hit the road, led and managed by Virgil's brother, Frank.[16] By 1940, the Stamps-Baxter Company was sponsoring over forty touring quartets.[17] Piano accompaniments in the earlier Vaughan Quartets had been provided by one of the four singers, but as performances inevitably became more theatrical the role of the keyboardist as a performer in his own right became an important element in quartet appearances. In 1926, the Frank Stamps Quartet began bringing along a fifth man to accompany. Ultimately, "four men and a piano" became the traditional standard for white gospel quartets.[18]

James Vaughan's intuition had been correct. The touring quartets were a popular addition to his company's promotional toolbox. The best of them developed their own fan base, drawing hundreds to events where they performed. In the short term, as noted above, sales benefited. Unfortunately, the popularity of the quartets over time changed the dynamic of conventions. By the mid-1930s, the take from ticket sales had mushroomed as

---

15. Wolfe, "Vaughan Quartet," 409–10.
16. Goff, *Close Harmony*, 120.
17. Goff, *Close Harmony*, 122.
18. Wolfe, "Vaughan Quartet," 409–10.

people came to hear the music, but fewer were buying songbooks. Churches were critical because the star power of the quartets drew attention away from what they felt was the convention's root purpose—the improvement of church music and communal music-making.

Adger M. Pace (1882–1959), a prominent composer and singing master of the period, was one of James Vaughan's loyal supporters. He taught at the Vaughan Normal School and sang in the Vaughan Radio Quartet. Despite this, he was disturbed by the trends occurring in the 1930s and wrote convincingly about it in a letter to *Vaughan's Family Visitor*:

> I realize that I have a very delicate subject to deal with, but I have it in my system and I must get it out. . . . we are having too much quartet singing in our conventions . . . I have seen a number of conventions ruined this year by this very thing. It seems that they are turned into a contest between quartets, each one trying to outdo the other . . . Many times, if they can't beat by singing gospel songs, they will resort to some frivolous, comic, suggestive song that is an abomination in the sight of God . . . There is nothing so great and grand as good chorus singing, and in this part of the worship everybody can take part.[19]

Knowing his critique would draw the rancor of some, Pace closed by defending his right to speak out and underlining the fact that there were spiritual and religious ramifications to his plea.

> I dare say that there is not a man in the whole country that has done more quartet singing than the writer. Seventeen years straight holding down my end of the Vaughan Radio Quartet is no short time to be at the same job, and I think I know something about its advantages as well as its disadvantages . . . There is nothing that pleases me more than to sing with or direct a great chorus . . . This is the kind of singing the Good Book says we shall have in the glory world, when [the] teeming millions from every nation come forth and join the heavenly choir under the direction of Moses. As the voice of many waters, we shall sing that new song of praise to our Lord and Savior Jesus Christ. Glory be to God! I want to be there, and by his grace I expect to be there and join that chorus![20]

Particularly touching are Pace's references to worship and his sense that the sacred purpose undergirding all his work was slipping away.

---

19. Pace, "Give Us More Chorus Singing," 9.
20. Pace, "Give Us More Chorus Singing," 10.

Black Gospel Music, the Developing Years

The variety of music falling under the label "Black gospel" can be bewildering. Al Hobbs, chairman of the Announcer's Guild of the Gospel Music Workshop of America, an organization dedicated to the encouragement of African American gospel music in the United States,[21] wrote in 1992 that education was needed regarding the different styles of gospel music, their purposes, and when their use was most effective. He listed three styles then prevalent: *traditional gospel, contemporary gospel,* and *urban gospel.* "Traditional gospel," he explained, "is used to set the mood for a worship service; contemporary gospel can be used in a worship service but is primarily heard at a concert; urban gospel goes out to people who may never hear the gospel message unless they hear it in a song played on a soul station or through a gospel music video on television."[22]

Joyce Marie Jackson, director of African and African American studies at Louisiana State University, has broken down the development of Black gospel music in the twentieth century into three periods:

- The early or transitional period, 1900-1929, in which the music of Black Pentecostal worship moves from the urban storefront churches to being grudgingly embraced by many large traditional congregations.
- A middle period, 1930-1945, beginning with the work of Thomas A. Dorsey, when Black gospel music actually can be identified with a particular style and sound.
- And a late period, 1946 to the present, when gospel singing becomes a successful commercial enterprise, more and more aligned with popular culture.[23]

One must remember that while the development of African American gospel music largely occurred in the urban centers of the North, especially Chicago, pioneers in that development migrated from the South. W. C. Handy (1873-1958), the legendary "Father of the Blues," in one of his autobiographical writings recalled his early music education in Florence,

---

21. The Gospel Music Workshop of America was founded in 1967 by the prominent singer/composer/music director James Cleveland (1931-1991). The organization's website states that its purpose is to sponsor annual conventions in which "national recording artists, new and inspiring songwriters, educators, liturgical dancers, the young and old, pastors, and others minister to each other and to the needs and directions within the African American religious experience." See https://www.gmwanational.net/History.htm.

22. Haynes, "Gospel Controversy," 80.

23. Jackson, "Changing Nature of Gospel Music," 189-92.

Alabama. The teaching method was identical to that used in singing schools a century earlier except the notation had seven shapes instead of four, and the tunes sung were from Ira Sankey's *Gospel Hymns, 1–6*.

> My introduction to the rudiments of music was largely gained during the eleven years I spent under this quaint instructor in the Florence District School for Negroes. I began in the soprano singing section, progressed to the alto and then shuttled back and forth between the tenor and bass as my voice cut up and played pranks.
>
> There was no piano or organ in our school, just as there were few instruments in the homes of the pupils. We were required to hold our books in our left hand and beat time with our right. Professor Wallace sounded his A pitch pipe or tuning fork, and we understood the tone to be *la*. If C happened to be the starting key, we made the step and a half in our minds and then sang out the keynote in concert. We would then sound the notes for our respective parts, perhaps *do* for the basses, *mi* for the altos, and *sol* and *do* for the sopranos and tenor, depending of course on the first note of the sopranos. Before attempting to sing the words of any song, we were required to work out our parts by singing over and over the proper sol-fa syllables. In this way we learned to sing in all keys, measures and movements. We learned all the songs in *Gospel Hymns, One to Six*.[24]

Louis Daniel Armstrong (1901–1971), the great "Satchmo," had similar experiences. He was born and raised in New Orleans, lived there to the age of twenty-one, and was mentored by jazz great Joe "King" Oliver. Often overlooked, however, is the fact that his musical career was rooted in church music and quartet singing.

> In those days, of course, I did not know a horn from a comb. I was going to church regularly for both grandma and my great-grandmother were Christian women, and between them they kept me in school. In church and Sunday School I did a whole lot of singing. That, I guess, is how I acquired my singing tactics . . . At church my heart went into every hymn I sang.[25]

The free church, evangelical flavor of his early worship experiences comes through in this remembrance:

---

24. Handy, *Father of the Blues*, 13.
25. Armstrong, *Satchmo*, 17.

> Across the street from where we lived was Elder Cozy's church. He was the most popular preacher in the neighborhood, and he attracted people from other parts of the city as well. I can still remember the night mama took me to his church. Elder Cozy started to get warmed up and then he hit his stride. It was not long before he had the whole church rocking. Mama got so happy and excited that she knocked me off the bench as she shouted and swayed back and forth. She was a stout woman, and she became so excited that it took six of the strongest brothers to grab hold of her and pacify her . . . I laughed myself silly, and when mama and I reached home she gave me hell. "You little fool," she said. "What did you mean by laughing when you saw me being converted?"[26]

Handy and Armstrong both sang in street quartets in their youth and had similar recollections. As Handy wrote,

> The Baptists had an organ in their church but no choir. They didn't need any. The lusty singers sat in the amen corner and raised the songs, raised them as they were intended to be raised, if I'm any judge. None of the dressed-up arrangements one sometimes hears on the concert stage for them. They knew a better way. Theirs was pure rhythm. While critics like to describe them as shouting songs, rhythm was their basic element. And rhythm was the thing that drew me and other members of our hometown quartet to attend the Baptist services.[27]

Vic Hobson in his magnificent book *Creating the Jazz Solo: Louis Armstrong and Barbershop Harmony* did a definitive study showing how much of Armstrong's technique was rooted in singing. He quotes Armstrong saying, "Singing was more into my blood than the trumpet . . . I had been singing all my life in churches, etc."[28] According to Hobson, Armstrong "thought of himself first and foremost as a singer who played the trumpet . . . However much he loved his horn, to Armstrong his instrument was an extension of his voice."[29]

---

26. Armstrong, *Satchmo*, 31–32.
27. Handy, *Father of the Blues*, 157–58
28. Hobson, *Creating the Jazz Solo*, 26.
29. Hobson, *Creating the Jazz Solo*, 26.

The Great Migration—A Collision of Cultures

In 1922, Louis Armstrong followed his mentor King Oliver to Chicago. In doing so, he became part of the Great Migration. That great city, which has been the focus of previous chapters, would come to be known as the birthplace of African American Gospel Blues. African Americans were active in *all* of the mainline denominations, not just those which were Pentecostal. By far the largest number of Blacks in mainline denominations were Baptists and Methodist Episcopalians.

Many Blacks migrating north found worship practiced differently from that to which they had been accustomed. Given the church's role in the African American community as an essential anchor, some Blacks sought to either organize their own less-structured churches or bring change to the old-line churches they joined.

> The Black man's religion is served as the organizing force around which his life was structured. The church was his school, his forum, his political arena, his social club, his art gallery, and his conservatory of music. It was lyceum, gymnasium, and inner-sanctum—all at the same time. The Black man's religion was his fellowship with his fellow man and his audience with God, giving him the strength to endure when endurance gave no promise.[30]

Blacks had to adapt. As Joyce Marie Jackson has written, African American gospel music developed as a reaction to "a multitude of new conditions in their lives . . . The African American 'folk' church has historically represented the single cultural institution through which African Americans have been able to express themselves freely and without constraint."[31]

Initially, many Blacks were drawn to the songs of the Great Urban Revival—by Fanny Crosby, Sankey, and others. By the time of the First World War, the music of the Billy Sunday revivals was being co-opted. Thomas Dorsey, still a twelve-year-old boy living in Georgia, attended a Billy Sunday revival in Atlanta in 1911. White-led revivals in the South were segregated. Some had designated seating for Blacks while others offered "colored nights" for Blacks only. The preacher for Billy Sunday's colored night was the Rev. Calvin P. Dixon, who was known as the "Black Billy Sunday" for his fiery brand of preaching.[32] Dorsey, singing in the mass choir under Homer Rodeheaver's direction, remembered the experience as one of the most

---

30. Southall, "Black Composers and Religious Music," 50.
31. Jackson, "Changing Nature of Gospel Music," 189.
32. Broughton, *Black Gospel*, 33.

exciting of his youth. Rodeheaver's mix of religion and showmanship was long remembered by Dorsey and likely shaped some of his views on the effective use of music in worship. A number of songs from the Rodeheaver/Sunday revivals have become standards in the lexicon of African American hymnody. They include "Brighten the Corner Where You Are," "His Eye is On the Sparrow," and "Since Jesus Came Into My Life," all with music composed by Charles H. Gabriel.

The growing number of Pentecostal and storefront churches in Chicago tended not to use hymnals, but rather relied on song leaders to teach songs using the call-and-response approach. Song sheets utilized the seven-shape notation the migrants brought with them from the South. The first shape-note hymnal specifically for use in Black churches was Judge Jackson's *The Colored Sacred Harp*, published in 1932. Seven-shape hymnals and tunebooks were used by churches affiliated with the Church of God in Christ (COGIC), the African Methodist Episcopal Church (AME), the Colored Methodist Episcopal Church (CME),[33] and the Baptist Church.

Thomas A. Dorsey—the Early Years

Thomas A. Dorsey, ca. 1945.
Image courtesy of Hogan Jazz Archives, Tulane University. Digital ID OPH000521.

When Thomas A. Dorsey died in 1993, Janita Poe of the *Chicago Tribune* wrote that "because of Mr. Dorsey's influence as a songwriter, music

---

33. The denomination was renamed the Christian Methodist Episcopal Church in 1954.

publisher, and performer, Chicago became and has remained the gospel capital of the world."[34] Dorsey's influence, however, goes far beyond the city of Chicago or even the gospel blues style that he perfected. Like the white southern gospel tradition, Dorsey's life and work exemplified the blurring of traditional lines between church music and popular culture.

Thomas Andrew Dorsey (1899–1993) was the son of Thomas M. Dorsey and his wife Etta in the rural town of Villa Rica, Georgia. His father divided his time between sharecropping and serving as an itinerant Baptist preacher. The Dorseys were musical. Etta played the organ for her husband's worship services, and the family had a reed organ in their home, a rarity for poor rural Black families. Thomas began piano lessons in early childhood, probably taught by his mother, and soon graduated to the organ. His upbringing exposed young Thomas to a variety of musical experiences. His father preferred traditional Protestant hymns in worship, but the wailing and moaning of slave spirituals could still be heard around the countryside. When the elder Dorsey was away preaching, Thomas and his mother attended a local church where shape-note singing was practiced. The fact that the congregation sang in full harmony made an impression on him that he would never forget.

When Thomas was eight the family moved to Atlanta. At age eleven he dropped out of school to focus on his music and took several jobs in the theater district, selling drinks and popcorn during intermissions and rubbing shoulders with prominent Black jazz performers like Ma Rainey and Bessie Smith. By 1911, the twelve-year-old Thomas Dorsey had developed sufficient musical skill to perform in cabaret shows and had a growing reputation as a party pianist.[35]

The Influence of African American Preaching

Much has been written in recent years about the close relationship between African American preaching and the rise of Gospel music. Thomas Dorsey was, after all, the son of a Baptist preacher and was in his younger years clearly torn between pursuing a career as a jazz artist or writing and performing sacred music. When he arrived in Chicago he was on the cusp of a successful career as a blues man. Regarding the relationship between preaching and the birthing of the blues as a jazz form, Michael W. Harris wrote:

---

34. Poe, "Thomas A. Dorsey," 66.
35. Clark, "Thomas Andrew Dorsey."

> Upon superficial investigation, one could conclude that these figures were the antithesis of one another. One [the jazz/gospel artist] sang in a secular setting and the other spoke in a religious setting. But the bluesman and the preacher, beyond surface distinctions, were cultural analogues of one another. The structure and delivery of sermons and blues songs bear more resemblance than dissimilarity. At the foundation of the art of each was a common creative mode: improvisation.[36]

Pearl Williams-Jones further elaborated on this in the journal *Ethnomusicology*:

> There are two basic sources from which gospel singing has derived its aesthetic ideals: the free-style collective improvisations of the Black church congregation and the rhetorical solo style of the Black gospel preacher. In seeking to communicate the gospel message, there is little difference between the gospel singer and the gospel preacher in the approach to his subject. The same techniques are used by the preacher and the singer—the singer perhaps being considered the lyrical extension of the rhythmically rhetorical style of the preacher.[37]

The creative use of rhythm and accentuation in Black preaching was demonstrated by Andrew Legg and Carolyn Philpott by analysis of an excerpt from a sermon by Dr. Anthony Campbell delivered in Tuscaloosa, Alabama, in 1976. Campbell drew some of his text from the C. A. Tindley song "Leave It There."

> If the world from you withhold of its silver and its gold,
> And you have to get along with meager fare,
> Just remember, in His Word, how He feeds the little bird,
> Take your burden to the Lord and leave it there.
>
> *[Refrain:]*
> Leave it there, leave it there,
> Take your burden to the Lord and leave it there.
> If you trust and never doubt, He will surely bring you out.
> Take your burden to the Lord and leave it there.[38]

Campbell closed his sermon by repeating the closing line of Tindley's refrain, "Take your burden to the Lord and leave it there." Building to a climax, "the dynamic level and amount of 'gravel' in his voice increased dramatically,

---

36. Harris, *Rise of Gospel Blues*, 154.
37. Williams-Jones, "Afro-American Gospel Music," 381.
38. Charles A. Tindley, "Leave It There," no. 78 in *Gospel Pearls* (1921).

the pitch of his voice rose, and, finally, he over-emphasized different words within that phrase":

> Take your <u>burden</u> to the Lord and leave it there.
> <u>Take</u> your burden to the Lord and leave it there.
> Take your burden to the <u>Lord</u> and leave it there.
> Take your <u>burden</u> to the Lord and leave it there.
> <u>Take</u> your burden to the Lord and leave it there.
> Take your burden to the <u>Lord</u> and leave it there![39]

Dorsey and Chicago

In 1916 Dorsey, like so many of his generation, decided to leave the South in hopes of better job prospects in the North. Arriving in Chicago that summer, he eked out a living by continuing to take gigs playing for house parties and accepting odd jobs. He also joined the Pilgrim Baptist Church. At first Dorsey was a snowbird, traveling back to Atlanta in the winter to reconnect with family, but in 1919 he moved his residence permanently to the Windy City. Making a living there, however, continued to be a challenge, and Dorsey suffered the first of two nervous breakdowns.

The publication by the National Baptist Convention on January 1, 1921, of the hymnal *Gospel Pearls* is a landmark in the history of African American sacred music. Many of Charles A. Tindley's songs were included, giving them a visibility far beyond Tindley Temple in Philadelphia. They were soon being used by Black churches in the Chicago area. Ethnomusicologist and singer Terri Brinegar has ranked the publication of *Gospel Pearls* in importance with Richard Allen's 1801 *A Collection of Spiritual Songs,* the first Black songster published in the United States.[40] It was a momentous occasion, and when the National Baptist Convention met in Chicago for its forty-first annual convention on September 7 through 12 of 1921, promotion of the new hymnal was prioritized.

Thomas Dorsey was in attendance. Singing songs from *Gospel Pearls* was William Nix Jr., a prominent Black evangelist and gospel singer. An advertisement in the *Chicago Defender* described Nix as "one of the most powerful gospel singers in the country today."[41] Nix sang four selections from *Gospel Pearls*, two of which had the convention-goers on their feet: "I Am Going Through, Jesus," with words and music by Herbert Buffum, and

---

39. Legg and Philpott, "Analysis of Performance Practices," 207.
40. Brinegar, "Recorded Sermons of Reverend Andrew William (A. W.) Nix," 109.
41. Brinegar, "Recorded Sermons of Reverend Andrew William (A. W.) Nix," 108.

"I Do, Do You?," with music by E. O. Excell. *Gospel Pearls* is of historic importance because of the significant number of songs and hymns composed or arranged by African Americans, but Buffum and Excell were both white revivalist song leaders. At any rate, it was Nix's singing of "I Do, Do You?" that lived on in Dorsey's memory.

> My inner being was thrilled. My soul was a deluge of divine rapture; my emotions were aroused; my heart was inspired to become a great singer and worker in the Kingdom of the Lord—and impress people just as this great singer did that Sunday morning . . .
>
> These turns and trills—he and a few others brought that into church music. Hymn singers, they couldn't put this stuff in it. What he did, I wouldn't call blues, but it had a touch of the blue note there . . .[42, 43]

What Dorsey was describing was the improvisatory characteristic that went to the very heart culturally and musically of African American music. It was a characteristic largely missing from the arranged spirituals of the Jubilee tradition.

Dorsey described William Nix's singing as being akin to a conversion experience for him and it inspired him to write his first gospel song, "If I Don't Get There," which appeared in the second edition of *Gospel Pearls*. Dorsey at this point did not, however, change careers. The 1920s in fact took him to the height of his career as a jazz pianist and composer. Once in Chicago he enrolled in the Chicago School of Composition and Arranging, where he sharpened his sight-reading skills and learned to arrange songs for performance on the jazz circuit. One of his songs, "Riverside Blues," was recorded that year by King Oliver's Creole Jazz Band, bringing him further celebrity, and in 1924 he became principal accompanist for the legendary blues singer Gertrude "Ma" Rainey. Dorsey wrote her theme song, "The Stormy Sea Blues," and toured with her for the next two years.[44]

In 1926, Thomas Dorsey suffered a second nervous breakdown which ended his collaboration with Ma Rainey. A busy schedule of performing and

---

42. Harris, *Rise of Gospel Blues*, 69–70.

43. There has been considerable confusion about who Thomas Dorsey actually heard singing at the National Baptist Convention and related issues concerning William Nix Jr. The confusion is understandable. William Nix Jr. (1878–1941) was indeed the singer Dorsey heard. But Nix had a more famous brother, Arthur William ("A. W.") Nix who was also a singer/preacher. Both brothers were present at the September convention, had official roles, and were listed in the convention program.

44. Clark, "Thomas Andrew Dorsey," 106.

composing resumed, however, and in 1928 under the stage name "Georgia Tom," Dorsey partnered with guitarist Tampa Red (Hudson Whittaker) to record "It's Tight Like That." It sold over a million copies, making it one of the best-selling blues recordings of the era. The two went on to make over sixty recordings between 1928 and 1932, but the period was not without its dissonant voices. Powerful voices within the Baptist church spoke out condemning the risqué lyrics of songs like "It's Tight Like That." Even W. C. Handy joined the chorus, saying of such songs, "A flock of dirty blues appeared on records, not witty double entendre but just plain smut."[45]

One senses that from early on Dorsey had felt an unrelenting pull toward active involvement in sacred music.[46] Even when away performing he chose to maintain his membership at the Pilgrim Baptist Church.[47] He also offered his services to other churches occasionally and, throughout the years of blues performing and touring, continued to write gospel songs that he hoped to sell.

When the National Baptist Convention returned in Chicago in August of 1930, Dorsey was asked to address the convention about his music and was permitted to set up a sales table on the convention floor. He sold over four thousand copies of his songs in the remaining days of the gathering.[48] Perhaps of even more consequence was the acquaintance Dorsey struck up with a fellow pianist, bluesman, and gospel singer, Theodore Frye. The partnership that ensued would result in the first modern gospel choirs.

Dorsey, Frye, and the Birth of the Black Gospel Chorus

The concept of a gospel chorus had been around through most of the 1920s. The Reverend Charles Henry Pace (1886–1963), a Baptist minister from Mississippi, had lived in Chicago since the age of thirteen. Pace, like Dorsey, had a jazz background. He was a trumpeter and had arranged over a hundred spirituals for choirs he directed at Beth Eden and Liberty Baptist churches. Between 1926 and 1929 Charles Pace with his "Pace Jubilee Singers" made over eighty-five recordings of spirituals at a Chicago recording studio. Thomas Dorsey accompanied some of those recording sessions. Pace did not aspire to a polished sound. Rather, some of his singers were

---

45. Handy, *Father of the Blues*, 209.

46. Despite his successes as a jazz performer, Thomas Dorsey had a deep Christian faith which repeatedly forced him to question his career choices. He would later speculate that his breakdowns may have had a spiritual rather than physical origin, the result of the conflicts within him.

47. He kept his membership at Pilgrim for the rest of his life.

48. Marovich, *City Called Heaven*, 85.

drawn from his Beth Eden choir, giving a slightly rough sound to the enterprise with individual voices being heard within the choral texture. In the recordings soloists were often featured, the most famous of whom would be the contralto, Hattie Parker. It is very likely that her singing quality became the prototype for what Dorsey would later seek for the ideal singer of gospel blues—a rich low and beautifully rounded female voice. (He would find that ideal in Mahalia Jackson.) Also important was the fact that Pace's spirituals were accompanied by piano with improvised embellishments, a complete departure from the Jubilee's traditional a cappella.[49]

Chicago's African American community was centered on its south side in the area known as Bronzeville. For Bronzeville's large and established old-line congregations in the first quarter of the twentieth century, choirs, vestments, liturgical display, and music of European masters was *de rigueur*. Nonetheless, there had been a gradual warming to the jubilee-style spirituals that were commonly heard at fellowship events and other gatherings outside of morning worship. For those old-line churches, the summit of musical leadership was personified in the great singer, teacher, arranger, and conductor Edward Boatner (1898–1981). He resided in Chicago from 1925 through 1933 and was both a nationally known operatic baritone and recitalist. Boatner published almost three hundred arrangements of slave songs over the course of his career, many of which are classics and standard recital repertoire to the present day. So highly esteemed was Boatner by Chicago's old-line Baptists that soon after his arrival in the city he was made director of music for the National Baptist Convention.[50]

Pilgrim Baptist and Ebenezer Missionary Baptist were not technically old-line churches. Both had come from humble storefront beginnings around the time of the First World War, and both had grown significantly larger in the early twenties. Both also sought to emulate the more tasteful worship practices and music of Bronzeville's Quinn Chapel. Pilgrim, where Thomas Dorsey was a member, had had for years a Sunday morning prayer meeting that was characterized by spontaneous singing and emotive praise. In 1925, Pilgrim pastor James C. Austin moved the prayer meeting to the

---

49. Marovich, *City Called Heaven*, 50–51. Keyboard accompaniments, of course, had been standard in gospel singing since the days of Ira Sankey. What was different was the incorporation of improvised embellishments to jazz up the straight doubling of voice parts. A pioneer in this style of playing was the Australian pianist Robert Harkness (1880–1961). Charles Alexander, when on tour in the outback with evangelist Reuben Torrey in 1902, hired Harkness as his accompanist. His percussive style and free ornamentation brought new vitality to the revival's music. Inspired by Harkness's example, the Moody Bible Institute launched a course in evangelistic piano playing in 1926.

50. Glover, "Life and Career of Edward Boatner," 89–90.

church basement and hired none other than Edward Boatner to be the church's new director of music.[51] Meanwhile, Ebenezer Church under the dynamic leadership and preaching of Charles H. Clarke had increased its membership to over three thousand members. Clark, whose musical preferences were oriented to classical, hired Mabel Sanford Lewis, a Boatner student, to direct its music program.

In 1931, the Reverend Dr. James Howard Lorenzo Smith was called to be pastor of Ebenezer Church. The heady optimism of the 1920s had been replaced by the dark foreboding of the Great Depression. Smith saw the need for a "livelier and more familiar" kind of music and wanted to move the choir from its traditional perch in the balcony to behind him on the rostrum. He preferred "good old-fashioned songs that were born in the hearts of their forefathers down in the southland."[52] To accomplish this Smith contacted Theodore Frye (1899–1963), a church member, and asked him to organize and direct a secondary choir. With it, he was to explore a new, more upbeat style of singing.[53] To keep critical outcry to a minimum, the group at least at first did not sing in the tradition-bound Sunday morning service. It had its first rehearsal on October 31, 1931, and Theodore Frye asked his friend, Thomas Dorsey, to accompany.[54]

The Ebenezer Gospel Choir had its Sunday morning worship debut on January 10, 1932. It marked a radical change. The make-up of the ensemble was different from a traditional church choir. Frye, a high baritone, functioned as lead singer with the chorus singers backing him up. To open the service, Frye came singing and strutting down the center aisle, not unlike the prancing gait of a minstrel "walk-around."[55] He was followed by his choir with Dorsey at the piano. To Pastor Smith's relief the service was well received.

The very next Sunday was a celebration marking the sixth anniversary of Pastor James Austin's coming to Pilgrim Baptist, and Ebenezer's Pastor Smith had been invited to preach. Typically, a guest preacher brought along his own choir and so Frye, Dorsey, and the singers accompanied Smith to Pilgrim Church. Again, the spirited music delighted many in the

---

51. Jackson, *Singing in My Soul*, 55.

52. Marovich, *City Called Heaven*, 90.

53. Frye's choir would be referred to as the "Junior Choir," but it was made up of adult singers.

54. Marovich, *City Called Heaven*, 90.

55. The "walk-around" was a standard part of minstrel shows. As the finale to a performance or at some other climactic point, the entire cast of the variety show dances or high-steps around the stage with each performer taking a solo turn when reaching the center.

congregation. James Austin, while still preferring a traditional worship format with classical music, asked Thomas Dorsey to organize and direct a gospel choir at Pilgrim. Austin's son later recalled that "My dad could see times changing and people desiring another type of music."[56]

The Reverend Austin's openness to change was not shared by many fellow Baptists, especially church musicians of the time.

> The supplanting of spirituals by gospel songs was a major controversy within the Black churches . . . Gospel, you see, was the great usurper, the new wave of youthful Black worship, the defiler of sacred hymnody with downhome blues, the sweet sounds of heaven thrown together with the noise of hell.[57]

The conservatory-trained Edward Boatner, of course, had little patience for Dorsey or his music. Recalling his first encounter with him, Boatner wrote:

> At the time I never knew what a gospel choir was. But I know that when I heard him play the piano, I knew what was happening. He was sitting in the church one day and he was playing a gospel hymn or song for some lady who was sitting there. And it was nothing but jazz. You can look at any of them today, of the gospel songs. They have that same jazz type of form.[58]

The decision, of course, to form a gospel choir at Pilgrim incensed Boatner and he vociferously condemned it:

> I felt it was degrading. How can something that's jazzy give a religious feeling? If you're in a club downtown, a nightclub, that's alright. That's where it belongs. But how can you associate that with God's Word? It's a desecration. The only people who think it isn't a desecration are the people who haven't had any training, any musical training—people who haven't heard fine religious anthems, cantatas, [and] oratorios.[59]

And, well, Boatner would have been incensed. Dorsey's choir would be radically different than ensembles he had worked to build. No auditions

---

56. Marovich, *City Called Heaven*, 94.

57. Broughton, *Black Gospel*, 46.

58. Jackson, *Singing in My Soul*, 56.

59. Harris, *Rise of Gospel Blues*, 198. Boatner left Chicago for good in 1933 to become director of music at Samuel Husten College in Austin, Texas (now Huston-Tillotson College). In the late 1930s, he moved permanently to New York City and opened his "Edward Boatner Studio" as well as becoming director of music at Concord Baptist Church in Brooklyn. See Glover, "Life and Career of Edward Boatner," 94.

were required to sing nor did the singers have to read music. "Making choir membership egalitarian had a sociological impact. It ensured that the gospel choir was, like its music, for the masses. It was a club that members, especially new southern migrants, could call their own."[60] Dorsey himself provided vocal instruction for each singer and taught the very basic music-reading skills he or she would need. The majority of "Dorsey songs," as they were called, required a strong lead singer with choral back-up. The phrases of the lead vocal line often featured held notes under which the chorus would echo, achieving a call-and-response effect. The *Chicago Tribune*, in its 1993 obituary and tribute to Dorsey, interviewed singers who had sung under him during his many years at Pilgrim. They remembered him as "a strict but caring director who demanded promptness and preparation," and one who had "a uniquely intense style" that other choir directors unsuccessfully tried to imitate. He was, one former choir member was quoted as saying, "one of a hundred to work with. Nobody had the way of directing that he had. He was a God-sent man."[61]

The introduction of the Frye and Dorsey gospel choirs had an almost immediate and stunning impact on African American church music in Chicago and later nationally. Most old-line churches were not ready to jettison traditional worship, but it was the Depression, and they saw in gospel choruses the potential both to attract new members and increase revenue. One of the ways the choruses were introduced was through featuring them in the monthly musicales that had become common during the 1920s. Held on Sunday afternoons, the musicales had been an opportunity to present choral music not practical during a Sunday morning service—oratorios or works in foreign languages, for example. They often also had featured touring jubilee choirs and quartets and even solo performers. In short, churches applied a more relaxed standard that allowed for music that was less rigidly traditional.[62] The musicale provided an ideal vehicle to introduce, with minimal friction, a gospel choir into the life of the congregation.

By May of 1932, just over four months since gospel choirs had been debuted at Ebenezer and Pilgrim, there were twenty Chicago churches with such ensembles. In August of that year, Dorsey and directors from other churches joined together to form the Gospel Choral Union of Chicago. A year later, the Union had 3500 in its membership and had gone national, becoming the National Convention of Gospel Choirs and Choruses and Smaller Musical Groups, or NCGCC.

---

60. Marovich, *City Called Heaven*, 96
61. Poe, "Thomas A. Dorsey," 66.
62. Harris, *Rise of Gospel Blues*, 108.

Gospel Metamorphosis

The year 1932 was a pivotal one for Thomas Dorsey. It began with the remarkable success of his gospel choir activities. Moreover, he was still aglow from the reception his songs had received at the National Baptist Convention. He now could now walk in front of any number of storefront churches "and not be too surprised to hear one of his tunes filtering through the door."[63] In the summer of that year, with his wife Nettie in the final term of her pregnancy, Dorsey boarded a train for St. Louis to attend a revival and promote his music.

While there, he received a telegram saying his wife had died on August 26 and the baby was in danger.

> They said for me to come to the door of the hall where I received a telegram. I read it—I almost fell out. "Hurry home. Your wife just died." I don't know how you accept that. I couldn't accept it at all. A friend of mine put me in a car and dropped me right at home. When I got home I just ran in to see if it was true and someone goes, "Nettie just died, Nettie just died, Nettie just died." The baby was still alive but within the next two days the baby just died.[64]

Overwrought with emotion, Dorsey sought out his friend Theodore Frye, who encouraged him to find solace in his music. Retreating to his music room, he found himself drawn to the old hymn "Must Jesus Bear the Cross Alone" with its tune "Maitland," by George N. Allen. By slowing it down and stretching a note here and there, a new song emerged—Dorsey's greatest and most remembered—"Precious Lord, Take My Hand." The loss of his wife and child and that song settled once and for all for Dorsey the conflict that had raged in him. He gave up his career as a jazz artist, and the "Father of Gospel Blues" was born.

Black Women and Gospel Music

One of the most striking differences between the African American gospel tradition and the white southern gospel tradition, as the two developed in the first half of the twentieth century, was the role of women. Except for a few family ensembles, the southern gospel scene was dominated by male quartets. But strong female musicians like Arizona Dranes, Mahalia Jackson, Rosetta Tharpe, and Roberta and Sally Martin would have an indelible

---

63. Broughton, *Black Gospel*, 49.
64. Broughton, *Black Gospel,* 49.

impact on the form Black gospel music was to take and, whether by fortune or fate, would all coalesce around Chicago during the Dorsey years.

African American churches did not allow female pastors during the first decades of the twentieth century and to this day the pastorate is mostly male. During the 1920s and '30s women in old-line Black churches were active mostly in social reform and uplift programs—training for domestics and teaching parenting skills, for example. [65]

It was different in the storefront and Pentecostal churches. The Church of God in Christ (COGIC) was dominated by women. They outnumbered men two to one, and music was viewed as a divine gift.[66] There, women were often assigned missionary responsibilities, and music was regarded as an essential component of mission. A prominent example of this was Sister Katie Bell Nubin (1880–1969), a COGIC preacher and mandolinist who toured with her daughter, Rosetta. "Little Rosetta Nubin," a prodigy of the guitar at age four, would mature to become one of gospel music's great singers, Sister Rosetta Tharpe.

> As a woman preacher in the sanctified church, [Katie Bell Nubin] was not able to call herself "elder," the title used by ministers, nor was she able to oversee a congregation as the senior spiritual officer. Yet she felt that she was "called to preach." The one avenue left open to her was to teach. A female preacher who taught was called a missionary or an evangelist and could teach in any sanctified church and even conduct revivals... Her hook for drawing people to her services was "Little Rosetta Nubin, the singing and guitar-playing miracle"... As members of the tent-meeting troupe of male evangelist F. W. McGee, [they] preached and sang their way through Arkansas, Mississippi, Florida, Georgia, and Tennessee before settling in Chicago in the late 1920s.[67]

Among those African American women who took a leading role in the development of Black gospel music in the Pentecostal tradition, three names stand out: Arizona Dranes, Sallie Martin, and Roberta Martin.

---

65. Jackson, *Singing in My Soul*, 27.
66. Jackson, *Singing in My Soul*, 29–30.
67. Boyer, *Golden Age of Gospel*, 154.

Arizona Dranes

Arizona Dranes, ca. 1945.
Image courtesy of Michael Corcoran. (https://www.michaelcorcoran.net/
he-is-my-story-the-sanctified-soul-of-arizona-dranes-excerpt/)

The blind COGIC pianist Arizona Juanita Dranes (1889–1963)[68] is largely unknown today, and yet her fiery barrelhouse piano style was a major influence on gospel stars from Mahalia Jackson to Roberta Martin, not to mention pop singers Fats Domino and Jerry Lee Lewis. Dranes learned to play the piano at the Institute for Deaf, Dumb, and Blind Colored Youths in Austin, Texas between 1896 and 1912. Later, along with the Nubins, she joined the evangelistic team of Black COGIC preacher F. W. McGee. She arrived in Chicago in 1926 with a note from a Dallas pastor pinned to her sweater and addressed to the owner of Okeh Records.[69] It read, "Since she is Deprived of Her Natural Sight, the Lord Has Given Her A Spiritual Sight that all Churches Enjoy. She is Loyal and Obedient, Our Prayers Ascend for her."[70] On June 16, 1926, Dranes recorded six sides of gospel tunes at Chicago's Okeh Studios. The influence of ragtime—"fast Texas boogie-woogie"—was obvious in her playing. "The template Dranes created with six tracks in one day came

---

68. Her birth certificate lists her name as "Drane" but at some point early on the s was added, and she was known as Arizona Dranes for her entire career.

69. Okeh Records was a subsidiary of the General Phonograph Corporation found in 1916 and named for its founder, Otto K. E. Hennemann. It was started to produce recordings directed to niche groups of customers, particularly minority communities. At the start, they made successful recordings of New Orleans jazz artists including King Oliver's Band and Louis Armstrong. In 1920, Okeh's recording of the Black blues singer Mamie Smith became a bestseller and inspired the development of a "race recording division" devoted specifically to Black artists. The 1926 Arizona Dranes recordings would be the first by a female gospel soloist. Okeh was bought out by Columbia Records later in 1926.

70. Corcoran, "Praising Arizona."

to be called 'the gospel beat'; it's still played against a polyrhythm of hand claps in Black church services today."[71]

Sallie Martin

Sallie Martin.
Public domain image. (https://aaregistry.org/story/sallie-martin-was-great-for-the-business-of-gospel/)

Sallie Martin (1895–1988) arrived in Chicago just a year after Dranes's history-making recording session. Martin was raised a Baptist in Georgia, but in her twenties became drawn to the more emotive and charismatic worship of the Pentecostals. She joined the Fire Baptized Holiness Church in Atlanta in 1916 and moved north to Cleveland, Ohio, a year later. Sallie Martin embodied the aggressive, rough-hewn singing style and sheer physicality of sanctified worship and rose quickly in popularity among Pentecostals. In 1927, however, when she moved to Chicago and approached Thomas Dorsey about being one of his soloists, he was reluctant to use her because of these very characteristics. She also did not read music. Not to be deterred, Martin purchased copies of Dorsey's songs and began promoting them, and in 1932, when the Gospel Choir at Pilgrim Church was organized, she was among its first members. A year later, Thomas Dorsey assigned Sallie Martin her first solo. She would be his principal soloist through the rest of the 1930s and until Mahalia Jackson took her place. Martin's importance to future generations was not in her singing, but in her administrative skills. Before anyone else, she recognized the marketability of "Dorsey songs." She helped him establish his own publishing company as well as the National Convention of Gospel Choirs and Choruses, and tirelessly traveled

---

71. Corcoran, "Praising Arizona."

throughout the country advocating for gospel choirs with Dorsey's music in their repertoire.⁷²

Roberta Martin

Roberta Martin.
Public domain image. (https://aaregistry.org/story/
roberta-martin-gospels-true-voice/)

Another female musician whose career had huge implications for African American gospel music was Roberta Martin (1907–1969). Martin (no relation to Sallie) grew up in Helena, Arkansas, where she studied piano from the age of six and aspired to a career as a concert pianist. Her family had migrated north to Chicago where she continued her piano studies. In 1932, Roberta was hired by Theodore Frye for five dollars a Sunday to accompany the new gospel choir at Ebenezer Church.⁷³ It was her first encounter with gospel music, and she liked it. A year later, Frye asked Roberta to help him organize a male quartet with her as accompanist and occasional soloist. In 1936, the group was renamed the Roberta Martin Singers and after 1940 treble voices were added, making them one of the first successful mixed-voice African American gospel groups. Over the forty years of their existence, they recorded over three hundred songs and toured extensively.⁷⁴ According to Pearl Williams-Jones, "the Roberta Martin sound defined an

---

72. Price, "Sallie Martin." The Sallie Martin /Thomas Dorsey collaboration ended in 1940, after which she toured as solo blues artist with one Ruth Jones as her accompanist. Ruth would eventually become famous under the stage name Dinah Washington. After parting ways with Dorsey, Sallie Martin established her own publishing company, the Martin and Morris Company, which published the first print version of the gospel hymn, "Just a Closer Walk with Thee." Martin also organized the very successful Sallie Martin Singers, which is thought to be the first touring all-female gospel quartet.

73. Boyer, "Roberta Martin."

74. Martin was also a highly respected and popular gospel singer.

entire musical era."[75] It would become a model for future Black gospel ensembles and was distinguished by a careful blending of voices supporting a lead singer. The timbre tended to be light and treble-oriented, the lowest voice being a high baritone. Piano or organ provided the harmonic foundation so a low bass singer was not needed.

The influence of Arizona Dranes, Sallie Martin, and Roberta Martin was felt largely within the Black church. It fell to two other women to break long held barriers—performing in both sacred and secular venues and building a following among both Black and white audiences.

Mahalia Jackson

Mahalia Jackson (1911–1972) was raised by her "Aunt Duke" in New Orleans's Sixteenth Ward. The family attended the Plymouth Rock and Mount Moriah Baptist churches. In them, traditional hymns—many by Isaac Watts—were still lined-out and from the age of four little "Halie" sang in the children's choirs. Next to Aunt Duke's house, however, was a sanctified church, and its music also made an impression. From early childhood Halie had loved to sing and was known for the power and strength of her voice. Her childhood idol was the famed blues singer Bessie Smith, and her favorite song—sung over and over at every opportunity—was W. C. Handy's "St. Louis Blues."

Mahalia Jackson.
Public domain image courtesy of Wikimedia Commons and ETH-Bibliothek Zürich, Bildarchiv/Fotograf: Comet Photo AG (Zürich) / Com_L10-0125-0004 / CC BY-SA 4.0.

Mahalia arrived in Chicago after Thanksgiving in 1927 and initially worshipped at the Greater Salem Baptist Church. Unfortunately, her uninhibited exuberance and body movement was off-putting to the traditional congregation, and she was not welcomed into the choir. She did, however,

---

75. Williams-Jones, "Roberta Martin," 255.

receive an invitation to sing with the church's male quartet, the Johnson Singers, one of Chicago's earliest gospel groups. The Johnson Singers would be Jackson's last experience as an ensemble singer. For the rest of her career she would devote herself exclusively to being a soloist.[76]

Pilgrim Baptist pastor James Austin was *not* put off by Mahalia's performing style. After hearing her sing, he invited her to assist him in his ministry as a "singing evangelist." Thus, Mahalia Jackson became acquainted with Thomas Dorsey and his music. She helped him sell his songs by singing them on street corners and at funeral homes where she was an on-call singer. She didn't work with Dorsey on a consistent basis, however, until the late 1930s, when he became for a time her accompanist and mentored her in the techniques of gospel singing. She had recorded four songs for Decca records in 1937 but sales were modest at best. She was basically unknown outside the city limits of the Windy City. By the outbreak of World War II, Jackson had become one of Chicago's most sought-after singers.

Breaking Boundaries: Sister Rosetta Tharpe

At the age of four in her hometown of Cotton Plant, Arkansas, Rosetta Nubin (1915–1973) stood on boxes playing a guitar only slightly smaller than herself, and sang "Jesus on the Main Line, Tell Him What You Want." While there was no doubt that she had an extraordinary voice—bright and clear, sonorous, warm, slightly brassy, and an easy delivery—she also knew at that tender age how to sing. Her pitch was solid, she knew the melody, and could even add extra notes of her own. Her rhythm was as accented, syncopated, and as intricate as any of the blues singers "in the bottoms." None of these vocal qualities, however, matched her guitar playing.[77]

Rosetta and her mother were devout members of the Church of God in Christ. Settling in Chicago in the mid-1920s, they were and would remain outside the Baptist coterie of Thomas Dorsey. The free-form nature Pentecostal service was based on the notion that God and the Holy Spirit, acting among believers, was in control. According to Boyer, "This was the birth of gospel music. Its purpose was not to entertain, not to satisfy, not to merchandize, but to express the pent-up emotions, whatever they might have been, of the participants."[78] Spiritual ecstasy was the objective.

According to Jerma Jackson, Rosetta and her mother drew "upon their religious fervor to fashion a powerful female culture that nurtured musical

---

76. Boyer, *Golden Age of Gospel*, 86.
77. Boyer, *Golden Age of Gospel*, 154.
78. Boyer, "Contemporary Gospel Music," 7.

talent and sought to turn worldly institutions to spiritual ends."[79] For Katie Bell Nubin that meant performance and witness at revivals beyond the purview of the local church. For the mature Rosetta, however, it meant taking her music deep into the jazz clubs and concerts of popular culture. She would seize "upon the new technologies of mass communication that infused commercial culture, recognizing that these technologies might be harnessed to spread religion to vast numbers of people."[80]

Sister Rosetta Tharpe.
1938 publicity photo by James J. Kriegsmann.
Public domain. (https://commons.wikimedia.org/wiki/File:Sister_Rosetta_Tharpe_
(1938_publicity_photo_with_guitar).jpg)

Mahalia Jackson and Rosetta Tharpe were almost exact contemporaries, and both grew up inspired by the jazz and blues artists of the 1920s. Both women committed themselves to solo careers and started out as exciting, energetic, but rough-around-the-edges singers who became extremely popular performers and recording artists in the late 1940s and '50s. Yet their views on gospel music as a performance medium were radically different. Jackson from early on had been encouraged to branch out into jazz blues singing, but refused. Decca Records, in fact, with whom Jackson had made her first recordings, terminated their contract with her because of that. On the other hand, Rosetta even as a teenager was an independent spirit. In private and before friends and family, she sang and played blues and jazz charts. When performing in public during the Chicago years, "she accepted every

---

79. Jackson, *Singing in My Soul*, 27.
80. Jackson, *Singing in My Soul*, 27.

opportunity offered. She began appearing [as a gospel singer] in multi-act concerts with performers of blues, jazz, and folk."[81]

Tharpe[82] moved to New York City in 1938. In October, Rosetta too made recordings with Decca. When the studio asked her to perform a mixed gospel and pop repertoire, she agreed. Four sides were recorded: Dorsey's "Hide Me in Thy Bosom," and three blues selections, "That's All," "Lonesome Road," and "My Man and I." [83] Tharpe's sanctified church family was scandalized, but the recordings were bestsellers.

From Spiritual Business to Show Business

In surveying populist sacred music in America from the 1870s forward, one sees a conflict of objectives: *ministry versus the marketplace* and *worship versus entertainment*. A certain tipping point seems to have been reached in the late 1930s for both African American and white southern gospel music. For African American gospel music, the transition from churchly ministry to entertainment revolved around Sister Rosetta Tharpe. After arriving in New York City in October of 1938 and her historic Decca Records recording session, she immediately began singing at various jazz clubs, including Café Society in Greenwich Village and the famous Cotton Club. The latter was an elaborate jazz club focused on Black entertainment for an all-white clientele. The famed singer and band leader Cab Calloway was the club's featured performer and Duke Ellington's band regularly appeared. Rosetta's performance was so well received that she was offered a $500 per week salary to be one of the club's regular performers. Performances at the club were aired nationally on the radio, giving Tharpe a celebrity far beyond New York City.[84]

The Cotton Club was only the first of several triumphs accrued to her in the last two months of the 1938. In early December, she performed with Count Basie and his band, and then she was invited to perform at the Apollo Theater for a Christmas fundraiser with a star-studded lineup including Fats Waller, Lionel Hampton, the Ink Spots, and Artie Shaw. But the truly life-changing engagement for Rosetta came with an invitation from the

---

81. Boyer, *Golden Age of Gospel*, 155.

82. In 1934, Rosetta Nubin married the COGIC pastor Thomas J. Thorpe. According to Boyer, the marriage was short-lived. Thorpe did not approve of her performing secular music in secular venues, and—the final blow—insisted she wear a hat when singing. After the divorce, Rosetta altered the spelling of her married name to Tharpe and used it for the remainder of her career.

83. Boyer, *Golden Age of Gospel*, 155.

84. Wald, *Shout, Sister, Shout!*, 33–36.

legendary promoter John Hammond to be a featured performer in a concert on December 23. It was to be at Carnegie Hall, and it was to be called "From Spirituals to Swing."[85]

Hammond intended "From Spirituals to Swing" to be a challenge to racism in America through the arts. He envisioned presenting a variety of the best African American performers before a fully integrated audience. Rosetta sang two gospel songs before a sold-out crowd in a segment of the concert entitled "Spirituals and Holy Roller Hymns." Basie later recalled that:

> She sang some gospel songs that brought the house down. She sang down-home church numbers and had those old cold New Yorkers almost shouting in the aisles. There were a lot of people out there who had never heard that kind of singing, but she went over big.[86]

Rosetta's sudden celebrity created a huge stir in far-away Chicago, not all of it positive. Thomas Dorsey was livid that she had rearranged one of his songs, "Hide Me in Thy Bosom," gave it a new title, "Rock Me," gave him no credit as the original composer, and sang it at such a den of iniquity as the Cotton Club! He groused that Tharpe's use of the song was a desecration.[87]

Emergence of Independent Gospel Recording and Performing Artists

With regard to white southern gospel music during the late 1930s, the symbiotic relationship between the top-tier quartets and their publisher-sponsors was weakening. Singers balked at sitting through reading sessions at singing conventions and performing for meager commissions. They recognized that more and more, audiences were coming to hear them sing and not to buy songbooks. They sensed the combination of inspiration and entertainment that ticket holders hungered for, and they wanted to provide it. This included adding popular country and western tunes along with gospel tunes to their repertoire. The quartets also realized that, by taking the publishers out of the equation, they could forge their own contractual agreements with radio stations and recording companies and benefit financially. The Homeland Harmony Quartet, which had been formed in the 1930s, struck a contract with Atlanta radio station WAGA that guaranteed $15 per

---

85. Wald, *Shout, Sister, Shout!*, 43.
86. Wald, *Shout, Sister, Shout!*, 45.
87. Wald, *Shout, Sister, Shout!*, 47.

day per man to perform three fifteen-minute shows a week. The shows were prerecorded so their radio work did not have to interfere with their schedule of performances on the road.[88]

A parallel sequence of developments happened with African American gospel quartets. There had been a tradition of quartet contests extending back at least to 1894. The format for these events required a panel of trained musicians as judges, cash prizes, and a detailed scoring system. Groups were graded on rhythmic accuracy, harmony or blend, articulation, and appearance on stage. The contests were often well attended, but their purpose was to improve the skill and performance of the singers.[89] That being said, the events were widely covered in the Black press, and as the 1930s progressed the coverage became progressively more focused on winners and losers. The invention of the applause meter in 1936[90] would change the character of the quartet contests completely. After World War II, judges were eliminated in favor of a philosophy that said, "Let the audience decide."[91] Any pretense of education or higher purpose had disappeared. The thumbs up/thumbs down of the Roman coliseum comes to mind.

The gospel soloist equivalent to the quartet contest was the "song battle." In 1936, Thomas Dorsey engineered a program he promoted as a song battle between two popular singers, Sallie Martin and Roberta Martin. It was not intended to be a duel really, but a means to drive up interest in selling from Dorsey's catalog of gospel songs. The program, however, drew a sizable audience and contests between other star performers and individual quartets were soon being promoted. The first of two legendary song battles pitted Mahalia Jackson against Roberta Martin at the Ebenezer Baptist Church in Chicago in 1947. A second was held at the Harlem's Golden Gate Auditorium between Jackson and Ernestine Washington for the title "America's Gospel Singing Queen." It was touted as a contest between East and West, the Brooklyn-based Washington, "Songbird of the East," versus Jackson, the "Empress of Gospel Singers" from Chicago.

At this point, gospel music in America had become one with popular culture. The implications would be long term. Populist sacred music in post–World War II America would become more and more in the embrace of radio, television, and social media—and less and less driven by the needs of the local church.

---

88. Wolfe, "Gospel Boogie," 75.

89. Burford, *Mahalia Jackson and the Black Gospel Field*, 107.

90. By the post-war years, the applause meter was a standard feature of radio variety programs, including *The Arthur Godfrey Show*.

91. Burford, *Mahalia Jackson and the Black Gospel Field*, 114.

Chapter 18

COLLAPSE AND CONFLICT
Cultivated Church Music during the Great Depression and World War II

Signs of trouble had surfaced a month earlier, but the stock market crash on "Black Tuesday"—October 24, 1929—was catastrophic. Share prices fell by fourteen billion dollars that day and by over thirty billion dollars in the week to come. The loss was ten times the total federal budget. It exceeded the total cost of American involvement in the First World War. Unemployment at the depths of the Depression in 1933 has been estimated at anywhere from 22.5 percent to 24.9 percent. Histories of the Great Depression typically focus on bank failures, the cost in human suffering, the failure of the Herbert Hoover administration to deal aggressively with the situation, and Franklin Delano Roosevelt's New Deal. The Great Depression's impact on American church life was devastating.

The Church in the Great Depression

During the 1920s—a decade of unbridled optimism—many congregations, Black and white, had built new, larger edifices. In doing so, they had amassed huge debts that, with the onset of the Depression, became burdens of crisis proportions. Episcopal cathedrals planned for Philadelphia and Olympia, Washington, had to be put on hold. Construction that had been continuing on the Cathedral of St. John the Divine in New York City experienced repeated delays, causing it to be called "St. John the Unfinished."[1] While many were able to weather the financial downturn, many others defaulted on obligations. Churches with endowments suddenly found they had lost them and had to either close or cut back drastically on programs.

Church-related colleges, publishing houses, missionary activities, and innumerable social services were all impacted.[2] The Estey Organ Corporation, one of America's principal pipe organ builders, was forced into bankruptcy and restructured. The Hope Publishing Company, purveyors of innumerable gospel song collections, had undergone tremendous growth during the 1920s. With the onset of the Depression, Hope Publishing's staff was reduced to twelve employees who were required to take an additional two weeks of vacation without pay. Demand for hymnals had not abated, but during the entire decade the company was able to produce only one, the *Service Hymnal* of 1935.[3]

The religious and social divisions of the 1920s only became sharper with the onset of the Great Depression. "Americans of every type sought and found scapegoats and panaceas; racist attitudes and ethnic animosities intensified; class antagonism sharpened."[4] The brutal dissonance between fundamentalists and modernists resulted in schisms. The dissension that had started years earlier over Fosdick's sermon "Shall the Fundamentalists Win?" expanded to a full-blown fight between conservative evangelicals and liberals, and resulted in the 1933 founding of the Orthodox Presbyterian Church. A similar controversy erupted in the Northern Baptist Church (now the American Baptist Convention). Conservatives, who insisted on literal interpretation of Scripture and tended toward premillennialism, separated from the main body to form the General Association of Regular Baptist Churches (GARBC).

While most mainline denominations avoided schism and most of their individual churches avoided bankruptcy and closure, those were not

---

1. The Cathedral of St. John the Divine is still referred to as "St. John the Unfinished" and likely will always be. The original plans called for a central steeple soaring 445 feet into the sky. Unfortunately, the rock formation on which it was built hid an underground spring, making a stable foundation for such a mammoth structure impossible. See Kirby, "St. John the Unfinished," and Broad, "Cathedral tried to Approach Heaven, but Earth Held a Secret."

2. Brauer, *Protestantism in America*, 265.

3. During the boom years of the 1920s, Hope Publishing had bought out the country's first, and for years its most successful, music publisher, Biglow and Main, as well as the revival music purveyor Tabernacle Publishing. They had also acquired copyrights to all of Charles A. Tindley's hymns. See: https://www.hopepublishing.com/content/AboutUs.

4. Ahlstrom, *Religious History of the American People*, 920.

the only devastating aspects of the Great Depression. The social gospel movement, for all its noble aspirations, had been based on a hopelessly naïve view of unbounded human potential with a promised new Jerusalem virtually just around the corner. With the financial collapse, the ebullient self-confidence of the 1920s gave way to despair.

> Suddenly the Protestant Churches were confronted with the stark reality of the failure of their dreams. Under all the supposed goodness and friendliness of the prosperous '20's were to be found greed and pride. Man suddenly was shown to be no higher on the moral scale, no less selfish than his medieval brethren. In place of a new stage in the Kingdom of God men had arrived at a shattered economy. The consequence was a new look at some old Protestant doctrines that had been largely ignored—sin, faith, and justification were once more relevant.[5]

Nevertheless, there was reason for optimism in some quarters. Pentecostal, Seventh-day Adventist, and Jehovah's Witnesses more than doubled in membership during the Depression, while mainline church rolls experienced only moderate reductions.[6] There was also a palpable and growing understanding that suffering and sacrifice should be an expected part of Christian living. No longer to be avoided was the recognition that greed and self-interest were driving forces in American society. The old Calvinistic perspectives on sin, the ultimate authority of God, and repentance—ideas that liberal theology had largely ignored—now seemed more relevant and gave rise to a new trend in theology, namely neo-orthodoxy. [7]

Spearheading the wave of neo-orthodoxy were the brothers Karl Paul Reinhold Niebuhr (1892–1972) and H. Richard Niebuhr (1894–1962), two of the most important Christian ethicists and theologians of the twentieth century. Writing in the *Christian Century* in 1939, Reinhold Niebuhr revealed that "about midway in my ministry, which extends roughly from the peace of Versailles to the peace of Munich[8] . . . I underwent a fairly complete conversion of thought which involved rejection of almost all the liberal theological ideals and ideas with which I ventured forth in 1915."[9] This

---

5. Brauer, *Protestantism in America*, 267.

6. Ahlstrom, *Religious History*, 920.

7. Christian Darwinism, which had helped to shape liberal theology in the late nineteenth century, had the unfortunate tendency to view humankind as evolving inevitably toward perfection (see chapter 9). The Great Depression forced an unvarnished reappraisal and reality check resulting in what is called neo-orthodoxy.

8. Niebuhr was referring to the years between the end of World War I (1918) and the disastrous Munich Peace Accord with Nazi Germany prior to World War II (1938).

9. Niebuhr, "Ten Years That Shook My World," 542.

reassessment began with his 1924 book *Does Christianity Need Religion?;* continued with 1932's *Moral Man in an Immoral Society: A Study of Ethics and Politics;* and reached its final distillation in his 1939 Gifford Lectures, later published as *The Nature and Destiny of Man: A Christian Interpretation* (1942).

One cannot maintain, Niebuhr argued, that the progress of humankind is steadily upward or that, in the words of a popular cliché of the 1920s, "every day in every way we are getting better and better." One can hold such a position, Niebuhr declared, only by ignoring reality. The reality is that human nature is perverse, and that society tends toward evil. Science, sanitation, and education cannot, will not, produce a perfect world, Niebuhr asserted; neither will a sentimental Protestantism that refuses to confront the undeniable realities of war, greed, exploitation, prejudice, poverty, cruelty, injustice, and lust. We tell people to love and imitate Christ, assuring them, Niebuhr wrote, that all will be well. "But Christ loved, and all was not well: he ended up on a cross. So a kind of 'Christian realism' is called for . . ."[10]

H. Richard Niebuhr on "Culture Protestantism" and Denominationalism

While Reinhold is most well-known, his younger brother Richard is regarded by many to be his equal as a theologian. He enlisted to be a chaplain in the United States Expeditionary Forces during World War I, but the war ended before he had an opportunity to serve. Of the two brothers, H. Richard appears to have been the more musically minded and wrote a hymn to be used by the chaplain's corps, "Fling Out, Fling Out the Banner." Richard Niebuhr returned to Missouri to teach at Eden Seminary from 1919 to 1924. From 1924 to 1927, he served as president of Elmhurst College. While at Elmhurst, he oversaw the founding of the school's music department.[11]

H. Richard Niebuhr saw inherent weakness in the Depression-era church's interaction with societal norms of the time. In his view, God had not abandoned the church during the Depression, but the church was failing to follow God's call to discipleship. He felt the church needed to disengage from rather than embrace the culture of the time.

> Christendom has often achieved apparent success by ignoring the precepts of its founder. The church as an organization interested in self-preservation and in the gain of power, has sometimes found the counsel of the Cross quite as inexpedient

---

10. Gaustad and Schmidt, *Religious History of America,* 281–82.
11. Diefenhaler, *H. Richard Niebuhr,* 9–10.

> as have national and economic groups. In dealing with such major social evils as war, slavery, and social inequality, it has discovered convenient ambiguities in the letter of the gospels which enabled it to violate their spirit . . .[12]

Richard Niebuhr had come to view the concept of textual criticism as too often being used as a justification to acquiesce to the norms of society. He coined a term for this perversion, "Culture Protestantism." It was based in part on his observations of Lutheran churches in Germany and their acquiescence to the rise of Nazism, but it was also rooted in what he saw taking place in America. He reasoned that the erosion of faith coming from the hardships of the Depression was the result of misplaced faith in humanity rather than God. "Unless we get out of our planetary provincialism, our narrow selfish way of thinking and looking at things, and cultivate a cosmic faith," he had written, "we can never understand much less solve the many problems we are facing, nor realize the brotherhood of man."[13]

By 1929, ritualism and cultivated church music in the United States had experienced tremendous progress across the mainline denominations. Much of it had been inspired by the pioneering ritualistic innovations in the Protestant Episcopal Church. Pipe organ sales were at an all-time high. Dudley Buck and Horatio Parker, the two most prominent anthem composers at the turn of the century, fell within the Episcopal fold, but their choral music was widely used by cultivated churches of all stripes. Smaller churches aspiring to a cultivated status bought hymnals, began to use vestments, gave varying attention to liturgical seasons, colors, and symbolism, and developed choral programs. Many in the mainline churches saw this as a hopeful sign that further unification of Protestant faith groups was possible.

> Yet amid these fallen idols a many-sided revival of spirit also occurred. Realizing that the whole country was in trouble, Americans gained a new kind of self-awareness. Mutual distress drew people together. As neighbor discovered neighbor, a great many Americans found a new sense of solidarity.[14]

But long-held divisions remained regarding theology, polity, and how churches related to the society around them. Adopting the trappings of ritualistic worship was often a superficial veneer cloaking division among Protestants.

---

12. Niebuhr, *Social Sources of Denominationalism*, 3.
13. Niebuhr, *Social Sources of Denominationalism*, 38.
14. Ahlstrom, *Religious History*, 920.

For Richard Niebuhr, denominationalism itself was simply a byproduct of the class and caste system that permeated American society. He theorized that denominationalism was the result of a pernicious repeating cycle. A group of believers with a common need would band together, over time become institutionalized, and then adopt an exclusive culture allowing entry only to the indoctrinated. For Niebuhr, this ran diametrically counter to the inclusiveness of Jesus's ministry as reflected in the parable of the good Samaritan.[15]

> The road to unity which love requires denominations, nations, classes, and races to take is no easy. There is no short cut even to the union of churches... The road to unity is the road of repentance. It demands a resolute turning away from all those loyalties to the lesser values of the self, the denomination, and the nation, which deny the inclusiveness of divine love. It requires that Christians learn to look upon their separate establishments and exclusive creeds with contrition rather than pride. The road to unity is the road of sacrifice which asks of the church as of individuals that they lose their lives in order that they may find the fulfilment of their better selves. But it is also the road to the eternal values of a Kingdom of God that is among us.[16]

Reinhold and Richard Niebuhr said little in their writings about church music per se, yet their highly influential works forced reassessment of the church's structure, priorities, and role in society. When Reinhold Niebuhr warns of the dangers implicit when the church allows its mission to be controlled by the societal pressures around it, the implications for church music are obvious. Like today, Depression-era churches had to wrestle with pressures being exerted by popular culture in their music—whether to embrace culture or, as Archibald Davison suggested, completely divorce themselves from it.

Richard Niebuhr's thoughts on denominationalism were and are thought-provoking. To what extent, he was asking, should cherished denominational doctrines and traditions be retained before they become prioritized over basic Christian ministry and servanthood? For many church musicians and clergy in the 1930s it had become clear that, for music to be a ministry, training needed to include biblical, theological, and liturgical studies *as well as* musical instruction. Even though future church musicians would minister in one denomination or another, their music would likely be drawn from multiple denominations and traditions. An openness to

---

15. Niebuhr, *Social Sources of Denominationalism*, 7.
16. Niebuhr, *Social Sources of Denominationalism*, 284.

a holistic approach to sacred music training would shape the ministry of coming generations of church musicians.

Archibald Davison and "Protestant Church Music in America"

The divisiveness that roiled society and the church during the Depression years extended predictably to the church's music. In 1933, Archibald Davison published what would become one of the most controversial books in the history of American church music. Davison's *Protestant Church Music in America* was a distillation of lectures he had given during the previous decade for the Unitarian Laymen's League of Baltimore, the student body at Princeton Seminary, and the Boston Chapter of the American Guild of Organists. Davison set the tone for his entire book in one of the opening paragraphs:

> Many musicians who live by a high professional standard refuse to associate themselves with the music of the church. They recognize that among the major branches of musical activity, ecclesiastical music occupies the lowest station, and rather than exert themselves in a field that is traditionally unfriendly to idealism, they remain at a safe distance lest they be counted among the opprobrious company of "church musicians." It is no exaggeration to say that the better educated musician looks with suspicion upon any member of his profession who holds a church position, for he knows in practically every case that to be in the pay of a Protestant congregation means subscription to a situation which no musician of ideals could possibly tolerate.[17]

In the book, Davison provided unvarnished criticism of the church music of his time and demands for reform. Among them:

1. The poor music heard in worship and the poor musical taste that encouraged it was a direct result of lack of education in the arts. Nothing would improve, he believed, unless churches, refusing to be bound by popular taste, insisted on a higher standard of music.

2. All children's hymns of the gospel variety needed to be replaced with timeless melodies of the church (for example, "*Ein feste Burg*" or "*Nun danket alle Gott*").

3. The same standards of excellence applied to concert music needed to be applied to the music of the church.

---

17. Davison, *Protestant Church Music*, 2.

4. Churches that reject polyphonic music, plainchant melodies, and Latin texts simply because of Roman Catholic associations needed to realize that such music is universal and rejecting it is indefensible.

5. The ideal church music, according to Davison, needed to be impersonal and God-centered, not the individual-centered, overly sentimental offerings of the Victorians and evangelicals.

The tone of Davison's words came across as overbearing and elitist. "Many of Davison's barbed comments probably elicited small chuckles from audiences when they had been delivered by the author personally with his characteristically rapid-fire delivery; in print, however, the humor of such comments was obscured, and Davison's comments seemed all the more caustic."[18]

Davison's strongly opinionated take-no-prisoners writing raised the hackles of the book's *New York Times* reviewer, Richard Aldrich, who wrote:

> Now comes Professor Davison of Harvard in a book embodying very positive views of his own as to what music should and should not be sung in the Protestant Church, and as to how, when and where it should and should not be. He comes into direct and aggressive conflict with many who regard themselves as authoritative in the Episcopal Church and still more strongly opposes many who are influential in the evangelical communion . . . He will have naught to do with Wesley's principle of not letting the devil have all the good tunes.[19]

An objective reading of *Protestant Church Music in America* reveals that most of Davison's criticisms were not new. Unfortunately, his biting and occasionally outrageous pronouncements may have overshadowed more important thoughts and even real profundities within the text. In a section on society's need for better music education, he wrote at length on the music-related training needed for church musicians and ministers. The following passage, while intended for clergy, certainly was applicable to

---

18. Tovey, "Archibald T. Davison," 211.

19. Aldrich, "Protestant Church Music." Aldrich was referencing the familiar saying "Why let the devil have all the good tunes?" The saying's origin is tantalizingly obscure. Its source has been attributed variously to Martin Luther, John Wesley, William Booth (the founder of the Salvation Army), Rowland Hill (a nineteenth-century British pastor), and even Larry Norman (a pioneer of the contemporary Christian music movement). There is no definitive evidence to support any of those conjectures. What can be said is that St. John Chrysostom in the fifth century declared, "Where dance is, there is the Devil," and by dance, we can assume he meant all the secular music of his time. A frequent criticism of the early Methodists was that their boisterous singing came from Satan (hence the Wesley and Methodist connection).

church musicians as well and reveal an awareness of a specialized skill-set for those seeking to work in the church.

> To this instruction should be added a study of the significance of music in liturgy; work in the psychology and aesthetics of church music; and one in its administration, dealing with various types of choirs, church music finances, and the thousand and one kindred problems that young ministers now solve by bitter experience.[20]

Tucked away on page fifty-five is a deeply moving statement regarding the nature and purpose of music in worship:

> Now, from the lay point of view, the most satisfactory definitions of religion are those which emphasize the elements which no wisdom can explain ... And it is exactly here, where the logic of human speech is futile, that the language of music is most eloquent. ... Indeed, the more worship points man away from earth and towards God, the greater is its power; and in the same way the more music shuns the everyday idiom of man's musical experience, the more efficient partner of worship it becomes. *For music, like religion, is fundamentally a mystery* ... .[21]

Most intriguing is Davison's embrace of an austere, mystical, almost medieval ideal for worship. How is it that Davison, raised a Baptist, who had only one rather brief and unsatisfying experience with high Episcopal worship, came to favor such a high liturgical ideal for Protestant worship? The years of service at Appleton Chapel certainly helped shape his views, but a university chapel is far different from a local church. And no doubt, Davison's Harvard credentials left him open to criticism by church leaders as an ivory tower idealist. Nevertheless, much of his thought parallels that expressed by Pius X in the 1903 *Motu proprio*. Davison cited Renaissance polyphony as "the ideal anthem style in that it is essentially impersonal, implying the equal cooperation of all voices instead of the exploitation of one at the expense of the others. It is, moreover, undramatic, since its full effect is almost never felt at any given second due to the constantly shifting melodic emphasis ... ."[22]

In *Protestant Church Music* Davison repeatedly called for worship to return to an impersonal, God-centered rather than individual-centered aesthetic. In a later book, *Church Music: Illusion or Reality* (1952), he reframed

---

20. Davison, *Protestant Church Music*, 20.
21. Davison, *Protestant Church Music*, 55.
22. Davison, *Protestant Church Music*, 120.

the discussion as the tension between "humanistic reality" versus "spiritual reality." The problem with the sermon-centered worship so common among the nonliturgical denominations, he felt, was that it shifted the focus away from worship to teaching. Tovey writes that for Davison, "Man's concern for his own spiritual welfare [has] superseded the importance of the glorification of God in most Protestant services."[23] The most essential components of true worship—"awe, detachment, exaltation, inner peace, contemplation, reverence, a sense of God's mercy, and, by no means least, mystery"—were being lost.[24] Hymns like "Onward, Christian Soldiers" and "I Need Thee Every Hour" were totally foreign to his vision of what worship should be. Awe, reverence, and mystery, Davison lamented, "To all of these the best sacred music gives voice."[25] If music no longer was directed to God, why have it at all in worship? Davison's rigid preference for worship that embodies the *mysterium* was a direct challenge to the very "personalized devotion" of evangelicals.

Protestant Church Music in America, despite the critical outcry it generated in 1933, was not revolutionary. It was reactionary. However, the book was important if for no other reason than it continued the conversation about the nature and value of music within worship. Was the awe, reverence, and mystery Davison feared losing essential to Protestant worship in general or just to a select group of high church Anglo-Catholics? Could there be a common standard for effective worship that transcended denominational boundaries? In fact, was denominationalism itself part of the problem hindering the development of music as a ministry in America?

Winds of Change

One needs to remember that in *Protestant Church Music in America*, Davison was reacting to the terrain of church music in the late 1920s and early '30s. The repertoire of hymns, anthems, service, and organ music used in most churches was reactionary. Victorian-influenced anthems of Stainer, Goss, Gounod, and others—over a half century old—were still standard fare to the exclusion of more progressive musical choices. The Depression-era church seemed not to be a place where Davison's musicians with a high professional standard could hope to work creatively. The leading lights of choral composition in 1930 were not church musicians. Aaron Copland

---

23. Tovey, "Archibald T. Davison," 234.
24. Davison, *Church Music: Illusion and Reality*, 75–76.
25. Davison, *Church Music: Illusion and Reality*, 76.

(1900–1990), Randall Thompson (1899–1984), Howard Hanson (1896–1981), and Virgil Thomson (1896–1989) are prime examples.

To be sure, there *were* church musician/composers providing serviceable choral and organ repertoire during the Depression era. Among them, in addition to Davison and Clarence Dickinson, were Seth Bingham (1882–1972), Edward Shippen Barnes (1887–1958), Joseph W. Clokey (1890–1961), Garth Edmundson (1895–1973), Katherine K. Davis (1892–1980), and Van Denman Thompson (1890–1969). It would take years, however, for their works to come into general use.

Church Music Reform and the Episcopalians during the Depression Era

Four composer/church musicians that did stand out were Episcopalians: Canon Charles Winfred Douglas (1867–1944), Everett Titcomb (1884–1968), David McK. Williams (1887–1978),[26] and Leo Sowerby (1895–1968). And indeed, the greatest momentum for change in church music in the years prior to World War II was in the Protestant Episcopal Church in the United States.

Canon Charles Winfred Douglas.
Public domain image. (http://anglicanhistory.org/music/douglas/)

---

26. The organist/composer David McKinley Williams used the abbreviated version of his middle name, "McK.," both as a performer and a composer. Therefore, it will be used wherever Williams's name appears in this text.

Canon Winfred Douglas represented the high church and Anglo-Catholic aspirations of American Episcopalians. Dorothy Mills Parker in *The Living Church* wrote that Douglas "was largely responsible for bringing plainsong, the ancient music of liturgical worship into general use, and with it the full choral service." With due deference to American priest/musicians of the nineteenth century such as Morgan Dix and John Ireland Tucker, Douglas's contribution was significant.[27] He saw the reforms sought by Pope Pius X in his *Motu Proprio* of 1903 as not exclusively Roman but applicable to the universal church. He defended the papal decree in a 1937 lecture:

> The world became aware of all this when Pius X issued in 1903 his famous and much misunderstood *Motu Proprio* on church music, which does *not* banish all music from the Roman Church save plainsong, but, in its own words, "admits to the services of religion everything good and beautiful discovered by geniuses in the course of the ages (!), but always with due regard to the purposes of the liturgy itself."[28]

Douglas himself made a pilgrimage to Solesmes in France, studying there from 1903 to 1906. He later served as president of the American Plainsong Society and was a member of the Joint Commission on the Revision of the Hymnal of the Protestant Episcopal Church (1940).[29] Dorothy Mills Parker, in *The Living Church*, wrote that "He was Catholic in the complete sense of the word, a member of the Universal Church who was happily at home in all parts of it."[30]

---

27. Parker, "Musician, Priest, Linguist and Poet."
28. Douglas, *Hale Lectures*, 210.
29. Armstrong, "Legacy of Everett Titcomb," 14.
30. Parker, "Musician, Linguist, Priest and Poet."

David McK. Williams,
ca. 1920 in Canadian Army uniform. Public domain image. (https://hymnology.hymnsam.co.uk)

David McK. Williams was born in Carnarvonshire, Wales, but his family immigrated to the United States while he was still in infancy. A prodigy at the organ, Williams was working as organist/choirmaster at a church in Denver in 1900 at the age of thirteen. In 1908, he moved to New York City and served as organist at the Grace Free Church. Three years later, Williams undertook organ and composition study in Paris with Vincent d'Indy, Louis Vierne, and Charles Marie Widor. Upon his return to New York in 1914, Williams was sought out by two of the city's leading Episcopal parishes. He first became organist/choirmaster at the Church of the Holy Communion, and then in 1920 at St. Bartholomew's, with its magnificent organ and outstanding chorus choir with a professional nucleus.[31] It would be a long and fruitful ministry of twenty-six years. In addition to being one of the country's premier organists, Williams was a talented and successful composer, a number of whose works are still being sung in the twenty-first century. His "In the Year King Uzziah Died," while clearly cast in a romantic idiom, remains one of the outstanding settings of the vision of Isaiah (Isaiah 6). It was at St. Bart's that Williams became a close friend of Amy Beach and premiered many of her anthems and other choral works.[32]

---

31. Ogasapian, *Church Music in America*, 245.

32. Note: When it became known that McK. Williams was homosexual, he was dismissed from the staff of St. Bartholomew's in 1947 using a fabricated reason that "he suffered from hearing loss." Undeterred, McK. Williams remained in the New York area, serving on the music faculty at Union Theological Seminary School of Sacred Music and as head of the organ department at Juilliard.

H. Everett Titcomb.
Public domain image, *The Tracker*, 31:1 (1987) p. 23.

Howard Everett Titcomb, like Canon Douglas, fell squarely in the high Episcopal-Anglo-Catholic tradition. He lived his entire life in or near Boston. While raised in a Unitarian family, Titcomb sang in a choir of men and boys at St. James Episcopal in Amesbury. It was there he began a lifelong connection to Episcopal liturgy and music.

In 1910, Everett Titcomb accepted the position of organist/choirmaster at the Church of St. John the Evangelist in Andover, Massachusetts, a mission church of the Society of St. John the Evangelist, an Anglican monastic order founded in 1866 in England and known colloquially as the "Cowley Fathers." Titcomb said of the appointment:

> Musically, it was not a step in advance, for the choir and music here had been greatly neglected, but there was something else, the atmosphere of Catholic worship, and the real presence of Almighty God. I knew that these were the essentials and felt that given time enough and the opportunities, I could build up an efficient choir and render music which was beautiful and of artistic merit ... without sacrificing that quality of devotion and worship.[33]

Titcomb remained at the Church of St. John the Evangelist for a record fifty years, retiring in 1960.

Though committed to the principles of the Oxford Movement, Titcomb had an intense dislike for Anglican chant and "pointing." He saw it as a clumsy and poor substitute for the lyricism of traditional plainsong. The

---

33. Armstrong, "Legacy of Everett Titcomb," 10. (Quoted from R. C. Smith, "The Shrine on Bowdoin Street: 1883–1958" in *Cowley Fathers Anniversary Issue*, 1958.)

congregational singing of chant that some church musicians were struggling to make possible, Titcomb saw as an anathema. Instead, he advocated the singing of chant as it was done in the Middle Ages by a trained choir. Titcomb would become one of the twentieth century's foremost authorities on the practice of plainchant and a strong advocate for the use of high Renaissance polyphony in worship. He was a master of improvisation at the organ and was known for his improvisations on chant melodies. During the 1930s he taught at both Boston University and the New England Conservatory. At the Conservatory, Titcomb used the Catholic *Liber usalis* as a text and required students to sing chants in the original neumatic notation. A fixture at the summertime Wellesley Church Music Conferences, he lectured on liturgical music, choral worship practices, plainsong, and other sacred music-related subjects. Trevor Rea, who attended those conferences recalled later that "He was a genuinely devout man, and the music of the church was surely the most important thing in his life."[34]

A composer of eighty-four anthems, seventy-nine of which were published, and nine settings of the mass, Titcomb was proudest of his unaccompanied anthems in the motet style. His *Eight Motets*, published in 1934, are most distinctive and creative. Here Titcomb, who had immersed himself in the music of the medieval church, used techniques of first practice counterpoint to craft anthems for modern worship that evoked the mystical devotion of the historic liturgy. Titcomb's *Eight Motets* were short choral pieces intended to fit seamlessly into the liturgy. Of the eight, by far the most well-known is number six, "I will not leave you comfortless," a miniature masterpiece. It was selected to be performed at the annual choir festival at London's Crystal Palace in 1936, the first piece by an American to be so honored.[35]

---

34. Armstrong, "Legacy of Everett Titcomb," 92.

35. Unlike the music of many of Titcomb's contemporaries, "I will not leave you comfortless" is truly timeless. It should be a staple in every church choir library, and when sung provides a great opportunity to teach singers a forgotten vignette regarding American church music during the Depression era.

Leo Sowerby.
Image courtesy of the Leo Sowerby Foundation.

The most important church musician/composer to arise during the Depression era was Leo Sowerby (1895–1968). Born in Grand Rapids, Michigan, in 1895, Sowerby was the child of immigrants. His father John Sowerby was an Englishman who worked for the Post Office in Grand Rapids. Gertrude, his mother, was Canadian. She died when Leo was four years old, and John remarried a Dutch woman, Mary Hennink. It was Mary who recognized Leo's musical talent and encouraged him to begin piano lessons at the age of seven. Though Leo Sowerby would one day be regarded as among the nation's finest organists, he was entirely self-taught.

> Sowerby first became interested in the organ at the age of fifteen and, naturally enough, turned for advice to Calvin Lamport, who offered to give him lessons. There followed but six periods of instruction, for the organ practice fee of twenty-five cents an hour at Old South Congregational Church was beyond the pupil's means.... Rather than give up his new interest because of financial considerations, Sowerby devised a simple but ingenious method by which pedal technique could be acquired while acquainting himself with organ literature on his piano at home. Procuring a large sheet of brown wrapping paper from a nearby butcher shop, he returned to the church where he had been practicing and made an accurate sketch of the organ's straight pedal board. This dummy clavier, placed on the floor beneath his piano, became a highly original, if in some ways ineffective, substitute for work at an organ console or pedal piano.[36]

---

36. Huntington, "Study of the Musical Contributions," 10–11. As pointed out earlier, Dudley Buck used the same means as a youth to acquaint himself with pedal usage.

When the United States entered World War I in April of 1917, Sowerby tried to enlist but was rejected due to his poor eyesight. A second attempt to enlist was successful, however, and Private Leo Sowerby became a clarinetist in the 332nd Field Artillery Band, then stationed at Camp Grant near Chicago. Within months Sowerby's musicianship gained notice. He was quickly promoted to the rank of sergeant and made bandmaster. The war, however, ended in November of 1918 and in February of the following year Leo Sowerby was back in Chicago as organist/choirmaster at Fourth Presbyterian Church. One of his first acts was to compose an anthem, "The Risen Lord," which was sung for worship on Easter Day, April 20, 1919.[37]

In 1921, Leo Sowerby was awarded the first fellowship by the American Academy in Rome and studied abroad through 1924. He became full-time organist/choirmaster at St. James Episcopal Church, Chicago, in May of 1927. St. James Church had a remarkable history, as we have already seen in this study. Dudley Buck had served as organist there from 1869 until the Great Chicago Fire of 1872. Peter Christian Lutkin was organist/choirmaster from 1891 to 1897 and Clarence Dickinson from 1903 to 1909, just prior to his fateful move to New York City. The move to St. James impacted Sowerby both musically and spiritually. Sowerby found himself deeply and spiritually moved by the Episcopal liturgy.[38]

St. James Episcopal Church, later St. James Cathedral, would have Leo Sowerby as its organist/choirmaster from 1927 to 1962. Early on he wrote about his work there in *The American Organist*.

> I try to do the good things of all schools, avoiding all sentimental slush in the form of anthems, and keeping away as far as possible from the threadbare Victorian stuff used in so many churches, though the best of it—Wesley, for example[39]—is not beneath anyone's notice. Perhaps I lay a little more insistence than do some choirmasters on doing things written in our own day, but that would be natural for me to do. I know there are some who think I do some things in an unusual way (in the matter of tempi, etc.), but this, of course, is a matter of personal opinion to which everyone has his right.[40]

Over the course of his career Sowerby produced five sacred cantatas, seven anthems, eight works for solo organ, and six works for organ and

---

37. Huntington, "Study of the Musical Contributions," 23–24.

38. Huntington, "Study of the Musical Contributions," 34–35.

39. Sowerby is referring to the works of the nineteenth-century British composer and organist, Samuel Sebastian Wesley (1810–1876).

40. Quoted in Parks, *Critical Analysis of the Works of Leo Sowerby*, 8–9.

orchestra, including two concerti. His *Canticle of the Sun,* which received its debut at Carnegie Hall in 1945, was awarded the Pulitzer Prize. The work, like much of Sowerby's later output, is in a massive, heroic style that is both challenging and requiring a large and well-trained choral ensemble. His 1933 cantata *Great Is the Lord* is similar in concept.

In 1956 Sowerby was asked to prepare a position statement for the Joint Commission on Church Music of the Protestant Episcopal Church. He titled it *Ideals in Church Music,* and it represented a synthesis of what he had learned over a long and productive career. In *Ideals,* Sowerby enunciated important principles every church musician must confront. Music in worship, he felt, however useful it might be to inspire and edify, must always be subservient to the liturgy, a corporate act of worship and an offering to God.

> The purpose of music in worship, it has been said, is to strengthen the ideas and feelings that the worshipper already has and to release the mind from life's ordinary activities. This may be true, but it puts the accent in the wrong place—on the worshipper. In reality, music in worship is essentially a part of the corporate act of worship and a direct means of approach to God. Thus music, then, is not primarily a means of edifying or even inspiring the worshipper but is a part of his offering to the Deity.[41]

The role of choirs and choral music in Sowerby's eyes was consistent with this:

> The choir does not sing *to* the people, but the people come to take part in a corporate act of worship and praise. Too frequently, people do come to church with the idea of getting rather than of giving—giving themselves to their Maker and in service to their fellow man, as an act of dedication.[42]

Sowerby's antipathy toward the Victorian music then prevalent in much Episcopal worship has already been noted.

> It was only natural that our churches should have looked to England for their music, since that music was set to the language we knew . . . and since we had too few composers of our own

---

41. Sowerby, "Ideals in Church Music," 5. Here Sowerby seems to be echoing Kierkegaard's concept of "worship as theater." (See Kierkegaard, *Purity of the Heart Is to Will One Thing,* 181.) Kierkegaard notes that much worship is performed as if God were the prompter, the clergy were actors, and the congregation functions as the audience. For true worship to take place, according to Kierkegaard, the clergy are prompters, those in the pews are the actors, and God is the audience. In other words, worship requires full participation with all directed to God.

42. Sowerby, "Ideals in Church Music," 17.

of any degree of excellence or fame. It was unfortunate that the music we took over—and we took it right heartily—should have been the music of Barnby, Stainer, and the Victorian school, for it is this music and the American imitators of it—rather worse for the imitating—that retarded, and in some quarters is still retarding, the development of the appreciation for what is most proper and fitting in the Church's music . . . It continues to be the staple offering of many of our American churches . . .[43]

Sowerby had mixed feelings about the effect of Anglo-Catholic ritualism on the music of the church. Oxford Movement ritualism, he believed, had inspired a renaissance of church music in the United States in the nineteenth century through its focus on historic liturgy and ritual. The movement, in his eyes however, stifled musical creativity. "The implication," he wrote, "is that there is no hope for growth and that music cannot and shall not be reflective of the changes that time imposes."[44] It was a grievance composers of sacred music would continue to voice: that the church with its unbending adherence to protocol and tradition stifled creativity.

Citing the writings of his friend David McK. Williams, Sowerby said that "proper church music" must meet three essential criteria. First, it must inspire devotion in the devout, whether or not they are musical. At the same time, however, it must uplift the musical person, whether or not they be devout.[45] There also should be absolutely no doubt that music in worship was *sacred* music. "It should be quite evident that profane and worldly influences should be eliminated." He immediately contradicts this powerful and direct statement by saying, "It is not demanding too much to expect that it [i.e., church music] shall be of the same standard of excellence as that of music heard in the concert hall."[46]

One senses that for Sowerby, his career as a church musician required finding a balance between artistry and servanthood. He prided himself in being a modern composer and, over the course of his career, chose unbridled creativity over the practicalities of work in church music. He did not apologize for this. "There has always been modern music," he wrote. "The art one generation calls new or modern comes to be accepted generally by the following generation, and it has always been so."[47] He had little patience for critics.

---

43. Sowerby, "Ideals in Church Music," 11.
44. Sowerby, "Ideals in Church Music," 12–13.
45. Sowerby, "Ideals in Church Music," 5–6.
46. Sowerby, "Ideals in Church Music," 6.
47. Sowerby, "Ideals in Church Music," 14.

Many churchgoers of today use the term "modern music" to refer disparagingly to an idiom as yet unfamiliar to them. These people "know what they like," as the old saying goes, and it always turns out that they like what they are accustomed to. If they are not accustomed to fine church music, it is the fault of the musician in charge and of the clergyman whose deputy he is.[48]

Sowerby was uncompromising in the demands he placed on organists and choral ensembles. At the same time, the balance between artistic integrity and ministry he sought is the same balance all church musicians must seek. To ignore either should always be unacceptable.

The organist and professor of church music at Wheaton College, Harold M. Best,[49] wrote of Sowerby:

> Beauty cannot equal truth. Every church musician must therefore pray that the two will be congruent in his ministry, through the upward call of the Word and the pressing on of artistic activity. Certainly, there have been excelling church musicians who have not subscribed to this, but there have been and are some who have edged delightfully close. God allows men at cross purpose with him to do beautiful things, but it is always necessary to distinguish between man's heart and man's art. While the former is uniquely God's business, the latter is ours . . .

> Those who make up the body of Christ have the right to pray for gifted artists and fearlessly welcome those whom God leads into the width and celebration of their worship. From all that can be gathered, Sowerby was gracious, self-giving, and humble. In the words of the Very Reverend Francis H. Sayre, Jr., at a memorial service for him in 1968, "his whole being was a psalm . . ."[50]

The Hymnal 1940

It bears repeating that prior to 1916, there was no single authorized musical edition of the Episcopal hymnal. Instead, there was a plethora of independently produced tunebooks. The first authorized denominational hymnal

---

48. Sowerby, "Ideals in Church Music," 17.

49. Harold M. Best (bn. 1931) was graduated with an SMD degree from Union Theological Seminary School of Sacred Music. He has been active as a church musician and is the former dean of the Conservatory of Music of Wheaton College. He served as president of the National Association of Schools of Music (NASM) in the 1980s.

50. Best, "Leo Sowerby."

with music was *The Hymnal of the Protestant Episcopal Church*, often referred to as the "1916 hymnal" because that was the year the General Convention accepted the initial draft. In actuality, the work on the hymnal was not completed until 1918, with the musical edition published in 1920.

The 1916 hymnal was a distinct improvement over its predecessors. It included much standard classic hymnody still in regular use and introduced several hymn settings by the then still living Boston composer, Horatio Parker. Nevertheless, the hymnal was weighted down with Victorian hymns. Characteristic of many such hymns was a cloying sentimentality or a triumphalism smacking of British colonialism.

By the 1930s, it had become obvious that a new hymnal was needed. Canon C. Winfred Douglas, who had helped edit the 1916 hymnal, was chosen to chair a hymnal revision commission for the *Hymnal 1940*. Serving with him on the commission were, among others, David Mck. Williams and Leo Sowerby. Douglas made a huge contribution to the hymnal, either translating or co-translating twelve classic hymn texts, providing two hymn tunes of his own, and arranging eighteen others. He also provided two settings of the communion service drawing from plainsong sources. Sowerby and McK. Williams were likewise well represented: Sowerby with two original hymn tunes and three carol arrangements; Mck. Williams with six original hymn tunes. The *Hymnal 1940* stands along with Henry Ward Beecher's *Plymouth Hymnal* as a landmark in American church music history. It provided a model for other denominational hymnals for almost two decades after World War II and made customary the singing of a wealth of classic hymnody from German chorales, Genevan psalm tunes, and plainsong melodies to modern classics by Ralph Vaughan Williams and others.

The Broadman Hymnal, a Milestone for the Evangelical Wing

As important as the *Hymnal 1940* was as a model for classic hymnals of the mainline traditional denominations, one must remember that the largest Protestant denomination in the United States during the 1930s and '40s was the white and evangelical Southern Baptist Convention. During the depression years, Southern Baptists used a variety of commercially produced hymnals in both shape- and round-note notation. The popular James Vaughan and Stamps-Baxter collections, however, were sometimes identified with Pentecostalism. Moreover, the newer gospel tunes constantly being added to generate sales held little interest for older traditional Southern Baptist congregations.

B. B. McKinney.
Public domain image. (https://www.findagrave.com/memorial/11312825/baylus-benjamin-mckinney)

Baylus Benjamin McKinney (1886–1952) was a successful gospel song writer, evangelistic singer, teacher, and music editor. Musically he was well-educated, holding a degree from the Bush Conservatory of Music in Chicago and seminary training from Southwestern Baptist Theological Seminary, Fort Worth, where he taught voice, harmony, and composition in its School of Sacred Music from 1919 to 1931. In 1935, McKinney was appointed music editor for the Baptist Sunday School Board and in 1941 he was made secretary of the newly created Department of Church Music.

It was under McKinney's leadership that the decision was made to authorize a standard hymnal for use in all Southern Baptist churches. Baptist music historian William J. Reynolds theorized that McKinney, from the start of his work with the Sunday School Board, had "carried in his heart his dream of publishing a major collection of hymns and gospel songs."[51] While he apparently did a survey of music directors across the South and may have had a committee to assist him, the *Broadman Hymnal* was largely a McKinney creation.

> Surely no one in 1940 could have predicted how phenomenally successful The Broadman Hymnal would be in the years ahead,

---

51. Reynolds, "Contributions of B. B. McKinney," 45.

or the extent to which it would have a positive influence on the congregational singers in Southern Baptist churches. Even with its unusual inclusion of several choral works and a substantial number of solos and duets, it was largely because of the gospel songs and the standard hymns that the Board's new product became a unifying force for congregational singing.[52]

Several features of the *Broadman Hymnal* are noteworthy. The hymnal was published in both round- and shape-note notation, making it eminently marketable and competitive with the Vaughan and Stamps-Baxter books. Its contents included core hymnody from traditional and evangelical American Protestantism: "A Mighty Fortress," "How Firm a Foundation," and "All Hail the Power of Jesus' Name," for example. Eleven Isaac Watts hymns, eight by Charles Wesley, and a selection of well-known Christmas carols appeared. While many gospel songs of the Moody/Sankey era were over fifty years old in 1940, McKinney's choices show a preference for even older selections. Nine hymns of W. B. Bradbury are listed and sixteen by Fanny Crosby. Sankey, Excell, and Gabriel are represented by only fourteen hymns between them.

The makeup of the *Broadman Hymnal* reflected a tension that still exists among established evangelical denominations between moderately liturgical, spoken word-centered worship, and the unbounded freedom of the Pentecostals. Its contents, a mix of traditional and cherished Protestant hymnody with older gospel repertoire, were perfectly suited to the time.

Depression Era Advancement of Sacred Music Education

By 1930 it had become commonly accepted that purely performance-based music instruction was insufficient if musicians were to be trained for ministry in the church. Theretofore, the only denominational schools offering degrees in sacred music had been affiliated with the Baptist church and were largely focused on gospel music. The sacred music curriculums of Westminster Choir College, Union Theological Seminary School of Sacred Music, and a number of other schools would change the face of American church music for the decades after World War II. David McK. Williams and C. Winfred Douglas taught at Union and Everett Titcomb at the New England Conservatory. Leo Sowerby was a long-time professor at the American Conservatory in Chicago and the founding director of the College of Church Musicians at Washington's Nation Cathedral in the 1960s. Both Union and

---

52. Fields, "Hymns and Gospel Songs."

Westminster, each affiliated with prestigious seminaries, were founded in the prosperous 1920s and managed to survive the Great Depression.

At UTS during the Depression, the seminary faculty had to take a 20 percent reduction in salary. The music school, at the urging of seminary president Henry Sloane Coffin, however, was allowed to continue operations at a deficit.[53] From the first, several core subjects were required of UTS church music students. Included were history of sacred music, the musical numbers in the great liturgies, hymnology, plainsong, and history of sacred art. A conscious effort was always placed on the "interdenominational" aspect of the school by exposing students to traditions and worship practices beyond mainline Protestantism and Roman Catholicism to those of less familiar faiths. It was common for Jewish, Eastern Orthodox, Roman Catholic, Lutheran, Calvinist, Anglican, Reformed, and "free" church musicians and clergy to be brought in to lead classes and seminars.[54] Courses related to choral music in the church included semester-long courses in choral organization and training, conducting, and choral score analysis. Specialized classes devoted to boy choir training, mixed children's choir training, and music in the church school were also offered.

Applied instruction in both organ and voice was central to the curriculum of the UTS School of Sacred Music. When the school opened there were only two pipe organs on campus for practice, one in the seminary chapel and one in a classroom. A third instrument was added soon thereafter. According to Ellouise Skinner, for a rapidly growing student body, among whom eight out of ten students were organ majors, this was a problem.[55] Organ students were provided instruction in conducting from the console, adapting piano and orchestral scores to the organ, hymn-playing, and sacred organ repertoire. Classes in voice were required of all music students at UTS. "We do not expect to make soloists out of all our organists," Clarence Dickinson observed, "but we do expect all our organists to learn how to sing decently and correctly and be able to pass this on to their choirs." In addition, applied voice lessons were required of voice majors.[56]

UTS was distinctive in its requirement of theological training for church musicians. Initially these were from the seminary curriculum, but over the years specialized classes designed especially for church musicians

---

53. Skinner, *Sacred Music at Union*, 30.

54. Skinner, *Sacred Music at Union*, 37.

55. Skinner, *Sacred Music at Union*, 45. According to Skinner, by the 1950s there were seven practice organs on the UTS campus, hardly enough for the large student body. Fortunately, students were required to work in a church during their time in UTS, which gave many of them access to off-campus instruments.

56. Skinner, *Sacred Music at Union*, 38.

were added. One sixth or ten semester hours of class work were required to earn a master of sacred music degree at UTS. Students enrolling in the program during its early days were directed to choose between courses in Bible, church history, and religious education. Classes in church polity or governance and liturgics were also included. Virtually all courses offered in the School of Sacred Music were open to divinity students as well, but the administrations of the two schools were never able to agree on any music course requirements for seminarians.[57] "The school's curriculum reflected Dickinson's belief that the church musician was to be a churchman or churchwoman, not simply a hired musician. . . . [The master of sacred music degree] was not primarily a theological degree, it was a musical degree with a theological emphasis placed within the context of a seminary environment."[58] Robert Baker, a graduate of the School of Sacred Music who replaced Dickinson as dean, recalled, "We were to be servants of the church, servants of the art, and to do all that we possibly could to make worship within the church worthy of the calling."[59]

Dickinson biographer Stephen Garner noted that in the aftermath of the stock market crash in the fall of 1929, many students' families were devastated financially. Dickinson was known to have personally covered the cost of a student's tuition and music lessons that their studies might continue.[60]

The School of Sacred Music faculty included some of the most prominent leaders in the sacred music of the twentieth century. These included: Searle Wright, Robert Crandell, David McK. Williams, and Seth Bingham, instructors in organ; C. Winfred Douglas teaching courses on chant and liturgical subjects; the composer Harold Friedell; H. Beckett Gibbs, boys' and children's choir methods; and of course, Clarence Dickinson himself.

For Westminster, the onslaught of the Depression came at a particularly critical time in the school's history. The Choir College, then located on the campus of the Ithaca Conservatory of Music in New York State, had expanded to a four-year curriculum. It conferred its first bachelor's degrees in 1930. WCC soon outgrew the space allotted to it at Ithaca and in 1932,

---

57. The mainline denominational seminaries continue to treat sacred music education and related subjects haphazardly, and uninformed pastoral leadership was often a factor crippling music ministry.

58. Weadon, "Clarence Dickinson," 431. David Allan Weadon died prematurely in 1996 at the age of thirty-nine. He had been organist at Brick Church, organist/choirmaster at Riverside Church, and director of music at the Princeton Theological Seminary.

59. Garner, *Clarence Dickinson*, 115.

60. Garner, *Clarence Dickinson*, 112–13.

at the depth of the Depression, a fateful decision was made to move the college to Princeton, New Jersey. Classes were held at first in a mix of nearby churches and buildings on the Princeton University campus, while options for permanent placement were explored. In 1934 the Westminster Choir—just returning from a major tour of Europe—sang for commencement at Princeton Seminary. Rhea Williamson recalled the encounter, which would wed the Westminster Choir College to the campus of Princeton University for decades to come:

> At the Seminary Commencement for which our choir sang, Mrs. Sophia Taylor of Cleveland, Ohio sat next to me and asked me if Jack [i.e., John Finley Williamson] and I would have dinner with her that evening at the Princeton Inn. We had met her only once before briefly, but she liked the way our choir was received and had listened weekly to our broadcasts with Mr. Walter Damrosch. We met her at the Inn, were seated and served our soup course when she said, "I want to give you four hundred thousand dollars with which to build your college buildings"—and this in the heart of the Depression with banks closed and bread lines everywhere. Then she added, "I want to give it to you tonight. I have a heart that may take me to glory anytime." Well, we called the presidents of two banks, every real estate man in town, who came hurrying . . .[61]

Thanks to that lavish gift from the department store heiress and philanthropist, Sophia Strong Taylor (1861–1936), Westminster Choir College was able to move to its own campus in 1934. A long-term association with Princeton Seminary provided a valuable interchange between church musicians and seminarians, which would be a model for college-level church music education for years to come. Once in Princeton, the Choir College's curriculum was once again expanded to include graduate level training, and Westminster's first master of sacred music (MSM) degrees were awarded in 1936.

Joseph G. Beck, a former Williamson student and disciple, evoked what it must have been like for incoming freshmen experiencing their first opening assembly at the Choir College. "The school formally opened each year with the student body and faculty attending a service in the college chapel . . . You can imagine how impressive and thrilling it was to hear for the first time the student body raising their voices in song . . . The hymns

---

61. Williamson, "My Career," 28.

were led by Dr. Williamson and accompanied by Alexander McCurdy on the magnificent Aeolian Skinner organ."[62]

Like UTS, Westminster Choir College had an outstanding faculty. In addition to Williamson, there were George Krueger, who would later found the "Singing Hoosiers" at Indiana University, Henry Pfohl, who would go on to be director of music at Brooklyn's fabled Plymouth Church, and John Kemp. All taught subjects related to choral and sacred music. Instructors in organ included Alexander McCurdy, Carl Weinrich, David Hugh Jones, and C. Harold Eineke.

Thanks to the quality of instruction at Union and Westminster and the fact that they were nonsectarian, students ranged across all the mainline denominations. Prominent among the male graduates of the School of Sacred Music in the 1930s and '40s were:

Donald Allured, handbell pioneer (MSM, 1947)
Walter Buszin, composer and Lutheran pastor (MSM, 1937)
W. Lawrence Curry (MSM, 1931; SMD, 1945)
Donald D. Kettering (MSM, 1931)
Robert S. Baker, future dean of UTS School of Sacred Music (MSM, 1940; SMD, 1944)

Olaf Christiansen, choral conductor/composer (MSM, 1940)
Austin Lovelace, organist/composer (MSM, 1941)
V. Earle Copes, composer (MSM, 1944)
Hugh Porter (SMD, 1944)
T. Charles Lee, composer (SMD, 1945)[63]

Well-known male graduates of Westminster during the period in question included the composer George Lynn (1938), and conductor/composer Warren Martin (1936).

Graduates of Westminster and Union, however, were not limited to men. While women had had opportunities for training in applied music since the 1890s—particularly performance degrees in piano and organ—sacred music training had been limited to denominational seminaries that only admitted men. The founding of the School of Sacred Music and Westminster Choir College was a watershed for women who wished to pursue a career as church musicians. At UTS, of the 278 individuals graduating between 1930 and 1946, 112 were women.[64] During the same period Westminster Choir College graduated 304 women with degrees in music

---

62. Beck, *America's Choral Ambassador*, 42–43.

63. Degree designations: MSM—Master of Sacred Music; SMD—Doctor of Sacred Music

64. Figures drawn from Tryon, ed., *Union Theological Seminary in the City of New York Alumni Catalogue, 1836–1947*.

education, organ performance, vocal performance, choral conducting, and church music.[65] Roberta Bitgood (1908–2007), who received her master's in sacred music from UTS in 1935 and her doctorate in 1945, was the first female doctor of sacred music in American history. She went on to an impressive career as a composer and was the first female president of the American Guild of Organists. Other distinguished female graduates from UTS included composers Nancy Poore Tufts, Ruth Bampton, and Eunice Lea Kettering. Elaine Brown, the fabled director of Philadelphia's "Singing City," received her bachelor's degree from Westminster in 1934 and received her master's there in 1945. Helen Kemp, possibly the most important authority on children's music in the second half of the twentieth century, graduated from the Choir College and taught on the faculty there. Moreover, on John Finley Williamson's insistence, a significant number of African Americans were graduates, including the Black soprano and founder of the Harlem School of the Arts Dorothy Maynor (1910–1996), and the composer Julia Perry.

The student bodies of the Union Theological Seminary School of Sacred Music and Westminster Choir College also represented a cross section of American Protestantism. Presbyterians were well represented given that denomination's ties to both seminaries. Episcopalians, Methodists, and American Baptists too would draw much music leadership from graduates of the two schools. The Southern Baptist Church, as previously noted, had its own seminary-affiliated schools of sacred music, but even they were impacted by the work done at Union and Westminster. The Rev. Ellis A. Fuller (1891–1950), pastor of Atlanta's First Baptist Church, had been an early admirer of John Finley Williamson and embraced his concept of graded choir programs, a concept passionately advocated through Westminster's curriculum. Fuller hired Westminster graduates Donald and Frances Winters to lead the music program at his Atlanta church in 1941. Later, at Fuller's encouragement, the Winters moved to Louisville, Kentucky, where they spearheaded the founding of the School of Church Music of Southern Baptist Theological Seminary.[66] In part because of Ellis Fuller's influence, graded choirs—primary, elementary, intermediate, and youth—would become ubiquitous in Southern Baptist churches in the 1950s. Alice Berman, another Westminster graduate, arrived at Charlotte, North Carolina's Myers Park Baptist Church in 1943 and later established the Charlotte Choral Society.

---

65. Figures provided to the author by Natalie M. Pollard, director of Alumni Relations, Ryder University, May 6, 2021.

66. Reynolds, "Baptists, Music, and World War II."

The Coming of War

The realization that the United States would most likely become enmeshed in the global crisis of World War II came well before December of 1941. The inevitability of US involvement was further augured by the institution of the draft or Selective Training and Service Act of 1940, which required all men between the ages of twenty-one and forty-five to register.

The war, of course, would be extremely taxing on church music programs. Everett Titcomb at the Church of St. John the Evangelist, like many church musicians, saw his choir shrink. By 1944, Titcomb had only two men still singing in his choir. The rest had all enlisted. To commemorate their sacrifice, he composed a "Victory Te Deum," dedicated "To the organists, choir directors, and singers—now serving in the Armed Forces of the Nation, with a prayer for their safe return . . ."[67]

Church music historian Talmage W. Dean actually was attending classes on the Princeton campus during the war and recalled the pallor the conflict put on campus life at Westminster Choir College:

> World War II was difficult for all schools of the arts, and Westminster was no exception. While enrolled in a special military training school of Princeton University, I was privileged to attend the First Presbyterian Church where Dr. Williamson was directing a very small choir and to attend the Princeton Chapel where Carl Weinrich was organist. There were many echoes of the pre-war vespers and choral activities, but . . . the emergence of church music as an academic discipline and church ministry was hardly imaginable during those bleak years.[68]

The sheer immensity of the war effort begged comparison with the Civil War. Approximately three-quarters of all US males between the ages of twenty and twenty-nine enlisted.[69]

Soldiers had the most opportunities to worship regularly when stationed stateside. During the military build-up prior to Pearl Harbor, hundreds of military chapels were constructed. Congress had authorized twelve million dollars for chapel construction on army bases. Ten thousand chaplains, drawn from each of the mainline Protestant denominations as well as Judaism and Roman Catholicism, were recruited to serve over the course of the war. Each one was responsible for organizing services each week in the dominant faith traditions—Protestant and Roman Catholic—plus

---

67. Armstrong, "Legacy of Everett Titcomb" (diss.), 129.
68. Dean, *Survey of Twentieth Century Protestant Church Music*, 191.
69. Walters, "Beyond the Battle," 3, 11–12.

officiating in a third service in whichever denomination they had been ordained. Still, soldiers could find it challenging to find worship based on their religious preference. Further complicating things was the segregation of African Americans, which still existed in the military. While the Army had appointed over three hundred Black chaplains, it was not always possible to find one. Seating in regimental worship tended to be segregated, and in many cases, Blacks were excluded entirely.[70]

Once soldiers shipped out for distant fields of conflict, as in the Civil War, when and how worship was celebrated could vary. Worship, if dependent upon the presence of chaplains, often took place on days other than Sunday. In the South Pacific, whatever day worship was to occur was referred to as "G. I. Sunday" regardless of when it was during the week.[71] There was a practical reason for this as well. The Office of War Information encouraged moving religious observances around as it "made it difficult for the Japanese to schedule an attack knowingly on a day when U. S. troops might be less prepared."[72] The Sunday morning surprise attack on Pearl Harbor was a painful reminder of what could occur.

Worship did take place, of course. Captain Charles P. Roland, who later became a distinguished professor of history at the University of Kentucky, remembered a stormy crossing of the English Channel in an LST[73] with his unit just three weeks after D-Day.

> The most memorable event of the crossing was a Sunday morning worship service the first day out. It was conducted by my battalion chaplain, First Lt. Edwin Hampton, down in the ship's tank hold. The altar from which he spoke and served the elements of Communion rested on the hood of a jeep. The soldier audience sat in vehicles or half-sat leaning against the barrels of cannons, which stood like silent, menacing beasts awaiting their prey . . . The chaplain spoke briefly and quietly, but with deep emotion, of the mighty crusade on which we were engaged. He called it a worthy cause, blessed by heaven. Then elevating his right hand in a gesture of beatitude, he said, "The Lord be with you and keep you. The Lord give you strength in the day of battle."[74]

---

70. Walters, "Beyond the Battle," 51–52, 55.
71. "Chaplains Surmount Obstacles in Reaching Lonely Outposts," 7.
72. Walters, "Beyond the Battle," 60.
73. The LSTs or "Landing Ship, Tanks" were ships designed to support amphibious operations by carrying tanks, vehicles, cargo, and landing troops directly onto the shores with no dock or pier.
74. Roland, *My Odyssey Through History*, 46.

Tragically, Chaplain Hampton was killed six weeks later during an artillery barrage. He was standing next to Roland's jeep.[75]

Music was often the most spiritual aspect of such services and was fondly remembered by veterans. John Hogan, an army private who later died in battle on Okinawa, remembered a Christmas Eve spent in Hawaii after fighting in the Aleutian Islands.

> You can picture ten or fifteen of us "rugged" soldiers gathered around in our tent singing "Away in a Manger." As we sang, my eyes traveled around the tent walls where our rifles hung in readiness as grim reminders of the world as it is. And I thought how completely and infinitely greater is the power of Christ than the power of the world, and of the symbol of the manger that will endure in time long after war and destruction and material things have passed away. I know that the cradle will outlast the cannon.[76]

When organists and choirmasters enlisted, many were assigned to nonmusical duties within the services. Lieutenant Herbert B. Nanney, organist at the First Congregational Church of Los Angeles and later on the music faculty at Stanford University, was assigned to a medical battalion in France.[77] Nevertheless, choral and organ music were a welcome diversion from the anxieties of wartime service, and *The Diapason* regularly reported on organists serving at military base chapels. Despite stringent black-out regulations in Hawaii, organist R. Kenneth Holt was able to perform recitals for the troops stationed there in darkened sanctuaries using only ambient light from the moon filtering in the windows. Resourcefully, he had recital programs printed in silver ink on black paper.[78]

Choirs were also organized among the recruits wherever practicable. Military base chapels usually had organized ensembles, especially stateside. Camp Lejeune in North Carolina had an excellent choir. For one thing, attending church was one of the few ways young women could leave the restricted women's area of the camp to be with the opposite sex. The sexes could commingle even more closely by joining the choir.[79] Even in less forgiving circumstances, choral groups were organized. A Red Cross volunteer, Jean Holdridge Reeves, wrote to her parents about worship on a troop ship

---

75. Walters, "Beyond the Battle," 49.
76. Hogan, *I Am Not Alone*, 38.
77. Woolley, "Lieutenant Nanny in Recital," 10.
78. "Organ Music Popular with Pacific Forces," 13.
79. Walters, "Beyond the Battle," 57.

headed for New Guinea. "We sing in the choir with very little practice—don't bother [with] the high-style singing—just the song book variety."[80]

Of the many trials and sacrifices experienced by church musicians during the Second World War, those of Richard Purvis (1913–1994) were memorable. Purvis, one of the more prominent American organists and church music composers of the twentieth century, enlisted in the US Army on June 20, 1942, and was stationed at Fort Meade in Maryland.[81] While there he served as a clerk and organist to the base chaplain. He also organized a choir to assist with regimental worship services. Because of Purvis's musical proclivities, he was soon assigned for training at the Army Music School in Arlington, Virginia. Paul Calloway, who would become the famed organist at Washington's National Cathedral, was a fellow student with Purvis during training at Arlington.[82]

In May of 1943, Richard Purvis graduated with honors and was made bandmaster for the Army 28th Infantry Division. In that capacity, he and his musicians marched in the celebration marking the liberation of Paris in August of 1944.[83] On November 10 of that year, Purvis and the band were present on the front lines during a massive German attack, part of what is now known as the Battle of the Bulge. Bandsmen were commanded to put aside their instruments and fight the brutal onslaught. Many of them were killed. Purvis was captured and imprisoned at the notorious Stalag 13B, where he would remain until the war ended. While Purvis never talked about his experiences in detail, he suffered from starvation and the filthy conditions of the camp and may have been tortured. Upon his return to the states, he underwent months of rehabilitation to restore strength to his hands. In February of 1947, Purvis was called to be organist at San Francisco's Grace Cathedral where he would have a storied twenty-four-year career.

Evangelism in World War II

The parallels between America's Civil War and the Second World War are striking. This is especially true with regard to evangelistic efforts that began in time of war but affected American Christianity long after peace was declared.

Ministry to children had long been a focus of Sunday schools and Christian education, but with thousands of men and women in their late

---

80. Walters, "Beyond the Battle," 209.
81. Welch, *Richard Purvis, Organist of Grace*, 81.
82. Welch, *Richard Purvis, Organist of Grace*, 83.
83. Welch, *Richard Purvis, Organist of Grace*, 83.

teens and twenties being recruited to fight in a foreign war, ministry to older youth and young adults now took precedence. Mainline denominations in the 1940s tended to support the Service Men's Christian League, the equivalent of the United States Christian Commission of the Civil War era. Established in 1942 at the outset of hostilities, its primary focus was providing devotional literature and other material support to the military chaplaincy. Conservative Protestants, on the other hand, seeking a more aggressive emphasis on evangelistic witness, preferred to work with emerging organizations like Youth for Christ.

Of the various religious movements to come out of World War II, by far the most influential regarding American sacred music was Youth for Christ. From the late 1930s on, revivalistic activities had been mounted to attract young people in major cities including New York, Philadelphia, Chicago, and Los Angeles. As with all the earlier revivals, attendees were encouraged to commit their lives to Christ, but there was a deliberate effort to avoid the appearance of church services. They featured "popular [Christian] music, short attention-grabbing skits, and . . . brief, clear sermons in everyday language on the concerns of young people."[84] In 1944, the movement coalesced into the founding of Youth for Christ. Chicago minister Torrey M. Johnson was made president, and a young, unknown evangelist from North Carolina—Billy Graham—was made its full-time evangelist.

Reproduced from "The Story of the Far Eastern Bible Institute and Seminary." Pamphlet. St. Paul, MN: Lincoln Printing, n.d. (https://www2.wheaton.edu/bgc/archives/bulletin/bu1203) Courtesy of Wheaton Archives & Special Collections, Wheaton College, IL.

---

84. "Greatest Youth Gathering in History, Background."

Evangelistic gatherings, both informal and formally organized, were common across the US military during World War II. Word of the success of the Youth for Christ movement quickly reached troops overseas. An Army nurse, Lieutenant Alice Schmidt, wrote of the weekly evangelistic meetings being held in the Philippines called G. I. Gospel Hours. "The singing set the rafters ringing and many accepted Christ as their personal Savior, truly, a bit of heaven here on earth."[85] A leader of the G. I. Gospel Hour meetings provided further details:

> The GIs came from all sorts of denominations—in fact, denominations were hardly mentioned. It was a mighty revelation of what great things could be done for the Lord when all worked together for a single purpose, the *salvation of souls*.[86]

Similar evangelistic activities were held on the military base on Guam. There, Cornelius Van der Breggen, a chemical officer who helped lead the rallies, "purposefully deemphasized identity with particular denominations or even churches because he felt that such emphasis confused people about the path to salvation. Rather than salvation through affiliation, he stressed salvation through an individual relationship with Jesus Christ."[87]

Wartime and the Manufacture of Organs and Keyboard Instruments

The impact of World War II was felt acutely by the piano and pipe organ industries. Most pipe organ manufacturers had to suspend production since the metal needed for pipework had been diverted for battlefield materiel, and their very specialized industry did not lend itself to being retooled to manufacture implements of war. A 1945 article in *The Diapason* provides a helpful overview of the situation:

> Efforts on the part of organ and piano manufacturers to obtain war contracts continue to be largely unsuccessful because of the types of military items that can be made with the facilities and labor on hand in the industry are extremely limited, members of the organ manufacturers', piano manufacturers', and piano supplies industry advisory committees emphasized at a recent joint meeting. Only pianos and organs for the armed forces, glider spars and other aircraft parts for which the woodworking

---

85. Walters, "Beyond the Battle," 210.
86. "Story of the Far Eastern Bible Institute and Seminary."
87. Walters, "Beyond the Battle," 211.

facilities of a small percentage of the industry are adaptable, and, to a limited extent, tools and tow ropes and slings for the army transportation corps are the principal types of war items now being made in the industry . . .[88]

Nonetheless, there was a need for portable keyboard instruments in base chapels and in the theater of conflict. The Estey Organ Company, which had been forced into bankruptcy during the Great Depression, was able to reform itself as the principal manufacturer of folding organs for the US Army Chaplain's Corps. These small but functional reed organs folded into wooden shipping crates when not in use and for transport. The organ had a four-octave keyboard, a treadle-activated bellows, and, in its crate equipped with leather carrying straps, weighed only one hundred pounds. Estey advertised the organ as "a treasure for missionaries or traveling singers" and "easily transported and always adequate." [89]

Estey Folding Organ.
Public domain image. (https://offerup.com/item/detail/49992185)

Meanwhile, Steinway contracted with the government to produce thousands of Victory Verticals. They were miniature upright pianos, "hardy enough to withstand the trying conditions out in the field—including being packed into a crate and dropped out of a plane." The Verticals were designed without legs, which would have been snapped off in air drops. They were built with water-resistant glue and insect-repellant materials, and painted olive green. The small pianos were designed to contain only a tenth as much metal as a normal piano and weighed about 455 pounds. Handholds built into them made it possible for four servicemen to easily carry

---

88. "Outlook for Organs in 1945 Not Hopeful," 2.
89. "Chaplain's Folding Organ, Model 42" (The Estey Organ Museum).

the instruments to and from playing locations. By war's end, about 2,500 Victory Vertical pianos were in use by the US military.[90]

GIs relaxing around a Steinway Victory Vertical.
Public domain image. (https://www.messengernews.net/life/local-lifestyle/2019/06/the-steinway-victory-vertical-piano-project)

The Long-Term Impact of the Second World War on Church Music in America

World War II affected church music and ministry in myriad ways extending well into the 1960s. Just as in the Civil War, the substantial military build-up resulted in an economic watershed for the nation. Returning combatants were anxious to resume normal lives and start families. This led to the greatest birth increase in American history and the so-called baby boomer generation. This return to normalcy also resulted in explosive growth among the mainline denominations. Pipe organ manufacture resumed at its prewar levels. Choir lofts often had to be expanded to handle the increased numbers wishing to sing. For composers of sacred music, it would be a time of peak creativity.

The war officially ended with the signing of formal surrender documents between the Allies and Japan on the *USS Missouri* on September 2, 1945, but the work of evangelism, which had gained in urgency during the conflict, continued. Youth for Christ would become a national and international phenomenon, and Billy Graham would witness to millions through his crusades. Aided by broadcast media, recordings, and later television, the line between sacred music and popular culture would become ever more blurred.

---

90. Lee, "When the Pianos Went to War."

CHAPTER 19

SACRED MUSIC IN THE POST-WAR ERA, 1946 TO 1965

Return to Peacetime, 1945–1950

WITH THE TREATY OF Paris in February of 1947, marking the formal end of World War II, and the Marshall Plan to provide relief to war-torn Europe, the United States took on the role of a global superpower, brimming with confidence and wealth. There was a deep desire, not just to relish the peacetime, but to recapture the normalcy of pre-Depression days. Returning military personnel were, of course, eager to marry, purchase homes, and grow families, and this is amply evidenced by statistics from the era. The US birthrate had soared by 1950 to an all-time high of twenty-four babies per one-thousand women.[1] The resulting "baby boom generation," as it approached adulthood in the 1960s, would be a key driving force in determining the future of American church music.

For a large percentage of Americans, raising a family in a proper home presupposed active participation in a church. Between 1945 and 1950, money spent for new church construction went from $26 million to $409 million. Between 1955 and 1958 church membership peaked at 47 percent of all Americans. The Protestant Episcopal Church grew from 2.5 million members in 1946 to 3.1 million in 1950; the Methodists, from 8.9 to 9.8 million; the Presbyterians, 2.3 to 3.1 million; and Southern Baptists, from

---

1. Carnes, ed., *Columbia History of Post-World War II America*, 22.

7 to 9.4 million.[2] Fastest growing of all was the Roman Catholic Church, bringing in a million new members in 1950 alone.[3]

> All of this was set against a distinctive fifties cultural milieu dominated by the immense fact of the recently ended Second World War and what it meant for the United States: a new post-war affluence, a younger and rapidly growing population, . . . the great internal migration to the suburbs, a typical post-war interest in traditional and religious values, and the shadow cast by the United States' new post-war status as a world power in conflict with communism.[4]

Regrettably, the Allied victory did nothing to end the class and caste divisions that had plagued America from the earliest days.

Charles C. Hirt, a Choral and Sacred Music Giant of the Post-War Era

Any listing of the pantheon of great choral conductors of the twentieth century will most assuredly include a Robert Shaw, a Williamson, the Christiansens, a Roger Wagner, and perhaps a Joseph Flummerfelt. One name likely to be missing, however, is that of Charles Carleton Hirt (1911–2001). Physically, Hirt was an imposing presence, and the scope of his contributions as a conductor, teacher, musicologist, and church musician are almost mythic in proportion. Yet, he was not prone to self-promotion and perhaps that is why his work has been habitually overlooked.

A native of Glendale, California, Hirt received his undergraduate training in education in English and music from Occidental College in 1934. After a number of years of successful public school and community college teaching, Hirt in 1941 became director of music at the First Presbyterian Church of Hollywood, or Hollywood Presbyterian. He would remain in that position for thirty years and build one of the most remarkable music ministries in the United States. Four hundred singers spread over five choirs—two adult and five for children and youth—were participating in the program at any given time. It was a flagship example of the Westminster Plan put into action and as such, served as a model for church music programs across the nation.[5]

---

2. Elwood, *Fifties Spiritual Marketplace*, 5.
3. Elwood, *Fifties Spiritual Marketplace*, 23.
4. Elwood, *Fifties Spiritual Marketplace*, 6.
5. Stewart, "Charles C. Hirt," 20.

Charles and Lucy Hirt with their Hollywood Presbyterian choristers.
Reprinted by permission from the American Choral Directors Association, original photo, Charles C. Hirt Collection, American Choral Directors Association Archives, Box 1, Series 3.

The Hollywood Presbyterian music ministry and its director were almost immediately the talk of the Los Angeles area. For his vaunted adult choir, Hirt demanded capable singers with above-average musicianship. "Each new or returning member was given a small, blue-printed booklet stating the objectives, rules, and requirements of the choir." Exemplary attendance was expected, and members who did not measure up knew that there was a waiting list of eager singers hoping to replace them. Soloists regularly singing with the choir included Harve Presnell (1933–2009), then performing as a classical baritone but who would reach stardom in the 1960 Broadway production of *The Unsinkable Molly Brown*. The tenor, Dennis Morgan (1908–1994), was a Hollywood mainstay, appearing in movies for Paramount and Warner Brothers throughout the 1940s and '50s.[6]

Charles Hirt continued his musical studies. After graduation from Occidental in 1934 he enrolled for graduate study in music at the University of Southern California. There he earned a master's degree in music education,

---

6. Stewart, "Charles C. Hirt," 21.

which would be followed by a PhD in musicology in 1946. His dissertation, focused on Russian choral music, made him a nationally known authority on the subject.[7] In 1942, he joined the faculty of the University of Southern California as a lecturer in music education and director of choral activities.

By the summer of 1945, the School of Sacred Music at Union Theological Seminary had been in existence for nearly twenty years. Its programs were nationally known and respected. Charles Hirt was well aware of the work being done at Union and invited Clarence and Helen Dickinson to the USC campus to provide input on the Union-style church music curriculum that would be introduced that very fall at the university. The program would culminate in bachelor's and master's degrees in sacred music. It was Hirt's plan to create a program that complemented the one offered at Union, but with emphasis placed on choral music rather than organ. Core classes for that first term were church music administration, music and worship, hymnology, and music of the great liturgies—all indicative of Clarence Dickinson's guidance. USC would later herald its department of sacred music as the first of its kind at a major American university.[8]

Cultivated Church Music in 1950s America

God of glory, around whose eternal throne all the heavenly powers offer their ceaseless songs of praise, grant that we may overhear these songs and with our own lips and lives interpret them to all in whose presence we play or sing, that your church may behold the beauty of its King and see with mortal eyes the land that is afar off, where all your promises are celebrated and where all your love in every sight and sound is the theme of eternal rejoicing. Through Jesus Christ our Lord . . .
(Erik Routley, composed for worship services in the chapel of Westminster Choir College)[9]

The 1950s, like the 1870s, has often been portrayed as a time when Americans paused to take a collective deep breath of relief after coming out of a great war. In both epochs, prosperity returned for the nation's middle and

---

7. Stewart, "Charles C. Hirt," 11.
8. Stewart, "Charles C. Hirt," 27.
9. Leaver, Litton, and Young, eds., *Duty and Delight*, 18.

upper classes. Ronald Steele, author and professor of international relations at the University of Southern California in the 1960s, wrote:

> Of all the blessings of the Eisenhower years, that historical intermission when America stopped off for a snooze while the world churned inconsiderately on, surely the most wonderful was that we were in such safe hands. Ike was in his castle, and all was right with the world.[10]

Nevertheless, it was not a period devoid of problems. The dropping of the atomic bomb, the Korean conflict, and the Cold War were all reasons for deep concern. Anti-Communist sentiment boiled over as evidenced in the McCarthy hearings and blacklists. There was an intensification of the struggle to gain civil rights for African Americans[11] and women.

A "Golden Age" for Sacred Choral and Organ Music

Thanks to work that had been done over the previous decade by the Union Theological Seminary School of Sacred Music, Westminster Choir College, and several state and private institutions offering church music-related instruction or applied training in organ or choral conducting, American churches now had far greater access to capable musical leadership. An important development for church music education was the decision in 1943 by the National Association of Schools of Music to begin certifying church music degrees and the curricula required to receive them. Once certification was possible a number of schools began offering sacred music degree programs. This included Boston University, the University of Southern California, the Southern Baptist Theological Seminary in Louisville, and Southern Methodist University.

Morgan Simmons, a graduate student at UTS who received his master's in sacred music in 1953, recalled what it was like to study amid New York's once again thriving church music scene in 1950. One had his or her choice of programs led by some of the nation's most esteemed church musicians. The shadow that had hung over the campus during the war had definitely faded.

---

10. Ronald Steel, "Mr. Clean." Dwight Eisenhower was elected president of the United States and served from 1953 to 1961.

11. As we have already seen, the struggle for civil rights began during Reconstruction and gained momentum with the work of W. E. B. Du Bois, among others. The advent of the modern civil rights movement, however, is usually dated to the passing of *Brown vs. Board of Education* on May 17, 1954.

> In New York, one could experience an oratorio every Sunday. At that time, Dickinson was at Brick Church, Frederick H. Candlyn was at St. Thomas, Harold Friedell was at St. Bartholomew's, Norman Coke-Jephcott was at the Cathedral of St. John the Divine, Robert Baker was at First Presbyterian in Brooklyn, and Vernon DeTar was at Ascension. DeTar was very smart. He presented his oratorios on Monday evening, thus avoiding competition.[12]

The influence of John Finley Williamson and his Westminster Choir College could be seen in the wide acceptance of his "Westminster Plan" for a full graded choir programs in churches. Graded programs for multiple choirs, at least one for each age range—primary, elementary, youth, and adult—were at their height in the 1950s.[13] Earlier boys' and children's choirs had "existed to lead congregational psalmody or to sing the service music after the fashion of European or English cathedrals. As such, they fulfilled their full purpose in the Sunday morning service."[14] The new graded choirs based on Williamson's model, however, had a primary focus on music education. While they sang in worship occasionally, their chief objective was to engender a love of singing while training for a lifelong involvement in music. Williamson elucidated his Westminster Plan in a 1925 speech to an Organ and Choral Music Conference sponsored by the Music Teachers National Association.

> We must find for our churches a plan that will coordinate a program of education for the individual, service to the community, and a program of worship for the church. For such a program I would suggest the following: that a department of music be formed in each church, this department to be formed under the control of one head and to include in each church a junior choir, ages 6–12, intermediate choir, ages 12–18, and an adult choir. In churches whose membership exceeds six hundred, a high school choir, ages 16–21, should be organized and the adult choir started at the age of 21 instead of 18 . . . Every member of the adult choir should receive free voice lessons each week and the other choirs, regular group training.[15]

With the hundreds of younger choirs then being organized, a new market was created for choral music written specifically in unison, two-part treble,

---

12. Egler, "Conversation."
13. Ogasapian, *Church Music in America*, 247.
14. Ogasapian, *Church Music in America*, 247–48.
15. Beck, *America's Choral Ambassador*, 91–92.

and three-part mixed voicings. Among the composers specializing in choral music for young singers were Natalie Sleeth (1930–1992) and Marie Pooler (1928–2013).

In 1964, after two years of lecturing on this side of the Atlantic, the English pastor and hymnologist Erik Routley made the following observations about church music in the United States:

> An assessment of church music in the U.S.A. is, however, even more difficult than in Britain because of the many religious and cultural streams which are mingled in the evolving culture of the American nation . . .
>
> Taking the picture as a whole, it ought to be true that the enormous amount of church music now pouring from American presses is of a better quality than the correspondingly enormous amount that was printed over here fifty to a hundred years ago. There is, equally, every possibility of over-writing and over-publication, of platitudinous degeneracy, if the American composers and publishers do not discipline themselves to learn from the errors of their European cousins . . .
>
> Economic expansion has yielded many advantages even to church music. It has provided fine modern churches with large organs, massive congregations, and enthusiastic choirs. To meet this demand, the publishers are now working at high pressure. Moreover, the universities are operating courses in sacred music which qualify for academic credit—a thing absolutely unheard of in Britain . . .[16]

At the same time, Routley noted "a vast and amiable vulgarity about much that goes on in the practice of church."[17] He decried a "virtuoso cult" that risked transforming "churches into concert halls for the connoisseur."

> In one very famous church of cathedral-like proportions and academic associations, the programme on one July Sunday in 1962 included Byrd's *Ave verum,* a complex aria from a Bach cantata, and Brahms' "How Lovely are Thy Dwellings" sung with masterly and enthusiastic skill by a first-class choir, accompanied by an organist who would give good run to the best English players, but if anybody asked why these things were sung together and at that time, an answer would be hard to find.[18]

---

16. Routley, *Twentieth Century Church Music,* 87–88.
17. Routley, *Twentieth Century Church Music,* 88.
18. Routley, *Twentieth Century Church Music,* 88–89.

Routley's comments were astutely perceptive regarding the amount of sacred choral (and organ) music coming from American publishers in the 1950s and '60s. A wealth of new repertoire was needed. Organists tended to be better trained and more numerous than in the years prior to World War II. The church choir of the 1950s was a wholly different ensemble from that of previous generations. Quartet choirs had gone out of fashion. Anthems written for chorus choirs with a sequence of sections alternating between soloists and chorus were a thing of the past. Modern, through-composed anthems[19] had taken their place in which solo parts, if there were any, were generally woven into the choral texture. Even the designation "chorus choir" had fallen out of favor. A choir was simply *a choir* and much of the new anthem repertoire was conceived to be sung whether or not soloists were available.

In previous generations, as we have seen, much of the choral and organ music for church use arose out of the Protestant Episcopal Church. By the 1950s and '60s, the increased opportunities for training had changed that. The list following is by no means complete:

Choral Composers

Baptist
Warren M. Angell (1907–2006)

Episcopal
Richard Dirksen (1921–2003)
Richard Purvis (1913–1994)
Ronald Arnatt (1930–2018)

Lutheran
Daniel Moe (1926–2012)
Carl Schalk (1929–2021)
Donald Busarow (1934–2011)
James E Fritschel (1929—)
Walter Pelz (1926—)
Richard Hillert (1923–2010)
Paul Christiansen (1914–1997)

Unitarian
Daniel Pinkham (1923–2006)

Methodist
Alice Jordan (1916–2012)
Eugene Butler
Austin Lovelace (1919–2010)
Lloyd Pfautsch (1919–2011)
Natalie Sleeth (1930–1992)
Jane M. Marshall (1924–2019)

Presbyterian
Carl F. Mueller (1892–1982)
Joseph W. Clokey (1890–1960)
Kent Newbury (1925—)

Roman Catholic
C. Alexander Peloquin (1918–1997)
Joseph Roff (1910–1993)

---

19. I use the term "through-composed" to distinguish anthem styles, commonly used from the 1950s forward, from typical chorus choir pieces of Buck and others. The latter were generally sectional in nature with parts clearly for soloist(s) only and parts assigned to the full chorus.

Composers for the Organ

Edward Shippen Barnes (1887–1958)
at First Presbyterian Church, Santa Monica
Seth Bingham (1882–1972)
at Madison Avenue Presbyterian, New York
Roberta Bitgood (1908–2007)
Served Lutheran and Presbyterian churches in New York, California, New Jersey, and Connecticut
Robert Elmore (1913–1985)
At Trinity Episcopal, Philadelphia, and Central Moravian, Bethlehem, PA
David N. Johnson (1922–1987)
Taught at Syracuse University, St. Olaf College, and Arizona State

Paul Manz (1919–2009)
at Evangelical Lutheran and Mount Olive Lutheran in Chicago area; taught church music at Christ Seminary, Lutheran School of Theology, and at Concordia University. Pioneered the modern "hymn festival" concept.
Vincent Persichetti (1915–1987)
Daniel Pinkham (1923–2006)
at Kings Chapel, Boston
Richard Purvis (1913–1994)
at Grace Cathedral, San Francisco
Ned Rorem (1923–)
Leo Sowerby (1895–1968)

What can be said about the vast quantity of choral and organ music published by these and other composers between 1946 and the mid-1960s? When asked, the great organist and acerbic raconteur Alec Wyton listed only Sowerby, Pinkham, Rorem, Dirksen, Pfautsch, and Moe to be choral composers of true artistic merit during that time. But if church music were to be judged solely on its effectiveness as a component of worship and not whether it passes muster for concert hall performance, many names could be added to Wyton's list.

In any period of music history one can find examples of shoddy workmanship and lack of creativity. Taken as a whole, however, the post-war years produced a great quantity of well-crafted, original sacred music, created not for paid professional choirs and concert organists, but for worship use in churches small and large the country over. This was not bad music, or hackneyed music, or cheap music—but it was *practical* music. The organist/composer Robert J. Powell, in an interview in *The Diapason,* stated well the perspective of many composers: "[I write for] choirs of twenty-five because that's what most choirs are. When you come right down to it, most choirs are not of cathedral ability or size. My pieces are all *practical things* and useful for specific occasions."[20]

So, how does one define the boundaries between that which is merely practical and that which is practical yet also artistically and spiritually worthy? Victor Gebauer wrestled with the conundrum in a tribute to the great conductor Leland B. Sateren (1913–2007):[21]

---

20. Overall, "Interview with Robert Powell."

21. Leland Sateren, a master composer and choral conductor, was director of choral activities at Augustana College from 1946 to 1979.

Sateren's insistence on artistic value and commitment to faith remind us of the careful balance which all church musicians struggle to discover for themselves in every generation. On one side, we can define the "sacred" so mechanically by idiom (perhaps a *safe* church song), nature of text, or liturgical function, that God's good gift of musical expression fades out. Too much "church music," including the stream of "easy to learn" anthems from today's publishers, flirt with this hazard. The theologian-cum-musician [Jeremy] Begbie might label such music "atrociously harmless," [and] unengaged with the world addressed by the Gospel. Art (here referring to musical values) and the church dare never be enemies.

Conversely, identifying the sacred music with the highest artistic expression (perhaps defined by a cultural elite) which is accessible only to an obediently awed audience, risks losing its soul . . . There is a difference between the "beauty of holiness" and the holiness of beauty. One draws forth our worship; the other, our idolatry.[22]

Another key development in the post-war years was the rise of support organizations, both denominational and nondenominational, for the advancement of church music among Protestants. The Fellowship of Methodist Musicians (now, the Fellowship of United Methodist Musicians and the Worship Arts, or FUMMWA) was established in 1955. Episcopalians followed with the founding of the American Cathedral Organists and Choirmasters Association in 1968. Its name was later changed to the Association of Anglican Musicians, in 1974. The Presbyterian Association of Musicians (or PAM) was founded in 1970. Each of the mainline denominations began sponsoring summer music conferences during this period—the Lutherans at Lutheridge, the Southern Baptists at Ridgecrest, and the Presbyterians at Montreat—all in the mountains of western North Carolina near Asheville.

Traditional Mainline vs. Evangelical; Cultivated vs. Populist— Southern Baptists Occupy the Middle Ground

In the 1950s, as now, the largest Christian body other than the Roman Catholic Church in the United States is the Southern Baptist Church. While Baptist worship is sermon-centered and places a high value on congregational singing, worship style can vary greatly. In the twenty-first century, many leading churches model the formal practices of the Baptist Union of

---

22. Gebauer, "Cantor of the Church," 11.

Great Britain while others, more entrenched in the revivalist tradition, have embraced a free-church approach including contemporary Christian music. One unidentified Baptist preacher has been quoted as saying, "Some burn incense, others bay at the moon."[23]

This divergence in worship styles and especially with music for worship became pronounced during the first half of the twentieth century, and was clearly reflected in the 1931 change of musical leadership at the Southwestern Baptist Theological Seminary in Fort Worth. Bayus Benjamin (B. B.) McKinney (1886–1952), whose work in relation to the *Broadman Hymnal* was discussed previously, had served as assistant director of the Southwestern School of Sacred Music from 1919 to 1931. The school, founded in 1915, was the first of its kind affiliated with the Baptist church. It had been originally called the School of Gospel Music, and its orientation musically had long been oriented toward revivalist music and the skills needed to lead in that area. By 1931, the school's director, Isham (Ike) Emmanuel Reynolds (1879–1949), himself a church musician, teacher, composer, and conductor, felt a change was needed from the gospel music focus of the curriculum.[24]

The shifting currents in Baptist music was further exemplified by the contributions a few years later by another Reynolds. William Jensen Reynolds (1920–2009) was I. E. Reynolds' nephew. Better known as "William J.," he would be called "the most influential Southern Baptist musician in the second half of the twentieth century."[25] W. J. Reynolds received his master of church music degree from Southwestern in 1945[26] and soon became director of music at the First Baptist Church of Oklahoma City. There he established a fully graded musical program modeled upon John Finley Williamson's Westminster Plan, which included a summer music camp for youth and annual multi-church performances of Handel's *Messiah* that would become an Oklahoma City tradition. Reynolds would go on to a memorable career, serving on the Baptist Sunday School Board from 1955 to 1979, chairing the hymnal committees for the 1956 and 1975 Baptist hymnals, and as editor of the influential Baptist periodical *The Church Musician*.[27] William J. Reynolds received his doctorate in music education from George Peabody College for Teachers in 1961.

Reynolds's career exemplified for many Baptists the need for sacred music education as it was being pioneered at UTS and Westminster Choir

---

23. Shoemaker, "Overview of Worship."
24. Pullin, "Isham Emmanuel Reynolds (1879–1949)."
25. Music, "William J. Reynolds, Extraordinary Church Musician."
26. Music, *William J. Reynolds, Church Musician*, 17.
27. Music, *William J. Reynolds, Church Musician*, 45, 51–52, 54.

College. Even before Reynolds arrived in Nashville, B. B. McKinney had outlined essential commitments Baptists needed to make to improve their musical ministry. The UTS/Westminster influence is obvious:

- "We can't have better church music until we train our people."
- "We reaffirm our belief in graded choirs."
- "We urge our Baptist colleges, universities, and seminaries to place in their curriculum a Department of Church Music and to require certain definite courses of all ministerial students."[28]

Westminster Choir College graduates were hired to serve at some of the nation's most prestigious Southern Baptist churches, including James Berry at First Baptist Church, Dallas, and Alice Berman at Myers Park Church in Charlotte, North Carolina. Donald and Frances Winters, who began their ministry of music at the First Baptist Church of Atlanta, went on to oversee the establishment of the School of Church Music at the Southern Baptist Theological Seminary in Louisville.[29] It was during the 1940s and '50s that many Southern Baptist choirs began donning choir robes. Processionals, recessionals, and other accoutrements associated with ritualistic worship became more common.

---

28. Reynolds, "Baptists, Music, and World War II."
29. Reynolds, "Baptists, Music, and World War II."

Introducing the Evangelistic Cantata

John W. Peterson.
Image courtesy of John W. Peterson Music Co.

Savvy marketing techniques actually made possible the introduction into evangelistic worship of a new musical form—one that would become ubiquitous in future years—the evangelistic cantata. Cantatas, relatively brief multi-movement works designed to fit within a worship service and highlight either a sermon theme or a Protestant feast day, had been around since the late sixteenth century. In America, mainline churches had been programming cantatas for years. Stainer's *Crucifixion*, J. H. Maunder's *Olivet to Calvary*, and Theodore Dubois's *Les Sept Paroles du Christ* (The Seven Last Words of Christ) had long been staples of cultivated worship. The American Dudley Buck composed five church cantatas between 1865 and 1900 and nine multi-movement settings of the *Te Deum,* but all of those predated the introduction of choral music into most evangelical worship and did not mesh well with its spirit.

Unlike earlier examples, a common characteristic of the evangelistic cantatas of the 1950s and '60s was the incorporation of well-known gospel and revival hymn tunes. While earlier examples can be cited, the composer who brought the evangelistic cantata to broad popularity was John Willard Peterson (1921–2006) or, more commonly, "John W."

In 1954, Albert B. Smith, founder of Singspiration Music, purchased a block of Peterson songs, and asked John to come to Montrose, Pennsylvania, as the company's music editor. When the decision was made for Singspiration to move into sacred choral music, Peterson was at the helm, and working with him was a young Harold DeCou (1932–2008) who would later become a principal composer/arranger in the evangelical fold. As Peterson related the story, "We were discussing the choir needs of the nation and talking about the arrangements and anthems we had produced. Suddenly someone said, 'Along with these things, we ought to produce a cantata.'"[30] Peterson was intrigued. He had been mulling over the possibility of composing a full-scale Christian musical for the stage, but the conversation inspired him to create a smaller scale work—a cantata based on an old Phillip P. Bliss gospel song. The cantata, *Hallelujah! What a Savior!*,[31] was published in 1957 and became an immediate bestseller. It was a pioneering effort not only in its gospel hymn-oriented style, but also in the company's approach to promotion. Churches were sent a complimentary copy of the work with a full-performance recording by professional singers. Hundreds of future cantatas would be released following this same successful marketing plan.

The success of *Hallelujah! What a Savior!* was such that both its format and how it was promoted became a model for dozens of such works in future years. Annual presentations of evangelistic cantatas featuring choirs and soloists with a variety of accompaniment options became an expected part of much Baptist worship during the 1960s and '70s, as well in other denominations.

In 1955, John W. Peterson became president and editor-in-chief of Singspiration Music—a post he held for fifteen years. It was there that Peterson edited one of the more popular nondenominational hymnals, *Great Hymns of the Faith* (1961). Collaborating with him at Singspiration were Harold DeCou, Don Wyrtzen, and Ralph Carmichael, all of whom had deep connections with the evangelist Billy Graham (1918–2018) and the Billy Graham Evangelistic Association.[32]

Shea, Barrows, and the Billy Graham Crusades

The biographer Grant Wacker wrote of William Franklin (Billy) Graham that he ranked "with Martin Luther King and Pope John Paul II as one of the most creatively influential Christians of the twentieth century."[33] This could not have been known, of course, when Graham first began his ministry in 1940s Illinois. One cannot, in reading Graham's biography, miss the significant role played by music in his rise to fame.

In 1944, Graham received a call from a friend Torrey Johnson, who had been hosting a gospel music radio program, *Songs in the Night*. The program was in danger of being dropped because of lack of funding. Graham

---

30. Peterson and Engquist, *Miracle Goes On*.
31. Peterson, *Hallelujah! What a Savior!*, 170.
32. Ruark, *House of Zondervan*, 147.
33. Wacker, *America's Pastor*, 2.

agreed to take over hosting the show and tapped members of his First Baptist Church in Western Springs, Illinois, to contribute. Torrey Johnson was also a Chicago leader for Youth for Christ and soon approached Graham about also becoming the movement's principal evangelist. The year 1944 would be one of frenzied activity and decision-making that would determine the course of Graham's ministry in the future.

One of his first actions as host of *Songs in the Night* was to hire the Canadian gospel singer, baritone George Beverly Shea (1909–2013), to be a regular on the program. At the time, Shea was the better known of the two men. He had already established a career as a gospel singer and had been singing regularly on WMBI, the radio station of the Moody Bible Institute. The same year Shea partnered with Graham, he had also been contracted by ABC and the Armed Forces Radio Network to host a show called *Club Time*. There he was billed as "America's Beloved Gospel Singer."[34] Shea would have a robust independent singing career, making dozens of recordings and hosting his own radio and television programs in addition to concert and revival appearances, but would remain closely aligned with Graham's ministry through all of it. "I've been listening to Bev Shea sing for more than 50 years," Graham said in 1997, "and I would still rather hear him sing than anyone else I know."[35]

Through his work for Youth for Christ, Graham met a second person who, like Shea, would be a lifelong musical collaborator in his ministry. Cliff Barrows (1923–2016) had graduated in 1944 from Bob Jones College (now Bob Jones University). He was the first student to complete studies in the school's new sacred music program. One year later, in 1945, he met Billy Graham. Graham was impressed with the young man and his potential.

That same year, 1945, Billy Graham made the fateful decision to strike out on his own as an evangelist. He invited George Beverly Shea and Cliff Barrows to join him, and the trio traveled to England to explore the possibilities for future evangelistic work. Upon their return, Graham and the two musicians toured widely, with Graham hosting numerous citywide revivals. Along the way, they sought to perfect an approach to revivalism that would be successful for post-war Americans. Graham studied in detail the revival process used by Dwight Moody and hired Willis Haymaker, who had organized many of Billy Sunday's rallies as an administrative resource.[36] Following Sunday's example, Graham favored tents, municipal auditoriums, custom-built tabernacles, and outdoor venues such as parks for these early

---

34. Blumhofer, "Singing to Save," 66–67.
35. Fox, "George Beverly Shea Dies at 104."
36. Wacker, *America's Pastor*, 140.

revivals. Meanwhile Cliff Barrows, while thoroughly conversant in the repertoire of gospel hymnody, sought input from seasoned song leaders of the past. In Winona Lake, Indiana, he spent hours with the now-retired Homer Rodeheaver.[37]

The crucial turning point in Billy Graham's career came with his Los Angeles revival in October of 1949. A huge tent was erected, capable of seating five thousand, which promotional material referred to as "the Canvas Cathedral with the Steeple of Light."[38] Whether due to the presence of some Hollywood celebrities or the support of newspaper tycoon William Randolph Hearst, the planned three-week event had to be extended to eight weeks because of the crowds assembled. Its success, and the media attention that it drew, almost instantly catapulted Graham to national prominence. Soon, tents and tabernacles were no longer adequate for Graham crusades. They would typically have to be staged in the largest indoor coliseums such as Madison Square Garden or the Cow Palace in San Francisco. Sports venues such as Yankee Stadium in New York, Soldier Field in Chicago, and the Pasadena Rose Bowl also became sites. Between 1947 and 2005, the Graham team conducted over four hundred crusades in 185 countries.

Cliff Barrows, Billy Graham, and George Beverly Shea.
Image courtesy of the Billy Graham Evangelistic Association.

The three members of the Graham team—Shea, Barrows, and Graham himself—each had carefully defined functions: Graham, the evangelist; Shea, the soloist; and Barrows, basically doing everything else. To the public, Cliff Barrows was the energetic chorus master and congenial master of ceremonies. Behind the scenes, however, he was stage manager and technical director. He was responsible for everything from determining what

---

37. Blumhofer, "Singing to Save," 68.
38. McLoughlin Jr., *Modern Revivalism*, 489–90.

notables would be seated on the platform with Graham, to being sure there was adequate parking.

Like Rodeheaver before him, Barrows played the trombone and was a showman perfectly suited to doing whatever was needed. For a pre-crusade promotion in Fort Worth, Texas, he postured for children as "Uncle Cliff" and acted out single-handedly the story of Commander Naaman and the prophet Elisha (2 Kings 5:1–19). "He dusted the platform in the role of a servant girl, galloped across the stage as an army of horses, and held his nose and ducked into the imaginary water of the [Jordan] river."[39]

As with all previous revivalists, music was a critical component of the Billy Graham crusades and, like Moody, Billy Graham apparently couldn't (or, at least, wouldn't) sing.

> When interviewers asked why Mr. Graham did not simply lead his flock in song himself, as many preachers do, Mr. Shea suggested that the status quo was better for all concerned: Mr. Graham, as Mr. Shea put it with true Christian charity, suffered from "the malady of no melody."[40]

While Graham would occasionally request a particular song or ask for music focused on a particular topic, it was Barrows and Shea who planned and implemented music for each crusade. The hymn choices tended toward the traditional and familiar. From the beginning of their partnership, Graham had indicated to Shea and Barrows his preference for "the old hymns of revival, consecration, and salvation."[41] The old hymn, "Just as I Am Without One Plea," with music by W. B. Bradbury, for example, would close each rally on a contemplative note.

Shea and Barrows were not, however, averse to programming less familiar songs and hymns, and some of them would become popular additions to the Protestant repertoire because of their exposure in the Graham crusades. The Fanny Crosby hymn "To God Be the Glory" (1870) had been popular in England since Dwight Moody's revivals in the nineteenth century, but was basically unknown in the United States until Barrows and Shea programmed it in the 1950s. The hymn "How Great Thou Art," set to an arrangement of the Swedish hymn tune, "O Stor Gut," came into national prominence as a signature song of George Beverly Shea in his crusade appearances.[42]

---

39. "Acts Out Story."
40. Fox, "George Beverly Shea Dies at 104."
41. Blumhofer, "Singing to Save," 66.
42. The hymn choices reflected not only Graham's personal preferences, but also those of his core audience, which was middle aged and older.

Billy Graham and the Media

Biographer Grant Wacker referred to Billy Graham's crusades as the cornerstone of his evangelistic empire.

> It is easy to imagine him without one or another of his publications, fairly easy to imagine him without his radio and TV broadcasts, difficult but theoretically possible to imagine him without access to the highest echelons of political and social power, but absolutely impossible to imagine him without the crusades.[43]

There is truth to Wacker's statement, but it fails to take into account the critical importance of the media to Graham's success. It is true that his early revivals were self-supporting, but as attendance grew and programming and staging became more varied and sophisticated, production costs increased dramatically. By 1956, the annual budget of the Billy Graham Evangelistic Association had ballooned to two million dollars a year. Only one-fourth to one-third of the costs generated by a single crusade rally came from attendee donations. The rest came from independent solicitations and from fundraising appeals on Graham's popular radio program, *The Hour of Decision*.[44]

The Hour of Decision—with Cliff Barrows as its program director and emcee and George Beverly Shea a frequent soloist—began airing on November 5, 1950. The weekly show had five component parts: a Scripture passage read by Graham associate Grady B. Wilson, Graham's sermon, a solo usually by Shea, a choir piece directed by Barrows, and a Crusade Update read by Jerry Beavan. *Hour of Decision* went through three iterations on television beginning in 1951 (and continuing through 2014).[45] In addition, Graham's media presence was bolstered by George Beverly Shea's highly successful career as an independent performer.[46]

One cannot separate the Billy Graham of crusade fame from Billy Graham the media personality. The two were mutually dependent on each other. The same was true in the budding gospel music business. By the mid-1950s, gospel music had become so wedded to the broadcast and recording industries and secular entertainment that its roots in worship were easily forgotten.

---

43. Wacker, *America's Pastor*, 140.
44. McLoughlin Jr., *Modern Revivalism*, 494.
45. Blumhofer, "Singing to Save," 157.
46. Shea was a frequent guest on other programs both on radio and television and became a contracted recording artist under the RCA Victor label in 1951. His 1965 album *Southland Favorites* won a Grammy for Best Gospel or Other Religious Recording.

Radio and Recording Become the Engine Driving White and Black Gospel Music in the Mid-Twentieth Century

Both white and Black gospel music had made significant inroads into secular music making before the Second World War began. Where white gospel was concerned, the dabbling of both James Vaughan and Virgil Stamps in record studios, the popular radio programs featuring professional male quartets and mixed ensembles, the Stamps-Baxter "All-Night Singings"—all of these acted to change the public perception of gospel music. Gospel could no longer be viewed as simply a form of church music. Rather, it had to be seen as a part of the popular culture of the time. Black gospel had begun a similar transformation with the nightclub forays of Sister Rosetta Tharp, the "Spirituals to Swing" concerts at Carnegie Hall, and "song battles" between the likes of Mahalia Jackson and Roberta Martin.

The Blackwood Brothers.
Public domain image. (https://www.last.fm/music/The+Blackwood+Brothers/+images/183fd345b68141e6a40f4168fed78e60)

These trends only intensified at war's end. The recording industry, which had largely shut down during the war years, came roaring back in 1946. By that time the whole nature of white gospel quartet singing was changing. Where quartets had once existed primarily to travel from one church or singing convention to another performing and selling songbooks, now a recording contract was the essential measure of a group's success. The Blackwood Brothers were America's top quartet in the late '40s, recording both on their own Blackwood label and for RCA. Other successful recording groups included Homeland Harmony and the Harmoneers, recording on the Bibletone label; The Sunshine Boys and the Blue Ridge Quartet on Decca Records; and the soon to be famous Statesmen on Capitol.[47]

The Soul Stirrers.
Public domain image. (https://www.discogs.com/es/artist/406831-The-Soul-Stirrers)

The most famous Black gospel vocal ensemble at the end of World War II was the Soul Stirrers. The group had originally been formed in Texas in the 1920s and went through several changes in personnel. They made their first recordings in Chicago in the 1930s, eventually moving there in 1937. By 1946, the group's fame rested on a popular weekly radio show, best-selling recordings, and national tours.[48] A key difference between white and Black gospel groups was the willingness of the latter to experiment. While white groups had long been performing with piano accompaniment, Black quartets had traditionally sung a cappella. In 1952, the Soul Stirrers made their first recordings with instrumental accompaniment—initially various combinations of piano, bass, organ, or guitar. Full orchestrations would follow. The Soul Stirrers introduced several innovations. By increasing their personnel to six—an accompanist and a fifth singer, a tenor—they could feature a soloist with full four-part harmony in support. Robert Harris, the group's lead tenor until 1950, perfected the use of falsetto in pop and gospel singing. Later, mainstream pop groups including the Temptations, the Four Tops, and the O'Jays all claimed they were influenced by the Soul Stirrers.[49]

---

47. Terrell, *Music Men*, 166, 170.
48. Burford, "Soul Stirrers," 356.
49. Burford, "Soul Stirrers," 357.

This was no idle claim. Certainly the musicality and creativity of the Soul Stirrers made other artists want to emulate them, but their media presence on the radio and in recordings also played a role.

Black "Crossover" Artists and Sam Cooke

From Sister Rosetta Tharp forward, as Black artists like the Soul Stirrers gravitated to secular performance venues and began mixing pop song selections with gospel tunes in live performance and recordings, there was an inevitable blurring of the line between sacred and secular. Viv Broughton wrote of the direction being taken by Black gospel music in the 1950s in her book, *Black Gospel: An Illustrated History of Gospel Sound*:

> Just where devotive music leaves off and sensual pleasure begins is anyone's guess, but the elders and pastors will draw arbitrary lines and stick to them ... For many though, it is this very inclusion of temporal pleasures into the religious sphere that makes the Black Church so down to earth and full of humanity. There is no false asceticism, and worship is a thing of riotous exuberance that extends over long periods.[50]

The apparent embrace of popular culture by supposedly sanctified artists was roundly condemned by some in the African American church. "The story of the gospel singer or group that 'crosses over' in the pursuit of fame and economic accolade is painfully familiar within the gospel community and is commonly regarded as a betrayal to the ideals of the church."[51] In 1950 Robert Harris, the Soul Stirrers' popular tenor, resigned due to the increasing secularization he saw happening in the gospel music business. Replacing him would be Sam Cooke, one of the most important transitional figures of the 1950s as gospel music moved toward soul gospel and pop.

---

50. Broughton, *Black Gospel*, 93.
51. Moore, "Soul Gospel", 355.

Sam Cooke.
Public domain image. (https://en.wikipedia.org/wiki/Sam_Cooke)

Samuel Cooke (1931–1964) was born in Mississippi. In his mid-teens, his pristine tenor voice caught the notice of Soul Stirrers' tenor, J. W. Alexander. He had "something special", Alexander recalled. "He had a particular charisma. People just liked the guy; they could relate to him."[52] Cooke was invited to join the Soul Stirrers as one of their lead singers in 1951 and remained with them through 1957. During that time, the group contracted with Specialty Records and recorded Dorsey's "Peace in the Valley" and other gospel standards with Cooke's voice featured. On records Sam Cooke's lead predominated, and in performance his handsomeness and charisma made him a heartthrob for young girls and a magnet for youth in general. In 1957 Cooke left the Soul Stirrers to embark on a solo career. He had thirty Top 40 hits between 1957 and 1964, including "You Send Me," which spent six weeks at number one on the Billboard Rhythm and Blues chart. In 1964, Cooke recorded what is generally regarded as his greatest song and an anthem of the civil rights era, "A Change Is Gonna Come," which he said was inspired by Bob Dylan's "Blowin' in the Wind."

Sam Cooke's importance for this study was his success as a crossover artist from gospel music to pop. He is regarded by many also as a pioneer of the soul-gospel genre. The choice to be a crossover artist often had repercussions, but Cooke was able to avoid or weather the scathing criticism experienced by Rosetta Tharp because he had the support of his minister

---

52. Guralnick, *Dream Boogie,* 36.

father. When he had left the QC's to join the Stirrers, the Reverend Cooke recalled their conversation:

> Oh, the church folks raised some sand! I told him, ". . . You working for money! You're out there making money, boy! That's your living. Don't let anybody tell you nothing about no church song!"[53]

James Baldwin, who was a devoted admirer of Cooke, wrote, "It should always be remembered that soul music in all its forms is the aesthetic property of a race of people who were brought to this country against their will and were forced to make dramatic adjustments in order to survive in a hostile environment."[54] In that sense, the Black gospel tradition was the direct descendant of the slave spiritual with all of its heartache and yearning.

Hilary Moore of the Royal College of Music in London, an authority on the subject of gospel pop, provided another perspective in 2005, which was focused on music style. Soul gospel according to Moore was a gospel-influenced pop style, more contemplative and lyrical than, for example, be-bop or jazz in general. Very often, the only audible difference between 1950s gospel hymn renditions and those of soul music was in the secular text. The approach to interpretation was exactly the same. [55]

Sam Cooke also had the distinction of being one of the mentors for another crossover singer, one who in a long and illustrious career would become known as the undisputed "Queen of Soul"—Aretha Franklin (1942–2018). She was the daughter of the famous Black preacher C. L. Franklin, pastor of the 4,500-member New Bethel Baptist Church in Detroit. His over seventy recorded sermons brought his aggressive preaching to national attention. At New Bethel, it was said that Franklin "would preach so hard that they had two white-uniformed nurses standing permanently by to revive the overcome parishioners!"[56] From the age of twelve, Aretha accompanied her father on revival tours as a featured singer. She recorded her first album of gospel songs and spirituals in 1956 and appeared occasionally after that as a guest artist with the Soul Stirrers.

Aretha Franklin soared to fame with "I Never Loved a Man" in 1967, which was followed by many other pop hits, but she returned briefly to gospel music in 1970 with a double album, *Amazing Grace,* recorded in Los Angeles with James Cleveland's Southern California Community Choir. It

---

53. Wolff, *You Send Me,* 153.
54. Lordi, "James Baldwin and the Sound of Soul," 34.
55. Moore, "Soul Gospel," 355.
56. Broughton, *Black Gospel,* 97.

would be one of the highest selling gospel LPs of all time, a *tour de force*. She would return a last time to gospel for her 1987 album, *One Lord, One Faith, One Baptism*. When asked about Aretha's move to fame as a popular singer, her father said, "If you want to know the truth, Aretha has never left the church. If you have the ability to feel and you have the ability to hear, you know that Aretha is still a gospel singer."[57] The legacy of Aretha Franklin was carried forward into the twenty-first century by crossover singers like Whitney Houston (1963–2012), Kelly Price (b. 1973), and Fantasia Barino-Taylor (b. 1984).

The crossover phenomena from pure gospel to gospel pop was hardly restricted to African American performers. Stylistic traits both improvisatory and ornamental of Black performers were absorbed into the styles of white pop musicians. Perhaps the best example to cite here is the legendary collaboration between Sam Phillips and Elvis Presley—two men, both of them Caucasian but both of whom were smitten with Black gospel music—who would change the trajectory of gospel music, Black *and* white, forever.

The underlying themes of this chapter have been twofold. First there was the growth of mainline, mostly white Protestantism in the years following the Second World War, and the almost astonishing progress of cultivated sacred music. As a part of that progress, there was an increase in options available for sacred music education. More schools began to offer graduate degrees in church music. In addition, denominations and independent organizations were offering a plethora of workshops, conferences, and summer musical retreats. All of this led to a greater availability of trained leadership, and there was a corresponding increase in the number of churches with choirs and even full *departments* of music offering musical opportunities for all ages. This led in turn to a mushrooming of sacred music publication for both organ and choirs. Looking back, we can now see that the period 1946 to 1966 was a golden age for cultivated church music in America.

Second, in the area of populist sacred music, there was an ever-increasing dependency on media (radio, recordings, and later television) rather than live performance. This was true with regard to the Graham Crusades as well as the activities of white and Black gospel entertainers. All of this would serve to weaken once rigid views on what was and was not appropriate in worship. Using Sam Cooke, Aretha Franklin, and Elvis Presley as examples—singers who regularly juxtaposed secular and sacred selections in performance and recordings—we can also see a gradual erasure of the lines traditionally setting apart sacred music from pop.

---

57. Darden, "Aretha's One Faith."

In essence there was a sort of Janus-faced, bipolar aspect to the period in question. The fifties is often characterized as a decade of stability and peace, yet deep concerns regarding "the bomb," Communism, civil rights, and military conflicts—first in Korea and then in Vietnam—smoldered just below the surface. Similarly, church life was largely focused on growth and bonhomie, and yet just below that same surface were long-ignored social justice issues needing to be addressed. The mix of gospel and pop music over the airways and on records was generally welcomed as wholesome entertainment. Unfortunately, though, the power and influence of recorded and broadcast media would only continue to grow and would eventually threaten once and for all to smash the barriers dividing music of the church from that of the commercial arena. These divisions would come into full view in the decade to come—the 1960s.

Chapter 20

A TIME OF TURBULENCE

The historian Sandra Opdycke cataloged many factors impinging upon communal living as America entered the decade of the 1960s.

> Today most commercial business takes place elsewhere—in suburban shopping malls and office parks located well beyond the reach of the inner-city neighborhoods where most people of color live. Jim Crow no longer rules, yet many of these suburban facilities are insulated against diversity as effectively as any "Whites Only" restaurant of the 1950s.[1]

Before World War II, Opdycke noted, the typical American home was oriented toward the street. A "living room" in the front of the house would likely have large windows for a view of passersby, and a generous front porch offered a place to relax and socialize with neighbors. In the post-war years, a typical home's primary living space was moved to the rear and a private, fenced-in deck or patio became the center for relaxation and socializing with select friends.[2] Connecting with the surrounding community was no longer a priority.

Opdycke's observations were, of course, generalized. Not every middle-class home in the 1960s was suburban and hundreds of downtowns continued to be vital hubs of community. Still, there was a certain self-satisfied, claustrophobic stagnation, and a preference to surround oneself with those of the same race and like mind. The desire for a return to normalcy and tranquility took precedence over confronting troubling issues and trends in

---

1. Opdycke, "Spaces People Share," 11–12.
2. Opdycke, "Spaces People Share," 29.

the nation and world at large. A long-standing division between classes in American church life was troubling to many church leaders who continued to seek solutions.

The Church at Mid-Century

> Every clergyman, pastor, or minister who takes his work seriously is uncomfortably conscious of the gulf between the members of his church, who are those of a Christian upbringing, and the ordinary people of the surrounding world. He knows that the church in its preaching and its writing is very often speaking to no more than its own members and hangers-on.
>
> I believe I am not alone in believing that this unwilling insularity, this failure in communication, is due very largely to the failure of the church to use the right language and thought-forms . . .
> The Christian religion was never meant to be a secret recipe for living, held by a few, it is good news for all mankind.[3]

The minister, Bible translator, and prolific author John Bertram ("J. B.") Phillips (1906–1982) was writing about the use of churchly or theological language in the pulpit. His concern for making Christianity more accessible to the uninitiated and unchurched, however, would be echoed by many in the coming decades, and a whole nondenominational branch of evangelical Protestantism, more powerful than any before it, would arise with witness to the unchurched as its mission.

At the same time, over the course of the 1960s, society's view of the traditional mainline church would become increasingly cynical. The 1960s and early '70s were a chaotic, often fearsome time for mainstream American Christianity. The self-inflicted myopia of the 1950s infected the church as well as society at large. One of the most inflammatory bestsellers of the post-war era was Pierre Berton's *The Comfortable Pew* (1965). In it Berton, a Canadian newspaper columnist, criticized organized religion for being elitist, failing to relate to real-world problems, and for being handicapped by multiple denominational groups, each claiming a monopoly on truth. It was clear, he wrote, that the world of the 1950s had changed, yet worshipping in the Anglican Church of Canada had not:

> We were all about to enter a New Age; yet there was nothing in that service to indicate the world was different, that the language

---

3. Phillips, *Is God at Home?*, 5–7.

was different, that men were different. Sermon and all, it was a carbon copy of those Sunday rituals in the pro-cathedral in Dawson City in the 1920s.[4]

Listing world peace, racial brotherhood, and the confusing of justice with revenge as the great issues of his time, Berton said that "the voice of the church, when it has been heard at all, has been weak, tardy, equivocal, and irrelevant."[5]

Perhaps most damningly, Berton sensed the church had not only acquiesced but had chosen to embrace a mass-market, commercially influenced definition for success. He wrote, "A successful church [was becoming viewed] like a successful business. If its membership is growing, its budget growing, and its program is growing, then it is said to be 'progressive.'"[6] Likewise clergy, in order to be successful, were encouraged to model qualities of successful persons in business. The successful minister was expected to be "success-oriented." He brought luster to his church and reputation through building programs paid for through his successful solicitation of funds from members.[7]

The Comfortable Pew, while intended as a critique of the Church of Canada, had implications not only for all denominations in the Anglican Communion, but also for Western Christianity as a whole. As a result, it was a major bestseller in the United States.

Hymn Explosion

Despite Berton's bleak assessment, there were hopeful signs for the American church in the early 1960s. For "high church" and "broad church" Episcopalians, there was a notable rise in interest in creating new and socially conscious hymnody. A movement in Great Britain often referred to as the Hymn Explosion was being led by several prominent hymn writers and composers. One of them, Erik Routley (1917–1982), would have a significant influence on hymnody and hymn singing in the United States.[8]

Hymn Explosion originated out of a series of workshops, sponsored by the ecumenical wing of the Church of Scotland, which were held in Dunblane, about forty miles from both Edinburgh and Glasgow. One of those workshops was organized around the topic of church music. "It should be

---

4. Berton, *Comfortable Pew*, 10.
5. Berton, *Comfortable Pew*, 16.
6. Berton, *Comfortable Pew*, 57.
7. Berton, *Comfortable Pew*, 59.
8. Luff, "Twentieth Century Hymn Explosion," 12–13.

understood," Routley wrote, "that the background of this was a feeling that the church must change its shape, its manner, and its attitudes. They were saying the same thing at the time at the Second Vatican Council in Rome . . ."[9]

At Dunblane, twenty-four individuals representing a variety of denominations, half clergy and half musicians, were broken down into working parties to produce new materials for contemporary worship. They included Congregationalists Fred Kaan, Brian Wren, and Ian M. Fraser; Methodists Fred Pratt Green and Richard G. Jones; the Anglican Timothy Dudley-Smith; and Father William Brian Foley, a Roman Catholic priest/composer. Out of the meetings came revolutionary collections of new hymnody, *Dunblane Praises I* (1964), *Dunblane Praises II* (1967), and an expanded version published later by Stainer & Bell/Galaxy that included the contents of both collections, *New Songs for the Church I and II*. The Richard Jones hymn "The Earth Is the Lord's" (1969), often sung to the tune "Minterne" by Cyril Taylor, is an excellent example of the contemporary thrust of the work done at Dunblane:

God of concrete, God of steel,	God, whose glory fills the earth,
God of piston and of wheel,	Gave the universe its birth,
God of pylon, God of steam,	Loosed the Christ with Easter's might,
God of girder and of beam,	Saves the world from evil's blight,
God of atom, God of mine,	Claims mankind by grace divine,
All the world of power is thine.	All the world of love is thine.

The hymnody coming out of Dunblane was both fresh and reflective of the societal conditions of 1960s America. As such it was soon embraced by mainline churches. The hymns of Kaan, Wren, Pratt Green, and Dudley-Smith began appearing in denominational hymnals as early as 1971.

The Promise of Vatican II

For those seeking change, by far the *most* hopeful sign was the Second Vatican Council of the Roman Catholic Church, which met from 1962 through 1965. The reforms put in place by Vatican II would change forever the face of worship for America's Roman Catholics. For Protestants, it suggested the nation might be on the cusp of a new era of ecumenical cooperation with Christians taking a more active role in social justice issues. Vatican II would be reflected in a flood of new liturgies, new ways of making music in the church, and new hymnody. "Dissatisfied with the complacent 'religiosity'

---

9. Routley, *Panorama of Christian Hymnody*, 398.

of the Dwight Eisenhower years, younger historians and theologians celebrated the ferment of the decade as foretelling a deeper, more authentically spiritual wakening."[10]

This desire for and openness to change extended to church musicians. Writing in 1966 when the many reforms coming out of Vatican II had yet to be put into practice, the Lutheran composer, conductor, and organist Robert Wetzler (b. 1932) referenced Manfred Bukofzer's *Music in the Baroque Era* (1947) to say that the style consciousness of the church in the twentieth century did not originate in the early church but rather in the fifteenth to eighteenth centuries. "The misleading idea that a certain style is in itself more proper for the Church than any other," Wetzler wrote, "came forth in the style-conscious Baroque period, and the same idea continues to afflict us today." The Catholic Church at that time, Wetzler noted, was seeking to recapture the glories of Renaissance polyphony by insisting composers write in the *stile antiquo*. The twentieth-century church, he warned, must not go down the same path.

> J. B. Phillips somewhere has pointed out that it was not times of persecution that ate away the strength of the church. Those were the times when men had to stand up and be counted. Rather, the dangerous times are when the church rots from within by becoming established and comfortable in the world.[11]

From a musical standpoint, Vatican II would most certainly confront a recalcitrant establishment and seek to rectify the misconceptions Wetzler cited.

The Roman Catholic Church in the United States after World War II was not the same institution it had been in when Pius X drafted his *Motu Proprio* in 1903. Catholics could no longer be stereotyped as a lower-strata, immigrant, working-class population. They were solidly middle-class with significant political and economic clout. While the *Motu Proprio* met with some resistance from American churches, leaders proceeded dutifully to carry out its mandates. By the 1960s, there was a recognition on the part of Rome that such all-encompassing edicts as the *Motu Proprio* could no longer be effective in diverse populations such as that in the United States. Perhaps the most important contribution of the Second Vatican Council, though one seldom mentioned, was that it limited Rome's ability to dictate and shape how worship would be practiced in the local church and gave clergy the flexibility

---

10. Cited in Ahlstrom, *Religious History of the American People*, 1097.
11. Wetzler, "Music for Worship," 6.

to utilize music best suited in their local community to achieve full congregational participation (*participatio actuosa*) in the liturgy.

During the first half of the twentieth century, the Roman Church had sought to reform its music and liturgy. It struggled diligently to achieve this, legislating that the church return to its roots in the Latin liturgy, Gregorian chant, and Renaissance polyphony. There had been some progress in the United States. Catholic University in Washington, DC, DePauw University in Indiana, and Alverno College in Wisconsin had begun awarding degrees in sacred music. Church music workshops at Boy's Town in Nebraska, founded by Msgr. Francis Schmitt, featured some of the most prominent boy choir trainers and composers, such as Flor Peeters.[12] Nevertheless, what progress there was had been impeded by a severe shortage of trained leadership. Unlike Europe, the melting pot which was America presented unique challenges. The sheer number of ethnic groups claiming a Catholic identity—while not speaking the same language and not able to read from the same Bible or prayer book—made insistence on a common liturgy daunting. In addition, each of those groups came with their own unique liturgical practices, ingrained over centuries, which would be difficult to change.

There had long been dissension between traditionalists and those seeking more robust reform of the church's worship practice. The Reverend Pius Parsch (1884–1954), a Moravian Catholic priest seeking reform, was a highly respected clergyman. He had served as a chaplain during the First World War and found the Latin Mass ineffective in ministering to soldiers on the front lines who were unfamiliar with it. "I often said Mass for the soldiers, at times for the whole division, as well as for a small group, and for the sick and wounded. I found it distressing that the soldiers understood nothing of the Mass." The experience led him to devote his life to liturgical reform. Regarding the movement toward liturgical reform, already active in the early 1950s, Parsch wrote that "The laity must realize then that much of the Mass has become set and fossilized. The movement recognizes the fact that the instruction part of the Fore-Mass[13] has completely lost its purpose of bringing the word of God to the hearer. It realizes that the laity were left almost entirely out of consideration and were represented (solely) by the choir and the ministers."[14]

---

12. Schaefer, *Catholic Music Through the Ages*, 141–42.

13. In citing the "Fore-Mass," Parsch was referring to the Liturgy of the Word or Service of the Word. In a concept likely inherited from pre-Christian synagogue, it includes a greeting, opening prayer, Psalm and Scripture readings, the sermon, and a recitation of a creed. In Roman Catholic tradition, this was the part of Sabbath worship open to all including, the catechumens who had not yet been confirmed into the faith..

14. Parsch, "Rev. Pius Parsch."

A Time of Turbulence

From the 1903 *Motu proprio* forward, a principal goal had been *"participatio actuosa"* or "active participation" of the congregation. One important way *participatio actuosa* was to be achieved was through congregational singing. Pius X envisioned congregations joining actively in the singing of at least the less complicated Gregorian chants with a trained *schola* to support as needed. The commitment to *participatio actuosa* never faded. In 1955 the papal encyclical *Musicae sacrae disciplina* (tr. "The Discipline of Sacred Music") acknowledged that music, "sung in the language of the people," could exert a "great and salutary force and power on the souls of the faithful." It therefore, for the first time, permitted and even encouraged singing of hymns and other music in the vernacular "during non-liturgical services and ceremonies, or when it is used outside [the] churches at various solemnities and celebrations."[15] Paul Hume in 1960 wrote ecstatically about what the *Musicae sacrae disciplina* could mean for Catholic worship. Speaking of Pius XII, he wrote, "No Pope before him had ever written so explicitly and so extensively on the importance which the Church herself attaches to hymns."[16] The encyclical, however, was but a foretaste of things to come.

In January of 1959 Pope John XXIII, Pius XII's successor, announced he would convene a council to be called "Vatican II."[17] The council formally opened on October 11, 1962.

Vatican II in progress. Public domain image from Creative Commons.

Four principal documents came out of the council over its four years in session:

1. *Sacrosanctum Concilium* (Sacred Liturgy)

---

15. Pope Pius XII, *Musicae sacrae disciplina*, December 1955.
16. Hume, *Catholic Church Music*, 81.
17. The name "Vatican II" was chosen to distinguish it from "Vatican I," a council held in the nineteenth century.

2. *Lumen gentium* (The Church)

3. *Dei verbum* (Divine Revelation)

4. *Gaudium et spes* (The Modern World)

The document most germane to this study was the first, *Sacrosanctum Concilium* (*SC*). In bringing the document before the council, Cardinal Ferdinando G. Antonelli stated that a great concern had arisen that the Catholic worshipping faithful were becoming "mute spectators" rather than active participants in the rites of the Church. (*Note: Items are grouped out of sequence according to subject matter. Bracket number indicates actual placement of each article.*)[18]

On that all-important topic of active participation, *SC* had this to say:

> [21.] . . . both texts and rites should be drawn up so that they express more clearly the holy things which they signify; the Christian people, so far as possible, should be enabled to understand them with ease and take part in them fully, actively, and as befits a community.
>
> [30.] To promote active participation (i.e., *participatio actuosa*), the people should be encouraged to take part by means of acclamation, response, psalmody, antiphon, and songs . . .

On the use of Latin versus the vernacular:

> [36.1] . . . The use of the Latin language is to be preserved in Latin rites. [36.2] But since the use of the mother tongue, whether in the Mass, administration of the sacraments or other parts of the liturgy, frequently may be of great advantage to the people, the limits of its employment may be extended. [36.3] These norms being observed, it is for the competent territorial ecclesiastical authority . . . to decide whether, and to what extent, the vernacular language is to be used.

On the use of hymnody in the observance of the Mass:

> [93.] To whatever extent may seem desirable, the hymns are to be restored to their original form . . . Also, as occasions may arise, let other selections from the treasury of hymns be incorporated.

On the use of Gregorian chant:

---

18. Following are excerpted texts from "*Constitution on the Sacred Liturgy, Sacrosanctum Concilium*, Solemnly Promulgated by His Holiness Pope Paul VI on December 4, 1963."

> [116.] The Church acknowledges Gregorian chant as specially suited to the Roman liturgy: therefore, other things being equal, it should be given pride of place in liturgical services. But other kinds of sacred music, especially polyphony, are by no means excluded from liturgical celebrations, so long as they accord with the spirit of liturgical action . . .

Regarding choirs in worship:

> [29.] Servers, lectors, commentators, and members of the choir also exercise a genuine liturgical function. They ought therefore to discharge their office with sincere piety.

> [114.] The treasure of sacred music is to be preserved and fostered with great care. Choirs must be diligently promoted, especially in cathedral churches; but bishops and pastors of souls must be at pains to ensure that, whenever the sacred action is to be celebrated with song, the whole body of the faithful may be able to contribute that active participation which is rightly theirs.

On liturgical and musical training for clergy:

> [16.] The study of sacred liturgy is to be ranked among the compulsory and major courses in seminaries.

> [115.] Great importance is to be attached to the teaching and practice of music in seminaries, in the novitiates, and . . . in other Catholic institutions and schools. To impart this instruction, teachers are to be carefully trained and put in charge of teaching sacred music. It is desirable also to found higher institutes of sacred music whenever this can be done.

The use of organs and other instruments:

> [120.] In the Latin Church, the pipe organ is to be held in high esteem, for it is the traditional musical instrument which adds a wonderful splendor to the Church's ceremonies and powerfully lifts up man's mind to God and to higher things.

> But other instruments also may be admitted for use in divine worship, with the knowledge and consent of the competent territorial authority . . . This may be done, however, only on condition that the instruments are suitable or can be made suitable for sacred use, accord with the dignity of the temple, and truly contribute to the edification of the faithful.[19]

---

19. Both the 1903 *Motu Proprio* and Vatican II's *Sacrsanctum Concilium* note the

The need for newly composed music:

> [121.] Composers, filled with the Christian spirit, should feel that their vocation is to cultivate sacred music and increase its store of treasures. Let them produce compositions which have the qualities proper to genuine sacred music, not confining themselves to works which can be sung only by large choirs but providing also for the needs of small choirs and for the active participation of the entire assembly of the faithful.

Owing to the gravity of the need for reform, Pope Paul VI put *Sacrosanctum Concilium* into effect as church law on December 4, 1963.[20] American bishops, knowing the action was eminent, designated November 29, the first Sunday in Advent, to introduce the new Mass liturgy in English.[21]

> So much changed so fast. On one Sunday in 1964, Catholics worshipped as they had for 400 years: in silence, on their knees, looking up to the altar at their priest as he prayed softly in Latin, his back to the congregation. The next week, this same priest faced the people, addressed them clearly in English, and encouraged them to sing together. Accustomed to silence, American Catholics joined in song reluctantly, if at all. That too, changed when young musicians brought their guitars and enthusiasm into the liturgy. Suddenly, the Church was rocking as Catholics discovered the *unifying power of congregational singing*.[22]

---

organ's historic importance in the church's worship history, but there are few specifics about the role of organ music as art in worship. To think Pope John XXIII viewed the organ negatively would be a misconception. "Yet it should be noted that only a few months before the official opening of this important event, John XXIII had used the blessing of the new organ at St. Peter's in Rome to deliver an enthusiastic tribute to Christian art and to make clear that, in a place so renowned for 'matchless expressions of human genius,' it was 'natural that music—the most spiritual of the fine arts—should make its own contribution toward lifting men up to the throne of the Most High, and toward suggesting to them sentiments of adoration, of exultation, and of gratitude.' In the same sense, the sovereign pontiff next observed that the pipe organ, which he referred to as the 'King of sacred musical instruments,' must become 'the spokesman for the feelings of all, for their noblest and holiest flights,' that it constitutes the symbol of the Church herself ('unity amid variety'), and that its prelude, played as the council opened, would invoke 'the Spirit of the Lord.'" Quoted from Sabatier, "Interrelations Between Liturgy, Music, and Organbuilding in France from the Middle Ages to Vatican II," Part 3.

20. Pope John XXIII, who had convened Vatican II, died in June of 1963. He was followed by Pope Paul VI.

21. Canedo, *Keep the Fire Burning*, 33.

22. Canedo, *Keep the Fire Burning*, 11.

Change was a gradual process in the US. First came the introduction of the Mass in English. Dennis Fitzpatrick, an American with a master's in organ and choral conducting from DePaul University in Chicago, was asked by Msgr. Reynold Hillenbrand, a longtime advocate of liturgical reform, if he might produce a traditional Roman Mass utilizing chant but in the English language appropriate for use in the United States when *SC* became official. Fitzpatrick gave his creation the uninspired name *Demonstration Mass English*, and it was first utilized at the National Liturgical Conference of the Roman Catholic Church in St. Louis on August 24, 1964.

Overall, the initial reaction among church musicians to *SC* was glowing. Msgr. Richard J. Schuler summed up the prevailing attitude:

> Truly, *Sacrosanctum Concilium* was a *magna carta* for the church musician reenforcing the historical developments of liturgical music from the Gregorian to modern works, openly allowing all styles of sacred music as long as they were appropriate to the occasion, encouraging and even demanding new works, both in the vernacular and in Latin, both for choirs and fore congregations, permitting the use of various instruments but ensuring the honored position of the pipe organ.[23]

Unfortunately, Schuler's optimism and that of others was short lived. While the vision implicit in *SC was* unfailingly hopeful, it was short on detail as to how reform was to be accomplished. It would fall to bishops and regional authorities to flesh out how the document's objectives were to be achieved. What soon became obvious was the wide gulf separating the Church's musicians from the Church's liturgical leadership and much of its clergy regarding how those objectives were to be prioritized.

Discordant Voices

Differences between Catholic musicians and liturgists were nothing new. The French composer and organist Jean Langlais (1907–1991)[24] had rued the progressive views of the church's liturgical leadership since the early 1950s. He saw them as seeking to remove the mystical, supernatural, and distinctly holy aspects of worship to replace them with the common and ordinary. "All religious composers, of which I am one," Langlais wrote, "are deeply discouraged by this movement which is the negation of art. In my opinion nothing is beautiful enough for God. Our forebears knew this and

---

23. Schuler, "Chronicle of Reform," 367.

24. Langlais became organist in 1945 at the *Basilica of Sainte-Clotilde*, where Cesar Franck had been organist in the nineteenth century. He served there until 1988.

held that to pray surrounded by beauty was central to worship, according to the holy word of Saint Pius X,[25] who was himself a great musician. Where is his thought, and what has become of his teaching?"[26] Particularly vexing to Langlais, one of the twentieth century's great masters of organ improvisation, was that the council's focus on *participatio actuosa* (and the liturgical wing's interpretation of it) would practically eliminate the extended improvisations that were central to his vision of ministry at the organ.

In 1978, ten years after *SC* became official, the eminent French composer Maurice Duruflé penned this scathing indictment of Vatican II: "The experiments attempted during these last twelve years have often been the pretext for the introduction of unbearably vulgar songs. This new music, played with the accompaniment of guitars and drums . . . was introduced into our sanctuaries for the express reason of attracting crowds . . ."[27]

Sacrosanctum Concilium was the first of the reform documents to be presented to the council when its deliberations began in 1962. The spirit of reform implicit in *SC* to facilitate full and active congregational participation, however, was the product of years of experimentation by forward-looking liturgical leaders. The most prominent of them was Father Joseph Gelineau (1920–2008), a French Jesuit priest.

Joseph Gelineau.
Public domain image. (https://www.discogs.com/
artist/1678759-Joseph-Gelineau?filter_anv=1&anv=J.+Gelineau)

---

25. Referring to Pope Pius X, author of the 1903 *Motu Proprio*.
26. Labounsky, *Jean Langlais*, 213.
27. Schubert, Review of "Reflections on Sacred Music", 25.

A Time of Turbulence

In 1943, Pius XII had charged biblical scholars with producing translations of the Bible based on the original Hebrew and Greek texts. The result in France was *The Jerusalem Bible*, first published in 1950. Following its publication, Gelineau collaborated with two other scholars to produce the *Psautier de la Bible de Jerusalem* in 1953, a translation of the Psalter into French that reflected the actual form and accentuation of the original Hebrew. Publication of musical settings for Gelineau psalms followed in 1957, however, individual psalms sung in French were appearing in Catholic worship well before that. By 1963, individual Gelineau psalms sung in English were being used in both England and the United States. The *Psautier de la Bible de Jerusalem* continues in use to the present day and made Joseph Gelineau a leader in Catholic liturgical reform in the era of Vatican II.

During the course of Vatican II, two international organizations took on the responsibility of interpreting in practical terms the wishes of the council, determining how they should be prioritized, and then mapping out steps for making the reform a reality. The *Consociatio Internationalis Musicae Sacrae* (or "International Society for Sacred Music") was authorized by Pope Paul VI in 1963 with Msgr. Johannes Overath (1913–2002) of Cologne as its president. In the United States, the society's affiliate organization was the Church Music Association of America (CMAA), established in 1965. The second organization seeking to shape the reform effort was *Universa Laus* (or "Universal Praise"), established in Lugano, Switzerland in 1966. Joseph Gelineau was one of its chief spokesmen. Its membership was largely made up of liturgists and liturgist-musicians, and its stated function was to study "the ritual function of music in liturgy, and the relationship between form, function, and signification."[28]

The Church Music Association of America took a conservative stance on reform, hoping to retain as much of Catholic worship traditions as possible—preserving the Latin liturgy of the Mass, continuing the use of Gregorian chant and the ongoing use of choirs dedicated to the performance of polyphonic music. They were quick to point out that much of the traditional repertoire was conceived for performance by a trained *schola* or choir and to be passively *listened to* by officiating clergy and congregation. A key argument posed by the CMAA centered on how *participatio actuosa* was to be defined. In their view, spiritually focused listening *was* active participation. Overath himself issued this explanation:

> If external activity (i.e., congregational participation) were demanded absolutely and in every single moment, then a death sentence would fall upon wide reaches of church music. With

---

28. Inwood, "History" (of Universa Laus).

> polyphonic mass parts and many compositions of Gregorian chant, singing along by the people is simply not possible. The concept of *participatio actuosa* cannot be narrowly restricted unless one completely misunderstands the spiritual nature of humanity. There is a real, indeed very elevated action, even when all external activity is missing ...
>
> Certainly, there is alongside this a *participatio actuosa* in which the faithful rise up out of their silent following along and reach the external activity of speaking along or singing along, but this changes nothing in the fact that silent listening to the choir singing Gregorian chant or polyphonic mass parts represents an entirely legitimate form of *participatio actuosa*.[29]

Sister Miriam Therese Winter (b. 1938), now famous for her songs including "Joy is Like the Rain," gained prominence through her work with the Catholic nursing order, the Medical Mission Sisters. Her folk-like, guitar-accompanied spiritual songs, recorded by the sisters in bestselling albums beginning in 1966, placed her squarely in the middle of the controversy roiling the Catholic Church. She later explained her perspective on the issues at stake. The polarization she saw was between the "song of the people" and the "artist's song"—between folk singers with guitars and professional musicians.[30]

> The Council's call for full, active participation by congregations created the context for the present problem ... The pastoral goal was closely linked to the need for comprehension, which resulted in a swift transition to a vernacular liturgy throughout the United States. Along with the loss of Latin there was the loss of all that music in which the Latin language played so integral a part. Gregorian Chant and classical polyphony ceased to be the norm or the goal of the average Catholic parish, a traumatic adjustment for professional musicians and all those sensitive to and appreciative of the art treasures of the past.[31]

A penultimate point in the battle between traditionalists and proponents of liturgical reform came in August of 1966 with the Fifth Annual Church Music Congress. The Church Music Association and *Universa Laus's* American arm, the National Liturgical Conference, were both well represented. The progressives in *Universa Laus* carried the day, and a new

---

29. Ruff, *Sacred Music and Liturgical Reform*, 362.
30. Winter, *Why Sing?*, 3.
31. Winter, *Why Sing?*, 5.

era of folk-based sacred music was quickly assimilated into the worship of American Catholicism.

Monsignor Richard J. Schuler (1920–2007) addressed the profound issues raised by the radical reforms of Vatican II in a lecture delivered at the University of Wisconsin in 1968. The word *religion*, he explained, was derived from the Latin *religere*, to bind. The purpose of religion therefore was to bind man to God. "Art can be sacred or secular," Schuler continued, "depending on its purpose."

> Secular art exists to imitate nature, to entertain, to create moods, to rouse passions, to aggrandize man. It may have a hundred different purposes. Sacred art, on the other hand, as the Vatican Council has recalled, exists to glorify God and edify the faithful.[32]

Schuler spoke passionately of priestly role church musicians should be playing.

> The work of art that the Church seeks will come from the trained and talented craftsman who has a vision of faith, is humble before the creativity of God in which he shares, and who has conceived in the depths of his soul a concept that he expresses in the material, but in which shines forth the majesty of God.[33]

Schuler was particularly troubled by a statement issued by the Bishop's Committee on Liturgy in 1968 that declared that "the primary goal of all eucharistic celebration is to make a *humanly attractive experience.*" This, he warned, threatened to replace "God with man as the end of sacred music."

> The basic problems of sacred music today do not lie in selection of repertoire or in the encouraging of congregational participation. The disputes over Latin and the vernacular, the choir, the use of various instruments besides the organ are not the essential points ... It is not a question of composers or performers or even of money to encourage them. The problem lies in the theological concept of "sacred." It is fundamentally a question of faith, and it touches every section of the church—the clergy, the musicians, the congregation.[34]

Schuler's observations were and still are profound, not only for Roman Catholicism in the post-Vatican II era, but for Protestants as well. The gulf

---

32. Schuler, "Sacred," 25.
33. Schuler, "Sacred," 23.
34. Schuler, "Sacred," 27.

separating populist/vernacular sacred music from that of cultivated religion had only widened in the decades leading up to 1963. As Schuler stated so eloquently, musicians with "a vision of faith," excellent training, and the humility to serve were desperately needed.

Sacred Troubadours, Guitars, and the Rise of the Folk Mass

The idea of re-dressing a traditional Christian liturgy of the Eucharist in the garb of popular culture did not originate with Vatican II or within Roman Catholicism. The Protestant Episcopal Church, born out of Anglicanism, had been celebrating the Eucharist in English since the sixteenth century, so worship in the vernacular was not an issue. Rethinking the role and kind of music that was appropriate, however, was a point of contention.

The Anglican priest Geoffrey Beaumont (1903–1970) was a composer of popular songs and pop-tinged hymn tunes. He was chaplain at Trinity College, Cambridge from 1947 to 1952. Beaumont was a strong advocate for congregational music drawn from popular music styles that might better relate to the general public, especially youth and young adults. In 1956, Beaumont's *A Twentieth Century Folk Mass* was published by the Josef Weinberger Company in London and soon was imported to the United States. While Beaumont labeled the work a "folk mass," it was not folk music in the sense of the American folk revival a decade later. Rather, by "folk" he simply meant "music of the people" or music in a popular style.

Excerpt from "Gloria," *A Twentieth Century Folk Mass,* **Geoffrey Beaumont. Used by permission of Josef Weinberger LTD (UK).**

In an article in *The Choral Journal,* James Evans listed characteristics of Beaumont's writing, including: a strong basic rhythm or beat under a syncopated melody, use of two vs. three hemiolas, repeated chordal patterns, and improvisatory riffs, etc.[35] All of these characteristics could be applied to 1950s jazz, and indeed Beaumont's *Twentieth Century Folk Mass* was often referred to as a jazz work in its time but it bore little resemblance to Charlie Parker or even Benny Goodman. Rather, according to Evans, movements of the mass sounded like "music hall ballads of the pre-war years. Poor imitations of Cole Porter immediately come to mind."[36]

Nevertheless, *A Twentieth Century Folk Mass* was a significant development because it represented a break from traditional practices for writing Anglican liturgical music, and most significantly, because it was conceived not for choral performance, but for full congregational participation. Unison writing was employed throughout with cantor and congregation interacting in a "call-and-response" pattern. This insured that even longer movements of the liturgy, the "Gloria" for example, which is excerpted above, could be readily sung by worshippers with no need of prior rehearsal. While it appealed for a time to the students at Cambridge and was "shocking and terrifying" to evangelical conservatives according to Erik Routley, that was not the reason for its significance. "It is significant," Routley wrote, "because it started something, and awakened the minds of church musicians to a quite new situation and a series of quite new questions. It is quite enough praise for any innovator in church music if we can say he did as much as this."[37]

A decade after Beaumont, in the United States, Episcopal composers led the way in producing some extremely popular and truly folk-inspired "guitar masses." The great organist at the [Episcopal] Cathedral of St. John the Divine in New York from 1954 to 1974, Alec Wyton (1921–2007), was also an astute, often acerbic, commentator on all things musical in the denomination. Regarding "tradition" in the church, Wyton delighted in quoting the concert pianist Arthur Schnabel who said "when we talk about tradition in art, we usually mean a collection of bad habits."[38] In an address to the American Guild of Organists in 1969, Wyton used Schnabel's pithy comment to expand upon his own views regarding the tyranny of tradition in the church:

> I want to submit to you that when we talk about tradition in
> the church that is exactly what we mean too, because so often

---

35. Evans, "Some Thoughts on Jazz," 14.

36. Evans, "Some Thoughts on Jazz," 14.

37. Routley, *Twentieth Century Church Music*, 167.

38. Edward Crankshaw, in his introduction to Schnabel's autobiography, *My Life and Music* (1961), states that Schnabel used this quote frequently in speaking publicly about music. He was a master of the pithy musical quote, many of which are legendary. "I know two kinds of audiences only," Schnabel once observed, "one coughing, and one not coughing."

we have gotten ground down in little sorts of ceremonies which are ours in our particular denomination. We are in love with Anglican Chant or *Hymns Ancient and Modern*, or plainsong, or call it whatever you like, and we cannot see that there is much more. There are millions of people who are not touched by these things. In New York City, whose population is nearly ten million, there are four million people who are utterly untouched by any denomination at all. I mean Protestant, Catholic, Jewish, you name it—absolutely untouched. And these are the people whom we are to be concerned about and the people whose minds have grown beyond our precious little ivory towers—Because, you see, often those who have grown up in the church, as indeed I did, love it and rightly so, but tend to get into the great danger of worshipping the liturgy rather than God through the liturgy.[39]

We've got to break down this sort of ivory tower thing. I'm not particularly worried about guitar masses. I don't care for them myself, but if pop masses have something to say or pop settings have something to say, then they should be allowed to say them. If they don't, they'll quickly die, and I can promise you that the more we resist these innovations, the longer they will be with us . . .[40]

Wyton's reference to guitar masses was likely inspired by the growing popularity of Herbert G. Draesel's *Rejoice! Music for the Worship of God in the Twentieth Century* (1964).

---

39. Wyton, "Thoughts on Music in the Church," 9.
40. Wyton, "Thoughts on Music in the Church," 14.

From *Hartford Courant,* January 9, 1965.

Rejoice! Music for the Worship of God in the Twentieth Century (1964) was scored for unison voices, guitar, optional keyboard, and bass. Draesel was a 1961 graduate of Trinity College in Hartford, Connecticut, followed by studies at General Theological Seminary (GTS). He was pastor of the House of Prayer Episcopal Church in Newark, one of the oldest Episcopal congregations in New Jersey, from 1965 to 1972. *Rejoice* was originally written for performance at GTS but became a favorite on college campuses and at Protestant churches of all denominations over the course of the decade.

Like the Beaumont, *Rejoice* was scored for unison voices, but the melodic lines are far more supple and memorable. The Nicene Creed example below was conceived to be sung over a strong beat in the bass and driving folk guitar providing energy and thrust

Nicene Creed (from "Rejoice") - Excerpt

Herbert G. Draesel

[Musical notation with lyrics:]

I be-lieve in one God, the Fa-ther Al-migh-ty, Ma-ker of hea-ven and earth, and of all things vis-i-ble and in-vis-i-ble; And in one Lord Je-sus Christ, the on-ly be-got-ten Son of God, be-got-ten of the Fa-ther be-fore all worlds; God of God, Light of Light, Ve-ry God of ve-ry God, be-got-ten not made be-ing of one sub-stance with the Fa-ther, by whom all things were made...

Copyright © 1964

Excerpt, *Rejoice! Music for the Worship of God in the Twentieth Century*, Draesel. Courtesy of Kaiser Southern Music Inc.

A second highly popular Episcopal guitar mass was the *American Folk Song Mass* of Father Ian David Mitchell, a guitar-playing, social activist priest who would eventually be dismissed from his Los Angeles parish for actively seeking homosexuals and Latinos to join the congregation.

In the Roman Catholic Church, any discussion of the introduction of folk-style Mass settings in English with guitar accompaniment must begin with Ray Repp.

Ray Repp.
Public domain image. (https://www.legacy.com/us/obituar-ies/stltoday/name/raymond-repp-obituary?id=1835121)

Raymond Robert Repp (1942–2020), while in seminary at Cardenal Glennon College Seminary in St. Louis in the early 1960s, began writing folk and folk-like melodies. He had been attracted to the music of the Kingston Trio and other popular folk-revival singing groups of the time. In 1965, Repp was asked to lead the music for a celebration of the Mass with a chorus of four hundred college-age youth at the Catholic Church Extension Society's Lay Volunteer Program in Chicago. This led to a request by the "Friends of the English Liturgy" (FEL)[41] to make a recording. The resulting album, *Mass for Young Americans* (1966), was a hugely popular success and inspired other writers to compose similar works. An excellent example of a Repp worship song is "Peace I Leave with You, My Friends."

---

41. The Friends of the English Liturgy was a Catholic organization founded in 1963 to advocate for liturgical reform.

Peace I Leave with You, My Friends

Ray Repp (1967)

[Musical notation with lyrics:]

Peace I leave with you, my friends, sha-lom, my peace, in all you do.
Peace I leave with you, my friends. I give to you so you can give to oth-ers too. To share God's love is why I came, to show God's kind-ness with-out end. Go now, my friends, and do the same, un-til I come a-gain.

Ray Repp, "Peace, My Friends" © 1967, 2015, Otter Creek Music. All rights reserved. Exclusive agent: OCP. Used with permission.

Social consciousness was a key ingredient in Ray Repp's faith, which he wrote of in later years:

> There is a great potential for liberation and evangelization (in the best sense of the word) in our musical texts. To deny this potential is not only naïve but irresponsible. We can help call each other forth—as God has been doing since the beginning—to be the loving, responsible, and just people we are capable of being. If the actions of the liturgy are at times vague, or the sermons sometimes meandering, people can still leave church with melodies and words of encouragement and challenge echoing in their hearts. It is not enough to leave people with pious platitudes and self-serving scripture quotes taken out of context. What does "Praise of the name of the Lord" have to do with the challenge of the Gospel? Does the Lord really like to be praised and entertained and sung to? Doesn't it make more sense that we sing together with the Lord (always present) about our willingness to live out our baptismal promise?[42]

---

42. Repp, "Current Trends."

Critics of the new folk masses were numerous. Joining in a chorus of dissent were conservative clergy, laity, and choirmasters desperate to preserve the legacy of Gregorian chant, retain Renaissance polyphony in worship, and save themselves from liturgical obsolescence. Many individual parishes found themselves divided by warring factions. Among those resisting change, a sort of nostalgia that was not based in reality set in about worship in pre-Vatican II days.[43]

But the growing popularity of guitar-accompanied worship songs and folk masses could not be ignored by the institutional church. It was discussed as early as April of 1965 at a meeting of the National Catholic Education Association. The following February, at a Catholic Music Advisory Board Meeting in Chicago, a proposal to authorize guitars and folk-oriented music in the celebration of the Mass was put up for a vote and passed. It was purely a symbolic victory. The board had no authority to make church policy, but once this measure passed, folk music in the church took on a life of its own.[44]

The folk masses of Ray Repp and others were but the earliest musical inheritance from the liturgical reforms of the Second Vatican Council. The folk character of much of music still permeating Catholic worship in the twenty-first century stems from this era. Perhaps most influential of all was a group of composer/singers who, like Repp, began their work in St. Louis—"The St. Louis Jesuits." Bob Dufford, John Foley, Tim Manion, Roc O'Connor, and Dan Schutte were all students at the Jesuit St. Louis University.

The conflict between the Church Music Association of America, representing the interests of the church's professional musicians, and *Laus Dei*, representing the church's liturgical contingent, would have ramifications still with us in Catholic musical circles. It was not unlike the many other polarizations surveyed in these pages, *all* reflecting a contest with winners and losers and the winners casting out all with which they disagree. Compromise, the hard work of finding common ground, was never pursued and the ramifications of *that* are still being felt in Catholic church music today.

Baby Boomers and the Folk Revival

In the 1960s, the United States was in the midst of a "folk music revival." Actually, calling it a folk music revival is a bit of a misnomer. While some true American folk music was sung, music composed in the "folk style"

---

43. Reagan, "Beautiful Noise," 108.
44. Schuler, "Chronicle of Reform," 379.

and performed with acoustic instruments—guitar, bass, banjo, and other instruments—is what would predominate and energize popular appeal. Historians generally trace the origins of the folk music revival to the Black singer, virtuoso guitarist, and prison convict Huddie William Ledbetter (1888–1949), better known by his stage name, Lead Belly. Beginning in the 1930s, Huddie Ledbetter made numerous historic recordings in New York City and tried to break into the burgeoning Black blues-gospel scene, performing at the Apollo Theater. He found his niche, however, playing smaller venues to aficionados of folk music.

Between September 1940 and January 1941, CBS radio aired a groundbreaking series of programs hosted by folk music legend Woody Guthrie (1912–1967). Guthrie personally insisted on Lead Belly's participation along with Burl Ives, Pete Seeger, and the Golden Gate Quartet of Southern gospel fame. Leadbetter, Guthrie, and Seeger became good friends and left a legacy of folk-influenced songs of social consciousness. Pete Seeger carried the legacy a step further by organizing the folk music quartet the Weavers in 1948. Following were the Kingston Trio and the Chad Mitchell Trio (both organized in 1958), the Limelighters (org. 1959), Peter, Paul, and Mary (org. 1961); and Joan Baez (first recordings, 1960).

By the opening of the Second Vatican Council in the fall of 1962, the folk music revival was in full swing and had been embraced by America's college-age youth, most of whom were Caucasian. The significance of the revival for American church music can only be understood by looking briefly at the baby boomer generation as it approached adulthood. The explosion of infant births following World War II was the largest in US history.

The 1950s had been for most white Americans a time of relative goodwill; a time to focus on family and to enjoy the comforts long denied them because of the Great Depression and wartime sacrifice. The 1960s, however, were an era of stark contrasts. While it was a period of increased prosperity, there were also widespread social tensions that tended to polarize American society. During the first four years of the decade the violent struggle for civil rights reached its pinnacle, leading to the historic passage of the Civil Rights Act of 1964. When the new decade dawned in 1960, most Americans were unaware that the United States had been funding a French military effort to defend the small nation of South Vietnam from the communist North Vietnamese for over six years. During the last half of the decade US military intervention in Vietnam continued to escalate with protests against the conflict dominating the news.

Out of this ferment came the distinct stratification between conservative Right and liberal Left, which remains with us today. "The right's goals included preserving social and moral order, promoting 'traditional values' such as family, patriotism, and the work ethic; and encouraging self-reliance, distrust of [big] government, and a tough stand on communism."[45] On the Left, there was a largely youth and young adult-led counterculture founded on idealism and a struggle for a new and more egalitarian society.

The peace activist Abbie Hoffman spoke for the newly emerging 1960s Left and its music when he said, "I am interested in fundamental changes to American society, in building a system of love, trust, brotherhood, and all the other beautiful things we sang about."[46] Music was a prominent feature of the counterculture. The folk music revival, since the times of Lead Belly, Woody Guthrie, and a youthful Pete Seeger, had roots in the Bohemian culture of New York's Greenwich Village. The anti-war and social justice themes of its music—a stark contrast to the shallow lyrics of commercial rock—matched perfectly the angst of the boomers. The musical style itself—folk-like with acoustic accompaniment—seemed the antithesis to the lush orchestrations of pop and the big band era.

The Origins of "Praise and Worship"

The near universal acceptance of contemporary Christian praise and worship music by American evangelicals by the late decades of the twentieth century was revolutionary. But what were its origins? Writers have usually dated its birth to the Jesus People, Chuck Smith, and the Calvary Chapel in Costa Mesa, California. The research of church historian Lester Ruth has shown the origin of concepts leading to Contemporary Christian Music (or CCM) came much earlier. The Latter Rain[47] preacher, theologian, and reviv-

---

45. Walsh, "1960s."

46. Hoffman, "Press of Freedom."

47. "Latter Rain" was a radical holiness group originating in western North Carolina and Tennessee in the 1880s that was founded on the belief that the "last days" had come upon the earth, that spirit baptism was to be encouraged as well as speaking in tongues and other spiritual gifts. It predated American Pentecostalism but shared much with it theologically. The movement took its name from the prophecy of Joel 2:23, "Be glad then, ye children of Zion, and rejoice in the Lord your God: for he hath given you the former rain moderately, and he will cause to come down for you the rain, the former rain, and the latter rain in the first month." In the twentieth century Latter Rain became a faction within the Assemblies of God denomination. Latter Rain's proponents preached that "the Christian Church must restore and equip a 'five-fold ministry' which included modern-day apostles, prophets, evangelists, pastors, and teachers." A more radical branch calling itself the "New Order of the Latter Rain" viewed mainstream Christianity as hopelessly corrupt and in need of purging. The ensuing controversy led to schism within the Assemblies of God. Latter Rain teachings were deemed heretical and ties to Latter Rain were severed in 1949. Other Pentecostal groups followed suit. While the term "Latter Rain" is seldom used today, most Charismatics adhere to aspects

alist Reg Layzell (b. 1904) accepted a call to Abbottsford, British Columbia, in 1946 where he birthed a powerful philosophy of worship based on Psalm 22:3, "But thou art holy, O thou that inhabitest the praises of Israel" (KJV), and Hebrews 13:15, "By him therefore let us offer the sacrifice of praise to God continually, that is, the fruit of our lips giving thanks to his name" (KJV).[48]

One facet of charismatic and Pentecostal theologies of worship has always been a desire to recapture the essence of worship in the first centuries of the Christian faith. It is a passion within the contemporary worship movement to the present day. The Reverend James Lee Beall (1924–2013), Latter Rain pastor at Bethesda Missionary Temple in Detroit, wrote:

> The [worship of God in the book of Revelation] is a far cry from what nominal Christianity calls "praise"! The majority of Sunday morning services has degenerated to the singing of two traditional hymns (and that by only a portion of the congregation), a prayer or two, a sermon, and a benediction ... I want to openly declare I DO NOT accept the apostate order of Protestantism worship as divine order. In fact, it is my firm contention that the church general has drifted so far from the Bible pattern that she wouldn't know divine order if she saw it and heard it![49]

Four basic themes stood out in Layzell's theology: (1) that the object of worship was to be in God's divine presence and the way there was through praise; (2) that a life of praise is mandatory for the believer regardless of personal circumstances; (3) that only through continual praise is one shielded from carnal sin; and (4) that praise is the ultimate declaration of love for God.[50]

Initially, Latter Rain music was completely improvisatory. There were no songbooks and the melodies, unaccompanied with some sung in harmony, were credited to the movement of the Spirit. This changed in 1949 with the publication of Phyllis Spiers's *Spiritual Songs by the Spiers,* and in 1952 with *Scripture Set to Music* by Rita Kelligan. Songs in Kelligan's collection, short musical settings of texts taken verbatim from Scripture, were a prototype for many of the earliest praise choruses of the 1960s and '70s.

---

of Latter Rain theology. The origins of praise music in Latter Rain worship are another example of that continued influence.

48. Ruth and Lim, *History of Contemporary Praise and Worship,* 8–11.
49. Ruth and Lim, *History of Contemporary Praise and Worship,* 41.
50. Ruth and Lim, *History of Contemporary Praise and Worship,* 21.

A period of continual praise through singing lasting up to an hour was an essential component of worship for Layzell and his followers.[51] The singing was intended to move from exuberant praise to a period of heartfelt adoration in God's presence. To achieve this, techniques were gradually developed to move from song to song and theme to them, seamlessly through tempo changes and key relationships.

One of the most striking characteristics of Latter Rain worship as advocated by Layzell was the place of prominence given to music and those leading it. As we have already seen, Latter Rain theology was based both in Old and New Testament Scripture. The Feast of Tabernacles (Deuteronomy 16:12–14) and the day of Pentecost were both seen as leading to the "end times" or final fulfillment. Therefore, worship as it was practiced in the tabernacle of David is key to understanding Latter Rain's ideas about music. In 1 Chronicles 25:1–7, priestly musicians are tasked with leading in worship with their voices and prophesying with instruments. From the first, Latter Rain praise and worship was usually accompanied by guitar and/or piano. Later drums were often added.[52] These concepts again foreshadow the prominent position in worship that song leaders and praise bands will occupy in contemporary Christian music to come.

The "Jesus Movement"

It's morning, Jesus. It's morning,
and here's that light and sound all over again.
I've got to move fast . . . get into the bathroom, wash up,
grab a bite to eat, and run some more.
I just don't feel like it. What I really want to do is get back into bed,
Pull up the covers, and sleep. All I seem to want today is the big sleep,
and here I've got to run all over again.
Where am I running? You know these things I can't understand.
It's not that I need to have you tell me. What counts most is that somebody
*   knows, and it's you. That helps a lot.*
So I'll follow along, OK? But lead, please. Now I've got to run.
Are you running with me, Jesus? (Malcolm Boyd)[53]

---

51. The term "praise and worship" has often been treated as a single concept, but in the Latter Rain view, they were separate ideas, worship always related to experiencing God's divine presence.

52. Ruth and Lim, *History of Contemporary Praise and Worship*, 27.

53. Boyd, *Are You Running with Me, Jesus?*, 2–4.

The term "Jesus People" was likely coined by the activist Episcopal priest Malcolm Boyd (1923–2015). Boyd, in 1965, published a book of prayers, *Are You Running with Me, Jesus?*, which became a national bestseller. During the 1960s, he became known as the "Espresso Priest" for his religious poetry readings at the Hungry I nightclub in San Francisco. He would later become a clergy icon of the American civil rights movement. In his travels, Boyd had become aware of a developing "underground church," and Dan Thrapp—a reporter for the *Los Angeles Times*—interviewed him on the subject:

> The underground church he described is not formally organized, has no bishop or anything comparable, and no rites or membership laws . . . He said members of the underground church include people "in no church," Catholics, and Protestants who have ceased to be active in their own church life. And Catholics and Protestants who have no intention of leaving their churches but deplore their inertia. They seek to renew it, to revitalize it.[54]

What Boyd was describing was quite likely an iteration of what would become the "Jesus Movement." It has often been conjectured that this countercultural movement among youth in the 1960s was descended from the Beat generation of the post-World War II years. There were similarities. Both were amorphous movements that rejected the traditional American values of the 1950s, experimented with psychedelic drugs, advocated for sexual liberation, and adopted styles of dress which clearly set them apart. Each was engaged in a spiritual quest, some with various strains of Christianity, others with a variety of Eastern religions. Leading figures of the Beat or beatnik counterculture of the 1950s included Jack Kerouac and Allen Ginsberg.

Music was also central to both movements. The Beats gravitated more toward underground and avant-garde jazz, but the early stages of the folk music revival also found their voice in the clubs of Greenwich Village. Bob Dylan, one of the most influential singer/composers for the 1960s counterculture, had in his youth been a disciple of the Beat generation's Allen Ginsberg.

The catalyst bringing the many diverse elements of the youth counterculture of the 1960s together was the notorious Summer of Love of 1967. Setting the stage for it was the Human Be-In on January 14, which was attended by up to thirty thousand people. It was there that Timothy Leary uttered the catch phrase that would help to shape the entire countercultural movement going forward: "turn on, tune in, drop out."

---

54. Thrapp, "New Underground Church," 3, 17.

As Malcom Boyd indicated, it was not a formally organized movement. A religious movement among white American youth, the Jesus Movement emerged in California around 1967 and ended abruptly in 1973. There was no central organizing figure or overarching organizational structure, but groups within it tended to live communally, be socially conscious, passionately evangelical, and share the values of the counterculture and hippiedom. Jesus People became famous for their aggressive street ministry, and the movement became increasingly Pentecostal over the years. A 1971 issue of *Time* magazine had as its cover story, "The Jesus Revolution," and had this to say about the Jesus People:

> WARNING: HE IS STILL AT LARGE!
>
> HE is indeed. As the words of this wanted poster from a Christian underground newspaper demonstrate, Jesus is alive and well and living in the radical spiritual fervor of a growing number of young Americans who have proclaimed an extraordinary religious revolution in his name. Their message: the Bible is true, miracles happen, God really did so love the world that he gave it his only begotten son . . .
>
> It is a startling development for a generation that has been constantly accused of tripping out or copping out with sex, drugs and violence. Now, embracing the most persistent symbol of purity, selflessness and brotherly love in the history of Western man, they are afire with a Pentecostal passion for sharing their new vision with others. Fresh-faced, wide-eyed young girls and earnest young men badger businessmen and shoppers on Hollywood Boulevard, near the Lincoln Memorial, in Dallas, in Detroit and in Wichita, "witnessing" for Christ with breathless exhortations.
>
> Christian coffeehouses have opened in many cities, signaling their faith even in their names: "The Way Word" in Greenwich Village, "The Catacombs" in Seattle, [the] "I Am" in Spokane. A strip joint has been converted to a "Christian nightclub" in San Antonio.[55]

The Jesus Movement had indeed spread nationally by 1971, but it was born of more humble origins. Converts to the movement commonly had a deep disenchantment with the established church, largely because of what they viewed as its unwillingness or inability to address the issues of contemporary society. The controversial leader of the Jesus People group "Children of God," David Berg, reflected this in a published screed:

---

55. "New Rebel Cry," 56.

Church members were a bunch of old hypocrites . . . [they were] much more interested in getting a fancier church building, swankier preacher, and more high-falutin' choir and organ music, and showing off fancy clothes at meetings . . . Membership had become a status symbol and a business necessity for the affluent society, a social club for the rich and well-to-do, to do their dainty little duty for God to the tune of dainty little ditties to God . . . Most of them were whited sepulchers full of dead men's bones, and the only way they reached heaven was by their stench.[56]

Nevertheless, some of those same established churches reached out to the displaced youth of the Summer of Love; among them, the First Presbyterian Church of Hollywood and St. Luke's Episcopal Church in Seattle. The Rev. Don Williams,[57] called to served First Presbyterian/Hollywood as its college pastor in 1968, was a fan of Bob Dylan, whose music he felt personified aspects of the '60s youth culture—"idealism on the one hand . . . and then anger on the other hand."[58]

Williams, with the input of his college-age Bible classes, came up with the idea of opening a coffee house patterned after folk music clubs in Greenwich Village. With the church agreeing to provide seed money and donated labor, a floor of an adjacent apartment building was remodeled to become "the Salt Company." An essential component, Williams insisted, had to be the "best sound system that money could buy at the time."[59] When the Salt Company opened its doors in the summer of 1968, it became a prototype for similar gathering places throughout the country.

Calvary Chapel

Calvary Chapel, in Costa Mesa, California, unlike the church in Hollywood, was new and not affiliated with a particular denomination. It was founded in 1965, just two years before the Summer of Love. An independent, Pentecostal church, Calvary started with only twenty-five in its membership and a very traditional worship format—"three hymns, a responsive scripture

---

56. Berg, *MO Letters*, No. 167.

57. Williams attributed his conversion to Christianity to membership in Young Life during his youth. He received his Master of Divinity degree from Princeton Theological Seminary and his PhD from Columbia University. Following his years at First Presbyterian Hollywood, he taught at Fuller Theological Seminary and became associated with John Wimber's the Vineyard.

58. Eskridge, *God's Forever Family*, 60.

59. Eskridge, *God's Forever Family*, 60.

reading, baby dedication, sermon, prayer and dismissal."[60] Costa Mesa, however, located near popular beach communities—Huntington Beach, Newport Beach, and Venice—was a magnet for hippiedom. Pianist and guitarist Tom Stipe recalled that "compressed into the area's cities and beaches were swarms of culturally orphaned young people looking for love, peace, sex, drugs and rock n' roll. They were called by many, 'the hippies'. A recipe for revival existed for every side of the spiritual spectrum in that assortment of youthful humanity."[61]

Calvary's pastor, Charles Ward ("Chuck") Smith (1927–2013), preached a message that appealed to the disaffected teenagers and young adults: the end times and the coming of the apocalypse. He pioneered a less formal, contemporary approach to worship including services on the beach and baptisms in the Pacific Ocean. Smith would later recall a sign posted in the church reading, "No bare feet allowed in the church" after hippie worshippers had dirtied the floor. He immediately called a church board meeting and had the sign taken down. "No one, hippies included," he declared, "would be turned away."[62]

The music of the Jesus People, at least initially, was simple, folk-influenced, and ideally suited to informal group singing and evangelistic witness in the outdoors. Some songs, now well-known even in non-Pentecostal circles, became theme songs for the movement. One of them, "They'll Know We are Christians by Our Love," by the Roman Catholic priest Peter Scholtes, was composed for St. Brendan Parish Church in Chicago in 1966.

---

60. Stipe, "Calvary Chapel Chronicles."
61. Stipe, "Calvary Chapel Chronicles."
62. Reagan, "Beautiful Noise," 160.

Peter Scholtes, "They'll Know We Are Christians by Our Love."
© 1966 F.E.L. Publications. Assigned 1991 Lorenz Publishing Company (admin. by Music Services). All Rights Reserved. ASCAP. Used by Permission.

Such songs were relatively short, often with a traditional verse/chorus format. The repeating chorus was easily memorized even for those new to the group. The guitar accompaniments were built entirely on primary chords and could easily be strummed by inexperienced players.[63]

Calvary Chapel soon became known as the "hippie church." Pastor Smith not only welcomed in the young people with their unconventional lifestyle and dress, but also innovated a worship style referred to later as "soft Pentecostalism." At Calvary, overt physical manifestations common to charismatic worship were prohibited. Smith felt they drew attention to individuals and away from Jesus, the object of their worship. Coincidentally, this would make Calvary's approach to worship more palatable to mainstream Protestants. In the long term, worship as practiced at Calvary Chapel would have wide influence and lead to what some have called "the Pentecostalization of American Christianity."[64]

The hiring of Lonnie Frisbee (1949–1993) and his wife Connie in May of 1968 was a key development in the music ministry of Calvary Chapel. Once in the employ of the church, Frisbee immediately began canvassing nearby beaches each morning, wearing a robe and carrying a Bible. It was under his leadership that guitars were introduced into the church's youth Bible study, after which attendance increased exponentially. Frisbee's Bible

---

63. The F# minor and B minor chords in "Pass It On" lend color to the song but are totally optional. A less capable player simply substitutes a D chord.

64. Reagan, "Beautiful Noise," 164.

study meetings quickly became "a major hub of the Jesus Movement."[65] Many of the songs such as "Rise and Shine" (the "Arky, Arky" song) had a campfire quality to them. Others were familiar because of their commercial origins: from Disneyland, "It's a Small World," and the Coca-Cola Song ("I'd Like to Teach the World to Sing").

Lonnie Frisbee in the 1960s.
Fair use. (https://en.wikipedia.org/w/index.php?curid=14973511)

During the four years he was at Calvary, Frisbee introduced alternative weeknight worship services, and many of the new converts brought in by Frisbee were musicians.

> A service at Calvary Chapel resembled a rock concert more than it did the traditional liturgy of that period. The pastoral staff was often indistinguishable from the congregation because of their casual attire. The worship service was led by guitar-playing young musicians wearing tee shirts and bell-bottom trousers . . . The new songs had contemporary melodies that expressed a relevant message, reflective of the author's spiritual experiences.[66]

A critical step, which would have long-term impact, both for Calvary and for the future of contemporary Christian music, was the forming of a band for these services. It would be called "Love Song." Love Song quickly became much more than a house band for Calvary Chapel. They performed widely,

---

65. Reagan, "Beautiful Noise," 165.
66. Reagan, "Beautiful Noise," 165.

often accompanied by Frisbee, who would preach. They were featured performers at Disneyland and even toured internationally.

The high-water mark of the Jesus Movement was a mammoth gathering, "Explo '72," in Dallas, Texas, June 12–17, 1972. Drawing seventy-five thousand people and sponsored by Campus Crusade for Christ, it has been referred to as "the religious Woodstock." The Campus Crusade sponsorship and the meeting's featured speaker, Billy Graham, are an indication that many unique features of hippiedom and Pentecostalism were falling away. The movement was melding into the broader stream of American evangelicalism. The theme song for the event was not one of the simple folk-like songs of the Jesus People. Rather, it was the pop gospel hit of the previous year, "Put Your Hand in the Hand of the Man from Galilee," by Canadian composer Gene MacLellan.

> Put your hand in the hand of the man who stilled the water
> Put your hand in the hand of the man who calmed the sea
> Take a look at yourself and you can look at others differently
> Put your hand in the hand of the man from Galilee.

Johnny Cash warmed up the crowd before Graham's sermon on the final day of Explo '72. He closed his set with MacLellan's song, and Graham rose to preach. The core of his sermon came from the song:

> Put your hand in the hand of the man from Galilee! When you do, you'll have a supernatural power to put your hand in the hand of a person of another race. You'll have a new love in your heart that will drive you to do something about poverty, the ecology question, the racial tension, the family problems and, most of all, to do something about your own life.[67]

Sacred Pop Goes Mainstream

In the 1950s, white Protestant worship had largely fallen along traditional lines. Hymns, choirs, and organs were standard fare in mainline parishes. Evangelical churches had much the same, though they gravitated more toward a gospel song repertoire with piano accompaniment. The maturing of the boomer generation in the 1960s and Vatican II brought with them a new perception of what appropriate worship music should look like. First there

---

67. Eskridge, *God's Forever Family*, 173. From a musical standpoint, Graham's crusades had always been formulated to appeal to his and earlier generations of Christians. Graham's appearance at Explo '72 could be seen as a recognition that there was a new generation that would require a different musical witness to reach it evangelically.

were the Episcopal folk masses with Ray Repp and the Roman Catholics following soon thereafter. The Jesus People took the new music a step further, reducing it to short, easily remembered choruses that could be used wherever ad hoc gatherings might take place. An essential element of all of this was a melding of religious themes with folk and popular music. Evidence of the extent to which this had become mainstream is revealed in two groundbreaking Broadway musicals that premiered during the period in question: *Jesus Christ Superstar* (1970) and *Godspell* (1973). Songs from both became recorded hits and even appeared in songbooks used in many denominations.

"Up with People," an American organization combining youth-focused music with a message of intercultural cooperation and communication, helped to soften the disdain with which many mainline churches viewed youth-oriented music. It began its five-month annual tours in July of 1968. Up With People utilized a combination of pop- and folk-influenced choral music, much of it with accompaniment of guitars and other instruments. The clean-cut image presented by Up with People, girls in skirts and guys often in shirts and ties—eschewing hippie beads, bell bottoms, and peasant dresses—made them more palatable to middle-class Protestants.

The group's nonsectarian message gave them much cross-denominational support and inspired the organization of youth choirs in hundreds of churches. Unlike most adult choirs, which were focused mainly on their weekly worship offerings, many of these youth choral groups combined music, Christian education, and fellowship into a single program, suggesting a kinship with the musical ministry at Calvary Chapel. The use of music from the Jesus Movement like "They'll Know We Are Christians" and "Pass It On" was common.

The influences of the folk revival and pop were also reflected in the popular youth musicals of the non-Pentecostal Southern Baptist Church. Among them: "Good News" (1967), "Tell It Like It Is" (1970), "Natural High" (1971), "If My People" (1974), and perhaps the most popular of all, "Celebrate Life" (1972). Such large-scale youth productions reached their peak of popularity between 1970 and 1972 and had largely faded out by 1975. Nevertheless, they were important for introducing and gaining acceptance for a variety of pop styles and instrumentations to evangelical worship.

By the early 1970s, the discord between a youth counterculture and a conservative "silent majority" had come to a head and would gradually moderate. The evangelical/Pentecostal movement that had originated in the 1960s as a mission effort to reach young people had, by the 1980s, morphed into an all-encompassing "church growth movement" affecting all of American Protestantism. It would have a major impact on church music.

Chapter 21

THE DECLINE OF THE CULTIVATED TRADITION IN AMERICAN CHURCH MUSIC

As noted in the preface, *Servanthood of Song* was conceived to be a survey of American church music history from the eighteenth through the end of the twentieth century. This chapter, which completes the historical aspect of the study, looks at the three decades following Vatican II. I struggled with using the word "decline," given its negative connotations, because much that is positive happened during those years. Nonetheless, I firmly believe that decline from the heady days of church music in the 1950s was inevitable, and from that decline we are now able to see signs of hope—hope for a new and more inclusive approach to church music ministry in the twenty-first century.

The last quarter of the twentieth century was by no means a musical wasteland for cultivated church musicians. Many churches across the nation continued to support traditional music programs with trained choirmasters, organists, and organist/choirmasters. In larger parishes—liberal, middle of the road, and evangelical—many such positions were full time. Sacred music repertoire had become quite expansive—from choral and organ masterworks of European and American origin to settings of folk tunes and spirituals. Hymnody expanded too, with profound and inspiring texts by British Hymn Explosion writers like Brian Wren and Fred Pratt Green. Americans including David Johnson, Carl Schalk, Lee Hastings Bristol, Richard Dirksen, and Harold Friedell contributed hymn tunes still in use in mainline churches. The Presbyterian poet Jane Parker Huber (1926–2008), among others,[1] did much to preserve traditional hymnody by making texts more inclusive[2] and by composing dozens of new hymns for the church in a new age.

Choral and organ music continued to be the primary focus of music ministry in most mainline churches with special musical services and concerts a common occurrence. My personal experience in ministry during the 1980s and '90s included multiple children's, youth, adult, and handbell choirs, each rehearsing weekly.

Beginning in the late 1980s, contemporary praise music was making inroads into traditional Presbyterian and Methodist congregations where I served. The music, initially led by a single songleader and perhaps a guitar or two, gradually morphed into singing "praise teams" and full instrumental combos with keyboard and percussion. The progression from something akin to informal group singing to a whole new area of music ministry requiring specialized instruments, rehearsals, and trained leadership meant additional expense in spite of often shrinking music budgets.

Choral repertoire for mixed voice adult choirs included a wide variety of anthems and service music appropriate to liturgical needs and the church year. In addition, there were the special annual presentations—many *Messiahs,* choral cantatas, *Tenebraes,* and major oratorios. I was fortunate to oversee large pipe organ installations, formed and grew excellent handbell programs, and even helped two churches acquire custom-built harpsichords to support the performance of early music repertoire. None of this was particularly unusual. Hundreds of music ministry colleagues had similar experiences. It was the life of a career church musician in the late twentieth century.

I doubt, however, that any church musician active in recent decades could have been unaware that a serious decline was in progress. Certainly, there were—and continue to be—flagship music programs in a few large

---

1. For a selection of Parker Huber hymns, see Huber, *Singing Faith.*

2. The issue of inclusive language in hymnody as well as other areas of worship was heavily debated during the last quarter of the twentieth century. At issue were whether the use of "man" or "mankind," for example, as gender-specific words or to be understood generically to mean "people" or "humanity." For proponents of inclusive language, there was a broader underlying issue that has been termed "linguistic racism." (See "Q & A.") *The New Century Hymnal* (1995) was one of the first to adopt inclusivity throughout. United Methodist and Presbyterian hymnals, published in the 1990s, took a more moderate approach, adjusting language in lyrics of well-known hymns where it fit naturally with the poetry and including newer hymns with inclusive texts. Jann Aldredge-Clanton (bn. 1946), a Baptist minister and feminist, carried forward the work of Parker Huber with her *Earth Transformed with Music! Inclusive Songs for Worship* (2018). Another resource: *God Is Still Speaking, We Are Still Singing* (2018) by Elizabeth A. Moore.

urban parishes, but for those of us serving in the trenches in middle America, something was happening. It affected everything—church budgets shrank; there seemed to be more cynicism in church politics; the number and makeup of choirs we were working with was changing. Also concerning was a tendency by many church pastors and administrators to distance themselves from their denominational leadership, choosing a decidedly more conservative theology than that espoused by the denomination as a whole. Because of this, many churches declined to purchase denominationally authorized hymnals when they were published. Some congregations opted for commercial, nondenominational collections while others chose to dispense with print hymnals entirely. Interest in children's music was on the decline by the mid-1990s and choirs for high school youth—which had enjoyed a boom during the late 1960s and early '70s—were becoming rare. The adult choir, usually the principal ensemble of any church music ministry, had entered a trying time as well. Recruitment of adult singers had become more challenging, and there was a general graying of choir membership rolls as demands of work and family prevented many of the younger from volunteering. Many larger congregations, polarized over musical preferences and determined to avoid schism, formed separate worship services, one for those in the church family wishing to retain traditional worship practices and trappings, and one for those wanting a less structured worship experience. In essence, the community was being split in two, upending the idea of communal worship as a unified body of believers.

Statistics accumulated during the period bear out that a serious decline was underway. Gallup polls over the years show that church and synagogue membership among Americans hovered around 70 percent between 1937 and 1976. Between 1976 and 1999 the membership percentage declined modestly to 68 percent,[3] but noticeable changes were occurring in the balance between mainline and evangelical denominations. In 1970 the percentage of the total population belonging to mainline Protestant churches (United Methodist, Presbyterian–PCUSA, Evangelical Lutherans, Episcopalians, etc.) outnumbered evangelicals 30 percent to 20 percent. By 1983, that balance had shifted with evangelical church membership outnumbering that of mainline churches. As of 1993, evangelicals comprised about 27 percent of the population while mainline church memberships seem to have plateaued at 20 percent. Also, between 1976 and 2021 just over 55 percent of people raised in a mainline church remained so in adulthood while the rate of retention for evangelicals was 70 percent.[4] This rate of decline would

---

3. Jones, "U.S. Church Membership Down Sharply."
4. Burge, "Mainline Protestants Are Still Declining."

The Decline of the Cultivated Tradition in American Church Music

radically increase in the first two decades of the twenty-first century.[5] Most worrisome, the percentage of Americans claiming no religious affiliation had increased from just 5 percent in 1970 to 30 percent in 2020.[6]

Only now can one look back and see the extent to which widespread change in American church life was taking place. Lester Ruth has listed various "plot lines" that may have triggered the rise of contemporary Christian music and the turn away from traditional worship by many in the late twentieth century. These include:

- The Jesus People and the introduction of popular music and popular music styles into worship.
- The church growth movement.
- God's means of renewing the church.
- The church's desire to be attractive to youth.
- A connection to frontier revivalism.[7]

Ruth noted two distinct musical forms that together define contemporary[8] Christian music: the "Praise and Worship Chorus" and the "Contemporary Worship Song." The short, easily learned and repeated praise and worship choruses were descended from the spiritual songs of the Latter Rain Pentecostal Movement discussed above. There were at least four key differences between Latter Rain choruses and those of 1960s and '70s praise and worship. First, lyrics for Latter Rain songs were generally verbatim quotes from Scripture in the King James Version of the Bible. The newer praise and worship texts, however, were often freely paraphrased from Scripture or completely original. Keith Green's "O Lord, You're Beautiful" from 1980 is an example:

---

5. Jones, "U.S. Church Membership Down Sharply."

6. Burge, "Mainline Protestants Are Still Declining." The accelerated decline in mainline church worship that has occurred since 2000 is reflected in the "National Congregations Studies" conducted in 1998, 2006, 2012, and 2018.

7. Ruth, *Essays on the History of Contemporary Praise and Worship*, 4.

8. The use of the adjectives "contemporary" and "traditional" in this and the previous chapter is regrettable yet, in my view unavoidable, because of their common usage. Neither term accurately describes the types of music to which it refers. Using the word *contemporary* in relation to praise music begs confusion with music of avant-garde classical composers like Györgi Legeti. *Traditional* is used too often to suggest something old, boring, and antiquated while, in actuality, worship retaining historic practices and liturgies often utilizes music and styles of modern and sacred/pop composers to be spiritually engaging.

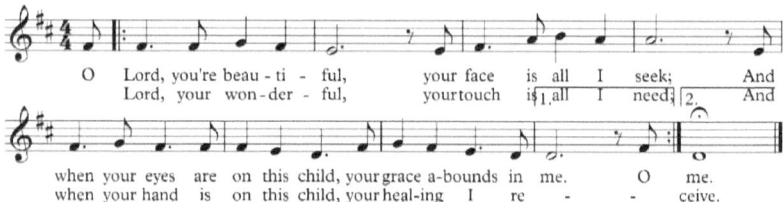

Keith Green, "O Lord, You're Beautiful," copyright 1980, Universal Music-Brentwood Benson Publishing and Birdwing Music. Used by permission.

Praise song composers, unlike their Latter Rain predecessors, stylized their music based on popular music idioms of the time—folk, pop, and later rock. Looking to pop as their style guide, they were much more expansive in their choices for instrumental accompaniments. Where Latter Rain song accompaniments were limited generally to keyboard or acoustic guitar, contemporary worship musicians, like the recording artists they modeled, soon branched out into electric guitars, basses, keyboards (often synthesizers), and drum sets, as well as a variety of other instruments. Finally, while Latter Rain's theology of worship drew inspiration from the Feast of Tabernacles of the Old Testament, praise and worship was exclusively New Testament based and focused on building a personal relation or "intimacy" with God. Songs of adoration *to* God and Jesus were favored over songs *about* them.

The more extended and complex contemporary worship songs that embraced styles of popular recording artists originated with the Youth for Christ movement[9] and highly visible events such as Explo '72. The style was eventually assimilated into the Vineyard and Maranatha! repertoires. "Lord of All" (1989), by Vineyard composer Danny Daniels, is an example. It would require a solo singer/song leader to be taught initially.[10]

---

9. Ruth, *Essays on the History of Contemporary Praise and Worship*, 5–7.

10. See Doucette, "Historical Development of the Modern Worship Song," for an excellent discussion of worship song form and content.

Lord of All

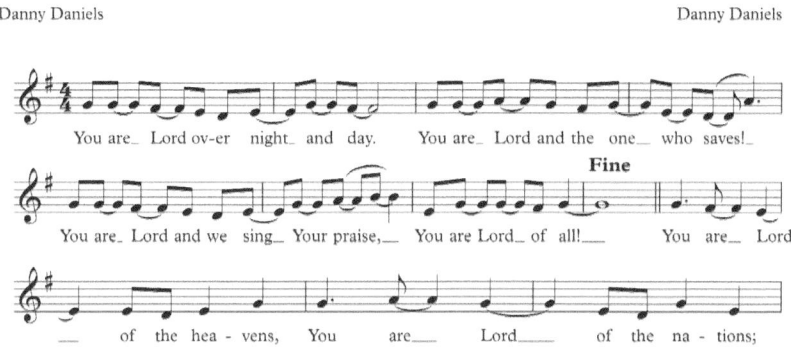

Copyright © 1989, Mercy Publishing, ARR/ICS

Danny Daniels, "Lord of All," © 1989 **Mercy/Vineyard Publishing (ASCAP) (adm at IntegratedRights.com). Used by permission.**

The two types, "praise and worship choruses" and "contemporary worship songs," would eventually merge around 2000. To understand any of this, we need first to assess the evolving roles of contemporary Christian music, the church growth movement, popular culture, electronic media, and how each of those has affected the church's theology and worship practice.

The Maturation of Contemporary Christian Music: Calvary Chapel and Maranatha! Music

In the 1970s, the songs of the Jesus Movement and the ministry of Chuck Smith at Calvary Chapel had coalesced and become a key component of worship both at Calvary and at a growing number of Calvary satellite locations. As Calvary's ministry expanded, Smith hoped to retain the authenticity of the church's worship music as it had been from the beginning. That included (seemingly) spontaneous song leading by worship leaders acting in the moment, and music, much of it never written down and created in the moment by Calvary musicians and congregation members.

Jesus music and the early, live, hands-on singing at Calvary Chapel, like much of the music of the folk revival, would eventually become commercialized. The British sociologist Simon Frith's views of the transition of folk music to commercial pop are useful. According to Frith (b. 1946), the transition can be viewed as a three-stage process: a "folk" stage, an "art" stage, and a "pop" or commercial stage. In its folk stage, music can only be retrieved in performance. Whether a work song, a play song, a lullaby, or a part of worship, it is spontaneous. In the second or "art" stage, the music is written down and notated. To be heard, it still requires performance, but spontaneity is replaced with a uniform, idealized version that can be repeated in a variety of places by a variety of performers. In the third "pop" or commercial stage, the music is stored on a record, tape, or compact disc. Now, live performance is no longer necessary. Instead, we have an idealized presentation by select performers which can be repeated *ad infinitum* for passive listeners.[11]

The transition of the Calvary Chapel's music to commercial "praise and worship" follows exactly this trajectory. In its early authentic stage (or "folk stage"), it was experienced totally in live, spontaneous performance in worship. With the incorporation of Maranatha! Music and the printing and distributing of song collections and companion recordings ("art stage"), the music of Calvary Chapel moved inexorably to the status of commercial commodity ("pop stage"). The casual listener need not even sing along, and an aspiring singer/performer now needed only to mimic the presentation to which he or she is listening. As a consequence, worshippers who purchased the recordings often expected their Sunday morning praise teams to mirror exactly the recorded renditions they loved. Inevitably, the folk-like, live-worship authenticity Chuck Smith cherished would have to be discarded for it to become the successfully mass-marketed commercial product we now know as contemporary Christian music (CCM).

A successful transition to the commercial marketplace would not come without resistance. Before 1970 the popularity of this music was largely confined to the West Coast. The music coming out of Calvary Chapel was either ignored entirely or regarded as an unwelcome threat by the leadership of the Gospel Music Association in Nashville.[12] Record labels open to Christian artists in the East would not front recordings of the new Christian music from the West Coast. Nevertheless, Calvary Chapel's entry into commercial recording and publishing is generally regarded as the beginning of CCM in the United States. For many years after 1971, their "Maranatha! Praise" albums and songbooks were essential tools for churches of all denominations attempting to form praise bands after the Love Song model. Its embrace

---

11. Frith, *Performing Rites*, 226–27.

12. In 1964 the Gospel Music Association was founded in Nashville, as an offshoot of the National Quartet Convention, which had been established a decade earlier to support the many white southern gospel quartets as touring and recording artists.

of the corporate interests of the recording industry presaged the demise of the Jesus Movement, whose idealistic converts had prioritized rejection of commercialism and materialism.

The Vineyard

John Wimber.
Use of Image courtesy of Vineyard, USA.

John Wimber (1934–1997) was a successful musician, songwriter, and band member with the pop recording duo the Righteous Brothers. In the early 1970s, Wimber began taking courses at Fuller Theological Seminary in Pasadena. He became an evangelist and was hired to be director of Fuller Institute of Evangelism and Church Growth.[13] Meanwhile, Wimber and his wife, Carol, had continued to attend the Friends Church in Yorba Linda and became active in a home-based Bible study group with an emphasis on encouragement, "spiritual refreshment," and spiritual healing. Carl Tuttle (b. 1953), a music leader for the group, recalled that it had been meeting in the home of his older sister, Candy.

> Vineyard worship informally began in my sister's living room ... I was asked if I would bring my guitar the following week, and from these early meetings, our worship began to evolve. I knew a handful of choruses that came out of the Jesus Movement and in particular Maranatha! Music, so we sang those. I didn't have a list; we didn't have lyrics. I just sang what came to mind and they all joined in. At first it was a few minutes, but over a few months, and as the group exploded, it would go

---

13. The church growth movement, which will be discussed later in this chapter, arose out of this program at Fuller Seminary.

> on for at least 45 minutes. Again, we had no lyrics, no list, and frankly no plan but to try to be sensitive to God and not get in the way. It was clear He was doing something very special with this group of people.[14]

Something important *was* happening, and in 1977, a worship space was rented at the nearby Masonic Temple. Ties severed with Friends Church, the study group became a satellite church of Calvary Chapel.[15]

Over the next five years, the Calvary Chapel of Yorba Linda grew to two thousand members. Musical leadership had changed from just Carl Tuttle and his guitar to a four-member combo with Tuttle leading and John Wimber on keyboard. Wimber also pastored the growing congregation.

> On Sunday mornings we did about 30 minutes of worship and Sunday nights about 45 minutes. . . . Our approach didn't vary during this time; we would get together and tune our instruments, pray, and then I would simply start a song and the guys would follow. In all that time we never rehearsed, never had a set list, never had any monitors, and never provided lyrics for the congregation. The songs were all so simple back then and repertoire was only about 30 songs, so if you stuck around you learned them pretty quickly.[16]

A split with Calvary Chapel was inevitable, however, over charismatic worship. Wimber's approach allowed for more congregational freedom than that permitted by Smith. His congregation actively participated in the lifting up of prayer and even the choice of music on Sunday mornings. Physical manifestations and glossolalia were common and not discouraged. Also, Wimber's emphasis on spiritual healing was outside Chuck Smith's comfort zone. Finally, in May of 1980 Lonnie Frisbee, who had left Calvary Chapel to evangelize on his own, was invited to speak at Wimber's Yorba Linda church, leading to what has been called a "charismatic explosion," and Wimber chose to form a new affiliation, this time with a small network of Bible study groups in Beverly Hills led by the Reverend Ken Gulliksen (b. 1945). The network was known as "the Vineyard."[17] Gulliksen's work had received some notoriety because of the participation of various celebrities, including Bob Dylan, who credited the Vineyard with his conversion to evangelical Christianity. Gulliksen turned over leadership of the Vineyard to Wimber,

---

14. Tuttle, "Vineyard Worship—The Early Years," Part 1.

15. Chuck Smith's Calvary Chapel had by the late 1970s built a network of affiliated or satellite churches of which Wimber's Yorba Linda Chapel was one.

16. Tuttle, "Vineyard Worship—The Early Years."

17. Reagan, "Beautiful Noise," 233–34.

who renamed his Yorba Linda church the "Vineyard Christian Fellowship of Anaheim."[18]

While the Vineyard was and is charismatic, Wimber and his followers viewed it as a progressive faith rooted in mainstream evangelicalism rather than Pentecostalism. While committed to scriptural inerrancy, the Vineyard's Statement of Faith, drafted in 1994, is remarkably free of religious dogma and takes liberal positions on same-sex marriage and gender issues. Regarding worship practice, the Vineyard—as opposed to Calvary Chapel—valued intimacy with God and spiritual healing over religious enthusiasm. Chuck Fromm, worship leader/evangelist and nephew of Calvary Chapel's founder, provided this assessment of John Wimber:

> Wimber had risen to prominence and achieved success within the ranks of the contemporary Christian community and leadership because of his acknowledged gifts as a composer/musician—a worship leader who specialized in the performative gift of music and song who was expert at sensing the mood of the congregation and rhapsodizing in the joyful sense of intimacy with God.[19]

Carl Tuttle, Wimber's musical associate at Calvary Chapel Yorba Linda, continued that association at the Anaheim Vineyard Christian Fellowship. As much as anyone, Tuttle understood the style of worship John Wimber aspired to, and it was he who Wimber asked to flesh out an order of worship that might realize those aspirations.

> Our church services became marked by the ministry of the Spirit. We were eager to minister to people. We wanted sick people to be healed, broken people to become whole, and oppressed people to be delivered. A liturgy began to develop in our services... We would sing songs, often starting with several choruses strung together in a medley and speeding up. We were goofy and had fun, but we also really worshipped. The upbeat songs transitioned to [a] more intimate worship of Jesus.[20]

One of John Wimber's most enduring songs came out of this period.

---

18. Jackson, *Quest for the Radical Middle*, 86.
19. Reagan, *Beautiful Noise*, 259.
20. Tuttle, *Reckless Mercy*, chapter 5 (ebook, no page numbers).

John Wimber, "Spirit Song."
Copyright 1979 Mercy Vineyard Publishing (ASCAP) (adm at
IntegratedRights.com). Used by permission.

"Spirit Song" embodied in its text and lyric melody the heart of Vineyard worship. Note the repetitive phrasing in the melodic structure. "Lift your hands in sweet surrender" validates the freedom of Vineyard worshippers to express their faith physically in a way discouraged at Calvary Chapel.

The intimate and rapturous quality of Vineyard worship and its emphasis on corporate congregational singing has continued through the years even after John Wimber's death in 1997. The medical/psychological anthropologist Tanya M. Luhrmann visited a Vineyard worship service in Chicago around 2003. She wrote this about the experience:

> On Sunday, the service in this church begins with music. A mainstream Protestant church distributes hymns throughout a service like raisins in morning cereal. There, hymns aren't so much individual prayers as collective assertions in which the congregation stands up as a group and affirms to each other that they are there. But at a church like the Vineyard *music is prayer.*

> The church sets aside a full thirty minutes for the music at the beginning of the service, and they call this section "worship."[21]
>
> This God is intensely human in this music, and the singer wants him so badly that the lyrics sound like a teenage fan's crazed longing for a teen idol she can touch. Unlike older church hymns, you do not sing *about* God but *to* God, directly to him in the second person and with unbridled yearning.[22]

As with Calvary Chapel and Maranatha! Music, media presence played a significant role in the Vineyard's ongoing success. Both entities had access to outstanding rock and pop musicians, and both began recording with the intent of recreating an authentic worship experience on disc. While the Maranatha! catalog over time began to feature bands like Love Song, the Vineyard kept its focus almost exclusively on encouraging the use of its songs in congregational worship. In 1986, Carl Tuttle and Randy Rigby established Vineyard's Worship Resource Center. The concept was to collect Vineyard songs being used around the country, gather them in printed collections, record them on cassette, and distribute them as a packaged teaching device for Vineyard worship leaders. The recording and publishing arms of the Vineyard were called Mercy Music and Mercy Publishing respectively. According to Tuttle, "This was not meant to be a commercial endeavor, but it was established as a ministry to the churches."[23] The first recorded collection of songs, *Glory,* was a major success and was followed by the even more successful *Father's Heart* series. Up until about 1990, Vineyard's music and recordings continued to be congregationally focused. According to Tuttle that changed to more "performer/listening audience" model during the 1990s.

> Up until this time, the worship style was seamless and completely engaging in terms of congregational participation. This new style included long breaks from the people singing and they would in many cases disengage and watch what was taking place on the stage. This is neither good nor bad; it is just what I observed taking place and it impacted not just our movement, but also the church at large . . . Overall I think it was an important and good progression for us and was necessary to keep things fresh.[24]

---

21. Luhrmann, *When God Talks Back,* 4.
22. Luhrmann, *When God Talks Back,* 5.
23. Tuttle, "History of Vineyard Worship—1976–1997."
24. Tuttle, "History of Vineyard Worship—1976–1997."

The Megachurch and the Church Growth Movement

In the March 1990 issue of *Christianity Today,* Lyle E. Schaller (1923–2015), author of fifty-five books on church growth in the United States, observed that there were likely well over a thousand churches with an average worship attendance of a thousand or more operating in the country. Of them, about two hundred served primarily the African American community, while the rest were white. Such large churches had arisen in a variety of Protestant denominations. Schaller estimated that about one of every three hundred Lutheran and Presbyterian parishes were of such proportions; one out of two hundred among Southern Baptist churches; and one in six hundred among those of the United Methodists.[25] The ten largest churches in 1990, according to Schaller were:[26]

Church	Avg. Attendance
1. First Baptist Church, Hammond, IN [Independent Baptist]	15–30,000
2. Willow Creek Community Church, South Barrington, IL [Independent]	14,000
3. Calvary Chapel, Costa Mesa, CA [Independent]	12,000
4. Thomas Road Baptist Church [Independent Baptist]	11,000
5. First Assembly of God, Phoenix, AZ [Assemblies of God]	10,500
6. North Phoenix Baptist Church, Phoenix, AZ [Southern Baptist]	9,500
7. Second Baptist Church, Houston, TX [Southern Baptist]	8,500
8. Grace Community Church, Sun Valley, CA [Independent]	8,000
9. Mount Paran Church of God, Atlanta, GA [Church of God]	8,000
10. Chapel Hill Harvester Church, Decatur, GA [Independent]	7,500

To describe these large churches, Schaller used the term *megachurch.*[27]

---

25. Schaller, "Megachurch!," 20.

26. "Ten Largest Churches," 22.

27. It is important to note that there have been and will continue to be large churches which *are not* megachurches. Televangelist Rex Humbard's "Cathedral of Tomorrow" in Akron, Ohio, and large Baptist congregations led by star preachers J. Frank Norris, Dallas Billington, Lee Roberson, and Jack Hyles—among the largest congregations of the 1950s—were part of what Jerry Falwell called the "large church movement." The large church, according to Falwell, "was the last best hope, a bulwark against the rising tide of iniquity . . ." (Richardson, "Big Religion," 280). Falwell's Thomas Road Baptist in Lynchburg, Virginia, and the others were unapologetically fundamentalist and far too doctrinaire to be megachurches. Musically, they tended to gravitate toward traditional and contemporary gospel music and evangelical choral music, not praise songs and

The Decline of the Cultivated Tradition in American Church Music 699

According to the Hartford Institute for Religion Research, megachurches generally share the following characteristics:

- Two thousand or more persons in attendance at weekly worship, counting adults and children at all worship locations.
- A transformational, authoritative senior minister.
- A very active seven-day-a-week congregational community.
- A multitude of diverse social and outreach ministries.
- An intentional small group system or other structures of intimacy and accountability.
- Innovative and often contemporary worship format.
- and a complex differentiated organizational structure.[28]

While each is different, most megachurches are independent of any established denominational authority, or—in the case of Southern Baptist megachurches—they are independent simply by virtue of being Baptist.

While there had been large—even monolithic—churches before, megachurches were different. Most were evangelical but only some were charismatic. Megachurches tended to be centered around a very visible leader whose name and ministry are identified as one with the church itself. Perhaps most important, they tended to prioritize church growth over doctrine, emphasize positivity and self-help messages in their preaching, and embrace musical styles of popular culture to attract hitherto unchurched worshippers. "The emergence of the megachurch," Schaller wrote, "is one of the four or five most significant developments in contemporary American church history."[29]

The megachurch movement did not emerge out of thin air. The positivity preaching that went to the core of their identity came much earlier. In 1952, Norman Vincent Peale published his *The Power of Positive Thinking*, a pioneering self-help book that was on the *New York Times* bestseller list for 186 weeks, forty-eight of them as number one. The book combined Christian themes with popular psychology and encouraged readers to better their lives with a disciplined positivity. The following Peale quotes serve to illustrate:

---

rock-influenced contemporary worship music.

28. Thumma, "Megachurches."
29. Schaller, "Megachurch!," 20.

1. "Formulate and stamp indelibly on your mind a mental picture of yourself succeeding . . . *Always* picture 'success' no matter how badly things seem to be going at the moment."
2. "Whenever a negative thought concerning your personal power comes to mind, deliberately voice a positive thought to cancel it out."
3. "Do not build up obstacles in your imagination. Depreciate every so-called obstacle."
4. "Do not be awestruck by other people and try to copy them. Nobody can be you as efficiently as YOU can . . ."
5. "Ten times a day repeat these dynamic words, 'If God be *for* us, who can be *against* us?' [Romans 8:31]."
6. "Get a competent counselor . . . Learn the origin of your inferiority and self-doubt feelings which often begin in childhood. Self-knowledge leads to a cure."
7. "Ten times a day practice the following affirmation, repeating it out loud if possible. 'I can do all things through Christ which strengtheneth me.' [Phil. 4:13]"
8. "Make a true estimate of your own ability, then raise it 10 percent . . . Believe in your own God-released powers."
9. "Put yourself in God's hands. To do that simply state, 'I am in God's hands.' Then believe you are NOW receiving all the power you need."
10. "Remind yourself that God is with you and nothing can defeat you. Believe that you *now* RECEIVE power from Him."[30]

Peale's positivism was carried forward to a new generation by his disciple in the Reformed Church in America, Robert Harold Schuller (1926–2015).

---

30. Peale, *Power of Positive Thinking*, 14–15.

The Decline of the Cultivated Tradition in American Church Music

Robert Schuller.
Public domain image courtesy of Wikimedia Commons.

Schuller's rise from Iowa farm boy to world famous evangelist has often been told. His successful career began with the establishment of the Garden Grove (California) Community Church in a drive-in theater in 1955 and reached its peak with the dedication of the Crystal Cathedral in 1980. The Cathedral in its heyday drew an average Sunday attendance of ten thousand, and millions around the world watched Schuller's *Hour of Power* television program. Schuller embraced "principles of successful retailing: accessibility, surplus parking, inventory (i.e., having what people want), customer service, visibility, and good cash flow."[31] Following Peale's example, he formed his own positivistic theology, declaring that in following Jesus one could realize the life of one's dreams. He commonly charged listeners to his sermons to live by the mantra: "I *am* somebody. I *can* do something. I *will* do something."[32]

In 1965, Schuller founded an "Institute for Successful Church Leadership," which presented four-day institutes held three times a year for pastors. Out of that experience came his highly popular book *Your Church Has Real Possibilities* (1974). In it, Schuller expounded on what he saw as the failure of the church to be a viable force for ministry and witness:

> Assuming that we successfully bring unchurched people into our Sunday morning services, will they understand what we are talking about? If they are biblically illiterate, will they understand the biblical terminology? And if they fail to understand, will they not turn off?

---

31. Reagan, "Beautiful Noise," 273.
32. Hagerty, "Fast Fall for Once Mighty Megachurch."

> Many churches are so dignified they're dull! The music is dull, the messages are dull, the architecture is dull; there is no excitement in the air! The worship service might be described as sleepy, quietly meditative and a perfectly tranquilizing arrangement—guaranteed to produce yawning and boredom.[33]

He repeatedly emphasized that the way to reach the unchurched was to *impress* them.[34]

> The secret of willing unchurched people into the church is really quite simple. Find out *what* would impress the non-churched people in your community and find out *who* would impress them . . . Discover the *cultural tempo* of the unchurched people. Then forget what Christians may think. Forget what your denominational leaders might think. Go out and make a big, inspiring impression on these non-churched people! And they'll come in![35]

For Schuller, church growth was the only appropriate measure by which to evaluate success in evangelism. "And this brings up a principle from which our Institute for Successful Church Leadership never wavers," he wrote, "*the growth of the church is the only thing that matters.*"[36]

Schuller's Crystal Cathedral differed significantly from most modern megachurches. His theology was largely orthodox, and he eschewed the so-called "prosperity gospel" adopted by many conservative evangelicals. His worship musical preferences tended toward the traditional with magnificent choral music and a world-class pipe organ constructed by Fratelli Ruffatti and designed based on specifications by Virgil Fox (the organ was later enlarged based on the specifications of Frederick Swann).

Nevertheless, as one of the earliest successful proponents of church growth, Schuller's influence was substantial on the emerging megachurch movement. It is worth noting that the preface to *Your Church Has Real Possibilities* was written by C. Peter Wagner of the School of World Mission and Institute of Church Growth at Fuller Theological Seminary. The Fuller connection is important. We have already noted that John Wimber served as the founding director of the Fuller Institute of Church Growth from 1974 to 1978.

---

33. Schuller, *Your Church Has Real Possibilities*, 39.
34. Schuller, *Your Church Has Real Possibilities*, 127.
35. Schuller, *Your Church Has Real Possibilities*, 128.
36. Schuller, *Your Church Has Real Possibilities*, 125.

The Church Growth Movement

The church growth movement in the United States began at Fuller with the landmark research of Donald McGavran and his book *The Bridges of God* (1955). It was McGavran's consensus, based on years of experience on the mission field in India, that Christian evangelism could only succeed if it was culturally centered in local communities of the country in question. "If the expansion of Christianity in these countries depends on its being a model from the West, then the Gospel in the world may be given up as lost."[37]

It was a blending of Schuller's market-based approach to church growth with McGavran's cultural and people-based theories that led to the development of the megachurch in its modern iteration—large, *seeker-focused institutions*[38] that de-emphasize doctrinal complexities and ecclesiastical language, encourage informal dress, and embrace the music of popular culture to reach the unchurched.

In his 1990 *Christianity Today* article, Lyle Schaller listed twenty-four reasons for the rise of the megachurch. Among them were several directly affecting worship music:

- The growing demand for higher-quality physical facilities, preaching, music, nurseries, teaching, and youth ministries.
- The freedom of younger generations to ignore denominational labels and shop for a church that meets their needs.
- The shift in priorities in many long-established congregations and denominations from people and needs to institutions and traditions.
- More persuasive public relations and advertising.
- The inability of most Protestant churches in the late 1960s to welcome the Jesus People, many of whom helped form the nucleus for what subsequently became the megachurch.
- A greater preference for a faster pace of corporate worship.

---

37. McGavran, *Bridges of God*, vii.

38. "Seeker-focused church" refers to churches intentionally conceived to appeal to and make comfortable the unchurched. The Rev. Bill Hybels of Willow Creek Community Church claimed credit for coining the term. In seeker-focused churches, typically casual dress is welcomed, and pop-oriented music used. Some churches move unfamiliar rituals like communion to sometime other than the Sunday morning hour. Video, drama, and other elements of secular programing are often incorporated. Unfamiliar religious and theological terminology is avoided. Proponents of "seeker-focused" worship are known to use the word "seeker-resistant" to apply to traditional mainline and particularly liturgical denominations.

- The inability or unwillingness of many long-established churches to accommodate that growing number of self-identified charismatic Christians who seek a prayer and praise service.[39]

A significant factor Schaller did not mention was "generationalism." It has been defined as "the belief that all members of a given generation possess characteristics specific to that generation, especially so as to distinguish it as inferior or superior to another generation."[40] The idea that worship should be rethought and reconfigured to resonate with a specific age group of Americans—namely young people—was primarily a twentieth-century phenomena. Torrey Johnson, the founder of Youth for Christ in 1944, wrote that "if communism, materialism, or wide indifference capture our youth, we shall go down the road to Fascism."[41] Jim Rayburn, founder of Young Life in 1941, wrote similarly that if young converts to Christianity joined traditional mainline churches, it would be "the kiss of death to any excitement a new believer might be experiencing."[42] Evangelical singing groups like the Spurrlows (org. 1959) and the Continentals (org. 1963), both made up entirely of young people, toured extensively throughout the 1960s and '70s, helping to showcase youth-oriented sacred song.[43] Generationalism, of course, had and continues to have its detractors. The theologian Thomas Bergler, professor of Christian Thought and Practice at Huntington University in Indiana, has called it "the juvenilization of American Christianity."[44]

The cross-fertilization between Schuller and the Fuller Institute can be seen in the successes of two of the most prominent megachurches of the period and their pastors: Bill Hybels (b. 1951) and the Willow Creek Community Church of South Barrington, Illinois, near Chicago; and Rick Warren (b. 1954) of Saddleback Church, a multi-site church headquartered in Lake Forest, California. It was at Willow Creek and Saddleback that the concept of "seeker sensitive worship" was born, tested, fine-tuned, and perfected. Both Hybels and Warren have spoken of being indebted to Robert Schuller. They knew Schuller personally and attended training sessions led by him. Schuller spoke glowingly of each of their ministries and appeared as a speaker at both churches.

---

39. Schaller, "Megachurch!," 21. By services of "prayer and praise," Schaller was referring to contemporary Christian worship as practiced at Calvary Chapel and the Vineyard.

40. Rauvola, Rudolph, and Zacher, "Generationalism," 3.

41. Larson, *Youth for Christ*, 134.

42. Tanis, *Making Jesus Attractive*, 91.

43. Ruth and Lim, *Lovin' on Jesus*, 16.

44. Bergler, *Juvenilization of American Christianity*, 5.

Bill Hybels and Willow Creek Community Church

Hybels's wife, Lynne, recalled that in April of 1975, her husband read Robert Schuller's *Your Church Has Real Possibilities*. It was his introduction to Schuller and his ideas. So inspired was he by the book that he resigned his position as youth director at the South Park Church and set about founding a church of his own—what would become Willow Creek Community Church.[45] In the fall of 1976, Hybels and his entire Willow Creek staff made a pilgrimage to a worship leader's conference at Garden Grove, where he outlined for Schuller his plans for a "church for the un-churched" and "seeker worship."[46]

Lynne Hybels later recalled what Bill was aspiring to with his budding concept of seeker worship and the important role to be played by music:

> We desperately wanted to provide a place where unchurched people with a spiritual hunger—seekers we called them—could come and hear truth that could transform their lives both here and in eternity. We wanted to use contemporary Christian music with lyrics that would communicate real-life spiritual experience. Sometimes we used crossover music, secular songs with a message that addressed the frustrations and longings of lost people.[47]

Robb Redman in his excellent survey of late twentieth century worship, *The Great Worship Awakening* (2002), had this to say about seeker worship:

> The seeker service approach builds on a basic assumption: unchurched people have dropped out of church or have stayed away because of traditional liturgy and music. Seeker churches create instead an alternative environment in which to hear the Gospel by using styles of music and communication that the seekers already know. By setting aside the traditional styles of liturgy and music, pastors and service planners hope to appeal to seekers through creative communication media—drama and the visual arts, but above all music and non-traditional preaching.[48]

The sole purpose of seeker worship was to engage and draw in the unchurched—the unbeliever and the beginning believer, the individual who had fallen away from Christianity, and those who had no experience at all

---

45. Hybels, *Rediscovering Church*, 51.
46. Hybels, *Rediscovering Church*, 69.
47. Hybels, *Rediscovering Church*, 63.
48. Redman, *Great Worship Awakening*, 3.

with organized religion. Theologically, Hybels was an evangelical conservative who embraced biblical inerrancy, but, in his eyes, seeker worship was conceived to eliminate as much as possible those elements making worship uncomfortable. In terms of architecture, massive but inviting structures were created with no steeples or symbolism that might suggest traditional religion. Sin and God's judgment were de-emphasized while God's paternal love was lifted up. The benefits of believing—self-fulfillment and therapeutic wellness, for example—were proclaimed regularly.[49] Worship music, whether secular soft rock or contemporary worship songs, was carefully tailored to the unchurched culture of the surrounding area.

Rick Warren and Saddleback Community Church

Rick Warren (b. 1954) was also a Schuller disciple. He attended the Institute for Successful Church Leadership in 1979, his last year at Southwestern Baptist Seminary. According to Rick's wife, Kay, Schuller "had a profound influence on Rick. We were captivated by his positive appeal to nonbelievers."[50] While Warren and Hybels both embraced the concept of seeker worship to the unchurched, the Warren approach at Saddleback was mellower—a style intended to attract suburban professionals and their families stressed out from life near Los Angeles.

Many characteristics of Saddleback worship were identical to those at Willow Creek. Both employed marketing surveys to determine the most effective hook to draw in the unchurched. Both targeted twenty-five- to fifty-year-old males, well-educated professionals who once recruited would, in theory, bring wives and families with them.[51] To appeal to unchurched adults, Warren and Hybels felt a completely professional presentation was needed:

> The result of this commitment [to professionalism] is that Harry[52] comes to the weekend services knowing that he is going to see a professional production. He won't have to listen to a voice that is breaking while trying to hit a high note or have to see inept actors.[53]

---

49. Richardson, "Big Religion," 298.
50. Stafford, "Regular Purpose-Driven Guy," 45.
51. Reagan, "Beautiful Noise," 285
52. Hybels used "Unchurched Harry" and "Unchurched Mary" as generic names for the unchurched.
53. Pritchard, *Willow Creek Seeker Services*, 101–2.

Lee Strobel, a Willow Creek staff member who previously had been among the unchurched, recalled that "I didn't have to sit there and worry that somebody was going to sing really bad, and I was going to feel embarrassed for them."[54] (As we have seen, proponents of the old quartet choirs made similar comments in their defense and as an argument against amateur singers and volunteer choirs in church.)

Warren at Saddleback added to the formula taped background music playing during the pre-service gathering time. It was intended to blur "the line between sanctuary and retail store, putting the unchurched at ease when entering a religious building possibly for the first time."[55] Looking back, when asked what he might do differently in starting the Saddleback Church, Rick Warren wrote that, "From the first day of the new church I'd put more energy and money into a first-class music ministry that matched our target. In the first years of Saddleback, I made the mistake of underestimating the power of music . . . I regret that now."[56]

While he recognized music's power to inspire spiritually, it is clear from Warren's writings that he viewed it primarily from a utilitarian standpoint. It could only be effective if carefully chosen for the targeted audience. He learned this in the early days at Saddleback:

> I also made the mistake of trying to appeal to everybody's taste. We covered the gamut, "from Bach to Rock," hymns, praise choruses, and contemporary Christian songs . . . The crowd never knew what was coming next. The result: We didn't please anybody, and we frustrated everybody! . . .
>
> Again, it's impossible to appeal to everyone's musical preference and taste. Music is a divisive issue that separates generations, regions of the country, personality types, and even family members . . . You must decide who you're trying to reach, identify their preferred style of music, and stick with it. You're wasting your time if you're searching for a style of music that everyone in your church will agree on.[57]

Another issue raised here by Warren relates to inclusiveness and the meaning of "community." One of Donald McGavran's most hotly debated theories and one which underpins the entire church growth movement is the Homogeneous Unit Theory. McGavran famously wrote, "People like to

---

54. Reagan, "Beautiful Noise," 293.
55. Reagan, "Beautiful Noise," 302.
56. Warren, *Purpose Driven Church,* 279.
57. Warren, *Purpose Driven Church,* 280.

become Christian without crossing racial, linguistic, or class boundaries."[58] As we have seen with Willow Creek and Saddleback, an intensive effort was made to target a specific demographic within the surrounding community—urban professionals, who happened to be overwhelmingly white. Other churches embracing church growth concepts targeted youth and college-age young adults. The rationale in every case was, *"Since we cannot meet the needs of everyone, we will excel at meeting the needs of this one select group."*

The many negative implications of this are obvious, and one pertains to the meaning and importance of community. The early church ministered to the entire community of believers, not a select group. Diversity of thought, gender, race, and financial status among worshippers strengthened solidarity and faith. The Homogeneous Unit concept had implications for the church's music as well. The "one size fits all" approach embraced by megachurches simply added a new form of "pop music elitism," further reinforcing barriers between cultivated and populist worship music that had been around for centuries.

On the subject of "musical style," however, Warren's observations in *The Purpose Driven Church* seem radically inclusive and community oriented:

- I reject the idea that music styles can be judged as either "good" or "bad" music. Who decides this? The kind of music you like is determined by your background and culture . . .

- To insist that all "good" music was written in Europe two hundred years ago is cultural elitism. There certainly isn't any biblical basis for that view.

- Churches also need to admit that no particular *style* of music is "sacred." What makes a song sacred is its *message*. . . . There is no such thing as "Christian music," only Christian lyrics.

- It takes all kinds of churches, using all kinds of music styles, to reach all kinds of people. To insist that one particular style of music is sacred is idolatry.[59]

---

58. Redman, *Great Worship Awakening*, 110.
59. Warren, *Purpose Driven Church*, 280.

Issues Raised by the Megachurch and Church Growth Movements[60]

At this point, it should be obvious that a wholly new understanding of "church" was percolating in the last quarter of the twentieth century. Mainline churches found themselves panicking over declining memberships, poor worship attendance, and declining revenue. Megachurches and the church growth movement forced a reconsideration of long held assumptions about church membership and Christian living.

The respected Lutheran composer and hymnologist Carl Schalk (1929–2021) addressed the fraught relationship between the church and the marketplace in 1990. The church growth movement, he observed, was simply a reflection of traditional American values of pragmatism and consumerism. How were churches to compete in the denominational marketplace? Were they even supposed to? "We tend to shop around; if a church does not offer our kind of religiosity—and our kind of music—we will go down the block to one that does."[61]

> Pragmatism asks: Does it get results? Are we attracting people to our worship? If we are, we must be doing something right. If not, we must be doing something wrong. The devastating implications for the church musician are obvious. Such pragmatism, critics of the church growth industry say, tends to quantify success. For church musicians, a "successful" music program would thus be identified by the size and number of people involved and, most importantly, its attractiveness to outsiders. We aspire—as congregations and as church musicians—to emulate the fastest growing and the biggest. And whatever it takes, musically speaking, for that to happen is its own justification.[62]

---

60. According to the research of Warren Bird and Scott Thumma of the Hartford Institute for Religion Research, there were "roughly 1750 megachurches in the United States" in 2020 (Bird and Thumma, *Megachurch 2020*, 2). While the typical congregant is still white and college educated, many congregations are now multiracial. The trend has been away from huge, amphitheater style worship spaces to smaller ones seating 1,200 or so on average, with worship taking place in multiple locations or satellite churches. As was true of most mainline and liturgical denominations, weekly attendance at megachurches had declined. Some things, however, had not changed in 2020: the typical megachurch pastor was white, middle-aged, and had been with church at least fifteen years. "The majority of megachurches are still led by the person who was leader during the church's most significant growth" (Bird and Thumma, *Megachurch 2020*, 13).

61. Schalk, "Church Music in the '90s."

62. Schalk, "Church Music in the '90s."

Such a viewpoint, according to Schalk, reflected a "basic misunderstanding about worship and its music." The church growth movement called for a reshaping of worship to make it more attractive to the target community, a position with which Schalk passionately took issue. "We do not come to worship to shape it to our own ends, but to be shaped by God who calls us together to hear his word and share his meal."[63]

The beloved United Methodist composer and church organist Austin Lovelace (1919–2010) bewailed the secular/pop influences invading the organ loft in the 1990s. When asked, "What do you see happening in church music today?," he replied:

> A lot of bad stuff. There are very troubling signs. I think too many churches are treating music as entertainment, where music is designed to make everybody feel good. In fact, church[es] are designed that way: they have a living room you sit in and padded pews, and people come to see a good show. They want the choir to do something they can understand immediately, which is not true of most great music.[64]

Numerous studies have shown that since 1960 there has been a gradual but definite shift in Americans' perception of the role played by the church in Christian living. Church membership in mainline denominations has often become viewed as something voluntarily chosen rather than a social obligation. Many see large denominations as too bureaucratic. There has been a growing distrust and cynicism regarding the moral authority of clergy. The politicization of religion—as implicit in the anti-war movements of the 1960s, the Moral Majority (which was founded in 1979), pro-choice and anti-abortion movements—have been hugely divisive forcing pushing many Christians to either take sides or withdraw entirely from church participation. As of 1990, polls showed that 7 percent of all Americans claimed no religious preference. By 2015 the percentage would increase to 20 percent, and among those under the age of thirty-two it stood at 32 percent.[65]

Contemporary Worship Music and Mainstream Protestantism

If one follows the idea that church music is set apart from the secular or profane world, the position frequently held by many church authorities and church musicians in the past, then there is no problem in reaching the

---

63. Schalk, "Church Music in the '90s."
64. "Interview with Austin Lovelace."
65. Edgell and Robey, "Loose Connections and Liberal Theology," 650.

assessment of the "new" music. One simply rejects it and continues to use only music of former generations or new music that sounds like the old, achieving an effect in the Sunday morning worship that is frequently spoken of as "traditional or classical" church music, whatever that phrase may mean to various individuals. One cannot accept the new sounds of "secular" music in the church if one makes use of the worship service as a refuge from the world and its problems, where the worshipper seeks to escape the realities of life in a quest for peace of mind.[66]

Prior to the mid-1960s, less formal, *enthusiastic* worship in both the white and African American communities had largely been associated with Pentecostalism. By the late 1960s, however, the use of praise and worship songs had spread well beyond the confines of Jesus People, Calvary Chapel, and the Vineyard. It had found its way into both mainline and evangelical youth programs. "Many Protestant-supported church campgrounds had become collection points for guitar-based Christian 'choruses' that teenagers could enjoy singing even though (back in the church buildings) some of their own church leaders were complaining that any music played on guitar was inherently evil."[67] Teens raised on this music found spiritual meaning in it, and so inevitably negativity was replaced by acceptance in the next generation.

The Episcopal Church with its cherished and historic liturgy found itself especially vulnerable. Church leaders were loath to adapt to pressures arising out of popular culture. Moreover, a publication of the Association of Anglican Musicians noted in 1984 that "the Episcopal Church frequently finds itself today without adequate resources to meet the challenge presented by the appearance of charismatics in her ranks at all levels."[68]

National Congregations Studies[69] in 1998 and 2019 provided interesting statistics related to worship music in American churches. Fifty-three percent of American congregations still used organ music in their worship in 1998 but use of piano as an accompaniment instrument had risen to 69 percent. By that time, however, around one fifth of all American churches were also using guitar and/or percussion in worship exercises. By 2019, use of the organ in worship had fallen to 47 percent and the downward trend is largely continuing. Use of visual projection equipment was still at a modest 12 percent in 1998, but later surveys would show it increasing to a

---

66. Zetty, "New Sounds in the Church," 15.
67. Race, "Brief History."
68. Doran and Peterson, *History of Music in the Episcopal Church,* 154.
69. Note: National Congregations Studies (NCS) have been directed by Mark Chaves, professor of sociology and religious studies at Duke University, in association with NORC at the University of Chicago.

whopping 46 percent by 2019.[70] A concluding statement in the 2019 survey is supported by these figures:

> The nature of worship services has changed considerably in recent decades. One of the most fascinating and important changes is that more congregations have embraced a more informal and enthusiastic worship style. Contemporary musical styles, spontaneous speaking from people in the pews, unscripted bodily movements, and other developments that make worship more expressive and participatory have become steadily more common since 1998, and they are now more prevalent than ever.[71]

Statistics of course only tell part of the story regarding the decline of classically oriented worship music in America's mainline churches. As the drift toward more informal and enthusiastic worship gained steam in the last decades of the twentieth century, its effects were felt in many areas:

- A noticeable decline in the number of church choirs as well as the makeup and quality of music-making.

- A critical loss of educational opportunities for musicians to be trained in music as a ministry and a corresponding dearth of trained leadership.

- A de-emphasis of church music among professional organizations such as the American Guild of Organists and the American Choral Director's Association, which previously had been key resources for church musicians.

- A decline in the use of the organ in worship and a corresponding decline in pipe organ manufacturing and sales.

- A decline in print music publishing with a corresponding increase in digital and print-on-demand options.

Toward a New Century in African American Church Music

African American musical worship by the mid-1990s had expanded to embrace a variety of styles, from more recently arranged choral spirituals by composers like Undine Smith Moore (1904–1989), to gospel choirs, to aspects of the praise and worship/contemporary worship movement, and even "gospel rap." The composer/director Richard Smallwood (b. 1948) with

---

70. Figures drawn from Chaves, NCS Wave IV Report Draft, last edited June 9, 2021, and Chaves, Konieczny, Beyerlein, and Barman, "National Congregation Study."

71. Chaves, NCS Wave IV Report, 12.

his Smallwood Singers innovated a style of church music in which a variety of influences present in African American church music coalesced.

Richard Smallwood.
Image courtesy of Metropolitan Baptist Church, Largo, MD.

His music has been called a "hybrid" comprising the needs of both liturgical and free worship and melding the heritage of the spiritual with pop/gospel. In doing this, he developed a new approach to choral writing that pointed toward the contemporary gospel sound now prevalent in African American worship.[72]

At the turn of the twenty-first century, the gospel choir movement pioneered by Thomas Dorsey and Sallie Martin was still a significant force in Black worship. A NCS survey in 1998 indicated that 90 percent of all Black congregations included a gospel choir in their ministries. As among white Christians, debate and controversy continued about the incursion of secular pop influences into African American worship. Hymnals used by traditional older Black congregations still contained hymns and songs from Anglo-American and British composers and gospel hymns of the Moody/Sankey era, but Black composers and hymnwriters were better represented than in the past.[73]

The influence of the contemporary praise and worship movement and the megachurch, however, was becoming evident by the late 1990s. At least fourteen African American congregations in the Los Angeles area had an average worship attendance of over three thousand. For these and many

---

72. Shelley, "Gospel Goes to Church," 399.

73. Abbington, ed., *Readings in African-American Church Music*, 2:134–39. Abbington lists forty-four commonly used hymns by whites, ranging from "Amazing Grace" to the gospel hymn "Yield Not to Temptation," by Horatio Richmond Palmer. That being said, the music of Tindley, Dorsey, James Cleveland, Andraé Crouch, and many other Black composer/hymnwriters also have common usage.

smaller worshipping communities, the praise and worship concepts innovated by Calvary Chapel and the Vineyard were adopted, with periods up to an hour long of sung praise opening each service. African Americans had their own pioneer composers and singers of praise and worship music, including Thomas Whitfield (1954–1992) and Fred Hammond (b. 1960), the so-called "architect of urban praise and worship."

Also appearing tentatively in the 1980s but gaining steam in the '90s was "gospel rap." Rapping is one manifestation of the broader cultural phenomena known as "hip-hop." It is a vocal style in which the performer speaks in rhyme and verse, generally over a instrumental or synthesized beat. Sandra L. Barnes of the Divinity School of Vanderbilt University has pointed out that rapping comes directly from the same Black rhetorical tradition as traditional extemporaneous Black preaching.[74] The Black minister, singer, and songwriter Stephen Wiley (b. 1956) recorded the first full-length albums of Christian rap music in the 1980s. Among the most prominent Christian rappers during the first decades of the twenty-first century is Lecrae Devaughn Moore (b. 1979), known simply as "Lecrae."[75]

The White Protestant Church Choir in Decline

In 1962, Clarence Dickinson, then eighty-nine years old, said in a lecture to a symposium of the American Choral Director's Association, "It is perhaps easy to think choral music in churches as involving only the sort of choir we happen to be leading at the moment. We must expect that economic and social factors, as well as theological ones, can alter that picture radically."[76] Dickinson's statement was prescient.

During the first half of the twentieth century volunteer choirs of mixed voices had become an almost universal presence in American worship. According to a National Congregations Study, as late as the 1990s, 63 percent of all white conservative evangelical churches in the United States had active choral music programs. By 2014 the number had decreased to 40 percent. Mainline moderate and liberal churches with choirs shrank from 78 percent to 50 percent between 1998 and 2012.[77] The number of children's and youth choir programs also declined sharply. Due in large part to the work

---

74. Barnes, "Religion and Rap Music," 567.

75. Christian rap has also been adopted by white performance artists. Two notable examples are Kevin Michael McKeehan (b. 1964), known as TobyMac, and Jonah Kirsten Sorrentino (b. 1975), who performs under the moniker KJ-52.

76. Dickinson, "Music in the Churches," 25.

77. Brumley, "Debate."

of Thomas A. Dorsey, Theodore Frye, and Sallie Martin in the 1930s, Black gospel choirs remain an integral part of worship in 90 percent of the African American churches surveyed.

The church choir decline in white mainline denominations must not be seen purely as a change in musical tastes. Economics and pressures from popular culture are major factors. The largest mainline churches, because of their size and financial resources, tend to have an influential voice in setting denominational priorities. These churches, like the megachurches they often emulate, frequently embrace contemporary worship. Choral music frequently is abandoned in favor of worship bands with a staff member as song leader. Maintaining a choral music program is expensive. Organizing and directing such a program requires trained leadership, usually paid, and a healthy budget for supplies. Smaller churches struggling to keep these programs going, with limited finances and desperately needful of new and pledging members, find the temptation to move to a contemporary worship model inescapable.[78]

Music Ministry Education and Professional Standards, a Dream on Hold

A recurring theme going back at least to the writings of Thomas Hastings and Lowell Mason and articulated in every generation since has been the need for music ministry education. Concomitant to that was a recognition that effective musical leadership in the church required a special skill set, in many ways different from that in the secular arena. We followed the enormous progress made in this area during the first half of the twentieth century with music school/seminary partnerships like the Westminster Choir College and the Union Theological Seminary School of Sacred Music, as well as the College of Church Musicians at Washington's National Cathedral (Episcopal). During the same period the Southern Baptist Convention set about creating educational opportunities for its own church musicians. The Southwestern Baptist Seminary in Fort Worth offered a pioneering degree in sacred music in the 1920s, followed by programs at the SBC seminaries in New Orleans and Louisville. Some major universities also inaugurated degree programs—the University of Southern California and Boston University being prime examples. In addition, a host of seminaries, liberal arts colleges, and conservatories began offering church music-related course

---

78. Of course, the embrace of contemporary Christian worship music in worship almost inevitably leads to substantial investments in audio/visual equipment, electronic keyboards, etc., which may equal or surpass the cost of mounting a traditional choral program.

offerings such as hymnology and church music history, in conjunction with programs in organ and voice performance.

The drift in mainline American churches toward contemporary worship had painful ramifications for church music education. With interest waning in traditional worship music (choral anthems, classic hymnody, and organ music), college-level sacred music programs experienced a 40 percent decline in enrollment between 1990 and 2000, and dozens were canceled entirely. Schools offering such programs found themselves conflicted. Conservatory-trained faculty were often "reluctant to integrate contemporary praise and worship music forms [into their teaching regimen] which an increasing number of hiring churches expected their musicians to be skilled in."[79]

This intransigence of music faculty was both understandable and unfortunate. The eminent teacher, composer, and writer on sacred music Paul Wohlgemuth (1927–1987) wrote in 1985 of the trends toward praise and worship music as well as other contemporary styles in mainline churches:

> Even though education has facilitated and often pioneered significant changes in religious thought and worship practices, it has at times exhibited an inability to respond to changes that occur within the larger Christian community. In particular, the need is for trained leaders of the church's worship life who are at least informed about significant, new, and even threatening worship music and practices.[80]

The unwillingness of respected teachers to accept and validate new trends all too evident in the local church was of course communicated to their students. Music directors trained in the old Dickinson/Williamson mold found it difficult to adjust to the praise and worship style of service.

> Some resist contemporary worship music for aesthetic reasons; they think it is boring, repetitive, or musically uninteresting. Others view free-flowing praise as an affront to decency and order in worship. Still others trained in traditional church music have a hard time playing music that requires improvisational skill or the ability to follow a chord chart and melody line rather than a full piano score.[81]

Wohlgemuth wrote eloquently about the new style of worship leader that was needed:

---

79. Ottaway, "Rise of the Worship Degree," 160.
80. Wohlgemuth, "Church Music Education," 90–91.
81. Redman, *Great Worship Awakening*, 45–46.

> Since this movement may develop as one of the most significant ecumenical music and worship influences of the last quarter of the twentieth century, it is important to be aware that this style of worship demands a new type of song leader, choir director, keyboard performer, as well as instrumentalist. Their use of orchestras, usually of popular-music instrumentation, is not uncommon. No worship movement in recent years is so dependent upon music for the heart of its expression . . . While the traditional Protestant church leans upon the pastor for the major leadership role in its worship services, the renewal calls for a dual leadership of pastor and minister of music called the *Worship Leader*.[82]

Harold M. Best (b. 1931), himself a church musician and composer, was president of the National Association of Schools of Music (NASM) during the 1980s. He was well aware of the changes occurring in church music since Vatican II and the blending of sacred, secular, and pop styles being integrated into music for worship. Best addressed how he felt music schools and seminaries should respond in 1982.

> A good church music curriculum must first of all provide the theological, procedural, and artistic ways out of this long-term dilemma. Excellent church music training must be embedded, not primarily in the nature of music and musical types, standards of practices, and scholarly excellence, but in a *bedrock* of theological perspective. By this, I do not mean the usual outlay of theology courses and studies of liturgies, as necessary as they are. Rather, I mean the articulation of a theology of creativity, a theology of worship, a theology of communication and response, and a theology of excellence.[83]

He went on to say that the graduates should be trained to judge the quality of music *not based on style but its content.*

No better omens of the impending crisis in church music education in 1970s and '80s can be cited than the tragic closures of the College of Church Musicians of Washington's National Cathedral and the Union Theological Seminary School of Sacred Music. Also troubling were repeated curriculum and structural changes at the Westminster Choir College in a desperate effort to maintain its relevancy. This would eventually necessitate its leaving the campus of Princeton Seminary. In all three cases financial insolvency due to declining enrollment were the root cause of closure. The

---

82. Wohlgemuth, "Church Music Education," 89.
83. Brady, "Investigation," 26.

College of Church Musicians founded in 1962 was the first to go. It had offered a unique instructional plan, pairing a select group of students, one-on-one, with master composers, organists, and conductors. While housed at the (Episcopal) cathedral, the program was nonsectarian. Presbyterians, Baptists, and even synagogue musicians received training there. When Leo Sowerby, the founding director, died in 1968, it lost its most determined advocate. Faced with crippling financial burdens the school closed a year later.[84]

Union Theological Seminary faced challenges during the turbulent latter years of the 1960s. With enrollment flagging, the decision was made to close the School of Sacred Music in 1972. Robert Baker, then director of the school, joined the faculty of Yale University, where he helped found the Yale Institute of Sacred Music. A cooperative program operated jointly by the Yale School of Music and Yale Divinity School continues to offer graduate degrees in applied organ and voice as well as certificates for students electing a sacred music emphasis.

Westminster Choir College has so far survived the challenges of recent years, but not without serious wounding. The college first tried to bolster its enrollment by expanding course and degree offerings, focusing more on applied music, and adding a musical theater major. Nonetheless, by 1990 the college was floundering with $2.5 million in debt, and enrollment in decline. Finally in July of 1992 an agreement was struck with Rider College in nearby Lawrenceville, New Jersey, which would allow Westminster to stay at Princeton and provide badly needed funds to repair and upgrade facilities. Unfortunately, the challenges in bringing WCC to financial stability were insurmountable. In December of 2016 Rider President Gregory Dell'Omo announced that options were being considered, including selling the school or shutting it down and moving students and faculty to Lawrenceville. The College Choir held its first classes on the Rider University campus in the fall of 2020. As of 2024, it was renting out some facilities on the old Princeton campus, the sale of which remained in limbo.[85]

Music Merchandizing

Critics, usually advocates for traditional classical repertoire and hymnody, often note that by the 1990s contemporary Christian music had become a commercial industry needing to be profitable to survive. *The potential for profitability to take precedence over artistry and appropriateness in worship is*

---

84. Campbell, "College of Church Musicians at Washington National Cathedral."
85. Minore and Neukam, "Look Back."

very real. What those same critics fail to point out, however, is how industry and commercialism have also severely impacted traditional choral and organ music for the church, resulting in less creativity in programming, same-sounding music from week to week, and less room for the Holy Spirit to act.

With fewer churches purchasing traditional music, the cost per copy rose exponentially over the years. An octavo of Peter C. Lutkin's "The Lord Bless You and Keep You," which could be had for 15¢ in 1965, retailed for $2.00 or more in 2021. With sales of choral sheet music for church choirs plummeting, brick-and-mortar sheet music shops were no longer cost effective and most had to close their doors. Large and highly respected local sheet music retailers—Brodt Music in North Carolina, Morse M. Preeman's in New York, among many others—were bought out by large conglomerates. By the year 2000 sheet music sales were being done almost totally by phone or online.

After a century devoted to the development of the modern hymnal, many in the 1980s and '90s were questioning why traditional hymnals were even needed. Resistance to acquiring new hymnals was becoming more common in both mainline and traditional evangelical churches. For many churches, the drift toward contemporary experiential worship was a driving factor in decisions regarding hymnal purchases. Mainline denominations had been slow to embrace anything other than traditional hymnody. A few folksongs and spirituals began appearing in some hymnals in the late 1960s, but denominational leaders and hymnal committees were reluctant to recognize the growing Pentecostal and charismatic elements in many local parishes. As a result, numbers of churches—denominationally connected yet independent in worship practice—eschewed purchase of denominational hymnals, preferring instead commercially produced collections usually with a conservative evangelical bent. By the late 1990s the dynamic would change once again as many mainline churches embraced praise and worship songs. Hymnals would stay in the pew racks or disappear entirely with song sheets and, later, overhead projections taking their place. All of these factors combined in the late twentieth century to produce a catastrophic decline in hymnal publishing.

The decline in cultivated/traditional church music affected publishers not only of hymnals but of virtually all forms of printed sacred music. During the last quarter of the twentieth century, there was a virtual feeding frenzy of mergers as powerhouse publishers gobbled up smaller independents. For the church musician in the local church perhaps the greatest loss with the demise of brick-and-mortar retailers was depersonalization. The locally owned music shop, to be successful, had to know the wants and needs of the local community and keep repertoire on the shelf to meet them. Most shops also served as a hub for musicians and salespeople to meet, share information, and seek advice. As music sales transitioned from brick-and-mortar to phone and online ordering, the consumer could access virtually any music from any publisher that was in print. The personalized element, however, was lost. Faced with a virtual torrent of choices and limited time to choose, the harried church musician was more likely to opt for the "known quantity"—the highly promoted piece, the well-known and commercially successful composer. Too often the preferred musical style was both safe and utterly conventional.

Needless to say, this was not a congenial landscape for aspiring composers of traditional, classically oriented church choir music. Fewer choirs meant less demand with a small number of "name" composers dominating. Established in 1992, the St. James Music Press (SJMP), then headquartered in Hopkinsville, Kentucky,[86] offered a new publishing concept. The perennial problem of illegal photocopying was addressed by replacing the selling of ink on paper musical scores with an annual fee authorizing the purchaser to legally make copies of anything in the SJMP catalog.

Arlen Clarke, choirmaster at St. Mary's Catholic Church in Greenville, South Carolina, and a respected choral composer, spoke candidly of the challenges facing a working church musician/composer in recent years:

> Western culture has become disenchanted with the Church. This disenchantment is a result of postmodernity thought-speak, producing a nearly toxic public culture that is increasingly Christophobic . . . Within this no-man's land of liturgical quality and suitability has risen an opportunity to hone my limited compositional skills and gifts. I feel that because I have been writing for a certain occasion, a specific group of musicians, and unique liturgical space, the result has been a plethora of music—new tunes in Anglican chant style, anthems and motets for two, three, four and in some cases multiple voices, and polyphony in the renaissance style, as well as treatments of traditional hymnody.
>
> From nearly the start of their operations several of my compositions have been published by St. James Music Press. Although there is a degree of cross-over to Catholic liturgical needs, most of SJMP's large library of quality music is designed for Protestant traditions. SJMP is a breath of fresh air in the realm of publishing because it relieves the church musician from being

---

86. SJMP is now headquartered in Saginaw, Michigan.

held hostage to the large publishing houses that seek the bottom line and very little else.[87]

The vast technological advancement in music notation software also provided new options for composers of traditional church music to self-publish and exhibit their wares on internet sites like Score Exchange. Still others chose to establish their own in-house publishing enterprises to circumvent the commercial roadblocks imposed by the conglomerates.

The King of Instruments

No musical instrument historically is more wedded to the music of the church than the pipe organ.[88] Many of the factors enumerated above coalesced negatively to affect the use of organs and organ music in American churches:

- Demographics: Churches utilizing traditional liturgies and music tended to have shrinking membership rolls and budgets, making the cost of either purchasing or maintaining a pipe organ challenging.
- Contemporary Christian and pop-influenced music: For this repertoire piano or guitar, not organ, were the accompaniment instruments of choice. Much of the traditional choral music being written included accompaniments too pianistic to be effective on the organ. Moreover, the acoustical and architectural requirements for organ music (a warm reverberant space) versus contemporary praise music (a dry acoustic space with minimal reverb) were incompatible.
- Decline of traditional hymnody and its historic identification with the organ.
- Education: The last decades of the twentieth century saw a sharp decline in the number of students seeking college- and graduate-level training to be church organists and organist/choirmasters. This decline would only intensify after the year 2000. Those churches desiring

---

87. Clarke, "Thoughts on the State of Church Music, 2021."

88. The "joined-at-the-hip" relationship between the organ and the church is questionable. The antecedent of the pipe organ, the hydraulis, was used outside the church as a signaling device and hardly a musical instrument. The first organs installed in cathedrals appeared in the thirteenth and fourteenth centuries and were viewed with disdain by many in the Roman Catholic leadership, who still viewed unaccompanied chant polyphony as the only appropriate music to be used in the liturgy.

to fill organ positions would find it more and more difficult to attract qualified candidates.[89]

The effect of the above trends on the American pipe organ industry was chilling. The collapse of the country's largest pipe organ builder, the 117-year-old M. P. Moller Company, had repercussions for hundreds of churches nationwide. The company had prospered through the 1960s but began an inexorable decline in the '70s partially due to a failure to modernize and upgrade its manufacturing facility.[90]

The history of American church music, as we have seen, is beautifully complex, filled with contradictory currents, at once forward-looking and short-sighted, beautiful in parts, shocking in others. The last quarter of the twentieth century had all of those elements. Certainly, there were aspects that should be of deep concern to all. The classically trained musician wonders if a return to the traditional worship values of the past is even possible. Those whose focus is contemporary worship music should be asking, "What is the shelf life of a musical ministry so inextricably tied to popular culture?" I am convinced we can find lessons within the past that can provide hope.

---

89. A 2014/2015 survey by the American Guild of Organists added depth to the trends suggested above. The guild noted that 58 percent of its membership was born between 1940 and 1959 while only 11 percent were born after 1980—a graphic illustration of lack of interest among the country's youth. See "American Guild of Organists 2014 Survey."

90. Hetrick, "It's Not a Very Happy Story."

CHAPTER 22

LEARNING FROM THE PAST —HOPE FOR THE FUTURE

AMERICAN CHURCH MUSIC IN the twenty-first century is in a period of radical transition, and nowhere is the change felt more pointedly than among traditional congregations still embracing the cultivated traditions of the past. The 2012 National Congregations Study showed a 28 percent decrease in the number of choirs in mainline churches just since 2008. The dismantling of traditional music programs has only intensified in the years since.[1] A more esoteric piece of evidence comes from Fender Musical Instrument Corporation, which reported a record number of guitars sold during the 2020/2021 pandemic and that one out of three were purchased by players in praise bands.[2]

Religious pluralism goes to the very heart of what it means to be American. Our revered freedom of religion from the very first was a hoped-for ideal, but never could it be guaranteed that a multitude of sects and faith systems would coexist harmoniously. Any history of music in American church life that attempts to survey theology, polity, and music over a range of denominations will be humbling in its complexity.[3] Yet such histories are

---

1. Brumley, "Debate."

2. Silliman, "1 out of 3 New Guitars."

3. As I stated in the prologue to this book, I have necessarily limited my narrative largely to mainline traditional and evangelical denominations, omitting entirely any discussion of the rich musical heritages of the Latter-day Saints, the Moravian and Brethren sects, and other groups. These groups have made significant contributions to the history of American sacred music that must not be ignored. What I have tried to do here is to follow what I perceive to be the most widely influential currents of thought

needed for the very reason that we *are* a pluralistic society. Healthy, growing twenty-first century congregations should expect to be multiracial, multicultural, and multigenerational. Church musicians laboring in this environment need a broad-based understanding of their art. The struggle continues to define what the width and breadth of that art should be. The traditionalist insists on rigid adherence to time-honored liturgical practice and a musical repertoire based largely on the canon of European masterworks. Many evangelicals and Pentecostals operate at the other end of the spectrum, advocating the elimination of all strictures imposed by tradition.

It is my hope to frame this concluding chapter around the concept of the church as a *community*—not a handpicked group of believers of the same race or age group; not a membership limited to people of similar education, wealth, or status; but rather a beautifully diverse collection of believers, believing and growing in faith together. In a healthy congregation of the twenty-first century, we should assume that multiple perspectives on the meaning of worship are present, as well as a variety of musical tastes. The challenge for the church musician of today is one of *ministry*—to know and embrace the diverse musical and liturgical needs of the community to which he or she is called and revel in that diversity. To do that effectively, musicians in ministry in the United States need broad training, both in sacred music and worship-oriented studies—clear-eyed training that recognizes the musical landscape in the twenty-first-century American church and puts forth positive avenues to work within that landscape.

Over the years spent writing *Servanthood of Song*, certain themes doggedly asserted themselves. They included the importance of congregational singing, the role of the church musician professional, and the many challenges affecting music in the church of our day. Those thematic elements form a basis for discussing what history has to teach us about the current state of church music. The history of American church music, it seems to me, with all its successes and failures, points to one overriding truth: in a pluralistic society such as ours, a broader, less rigidly doctrinaire, and more inclusive approach to worship is needed. We should no longer expect that traditional liturgical and musical practices will be retained simply because of their historical importance, but *only* as they can be shown to be an effective vehicle for vital, engaging, Spirit-filled worship. Make no mistake—I believe it can be done and *is* being done by churches in our midst!

This study also shows another critical need common to all generations before us—that of liturgical and church music education, education of musical leaders and clergy, but also an intentional and aggressive approach

---

and action. I know full well that there is much still to be said.

to educating congregations. Too often congregations are expected to "go through the motions" of worship with little understanding of *why* we do what we do. Musician and pastoral leaders are needed who can communicate a passion for the nuts and bolts of our faith—be it the order and rationale of a worship service, elements of the liturgy, or the historical and theological substance of hymns and songs. Only when the need for education is taken seriously can we build a healthy ministry to the unchurched. *Only when a passion for liturgy and the church's music is aggressively and repeatedly shared can we expect it to be embraced by people in the pews—let alone the unchurched!*

Missed Opportunities for Consensus

In his book *Flow* (2020), Lester Ruth has listed elements of traditional worship that proponents of contemporary worship wished to see changed. Use of choral and organ music and hymns were, of course, near the top of the list, but other factors were also present. Contemporaries found printed bulletins to inhibit a more Spirit-led extemporaneous approach to worship. They saw rigid adherence to a prescribed order as encouraging worshippers to be both physically passive and emotionally restrained. Ceremonial acts and mystical symbolism that seemed to have no relevance to the common worshipper also caused contemporaries to react negatively.[4]

What advocates for contemporary worship ignored, however, were the changes which *were* occurring in traditional worship in the mainline Protestant denominations. Liturgies were being rewritten utilizing modern English. Liturgical churches were turning away from the old sermon-focused approach to worship and placing more emphasis on the regular observance of the Eucharist.[5] Also, while approached in different ways, mainline, contemporary, and Roman Catholic churches all recognized a need to achieve full corporate participation in worship. Many of differing perspectives sought to reform worship in the twenty-first century to conform with how it was practiced in the early church. To do this, they frequently turned to the *First Apology* of Justin Martyr (110–165 AD), which detailed worship practice in the second century:

> And on the day called Sunday, all who live in cities or in the country gather together to one place, and the memoirs of the apostles or the writings of the prophets are read, as long as time permits; then, when the reader has ceased, the president verbally

---

4. Ruth, *Flow,* 7–8.
5. Ruth, *Flow,* ix–x.

instructs, and exhorts to the imitation of these good things. Then we all rise together and pray, and, as we before said, when our prayer is ended, bread and wine and water are brought, and the president in like manner offers prayers and thanksgivings, according to his ability, and the people assent, saying Amen; and there is a distribution to each, and a participation of that over which thanks have been given, and to those who are absent a portion is sent by the deacons. And they who are well to do, and willing, give what each thinks fit; and what is collected is deposited with the president, who succours the orphans and widows and those who, through sickness or any other cause, are in want, and those who are in bonds and the strangers sojourning among us, and in a word takes care of all who are in need.[6]

As one reads Justin's account, one is immediately struck by the full corporate participation of the worshipping community. Justin repeatedly describes activity in the third person—what "we" do. There is also an extemporaneous quality to what Justin describes. Scripture is read "as time permits." The officiant delivers prayers, not as prescribed, but "according to his ability." In addition, the apostle Paul's epistles to the Colossians, Ephesians, and in 1 Corinthians all make reference to responsorial singing of psalms and sacred songs as a common component of early Christian worship. Extemporaneousness no doubt characterized worship in the disparate communities of Christians that spread across the diaspora in the century following Justin's time. Unfortunately, when it became necessary for such communities to coalesce into what would become a global faith under the leadership of Rome, standardization of language (worship in Latin) and liturgy was viewed as essential. Congregational singing was minimized and eventually replaced almost entirely by monastic choirs. The free-form worship of the early church was lost and even the Protestant Reformation could not bring it back.

The Congregational Singing Dilemma

The praise of God which constitutes the community and its assemblies seeks to bind and commit and therefore to be expressed, to well up and be sung in concert. The Christian community sings. It is not a choral society. Its singing is not a concert. But from inner, material necessity it sings. Singing is the highest form of human expression. It is to such supreme

---

6. Justin Martyr, "First Apology," 106–7.

> expression that the *vox humana* is devoted in the ministry of the Christian community...⁷

> What we can and must say quite confidently is that the community which does not sing is not the community... The praise of God which finds its concrete culmination in the singing of the community is one of the indispensable basic forms of the ministry of the community. (Karl Barth, 1953).⁸

Thomas Symmes subtitled his *The Reasonableness of Regular Singing* (1720) *an essay to revive the true and ancient mode of singing psalm-tunes . . . the knowledge and practice of which is greatly decay'd in most congregations.* His was the common complaint throughout the eighteenth and nineteenth centuries. Hastings, Mason, and Bradbury all recognized congregational singing to be a component essential to vital corporate worship. They spent their lives lecturing about, composing for, and innovating ways to address the problem. Nevertheless, the problem persisted. The first American church choirs were formed not to sing anthems, masses, and service music, but to support and encourage congregational singing. Choral leadership saw some success, most notably in the work of Lowell Mason and at Henry Ward Beecher's Plymouth Church. Nevertheless, by the middle of the nineteenth century many leading American churches had given up, abandoning congregational singing almost entirely for professional quartets and chorus choirs.

With all the progress made in the 1950s and '60s to recognize music ministry as a profession, with the publication of many outstanding hymnals and the writing of copious amounts of new and thought-provoking hymnody, I find it remarkable that so little thought was devoted to addressing the *quality* of congregational singing in churches or how it might be improved. It was a problem for the mainline churches and one that needed to be seriously addressed. Where sacred music education was concerned, the study of church music and liturgical history, choral organization and conducting, organ technique, and hymnology all took precedence over getting people in the pews to lift their voices in song.

It is no surprise then that the radical changes occurring in church music during the last decades of the twentieth century represented a crossroads. Suddenly elite, cultivated churches were not the dominant force they had been. Disaffected baby boomers and millennials were either leaving the church entirely or gravitating toward a new populist style of worship music, and they had the power and wealth of popular culture and the electronic

---

7. Barth, *Church Dogmatics* IV, 866.
8. Barth, *Church Dogmatics* IV, 867.

media to encourage them. Meanwhile, much of the philanthropy that had supported cultivated art music in the past was being diverted elsewhere. Most important, whatever might be said of the praise and worship/contemporary Christian worship movement, *people were singing.*

Music Ministry Education

Eurocentric dualism of course shaped the training being offered at the undergraduate and graduate levels for church musicians. Harold Best, for example, grew up in a musical family. While his father was rigidly opposed to any sort of popular music, Harold was drawn to musical styles of the early '50s, like boogie-woogie and swing.

> I simply knew that I needed all of these kinds of music as much as I needed the classical music that my father had personally singled out. To me, it was all one enchanting world, each part merging with the rest. Enchanting that is, until I began to hear that all of this popular stuff wasn't spiritual—that it was the music of the world, therefore of worldliness. Thus my one world of music became divided, not aesthetically but spiritually, into "good" music and "bad" music.[9]

Music ministry training on the graduate and undergraduate levels in the 1970s and '80s was typically guided by the same classically oriented philosophy. Students could expect training in choral organization and conducting, applied voice or organ, approaches to children's music, hymnology, worship planning, and electives such as handbell methods. Despite its growing presence in the real world of ministry, contemporary Christian music was frequently ignored entirely.[10] Best said of his years at UTS that they were imbued with "the very highest of high art practices."[11] The same dualistic perspective on sacred music applied:

> The split between "good" and "bad" music with precious little middle ground also occurred in my academic training. There was one kind of good music: the music of the great masters . . . And there were two types of bad music: low-quality classical music and almost everything else—popular, jazz, gospel, country, and so on . . .[12]

---

9. Best, *Music Through the Eyes of Faith*, 2.
10. Bearden, "Competencies for a Minister of Music," 79.
11. Best, *Music Through the Eyes of Faith*, 77.
12. Best, *Music Through the Eyes of Faith*, 3.

By the 1980s, with the explosion of interest in CCM, a new type of church music leadership was needed—one that seminaries and music schools were not providing. The worship model established at Calvary Chapel and the Vineyard was far less sermon-focused than traditional Protestant worship. Preaching tended to be loosely topical and often extemporaneous. Music occupied a far greater part in the service—as much as 50 percent—and the responsibility for planning and implementation of the service order was shared equally between preacher and musician. This meant the musician's role extended well beyond music. He or she was expected to guide the worshippers through the various parts of the service and even lead them in prayer. Consequently, it became common to give the contemporary Christian music leader the designation "worship leader" or "worship pastor," titles that now are in common use. The important role played by the church musician is well exemplified by Carl Tuttle. John Wimber entrusted Tuttle with not only song leading but also fleshing out how the church's theology would be acted out in worship at the Vineyard.

College-level sacred music education had not kept pace with these needs, and as a result most contemporary praise leadership in the 1980s and early '90s fell to self-taught volunteers and professional rock band players. Many had little experience in music ministry or worship leadership. The first serious efforts to develop degree programs focused on the unique skills required of contemporary music and worship pastors did not begin until the late 1990s. Regent University in Virginia Beach, Virginia, and affiliated with evangelist Pat Robertson's Christian Broadcasting Network, Jerry Falwell's Liberty University, and the Institute for Worship Studies at Wheaton College each were offering such training by 2020.[13]

Dualism and Postmodernism in the Twenty-First Century

The dualistic mind features essentially binary, either/or thinking. It knows by comparison, opposition, and differentiation. It uses descriptive words like good/evil, pretty/ugly, smart/stupid, not realizing there may be a hundred degrees between the two ends of each spectrum. Dualistic thinking works well for the sake of simplification and conversation, but not for the sake of truth or the immense subtlety of actual personal experience.

> We do need the dualistic mind to function in practical life, however, and to do our work as a teacher, a nurse, a scientist, or an engineer. It's helpful and fully necessary as far as it goes, but it just doesn't go far enough. The dualistic mind cannot process

---

13. Ottaway, "Rise of the Worship Degree," 162.

things like infinity, mystery, God, grace, suffering, sexuality, death, or love; this is exactly why most people stumble over these very issues. The dualistic mind pulls everything down into some kind of tit-for-tat system of false choices and too-simple contraries, which is largely what "fast food religion" teaches, usually without even knowing it. Without the contemplative and converted mind—honest and humble perception—much religion is frankly dangerous (Richard Rohr, 2017).[14]

We see examples of dualistic thinking throughout the history of American church music, always with class as a dimension. The regular singing controversy of the eighteenth century pitted elite educated clergy in Boston against the folkways of more rural New England meetinghouses where the old way of singing psalms was preferred. The advocates for regular singing were not wrong to want musically literate congregations and to organize singing schools to achieve that. One might ask, however, if it was really necessary to vilify those disagreeing with them. We now know that the so-called old way was not the result of ignorance and stupidity as the reformers had claimed. It was a centuries-old tradition brought over from the British Isles and a significant early form of American folk music.

The Wiley Hitchcock concept of two distinctive traditions dividing American music for generations—the "cultivated" and the "vernacular"—is first discernable in the postrevolutionary 1790s. We see elitist dualism in the treatment of the lowly singing school, once promoted as a solution to musical illiteracy, but later condemned and derided for its folkish, homegrown methods. It can be seen in the way northern elites dismissed the religious fervor of the camp meeting revival and the shape-note singing tradition as rustic nonsense. Eurocentric dualism caused well-meaning serious composers like George W. Chadwick and Amy Beach to deny there *could even be* such a thing as American music.

This dualistic, Eurocentric view had shaped how church music was practiced in most mainline American churches for two centuries. By the late twentieth century, however, the meteoric rise of contemporary Christian music had many Protestant churches with traditional worship reorienting their music toward the pop-influenced repertoire of Calvary Chapel and the Vineyard. Sacred music being co-opted by popular recording artists and television personalities, as we have seen, had already weakened the boundary between sacred and pop. The Roman Catholic Church's post-Vatican II break with plainchant and Renaissance polyphony, replacing it with contemporary and folk-inspired music, was also a break with the past.

---

14. Rohr, "Dualistic Mind."

Increased racial and cultural diversity within the general population was another force at play. Worship shaped exclusively by white culture could no longer to be considered the only viable option. Widely differing racial and ethnic worship traditions challenged once unchallenged assumptions about the appropriateness of certain musical styles. Unbreachable boundaries between sacred and secular were far less prevalent in the Asian, African American, Latin American, and Caribbean cultures now reshaping the American landscape. Latin American[15] and Black Pentecostal worship,[16] for example, commonly took a holistic approach toward music in worship, borrowing liberally from both sacred and secular sources.[17] In short, the precarious balance between church music in the cultivated tradition and that of the populist tradition was shifting with populist church music becoming dominant. History teaches us that the church of the future must be culturally aware—putting up welcome signs rather than creating barriers to inclusiveness. It must seek to minister to all classes and groups within the community. Church musicians must acquire a broad-based training and appreciation for the many musical traditions making up our pluralistic Christian culture.

---

15. Hispanic worship generally is shaped by the community it serves, not by a predetermined liturgical form. Rather it is community focused and draws from the cultural background of the worshippers. A word most commonly associated with Hispanic worship is *fiesta*. It is a celebration of what God has done, and what God is going to do. It is a family celebration with singing, clapping, and bodily movement. A broad mix of musical styles are used—sacred, secular, and folk. See Teja, "Worship as Fiesta."

16. We have already seen the melding of sacred and secular musical styles in worship among African Americans beginning with worship in the storefront churches of the early twentieth century.

17. Redman, *Great Worship Awakening*, 105.

The Crucible of Perfectionism, Elevation of Musical Taste, and Sacralization

Biagio, "The Apotheosis of Handel" (1787).
Public domain image. (https://www.meisterdrucke.uk/fine-art-prints/Biagio-Rebecca/112119/Apotheosis-of-Handel,-1787-.html)

Faith in the power and importance of education led Lowell Mason, Thomas Hastings, and many others to assert (1) that only music of the very highest quality was appropriate for church use (perfectionism), and (2) that as worshippers were exposed to the very best music, musical taste will be elevated. "The very best music" was thought, of course, to be European art music. The successful elevation of musical taste would become the gold standard for musical reform in the elite and cultivated Protestant churches of the nineteenth century. It was thought that the thorny problems of poor congregational singing and amateurish music making would go away as worshippers' artistic standards were raised.

The vestiges of perfectionism and sacralization are still with us today and create an unnecessary barrier to music ministry in worship. I personally stand in awe of J. S. Bach and find myself wondering how any human being could create such sublime art. I experience the same awe in conducting a symphony or mass of Mozart. Performing the Brahms German Requiem never fails to bring a tear to my eye. *But*, we must remember there is nothing inherently sacred about notes on a page. Vocal music with a religious text adds a sacred element, but ultimately music only becomes sacred when it comes as a sincere offering to God from the heart of the performer. Worship cannot be *about the music*. Whether attempting to raise a congregation's musical taste by exclusively offering high art or trying to achieve church growth through the musical styles of popular culture—either approach gives music an importance it should not have.

> What is faulty is the churches' assumption that if we choose the right kind of music, people will be attracted to Christ. It is idolatry to think our work makes the difference.[18]

Over a century ago Waldo Selden Pratt attempted to address the same factional divisiveness between the church's artistic and cultivated elite and proponents of the gospel song. He wrote, "The fitness of any example of musical production for use in public worship does not depend wholly upon its merely formal excellence. Some very poor music has proved itself liturgically useful; some very perfect music has proved itself liturgically pernicious."[19] Pratt's point was not to deny great music a place in the worship of the church; nor was it to either prohibit or promote gospel songs. In essence, he was saying that *ministry*—not musical style—must take precedence at any given time. That music which can bring the worshipping community closer to Christ is the *right* music. This then points us to another truth about the specialized path church musicians must follow. The principal objective of music for the concert performer or teacher is *artistic expression*. For the church musician, it must be *ministry*. They are two separate and distinct disciplines.

"The Call"

Will you come and follow me if I but call your name?

---

18. Dawn, *Reaching Out Without Dumbing Down*, 192.
19. Pratt, *Musical Ministries in the Church*, 42.

Will you go where you don't know and never be the same?
Will you let my love be shown; will you let my name be known;
Will you let my life be grown in you and you in me?[20]

The apostle Paul wrote eloquently about servanthood and the call to ministry in the first chapter of Colossians: "I became its servant according to God's commission that was given to me for you, to make the word of God fully known."[21] He went on to explain the life of sacrifice a call to servanthood requires. A sermon by the Rev. Canon Kristi Philip of the Cathedral of St. John the Evangelist in Spokane, Washington, referenced John Bell's Iona hymn "The Summons" to address the subject of ministerial calling. In it she alluded to Isaiah's vision, Paul's conversion on the Damascus Road, and Jesus's call to the fisherman. In each case, she noted, the recipient(s) of the call felt "a profound sense of unworthiness." This is certainly true for anyone accepting a call to music ministry. "Who we are called to be and what we are called to do," Philip preached, "is part of a larger, broader sense of vocation."[22] The church musician is called to be teacher, encourager, passionate advocate for worship, and prayer partner—a job description far beyond that of "musician in residence." No matter how well trained the church musician entering a new music ministry, there is a sense of stepping into the unknown. How that ministry unfolds will be shaped by the community served and its needs.

Stepping into the unknown? I suspect every church musician has had experiences—some thrilling, others different, and still others emotionally draining—but all unexpected. When I began my journey, little did I know:

- That I would be leading churches into often new and uncharted territory—having to justify musical choices all along the way.
- That I would be called upon, not only to minister through music but also as a spiritual guide and pastoral support figure: rushing to the ER, after receiving a midnight call, to assist with ministering to the family of a beloved soloist, tragically killed in a motor vehicle accident. I would also be called upon to provide comfort to the family of a children's choir member who died because of child abuse. Working closely with families, I would plan for and often lead music for memorial services for numerous singers and colleagues.

---

20. "The Summons," text by John Bell and Graham Maule, © G. I. A. Publications representing Wild Goose Resource Group/Iona Community, 1987. Used by Permission.

21. Colossians 1:25, NRSV.

22. Rev. Canon Kristy Philip, Sermon for February 10, 2019, Cathedral of St. John the Evangelist. Used by permission.

- That I would need to weather times of controversy over a range of issues from LGBTQ justice, to inclusive language and gender equality, to racial inclusivity, to clergy malfeasance—trying always to do so with integrity, patience, understanding, and love.

Certainly, dealing with such things was beyond the scope of my conservatory musical training. None of them were among my expectations when first stepping in front of a church choir in 1967. How to approach them was not in my "music ministry toolbox." Each had to be experienced and learned from.

We can see a glimmer of the concept of music as a *called ministry* in the early nineteenth-century writings of Lowell Mason and Thomas Hastings. We can see it fleshed out in mid-century by the pioneering work of Episcopal priests such as Morgan Dix and John Ireland Tucker. In the twentieth century, we see the idea expanded to include both liturgical and nonliturgical sects in the writings of Pratt and the mission of the UTS School of Sacred Music. Still, in the cultivated church the church musician is often viewed as a remote presence—too often hidden away on the organ bench or behind a music stand. In this the contemporary Christian movement has had much to teach us, with church musicians having a direct and pastoral presence that guides and nurtures congregational worship and singing.

Hopeful Signs

Church music in this first quarter of the twenty-first century is in a state of transition. After four decades of unbridled growth, there are signs that enthusiasm is waning for an exclusive diet of contemporary worship music. As early as 2014, voices within the music department of the Southern Baptist Church were saying that interest in CCM had peaked two years earlier and was now in decline. Reasons given included superficial song texts and oversaturation. The novelty of CCM was no longer there. Instead of being "hip" or "forward-looking," CCM had become commonplace.[23]

One of the most influential and positive voices providing guidance during a time of consternation and uncertainty was Robert E. Webber (1933–2007).

---

23. Gordan, "Imminent Decline of Contemporary Worship Music."

Robert E. Webber.
Courtesy of the Robert E. Webber Institute for Worship Studies.
(https://iws.edu/about/who/robert-e-webber/)

From 1968 to 2000 Webber served as a professor of theology at Wheaton College and founded the Institute for Worship Studies in 1998. He was a prolific author and devoted his life to bridging between mainline and evangelical Protestantism in the United States. To do that, Webber became an authority on Christian worship in the first and second centuries and convincingly argued that liturgical and contemporary worship practices need not be mutually exclusive. The concept of "blended worship" had been around years before Webber wrote this book and was not universally well-received. Too often, blended simply meant putting together a conglomeration of disparate musical styles to please various segments of a congregation rather than a carefully thought-out plan for musical and theological continuity. Achieving such continuity and spiritual effectiveness was Webber's goal in writing, and as a result he changed his terminology from "blended worship" to "convergent worship," and ultimately to "ancient-future." Webber challenged evangelical churches "to approach worship with a healthy respect for liturgical tradition while being fully committed to contemporary relevance."[24] Webber observed, "The theological systems and denominational particulars that at one time divided one church from another have become increasingly blurred. The priority of Christ-centered faith [is taking] precedence over theological rules and denominational confessions."[25]

Of congregational singing, Webber wrote:

> The challenge of future worship is to identify those choruses and spiritual songs that have lasting value, to retain music of the past

---

24. Powers, "Robert Webber," 97.
25. Webber, *Planning Blended Worship*, 14.

Learning from the Past—Hope for the Future

that is characterized by depth and power, and to combine these many forms of music into an order of worship that remembers, proclaims, enacts, and celebrates the story of salvation. While some churches will continue to remain hymn-singing churches only, and other churches will insist on being chorus-singing churches only, the majority of churches are likely to find ways to incorporate both the richness and dignity of the hymns of the church with the inspiration and relevance of gospel songs and contemporary choruses.[26]

To expand on Webber's thoughts on congregational singing—the days of pitting choirs vs. worship teams, praise bands vs. organs, hymns and anthems vs. choruses must end.

Contemporaneous with Webber's writing has been a discernible increase in interest among young adults to reconnect with the *mysterium* and awe of liturgical worship. A study among university students in Minnesota and Wisconsin in 2012 found that, while they were not accepting of dogmatic differences between denominations, they were drawn to ritual. The study found that "the most communal spiritual practice in the area [was] centering prayer, Evensong, and Taizé," each of which fostered "a contemplative religious experience."[27]

Taizé is the name given to a style of contemplative worship coming out of the Taizé Community, an ecumenical Christian monastic fraternity in Taizé, France. Brother Roger Schultz (1915–2005), a Reformed Protestant Christian, founded the Taizé movement in 1940 to model ecumenical Christ-centered communal living and break down the barriers dividing denominational Christianity. Its brothers come from both the Roman Catholic and Protestant traditions. The Taizé Community emphasizes ecumenical communal worship based on "the universal priesthood of all the faithful."[28] Worship in the Taizé style is intentionally simple, consisting of meditative chant, interspersed with prayer, Scripture readings, and a celebration of the Eucharist.[29] The format became formalized with the founding of the Church of Resurrection in 1962, specifically for the fraternity's use. Taizé's important identification with church music began with Brother Roger's meeting the composer/organist Jacques Berthier (1923–1994).

---

26. Webber, *Worship Old and New*, p203.
27. Edgell and Robey, "Loose Connections and Liberal Theology", 653.
28. Heijke, *Ecumenical Light*, 181.
29. Selles, "Taizé in the Fall."

Jacques Berthier. Public domain image. (https://www.discogs.com/artist/1835424-Jacques-Berthier)

A disciple of Fr. Joseph Gelineau, Berthier was fascinated with the Taizé concept of repetitive chant. Between 1975 and his death, Berthier composed 232 musical pieces for use by the brothers. His style of writing was uniquely lyrical and accessible to worshippers with little rehearsal. Taizé worship and its music, translated into English, arrived in the United States thanks to an agreement between Berthier and Robert Batastini, president of the G.I.A. Publishing Company, in 1978.[30]

Regarding contemporary Christian music, the years since 1995 have brought a significant increase in theological depth and musicality to the song repertoire. Songs of British songwriters Graham Kendrick ("Shine, Jesus, Shine!"), Brian Doerksen ("Come, Now is the Time to Worship"), Martin Smith ("I Could Sing Love Forever"), and Matt Redman ("Better Is One Day") continue to be sung regularly in worship. Singer/composer/lyricist Darlene Zschech, music director at Hillsong Church in Australia from 1995 to 2007, has produced a number of high caliber songs. Her unique, rhythmically driven style as reflected in "Shout to the Lord" has been eagerly embraced by American congregations. American songwriter Chris Tomlin (b. 1972) also stands out for songs like "How Great is Our God" (2004) and "Amazing Grace, My Chains Fell Off"(2008).

We must not miss the kindred needs both contemporary Christian worship and Taizé sought to satisfy. Both traditions have generated strong interest among youth and young adults. Both emphasize intense spirituality and full congregational participation in singing. The short, repetitive Taizé melodies, while entirely different in style, share with praise choruses

---

30. *G. I. A. Diamond Jubilee Collection*, xxiv.

an ease of accessibility with makes singing accessible and enjoyable for all congregants.

Taizé differs from CCM in its embrace of ritual. CCM, conversely, stands out for its embrace of popular culture. Efforts are being made to find common ground. Tara Isabella Burton provided an interesting perspective on the growing appreciation of ritual in a 2020 article in the *New York Times*. "More and more," she wrote, "young Christians, disillusioned by the political binaries, economic uncertainties and spiritual emptiness that have come to define modern America are finding solace in the decidedly anti-modern vision of faith . . . Old forms of religiosity offer a glimpse of the transcendent beyond the present."[31] Dr. C. Michael Hawn, director of the pastoral music degree program at Perkins School of Theology, Southern Methodist University, observed the same trend in another context at the Church of the Apostle in Seattle, Washington, in 2007. There, worshippers were led through a traditional Lutheran order of worship but with contemporary music from Scotland and composers within the church itself. Leading the musical portion of the service was a director of music backed up by a worship band and a large, mixed-voice chorus dedicated exclusively to supporting the singing of the congregation.[32]

To Revitalize Artistic Expression in Church Music—A Challenge for the Twenty-First Century

Where there has been a decline in the use of traditional choral and organ music in worship in the American church, it must not be seen as simply a musical problem. *It is a worship problem* and certainly nothing new.

History tells us to once again revisit the issue of *participatio actuosa*—full and engaged congregational participation. How may we achieve it? It is clear, I believe, from the study of church music in America, that *full participation in congregational singing* is one critical key to a rebirth of authentic and vital worship in America. Vatican II recognized this in 1965. The contemporary Christian movement embraced full participation from the time of its birth. I am convinced that the repertoire of traditional hymnody is an irreplaceable treasure for mainline Protestantism as well as Catholicism. *Hymn singing can be taught.* Congregations can be just as engaged and invigorated by singing hymns together as praise songs, but they need to do it more. The concept of extended times devoted just to singing with impassioned leadership should be a universal part of church life. But this often

---

31. Burton, "Christianity Gets Weird."
32. Hawn, "What Has Happened to the Church Choir?," 10–11.

requires a reorientation of priorities.³³ Choirs need to refocus their energies on leadership of hymn singing. Music directors need to gauge their success on the quality of singing in the pews rather than quality of anthem singing. As Karl Barth said, "the community which does not sing is not the community"—that should be the standard by which music ministry is judged. Also important in preparation, congregations need to know about what they are being asked to sing. A bit of teaching about the historical background of a hymn or song, highlighting key elements in a text—these can do wonders to answer the question, "Why are we singing this?" The too often mechanical running through of congregational music does little to encourage and may even discourage participation by the uninitiated.³⁴

The Tyranny of Labeling

A repeating theme throughout this study has been dualism, the unfortunate partisan divide between proponents of cultivated art in the church on one side and populist musical styles on the other. Hitchcock, Chase, and others greatly helped our understanding by pointing out and defining the conflicting currents running through the history of American music. *I believe that where music in the church is concerned, the time has come to put an end to dualistic thinking. We should no longer be talking about labels: "cultivated versus vernacular (or populist)" and "contemporary versus traditional"; there is only American sacred music.* All worship should be contemporary, whatever the style, in that it must effectively minister and engage those in the pews. All worship, whatever the style, should have a healthy respect for its traditional roots in Christian history. We should no longer dismiss an entire class or style of music as inappropriate but judge individual works on their own merit, musically and textually. As for European art music, it must and

---

33. In my own career, I can remember often pondering after a service how well the choir sang and what might be done to improve its performance. Post-performance evaluations are something all choirmasters should do. But I suspect there are other equally important questions that don't get addressed as often as they should: "How was the congregation's singing this morning? What needs to be done to improve it? If the hymns or songs were unfamiliar, the music challenging in some way, what can we do to address that?"

34. The hard truth is that, despite centuries of effort from the singing schools forward, the average congregant does not possess the skills needed to navigate an unfamiliar tune and absorb an unfamiliar text at the same time. As a result the singer in the pews struggles, totally missing the spiritual and musical intent of the hymn, and is relieved when the music stops. Others simply close their hymnal and refuse to participate. Worship planners must realize that a majority of people *want* to sing, if steps can be taken to make that an enjoyable and fulfilling experience.

should remain an important part of choral and organ repertoire in mainline Protestant worship, but church musicians will be wise to insist it share a place with music from our American heritage as well as that of other non-European cultures. Finally, I believe that to be truly inclusive, clergy and musicians must strive to understand and embrace the musical heritage of communities they serve. That should begin with a solid grounding in the history of the American church and its music.

A Final Word

A dream yet to be fully realized is the universal recognition of music as a career ministry essential to the church. Nevertheless, it has been an aspirational goal for much of this country's history. I close with words addressed to church musicians by the Episcopal priest and organist, the Reverend Victoria R. Sirota, formerly priest and vicar of the Cathedral of St. John the Divine in New York City:

> One person is all it takes to make a difference . . .
>
> You mold the spiritual life—the soul of your congregation—by your music and by the silence you create. When you get it right, you help us feel joy, you comfort us and feed us, you remind us of what is important, you allow us to rest in your spirituality, we can trust you with our frailty and our vulnerability, you help us to cry out and complain, weep and rejoice in new life and resurrection.
>
> And finally, you walk us to heaven, again and again. And we are grateful.
>
> Be who you are! Be the light! Amen.[35]

---

35. Sirota, "Musician's Struggle with Vocation and Call," 80.

EPILOGUE

Reflections and Appreciations

THE INSPIRATION FOR SERVANTHOOD *of Song* came from my almost fifty-year career as a church musician. Classically trained as a singer, voice teacher, and conductor, I had to learn that church music, if it is to be the powerful witness it can be, must be understood as a ministry with different priorities than those of the school, the concert hall, or popular culture. The more I researched, the more I realized that "music ministry" was not a new idea, but one that germinated early on in our country's history and grew as it threaded its way from one generation to another.

Yet another motivation was my desire to teach. I remember that, as I was about to leave a parish I had been serving, a nonmusician church member told me my leadership had been "transformational." I was, of course, flattered by the comment, but also taken aback. Upon reflection, I realized the individual was responding to my almost unconscious tendency not simply to perform, but to teach—to teach about liturgy, about the hymns, the historical background of the hymns—anything that might make the worship experience more relevant and meaningful. Communicating "why we do what we do" should be a priority for all of us in all our work.

The research for this book really began in the 1980s with the writing of my dissertation, *Church Song and the Cultivated Tradition in New England and New York*. My career, you see, has been as what H. Wiley Hitchcock would call a "cultivated church musician." It has been a life devoted largely to work as a choral conductor and singer working in traditional worship settings—Presbyterian, United Methodist, and Episcopal. The required conducting and directorial skills were wide-ranging—everything from classic hymns, anthems, to choral/orchestral works—and in later years helping to organize praise teams. The rich variety of experiences across denominations led me to a concentrated study, both formal and private of Christian liturgy, a subject about which I have since taught on the graduate level.

I was also inspired to undertake this study by a long-held passion for American music. I suspect it existed in me long before, but the incredible feast of music making during our nation's bicentennial celebrations in the 1970s was an eye-opening experience for me. I had already been directing choirs for nearly a decade, but had never heard of "lining out," or "shape-note singing," or William Billings. Where had this wild, often primitive, yet spiritual music come from? How could this repertoire not be a part of our musical DNA as American church musicians? Those are questions that I feel still need to be answered. How can we expect to reach a broad range of congregants on Sunday morning if we program largely Eurocentric repertoire and deny them their musical birthright?

The writing of *Servanthood of Song*, however, was for me more than an academic exercise. The subject matter repeatedly intersected with life experiences over the years:

- *Witness to change*

The period from the mid-1960s through about 1975 was when I began my career in church music, and, like many others of my generation, I witnessed firsthand the incursion of sacred folk style and pop-influenced youth music into worship. While still in college I took on my first director of music position at an American Baptist Church in northern Virginia. "What was a devout, rather left-wing Episcopalian doing in a Baptist church?," you might ask. I wonder sometimes what they really thought (with their Baptist ears), about Purcell's *Music for the Funeral of Queen Mary* in a worship service, but the pastor and congregation were unstintingly supportive.

I mention this because of another example of unconventional programming. My first summer in the position I organized a youth choir and taught them Herbert Draesel's *Rejoice! Music for the Worship of God in the Twentieth Century*. Again, due to inexperience, I had chosen something so liturgically Episcopalian, so foreign to Baptist worship sensibilities, yet it was received enthusiastically and without reservation. It was, I was told, the first time that guitars had been used in that sanctuary.

There was a lesson in that experience that I only recognized much later: the power of music to transcend denominational boundaries. What I remember most fondly, however, was their singing of Draesel's folk-style setting of the William Percy hymn, "They Cast Their Nets." The poignant text says much about the Christian life, and I suspect what writers of the "Hymn Explosion," the reformers of Vatican II, and the Jesus People all shared: a belief in the sacrificial aspect of ministry.

> Contented, peaceful fishermen, before they ever knew
> The peace of God that filled their hearts, brimful and broke them too.
> Young John who trimmed the flapping sail, homeless in Patmos died.
> Peter, who hauled the teeming net, head-down was crucified.
> The Peace of God—it is no peace, but strife closed in the sod.
> Yet, brothers, pray for just one thing, the marvelous peace of God.[1]

- *Church Music History in Small-Town Ohio*

An hour's drive east along the banks of Lake Erie from the great city of Cleveland is the town of Ashtabula (pronounced *ash-tuh-byoo-luh*) and the county which bears its name. It's a place with a colorful history, yet, safe to say, too obscure to be a featured destination in *National Geographic*. In my research on "musical conventions," I found that one famous person *did* set his sights on Ashtabula. W. B. Bradbury led conventions in 1858 and 1859 in Ashtabula County.

A far more significant and somber event, however, took place two decades later. Phillip P. Bliss, the famed gospel singer and composer of "It is Well with My Soul," his wife, Lucy, and their two children along with ninety-two other hapless passengers died in the Ashtabula train disaster. A monument to the Bliss family and the many others burned beyond recognition in the aftermath of the wreck still dominates the Chestnut Grove Cemetery, a reminder of a tragic December night in 1876.

- *The Symbolism of Two Hymnals*

My grandmother—we called her "Bingy"—moved north from Georgia during the Great Depression and eventually came to live with us, taking care of my sister and I while my mother, a secretary, and my dad, a railroader, worked during the day. Our family was Episcopalian, but Bingy was not a churchgoer. When asked, however, she would always proclaim her allegiance to the little Baptist church her family attended near Atlanta. As a child in the 1950s, I vividly remember the huge, old upright piano in our den with two well-worn hymnals nearby, the *Hymnal 1940* and that quaint little green book, the *Broadman Hymnal*. Grandmother played "by ear" and did not read music. I think she kept the *Broadman Hymnal* nearby just to thumb through and recall the

---

1. William Alexander Percy (1885–1942), "They Cast Their Nets in Galilee" (text public domain).

old, cherished hymns of her childhood. To this day I can still remember coming home from school and hearing her, alone in our den, playing "The Old Rugged Cross." Looking back, the juxtaposition of those two hymn collections, the *Hymnal 1940* and the *Broadman Hymnal*, were significant to my search for relevance as a church musician. Being able to find inspiration both in the high church contributions of C. Winfred Douglas and the sentimental faith of treasured gospel hymnody has shaped my view of ministry.

- *African Americans, the Church, and Sacred Music*

It might be asked why I should be the one writing about this difficult subject—the church's interaction with slavery and the relationship of that interaction to traditions of African American music and worship. As one whose life has been devoted to ministry through music, I see ministry and the need to understand history as interrelated. Perhaps despite the old saying, we can never truly "walk in another's moccasins," but we must aspire to it—to understand.

Back in the 1980s, I had been asked to coordinate and direct the music for a community-wide Thanksgiving service. Early in the planning, I visited the large African Methodist Episcopal church nearby. Their music director (I will call her Margaret) was well known for her passion, expertise, and the powerful ministry of music she had built. Our paths had not crossed, and I was looking forward to collaborating with her. We had a pleasant and productive conversation, and she too seemed excited about being a part of the project along with her choirs. One piece of that conversation, however, will always stay with me.

I had tentatively programmed a William Dawson choral arrangement of an African American spiritual to be sung by the massed choir at a central point in the service. "Margaret," I asked, "would you be willing to work with the choir to see that the spiritual is sung in a manner stylistically appropriate to your tradition?" She responded, "Stan, your people can never truly understand our music." I'm sure I was initially taken aback and a bit miffed. Her words stung. We moved on, though, and Margaret, bless her heart, did coach the chorus. While the chorus was made up largely of "white folks," they did a credible job. The music was inspiring and well received. Margaret's response to my question, nevertheless, haunted me.

Margaret, if you are reading this, it troubles me that, even today, decades after our conversation, many general histories of American church music treat the subject of African American sacred music lightly or skip over it entirely. Flawed though it may be, *Servanthood of Song* is my effort to address the omission.

And so, yes, I feel a personal connection to the writing on these pages, and I want to thank you the reader for joining with me on this journey.

In Appreciation

Isaac Newton once said, "If I have seen further it is by standing on the shoulders of giants." Most authors, I suspect, recognize that their efforts are indebted to others—giants of the profession, yes, but also teachers, mentors, friends, work associates, and parents.

First, my parents. Their lives were defined at least in part by living through the Great Depression. Neither had the luxury of pursuing educational advancement. My mother finished high school, but immediately had to take on secretarial work, not only to support herself but also her parents. Mother knew very little of music short of singing in a school choir in her teens, but she recognized early on that music was where my heart lies. She made every effort to encourage my dreams. Somehow, Mom and Dad stretched budgets to allow for the purchase of expensive musical instruments, music lessons, travel to competitions, and attendance at performances of the Cleveland Orchestra and the Metropolitan Opera when on tour. It was not enough to attend an opera for mother. The hour-long drive to Cleveland was always occupied with reading plot summaries by Milton Cross!

From my father I was gifted with a love of history. His schooling had ended with the seventh grade. Like Mom, he had to drop out to work and contribute toward his family's survival. Nevertheless, he loved history—not simply the national history most of us are taught in school, but local history. What I learned from my father, more broadly speaking, is that history is like a tapestry. On the one hand, if one concentrates only on the tiny details, one risks missing the majesty of the fabric as a whole. On the other hand, if one focuses only on the broad design of the needleworker, one risks missing the craftsmanship entirely. I firmly believe that knowing the historical context gives meaning to our lives and is essential to the work of church musicians.

Teachers and mentors . . . There were so many! I was blessed with incredible music teachers. Ms. Alfield Johnson (choir) and Mr. Norman Taylor (band) saw potential in me and pushed me to develop it. I will be ever thankful for Ruth Orn, my high school Latin teacher, who taught me so much more than a classical language. She instilled in her students a love of learning and a recognition of the benefits to be reaped from disciplined study, whatever the subject. At Shenandoah Conservatory, I will always be grateful for my voice teacher James Corbett, who gave me the courage to reorient my career goals from instrumental to vocal music. On the graduate level I was fortunate to study with some true giants of the profession: Dr. Wilton Mason and Dr. Lara Hoggard at the University of North Carolina/Chapel Hill; and Drs. James Vail, David Wilson, and Rodney Eichenberger at the University of Southern California. All of them have their imprint on the pages of this study.

My decision to dedicate my life to church music was made gradually, and some part of that decision must be credited to the wonderful, ordained clergy with whom I have partnered. Their self-sacrifice and commitment to servanthood not only led me to church work, but also provided for me a model for what a musician set apart for ministry should be.

My students at East Carolina University/Greenville! I learned much from them about the challenges of church music ministry in recent decades. Their input and concerns helped to shape my choice of content in this study.

I also would be remiss in not mentioning the hundreds of singers I have worked with over the years including most recently the personnel of Chorale Coeur d'Alene. Collectively, they have repeatedly shone the power of music to unite people of vastly diverse races, political persuasions, religious sensibilities, and musical tastes in creating something inexpressibly beautiful. It is that unifying potential of music in this time of worrying polarities that led me to write *Servanthood of Song*.

There is a legion of others whose contributions, small and large, made it possible for me to write this book. Judith Anne Horton, my original proof editor, devoted two years to sweating out with incredible patience and grace each chapter of *Servanthood of Song*. Reference librarians at Whitworth University, the University of Southern California, the University of Idaho, and the Newberry Library in Chicago all helped me access critical research materials. My friends at Opportunity Presbyterian Church, Spokane, the Spokane City and County Library Systems, Larry and Susan Almeida, John Cambareri and Kathleen Webb—all generously allowed me space for weeks of "off the grid" writing time. Dr. Amy Porter of the Gonzaga University Music Department went the extra mile to locate a needed reference source. Thanks to all!

Regarding specific individuals in the publishing process, I want to express deep appreciation to Dr. Wayne Wold, who contributed the beautiful foreword that opens *Servanthood of Song*. Thanks also to the Reverend Victoria R. Sirota, David W. Music, Colin Andrews, and Janette Fishell, all leaders in my profession, for their encouragement to pursue this project. My heartfelt gratitude also goes to Michael Thompson, Noel Snyder, Rodney

Clapp, and the editorial staff at Cascade Books for seeing promise in my work and their patience as I navigated through the editorial process.

Finally, I want to express my deepest appreciation to my wife, Cheryl, for her love, unbounded patience, and support during the writing of *Servanthood*. She too read the entire manuscript and gave invaluable input. A too-often grouchy husband, our loving but often challenging pugs, and a global pandemic—she weathered it all while never failing to buoy my confidence to see the project through.

It is my fervent wish that this book can be a resource and provide another layer of context for our spiritual witness through the art of music.

February 28, 2024
Spokane, Washington

BIBLIOGRAPHY

Abbington, James, ed. *Readings in African-American Church Music and Worship*. 2 vols. Chicago: G.I.A, 2001, 2014.
Abbott, Lyman. "The Lake Mohonk Conference on the Negro Question." Editorial in *The Christian Union* 41:24 (June 12, 1890) 830–31.
———. *Silhouettes of My Contemporaries*. London: George Allen & Urwin, 1922.
Abbott, Lynn. "Play That Barbershop Chord! A Case for the African-American Origin of Barbershop Harmony." *American Music* 10:3 (Autumn 1992) 289–325.
Acosta, Juan de. "Annual Letter of 1639." In *Records of the English Province of the Society of Jesus*, vol. 3, 378. London: Burns & Oates, 1878.
Addams, Jane. "Respect for the Law." *The Independent*, January 3, 1901.
Ahlstrom, Sydney. *A Religious History of the American People*. New Haven: Yale University Press, 2004.
Aikin, J. B. *The Christian Minstrel: A New System of Musical Notation: with a Collection of Psalm Tunes, Anthems and Chants Selected from the Most Popular Works in Europe and America: Designed for the Use of Churches, Singing-schools and Societies*. Philadelphia: T. K. Collins, 1851.
Albrecht, T. "German Singing Societies in Texas." PhD diss., North Texas State University, 1975.
Aldrich, Richard. "Protestant Church Music." *New York Times*, January 7, 1934.
Alexander, Helen C., and J. Kennedy Maclean. *Charles M. Alexander: A Romance of Song and Soul Winning*. London: Marshall Brothers, 1920.
Allen, Alexander V. G. *The Life and Letters of Phillips Brooks with Portraits and Illustrations*. Vol. 2. New York: E. P. Dutton, 1900.
Allen, Ray. *Singing in the Spirit: African-American Quartets in New York City*. Philadelphia: University of Pennsylvania Press, 1991.
Allen, William Francis. *A Yankee in Coastal South Carolina: William Francis Allen's Civil War Journals*. Edited by James Robert Hester. Columbia: University of South Carolina Press, 2015.
Allen, William Francis, et al. *Slave Songs of the United States*. New York: A. Simpson & Co., 1867.
Allwardt, Anton Paul. "Sacred Music in New York City, 1800–1850." PhD diss., Union Theological Seminary School of Sacred Music, 1950.
Alviani, Doric. "The Choral Church Music of Arthur William Foote." PhD diss., Union Theological Seminary, New York, 1962.

Anderson, George B. *Landmarks of Rensselaer County, New York.* Syracuse, NY: D. Mason & Company, 1897.

Anderson, Terry H. *The Movement and the Sixties: Protest in America from Greensboro to Wounded Knee.* New York: Oxford University Press, 1995.

Anderson, Toni. *"Tell Them We Are Singing for Jesus": The Original Fisk Jubilee Singers and Christian Reconstruction, 1871–1878.* Macon, GA: Mercer University Press, 2010.

Andrus, Helen. *A Century of Music in Poughkeepsie, 1802–1911.* Poughkeepsie, NY: Frank B. Howard, 1912.

Anson, Adrian C. *A Ball Player's Career: Being the Personal Experiences and Reminiscences of Adrian C. Anson, Late Manager and Captain of the Chicago Baseball Club.* Chicago: Era, 1900.

Anstice, Henry. *History of St. George's Church in the City of New York, 1732–1911.* New York: Harper & Brothers, 1911.

Armstrong, Anton. "The Musical Legacy of F. Melius Christiansen." *Choral Journal* 37:4 (November 1996) 9–14.

Armstrong, Louis. *Satchmo: My Life in New Orleans.* New York: Prentice-Hall, 1954.

Armstrong, Susan O. "The Legacy of Everett Titcomb." PhD diss., Boston University, 1990.

———. "The Legacy of Everett Titcomb." *The Tracker* 31:1 (1987) 23–28.

Asbury, Francis. *The Journal and Letters of Francis Asbury.* Vol. 1. Wesleyan Heritage Publications (1998). http://media.sabda.org/alktab-6/wh3-ref/ai-v1.pdf.

Askew, Thomas, and Richard Pierard. *The American Church Experience.* Eugene, OR: Wipf & Stock, 2004.

Atkins, John. *A Voyage to Guinea, Brazil, and the West Indies in His Majesty's Ships, the Swallow and the Weymouth.* London: Ward & Chandler, 1737.

Atwater, Lyman H. "Our Industrial and Financial Situation." *The Presbyterian Quarterly and Princeton Review*, July 1875, 517–29.

Ayers, Edward L. *In the Presence of Mine Enemies: The Civil War in the Heart of America, 1859–1863.* New York: W. W. Norton, 2003.

Ayres, Ann. *The Life and Work of William Augustus Muhlenberg, Doctor of Divinity.* New York: T. Whittaker, 1889.

Bacon, Margaret Hope. "Lucy McKim Garrison: Pioneer in Folk Music." *Pennsylvania History: A Journal of Mid-Atlantic Studies* 54:1 (January 1987) 1–16.

Bailey, Alfred Edward. *The Gospel in Hymns: Backgrounds and Interpretations.* New York: Charles Scribner, 1950.

Bailey, Ben E. "The Lined-Hymn Tradition in Black Mississippi Churches." *The Black Perspective in Music* 6:1 (Spring 1978) 3–17.

Baker, David N. "A Periodization of Black Music History." In *Reflections on Afro-American Music*, edited by Dominique-Rene de Lerma, 143–60. Kent, OH: Kent State University Press, 1973.

Baldwin, James. *Go Tell It on the Mountain.* Ebook ed. New York: Vintage, 2013.

Baldwin, Samuel A. "The American Guild Of Organists." *Musical Quarterly* 32:2 (April 1946) 289–95.

Ball, Thomas. *My Threescore Years and Ten: An Autobiography.* Boston: Roberts Brothers, 1891.

Balmer, Randall H. *Encyclopedia of Evangelicalism.* Louisville: Westminster John Knox, 2002.

Banville, Scott "The LeFevres." In *Encyclopedia of American Gospel Music*, edited by W. K. McNeil, 228. New York: Routledge, 2005.

Barnabee, Henry Clay. *Reminiscences of Henry Clay Barnabee*. Edited by G. L. Varney. Boston: Chapple, 1913.

Barnes, Sandra L. "Religion and Rap Music: An Analysis of Black Church Usage." In *Readings in African-American Church Music and Worship*, vol. 2, edited by J. Abbington, 563–86. Chicago: G.I.A, 2014.

Barth, Karl. *Church Dogmatics*. Vol. IV: *The Doctrine of Reconciliation*. Edited by Geoffrey Bromiley and T. F. Torrance. Edinburgh: T. & T. Clark, 1962.

Bartlett, Joseph. "Music as an Auxiliary to Religion." Address before the Handel Society of Dartmouth College, April 1841. Boston: Crocker & Brewster, 1841.

Basile, Salvatore. *Fifth Avenue Famous: The Extraordinary Story of Music at St. Patrick's Cathedral*. New York: Fordham University Press, 2010.

Bayley, Daniel. *The New Harmony of Zion*. Newburyport, MA: printed by the author, 1788.

Bealle, John. *Public Worship, Private Faith: Sacred Harp and American Folksong*. Athens, GA: University of Georgia Press, 1997.

———. "The Sacred Harp" In *Encyclopedia of Gospel Music*, 2nd ed., edited by W. K. McNeil, 327–28. New York: Routledge, Taylor, and Francis, 2010.

Bearden, Donald R. "Competencies for a Minister of Music in a Southern Baptist Church: Implications for Curriculum Development." PhD diss., New Orleans Baptist Theological Seminary, 1980.

Beck, Joseph G. *America's Choral Ambassador: John Finley Williamson*. Bloomington, IN: AuthorHouse, 2014.

Beecher, Henry Ward. "Poverty and the Gospel." (Sermon preached June 17, 1883.) In *Library of the World's Best Literature: An Anthology in Thirty Volumes*, edited by C. D. Warner et al. (1917). Bartleby.com, Great Books Online. https://www.bartleby.com/library/prose/652.html.

———. "The Religious Uses of Music." In *The Sermons of Henry Ward Beecher of Plymouth Church, Brooklyn, March–September 1872*, 287–301. New York: J. B. Ford & Company, 1873.

Beecher, Lyman. *Autobiography*. Vol. 2. Edited by Charles Beecher. New York: Harper & Brothers, 1865.

Begbie, Jeremy, D. K. Chua, and M. Rathey, eds. *Theology, Music, and Modernity: Struggles for Freedom*. London: Oxford University Press, 2021.

Beirne, Francis F. *St. Paul's Parish, Baltimore: A Chronicle of Mother Church*. Baltimore: St. Paul's Parish/Horn Schaeffer Co., 1967.

Bell, Marion L. *Crusade in the City: Revivalism in 19th Century Philadelphia*. Lewisburg, PA: Bucknell University Press, 1977.

Belmonte, Kevin. *D. L. Moody—A Life: Innovator, Evangelist, World Changer*. Chicago: Moody, 1994.

Bennett, William W. *A Narrative of the Great Revival which Prevailed in the Southern Armies*. Philadelphia: Claxton, Remsen, and Haffelfinger, 1877.

Benson, Louis. *The English Hymn: Its Development and Use in Worship*. Philadelphia: Presbyterian Board of Education, 1915.

Benson, Robin. A. *Jane Addams: A Biography*. Westport, CT: Greenwood, 2004.

Bereza, Sarah. "The Right Kind of Music: Fundamentalist Christianity as Musical and Cultural Practice." PhD diss., Duke University, 2017.

Berg, David. *MO Letters*, No. 167 (June 1972).
Berge, Albert W. "Vested Choirs." *The Bostonian* (April 1896) 34, 66.
Bergmann, Leola N. *Music Master of the Middle West: The Story of F. Melius Christiansen and the St. Olaf Choir.* Minneapolis: University of Minnesota Press, 1944.
Bergler, Thomas E. *From Here to Maturity: Overcoming the Juvenilization of American Christianity.* Grand Rapids: Eerdmans, 2014.
———. *The Juvenilization of American Christianity.* Grand Rapids: Eerdmans, 2012.
Berton, Pierre. *The Comfortable Pew.* Philadelphia: J. B. Lippincott & Co., 1965.
Best, Harold M. "Leo Sowerby: His Life Was a Psalm." *Christianity Today*, September 12, 1975, 25.
———. *Music Through the Eyes of Faith.* Ebook ed. New York: Harper Collins, 2013.
Beuttler, Fred. "Revivalism in Suburbia: Son City and the Origin of Willow Creek Community Church." In *Embodying the Spirit: New Perspectives on North American Revivalism*, edited by M. J. McClymond, 168–95. Baltimore: Johns Hopkins University Press, 2004.
Bianchi, Eugene. "John XXIII and American Catholicism." *The Annals of the American Academy of Political and Social Science* 387 (January 1970) 30–40.
Billings, John D. *Hardtack and Coffee: The Unwritten Story of Army Life.* Boston: George M. Smith, 1888.
Billings, William. *The Singing Master's Assistant.* Boston: Draper and Fulsom, 1778.
Bird, Warren, and Scott Thumma. *Megachurch 2020: The Changing Reality in America's Largest Churches.* Hartford Institute for Religion Research. http://hirr.hartsem.edu/megachurch/2020_megachurch_report.pdf.
Bjorlin, David. "Songs of the Kingdom: A Reappraisal of Social Gospel Hymnody." *The Hymn* 65:3 (Summer 2014) 18–25.
Blackwell, Lois S. *The Wings of the Dove: The Story of Gospel Music in America.* Norfolk, VA: printed by the author, 1978.
Blanchard, Annie R. "The Life and Works of Arthur Foote." MA thesis, Boston University, 1935.
Blanchard, Ira. *I Marched with Sherman: Ira Blanchard's Civil War Memoirs of the Illinois 20th Infantry.* Edited by N. A. Mattingly. Lincoln, NE: J. D. Huff & Co., 2000.
Blevins, Brooks. "Upbeat Down South: Where Everything New Is Old Again." *Southern Culture* (Winter 2016) 135–49.
Bliss, Philip P. *Gospel Songs: A Choice Collection of Hymns and Tunes, New and Old, for Gospel Meetings, Prayer Meetings, Sunday Schools, etc.* Cincinnati: John Church & Company, 1874.
Block, Adrienne F. *Amy Beach, Passionate Victorian: The Life and Work of an American Composer—1867–1944.* New York: Oxford University Press, 1990.
Blum, Edward J. *W. E. B. DuBois: American Prophet.* Ebook ed. Philadelphia: University of Pennsylvania Press, 2013.
Blumenthal, F. A. "The German Romantic Movement in Music in St. Louis." PhD diss., Washington University, 1983.
Blumhofer, Edith. "Fanny Crosby and Protestant Hymnody." In *Music in the American Religious Experience*, edited by Edith Blumhofer, Philip Vilas Bohlman, and Maria M. Chow, 215–22. New York: Oxford University Press, 2006.
———. "Singing to Save: Music in the Billy Graham Crusades." In *Billy Graham: American Pilgrim*, edited by Andrew Finstuen, Anne B. Wells, and Grant Wacker, 64–81. New York: Oxford University Press, 2017.

Boots, Cheryl C. "Earthly Strains: The Cultural Work of Protestant Sacred Music in Three Nineteenth Century American Popular Novels." PhD diss., Boston University, 2000.

Boss, Leon F. "Church Choirs: An Examination of Relevancy in 21st Century American Churches." DMin thesis, Liberty University, 2011.

Bowman, James. "How Church Reform Stilled the Voices of the Paulist Choir." *Chicago Tribune*, January 20, 1985.

Bowman, Sister Thea. "The Gift of African-American Sacred Song." In *Readings in African-American Church Music and Worship*, vol. 1, edited by James Abbington, 209–16. Chicago: G. I. A., 2001.

Boyd, Charles N. "Choir Development Since 1876 and the Preeminent Choirmasters." *Proceedings, Music Teacher's National Association*, vol. 23 (1928) 67–80.

Boyd, Malcolm. *Are You Running With Me, Jesus?* 40th anniversary ed. New York: Cowley, 2006.

Boyer, Horace C. 1983. "Charles Albert Tindley: Progenitor of Black-American Gospel Music." *The Black Perspective in Music* 11:2 (Autumn 1983) 103–32.

———. "Contemporary Gospel Music." *The Black Perspective in Music* 7:1 (Spring 1979) 5–58.

———. *The Golden Age of Gospel*. Urbana, IL: University of Illinois Press, 2000.

———. "Roberta Martin, Innovator of Modern Gospel Music." In *We'll Understand It Better By and By*, edited by Bernice Johnson Reagon, 275–86. Washington DC: Smithsonian Institute, 1992.

Boylan, Ann P. *Sunday School: The Formation of an American Institution*. New Haven: Yale University Press, 1988.

Bradbury, W. B. "Special Notices: Mr. William B. Bradbury." *New York Musical Review and Gazette* 9:21 (October 16, 1858) 329.

Bradbury, William B. *Bradbury's Golden Shower of S. S. Melodies, a New Collection of Hymns and Tunes for the Sunday School*. New York: W. B. Bradbury, 1862.

———. *Bright Jewels for the Sunday School*. New York: Biglow & Main, 1860.

Bradford, Sarah H. *Scenes in the Life of Harriet Tubman*. Auburn, NY: W. J. Moses, 1869.

Brady, Margaret M. "An Investigation of the Use of Contemporary Congregational Music in Undergraduate Sacred Music Programs." PhD diss., Northern Illinois University, 2002.

———. "When I Survey the Wondrous Cross: The Musical Styles of the Top 77 Songs—A Historical/Critical Analysis." In *The Message in the Music: Studying Contemporary Praise and Worship*, edited by Robert Woods and Brian Walrath, 156–59. Nashville: Abingdon, 2007.

Brauer, Jerald. *Protestantism in America: A Narrative History*. Philadelphia: Westminster, 1965.

Brewster, C. H. *When this Cruel War Is Over: The Civil War Letters of Charles Harvey Brewster*. Edited by D. W. Bright. Amherst, MA: University of Massachusetts Press, 1992.

Brinegar, Terri M. "The Recorded Sermons of Reverend Andrew William (A. W.) Nix: Black Voices and the Creation of a Modernized Tradition." PhD diss., University of Florida, 2019.

Britton, Allen P. "The How and Why of Teaching Singing Schools in Eighteenth-Century America." *Bulletin of the Council for Research in Music Education* 99 (Winter 1989) 23–41.

———. "Theoretical Introductions in American Tunebooks to 1800." PhD diss., University of Michigan, 1949.
Broad, William J. "A Cathedral tried to Approach Heaven, but Earth Held a Secret." *New York Times,* December 27, 2022.
Brobston, S. H. *Daddy Sang Lead: The History and Performance of White Southern Gospel Music.* New York: Vantage, 2007.
Brooks, Henry M. *Olden Time Music.* Boston: Ticknor & Co., 1888.
Broughton, Viv. *Black Gospel: An Illustrated History of Gospel Sound.* Poole, UK: Blandford, 1985.
Brumley, Jeff. "Debate: What (if anything) to Do About Choir Decline." Baptistnews.com. https://baptistnews.com/article/debate-what-if-anything-to-do-about-choir-decline/.
Bruns, Roger. *Preacher: Billy Sunday and Big-Time American Evangelism.* Urbana, IL: University of Illinois Press, 2002.
Buck, Dudley. "Hints for Young Organists." *The Song Journal,* February 1871.
———. *The Influence of the Organ in History.* London: W. Reeves, 1882.
———. "On Recital Repertoire." *The Musical Independent,* March 1869, 146–47.
———. *Studies in Pedal Phrasing.* Rev. ed. New York: G. Schirmer, 1894.
Buechner, Alan C. *Yankee Singing Schools and the Golden Age of Choral Music in New England, 1760–1800.* Boston: Boston University Press/Dublin Seminar for New England Folk Life, 2003.
Bungert, Heike. "The Singing Festivals of German Americans, 1849–1914." *American Music* 34:2 (Summer 2016), 141–79
Burford, Mark. *Mahalia Jackson and the Black Gospel Field.* New York: Oxford University Press, 2019.
———. "Soul Stirrers." In *Encyclopedia of American Gospel Music,* edited by W. K. McNeil, 356–58. New York: Routledge, 2005.
Burge, Ryan P. "Mainline Protestants Are Still Declining, but That's Not Good News for Evangelicals." *Christianity Today Research Newsletter,* July 13, 2021. https://www.christianitytoday.com/news/2021/july/mainline-protestant-evangelical-decline-survey-us-nones.html.
Burleigh, Henry Thacker. *The Celebrated Negro Spirituals Arranged for Solo Voice by H. T. Burleigh.* London: G. Ricordi & Company, 1897.
Burns, James MacGregor. *The American Experiment: The Vineyard of Liberty.* New York: Open Road Integrated Media, 2013.
Burroughs, Edwin G., and Mike Wallace. *Gotham: A History of New York City to 1898.* New York: Oxford University Press, 1991.
Burroughs, Wilson A. "The Amateur Chorister: His Faults and Virtues." *Etude* 33:3 (August 1915) 603.
Burton, Tara Isabella. "Christianity Gets Weird." *New York Times,* May 8, 2020.
Bush, Douglas Earl, and Richard Kassel. *The Organ: An Encyclopedia.* New York: Routledge, Taylor & Francis Group, 2006.
Bustraan, Richard A. *The Jesus People Movement: A Story of Spiritual Revolution Among the Hippies.* Eugene, OR: Wipf & Stock, 2014.
Butler, Dana H. *Standing Against the Whirlwind: Evangelical Episcopalians in Nineteenth-Century America.* New York: Oxford University Press, 1995.
Cade, John B. "Out of the Mouths of Ex-Slaves." *Journal of Negro History* 20:3 (July 1935) 294–337.

Calvin, John. *Institutes of the Christian Religion*. Vol. 2. Edited by J. T. McNeill. Philadelphia: Westminster, 1960.
Campbell, Eric A. "Civil War Music and the Common Soldier: The Experiences of Charles Wellington Reed." In *Bugle Resounding: Music and Musicians of the Civil War Era*, edited by B. C. Kelley and M. A. Snell, 202–28. Columbia, MO: University of Missouri Press, 2004.
Campbell, Norman "Giving Out the Line: A Cross-Atlantic Comparison of Two Presbyterian Cultures." *Scottish Reformation Historical Society Historical Journal* 1 (2011) 241–65.
Campbell, Neal. "The College of Church Musicians at Washington National Cathedral." *Journal of the Association of Anglican Church Musicians* (Reprint, 2016). https://nealfcampbell.wordpress.com/2016/01/14/the-college-of-church-musicians-at-washington-national-cathedral/.
Canedo, Ken. *Keep the Fire Burning: The Folk Mass Revolution*. Portland, OR: Pastoral, 2009.
Cannon, M. Hamlin. "The United States Christian Commission." *The Mississippi Historical Review* 38:1 (June 1951) 61–80.
Cantwell, Robert. *When We Were Good: The Folk Revival*. Cambridge: Harvard University Press, 1996.
Capps, Donald. "Norman Vincent Peale, Smiley Blanton, and the Hidden Energies of the Mind." *Journal of Religion and Health* (Abstract, 2009). https://link.springer.com/article/10.1007/s10943-009-9258-6.
Card, Edit. "William Walker's Music Then and Now: A Study of Performance Style." PhD diss., Florida State University, 1975.
Carden, Allen D., comp. *The Missouri Harmony, a Choice Collection of Psalms, Hymns, and Anthems*. St. Louis: E. Morgan and Son, 1837.
Carder, Polly Hinson. "George Frederick Root, Pioneer Music Educator: His Contributions to Mass Instruction in Music." EdD diss., University of Maryland, 1971.
Carnes, Mark C., ed. *The Columbia History of Post-World War II America*. New York: Columbia University Press, 2007.
Carr, Benjamin. *Masses, Vespers, Litanies, Hymns, Psalms, Anthems & Motets*. Baltimore: J. Carr, 1805.
Carter, Paul A. *The Spiritual Crisis of the Gilded Age*. DeKalb: Northern Illinois University Press, 1961.
Caswell, Austin C. "Social and Moral Music: The Hymn." In *Music in American Society, 1776–1976: From Puritan Hymn to Synthesizer*, edited by G. McCue, 47–72. New Brunswick, NJ: Transaction, 1977.
Chadwick, George Whitefield. *Horatio Parker, 1863–1919 (Address given at American Academy of Arts and Letters, July 1920)*. New Haven: Yale University Press, 1921.
———. "A Plea for Choral Singing." In *Source Readings in American Choral Music*, edited by David P. DeVinney, 95–96. Missoula, MO: The College Music Society, 1995.
Champion, Herman D. "A Rhetorical Analysis of Selected Sermons by Sam Jones During His Emergence as a National Figure, 1872–1885." PhD diss., Louisiana State University, 1980.

Channing, William Ellery "Likeness to God: Discourse at the Ordination of Rev. F. A. Farley, Providence, R. I. 1828." In *The Works of William Ellery Channing*, vol. III., 227–55. Boston: American Unitarian Association, 1903.

Chapman, J. Wilbur. *The Life and Work of Dwight L. Moody*. Toronto: The Bradley-Garretson Company, 1900.

Charters, Samuel. *Songs of Sorrow: Lucy McKim Garrison and the Slave Songs of the United States*. Jackson: University of Mississippi Press, 2015.

Chase, Gilbert. *America's Music, from the Pilgrims to the Present*. 2nd ed. New York: McGraw-Hill, 1966.

Chase, Lucy, and Sarah Chase. *Dear Ones at Home: Letters from Contraband Camps*. Edited by H. L. Swint. Nashville: Vanderbilt University Press, 1966.

Chaves, Mark, Mary Ellen Konieczny, Kraig Beyerlein, and Emily Barman. "The National Congregations Study: Background, Methods, and Selected Results." *Journal for the Scientific Study of Religion* (1999) 458–76.

Chaves, Mark. *American Religion: Contemporary Trends*. Princeton: Princeton University Press, 2017.

———. *National Congregations Study—Cumulative File for 1998, 2006, and 2012*. https://www.icpsr.umich.edu/web/ICPSR/studies/3471.

Cheeseborough, David H. *God Ordained This War: Sermons on the Sectional Crisis, 1830–1865*. Columbia: University of South Carolina Press, 1991.

Child, Lydia Marie. *Letters from New York*. New York: C. S. Francis & Company, 1844.

Chorley, E. Clowes. *The Centennial of St. Bartholomew's Church*. New York: St. Bartholomew's, 1935.

Clark, Joe C. "Thomas Andrew Dorsey." In *Encyclopedia of American Gospel Music*, edited by W. K. McNeil, 105–6. New York: Routledge, 2005.

Clark, Linda Jane. "Music in Trinity Church, Boston, 1890–1900: A Case-Study in the Relationship Between Worship and Culture." SMD diss., Union Theological Seminary, New York, 1973.

Clarke, Arlen. "A Few Thoughts on the State of Church Music, 2021." Unpublished essay.

Clayton, W. W. *The History of Davidson County, Tennessee, with Illustrations and Biographical Sketches of Its Prominent Men and Pioneers*. Philadelphia: J. W. Lewis & Co., 1880.

Cobb, Buell E. *The Sacred Harp: A Tradition and Its Music*. Athens: University of Georgia Press, 1989.

Coffin, Levi. *Reminiscences of Levi Coffin, the Reputed President of the Underground Railroad*. 2nd ed. Cincinnati: Robert Clarke & Company, 1880.

Cole, Ronald F. "Music in Portland, Maine, from Colonial Times Through the 19th Century." PhD diss., Indiana University, 1975.

Cole, Rosseter G. "Dudley Buck." In *Dictionary of American Biography*, edited by Allen Johnson, 222–23. New York: Charles Scribner's Sons, 1929.

Commager, Henry Steele. *The American Mind: An Interpretation of American Thought and Character Since the 1880s*. New Haven: Yale University Press, 1950.

Corcoran, Michael. "Praising Arizona." 2007 blog. https://www.michaelcorcoran.net/praising-arizona/.

Cornell, John H. "What Is Church Music?" *Music Teacher's National Association, Ninth Annual Meeting, Official Report (1885)* 96–104. N.p.: Music Teacher's National Association, 1885.

Cornwall, N. E. *Music: As it Was, and As it Is.* New York: D. Appleton & Company, 1851.
Costen, Melva. *In Spirit and in Truth.* Rev. ed. Louisville: Westminster John Knox, 2004.
Cotton, John. *Singing of Psalms, a Gospel Ordinance.* London, 1650. Reprint: Shropshire, UK: Quinta, 2011.
Crankshaw, Edward. "Introduction." In *My Life and Music* by Artur Schnabel, ix–xv. New York: Longmans, 1961.
Crawford, Richard. *America's Musical Life: A History.* New York: W. W. Norton, 2001.
———. *Andrew Law: American Psalmodist.* Evanston, IL: Northwestern University Press, 1964.
Cripe, Helen. *Thomas Jefferson and Music.* Charlottesville: University Press of Virginia, 1974.
Crumbley, Diedre H. *Saved and Sanctified: The Rise of a Storefront Church in Great Migration Philadelphia.* Gainesville: University Press of Florida, 2012.
Cunningham, W. Patrick. "Sacred Music in U.S. Catholic History: A Reassessment." *Sacred Music* 145:4 (Winter 2018) 21–33.
Curtis, Susan. *A Consuming Faith: The Social Gospel and Modern American Culture.* Baltimore: Johns Hopkins University Press, 1991.
———. "Scottish Communions, American Revivals (Review of L. E. Schmidt, *Holy Fairs: Scottish Communions and American Revivals in the Early Modern Period*)." *Reviews in American History* 19:1 (March 1991) 20–25.
Cusik, Don. *Saved by Song: A History of Gospel and Christian Music.* Jackson: University of Mississippi Press, 2002.
Daniel, R. T. *The Anthem in New England Before 1800.* Evanston, IL: Northwestern University Press, 1966.
Daniel, W. H. "The Christian Association: A Religious Society in the Army of Northern Virginia." *Virginia Magazine of History and Biography* 69:1, part 1 (January 1961) 93–100.
Daniels, W. H. *D. L. Moody and His Work.* London: Hodder and Stoughton, 1875.
Danker, Ryan N. *Wesley and the Anglicans: Political Division in Early Evangelicalism.* Downer's Grove, IL: InterVarsity, 2016.
Darden, Robert F. "Aretha's One Faith." *Christianity Today*, August 2018. https://www.christianitytoday.com/ct/2018/august-web-only/aretha-franklin-died-tribute.html.
———. "Happy Birthday, B-3: How the Hammond Organ Transformed Gospel Music." *Christianity Today*, May 14, 2015. https://www.christianitytoday.com/ct/2015/may-web-only/happy-anniversary-b-3.html.
———. *Nothing But Love in God's Water: Black Sacred Music from the Civil War to the Civil Rights Movement.* University Park: Pennsylvania State University Press, 2014.
Darlington, Marwood. *Irish Orpheus: The Life of Patrick S. Gilmore, Bandmaster Extraordinary.* Philadelphia: Oliver-Maney-Klein Company, 1950.
Davidson, Robert. *History of the Presbyterian Church in the State of Kentucky; with a Preliminary Sketch of the Churches in the Valley of Virginia.* New York: Robert Carter, 1847.
Davis, George T. B. *Dwight L. Moody, the Man and His Mission.* Chicago: K. T. Boland, 1900.
Davison, Archibald T. *Church Music: Illusion and Reality.* Cambridge: Harvard University Press, 1952.
———. *Protestant Church Music in America.* Boston: E. C. Schirmer, 1933.

Dawn, Marva. *Reaching Out Without Dumbing Down*. Grand Rapids: Eerdmans, 1993.
Day, Stephen. *The Whole Book of Psalms*. Cambridge, MA: printed by the author, 1640.
De Hart, Scott D. "The Influence of John Mason Neale and the Theology of Symbolism." In "Anglo-Catholics and the Vestment Controversy in the 19th Century with Special Reference to the Question of Authority." PhD diss., Oxford University, 1997. http://anglicanhistory.org/essays/dehart1.pdf.
De Lerma, Dominique-René, ed. *Reflections on Afro-American Music*. Kent, OH: Kent State University Press, 1973.
Dean, Talmadge W. *A Survey of Twentieth Century Protestant Church Music in America*. Nashville: Broadman, 1988.
Deebin, John. "Faith on the Firing Line: Army Chaplains in the Civil War." *Prologue Magazine, Official Journal of the National Archives* 48:1 (Spring 2016). https://www.archives.gov/publications/prologue/2016/spring/chaplains.html.
Delvin, Robert C. "A Tale of Two Organs: Henry Erben and Apalachicola, Florida." *Illinois Wesleyan University Scholarly Publications*, No. 106. https://digitalcommons.iwu.edu/ames_scholarship/106/.
DeMille, George E. *The Catholic Movement in the American Episcopal Church*. Philadelphia: Church Historical Society, 1941.
Dickens, W. E., Jr. "The Standardization of the Military Chaplaincy During the American Civil War." PhD diss., Southern Baptist Theological Seminary, 1998.
Dickinson, Clarence. "Choral Music and Choir Direction." In *American History and Encyclopedia of Music, Volume 11, "Essentials of Music*," edited by W. L. Hubbard, 325–75. Toledo, OH: Irving Squire, 1908–1910.
———. "Music and Worship" (Reprint of undated lecture). *The Diapason*, December 2009, 40–42.
———. "Music in the Churches." *Choral Journal* 2:5 (May 1962) 8, 25.
———. "Reminiscences by Clarence Dickinson (Series: "From the Dickinson Collection"). Edited by Lorenz Maycher. *The Diapason*, July 2008, 22–24.
Dickinson, Clarence, Helen A. Dickinson, and Paul A. Wolfe. *The Choir Loft and Pulpit: Fifty-Two Complete Services of Worship with Sermon Text, Psalter, Scripture Readings, Hymns, Anthems and Organ Numbers Related to the Theme of the Service*. New York: H. W. Gray, 1943.
Dickson, D. Bruce. *And They All Sang Hallelujah*. Knoxville: University of Tennessee Press, 1974.
Diefenhaler, Jon. *H. Richard Niebuhr: A Lifetime of Reflections on the Church and the World*. Macon, GA: Mercer University Press, 1986.
Dix, John A. *A History of the Parish of Trinity Church in the city of New York, Part 5: The Rectorship of Morgan Dix*. New York: Columbia University Press, 1950.
———. *A History of Trinity Church*. Edited by L. C. Lewis. New York: Putnam, 1950.
Dix, Morgan. "The Oxford Movement (Undelivered Sermon)." Chicago: The Living Church Company, 1884.
———. "A Sermon for the Times." New York: Pott & Amery, 1886. Online source: Project Canterbury.
Dollar, Kent T. "'Soldiers of the Cross': Confederate Soldier-Christians and the Impact of the War on Their Faith." PhD diss., University of Tennessee, 2001.
———. *Soldiers of the Cross: Confederate Soldier-Christians and the Impact of the War on Their Faith*. Macon, GA: Macon University Press, 2005.

Dooley, John Edward. "Thomas Hastings, American Church Musician." PhD diss., Florida State University, 1963.
Doran, Carol A., and William H. Peterson. *A History of Music in the Episcopal Church.* Norwalk, CT: Association of Anglican Musicians, 1984.
Dorsett, Lyle. *Billy Sunday and the Redemption of Urban America.* Macon, GA: Mercer University Press, 2004.
———. *A Passion for Souls: The Life of D. L. Moody.* Chicago: Moody, 2003.
Doucette, T. J. "The Historical Development of the Modern Worship Song Over the Past 100 Years." Honors senior thesis, Liberty University, 2008.
Douglas, Ann. *The Feminization of American Culture.* New York: Alfred A. Knopf, 1977.
Douglas, Charles Winfred. *The Hale Lectures: Church Music in History and Practice; Studies in the Praises of God.* New York: Charles Scribner's Sons, 1937.
Douglass, Frederick. *My Bondage and My Freedom.* New York: Miller, Orton & Milligan, 1855.
Doukhan, Lillianne "Historical Perspectives on Change in Worship Music." *Notes, Journal of the International Association of Adventist Musicians* (September 1996) 7–9. https://www.ministrymagazine.org/archive/1996/09/historical-perspectives-on-change-in-worship-music.
———. *In Tune with God.* Hagerstown, MD: Autumn House, 2010.
Downey, James C. "Revivalism, the Gospel Songs and Social Reform." *Ethnomusicology* 9:2 (May 1965) 115–25.
Drinker, Sophie. *Music and Women: The Story of Women in Their Relation to Music.* New York: Coward-McCann, 1948.
Du Bois, W. E. B. *The Souls of Black Folk: Essays and Sketches.* 2nd ed. Chicago: A. C. McClurg & Co., 1903. https://docsouth.unc.edu/church/duboissouls/dubois.html.
———. "Strivings of the Negro People." *Atlantic Monthly*, August 1897, 194–98.
Dvořák, Antonin. "Music in America." *Harper's New Monthly Magazine*, February 1895, 428–34.
Eames, Emma. *Some Memories and Reflections.* New York: D. Appleton & Co, 1927.
Earle, Alice Morse. *The Sabbath in Puritan New England.* 5th ed. New York: Charles Scribner's Sons, 1892.
Eaton, John. *Grant, Lincoln, and the Freedmen.* New York: Longmans, Green, and Co., 1907.
Ebaugh, Helen R., and James S. Chavitz. "Dilemmas of Language in Immigrant Congregations: The Tie That Binds or the Tower of Babel." *Review of Religious Research* 47:4 (June 2000) 432–52.
Eddy, Clarence. "The Organ as a Concert Instrument." Quoted in full in "National Association of Organists: Clarence Eddy Elected President," *The Musical Courier*, August 9, 1911, 23–24.
Edgell, Penny, and Derek Robey. "Loose Connections and Liberal Theology: Blurring the Boundaries in Two Church-Based Communities of Spiritual Practice." *Journal for the Scientific Study of Religion* 54:4 (December 2015) 649–67.
Edwards, Arthur C., and Thomas Marocco. *Music in the United States.* Dubuque, IA: W. C. Brown, 1968.
Egler, Steven. "A Conversation with Morgan and Mary Simmons." *The Diapason*, April 2018, 21–25.
Eiselen, F. C. *1 Corinthians.* The Abingdon Bible Commentary. Nashville: Abingdon, 1929.

Ellinwood, Leonard. "English Influences in American Church Music." *Proceedings of the Royal Church Music Association* (1953/1954) 1–13.

———. *The History of American Church Music*. New York: Morehouse-Gorham Co., 1953.

Elliot, James I. "Maranatha! Music." In *Encyclopedia of American Gospel Music*, edited by W. K. McNeil, 240–41. New York: Routledge, 2005.

Ellis, William T. *Billy Sunday, the Man and His Message*. Philadelphia: John C. Winston, 1914.

Elwood, Robert S. *The Fifties Spiritual Marketplace: American Religion in a Decade of Conflict*. New Brunswick, NJ: Rutgers University Press, 1997.

Entriken, William F. "The Guilmant Organ School at First Presbyterian Church, NYC." https://organfocus.com/the-guilmant-organ-school-at-first-presbyterian-church-nyc/.

Epstein, Dena. "Black Spirituals: Their Emergence into Public Knowledge." *Black Music Research Journal* 10:1 (Spring 1990) 58–64.

———. "Documenting the History of Black Folk Music." *Fontes Artis Musicae (International Association of Music Libraries)* 23:4 (October/December 1976) 151–57.

———. *Sinful Tunes and Spirituals: Black Folk Music to the Civil War*. Urbana: University of Illinois Press, 2003.

———. "A White Origin for the Black Spiritual? An Invalid Theory and How It Grew." *American Music* 1:2 (Summer 1983) 53–59.

Erskine, John *The Memory of Certain Persons*. Philadelphia: J. B. Lippincott, 1947.

———. *The Philharmonic Society of New York*. New York: Macmillan, 1943.

Eskew, Harry. "Eben Tourjée." Grove Music Online. https://doi.org/10.1093/gmo/9781561592630.article.28221.

———. "Joseph Funk's *Allgemein Nützliche*," 38–46. https://loyolanotredamelib.org/php/report05/articles/pdfs/Report32Eskew38-46.pdf.

———. "William Walker: Carolina Contributor to American Music." Essay adapted by Jesse P. Karlsberg from an article published in the *Journal of the South Carolina Baptist Historical Society* 29 (2005–2006). https://originalsacredharp.com/2013/12/31/william-walker-carolina-contributor-to-american-music/.

Eskew, Harry, and Stephen Shearon. "Gospel Music." Rev. ed. Edited by J. and R. Downey, 2013. Grove Music Online. https://doi.org/10.1093/gmo/9781561592630.article.A2224388.

Eskridge, Larry. *God's Forever Family: The Jesus People Movement*. New York: Oxford University Press, 2013.

Eslinger, Ellen. "Some Notes on the History of Cane Ridge Prior to the Great Revival." *The Register of the Kentucky Historical Society* 91:1 (Winter 1993) 1–23.

Evans, Christopher H. *The Social Gospel in American Religion: A History*. New York: New York University Press, 2017.

Evans, James. "Some Thoughts on Jazz in Church." *Choral Journal* 6:6 (July/August 1966) 14–15.

Evensen, Bruce J. *God's Man for the Gilded Age: D. L. Moody and the Rise of Modern Mass Evangelism*. New York: Oxford University Press, 2003.

Ewen, David. *Music Comes to America*. New York: Allen, Towne & Heath, 1947.

Farrelly, Maura Jane. *Anti-Catholicism in America, 1620–1860*. New York: Cambridge University Press, 2018.

Farwell, J. V. *Early Recollections of Dwight L. Moody.* Chicago: The Winona Publishing Company, 1907.
Faucett, Bill F. *George Whitefield Chadwick: The Life and Music of the 'Pride of New England.'* Boston: Northeastern University Press, 2012.
Faulkner, Quintin. *Wiser than Despair: The Evolution of Ideas in the Relationship of Music and the Christian Church.* Rev. ed. Santa Barbara, CA: Religious Affections Ministries, 2012.
Fellerer, K. G., and F. A. Brunner. *The History of Catholic Church Music.* Baltimore: Helicon, 1961.
Fenwick, Benedict. "Brief Account of the Settlement of Maryland." In *Woodstock Letters*, vol. 9, 167–80. Woodstock, MD: Woodstock College Press, 1880.
Ferguson, Charles W. *Organizing to Beat the Devil.* Garden City, NY: Doubleday, 1971.
Fielder, A. T. *Captain A. T. Fielder's Civil War Diary.* Ebook ed. Edited by M. T. Cathey. Creative Space/Amazon, 2012.
Fields, Warren. "Hymns and Gospel Songs in the Core Repertory of Southern Baptist Congregations as Reflected in Five Hymnals Published from 1940 to 2008." Colloquium on Baptist Church Music, Baylor University, September 24–25, 2009. https://www.baylor.edu/content/services/document.php/98386.pdf.
Finck, Henry T. *Success in Music and How It Is Won.* New York: Charles Scribner's Sons, 1927.
Finke, Roger, and Rodney Stark. *The Churching of America, 1776–1990: Winners and Losers in Our Religious Economy.* New Brunswick, NJ: Rutgers University Press, 1992.
Finn, William J. *The Art of the Choral Conductor. Volume 1: Choral Technique.* Boston: C. C. Birchard, 1939.
———. "Father Finn's Views on the Two-Fold Purpose of Church Music." *The Caecilia*, August 1934, 301.
———. *Sharps and Flats for Five Decades.* New York: Harper & Brothers, 1947.
Finn, William J., G. H. Wells, and F. J. O'Brien. *Manual of Church Music.* Philadelphia: Dolphin, 1905.
Finney, Charles Grandison. *Lectures on Revivals of Religion.* 2nd ed. New York: Leavitt, Lord, & Co., 1835.
Fishburn, Janet Forsythe *The Fatherhood of God and the Victorian Family: The Social Gospel in America.* Philadelphia: Fortress, 1981.
Fisher, Miles Mark. *Negro Slave Songs in the United States.* Ithaca, NY: Cornell University Press, 1953.
Fisher, Stanley Ross. "The Growing Importance of Music in American Church Life." In *National Federation of Music Clubs Book of Proceedings* (1939) 52–56.
Fitts, Elizabeth C. "Aspects of American Musical Life as Reflected in the New Music Review and Church Music Review, 1901–1935." PhD diss., University of Maryland, 2009.
Foote, Arthur. "A Bostonian Remembers." *Musical Quarterly* 23:1 (January 1937) 37–44.
Foote, Henry Wilder. *Annals of King's Chapel from the Puritan Age of New England to the Present Day.* Boston: Little & Brown, 1896.
Fosdick, Harry Emerson. *The Living of These Days.* New York: Harper & Brothers, 1956.

———. "Shall the Fundamentalists Win? (A Sermon Preached at the First Presbyterian Church, New York, 1922." Philadelphia, Presbyterian Historical Society, n.d. http://historymatters.gmu.edu/d/5070/.

Fox, Derrick. "African American Practice of Shape-Note Singing in the United States." *Choral Journal* 56:5 (December 2015) 38–51.

Fox, M. "George Beverly Shea Dies at 104; Stirring Singer at Billy Graham Revivals." *New York Times*, April 17, 2013.

Frazier, E. Franklin. *The Negro Church in America*. New York: Schocken, 1963.

Freeman, Andrew. "English Organ-Cases." In *Dictionary of Organs and Organists*, edited by F. W. Thornsby, 15–78. London: H. Logan & Co., 1912.

Fresne, Jeanette. "History of the Stamps-Baxter Singing Schools and Normal School of Music." *Journal of Historical Research in Music Education* 30:1 (October 2008) 21–38.

Frith, Simon. *Performing Rites: On the Value of Popular Music*. Cambridge: Harvard University Press, 1998.

Fry, Henry S. "From the Brattle Organ to ———?" *The Diapason*, June 1, 1919, 19.

Furman, Richard. "Exposition of the Views of the Baptists Relative to the Coloured Population of the United States in Communication to the Governor of South Carolina." Charleston, 1823. Reprinted in *Richard Furman: Life and Legacy*, by James A. Rogers, 274–86. Macon, GA: Mercer University Press, 1985. https://glc.yale.edu/exposition-views-baptists-relative-coloured-population.

Gallo, W. K. "The Life and Church Music of Dudley Buck, 1839–1909." PhD diss., Catholic University, 1968.

Garner, Stephen W. *Clarence Dickinson: Dean of American Church Musicians*. Columbus, OH: Gatekeeper, 2018.

Garrison, Lucy McKim. "Songs of the Port Royal Contrabands." *Dwight's Journal of Music*, November 8, 1862, 254–55.

Gasche, Pere Louis-Hippolyte. *A Frenchman, A Chaplain, A Rebel: The War Letters of Pere Louis-Hippolyte Gasche, SJ*. Edited by C. M. Buckley. Chicago: Loyola University Press, 1981.

Gates, J. Terry. "Music Education's Professional Beginnings in America: Early 18th Century New England Singing School Teacher Qualifications and Programs." *Visions of Research in Music Education*, vol. 16, article 9, 43–48. Courtesy of the University of Connecticut Library *Quarterly Journal of Music Teaching and Learning* (Spring 1990). https://opencommons.uconn.edu/cgi/viewcontent.cgi?article=1611&context=vrme.

Gaustad, Edwin A., and Leigh Schmidt. *The Religious History of America: The Heart of the American Story from Colonial Times to Today*. San Francisco: Harper San Francisco, 2002.

Geary, Gregg S. "George W. Chadwick and the Nineteenth-Century Te Deum." PhD diss., University of Hawaii, 2011.

Gebauer, Victor E. "Cantor of the Church: Leland Bernard Sateren (1913–2007)." *Grace Notes* (Journal of the Association of Lutheran Church Musicians) 25:4 (August/September 2009) 10–11.

George, Henry. *Progress and Poverty: An Inquiry Into the Cause of Industrial Depressions, and of Increase of Want with Increase of Wealth. The Remedy.* 50th anniversary ed. New York: Robert Schalkenbach Foundation, 1946.

Gersztyn, Bob. "Calvary Chapel, Costa Mesa." In *Encyclopedia of American Gospel Music*, edited by W. K. McNeil, 58–59. New York: Routledge, 2005.

Gibbs, Harold Becket. "Congregational Singing." *Church Music: A Magazine for the Clergy, Choirmasters and Organists* 1:1 (December 1905) 21–33.

Gilbert, Henry F. "Composer Gilbert on America's Music: Mother Europe Too Long an Autocrat; America, the Spoiled Child—Some Criticisms and Suggestions." *New York Times*, March 24, 1918.

Gilbert, Kenyatta. "Hidden Figures: How Black Women Preachers Spoke Truth to Power." https://theconversation.com/hidden-figures-how-black-women-preachers-spoke-truth-to-power-73185.

Gilman, Samuel. *Memories of a New England Village Choir with Occasional Reflections by a Member*. Boston: Benjamin H. Green, 1834.

Gilmore, Patrick S. *History of the National Peace Jubilee Held in the City of Boston, June 1869*. Boston: Lee and Shepard, 1871.

Ginsberg, Ruth Bader. *United States vs. Virginia* (1996). https://constitutioncenter.org/the-constitution/supreme-court-case-library/united-states-v-virginia-1996.

Gipson, Richard M. *The Life of Emma Thursby, 1849–1911*. New York: New York Historical Society, 1940.

Gladden, Washington. *Recollections*. New York: Houghton Mifflin, 1909.

———. *Working People and Their Employers*. Boston: Lockwood, Brooks, & Co., 1876.

Glover, Gisele. "The Life and Career of Edward Boatner and Inventory of the Boatner Papers at the Schonberg Center." American Music Research Center/ProQuest, 2013.

Goff, James R. *Close Harmony: A History of Southern Gospel Music*. Chapel Hill: University of North Carolina Press, 2002.

———. "The Rise of Southern Gospel Music." *Church History* 67:4 (December 1998) 722–44.

Goodstein, Laurie. "Conservative Churches Grew Fastest in the 1990's, Report Says." *New York Times*, September 18, 2002.

Gordan, T. David. "The Imminent Decline of Contemporary Worship Music: Eight Reasons." *Second Nature Journal*, October 27, 2014. https://secondnaturejournal.com/the-imminent-decline-of-contemporary-Christian-music/.

Gottschalk, Louis Moreau. *Notes of a Pianist*. Edited by Clara Gottschalk and translated by R. E. Peterson. Philadelphia: J. B. Lippincott, 1881.

Gould, Nathaniel D. *Church Music in America*. Boston: A. N. Johnson, 1853.

Graham, Sandra Jean "How African American Spirituals Moved from Cotton Fields to Concert Halls". Smithsonian Institution blog, October 29, 2018. www.whatitmeanstobeamerican.org.

———. *Spirituals and the Birth of the Black Entertainment Industry*. Urbana: University of Illinois Press, 2018.

Granquist, Mark. *A History of Luther Seminary, 1869–2019*. Minneapolis: Fortress, 2019.

———. *Lutherans in America*. Minneapolis: Fortress, 2015.

Green, Joseph. "Letter to Stephen Williams at Longmeadow, Massachusetts, October 22, 1722." Boston: Publications of the Colonial Society of Massachusetts, 1927.

Greene, William A. "Joel Harmon's Home on Bullard Road." In *The Harmon Family History* (1897 by William P. Harmon). http://www.alleganyhistory.org/places/

towns-and-villages/a-e274/andover24/andover-related-articles/3172-joel-harmon-s-home-on-the-bullard-road.

Grem, Daniel F. "Sam Jones, Sam Hose and the Theology of Racial Violence." *Georgia Historical Quarterly* 90:1 (Spring 2006) 35–61.

Grimes, Robert R. "The Emergence of Catholic Music and Ritual in Colonial Maryland." *American Catholic Studies* 114:2 (Summer 2003) 1–35.

———. "A Grand Selection of Sacred Music: Benjamin Carr and Early 19th Century Catholic Music in Philadelphia." *U.S. Catholic Historian* 30:4 (Fall 2012) 21–37.

Grimke, Charlotte Forten. *The Journals of Charlotte Forten Grimke*. Edited by Brenda Stevenson. New York: Oxford University Press, 1988.

———. "Life on the Sea Islands." *The Atlantic Monthly*, May 1864, 587–96.

Grimminger, Daniel J. "Singenberger, Johannes Baptist [John B.]." Grove Music Online. https://doi.org/10.1093/gmo/9781561592630.article.A2088739.

Griswold, Stephen M. *Sixty Years with Plymouth Church*. New York: Fleming H. Revell, 1907.

Grosheide, F. W. *Commentary on the First Epistle to the Corinthians*. London, 1954.

Grossman, Cathy Lynn. "Many Church Choirs Are Dying. Here's Why." September 17, 2014. https://www.ministrymatters.com/worship/entry/5414/many-church-choirs-are-dying-heres-why.

Guenther, Ellen. *In Their Own Words: Slave Life and the Power of Spirituals*. St. Louis: Morningstar Music, 2015.

Guralnick, Peter. *Dream Boogie: The Triumph of Sam Cooke*. New York: Little and Brown, 2005.

Hagerty, Barbara B. "A Fast Fall for a Once Mighty Megachurch." Transcript from *All Things Considered,* National Public Radio, October 9, 2010. https://www.npr.org/templates/story/story.php?storyId=130679470.

Halberstam, David. *The Fifties*. New York: Open Road/Integrated Media, 1983.

Hale, Philip. "Psychology of the Church Soprano, Part 2." *Choir and Choral Magazine* 4:12 (December 1904) 7–9.

Hall, David D. "From the Seventies to the Present." In *A Religious History of the American People*, by Sydney E. Ahlstrom, 1097–1117. New Haven: Yale University Press, 2004.

Hall, Rachel Wells. "Did Lucius Chapin write the Amazing Grace tune?" https://thesoundofnumbers.com/2015/05/did-lucius-chapin-write-the-amazing-grace-tune-2/.

———. "Philadelphia, Birthplace of Shapes and Center of Shape-Note Publishing." September 1, 2017. https://originalsacredharp.com/2017.

Hamm, Charles. "The Chapins and Sacred Music in the South and West." *Journal of Research in Music Education* 8:2 (Autumn 1960) 91–98.

Hammond, J. Pinkney. *The Army Chaplain's Manual Designed as a Help to Chaplains in the Discharge of Their Various Duties, both Temporal and Spiritual*. Philadelphia: J. & H. Lippincott, 1863.

Handy, Robert T. *A History of Union Theological Seminary in New York*. New York: Columbia University Press, 1987.

Handy, W. C. *Father of the Blues: An Autobiography*. New York: Macmillan, 1944.

Hannah, John D. "The Roman Catholic Charismatic Movement." From "Lecture Series: A History of Charismatic Movements." https://dpz73qkr83wop.cloudfront.net/en_US/transcripts/CH510-18.pdf.

Harlan, Louis R. *Booker T. Washington in Perspective: Essays of Louis R. Harlan*. Ebook ed. Edited by Raymond Smock. Jackson: University of Mississippi Press, 2011.
Harland, Marion. *Marion Harland's Autobiography: The Story of a Long Life*. New York: Harper and Brothers, 1910. UNC-CH Digitalization Project, 1998. https://docsouth.unc.edu/fpn/harland/menu.html.
Harley, Rachel A. "Ananias Davisson: Southern Tune-Book Compiler (1780–1857)." PhD diss., University of Michigan, 1972.
Harold, Claudrina N. *When Sunday Comes: Gospel Music in the Soul and Hip Hop Eras*. Urbana: University of Illinois Press, 2020.
Harris, Michael W. *The Rise of Gospel Blues: The Music of Thomas Andrew Dorsey in the Urban Church*. New York: Oxford University Press, 1992.
Harrison, Douglas. "Why Southern Gospel Music Matters." *Religion in American Culture: A Journal of Interpretation* 18:1 (Winter 2008) 27–58.
Harvey, Bonnie. *D. L. Moody: The American Evangelist*. Uhrichsville, OH: Barbour, 1997.
Hash, Phillip M. "George F. Root's Normal Musical Institute, 1853–1885." *Journal of Research in Music Education* 60:3 (October 2012) 267–93.
Hastings, Robert J. *Glorious Is Thy Name! B. B. McKinney, the Man and His Music*. Nashville: Broadman, 1986.
Hastings, Thomas. *Dissertation on Musical Taste, or General Principles of Taste Applied to the Art of Music*. Albany, NY: Webster & Skinners, 1822.
———. "Divisions of Labor." *Musical Magazine*, vol. 1. (December 1835) 210–13.
———. "Musical Authors and Publications of the United States." *Musical Magazine* (July 1835) 85–91.
———. "Organ Voluntaries." *Musical Magazine* (July 1835) 77–78.
———. "Want for Teachers." *Musical Magazine*, vol. 1. (October 1835) 159–62.
Hatchett, M. J. *A Manual for Clergy and Church Musicians*. New York: The Church Hymnal Corporation, 1980.
Hauptmann, Moritz. *The Letters of a Leipzig Cantor, Being the Letters of Moritz Hauptmann to Franz Hauser, Ludwig Spohr, and other Musicians*. Edited by Alfred Schöne and Ferdinand Hiller; translated by A. D. Coleridge. New York: Vienna House, 1892.
Haweis, H. R. *Music and Morals*. London: Daldy, Isbister & Company, 1875.
Hawn, C. Michael. "History of Hymns: Joy to the World." Discipleship Ministries of the United Methodist Church. http://www.umcdiscipleship.org/resources/history-of-hymns-joy-to-the-world.
———. "What Has Happened to the Church Choir? Strategies for Preparing Church Musicians for the 21st Century." *Choral Journal* 47:9 (March 2007) 8–21.
Hayburn, Robert F. *Papal Legislation on Sacred Music, 95 A.D. to 1977 A.D.* Collegeville, MN: Liturgical, 1979.
Haynes, Karima A. "The Gospel Controversy: Are the New Songs Too Jazzy and Too Worldly?" *Ebony* 47:5 (March 1992) 78, 80, 82.
Hehn, Jonathan J. "American Presbyterian Worship and the Organ." Doctor of Music treatise, Florida State University, 2013.
Heijke, John. *An Ecumenical Light on the Renewal of Religious Community Life: Taize*. Pittsburgh: Duquesne University, 1967.
Heilburt, Anthony. *The Gospel Sound: Good News and Bad Times*. Updated and rev. ed. New York: Simon and Schuster/Limelight Editions, 1997.

Henry, H. T. "How Shall the Reform in Church Music Be Effected?" *Church Music: A Magazine for the Clergy, Choirmasters, and Organists* 1:1 (December 1905) 1–10.

Hetrick, Ross. "It's Not a Very Happy Story. Organ Maker's Collapse Leaves Many in the Lurch." *Baltimore Sun*, November 8, 1992. https://www.baltimoresun.com/news/bs-xpm-1992-11-08-1992313159-story.html.

Hewins, James M. *Hints Concerning Church Music, the Liturgy, and Kindred Subjects*. Boston: Ide & Dutton, 1858.

Hiemstra, William. "Early Frontier Revivalism in Kentucky." *The Register of the Kentucky Historical Society* 59:2 (April 1961) 133–49.

Higginson, J. Vincent. "John Aitken's Compilation, 1787 and 1791." *The Hymn* 27:3 (July 1976) 68–75.

Higginson, Thomas Wentworth. *The Complete Civil War Journal and Letters of Thomas Wentworth Higginson*. Edited by C. Looby. Chicago: University of Chicago Press, 2000.

———. "Negro Spirituals." *The Atlantic Monthly*, June 1867, 685–94.

Hillis, Newell Dwight. *The Influence of Christ in Modern Life, being a Study of the Problems of the Church in America*. Toronto: Fleming H. Revell, 1900.

Hillman, Joseph and L. Hartsough. *The Revivalist*. Revised and enlarged ed. Troy, NY: Joseph Hillman 1872.

Hitchcock, H. Wiley. *Music in the United States: A Historical Introduction*. Englewood Cliffs, NJ: Prentice Hall, 1959.

Hobson, Vic. *Creating the Jazz Solo: Louis Armstrong and Barbershop Harmony*. Jackson: University of Mississippi, 2018.

Hodge, Charles B. *Clergy and Choir*. Milwaukee: Young Churchman Company, 1891.

Hodges, Faustina. *Edward Hodges*. New York: G. Putnam's Sons, 1896; AMS Reprint, 1970.

Hodges, John Sebastian Bach. "The Nature of Worship." Sermon, August 24, 1856. Project Canterbury. http://anglicanhistory.org/usa/hodges_worship1857.html.

Hodges, Judy. "The Evolution of Sacred Music and Its Rituals in Watauga County, North Carolina." MA thesis, Appalachian State University, 2010.

Hoffman, Abbie. "The Press of Freedom." *The Village Voice*, December 15, 1966.

Hoffman, Richard. *Some Musical Recollections of Fifty Years*. Detroit: Charles Scribner's Sons, 1910; Reprint, Information Coordinators, 1976.

Hogan, John. *I Am Not Alone: From the Letters of Combat Infantryman, John J. Hogan, Killed at Okinawa*. Washington, DC: Mackinac, 1947.

Holifield, E. Brooks. *Theology in America: Christian Thought from the Age of the Puritans through the Civil War*. New Haven: Yale University Press, 2003.

Hoogenboom, Olive. *The First Unitarian Church of Brooklyn: One Hundred Fifty Years*. Brooklyn: First Unitarian Church of Brooklyn, 1987.

Hopkins, John Henry, III. "The Reverend John Henry Hopkins Jr." *Historical Magazine of the Protestant Episcopal Church* 4:4 (December 1935) 267–80.

Hopkins John Henry, Jr. "The Cathedral System in the City." In *Transactions of the New York Ecclesiological Society*, 1–16. New York: Daniel Dana Jr., 1857.

———. *The Life of the Late Right Reverend John Henry Hopkins, First Bishop of Vermont and Seventh Presiding Bishop, by One of His Sons*. New York: F. J. Huntington & Co., 1873.

———. "Memoir of the Rev. Milo Mahan, D. D." In *The Collected Works of Milo Mahan, Volume 3.* Project Canterbury. http://anglicanhistory.org/usa/mahan/memoir.html.

Hopkins, John Henry, Sr. *Essay on Gothic Architecture in Various Plans and Drawings for Churches.* Burlington, VT: Smith & Harrington, 1836.

———. *A Scriptural, Ecclesiastical, and Historical View of Slavery from the Days of the Patriarch Abraham to the 19th Century.* New York: W. I. Pooley & Company, 1864.

Hopkins, Charles H. *The Rise of the Social Gospel in American Protestantism, 1865–1915.* New Haven: Yale University Press, 1940.

Horner, John B. "Sergeant Hugh Paxton Bigham: Lincoln's Guard at Gettysburg." Horner Enterprises. Emmitsburg, PA: Emmitsburg Area Historical Society, n.d. https://t.emmitsburg.net/archive_list/articles/history/civil_war/21st_penn/sgt_hugh_paxton_21st_penn_cav.htm.

Hotchkiss, W. A. *A Codification of the State Law of Georgia.* Savannah, GA: John M. Cooper, 1845.

Hovet, Theodore R. "The Church Diseased: Harriet Beecher Stowe's Attack on the Presbyterian Church." *The Journal of Southern History* 52:2 (Summer 1974) 167–87.

Howard, Jay. "Let the Weak Say I Am Strong: Contemporary Worship Music and God's Concern for Righteousness and Social Justice." In *The Message in the Music: Studying Contemporary Praise and Worship,* edited by Robert Woods and Brian Walrath, 65–76. Nashville: Abingdon, 2007.

Howard, John Tasker. *Our American Music: Three Hundred Years of It.* New York: Thomas Y. Crowell, 1939.

Howard, Katherine K. *Confessions of an Opera Singer.* New York: Alfred A. Knopf, 1918.

Howe, M. DeWolfe. "John Knowles Paine." *Musical Quarterly* 25:3 (July 1939) 256–67.

Howe, Solomon. *The Farmer's Evening Entertainment.* Northampton, MA: Andrew Wright, 1804.

Hubbard, W. L., ed. *The American History and Encyclopedia of Music: American Music.* Toledo, OH: Irving Squire, 1908–1910.

———. *The American History and Encyclopedia of Music: Musical Biographies, Volume 2.* Toledo, OH: Irving Squire, 1908–1910.

Huber, Jane Parker. *A Singing Faith.* Philadelphia: Westminster, 1986.

Hudson, Winthrop. *Religion in America.* New York: Charles Scribner's Sons, 1965.

Hughes, Rupert. *Contemporary American Composers.* Boston: L. C. Page & Co., 1900.

Hughes, Sarah M. "An Interview with Miriam Clapp Duncan." *The Diapason,* October 1999, 14–15. https://thediapason.com/interview-miriam-clapp-duncan.

Hume, Paul. *Catholic Church Music.* New York: Dodd, Mead & Co., 1960.

Hummel, Scott. "Music on Demand: Residential Pipe Organs in America." *Vox Humana Journal,* January 20, 2019. https://www.voxhumanajournal.com/hummel2019.html.

Humphreys, Charles A. *Field, Camp, Hospital, and Prison in the Civil War, 1863–1865.* Boston: George Ellis & Co., 1918.

Huntington, Ronald M. "A Study of the Musical Contributions of Leo Sowerby." Master of Music thesis, University of Southern California, 1957.

Hustad, Donald. *Jubilate! Church Music in the Evangelistic Tradition.* Carol Stream, IL: Hope, 1982.

Hutchinson, Tim. "The Theological and Political Evolution of Henry Ward Beecher." MA thesis, University of Arkansas, 1990.

Hybels, Lynne. *Rediscovering Church: The Story and Vision of Willow Creek Community Church.* Grand Rapids: Zondervan, 1995.

Inwood, Paul. "History." (Of Universa Laus, International Study Group for Liturgical Music.) https://universalaus.org/history/.

Irmen, Hans-Josef. *Gabriel Josef Rheinberger als Antipode des Cæcilianismus.* Regensberg, DE: Gustav Bosse, 1970.

Irving, Washington. "Christmas Day." From *The Sketchbook of Geoffrey Crayon* (1819), in *The Works of Washington Irving*, vol. 1, 54–58. New York: P. F. Collier, 1885.

———. "The Legend of Sleepy Hollow." From *The Sketchbook of Geoffrey Crayon* (1819), in *The Works of Washington Irving*, vol. 1, 89–98. New York: P. F. Collier, 1885.

Irwin, Joyce. "The Theology of Regular Singing." *The New England Quarterly* 51:2 (June 1978) 176–92.

Ives, Charles. "Epilogue." In *Essays Before a Sonata, The Majority, and Other Writings*, edited by H. Boatwright, 80–88. Rev. ed. New York: W. W. Norton, 1970.

Jackson, Bill. *The Quest for the Radical Middle: A History of the Vineyard.* Cape Town, ZA: Vineyard International, 1999.

Jackson, George Pullen. "Buckwheat Notes." *The Musical Quarterly* 19:4 (October 1933) 393–400.

———. *White Spirituals in the Southern Uplands.* Chapel Hill: University of North Carolina Press, 1933.

Jackson, Jerma A. *Singing in My Soul: Black Gospel Music in a Secular Age.* Chapel Hill: University of North Carolina Press, 2004.

Jackson, Joyce Marie. "The Changing Nature of Gospel Music, A Southern Case Study." *African-American Review* 29:2 (Summer 1995) 185–200.

Jackson-Smith, Irene. "Developments in Black Gospel Performance and Scholarship." *Black Music Research Journal* 10:1 (Spring 1990) 36–42.

James, William. *The Varieties of Religious Experience: A Study in Human Nature, being the Gifford Lectures on Natural Religion Delivered in Edinburgh in 1901–1902.* New York: Longman's, Green, & Company, 1917; digital edition, Project Gutenberg, 2014. https://www.gutenberg.org/ebooks/621.

Jefferson, Thomas. "A Bill for the More General Diffusion of Knowledge." In *The Papers of Thomas Jefferson*, vol. 2, 1777–1779, edited by Julian P. Boyd, 526–35. Princeton: Princeton University Press, 1950.

———. Letter to Giovanni Fabbroni, June 8, 1778. In *The Papers of Thomas Jefferson*, digital ed., edited by James P. McClure and J. Jefferson Looney. Charlottesville: University of Virginia Press, Rotunda, 2008–2022. https://rotunda.upress.virginia.edu/founders/TSJN-01-02-02-0066.

———. *Notes on the State of Virginia.* Philadelphia: Pritchard & Hall, 1788. Digital ed. 2006. https://docsouth.unc.edu/southlit/jefferson/jefferson.html.

Jenkins, Isabela A. "The Influence of the Oxford Movement on Church Music." MA thesis, Boston University, 1946.

Jerold, Beverly. "Glimpses of the American Organ and Its Use." *The Tracker* 53:4 (Fall 2009) 14–22.

Johansson, Calvin. *Discipling Music Ministry: Twenty-First Century Directions.* Peabody, MA: Hendrickson, 1992.

———. *Music Ministry: A Biblical Counterpoint.* 2nd ed. Peabody, MA: Hendrickson, 1998.

John XXII, Pope. "Papal Bull." (1324.) In *Teachings of the Holy Fathers in Their Own Words,* the Generalist Academy. https://www.cengage.com/music/book_content/049557273X_wrightSimms/assets/ITOW/7273X_10b_ITOW_John_XXII.pdf.

John Paul II, Pope. "Address of the Holy Father to the Bishops of Canada in their '*Ad limina*' Visit." September 25, 1999. The Vatican, Holy See Press Office Daily Bulletin. https://www.vatican.va/content/john-paul-ii/en/speeches/1999/september/documents/hf_jp-ii_spe_25091999_ad-limina-canada.html.

John, Robert W. "Origins of the First Music Educator's Convention." *Journal of Research in Music Education* 13:4 (Winter 1965) 207–19.

Johnson, Charles A. *The Frontier Campmeeting.* Dallas: Southern Methodist University Press, 1955.

Johnson, James Weldon. *The Book of American Negro Spirituals.* New York: Viking, 1925.

———. *Fifty Years and Other Poems.* Philadelphia: Cornhill, 1917.

Jones, Darius E. *Temple Melodies.* New York: Mason & Law, 1851. http://vmirror.imslp.org/files/imglnks/usimg/1/15/IMSLP460837-PMLP748473-templemelodies00jone_1851.pdf.

Jones, J. William. *Christ in the Camp, or Religion in Lee's Army.* Richmond, VA: B. F. Johnson, 1887.

Jones, Jeffrey M. "U.S. Church Membership Down Sharply in Past Two Decades." Gallup News. https://news.gallup.com/poll/248837/church-membership-down-sharply-past-two-decades.aspx.

Justin Martyr. "The First Apology, The Second Apology, Dialogue with Trypho, Exhortation to the Greeks, Discourse to the Greeks, The Monarchy or The Rule of God." In *The Fathers of the Church,* vol. 6. Edited by Thomas Falls. Washington, DC: Catholic University Press, 1948.

Kalm, Peter. *Travels in North America.* Translated by J. R. Forster. Warrington, UK: William Eyres, 1750.

Kaufmann, Charles H. "The Hodges and Newland Collections in the Library of Congress: A Preliminary Report." *Current Musicology* 18 (1974) 79–89. https://docslib.org/doc/13028747/the-hodges-and-newland-collections-in-the-library-of-congress-a-preliminary-report-charles-h.

Kearns, William K. *Horatio Parker, 1863–1919: His Life, Music, and Ideas.* Metuchen, NJ: Scarecrow, 1990.

Keck, G. R., and Martin, S. ed. *Feel the Spirit: Studies in Afro-American Music.* Ebook ed. New York: Greenwood, 2008.

Keene, James A. *A History of Music Education in the United States.* 2nd ed. Centennial, CO: Glenbridge, 2009.

Kelley, B. C., and M. A. Snell, eds. *Bugle Resounding: Music and Musicians of the Civil War Era.* Columbia, MO: University of Missouri Press, 2004.

Kemp, Kathryn. "The Father of Gospel Music Wanted to Be a Secular Star: How Thomas Dorsey Decided to Give Up a Thriving Jazz Career for 'Precious Lord.'" *Christianity Today,* May 24, 2018. https://www.christianitytoday.com/history/2018/may/father-gospel-music-thomas-dorsey.html.

Kendi, Ibram X. *Stamped from the Beginning: The Definitive History of Racist Ideas in America*. New York: Nation, 2016.
Kennedy, Rev. D. D. *A Sermon on Sacred Music Preached in the Second Presbyterian Church, Troy, New York, on Sunday Morning, March 19, 1865*. Troy, NY: A. Y. Scribner, 1865.
Kidd, Thomas, and Barry Hankins. *Baptists in America*. New York: Oxford University Press, 2015.
Kiel, Eleanor. "Vatican II Embraced the Role of Sacred Music in Liturgy." *The Catholic Messenger*, January 23, 2014. https://catholicmessenger.net/2014/01/vatican-ii-embraced-the-role-of-sacred-music-in-liturgy.
Kierkegaard, Søren. *Purity of the Heart Is to Will One Thing*. Edited by D. V. Steele. New York: Harper Torchbooks, 1948.
Kilde, Jeanne Halgren. *When Church Became Theater: The Transformation of Evangelical Architecture and Worship in Nineteenth-Century America*. New York: Oxford University Press, 2002.
Kimball, Gregg D. "The Musical Million: The Ruebush-Kieffer Company, Singing Schools, and the Birth of Southern Gospel." https://uncommonwealth.virginiamemory.com/blog/2018/12/03/the-musical-million-the-ruebush-kieffer-company-singing-schools-and-the-birth-of-southern-gospel/.
Kimberling, Clark. "American Bass Viol." In *The Canterbury Dictionary of Hymnology*. https://hymnology.hymnsam.co.uk/a/american-bass-viol.
King, William M. "History as Revelation in the Theology of the Social Gospel." *Harvard Theological Review* 76:1 (January 1983) 109–29.
Kirby, David. "St. John the Unfinished; Dean of Cathedral on Morningside Heights Vows to Fix What He's Got, Not Build More." *New York Times*, January 10, 1999.
Klein, Hermann. *Unmusical New York: A Brief Criticism of Triumphs, Failures, and Abuses*. New York: John Lane, 1910.
Klein, Nancy Kirkland. "The Roots and Development of Public School Music in the State of Kentucky." PhD diss., New York University, 1986.
Knauff, Christopher W. *Doctor Tucker, Priest-Musician: A Sketch Which Concerns the Doings and Thinkings of the Reverend John Ireland Tucker, S. T. B*. New York: A. D. F. Randolph, 1897.
Krehbiel, H. E., ed. *Review of the New York Musical Season, 1886–1890*. New York: Novello, Ewer & Co.
Kroeger, Karl, ed. *The Complete Works of William Billings*. Charlottesville, VA: American Musicological Society/Colonial Society of Massachusetts, 1986.
Kubicki, Judith M. "Taize (USA)." Grove Music Online. https://doi.org/10.1093/gmo/9781561592630.article.A2252419.
Labounsky, Ann. *Jean Langlais: The Man and His Music*. Portland, OR: Amadeus, 2000.
Lacy, Creighton. *Frank Mason North: His Social and Ecumenical Mission*. Nashville: Abingdon, 1967.
Lahee, H. C. "A Century of Choral Singing in New England." *New England Magazine* 26 (1902) 102–17.
Lahee, Henry C. *The Organ and Its Masters: An Account of the Organists of Former Days, as well as Some of the Prominent Virtuosi of the Present, with a brief Sketch of the Development of Organ Construction*. Boston: L. C. Page & Company, 1902.
Larson, Mel. *Youth for Christ*. Grand Rapids: Zondervan, 1947.

Law, Andrew. *The Musical Primer or the First Part of the Art of the Art of Singing.* 2nd ed. Cheshire, CT: printed by the author, 1804. http://vmirror.imslp.org/files/imglnks/usimg/5/57/IMSLP262790-PMLP426158-artofsingoolawa_1_musical_primer.pdf.

———. *The Rudiments of Music.* 4th ed. Cheshire, CT: W. Law., 1792. https://www.loc.gov/resource/muspre1800.100580/?sp=1.

———. *Select Harmony, Containing in a Plain Concise Manner the Rules of Singing.* Philadelphia: Robert & William Carr, 1812. https://vmirror.imslp.org/files/imglnks/usimg/4/48/IMSLP265723-PMLP430617-selconoolawa.pdf.

Lawrence, Brian D. "The Relationship Between the Methodist Church, Slavery and Politics, 1784–1844." MA thesis, Rowan University, 2018.

Lears, T. Jackson. *No Place for Grace: Anti-Modernism and the Transformation of American Culture, 1880–1920.* Chicago: University of Chicago Press, 1994.

Leaver, Robin A. "More than Simple Psalm Singing in English: Sacred Music in Early Colonial America." *Yale Journal of Music and Religion* 1:1 (2015) Article 5. https://elischolar.library.yale.edu/cgi/viewcontent.cgi?article=1012&context=yjmr.

Leaver, Robin A., James H. Litton, and Carlton R. Young, eds. *Duty and Delight: Routley Remembered, A Memorial Tribute to Erik Routley.* Carol Stream, IL: Hope, 1985.

Lee, Winnie. "When Pianos Went to War." Atlas Obscura. https://www.atlasobscura.com/articles/victory-verticals-steinway-pianos.

Legg, Andrew, and Carolyn Philpott. "An Analysis of Performance Practices in African American Gospel Music: Rhythm, Lyric Treatment, and Structures in Improvisation and Accompaniment." *Popular Music* 34:2 (May 2015) 197–225.

Levine, Lawrence W. *High Brow, Low Brow: The Emergence of Cultural Hierarchy in America.* Cambridge: Harvard University Press, 1990.

Liebergen, Patrick. "The Cecilian Movement in the 19th Century: Summary of the Movement." *Choral Journal* 21:9 (May 1981) 13–16.

Liebling, Emil. "Essentials of Music." In *American History and Encyclopedia of Music, Vol. 11 and 12,* edited by W. L. Hubbard. Toledo, OH: Irving Squire, 1908–1910.

Liemohn, Edwin. *The Organ and Choir in Protestant Worship.* Philadelphia: Fortress, 1968.

Lincoln, Abraham. "General Order Respecting the Observance of the Sabbath, November 15, 1862." In *The Writings of Abraham Lincoln, Vol. 6, 1862–1863,* edited by A. B. Lapsley, 170. New York: G. Putnam's Sons, 1906.

———. Preliminary Emancipation Proclamation. 1st ed. Washington, DC: Government Printing Office, September, 1862.

Lincoln, C. Eric, and L. H. Mamiya. "The Performed Word: Music in the Black Church." In *Readings in African-American Church Music and Worship, Vol. 1,* edited by J. Abbington, 39–76. Chicago: G.I.A., 2001.

Little, William, and William Smith. *The Easy Instructor or A New Method of Teaching Sacred Harmony.* Albany, NY: Webster, Skinner, & Steele, 1809.

Litwack, Leon F. *Been in the Storm So Long: The Aftermath of Slavery.* New York: Alfred A. Knopf, 1979.

Locke, Ralph P. "Music Lovers, Patrons, and the 'Sacralization' of Culture in America." *19th Century Music* 17:2 (Autumn 1993) 149–73.

Long, Kenneth R. *The Music of the English Church.* London: Hodder and Stoughton, 1971.

Lord, Walter. *The Good Years: From 1900 to the First World War*. Ebook ed. Open Road Integrated Media, 2015.

Lordi, Emily. "James Baldwin and the Sound of Soul." *The New Centennial Review* 16:2 (Fall 2016) 31–46.

Lorenz, Edmund S. *Practical Church Music: A Discussion of Purposes, Methods, and Plans*. New York: Fleming H. Revell, 1909.

Lorenz, Ellen Jane. "A Treasure of Campmeeting Spirituals." PhD diss., Union University, 1975.

Loughborough, Mary A. *My Cave Life in Vicksburg with Letters of Trial and Travel by a Lady*. New York: D. Appleton & Co., 1864; digitized 2009. https://archive.org/details/mycavelifeinvico1lougoog.

Lowell, James Russell. "The Present Crisis." In *The Poems of James Russell Lowell*, 96–98. London: Oxford University Press, 1917.

Lowens, Irving. "The American Tradition of Church Song." In *Music and Musicians in Early America*, by Irving Lowens, 279–86. New York: W. W. Norton, 1964.

———. "Daniel Read's World: the Letters of an Early American Composer." In *Music and Musicians in Early America*, by Irving Lowens, 159–77. New York: W. W. Norton, 1964.

———. "John Tufts' 'Introduction to the Singing of Psalm-tunes' (1721–1744): The First American Music Textbook." *Journal of Research in Music Education* 2:2 (Autumn 1954) 89–102.

———. "John Wyeth's 'Repository of Sacred Music, Part Second.'" *The Journal of the American Musicological Society* 5:2 (Summer 1952) 114–31.

———. *Music and Musicians in Early America*. New York: W. W. Norton, 1964.

———. *Music in America and American Music: Two Views of the Scene with a Bibliography of the Published writings of Irving Lowens*. Brooklyn: CUNY, 1978.

Lowens, Irving, and Allen Britton. "'The Easy Instructor' (1798–1831): A History and Bibliography of the First Shape Note Tunebook." *Journal of Research in Music Education* 1:1 (Spring 1953) 30–55.

Lucarini, Dan. *It's Not About the Music: A Journey Into Worship*. Darlington, UK: EP, 2010.

Ludwig, Charles. *Sankey Still Sings*. Anderson, IN: Warner, 1947.

Luff, Alan. "The Twentieth Century Hymn Explosion: Where the Fuse was Lit." *The Hymn, Journal of the Hymn Society of America*, Autumn 2007, 12–13.

Luhr, Eileen. *Witnessing Suburbia: Conservatives and Youth Culture*. Berkeley: University of California Press, 2009.

Luhrmann, Tanya. *When God Talks Back: Understanding the American Evangelical Relationship with God*. New York: Vintage, 2012.

Luker, Ralph E. *The Social Gospel in Black and White: American Racial Reform, 1885–1912*. Chapel Hill: University of North Carolina Press, 1991.

Luther, Martin. "Address to the Nobility of the German Nation." 1520. Internet History Sourcebooks Project. https://sourcebooks.fordham.edu/mod/luther-nobility.asp.

Lutkin, Peter C. *Music in the Church*. Milwaukee: The Young Churchman, 1910.

Maltby, Reba Broughton. "How Woman Organist Overcame Barriers Half a Century Ago." *The Diapason* 16:6 (May 1, 1950) 6.

Manning, William T. "Morgan Dix, Priest and Doctor (Unpublished sermon preached at Service Commemorating the Hundredth Anniversary of the Birth of Dr. Dix,

November 6, 1927.)" New York Diocese Archives/Project Canterbury, 2012. anglicanhistory.org/usa/wtmanning/dix1927.html.

Mansfield, Patti Gallagher. "It Is the Spirit Who Gives Life." *Spiritan Horizons: A Journal of the Congregation of the Holy Spirit* 10 (Fall 2015) 43–44.

Marini, Stephen A. "The New England Singing School: Sacred Music and Ritual Community in Revolutionary America." *Prism* 14:8 (May 2005) 2–3.

———. *Sacred Song in America: Religion, Music, and Popular Culture.* Urbana: University of Illinois, 2011.

Marks, Christopher. "Dudley Buck and the Evolution of American Pedal Technique." *Keyboard Perspectives* vol. 4 (2011) 61–62.

Marovich, Robert M. *A City Called Heaven: Chicago and the Birth of Gospel Music.* Urbana: University of Illinois, 2015.

Marsden, George M. *Fundamentalism and American Culture.* 2nd ed. New York: Oxford University Press, 2006.

Marsh, J. B. T. *The Story of the Jubilee Singers with Their Songs.* Boston: Houghton, Mifflin, 1880.

Martin, Robert F. *Hero of the Heartland: Billy Sunday and the Transformation of American Society, 1862–1935.* Bloomington, IN: Indiana University Press, 2002.

Martineau, Harriet. *Society in America.* Vol. 2. Paris: Baudry's European Library, 1837.

Martins, Daniel H. "Church Music After Vatican II." *The Living Church*, September 10, 2014. https://livingchurch.org/2014/09/10/church-music-after-vatican-ii/.

Mason, Elsie. *The Man: Charles Harrison Mason (1866–1961).* Memphis, TN: The Church of God in Christ, 1979.

Mason, Lowell. "Address on Church Music delivered by request on the evening of Saturday, October 7, 1826 in the Vestry of Hanover Church." Boston: Hillard, Little, and Wilkins, 1827.

———. *Book of Chants, Consisting Mostly of Selections from the Sacred Scriptures.* Boston: Wilkins, Carter, & Co., 1846.

———. *The Modern Psalmist: A Collection of Church Music.* Boston: J. H. Wilkins and B. K. Carter, 1841.

Massa, Mark S. *Anti-Catholicism in America.* New York: Crossroad, 2003.

Mather, Cotton. "The Accomplished Singer." Boston: Bartholomew Green, 1721.

———. *Rules for the Society of Negroes.* Boston: Bartholomew Green, 1714. Library of Congress digital ID: http://hdl.loc.gov/loc.rbc/rbpe.03302600.

Matthews, W. S. B. *A Hundred Years of Music in America: An Account of Musical Effort in America.* Chicago: G. L. Howe, 1889.

McBride, E. "Battle of Vicksburg Being Fought Again Over Recognition of Black Civil War Troops." *Jackson Advocate*, September 8–23, 2003.

McCarthy, Susan. "By Studying Vatican II, We Can Become Better Participants in Our Faith." *Understanding Our Church.* Catholic Diocese of Little Rock. https://www.dolr.org/article/studying-vatican-ii-we-can-become-better-participants-our-faith.

McClenachan, C. T. *Detailed Report of the Proceedings Had in Commemoration of the Successful Laying of the Atlantic Telegraph Cable by Order of the City of New York.* New York: Edmund Jones, 1863.

McCreless, Patrick. "Richard Allen and the Sacred Music of Black Americans." In *Theology, Music, and Modernity: Struggles for Freedom,* edited by Jeremy Begbie, D. K. Chua, and M. Rathey, 201–16. London: Oxford University Press, 2021.

McDaniel, Ruth Currie. *Carpetbagger of Conscience: A Biography of John Emory Bryant.* Athens: University of Georgia Press, 1987.

McDaniel, Stanley R. "Church Song and the Cultivated Tradition in New England and New York." DMA diss., University of Southern California, 1983.

McDowell, J., et al. *What D. L. Moody Means to Me: An Anthology of Appreciations and Appraisals of the Beloved Founder of the Northfield Schools.* Northfield, MA: The Northfield Schools, 1937.

McGavran, Donald A. *The Bridges of God: A Study in the Strategy of Missions.* New York: Friendship, 1955.

McGready, James. "Sermon III: On the Nature and Consequences of Sin." In *The Posthumous Works of the Reverend and Pious James McGready, Late Minister of the Gospel in Henderson, Kentucky*, edited by James Smith, 32–41. Nashville: J. Smith's Steam Press, 1837.

McIlvaine, Charles P. *Oxford Divinity Compared with that of Romish and Anglican Churches.* Philadelphia: Joseph Whetham & Son, 1841.

McKay, David, and Richard Crawford. *William Billings of Boston, Eighteenth Century Composer.* Princeton: Princeton University Press, 1975.

McLoughlin, William G., Jr. *Modern Revivalism: Charles Grandison Finney to Billy Graham.* Eugene, OR: Wipf & Stock, 1959.

———. *Revivals, Awakenings, and Reform: An Essay on Religion and Social Change in America, 1607-1977.* Chicago: University of Chicago Press, 1978.

McNeil, W. K. "The Chuckwagon Gang." In *Encyclopedia of American Gospel Music*, edited by W. K. McNeil, 80–88. New York: Routledge, 2005.

———. "Vaughan, James D." In *Encyclopedia of American Gospel Music*, edited by W. K. McNeil, 410. New York: Routledge, 2005.

McNemar, Richard. *The Kentucky Revival, Or, A Short History of the Late Extraordinary Out-pouring of the Spirit of God in the Western States of America.* Cincinnati: E. Hosford, 1808.

Meacham, John, and T. McGraw, eds. *Songs of America.* New York: Random House, 2019.

Merrill, William P. *Faith in Sight: Essays on the Relation of Agnosticism to Theology.* New York: Charles Scribner's Sons, 1900.

———. "A Noted Divine's Advice to Organists." *The Etude*, January 1922, 56.

Messiter, Arthur H. *A History of the Choir and Music of Trinity Church.* New York: Gorham, 1906.

Metcalf, Frank J. *American Writers and Compilers of Sacred Music.* New York: Russell & Russell, 1925.

Millard, Harrison. *Millard's Popular Mass in G with Latin and English Worlds Including a Veni Creator.* New York: S. T. Gordon, 1866.

Miller, Benjamin L. "In God's Presence: Chaplains, Missionaries, and the Religious Space of War and Peace." PhD diss., University of Florida, 2012.

Miller, Donald L. *City of the Century: The Epic of Chicago and the Making of America.* New York: Rosetta, 1996.

Miller, James. *Flowers in the Dustbin: The Rise of Rock and Roll, 1947-1977.* New York: Simon & Schuster, 1989.

Miller, Robert J. *Both Prayed to the Same God: Religion and Faith in the American Civil War.* New York: Lexington, 2007.

Miller, Randall L., Harry S. Stout, and Charles L. Wilson. *Religion and the American Civil War*. New York: Oxford University Press, 1998.

Minore, Lauren, and Stephen Neukam. "A Look Back at Westminster Choir College and Its History with Rider." *Rider News*, October 23, 2019. https://www.theridernews.com/a-look-back-at-westminster-choir-college-and-its-history-with-rider/.

Moody, William R. *The Life of Dwight L. Moody*. New York: Fleming H. Revell, 1900.

Moore, David A. "Victorian Anthems of the Oxford Movement: Composers and Theologians in Dialog." *Choral Journal* 34:5 (December 1993) 9–14.

Moore, Hilary. "Soul Gospel" In *Encyclopedia of American Gospel Music*, edited by W. K. McNeil, 355–56. New York: Routledge, 2005.

Moore, John W. "Anthem Singing." In *Complete Encyclopaedia of Music*, 54. Boston: Oliver Ditson, 1854.

Morris, Wesley. "Music." In *The 1619 Project*, edited by Nicole Hannah-Jones, Caitlin Roper, Ilena and Jake Silverman, 359–86. New York: New York Times Publishing Co., 2021.

Morrison, Larry R. "The Religious Defense of American Slavery Before 1830." *Journal of Religious Thought* 37 (1980) 16–29.

Moss, Lemuel. *Annals of the United States Christian Commission*. Philadelphia: Lippincott, 1867.

Mouw, R. J., and M. A. Noll. *Wonderful Words of Life: Hymns in Protestant History and Theology*. Grand Rapids: Eerdmans, 2004.

Mullin, Robert B. *Episcopal Vision/American Reality: High Church Theology and Social Thought in Evangelical America*. New Haven: Yale University Press, 1986.

Murison, Justine S. *The Politics of Anxiety in Nineteenth-Century American Literature*. Cambridge: Cambridge University Press, 2011.

Music, David W. "Ananias Davisson, Robert Boyd, Reubin Monday, John Martin, and Archibald Rhea in East Tennessee, 1816–1826." In *American Music* 1:3 (Autumn 1983) 72–84.

———. "The Origins of Lowell Mason's HAMBURG." *The Hymn* 68:1 (Winter 2017) 24–30.

———. *William J. Reynolds, Church Musician*. Nashville: By the Author/Smyth & Helwys, 2013.

———. "William J. Reynolds, Extraordinary Church Musician." ArtisticTheologian.com, November 15, 2013. https://artistictheologian.com/2013/11/15/william-j-reynolds-extraordinary-church-musician/.

Musselman, Joseph. "Mendelssohnism in America." *The Musical Quarterly* 53:3 (July 1967) 335–46.

Mussey, Mabel H. B., ed. *Social Hymns of Brotherhood and Aspiration*. New York: A. S. Barnes, 1914.

Nason, E., and J. Frank Beale. *Lives and Labors of the Eminent Divines*. Philadelphia: John E. Potter, 1895.

Nathan, Hans. *William Billings: Data and Documents*. Detroit: College Music Society, 1976.

Neilson, Peter. *Recollections of a Six Years' Residence in the United States of America*. Glasgow: David Robinson, 1830.

Ness, Marjorie. "The Role of the Musician in the Faith Community." *The American Organist* 54:8 (August 2020) 42–45.

Nichols, L. Nelson. *History of the Broadway Tabernacle of New York City.* New Haven: Tuttle, Morehouse, and Taylor, 1940.
Niebuhr, H. Richard. *The Social Sources of Denominationalism.* New York: Henry Holt, 1929.
Niebuhr, Reinhold. *The Nature and Destiny of Man.* 2 vols.; vol. 1, "Human Nature"; vol. 2, "Human Destiny." London: Nisbet, 1942/1943.
———. "Ten Years That Shook My World." *The Christian Century* 56:17 (1939) 542–46.
Norden, N. Lindsay. "The Boy Choir Fad." *Musical Quarterly* 3:2 (April 1917) 189–97.
———. "A Plea for Pure Church Music." *Musical Quarterly* 4:2 (April 1918) 196–208.
Norton, Herman A. *Struggling for Recognition: The United States Army Chaplaincy, 1791–1865.* Washington, DC: Office of the Chaplaincy, Department of the Army, 1977.
Norton, Kay. "Who Lost the South?" *American Music* 21:4 (Winter 2003) 391–411.
O'Brien, David. "America's Catholics." *Christianity Today*, November 7, 1986, 19–22.
Ochse, Orpha C. *The History of the Organ in the United States.* Bloomington: Indiana University Press, 1988.
O'Connor, Michael. "Hymns, Songs, and the Pursuit of Freedom." In *Theology, Music, and Modernity: Struggles for Freedom,* edited by Jeremy Begbie, D. K. Chua, and M. Rathey, 217–44. London: Oxford University Press, 2021.
O'Donnell, Catherine. *Jesuits in the American Colonies and the United States: Faith, Conflict, Adaptation.* Brill Research Perspectives in Jesuit Studies 2020. Open access ebook. https://www.jstor.org/stable/10.1163/j.ctv2gjwn2q.1.
Ogasapian, John. *Church Music in America, 1620–2000.* Macon, GA: Mercer University Press, 2007.
———. *English Cathedral Music in New York: Edward Hodges of Trinity Church.* Richmond, VA: Organ Historical Society, 1994.
Olds, K. "Privatizing the Church: Disestablishment in Connecticut and Massachusetts." *Journal of Political Economy* 102:2 (April 1994) 277–97.
Oliver, H. K. "Lecture on Church Choirs and the Relation of the Clergy Thereto delivered to the students of Andover Theological Seminary, November 1881." *The Musical Herald*, April 1882, 93–94.
O'Malley, John W. *What Happened at Vatican II.* Cambridge: Harvard/Belknap, 2008.
Opdycke, Sandra. "The Spaces People Share." In *The Columbia History of Post-World War II America,* edited by Mark C. Carnes, 11–35. New York: Columbia University Press, 2007.
Ord-Hume, Arthur W. J. G. *Harmonium: The History of the Reed Organ and Its Makers.* London: David & Charles, 1986.
Orr, N. Lee. *Dudley Buck.* Urbana: University of Illinois Press, 2008.
———. "Dudley Buck, Leader of a Forgotten Tradition." *The Tracker, Organ Historical Society* 38:3 (Fall, 1994) 10–22.
Osborne, William. *Clarence Eddy, Dean of American Organists.* Richmond: Organ Historical Society, 2000.
———. "Henry Dike Sleeper." Grove Music Online. https://doi.org/10.1093/gmo/9781561592630.article.A2092705.
Oshatz, Molly. *Slavery and Sin: The Fight Against Slavery and the Rise of Liberal Protestantism.* New York: Oxford University Press, 2012.
Osofsky, Gilbert. *Harlem, the Making of a Ghetto: Negro New York, 1890–1930.* New York: Harper & Row, 1966.

Ottaway, Jonathan. "The Rise of the Worship Degree: Pedagogical Changes in the Preparation of Church Musicians." In *Essays on the History of Contemporary Praise and Worship*, edited by Lester Ruth, 160–76. Eugene, OR: Wipf & Stock, 2020.
Otten, Joseph. "Franz Xavier Witt." In *The Catholic Encyclopedia, an International Work of Reference*, vol. 15, 678. New York: Encyclopedia, 1914.
Overall, Jason. "An Interview with Robert Powell." *The Diapason*, November 2002, 18–21.
Owen, Barbara. "Eighteenth-Century Organs and Organ Building in New England." In *Music in Colonial Massachusetts, 1630-1820: Music in Homes and Churches*, vol. 54, 655–714. Colonial Society of Massachusetts, 2017.
———. "The Goodriches and Thomas Appleton, Founders of the Boston Organ Industry." *The Tracker* 4:1 (October 1959) 2–6.
———. "The Maturation of the Secular Organ Recital in America's Gilded Age." *19th-Century Music Review* 12:1 (June 2015) 95–117.
Owen, Barbara, and A. Ord-Hume. "Orchestrion." Grove Music Online. https://doi.org/10.1093/gmo/9781561592630.article.20409.
Pace, Adger M. "Give Us More Chorus Singing (Letter to Editor)." *Vaughan's Family Visitor*, November 1934, 9.
Page, Paul Eric. "Musical Organizations in Boston." PhD diss., Boston University, 1967.
Palmer, Benjamin M. "On the first day of the new year and century." A Sermon, New Orleans Brotherhood of the First Presbyterian Church, 1901. https://www.logcollegepress.com/blog/2017/12/30/a-new-years-sermon-by-benjamin-morgan-palmer.
Panayiotou, Andrea C. "An Examination of Pre- and Post-Vatican II Music for the Roman Catholic Liturgy: Ethnic Diversity as a Vehicle of Unity." MA thesis, Florida Atlantic University, 2011.
Pappas, Nikos. "Patterns in the Sacred Music Culture of the American South and West 1700–1820." PhD diss., University of Kentucky, 2013.
Parker, Dorothy Mills. "Musician, Linguist, Priest and Poet." *The Living Church*, July 18, 1999, 13.
Parker, Horatio. "Contemporary Music." *The North American Review* 191:653 (April 1910) 517–26.
Parker, Theodore. *The Transient and Permanent in Christianity*. Edited by George W. Cooke. Boston: American Unitarian Association, 1908.
Parker-Semler, Isabella. *Horatio Parker: A Memoir for His Grandchildren Compiled from Letters and Papers*. New York: G. Putnam's Sons, 1942.
Parks, O. G. "A Critical Analysis of the Works of Leo Sowerby." MA thesis, North Texas State Teachers College, 1941.
Parsch, Pius. "Rev. Pius Parsch (Autobiographical Sketch.)" www.catholicauthors.com/parsch.html.
Paul VI, Pope. *Constitution on Sacred Liturgy, Sacrosanctum Concilium*. December 4, 1963. https://www.vatican.va/archive/hist_councils/ii_vatican_council/documents/vat-ii_const_19631204_sacrosanctum-concilium_en.html.
Pawtak, Kevin. "Music on the Spotsylvania Earthworks." Emerging Civil War, 2019. https://emergingcivilwar.com/2019/05/11/music-on-the-spotsylvania-earthworks/.
Payne, Daniel A. *Recollections of Seventy Years*. Nashville: A. M. E. Sunday School Union, 1888.

Peale, Norman Vincent. *The Power of Positive Thinking.* New York: Prentice-Hall, 1952.

Pecke, Edwin M. "The Choral Services of the Church." *New York Ecclesiologist,* September 1852, 142.

Pecklers, Keith F. "The Evolution of Liturgical Music in the United States of America." In *Renewal and Resistance: Catholic Church Music from the 1850s to Vatican II,* 151–70. Oxford: Peter Lang, 1965.

Pemberton, Carol Ann. *Lowell Mason: A Bio-Bibliography.* New York: Greenwood, 1988.

———. "Lowell Mason, His Life and Work." PhD diss., University of Minnesota, 1971.

Perrone, Fernanda. "'I Prayed and Sang in Every Tent,' Israel Silvers, USCC Delegate from New Jersey." *Journal of Rutgers University Libraries* 66 (2014) 81–90.

Peters, John Punnett. *Annals of St. Michael's.* New York: G. P. Putnam's Sons, 1907.

Peterson, John W. *Hallelujah! What a Savior!* Grand Rapids: Singspiration, 1957.

Peterson, John W., and Richard Engquist. *The Miracle Goes On: An Autobiography.* Grand Rapids: Zondervan, 1976.

Philip, Canon Kristy. "The Call." Sermon preached at Cathedral of St. John the Evangelist, Spokane, Washington, February 10, 2019.

Phillips, Christopher N. "Emily Dickinson's Hymnody of Privacy." In *The Hymnal: A Reading History.* Ebook ed. Baltimore: Johns Hopkins University Press, 2018.

Phillips, J. B. *Is God at Home?* Nashville: Abingdon, 1957.

Phillips, Leonard M., Jr. "The Leipzig Conservatory." PhD diss., Indiana University, 1979.

Phillips, Philip. *The Singing Pilgrim or Pilgrim's Progress Illustrated in Song.* Cincinnati: Phillips/Hitchcock & Walden Printers, 1866.

Phillips, Philip, and A. Clark. *Philip Phillips: The Story of His Life.* London: Wesleyan Methodist Sunday School Union, 1882.

Pichierri, Louis. *Music in New Hampshire, 1623–1800.* New York: Columbia University Press, 1960.

Pierce, R., ed. *Records of First Church, Boston, 1630–1868.* Vols. 19, 40, and 41. Boston: Colonial Society of Massachusetts, 1961.

Pitts, Charles F. *Chaplains in Gray: The Confederate Chaplains' Story.* Nashville: Broadman, 1857.

Pike, Gustavus D. *The Jubilee Singers: And Their Campaign for Twenty Thousand Dollars.* London: Hodder and Stoughton, 1873.

———. *The Singing Campaign for Ten Thousand Pounds; or The Jubilee Singers in Great Britain.* New York: American Missionary Association, 1875.

Pius X, Pope. *Tra le Sollecitudin* (Instructions on Sacred Music). 1903. https://adoremus.org/1903/11/tra-le-sollecitudini/.

Pius XI, Pope. *Divini cultus sanctitatem* (The Holiness of Divine Worship). 1928. https://adoremus.org/1928/12/on-divine-worship/.

Pius XII, Pope. *Mediator Dei* (Mediator between God and Mankind). 1947. https://www.vatican.va/content/pius-xii/en/encyclicals/documents/hf_p-xii_enc_20111947_mediator-dei.html.

———. *Musicae sacrae disciplina* (On Sacred Music). 1955. https://www.vatican.va/content/piusxii/en/encyclicals/documents/hf_p-xii_enc_25121955_musicae-sacrae.html.

Playford, John. *An Introduction to the Skill of Music.* 12th ed. London: W. Godbid, 1694.

———. *The Whole Book of Psalms with the Usual Hymns and Spiritual Songs Together with all the Ancient and Proper Tunes Sung in Three Parts, Cantus, Medius, and Bassus*. London: printed by the author, 1677. https://s9.imslp.org/files/imglnks/usimg/0/05/IMSLP278473-PMLP146642-tusalmooplay.pdf.

Poe, Janita. "Thomas A. Dorsey, Gospel Pioneer." *Chicago Tribune*, January 25, 1993.

Polman, Bert. "Praise the Name of Jesus: Are All Praise and Worship Songs for the Congregation?" In *The Message in the Music: Studying Contemporary Praise and Worship*, edited by Robert Woods and Brian Walrath, 127–37. Nashville: Abingdon, 2007.

Pope, Charles Henry. *The Cheney Genealogy*. Boston: C. H. Pope, 1897.

Porter, Noah. "The New England Meetinghouse (abridged version of lecture to the New England Society of Brooklyn, December, 1882)." New Haven: Yale University Press, 1933.

Porter, Wendy J. "Trading My Sorrows: Worshipping God in the Darkness—The Expression of Pain and Suffering in Contemporary Worship Music." In *The Message in the Music: Studying Contemporary Praise and Worship*, edited by Robert Woods and Brian Walrath, 76–91. Nashville: Abingdon, 2007.

Power, John C. *The Rise and Progress of Sunday Schools: A Biography of Robert Raikes and William Fox*. New York: Sheldon & Company, 1863.

Powers, Jonathan. "Robert Webber: Preserving Traditional Worship Through Contemporary Styles." In *Essays on the History of Contemporary Praise and Worship*, edited by Lester Ruth, 95–116. Eugene, OR: Wipf & Stock, 2020.

Pratt, James Bissett. *The Religious Consciousness: A Psychological Study*. New York: Macmillan, 1920.

Pratt, Waldo Selden. "The Choir." In *Parish Problems: Hints and Helps for the People of the Churches*, edited by Washington Gladden, 448–55. New York: Century Co., 1887.

———. *The History of Music: A Handbook and Guide for Students*. New York: G. Schirmer, 1907.

———. "The Isolation of Music." *Proceedings of the Royal Music Association*, 1894. https://www.jstor.org/stable/765376.

———. "The Liturgical Responsibilities of Non-Liturgical Churches." *The American Journal of Theology* 5:4 (October 1901) 641–65.

———. *Musical Ministries in the Church: Studies in the History, Theory, and Administration of Sacred Music*. New York: Fleming H. Revell, 1901.

———. "The Recent Ordination of Mr. H. D. Sleeper." *Hartford Seminary Record*, December 1891, 41–42.

———. "Status of Church Musicians." *Hartford Seminary Record*, June 1893, 208.

———. "Wanted, Specialists in Church Music." *Century Illustrated Monthly Magazine*, June 1893, 317.

Price, Emmett G. "Sallie Martin." In *Encyclopedia of American Gospel Music*, edited by W. K. McNeil, 243–44. New York: Routledge, 2005.

Pritchard, Gregory. *Willow Creek Seeker Services: Evaluating a New Way of Doing Church*. Grand Rapids: Baker, 1996.

Proctor, Edna Dean. *Life Thoughts Gathered from the Extemporaneous Discourses of Henry Ward Beecher by One of His Congregation*. New York: Sheldon & Co., 1863.

Pruett, Laura M. "Louis Moreau Gottschalk, John Sullivan Dwight, and the Development of Musical Culture in the United States, 1853–1865." PhD diss., Florida State University, 2007.

Pullin, Michael. "Isham Emmanuel Reynolds (1879–1949)." Online Handbook of Texas Historical Association. https://www.tshaonline.org/handbook/entries/reynolds-isham-emmanuel.

Purifoy, Lewis M. "The Methodist Anti-Slavery Tradition, 1784–1844." *Journal of the Methodist Historical Societies,* July 1, 1966, 3–16. http://archives.gcah.org/pdfpreview/bitstream/handle/10516/1445/MH-1967-07-%20Purifoy-%205-18.pdf?sequence=1.

Race, Paul D. "A Brief History of Contemporary Christian Music." School of the Rock (blog). https://schooloftherock.com/html/a_brief_history_of_contemporar.html.

Radano, Ronald. *Lying Up a Nation: Race and Black Music.* Chicago: University of Chicago Press, 2003.

Radloff, Nancy S. "The Organist's Role in the Colonial American Church." *Anglican Episcopal History* 73:3 (September 2004) 266–93.

Randolph, Peter. *From Slave Cabin to the Pulpit: The Autobiography of Rev. Peter Randolph.* Boston: James H. Earle, 1895. https://docsouth.unc.edu/neh/randolph/menu.html.

Rasmussen, Jane. *Musical Taste as a Religious Question in 19th-Century America.* Lewiston, NY: Edwin Mellen, 1986.

Rauschenbusch, Walter. *Christianity and the Social Crisis.* New York: Macmillan, 1907.

———. *A Theology for the Social Gospel.* New York: Macmillan, 1918.

Rauvola, Rachel S., Cort W. Rudolph, and Hannes Zacher. "Generationalism: Problems and Implications. Organizational Dynamics." 2018. https://www.researchgate.net/publication/325158163_Generationalism_Problems_and_Implications/link/5afb57fdaca272e7302c2efd/download.

Read, Daniel. *The American Singing Book.* 2nd ed. New Haven: printed by the author, 1786. https://s9.imslp.org/files/imglnks/usimg/f/ff/IMSLP459642-PMLP364041-americansingingbooread.pdf.

Reagan, Wen. "A Beautiful Noise: A History of Contemporary Worship Music in America." PhD diss., Duke University, 2015.

Reagon, Bernice J. *If You Don't Go, Don't Hinder Me: The African-American Sacred Song Tradition.* Lincoln: University of Nebraska Press, 2001.

Reagon, Bernice J., ed. *We'll Understand It Better By and By: Pioneering African-American Gospel Composers.* Washington, DC: Smithsonian Institute, 1992.

Redman, Robb. *The Great Worship Awakening: Sing a New Song in the Postmodern Church.* San Francisco: John Wiley & Sons, 2002.

Reid, J. K. S., ed. "Articles concerning the Organization of the Church and Worship at Geneva." In *Calvin: Theological Treatises,* 48–55. Philadelphia: Westminster, 1977.

Reigles, B. Jean. "The Choral Music of Amy Beach." PhD diss., Texas Tech University, 1996.

Repp, Ray. "Current Trends: A Modest Proposal to Composers of Liturgical Music." *Spirituality Today* 40:3 (August 1988). https://sicutincensum.wordpress.com/2020/04/29/ray-repp-founder-of-catholic-folk-a-modest-proposal/.

Reuben, Julie A. "Patriotic Purposes: Public Schools and the Education of Citizens." In *The Public Schools,* edited by Susan Fuhrman and Marvin Lazerson, 1–24. New York: Oxford University Press, 2005.

Reynolds, Helen W. *The Records of Christ Church, Poughkeepsie, New York*. Poughkeepsie, NY: Frank B. Howard, 1911.

Reynolds, William J. "Baptists, Music, and World War II." *Baptist History and Heritage* 36:3 (Summer/Fall 2001). https://www.thefreelibrary.com/Baptists%2c+music%2c+and+World+War+II.-a094160978.

———. "B. F. White: The Sacred Harp Man." In *Away Here in Texas* (March/April 1997) 1.

———. "The Contributions of B. B. McKinney to Southern Baptist Church Music." *Baptist History and Heritage* 21:3 (July 1986) 41–49.

Rhoads, Mark D. "Hymns in the Lives of American Soldiers." *Singing the Songs of Zion: Soldier's Hymn Collections and Hymn Singing in the American Civil War*. http://www.markrhoads.com/soldiershymns.

Rhodes, Elisha Hunt. *All for the Union: The Civil War Diary and Letters of Elisha Hunt Rhodes*. Edited by R. H. Rhodes. New York: Random House, 1985.

Rice, E. W. *The Sunday School Movement, 1780–1917*. Philadelphia: American Sunday School Union, 1917.

Rice, Kym S. *World of a Slave: Encyclopedia of the Material Life of Slaves in the United States*. 2 vols. Santa Barbara, CA: Greenwood/ABC-CLIO, 2010; ebook, https://archive.org/details/worldofslaveencyoooounse.

Rice, David. *Slavery Inconsistent with Justice and Good Policy*. Philadelphia: M. Guerney, 1792. Digital reproduction, Digital Commons/University of Maine: https://digitalcommons.library.umaine.edu/cgi/viewcontent.cgi?article=1328&context=mainehistory.

Richardson, Joe M. *Christian Reconstruction: The American Missionary Association and Southern Blacks, 1861–1890*. Tuscaloosa: University of Alabama Press, 1986.

———. "Fisk University: The First Critical Years." *Tennessee Historical Quarterly* 29:1 (Spring 1970) 24–41.

Richardson, Kip C. "Big Religion: The Cultural Origin of the American Megachurch." PhD diss., Harvard University, 2017.

Richey, Russell E., Kenneth E. Rowe, and Jean Miller Schmidt. *American Methodism: A Compact History*. 2nd ed. Nashville: Abingdon, 2012.

———. *The Methodist Experience in America*. Vol. 1. Ebook ed. Nashville: Abingdon, 2010.

Rigler, Ann Marie. "John Zundel as Pedagogue." MA thesis, University of Iowa, 1993.

Ritter, Frederic Louis. *Music in America*. New York: Charles Scribner's Sons, 1884.

Robinson, Alan M., Jr. "The Genesis of Cultivated Choral Tone in the United States, 1906–1928: Peter C. Lutkin, F. Melius Christiansen, and John Finley Williamson." PhD diss., Boston University, 2015.

Robinson, Charles S. "Worshipping by Proxy." Letter to the Editor. *Century Illustrated Monthly Magazine* (March 1884) 946–48.

Robinson, Ray. "John Finley Williamson: His Contribution to Choral Music." *Choral Journal* 12:1 (September 1981) 5–10.

Roche, Olin Scott. *Forty Years of Parish Life and Work: An Autobiography*. New York: Friebele, 1930.

Rockwood, George G. "Our Early Church Choirs." In *The New York Musical Directory and Encyclopedia*, 8. New York: Harrison & Co., 1882.

Rodeheaver, Homer. *20 Years with Billy Sunday*. Nashville: Cokesbury, 1936.

Rohr, Richard. "The Dualistic Mind." Daily Meditation, Center for Action and Contemplation, June 29, 2017. https://cac.org/about/richard-rohr/?gclid=CjoKCQjws4aKBhDPARIsAIWHoJX-gz2iBM1mYArvQnPkpUixE3pNW9e-jK5p_26QQfOuv5eF69ZDTjYaAtaWEALw_wcB.

Roosevelt, Franklin D. "Inaugural Address of President Franklin D. Roosevelt March 4, 1933." https://www.fdrlibrary.org/documents/356632/390886/First+Inagural+Address+Curriculum+Hub+Documents.pdf/55c42890-6b80-4d34-b68a-b4a30f2797d5.

Roland, Charles P. *My Odyssey Through History: Memoirs of War and Academe*. Baton Rouge: Louisiana State University Press, 2004.

Root, George Frederick. *The Story of a Musical Life: An Autobiography*. Cincinnati: John Church, 1891.

Rose, Anne C. *Victorian America and the Civil War*. Cambridge: Cambridge University Press, 1992.

Rosewall, Richard B. "Singing Schools of Pennsylvania, 1800–1900." PhD diss., University of Minnesota, 1969.

Routley, Erik. *A Panorama of Christian Hymnody*. Chicago: G. I. A., 1979.

———. *Twentieth Century Church Music*. New York: Oxford University Press, 1964.

Ruark, James E. *The House of Zondervan: Celebrating 75 Years*. Grand Rapids: Zondervan, 2011.

Ruff, Anthony. *Sacred Music and Liturgical Reform: Treasures and Transformations*. Chicago: Liturgical Training Publications/Hillenbrand, 2007.

Rugoff, Milton. *The Beechers: An American Family in the 19th Century*. New York: Harper & Row, 1981.

———. *The Gilded Age*. New York: Harper & Row, 1981; ebook, New Word City, 2018.

Rumburg, H. R. *The Songs of Southern Zion: Confederate Hymnology*. Spout Spring, VA: Society for Biblical and Southern Studies, 2011.

Rumer, Anna. "Elvis in the Heart of America." *Time*, August 21, 2017. https://time.com/4894995/elvis-in-the-heart-of-america.

Ruth, Lester. *Essays on the History of Contemporary Praise and Worship*. Eugene, OR: Wipf & Stock, 2020.

———. *Flow: The Ancient Way to Do Contemporary Worship*. Nashville: Abingdon, 2020.

———. "How Great Is Our God." In *The Message in the Music: Studying Contemporary Praise and Worship*, edited by Robert Woods and Brian Walrath, 29–42. Nashville: Abingdon, 2007.

Ruth, Lester, and Swee Hong Lim. *A History of Contemporary Praise and Worship*. Grand Rapids: Baker Academic, 2021.

———. *Lovin' On Jesus: A Concise History of Contemporary Worship*. Nashville: Abingdon, 2017.

Ryan, Edwin. "The Oxford Movement in the United States." *Catholic Historical Review* 19:1 (April 1933) 33–49.

Sabatier, Francois. "Interrelations Between Liturgy, Music, and Organbuilding in France from the Middle Ages to Vatican II." *The American Organist* 55:12 (December 2021) 74–91.

Sabatier, Paul. *Modernism*. New York: Charles Scribner's Sons, 1908.

Saenger, Oscar. "How to Succeed as a Public Singer." In *American History and Encyclopedia of Music*, vol. 11, "Essentials of Music," edited by Emil Liebling, 285–322. Toledo, OH: Irving Squire, 1908–1910.

Sammond, Herbert Staveley. "How Can a Young Organist Become an Efficient Choirmaster?" *Etude*, May 1914, 380–82.

Sandburg, Carl. *The American Song Bag*. New York: Harcourt, Brace, and Company, 1927.

Sankey, Ira D. *My Life and the Story of Gospel Hymns and Sacred Songs and Solos*. Philadelphia: P. W. Ziegler Company/Sunday School Times Company, 1907.

Sankey, Bliss, McGranahan, and Stebbins. *Gospel Songs, No's 1 to 6 Complete*. Chicago: Biglow & Main Company, 1894.

Saul, Eric A., ed. "United States and Anti-Slavery Timeline". AmericanAbolitionists.com. http://www.americanabolitionists.com/us-abolition-and-anti-slavery-timeline.html#US%20timeline.

Saxton, General Rufus. "Proclamation for a Day of Public Thanksgiving and Praise." *The Liberator*, December 26, 1862, 205.

Schaefer, Edward. *Catholic Music Through the Ages: Balancing the Needs of a Worshipping Church*. Chicago: Hellenbrand/Archdiocese of Chicago Liturgy Publications, 2012.

Schalk, Carl. "Church Music in the '90s: Problems and Progress." *The Christian Century*, March 21, 1990. https://www.religion-online.org/article/church-music-in-the-90s-problems-and-prognoses/.

Schaller, Lyle E. "Megachurch!" *Christianity Today*, March 5, 1990, 20–24.

Scharf, John Thomas. *History of Baltimore City and County from the Earliest Period to the Present Day*. Philadelphia: Louis H. Everts, 1881.

Schmidt, Paul G. *My Years at St. Olaf*. Northfield, MN: St. Olaf College, 1962.

Schmoyer, Helen C. "Contribution of the Westminster Choir Movement in American Choral Music." MA thesis, North Texas State Teachers College, 1942.

Schubert, Virginia A. Article Review: Maurice Duruflé, "Reflections on Sacred Music." *Una Voce*, November/December 1978, in *Sacred Music* 106:2 (Summer 1979) 25.

Schuler, Richard J. "A Chronicle of Reform." In *Cum Angelis Canere: Essays on Sacred Music and Pastoral Liturgy in Honor of Richard J. Schuler, 1920–1990*, edited by Robert A. Skeris, 349–416. St. Paul, MN: Catholic Church Music Associates, 1990.

———. "The Sacred." Reprint of lecture given at University of Wisconsin, July 1980. *Sacred Music* 107:3 (Fall 1980) 21–27.

Schuller, Robert H. *Your Church Has Real Possibilities*. Glendale, CA: G/L Regal, 1976.

Selles, Otto. "Taize in the Fall." *Books and Culture: A Christian Review*, November 29, 2005. https://www.booksandculture.com/articles/webexclusives/2005/november/051128.html.

Sernett, Milton, and C. Eric Lincoln. *Bound for the Promised Land: African-American Religion and the Great Migration*. Durham, NC: Duke University Press, 1997.

Sessions, Ruth Huntington. *Sixty Odd: A Personal History*. Brattleboro, VT: Stephen Daye, 1936.

Sheahan, James W., and George P. Upton. *The Great Conflagration: Chicago, Its Past, Present and Future*. Chicago: Union, 1871.

Shelley, Braxton D. "Gospel Goes to Church (Again): Smallwood's Hybridity as Liturgical Compromise." In *Readings in African-American Church Music and Worship*, vol. 2, edited by J. Abbington, 399–418. Chicago: G.I.A, 2014.

Shelton, Jason. "Music, Community, and Identity: Church Musician as Minister and Theologian." Treatise, Vanderbilt Divinity School, 2003.

Sheppard Moore, Ella. "Historical Sketch of the Jubilee Singers." *Fisk News*, October 1911. https://hbcudigitallibrary.auctr.edu/digital/collection/FUPP/id/1227/rec/1.

Shoemaker, Alfred L. "Stephen St. John." In *The Pennsylvania Dutchman* 4:13, 3.

Shoemaker, H. Stephen. "Overview of Worship in the Southern Baptist Convention." WorshipLibrary.com. https://www.worshiplibrary.com/blog/an-overview-of-worship-in-the-southern-baptist-convention/.

Shoemaker, Samuel M. *Calvary Church, Yesterday and Today*. New York: Fleming H. Revell Jr., 1936.

Silliman, Daniel. "1 Out of 3 New Guitars Are Purchased for Worship Music." *Christianity Today*, August 17, 2021. https://www.christianitytoday.com/ct/2021/september/guitar-industry-church-worship-music-gig-percentage.html.

Silverberg, Ann L. "American Catholic Liturgical Music in the Twentieth Century: Pius X's 'Motu Proprio.'" *American Catholic Studies* 115:1 (Spring 2004) 45–62.

Silverberg, Ann L. "Cecilian Reform in Baltimore, 1868 to 1903." In *Renewal and Resistance: Catholic Church Music from the 1850s to Vatican II*, 171–88. London: Peter Lang, 1965.

Simonds, M. N. "At the Sunday School." *National Magazine*, April 1909, 87.

Sims, Scott G. "Dissonance Treatment in Fuging Tunes by Daniel Read from The American Singing Book and The Columbian Harmonist." MA thesis, North Texas State University, 1987.

Sirota, Victoria R. "The Musician's Struggle with Vocation and Call." *The American Organist* 53:12 (December 2019) 78–80.

———. *Preaching to the Choir: Claiming the Role of Sacred Musician*. New York: Church Publishing Corp., 2006.

Sizer, Sandra. *Gospel Hymns and Social Religion: The Rhetoric of 19th Century Revivalism*. Philadelphia: Temple University Press, 1978.

Skeris, Robert A. "Sarto, the 'Conservative Reformer'—100 Years of the Motu Proprio of Pope St. Pius X." *Sacred Music* 130:4 (Winter 2003) 5–9.

Skinner, Ellouise W. *Sacred Music at Union Theological Seminary, 1836–1953*. New York: Union Theological Seminary, 1953.

Slaughter, Linda W. *The Freedmen of the South*. Cincinnati: Elm Street Printing, 1869.

Sleeper, Henry Dike. "Church Music." In *Recent Christian Progress: Studies in Christian Thought and Work During the Last Seventy-five Years*, edited by L. B. Paton, 382–89. New York: Macmillan, 1909.

Sleeper, Henry Dike, ed. *Songs of Harvard: A Collection of Songs and Glees as Sung by the Glee-Club and Students of Harvard College*. Cambridge: Charles Sever/Harvard Bookstore, 1890.

Sloat, William A. III. "George Whitefield, African Americans, and Slavery." *Methodist History* 33:1 (October 1994) 3–13.

Small, Abner R. *The Road to Richmond: The Civil War Memoirs of Major Albert R. Small of the Sixteenth Maine Volunteers, Together with the Diary He Kept When He Was a Prisoner of War*. Edited by Harold A. Small. New York: Fordham University Press, 2000.

Smith, David Stanley, and W. Oliver Strunk. "A Study of Horatio Parker." *Musical Quarterly* 16:2 (April 1930) 153–69.

Smith, Edward P. *Incidents of the Christian Commission*. Philadelphia: J. B. Lippincott, 1869.

Smith, Ryan K. *Gothic Arches, Latin Crosses: Anti-Catholicism and American Church Designs in the Nineteenth Century*. Chapel Hill: University of North Carolina Press, 2006.

Smith, Timothy Alan. "The Southern Folk-Hymn, 1800–1860." *Choral Journal* 23:7 (March 1983) 23–29.

Smith-Pollard, Deborah. *When the Church Becomes Your Party*. Detroit: Wayne State University Press, 2008.

Smylie, James H. "The American Sunday School Union Papers, 1817–1915." *Journal of Presbyterian History* 58:4 (Winter 1980) 372–76.

Sommerville, Murray F. "John Knowles Paine." *Harvard Magazine*, May 1, 2000. https://harvardmagazine.com/2000/05/John-Knowles-Paine.html.

Southall, Geneva. "Black Composers and Religious Music." *The Black Perspective in Music* 2:1 (Spring 1974) 45–50.

Southern, Eileen. *The Music of Black Americans: A History*. New York: W. W. Norton, 1983.

Sowerby, Leo. "Ideals in Church Music: Official Statement Prepared for the Joint Commission on Church Music of the Protestant Episcopal Church." Greenwich, CT: Seabury, 1956.

Spalding, Walter R. *Music at Harvard: A Historical Review of Men and Events*. New York: Coward-McCann, 1935.

Spangler, Michael. "Benjamin Brown French in the Lincoln Period." *White House History*, no. 8. https://www.Whitehousehistory.org/benjamin-brown-french-in-the-lincoln-period.

Spencer, J. Michael. *Black Hymnody: A Hymnological History of the African-American Church*. Knoxville: University of Tennessee Press, 1992.

———. "Hymns of the Social Awakening: Walter Rauschenbusch and Social Gospel Hymnody." *The Hymn* 40:2 (April 1989) 18–24.

Spencer, John. *A History of Kentucky Baptists: From 1769 to 1895, including more than 800 Biographical Sketches*. Vol. 1. Cincinnati: J. Baumes, 1885.

Spicer, Tobias. *Autobiography of Rev. Tobias Spicer Containing Incidents and Observations and Some Account of the Visit to England*. New York: Lane & Scott, 1859.

———. *Campmeetings Defended*. New Haven: T. G. Woodward, 1828.

Stafford, Tim. "A Regular Purpose-Driven Guy." *Christianity Today*, November 18, 2002, 42–48.

Stebbins, George C. "Mr. Moody as a Singer." *Congregational and Christian World*, November 14, 1914, 652.

———. *Reminiscences and Gospel Hymn Stories*. New York: George H. Doran Company, 1924.

Steel, Ronald. "Mr. Clean (Review of 'Waging Peace' by Dwight David Eisenhower)." *New York Review of Books*, January 6, 1966. https://www.nybooks.com/articles/1966/01/06/mr-clean/?lp_txn_id=1513283.

Steele, David W. "John Wyeth and the Development of Southern Folk Hymnody." In *Music from the Middle Ages Through the 20th Century: Essays in Honor of Gwynn McPeak*, edited by Carmelo P. Comberiati and Matthew C. Steele, 357–74. London: Gordon & Breach, 1988.

Steele, Daniel W., and R. H. Hulan. *The Makers of the Sacred Harp*. Urbana: University of Illinois Press, 2010.

Steere, Dwight. *Music for the Protestant Church Choir: A Descriptive and Classified List of Worship Material*. Richmond, VA: John Knox, 1955.

Stephens, Randall J. *The Fire Spreads: Holiness and Pentecostalism in the American South*. Cambridge, MA: Harvard University Press, 2008.

———. "The Klan, White Christianity, and the Past and Present: a response to Kelly J. Baker by Randall J. Stephens." Religion and Culture Forum, 2017. https://voices.uchicago.edu/religionculture/2017/06/26/the-klan-white-christianity-and-the-past-and-present-a-response-to-kelly-j-baker-by-randall-j-stephens/.

Stevenson, Robert. *Protestant Church Music in America: A Short Survey of Men and Movements from 1564 to the Present*. New York: W. W. Norton, 1966.

Stewart, Shawna Lynn. "Charles C. Hirt at the University of Southern California: Significant Contributions and an Enduring Legacy." DMA treatise, University of Southern California, 2013.

Stewart, W. R. *Grace Church and Old New York*. New York: E. P. Dutton, 1924.

Stipe, Tom. "The Calvary Chapel Chronicles: The Music." *The Phoenix Preacher*, blog. https://phoenixpreacher.com/the-calvary-chapel-chronicles-the-music-by-tom-stipe/.

Stone, Barton. *The Biography of Elder Barton Stone, Written by Himself*. Edited by John Rogers. Cincinnati: J. A. & U. P. James, 1847.

Stone, Duncan. "Deconstructing the Gentleman Amateur." *Cultural and Social History* 18:3 (2021) 315–36.

Stowe, Harriet Beecher. *Uncle Tom's Cabin, or Life Among the Lowly*. Boston: John P. Jewett & Co., 1852.

Strimple, Nick. *Choral Music in the Twentieth Century*. Rev. ed. Pompton Plains, NJ: Amadeus/Hal Leonard, 2005.

Strong, Josiah. *Our Country: Its Possible Future and Its Present Crisis*. New York: Baker & Taylor, 1885.

Stubbs, G. Edward. *Practical Hints on Boy Choir Training with an Introduction by Reverend Dr. J. S. B. Hodges*. 6th ed. New York: Novello/E. & J. B. Young, 1888.

———. "Secularization of Sacred Music." *Musical Quarterly* 2:4 (October 1916) 615–27.

———. "Why We Have Male Choirs in Churches." *Musical Quarterly* 3:3 (July 1917) 416–27.

Stuckenberg, J. H. W. *I'm Surrounded by Methodists: Diary of John H. W. Stuckenberg, Chaplain of the 145th Pennsylvania Volunteer Infantry*. Edited by Hedrik & Davis. Gettysburg, PA: Thomas, 1995.

Sunday, Billy. *The Sawdust Trail: Billy Sunday in His Own Words*. Ebook ed. Ames: University of Iowa Press, 2009.

Sutton, Matthew A. *American Apocalypse: A History of Modern Evangelicalism*. Cambridge: Belknap/Harvard University Press, 2014.

Swain, Joseph P. *Sacred Treasure: Understanding Catholic Liturgical Music*. Collegeville, MN: Liturgical, 2012.

Swan, Marcus Lafayette. *Harp of Columbia*. Knoxville, TN: printed by the author, 1848.

Sweet, Charles F. *A Champion of the Cross, being the Life of John Henry Hopkins, S. T. D., Including Selections from His Writings*. New York: James Pott & Company, 1894.

Bibliography

Sweet, William W. *Revivalism in America: Its Origin, Growth, and Decline.* Nashville: Abingdon, 1944.

Symmes, Thomas (attrib.). *The Reasonableness of Regular Singing.* Boston: Gerrish, 1720.

Talmadge, T. DeWitt. *Sports That Kill.* New York: Harper & Brothers, 1875.

Tanis, Gretchen S. *Making Jesus Attractive: The Ministry and Message of Young Life.* Eugene, OR: Pickwick, 2016.

Tawa, Nicholas E.. *Arthur Foote: A Musician in the Frame of Time and Place.* Lanham, MD: Scarecrow, 1997.

Taylor, James B . "Lewis Craig." In *Lives of Virginia Baptist Ministers*, 84–88. Richmond, VA: Yale and Wyatt, 1838.

Teja, Gary. "Worship as Fiesta: Hispanic Traditions Provide a Fresh Perspective." *Reformed Worship* 43 (March 1997). https://www.reformedworship.org/article/march-1997/worship-fiesta-hispanic-traditions-provide-fresh-perspective.

Temperley, Nicolas. *The Music of the English Parish Church.* Cambridge: Cambridge University Press, 1979.

Terrell, Bob. *The Music Men: The Story of Professional Gospel Quartet Singing.* Alexander, NC: Mountain Church, 2001.

Tesch, John W. "The Reception Accorded George Whitefield in the Southern Colonies." *Methodist History Journal* (January 1968) 17–26. https://archives.gcah.org/server/api/core/bitstreams/6edeocc9-a93b-4556-b1ba-4c11f21ae534/content.

Thomas, Andre J. *Way Over in Beula Lan'.* Dayton, OH: Heritage Music, 2007.

Thomas, H. G. "The Colored Troops at Petersburg." In *Battles and Leaders of the Civil War*, vol. 4, 563–67. New York: The Century Company, 1888.

Thomas, John L. "Romantic Reform in America, 1815–1865." *American Quarterly* 17:4 (Winter 1965) 656–81.

Thomas, Rose Faye. *Memoirs of Theodore Thomas.* New York: Moffat, Yard & Company, 1911.

Thompson, Noyes L. *The History of Plymouth Church.* New York: G. W. Carleton & Co., 1873.

Thorson, T. W. "A History of Music Publishing in Chicago, 1850–1960." PhD diss., Northwestern University, 1961.

Thrapp, Dan. "New Underground Church Reported Gaining Strength." *Los Angeles Times*, June 8, 1967, 3, 17.

Thumma, Scott. "Megachurches." Hartford Institute for Religion Research. http://hartfordinstitute.org/megachurch/megachurches.html.

Tilden, William S. "Early Life of Lowell Mason." In *Memories of a Musical Life*, by William Mason, 275–90. New York: Century Company, 1901.

Titcomb, Everett. "Twenty-Five Years at St. John's." *Cowley (Quarterly magazine of the Society of St. John the Evangelist)* 9:34 (1935) 61–67.

Tovey, David G. "Archibald T. Davison, Harvard Musician and Scholar." PhD diss., University of Michigan, 1979.

Towne, Laura M. *Letters and Diary of Laura M. Towne, Written from the Sea Islands of South Carolina, 1862–1864.* Edited by R. S. Holland. Cambridge: Riverside, 1912.

Treloar, Geoffrey R. *The Disruption of Evangelicalism: The Age of Torrey, Mott, McPherson, and Hammond.* Downers Grove, IL: IVP Academic, 2017.

Tresch John W., Jr. "The Reception Accorded George Whitefield in the Southern Colonies." https://pdfs.semanticscholar.org/f923/3f42c8b2f008e27af359d09a4fedf82001ff.pdf.

Trollope, Francis. *Domestic Manners of Americans*. 4th ed. London: Wittaker, Treacher & Company, 1832.

Trumbull, H. Clay. *War Memories of an Army Chaplain*. New York: Charles Scribner's Sons, 1898.

Tryon, H., ed. *Union Theological Seminary in the City of New York Alumni Catalogue, 1836–1947*. New York: Union Theological Seminary, 1948.

Tucker, George. *Letters from Virginia, Translated from the French*. Baltimore: Fielding Lucas/J. Robinson, 1816. https://www.google.com/books/edition/Letters_from_Virginia_translated_from_th/yrqmwQEACAAJ?hl=en&gbpv=1.

Tucker, John Ireland. *The Service Book: A Manual of Anglican Chants and Gregorian Tones Adapted to the Canticles*. New York: F. J. Huntington and Co., 1873.

Turner, Eldon. "Earwitness to Resonance in Space: An Interpretation of Puritan Psalmody in Early 18th Century New England." *American Studies* 25:1 (Spring 1984) 25–47.

Turner, Samuel H. *Autobiography of Samuel H. Turner, Late Professor of Biblical Learning and the Interpretation of Scripture in the General Theological Seminary*. New York: A. D. F. Randolph, 1864.

Tuthill, Burnet C. "Leo Sowerby." *The Musical Quarterly* 24:3 (July 1938) 249–64.

———. "Mrs. H. H. A. Beach." *Musical Quarterly* 26:3 (July 1940) 297–310.

Tuttle, Carl. "History of Vineyard Worship—1976–1997." https://worshiptherock.com/profiles/blogs/history-of-vineyard-worship.

———. *Reckless Mercy: A Trophy of God's Grace*. Oklahoma City: Coaching Saints, 2017.

———. "Vineyard Worship—The Early Years, Parts 1–3" http://www.carltuttle.com/wimber-years/2009/1/31/vineyard-worship-the-early-years-part-1.html.

Van Dyke, Henry. *Joy and Power: Three Messages with One Meaning*. New York: T. Y. Crowell and Company, 1906.

Vignone, Cristina. "A Long History of Community Service at the Church of All Nations." Virginia Commonwealth University (2013). https://socialwelfare.library.vcu.edu/settlement-houses/church-of-all-nations/.

Wacker, Grant. *America's Pastor: Billy Graham and the Shaping of a Nation*. Cambridge: Harvard/Belknap Press, 2014.

Wainwright, Jonathan, and G. K. Jackson. *A Set of Chants Adapted to the Hymns in the Morning and Evening Prayer, and to the Communion Service of the Protestant Episcopal Church in the United States*. Boston: Thomas Badger, 1819.

Wald, Gayle F. "From Spirituals to Swing: Sister Rosetta Tharpe and Gospel Crossover." *American Quarterly* 55:3(September 2003) 387–416.

———. *Shout, Sister, Shout!: The Untold Story of Rock-and-Roll Trailblazer Sister Rosetta Tharpe*. Boston: Beacon, 2007.

Walker, William. *The Christian Harmony Containing a Choice Collection of Hymn and Psalm Tunes, Odes and Anthems*. Philadelphia: E. W. Miller and William Walker, 1867. https://imslp.org/wiki/The_Christian_Harmony_(Walker,_William).

———. *The Southern Harmony and Musical Companion Containing a Choice Collection of Hymn and Psalm Tunes, Odes and Anthems*. Spartanburg, SC: Walker and King,

1840; Philadelphia: E. W. Miller, 1854. https://imslp.org/wiki/The_Southern_Harmony_(Walker,_William).

Walsh, Kenneth T. "The 1960s; Polarization, Cynicism, and the Youth Rebellion." *U.S. News and World Report*, March 12, 2010. https://www.usnews.com/news/articles/2010/03/12/the-1960s-polarization-cynicism-and-the-youth-rebellionredirect.

Walter, Thomas. *The Grounds and Rules of Musick Explained, or An Introduction to the Art of Singing by Note*. Boston: J. Franklin, 1721.

———. "The Sweet Psalmist of Israel." Boston: J. Franklin, 1722.

Walters, Kevin L. "Beyond the Battle: Religion and American Troops in World War II." PhD diss., University of Kentucky, 2013.

Warch, Willard. *Our First 100 Years: A Brief History of the Oberlin Conservatory of Music*. Oberlin, OH: Oberlin Conservatory of Music, n.d.

Ward, Andrew. *Dark Midnight When I Rise: The Story of the Fisk Jubilee Singers*. New York: Harper Collins, 2000.

Ward, Susan Hayes. *The History of the Broadway Tabernacle Church from its Organization in 1840 to the close of 1900*. New York: Broadway Tabernacle, 1901.

Waring, Dennis G. *Manufacturing the Muse: Estey Organs and Consumer Culture in Victorian America*. Middletown, CT: Wesleyan University Press, 2002.

Warner, Robert Austin. *New Haven Negroes: A Social History*. New Haven: Yale University Press, 1940.

Warren, Rick. *The Purpose Driven Church*. Grand Rapids: Zondervan, 1995.

Washington, Booker T. *Character Building: Being Addresses Delivered on Sunday Evenings to the Students of Tuskegee Institute*. New York: Doubleday, Page, & Company, 1902.

———. "Preface." In *Twenty-Four Negro Melodies, Opus 59*, by Samuel Coleridge-Taylor, vii–ix. New York: Oliver Ditson, 1904.

———. *The Story of My Life and Work*. Toronto, Ontario: J. J. Nichols & Company, 1901.

———. *Up from Slavery: An Autobiography*. New York: Doubleday & Company, 1901.

Watley, W. D. *Singing the Lord's Song in a Strange Land: The African-American Churches and Ecumenism*. New York: World Council of Churches, 1993.

Weadon, David A. "Clarence Dickinson (1873–1969) and the School of Sacred Music at Union Theological Seminary in the City of New York." PhD diss., Drew University, 1993.

Webber, Robert E. *Planning Blended Worship: The Creative Mixture of Old and New*. Nashville: Abingdon, 1998.

———. *Worship Old and New*. Grand Rapids: Zondervan, 1994.

Welch, James. *Richard Purvis: Organist of Grace*. Palo Alto, CA: printed by the author, 2013.

Wesley, John. *The Journal of John Wesley*. Edited by Percy L. Parker. Chicago: Moody, 1974.

———. *Thoughts Upon Slavery*. London: Joseph Cruikshank, 1774. Digital ed., Chapel Hill: University of North Carolina, 1999. https://docsouth.unc.edu/church/wesley/summary.html.

West, Edward N. "History and Development of Music in the American Church." *Historical Magazine of the Protestant Episcopal Church* 14:11 (March 1945) 15–37.

Westermeyer, Paul. *Let the People Sing: Hymn Tunes in Perspective*. Chicago: G.I.A., 2005.

Westermeyer, Paul, and David W. Music. *Church Music in the United States, 1760–1901*. St. Louis: Morningstar Music, 2014.

Wetzler, Robert. "Music for Worship." *Choral Journal* 6:6 (July/August 1966) 6.

White, James F. *Protestant Worship: Traditions in Transition*. Louisville: Westminster John Knox, 1989.

White, Newman Ivey. *American Negro Folksongs*. Hattboro, PA: Folklore Associates, 1965.

White, R. C., and C. H. Hopkins. *The Social Gospel: Religion, and Reform in a Changing America*. Philadelphia: Temple University Press, 1976.

Whitefield, George. "A Letter to the Inhabitants of Maryland, Virginia, North, and South Carolina." In *The Works of the Reverend George Whitefield*, vol. IV, 37–41. London: Edward & Charles Dilly, 1771.

Whiting, Arthur. "The American Composer." *The Outlook*, February 17, 1915, 400–405.

Whittaker, Will. "Church Choirs Shouldn't Be Declining Because of Lack of Interest." *Intergenerational Worship*, September 16, 2019. https://intergenerationalworship.com/2019/09/16/church-choirs-shouldnt-be-declining-because-of-lack-of-interes .

Whittle, Daniel Webster, ed. *Memoirs of Philip P. Bliss*. New York: A. S. Barnes, 1877.

Whyte, William. "What Victorian Churches Did for Us." *Church Times*, October 13, 2017. www.churchtimes.uk/articles/2017/13-October/comment/opinion.

Wicks, Sammie Ann. "A Belated Salute to the 'Old Way' of 'Snaking' the Voice on Its 345th Birthday." *Popular Music* 8:1 (January 1989) 59–96.

———. "Life and Meaning: Singing, Praying, and the Word Among the Old Regular Baptists of Eastern Kentucky." PhD diss., University of Texas/Austin, 1983.

Wienandt, Elwyn A. *Choral Music of the Church*. New York: Free Press, 1965.

Wienandt, Elwyn A., and Robert Young. *The Anthem in England and America*. New York: Free Press, 1970.

Wilder, Laura Ingles. "A Shelter in the Time of Storm." http://www.pioneergirl.com/blog/archives/4782.

Wiley, Bell I. *The Life of Johnny Reb: The Common Soldier of the Confederacy*. Louisiana State University Press, 1943; *The Life of Billy Yank: The Common Soldier of the Union*. Louisiana State University Press, 1952. Special Combined Edition. New York: Book of the Month Club, 1994.

Wilhoit, Mel R. "Ira D. Sankey: Gospel Roots—Remembering the Father of Gospel Music Part 1." *Cross Rhythms Magazine*, Thursday, October 1, 1992. https://www.crossrhythms.co.uk/articles/music/Ira_D_Sankey_Gospel_Roots__Remembering_the_Father_of_Gospel_Music_Part_1/36809/p1/.

Wilhoit, Bert H. *Rody: Memories of Homer Rodeheaver*. Greenville, SC: Bob Jones University Press, 2000.

Williams, H. W. *Thomas Hastings: An Introduction to His Life and Music*. New York: iUniverse, 2005.

Williams, Peter W. *Religion, Art, and Money: Episcopalians and American Culture from the Civil War to the Great Depression*. Chapel Hill: University of North Carolina Press, 2016.

Williams, Rachel. "The United States Sanitary and Christian Commissions and the Union War Effort." National Museum of Civil War Medicine. www.civilwarmed.org/commissions.

Williams, Richard G. "Chaplains in the Civil War." *Essential Civil War Curriculum*. Virginia Center for Civil War Studies—Virginia Tech (2010–2011). https://blog.uag-us.com/blog/chaplains-in-the-civil-war.

Williams-Jones, Pearl. "Afro-American Gospel Music: A Crystallization of the Black Aesthetic." *Ethnomusicology* 19:3 (September 1975) 373–85.

———. "Roberta Martin, Spirit of an Era." In *We'll Understand It Better By and By*, edited by Bernice Johnson Reagon, 255–74. Washington, DC: Smithsonian Institute, 1992.

Williamson, John Finley. "Choir Organization and Training." In *Selected Writings of John Finley Williamson*, edited by J. G. Beck. St. Louis: AuthorHouse, 2004.

———. "John Finley Williamson Defends Purpose of Church Music." *The Once-a-Week*, newsletter of Ithaca Conservatory of Music 7:2 (March 1929) 2–3.

Williamson, Rhea Parlette. "My Career." In *America's Choral Ambassador: John Finley Williamson* by Joseph G. Beck, 24–33. Bloomington, IN: AuthorHouse, 2014.

Wilson, K. P. *Campfires of Freedom: The Camp Life of Black Soldiers During the Civil War*. Kent, OH: Kent State University, 2002.

Wilson-Dickson, Andrew. "Jacques Berthier." Grove Music Online. https://doi.org/10.1093/gmo/9781561592630.article.52471

Wimber, Carol. *John Wimber—The Way It Was*. London: Hodder & Stoughton, 1999.

Wingard, Alan B. "The Life and Works of William Batchelder Bradbury, 1816–1868." PhD diss., Southern Baptist Theological Seminary, 1973.

Winslow, E. *Meetinghouse Hill: 1630—1783*. New York: Macmillan, 1952.

Winter, Miriam T. *Why Sing? Toward a Theology of Catholic Church Music*. Washington, DC: Pastoral, 1984.

Witherspoon, Edward. "Church Music: A Voice from the Choir Loft." *Century Illustrated Magazine*, November 1884, 474–76.

Witvlet, John D. "Discipleship and the Future of Contemporary Worship Music: Possible Directions for Scholarship, Songwriters, and Public Worship." In *The Message in the Music: Studying Contemporary Praise and Worship*, edited by Robert Woods and Brian Walrath, 167–92. Nashville: Abingdon, 2007.

Wolfe, Charles K. "Elvis Aaron Presley." In *Encyclopedia of American Gospel Music*, edited by W. K. McNeil, 303–4. New York: Routledge, 2005.

———. "Gospel Boogie: White Southern Gospel Music in Transition, 1945–1955." *Popular Music* 1 (1981) 73–82.

———. "Vaughan Quartet." In *Encyclopedia of American Gospel Music*, edited by W. K. McNeil, 409–10. New York: Routledge, 2005.

Wolfe, Richard J. *Early American Music Engraving and Printing*. Urbana: University of Illinois Press, 1980.

Wolff, Daniel. *You Send Me: The Life and Times of Sam Cooke*. New York: William Morrow, 1995.

Wohlgemuth, Paul. "Church Music Education in American Protestant Seminaries." In *Duty and Delight: Routley Remembered, a Memorial Tribute to Erik Routley*, edited by Robin A. Leaver, James H. Litton, and Carlton R. Young, 89–96. Carol Stream, IL: Hope, 1985.

Wood, Nathan E. *The History of the First Baptist Church of Boston, 1665–1899*. Philadelphia: American Baptist Publishing Society, 1899.

Woods, Robert, and Brian Walrath, eds. *The Message in the Music: Studying Contemporary Praise and Worship*. Nashville: Abingdon, 2007.

Woodson, Carter G. *A History of the African American Church*. New York: Diasporic Africa, 1990.

Woodworth, Steven E. *While God Is Marching On: The Religious World of Civil War Soldiers*. Lawrence: University Press of Kansas, 2001.

Woolley, Ethel. "Lieutenant Nanny in Recital." *The Diapason*, December 1, 1943, 10.

Woolverton, John F. "William Augustus Muhlenberg and the Founding of St. Paul's College." *Historical Magazine of the Protestant Episcopal Church* 29:3 (September 1960) 192–218.

Work, John Wesley, II. *Folk Song of the American Negro*. Nashville: Fisk University Press, 1915.

Worsham, John H. *One of Jackson's Foot Cavalry: His Experience and What He Saw During the War, 1861–1865*. New York: Neale, 1912.

Wright, Tim, and Jan Wright. *Contemporary Worship: A Sourcebook for Spirited Traditional, Praise, and Seeker Services*. Nashville: Abingdon, 1997.

Wyton, Alec. "Thoughts on Music in the Church (Reprint of Address to April 1969 A.G.O. Convention." *Choral Journal* 12:5 (January 1972) 9–14.

Yarmolinsky, A. *Picturesque United States of America, 1811, 1812, 1813: Being a Memoir on Paul Svinin, Russian Diplomatic Officer, Artist, and Author, Containing Copious Excerpts from His Account of His Travels in America*. New York: W. E. Rudge, 1930.

Yeo, Douglas. "Homer Rodeheaver: Reverend Trombone." http://www.yeodoug.com/articles/Yeo_HBSJ_Homer_Rodeheaver_2015.pdf.

Young, Carlton R., ed. *Companion to the United Methodist Hymnal*. Nashville: Abingdon, 1993.

Zabriskie, Alan. "Evolution of Choral Sound of the St. Olaf Choir and the Westminster Choir." PhD diss., Florida State University, 2010.

Zald, M. N., and P. Denton "From Evangelism to General Service: The Transformation of the YMCA." *Administrative Science Quarterly* 8:2 (September 1963) 214–34.

Zetty, Claude. "New Sounds in the Church." *Choral Journal* 8:5 (May-June, 1968) 15–17.

Zundel, John. *The Modern School for Organ: A New Progressive and Practical Method in Three Parts*. Boston: Oliver Ditson, 1860.

———. *Treatise on Harmony and Modulation being an Exposition of the Principles and Rules of Harmony, Thoroughbass, and Composition*. New York: Gordon & Son, 1862.

Author Unattributed

"1800 Revival at Red River and Gasper River." 2019. Romans1015.com/red-river.

"Acts Out Story: Graham Aide is Baby-Sitter for 10,000." *Fort Worth Star-Telegram*, March 18, 1951.

All Saints Church, Worcester, Massachusetts: A Centennial History, 1835–1935. Worcester, MA: Commonwealth/Worcester, 1935.

"American Guild of Organists 2014 Survey: Past, Present and Future Members." https://www.agohq.org/wp-content/uploads/2015/04/Complete-Survey-Report-3.24.15.FINAL_.pdf.

Bibliography

America's Great Revivals: The Story of Spiritual Revival in the United States, 1734–1899. Ebook ed. Grand Rapids: Bethany, 2002.

"The Annual Musical Festival of the Broadway Tabernacle Choir." *The Musical World* 3:16 (August 15, 1852) 247.

"April 30, 1862"—reprint from *National Intelligencer.* Vol. 5, in *The Rebellion Record, A Diary of American Events with Documents, Narratives, Illustrative Incidents, Poetry, etc.*, edited by F. Moore, 10. New York: G. Putnam, 1863.

"Cathedral Organ." Savannah, Georgia: Cathedral Basilica of St. John the Baptist, n.d. www.savannahcathedral.org/cathedral-organ/.

"Changes in Church Choirs." *New York Times*, April 9, 1899.

"Chaplains Surmount Obstacles in Reaching Lonely Outposts." *Protestant Voice*, January 28, 1944, 7.

"Charter of Privileges Granted by William Penn, esq. to the Inhabitants of Pennsylvania and Territories, October 28, 1701." The Federal and State Constitutions Colonial Charters, and Other Organic Laws of the States, Territories, and Colonies Now or Heretofore Forming the United States of America, Compiled and Edited Under the Act of Congress of June 30, 1906 by Francis Newton Thorpe, vol. 5, 3076–80. Washington, DC: Government Printing Office, 1909.

"Choir Candidating." *The Musical Herald*, April 1885, 88.

"The Choirs of New York." *American Church Review*, July 1890, 298–99.

The Choral Service: The Liturgical Music for Morning and Evening Prayer, the Litany, and the Holy Communion According to the Use of the Protestant Episcopal Church in the United States of America. Joint Commission on Church Music for the General Convention, Protestant Episcopal Church of the United States. New York: H. W. Gray, 1927.

"The Church Choirmaster." *The Musical Herald*, March 1886, 72.

"Church Choirs in America as Reported in the Scotch Guardian." *Dwight's Journal of Music*, November 25, 1876, 338–39.

"Church Music." *Dwight's Journal of Music*, June 2, 1860, 74.

"Church Music—Church of St. Francis Xavier." *The Arcadian*, February 6, 1873, 2.

"Church Music in New York." *Dwight's Journal of Music*, February 23, 1861, 380.

"Church Music in New York." *Dwight's Journal of Music*, March 9, 1861, 396.

"Church Music in New York." *Dwight's Journal of Music*, March 16, 1861, 404–5.

"Colportage as Conducted by the American Tract Society: Its Necessity, Efficiency, and Economy." New York: American Tract Society, 1859.

"Congregational Singing Schools." *The Musical Visitor*, February 12, 1841, 2.

"Contraband Singing." *Dwight's Journal of Music*, September 7, 1861, 182.

"Description of Music at Plymouth Church—H. W. Beecher and Choral Director Huntington." *Dwight's Journal of Music*, March 6, 1858, 369.

Dictionary of Organs and Organists. Edited by F. W. Thornsby. London: H. Logan & Company, 1912.

"Facts on File, 2003." www.fofweeb.com/electronic_images/Maps/populationchart.pdf.

"First School Here for Church Music." *New York Times*, July 22, 1913.

G. I. A. Diamond Jubilee Collection: Seventy-Five Years of Music for the Church. Chicago: G.I.A., 2016.

"Gospel Hymns, 80,000,000 sold. The Death of Ira D. Sankey." *The Nation*, August 20, 1908, 156–57.

"The Greatest Youth Gathering in History: Background." The Billy Graham Center. https://www2.wheaton.edu/bgc/archives/exhibits/YFC%201945/02%20background.html.

A Guide to the Spence Family Collection, 1812–1961. Fisk University Archives. https://www.fisk.edu/wp-content/uploads/2020/06/spence-familycollection1812-1961_revised.pdf.

"The Guild of Organists." *New York Times*, December 13, 1896.

"Henry Ward Beecher and the Fisk Jubilee Singers." *Marin Journal*, February 1890.

Historical Statistics of the United States: Colonial Times to 1970, vol. 1. Washington, DC: US Department of Commerce, 1975.

Hymnbook for the Army and Navy. New York: American Tract Society, 1863.

"Interesting from Port Royal." *New York Times*, January 9, 1863.

"An Interview with Austin Lovelace." *Online Newsletter of Selah Publishing*, April 2, 1993. https://www.selahpub.com/MusicInWorship/LovelaceInterview.html.

"Letters from the Clergy of the Anglican Church in South Carolina, ca. 1696–1775." https://speccoll.cofc.edu/wp-content/uploads/2016/06/Letters-from-the-Clergy-of-the-Anglican-Church-in-SC.pdf.

"Madame Sontag in Brooklyn." *The Musical World*, November 13, 1852, 162–63.

Minute Book of St. Mary's Church, Philadelphia, 1782–1811. Philadelphia: American Catholic Historical Society, 1893.

"Mr. Beecher Says So." *The Arcadian* 1:5, December 26, 1872, 5.

"The Music of the Church: Women in Choirs." *American Church Review*, October 1889, 319–21.

"Music at the Brick Church." Pamphlet, 1963.

"The Musical Convention." *Dwight's Journal of Music*; Part 1 (August 21, 1852) 157–58; Part 2 (August 28, 1852) 165–66.

"Musical Matters: The National Conservatory Throws Its Doors Open to Colored People." *Buffalo Sunday Morning News*, May 28, 1893.

"The New Rebel Cry: Jesus is Coming." *Time*, June 21, 1971, 56–63.

"News of the Day." *New York Times*, September 8, 1861.

Nickerson's Illustrated Church Musical and School Directory of New York and Brooklyn, Part 2. New York: Nickerson & Young, 1895.

"The Nineteenth Century." Editorial. *New York Times*, December 31, 1899.

A Noble Landmark of New York: The Fifth Avenue Presbyterian Church, 1858–1958. New York: Fifth Avenue Presbyterian Church, 1960.

"Opening of a New Organ." *The American Musical Times*, June 10, 1848, 28.

Organ Historical Society Database, 2012. https://pipeorgandatabase.org/.

"Organ Music Popular with Pacific Forces; Moonlight Recitals." *The Diapson*, December 1, 1943, 13.

"Organs, Organists, and Church Music in this Country." *The Musical Herald*, January 3, 1884, 110.

"Outlook for Organs in 1945 Not Hopeful." *The Diapason,* January 1, 1945, 2.

"Q & A: Why Inclusive Language Matters." *Duke Today.* https://today.duke.edu/2021/05/qa-why-inclusive-language-matters.

"The Quotable Moody." http://moodycenter.org/the-quotable-moody.

Records of Holy Trinity (Old Swedes) Church, Wilmington, Delaware, 1697–1773. Edited by H. Burr. Wilmington, DE: Historical Society of Delaware, 1890.

"Report of Committees to the Annual Meeting, April 25,1877; Church of the Disciples." Boston: D. B. Fletcher, 1877.

The Restless Church: A Response to the Comfortable Pew. Edited by William Kilbourn. Philadelphia: J. B. Lippincott, 1966.

"Review, John Henry Wilcox Organ Recital." *New York Musical Pioneer and Chorister's Budget*, September 1866, 93.

Revised United States Army Regulations of 1861 with an Appendix Containing the Changes and Laws Affecting Army Regulations and Articles of War to June 25, 1863. Washington, DC: US Government Printing Office, 1863.

"Revival Born in a Prayer Meeting." In *America's Great Revivals: The Story of Spiritual Revival in the United States, 1734–1899*, 57–70. Ebook ed. Grand Rapids: Bethany, 2002.

"Sunday's 19 Aids Draw Trail-hitters." *The New York Times*, January 28, 1917, 6.

"School Committee's Report." *Boston Musical Gazette*, December 26, 1838, 1–2.

"Selections: Proceedings of the Musical Convention Assembled in Boston, August 16, 1838." *The Boston Musical Gazette*, April 3, 1839, 193–94.

"Seraphima is in the Choir." *New York Times*, April 16, 1899.

Shenandoah University Historic Timeline. https://www.su.edu/about-us/history/.

"Singing in the Choir: Those Who Want Places and Those Who Get Them." *New York Times*, June 29, 1884.

Slave Narratives (Alabama). Vol. 1. Washington, DC: Works Progress Administration, 1941. https://www.gutenberg.org/ebooks/36020.

Slave Narratives (Georgia). Vol. 4, part 3. Washington, DC: Works Progress Administration, 1941. https://www.gutenberg.org/cache/epub/18484/pg18484-images.html.

Slave Narratives (Texas). Vol. 16. Washington, DC: Works Progress Administration, 1941. https://www.gutenberg.org/ebooks/35380.

"Slave Songs of the United States." Anonymous review. *Lippincott's Magazine of Literature, Science, and Education*, March 1868, 341–42.

"Slavery Law and Power in Early America and the British Empire." https//:slaverylawpower.org/barbados-side-by-side.

Soldiers' Hymnbook for Camp Worship. N.p.: Soldiers' Tract Society, Virginia Conference of the Methodist Episcopal Church South, 1862.

Songs of Harvard: A Collection of Songs and Glees as Sung by the Glee-Club and Students of Harvard College. Edited by H. D. Sleeper. Cambridge: Charles Sever/Harvard Bookstore, 1890.

"The Story of the Far Eastern Bible Institute and Seminary." Pamphlet. St. Paul, MN: Lincoln Printing, n.d. https://www2.wheaton.edu/bgc/archives/bulletin/bu1203.htm#:~:text=The%20tragedy%20of%20World%20War,for%20ministry%20in%20the%20Philippines.

"The Strange Tale of Robert Schuller and the Crystal Cathedral: A Conversation with Sociologists Mark T. Mulder and Gerardo Marti." https://albertmohler.com/2020/05/27/mark-mulder-gerardo-marti.

"The Temple Choir." *Musical Life*, December 1904, 12–13.

"The Ten Largest Churches." *Christianity Today*, March 5, 1990, 22.

Third Annual Report of the New York Ecclesiological Society, 1851. New York: Stanford and Swords, 1851.

"This Far By Faith: Daniel A. Payne." PBS blog. https://www.pbs.org/thisfarbyfaith/people/daniel_payne.html.

"Untitled Alumni Report on Activities of H. D. Sleeper." *Hartford Seminary Record*, 1892–93, 155.

"Untitled Description of Henry D. Sleeper's Graduation." *Hartford Seminary Record*, 1891–92, 71.

U.S. Census Bureau. "Historic Census Statistics on Population Totals by Race, 1790 to 1990, and by Hispanic Origin, 1970 to 1990. For the United States, Regions, Divisions, and States." 2002. https://www.census.gov/library/working-papers/2002/demo/POP-twps0056.html.

War of the Rebellion: A compilation of the Official Records of the Union and Confederate Armies. Series 3, vol. 1. Washington, DC: Government Printing Office, 1880–1901.

"The Week of Prayer: Revival Movements in the City." *Chicago Tribune*, January 10, 1866.

"What is Calvinism?—Understanding the History and Denominational Doctrine." Christianity.com, 2013. https://www.christianity.com/church/denominations/what-is-calvinism.html.

The Whole Book of Psalms. Cambridge, MA: Stephen Day, 1640.

"Women at Church." Editorial. *The Arcadian*, January 2, 1873, 5.

INDEX

A

Abbott, Lyman (1835–1922), 368–69, 374, 379, 399
   Lake Mohonk Conferences (1890, 1891), 399n65
Adams, John (1735–1826), 29
Addams, Jane (1860–1935), 364, 369, 374, 379n24, 399
African Methodist Episcopal Church (A.M.E.), 36n89, 165, 174, 381, 441, 569, 745
African Methodist Episcopal Zion Church, 40, 165, 381, 441
Aldredge-Clanton, Jann (bn. 1946), 687n2
Alexander, Charles M. (1867–1920), 458–59
Allen, Richard (1760–1831), 173–74, 572
Allen, William Francis (1830–1889), 192, 203–208
"All-Night Singings", 644
American Cæcilian Society, 310–11, 505, 509
American College of Musicians, 264, 344
American Conservatory in Chicago, 612
American Guild of Organists, 359, 457n44, 478, 485, 521n1, 531n26, 532
American Missionary Association (A.M.A.), 187, 385n37, 390, 392
American Sunday School Union, 63
American Tract Society, 223n18,19, 231
"Ancient Style" (Pappas), 137
Ancient-Future/Convergent Worship (Webber), 736
Ante-Communion, 97n7, 102
Anti-Catholicism, 93, 110–13, 115, 119, 306
Anxious seat, 121n4, 415n28
Applause Meter, 589n90
Ashtabula, Ohio, 82n62, 428n53, 744
Association of Anglican Musicians, 635, 711
Anthem singing,
   Late Eighteenth and Early Nineteenth Centuries, 22n55, 28–31, 56, 67
   Mid-Nineteenth Century, 105–106, 109, 261, 267, 272, 351–53
   Late Nineteenth and Twentieth Centuries, 487, 491–93, 529, 536, 542–43, 594, 598, 604, 606, 633, 727, 740
Arminius, Jacobus (1560–1609), 46
Arminianism, 46–47, 85, 128n27, 479
Armstrong, Louis (1901–1971), 566–68, 581n69
Army Chaplains' Manual (Civil War), 218, 241
Asbury, Francis (1745–1816), 35–36, 41, 62
Austin, Rev. James C. (1887–1968), 575–77, 585
Azusa Street Revival, 453n34

B

Baker, Benjamin Franklin (1811–1899), 82–83
Ball, Thomas (1819–1911), 318
Band Music, 214, 216, 237, 239–41, 430, 438, 460–61, 606, 621
Baptist Sunday School Board, 611, 636
Barnabee, Henry Clay (1833–1917), 118
Barrows, Cliff (1923–2016), 639–43
Barth, Karl (1886–1968), 727, 740
Bass Viol, 51, 53–56, 337, 429
Bassford, William Kipp (1839–1902), 331n59, 332
Batastini, Robert (bn. 1942), 738
Baxter, Jesse Randall (1887–1960), 558, 560
Bay Psalm Book (*The Whole Book of Psalms Faithfully Translated into English Meter*, 1640), 8, 16
Beach, Amy Marcy Cheney (1867–1944) [a.k.a."Mrs. H. H. A."], 483, 486–88, 494–95, 501, 602, 730
Beall, Rev. James Lee (1924–2013), 676
Beaumont, Geoffrey (1903–1970), 666–67
Beecher Family,
  Harriet Beecher Stowe (1811–1896), 212–13, 485
  Henry Ward Beecher (1813–1887), 249, 252–58, 290, 303, 319, 322–23, 342–43, 391–96
  Lyman Beecher (1775–1863), 47, 60, 75, 84, 113, 120, 120n2, 121–22, 213, 246, 413, 539
  Thomas K. Beecher (1824–1900), 391–92
Belcher, Supply (1751–1836), 27n66, 29
Berge, William (d. 1883), 307–308
Benson, Rev. Louis F. (1855–1930), 480n21
Berman, Alice H. (1911–2006), 617, 637
Berthier, Jacques (1923–1994), 737–38
Berton, Pierre F. M. (1920–2004), 651–53
Best, Harold M. (b. 1931), 609n49, 717
Biglow & Main Publishing Company, 591n3
Billings, William (1746–1800), 22–23, 27–30, 49, 53, 90, 138
Bitgood, Roberta (1908–2007), 617, 634
Blackwood Brothers, 644
"Blended" Worship, 736
Bliss, Phillip P. (1838–1876), 340, 422, 426–427, 428n53, 429
Boatner, Edward (1898–1981), 575–77
Boston Gregorian Society, 308, 505
Bowman, Edward Morris (1843–1913), 262–64, 344, 530
Boy choirs/Vested Choirs of Men and Boys, 95, 102–103, 109n27, 272, 293–99, 301, 303–304, 329, 348n81, 514–17, 542
Boyd, Malcolm (1923–2015), 677–79
Bradbury, William B. (1816–1868), 81–82n62, 86–91, 104, 122n5, 212, 261, 346–47, 387–88, 427, 430–31, 444, 477n15, 642, 744
Brattle, Thomas (1658–1713), the Brattle Organ (Boston), 52
Brewer, John Hyatt (1856–1931), 359
Brewster, W. Herbert (1897–1987), 446
Bronzeville (South Chicago), 441, 454, 575
Brooks, Phillips (1835–1893), 249, 300n84, 301, 303, 333, 487
Brown, Bartholomew (1772–1854), *Bridgewater Collection* (1802), 50
Brown, Elaine (1910–1997), 617
Brush Arbors, 171n17
Bryant, John Emory (1836–1900), 191
Buck, Dudley (1839–1905), 88 (79n), 259, 262, 264, 328, 336, 344, 349–59, 488, 530, 594, 605–606n36, 633n19, 638

Buckminster, Joseph (1784–1812), 46, 73–74,
The Brattle Square Collection (1805), 74
Bull, Amos (1744–1825), 29
Burleigh, Henry Thacker "Harry T." (1866–1949), 398, 494n56,
Bushnell, Horace (1802–1876), 49, 247, 249, 303, 351
Butler, Benjamin Franklin (1818–1893), 186–87, 190

C

Cæcilian Movement, 310–12, 505, 507, 509–10
Caecilian Choir (Newark, New Jersey), 263
Calvert, Cecil (1605–1675), 113
Calvin, John (1509–1564), Calvinism, 5n2, 6–7, 44–46, 97, 112, 121, 125, 128n27, 289
Camp Douglas (Chicago), 412n18
Camp meetings,
 Red River (June 13–17, 1800), 125, 126–27
 Cane Ridge (August 6–13, 1801), 120n2, 123n7, 124–25, 129–36
 Camp meeting songs and spirituals, 131–34
Cantatas, 387, 638–39
Carden, Allen (1792–1859), *Missouri Harmony* (1820), 151–52
Carl, William C. (1865–1936), 482
Carmichael, Ralph (1927–2021), 639
Carr, Benjamin (1768–1831), 6n4, 50, 116–19
 "Grand Selection of Sacred Music", 118–19
Chadwick, George Whitefield (1854–1931), 360–61, 483, 488–91, 495, 501–503, 530–31, 730
Chamberlain, William B. and School of Sacred Music, Chicago Theological Seminary, 534
Chambersburg, PA, 213–14
Channing, William Ellery (1780–1842), 46–48
Chant, Anglican style, 103–107, 237–238, 238 n57, 267, 269–270, 270n10, 280–82, 284–85, 290, 603, 668, 720,
 Mason's interest in, 104–107
 "Pointed" psalters, 269, 276, 280, 284
Chant, Gregorian, xviii, 114, 505–19, 656–61, 664, 673,
 Solesmes, 308, 507, 510–511, 511n14
 Regensberg (*Editio medecea*), 309, 507, 510, 516n28
Chapin, Lucius (1760–1842) and Amzi (1768–1835), 149n75, 156
Chapman, J. Wilbur (1859–1918), 416, 425, 458, 463
Chaplaincy
 Civil War, 216–22, 225–30, 241–42, 248, 364, 412, 423
 World War I, 481, 593, 656,
 World War II, 618–22, 624
Charity School Children, 94–96
Chase, Philander (1775–1852), 97
Cheney, Moses (1776–1856), 25, 81n60, 262
Chicago Fire, "The Great", 357, 424, 437, 514n23, 606
"Choir candidating", 324n41
"Choral Service, The" (Episcopal liturgy), 269n10, 269–70, 278, 280–81, 285, 287, 291, 298, 341n81, 601
"Chorus choirs", 255, 261, 264, 293, 295, 329, 349, 351, 354, 358, 491–92, 531, 602, 633n19, 727
Christiansen, F. Melius (1871–1955), 496–98, 498n69, 499n72
Christiansen, Olaf (1901–1984), 499n72, 616
Christiansen, Paul (1914–1997), 499n72, 633
Churches (individual)
 Bethel African Methodist Episcopal (Philadelphia), 40, 176
 Bethel African Methodist Episcopal (Chicago), 441
 Brattle Square Congregational (Boston), 46, 52, 74

Churches (individual) *(continued)*
  Brick Presbyterian (NYC), 52, 349, 530, 540–42, 545, 614n58, 631
  Broadway Tabernacle Church (NYC), 84, 85n70–73, 86, 88–89, 121, 122n5, 261, 481, 531,
  Calvary Chapel (Costa Mesa, CA), 675, 680–83, 685, 692, 694n15, 695–98, 711, 714, 729–30
  Cathedral of Tomorrow (Akron, OH), 698n27
  Church of the Advent (Boston), 272, 295, 487n37, 514, 531
  Church of the Holy Communion (NYC), 102, 294, 602
  Fifth Avenue Presbyterian (NYC), 79, 102, 482
  Ebenezer (Missionary) Baptist (Chicago), 575–76, 578, 583, 589
  Hollywood Presbyterian (Los Angeles), 627–28
  Holy Trinity Episcopal (Brooklyn, NY), 353–54, 358, 530
  "Old Buttonwood" Church, (Philadelphia), 18
  Pilgrim Baptist (Chicago), 572, 574, 575–76, 585
  Plymouth Church (Brooklyn), 252–53, 255–56, 261, 314, 319, 323, 342–44, 392, 396, 475, 616, 727
  Quinn Chapel A.M.E. (Chicago), 441–42, 575
  Riverside Church (NYC), 480–81, 614n58
  Saddleback Community Church (Lake Forest, CA), 704, 706–709
  St. James Episcopal (Chicago), 355, 357, 539–40, 606
  Silver Bluff Baptist (South Carolina), 39
  Tindley Temple (Philadelphia), 447, 572
  Tremont Temple (Boston), 551
  Trinity Church (Boston), 249, 300n84, 301, 333, 486, 491
  Trinity Parish (NYC), 52, 95–96, 99, 107–110, 271–78, 283, 287, 290–91, 294–95, 297n74, 314,
  Westminster Presbyterian (Dayton, Ohio), 500–501, 537–38
  Willow Creek Community Church (South Barrington, IL), 698, 703n38, 704–706.
Church Choral Society (NYC), 277–78, 285, 490
Church growth movement, 685, 689, 691, 693n13, 698–99, 702–704, 707–710, 733
Church Music Association of America (CMAA), 511, 663–64, 673
Civil War,
  Black Troops in the Civil War, 233–34
  Use of hymns and sacred music, 233–39
  Worship during, 223–29
Cleveland, James (1931–1991), 565n21, 648, 713n73
Coffin, Henry Sloane (1877–1954), 378, 545–47, 613
College of Church Musicians, 612, 715, 717–18
Colored Methodist Episcopal Church, 381, 569
Colporteur, 220, 222–23
Confiscation Act of 1862, 187
Congregational singing,
  Colonial and Late Eighteenth Century, 6–8, 10–12, 16–17, 21, 24, 50–51, 94, 114, 121
  Early Nineteenth Century, 59n5, 66–70, 74, 79, 87–89, 91, 102–103, 106, 122n5, 124, 135, 137, 141–42n63, 150, 152, 162, 168,
  Mid- to late Nineteenth Century, 226, 230, 252–56, 261, 267, 276, 281, 286, 306, 313, 329–30, 336–37, 343, 415–16, 420–21, 442, 456, 479,
  Twentieth Century, 507–508, 511–12, 517, 534, 537, 559, 604, 612, 635, 657, 660, 696, 724, 726–28, 736–37

Consociatio Internationalis Musicae Sacrae (est. 1963), 663
Contemporary Christian Music and Worship (CCM), 1, 439, 552, 675, 677, 683, 689, 691–95, 705, 707, 715n78, 718, 721, 728–30, 735–39
Continentals, The, 704
Contrabands, 187–90, 195, 208
Cooke, Sam (1931–1964), 646–49
Cotton, John (1564 – 1642), 7–9, 78
  Singing Psalms a Gospel Ordinance (1647), 8–9
Craig, Rev. Lewis (1737–1825), 135
Cravath, Erastus M. (1833–1900), 385n37, 389n44, 392
Crosby, Fanny J. (Frances Jane van Alstyne, 1820 – 1915), 212, 435, 439n69, 444, 450, 568, 612, 641
Cultivated and Vernacular Traditions (Hitchcock),
  Defined, 58
  Cultivated Tradition in American church music, 91, 246, 344, 359, 473, 477n15, 483, 508, 686, 730, 740
  Vernacular/Populist Tradition in American church music, 58, 121–22, 211, 243, 246, 340, 362, 438n67, 472–73, 509–510, 552, 587, 589, 649, 666, 708, 727, 730–31, 740
Cutler, Henry Stephen (1825–1902), 271–74, 276, 290, 297n74

D

Darwin, Charles (1809–1882), 247,
  On the Origin of Species (1851), 247
Darwinism, 248–50, 405, 471, 475n8, 506, 592n7
Davison, Archibald T. (1883–1961), 325, 520, 527–30, 595–600
  Protestant Church Music in America (1933), 596–599
Davisson, Ananias (1780–1857), 149–50
  The Kentucky Harmony (1816), 150

Dawson, William L. (1899–1990), 398, 745
Dearborn, Benjamin (1754–1838), 27
DeCou, Harold (1932–2008), 638–39
Denominationalism (Niebuhr), 593–99
Denominations and Religious Groups, Christian
  Assemblies of God, 453n34, 675n47, 698
  Baptist
    Eighteenth Century, 31n76
    Early Nineteenth Century, 37–39, 121, 123, 130, 134–35, 137–38, 184, 212,
    Late Nineteenth Century, 263–64, 312, 329, 337,
    Twentieth Century, 376, 441, 447, 567–69, 574–75, 610–12, 617, 626, 635–37, 685, 698, 698n27, 699, 715
  Church of England (Anglicanism), 6–7, 11, 17–18, 33, 52n17, 93–98, 98n9, 238n57, 265–267, 268n6, 272, 287, 289, 291, 336n62, 652–53, 652–54, 666–67
  Church of Scotland, 124, 652–54,
  Church of God in Christ (COGIC), 441, 452n29, 453–54, 456, 569, 580, 585
  Congregational Church, 41, 46, 52, 84–85, 122, 321, 391
  Episcopal Church, Protestant, 5, 52, 63, 92–96, 97n7, 98–99, 100–104, 107–110, 116, 165, 238n57, 257n31, 267–94, 311–12, 336n62, 491n46, 590, 594, 600–601, 607–610, 626, 635, 667–70, 711
  High Church and Anglo-Catholic Movements, 99n11,
  Latter Rain, 675n47, 676–77, 677n51, 689–90
  Lutheranism, 100, 304–306, 329, 336n62, 341, 496–99, 499n72, 594, 633–34, 698, 739

Denominations and Religious Groups, Christian *(continued)*
  Methodist/Methodist Episcopal, United Methodist, 31n76, 35–36, 36n92, 46, 52, 62–63, 121, 123–24, 130–132, 137, 212, 253–54, 312, 369–70, 374–75, 377, 452, 626, 633, 635, 654
  Pentecostalism, 447, 451–52, 452n29, 454–57, 459, 565, 568–69, 580, 582, 585, 592, 610, 612, 675n47, 675–77, 679–85, 689, 695, 711, 719, 724, 731
  Presbyterian Church, 10, 17–18, 31n76, 38, 52, 63, 92, 113, 121, 123n7, 124–26, 126n18, 127–28, 128n27, 130, 137, 213, 257, 285, 312, 329, 362–63, 373, 471, 474–75, 475n5, 480, 544, 591, 617, 626, 633–35, 687n2, 688, 698
  Roman Catholicism, 3, 4, 6n4, 7, 45, 50–51, 92–93, 97n7, 98, 110–11, 111n35, 112–118, 123–24, 165, 211–12, 219, 229, 257, 257n30, 272n14, 306–312, 504–519, 613, 627, 654–666, 670–73, 685, 725, 730, 739
    Motu Proprio/"Tra le Sollecitudini" (1903), 311, 504–14, 517–19
      Divini cultus sanctitatem (1928), 518
      Deus scientiarum Dominus est (1931), 518
      Mediator Dei (1947), 518
      Musicae sacrae disciplina, (1955), 518–19, 657
    Vatican II (1962–65), 654–666
  Unitarianism, 46–47, 103, 405, 485
Dickinson, Clarence (1873–1969), 298, 327, 357, 477, 482, 539–50, 600, 606, 613–14, 631, 714
Dickinson, Emily (1830–1886), 199, 258n32,
Dilworth, Rollo A. (bn. 1970), 398
"Dissenting Churches", 11, 18, 52n17, 94, 524,

Dix, Morgan (1827–1908), 99, 273–75, 278, 287–89, 290n53, 291, 601, 735
Dixon, Rev. Calvin P. (d. 1946), 568
Dorsey, Thomas A. (1899–1993), 445–46, 553n3, 565, 568–573n43, 574n46, 575–79, 582–83, 583n72, 585, 588–89, 713, 715
Douglas, Charles Winfred (1867–1944), 600–601, 610, 612, 614, 745
Douglass, Frederick (1818–1895), 40, 179n32, 403
Draesel, Herbert G. (bn. 1940), 668–70
Dranes, Arizona (1889–1963), 579–81, 581n68, 582
Dualism, Dualistic thinking, 523, 728–31, 740
Du Bois, William Edward Burghardt (1868–1963), 179–80, 366n5, 397, 399, 402–404, 442–43, 630n11
  "Strivings of the Negro People" (1897), 403
  The Souls of Black Folk (1903), 38–39, 39n98, 179, 366n5, 397, 403
Dudley-Smith, Timothy (bn. 1926), 654
"Dunblane Praises", 653–54
Dunham, Henry Morton (1853–1929), 478, 531
Duruflé, Maurice (1902–1986), 662
Dvořák, Antonin (1841–1904), 493–95n61
Dylan, Bob (bn. Robert Allen Zimmerman in 1941), 647, 678, 680, 694

E

"Easy Instructor, The" (Smith & Little, 1801), 143–44, 144n65, 145–46, 153
Eames, Emma (1865–1952), 320
Eastburn, Manton (1801–1872), 267
Eddy, Clarence (1851–1937), 359, 496, 527n18, 531, 539, 548

Edwards, Jonathan (1703–1758), 31n76, 47, 60, 120n2, 123n7
Eineke, C. Harold (1904–1979), 616
Emerson, Luther Orlando (1820–1915), 84, 144–45, 145n67
English parish church, 8, 27–28, 50, 53, 95, 289, 299
Erben, Henry (1800–1884), 110, 273–74, 343, 350
Eschatology, 248
Estey Organ Company, 338–39, 591, 624,
Excell, Edwin ("E. O.") Othello (1851–1921), 459–60
"Explo 72", 684n67, 690

F

Farwell, John V. (1825–1908), 410–11, 414n25, 416,
 Farwell Hall (Chicago), 419, 424, 427n51, 428n53
Fellowship of United Methodists in Music and Worship Arts (FUMMWA), 635
Fenwick, Fr. Benedict (1782–1846), 114
Finn, William J. (1881–1961), 295, 504–505, 508, 514–518
Finney, Rev. Charles G. (1792–1875), 47, 60, 70, 84, 85n68, 85n72, 86, 120n2, 121–22, 122n5, 413
First Day Schools, 62
Fisk Free Colored School, 383–384, 384n35, 385
Fisk Jubilee Singers, 364n2, 382, 385, 389–98
 Ensembles patterned after, 396n61
Fitzpatrick, Dennis, "Demonstration Mass English", 661
Flagg, Josiah (1737–1794), 22
 A Collection of the Best Psalm Tunes (with Paul Revere, 1764), 22
Flushing Institute for Boys (NY), 101–102, 278–79, 284, 294
Folk and guitar masses, 666–673
Foote, Arthur (1853–1937), 329n27, 333–34, 349, 483, 485, 531
Forrage, Stephen (1722–1785), 115

Forten-Grimke, Charlotte (1837–1914), 192, 201–202, 204
Fortress Monroe (Va.), 186–88, 233
Fosdick, Rev. Harry Emerson (1878–1969), 376, 479–80, 541, 591
Franklin, Aretha (1942–2018), 648–49
Freeman, Rev. James (1759–1835), 46
French, Jacob (1754–1817), 27, 29
Friends of the English Liturgy (F.E.L.), 671n41
Frisbee, Lonnie (1949–1993), 682–84, 694
"From Spirituals to Swing" (1938), 588
Frye, Theodore (1899–1963), 574, 576, 578–79, 583, 715
Fuller Theological Seminary/Fuller Institute of Church Growth, 680n57, 693n13, 702–704
Fundamentalism, 246n4, 470–72, 477, 591,
Funk, Joseph (1778–1862), 27, 150–51, 151n85, 163, 554
 Ein allgemein nützliche Choral-Music (1816), 150–51
 A Compilation of Genuine Choral Music (1832), 151
Furman, Richard (1755–1825), *Exposition of the Views of Baptists Relative to the Coloured Population of the United States* (1822), 37–38
Fux, Johann Joseph (1660–1741), *Gradus ad Parnassum,* 510

G

Gale, Walter Church (d. 1938), 481, 531
Gelineau, Fr. Joseph (1920–2008), 662–63, 738
General Theological Seminary (NYC), 99–100, 277–79, 283–85, 289, 291–93, 298, 669
"Generationalism", 662–63, 738
George, Henry (1839–1907), *Progress and Poverty* (1879), 366
Gettysburg, Pennsylvania, 141, 164n2, 174, 214n7

Gettysburg, Battle of (1863), 226–27, 233, 236–37
  National Consecration Chant or Hymn (1863), 237n57, 238–39
"G. I. Sunday", 619
"G. I. Gospel Hour", 622–23
"Gideonites", 192n67,
Gibbs, Harold Beckett (1868–1955), 511n14, 512
Gilbert, William Bond (1829–1910), 297n74
Gilmore, Patrick Sarsfield (1829–1892), 259–61, 323, 395, 420n36, 485, 488
  National Peace Jubilee (1869) 259–61, 420n36, 485
  World Peace Jubilee (1872) 261, 395, 420n36, 488
Gladden, Rev. Washington (1836–1918), 364–66n5, 368–72, 374, 378–79, 399
Gleason, Frederick Grant (1848–1903), 359
Glossolalia (Speaking in tongues), 452–53, 675n47, 694
Godspell (musical), 685
Good News! (youth musical), 685
Gospel Choral Union of Chicago, 578
"Gospel Pearls" (collection), 572–73
Gospel Music, History, Types and Characteristics, 4, 159n85, 440n3, 445–46, 452, 454–57, 552–53, 553n3, 559n9, 560n11, 561–649
  Southern Gospel, 553n3, 554–79, 587–89, 692n12
  Black Gospel, 451–57, 553n3, 559n9, 565–589, 644–650, 715
Gospel Music Association (founded 1964), 692n12
Gospel Music Workshop of America, 565n21
Gospel songs and hymns, 212, 366n7, 419n34, 428, 430, 433–39
  Formal, theological, and textual characteristics, 433–38

Graham, Rev. William Franklin "Billy" (1918–2018), 120n2, 622, 625, 639–43, 649, 684n67
"Great Awakenings" (See revivals),
"Great Migration, The", 440n1, 454, 553, 568–69
Green, Rev. Fred Pratt (1903–2000), 380, 654, 686
Green, Keith (1953–1982), 689–90
Gregorian Institute of America (G.I.A.), 511
Grosh, Rev. Aaron Burt (1803–1884), 139n53
Guilmant, Felix-Alexandre (1837–1911), 262, 482n27, 539
  Guilmant Organ School, 482n27
Gulliksen, Rev. Ken (bn. 1945), 694
Gunn, Abel (1800–1875), 20
Gustavus Adolphus College (St. Peter, MN), 499n72
Guthrie, Woodrow Wilson "Woody" (1912–1967), 674–75

H

Hairston, Jester (1901–2000), 398
Hale, Philip (1834–1954), 326
Hammond, Fred (bn. 1960), 714
Hammond, John (1910–1987), 588
Hammond, Laurens (1895–1973), Hammond Organs, 481
Hampton Institute Singers, 364, 396n61
Handel and Haydn Society (Boston), 79, 259, 318n15, 429, 486, 487n37, 491
  Handel and Haydn Society Collection of Church Music (1822), 75, 88
Handy, William Christopher "W.C." (1873–1958), 440n3, 565–67, 574, 584
Harkness, Robert (1880–1961), 575n49
Harmon, Joel (1772–1833), 141–42
Hastings, Thomas (1784–1872), 60–72, 74, 76–81, 87–88, 90–91, 103, 146–47, 344, 346, 477n15, 544, 550n70, 715, 727, 732, 735

Dissertation on Musical Taste,
  65–70, 74–75, 79–80, 477n15
Musical Magazine, 70, 146,
Henni, Fr. John Martin (1805–1881),
  310
Higginson, Thomas Wentworth
  (1823–1911), 192, 199–200, 202
Hirt, Charles C. (1911–2011), 627–29
  University of Southern California
  Dept. of Sacred Music, 629
Hobart, Rev. John Henry (1775–
  1830), 97, 99, 99n11, 277, 287
Hodges, Edward (1796–1876),
  107–110, 270–72, 277, 280, 283,
  291, 297n74, 314
Hodges, Rev. John Sebastian Bach
  (1830–1915), 278, 291–92,
  292n59, 293–94, 299–300
Hoffman, Abbie (1936–1989), 675
Hoffman, Richard (1831–1909), 85
Hogan, Moses (1957–2003), 398
Holden, Oliver (1765–1844), 29
Holy Fairs, 124, 126n18,
Homogeneous Unit Theory (Mc-
  Gavran), 707–708
Hook Organ Company (later Hook
  & Hastings), Elias Hook
  (1805–1881), and George G.
  Hook(1807–1880), 343–44
Hope Publishing Company, 591,
  591n3
Hopkins Sr., Rt. Rev. John Henry
  (1792–1868), 97, 282, 282n40,
Hopkins Jr., Rev. John Henry (1820–
  1891), 277–78, 282–87
Hopkinson, Francis (1737–1791), 116
Horner, Wilson G. (1834 – 1864), 237
Howard, Kathleen (1884–1956), 320
Howe, Solomon (1750–1835), 23
Huber, Jane Parker (bn. 1926),
  686–87, 687n1, n2
Humbard, Rev. Alpha "Rex" Em-
  manuel (1919-2007), 698n27
Humphreys, Rev. Charles A. (1838–
  1921), 218, 218n13, 219, 226,
  228, 240–41
Hybels, Rev. William "Bill" (bn. 1951),
  703n38, 704–706

Hymnals
  A Collection of Spiritual Songs and
    Hymns Selected (1801), 174
  Baptist Hymnal (1956, 1975), 636
  Broadman Hymnal, 610–12, 636,
    744
  Christian Psalter"(Hastings, 1836),
    86
  English Hymnal (1906), 529
  Hymnal 1940, 609–610, 744
  Hymnal Revised and En-
    larged(1903), 257n31, 491
  Hymnbook for the Army and Navy
    (1863), 231
  Hymn, Ancient and Modern (1869),
    276, 480, 668
  Hymnal of the Methodist Episcopal
    Church (1878), 480
  Hymns Selected and Original
    (1828), 305
  Plymouth Collection, 256–58
  Social Hymns of Brotherhood and
    Aspiration (1914), 377–78
  Soldiers' Hymnbook for Camp Wor-
    ship (1862), 231
  Gospel Hymns, 1–6, 430, 436–38,
    439n69, 444n13, 566
  Gospel Pearls, 572–73
  "Hymn Explosion", 653–54

I

Inclusive language, 687n2, 735
Inquiry Room, 415, 415n28
Instrumental Music in Churches,
  Introduction of, 51–56, 240
Invisible Institution, 170–71, 171n17
Irving, Washington (1783–1859), 24,
  56
Ives, Charles E. (1874–1954), *Essays*
  Before a Sonata, 457, 457n44
Ives, Elam (1802–1864), 63–64
  Manual of Instruction in American
    Sunday School Psalmody (1832),
    63
  American Sunday School Psalmody
    (Collection, 1832), 63

J

Jackson, George Knowil (1745–1822), 340
Jackson, George Pullen (1874–1953), 138–39, 154, 159–60
Jackson, Judge (1883–1958) and *The Colored Sacred Harp*, 569
Jackson, Mahalia (1911–1972), 575, 579, 582, 584–85
James, William (1842–1910), 476, 476n11
Jefferson, Thomas (1743–1826), 33n79, 57–58, 61,
Jesus Christ, Superstar (musical), 685
"Jesus Movement" and the "Jesus People", 675, 678–79, 681, 684–85, 689, 703, 711
John XXII, Pope (Jacques Duéze, 1244 – 1334), 6, 7n5
John XXIII, Pope (Angelo Roncalli, 1881 - 1963), 519, 657, 659n19, 660n20
John Paul II, Pope (Karol Józef Wojtyla, 1920 – 2005), 2, 3n1
Johnson, Hall (1888–1970), 398, 442
Johnson, Torrey (1909–2002), 639–40, 704
Joint Commission on the Revision of the Hymnal(Episcopal, 1940), 601, 607,
Jones, Rev. Charles Price (1865–1949), 452, 452n29
Jones, Darius Eliot (1815–1881), 156
Jones, Samuel Porter (1847–1906), 459–60
Jubilee Day, 392
"Juvenilization", 704

K

Kaan, Rev. Fred (1929–2009), 654
Katholisches Gesang-und Gebetbuch (1858) 512
Keble, John (1792–1866), 98
Kellogg, Clara Louise (1842–1916), 323
Kemp, Helen (1918–2015), 617
Kemp, John S. C. (d. 1997), 616
Kennedy, Rev. Duncan (1809–1889), 315–16

Kierkegaard, Søren (1813–1855), 607n41,
Kimball Organ Company, 339
Kimball, Edward (1823–1901), 407
King, Elisha J. (1821–1844), 160
Krueger, George Frederick (1907–1986), 616

L

Lamond, Felix (1862–1940), 535–36, 536n35
Langlais, Jean (1907–1991), 661n24, 661–62
Lanier, Sydney (1842–1881), 294
"Large Church Movement", 698n27
Latter Rain Movement, 675n47, 675–77, 677n51, 689–90
Layzell, Rev. Reg (bn. 1904), 676–77
Law, Andrew, 49, 143
  Select Harmony (1778), 49, 143
Lay preachers, 123n7, 124, 135, 220, 452
"Lecrae" (Lecrae Devaughn Moore, bn. 1979), 714
Le Jeune, George F. E. (1841–1904), 298–99n74
Ledbetter, Huddie "Lead Belly" (1888–1949), 674
Lee, Robert E. (0807–1870), 224
Liber usalis, 604
Liedertafeln or *Männerchor*, 259
Liele, Rev. George (ca.1750–1828), 39, 39n99
Leipzig Conservatory (Germany), 87–88
Lincoln, Abraham (1809–1865), 152, 190, 201, 203–204, 224, 237–38, 330n58, 410–11, 418
Lind, Jenny (Johanna Maria Lind, 1820–1887), 86, 319,
"Lining out", 8–9, 11, 132, 137, 167–68, 466, 743
"Litany of Loreto" (Litany of the Blessed Virgin), 114
Little, William, See *"Easy Instructor"*
Liturgical vs. Non-Liturgical Denominations, 312
Liturgy, 92, 97n7, 98–99, 99n11, 269n10, 293, 302, 504, 506–508,

518–24, 656, 656n13, 657–60, 665–66, 711
Locke, Warren A. (1847–1920), 295–96, 531
Lockwood, Rev. Lewis C. (1815–1904), 187–89
Lorenz, Edmund S. (1854–1942), 185, 533, 533n30, 534
Lovelace, Austin C. (1919–2010), 616, 633, 710
"Love Song" (CCM Band), 683–84, 692, 697
Lowell, James Russell (1819–1891), 367, 367n9, 378
Lutkin, Peter Christian (1858–1931), 297, 299, 357, 497n67, 499, 531, 536, 539, 606, 719
Lutheranism, 100, 304–306, 329, 336n62, 496–99, 499n72, 594, 688, 698, 739

M

M. P. Möller Pipe Organ Company, 722
Mahan, Rev. Milo (1819–1870), 277, 284, 292–93
Malibran, Maria (Maria Felcite Garcia, 1808–1836), 317–18, 317n11
Mann, Horace (1796–1859), 47–48
Männerchor *(See Liedertafeln)*
Manual for Clergy and Church Musicians (1980), 5, 269
Maranatha! Music, 690–93, 697
Martin, Roberta (1907–1969), 579–80, 583–84, 589, 644
Martin, Sallie (1895–1988), 580, 582–83, 583n72, 584, 589, 713, 715
Martyr, Justyn (110–165 A.D.), 725–26
Mason, Rev. Charles Harrison (1866–1961), 452, 454
Mason, Lowell (1792–1872), 28, 60, 65, 72–82, 90, 102, 104, 108n23, 122n5, 144n67, 146, 259, 318, 340, 344, 346, 361, 445, 477n15, 493, 533, 544, 551, 715, 727, 732, 735

Address on Church Music (1826), 65, 75–78, 80
Mather, Rev. Cotton (1663–1728), 12–13, 32, 41
The Accomplished Singer (1721), 12–13,
Rules for the Society of Negroes (1714), 32
Maynor, Dorothy (1910–1996), 617
McClellan, George B. (1826–1885), 224, 228
McCurdy, Alexander (1905–1983), 616
McGavran, Donald A. (1897–1990), 703, 707
McGranahan, James (1840–1907), 422, 429–30, 433n60, 435
McGready, Rev. James (1763–1817), 123, 123n7, 124–27,
McIlvaine, Rt. Rev. Charles Petit (1799–1873), 97, 267
McKinney, Baylus Benjamin "B.B." (1886–1952), 611–612
McKim - Garrison, Lucy (1842–1877), 192, 192n68, 194–98, 204–205
Megachurches, 698, 698n27, 699, 702–704, 709, 709n60, 713, 715
Meineke, Christoph (né Christopher, 1782–1856), 292n60
Mercadante, Saverio (1795–1870), 306, 308
Mercy Music/Mercy Publishing, 697
Merrill, Rev. William Pierson (1867–1954), 541, 541n43, 542, 545
Messiter, Arthur (1834–1916), 275–76, 287, 290, 298
Methodism, 31n76, 35–36, 36n89, 36n92, 46, 52, 62–63, 92, 96, 123–24, 131–32, 137, 165, 173–74, 253–54, 312, 369–70, 374–75, 452, 597n19, 626, 635, 687, 687n2
"Middle Passage", 178n31
"Minister of music" (professional title), 2, 546–550, 550n70
Ordination of church musicians, 547–48

Millard, Harrison (1830–1895), 307, 307n110, 330n58
Moody, Rev. Dwight Lyman (1837–1899), 61, 120n2, 122, 211, 220n15, 248, 405–17, 420–30, 433–39
Moody Bible Institute (Chicago), 430, 458, 575n49, 640
Moore, Undine Smith (1904–1989), 712
Morgan, Justin (1747–1798), 27, 27n66, 29
"Mourner's Bench" or "Anxious Bench", 121, 121n4, 415n28,
Muck, Karl (1859–1940), 501
Music Ministry Education, 532–50
Music Teachers National Association (MTNA), 264, 325, 360, 521, 521n1, 631
Muhlenberg, Rev. William Augustus (1796–1877), 100–103, 277–78, 284, 294
Musical conventions, 60, 81–84, 91, 161, 744
Mussey, Mabel H. B. (1873–1931), 377–78
  Social Hymns of Brotherhood and Aspiration (1914), 377–78
"*Mysterium*", 99, 99n10, 266, 508, 598–99, 730, 737

N

National Association of Organists, 541
National Association of Schools of Music (NASM), 609, 630, 717
National Baptist Convention, 381, 572, 573n43, 574–75, 579
National Congregations Studies (NCS), 689n6, 711, 711n69, 712n70, 714, 723
National Conservatory of Music (NYC), 493
National Convention of Gospel Choirs and Choruses (NCGCC), 578, 582
Neale, Rev. John Mason (1818 – 1866), 265–67, 277

Neidlinger, William H. (1863–1924), 359
New York Ecclesiological Society, 277, 285
Newman, Rt. Rev. John Henry (1801–1890), 98, 268n6
New England Conservatory, 260, 357, 360, 420n36, 478, 488–89, 530–31, 604, 612
Niebuhr, Rev. Reinhold (1892–1972), 592, 592n8, 593
Niebuhr, Rev. H. Richard (1894–1962), 592–96
Nix Jr., William (1878 – 1941), 572–73, 573n43,
Normal Schools of Music, 344
  Catholic Normal School of the Holy Family (St. Francis, WI), 310
  Normal School Academy of Music (Geneseo, NY), 429
  Normal Musical Institute (1853, NYC), 346–47,
  Southern Normal Institute of Music (1880, Dalton, GA)\, 560–61, 560n11
  Stamps-Baxter Normal School of Music (1924, Jacksonville, TX), 558
  Vaughan Normal School of Music (1911, Lawrenceburg, TN), 558, 560, 564
  Virginia Normal School of Music (1874, New Market, VA), 151n85, 554, 558, 560n11
North, Rev. Frank Mason (1850 – 1935), 369, 374–75,
North Market Street Mission School (Chicago), 409–10, 416, 421
Northwestern Conservatory of Music (Minneapolis, MN), 497, 497n67,
Northwestern University and Conservatory (Evanston, IL), 497n67, 536, 539
Nubin, Katie Bell "Mother Bell" (1880–1969), 580–81, 585–86

O

"Old way", 6, 8–11, 11n22, 12–13, 17, 78, 137–38, 730
Oliver, Henry Kimball (1800–1885), 28,
Oliver, Joseph Nathan "King" (1881–1938), 566
Oliver Ditson Company, 186, 206, 261, 429
Onderdonk, Benjamin T (1791–1861), 99
Oral Tradition, 114, 134, 134n38,
Organ, pipe
  Colonial era: 52, 292n60, 336
  Late Eighteenth and Nineteenth Centuries: 110, 117, 122n5, 245, 273–74, 292n60, 336–37, 350, 357
  Twentieth Century: 480–483, 591, 594, 613, 623–24, 659, 659n19, 661, 687, 702, 712, 721–22, 721n88
Organ, reed (Cabinet organs and Melodeons), 337–40, 357–58, 480–81, 624
  "Estey Folding Organ", 624
Oxford Movement, 98, 265–68, 268n6, 276, 282, 291, 306, 308, 328, 603, 608
  See also "Ritualism" and "Tracts for the Times".

P

Pace, Adger M. (1882–1959), 564
Pace, Charles Henry (1886–1963), 574–75
  Pace Jubilee Singers, 574
Pacific Lutheran University (Tacoma, WA), 499, 499n72
Paine, John Knowles (1839–1906), 88n79, 296, 344, 355, 528, 531–32, 532n29, 548
Palestrina, G. P. da' (1525 -1594), 309–10, 492, 506, 509–10, 528
Palmer, Rev. Benjamin M. (1818–1902), 474–76
Parker, Horatio W. (1863–1919), 257n31, 333, 478–79, 489–91, 491n49, 492–93, 495, 502, 531, 594, 610
Parker, James Cutler Dunn (1828–1916), 332–33
Parker, Rev. Theodore (1810–1860), 47–48, 368, 378
Parsch, Fr. John Bruno "Pius" (1884–1954), 656, 656n13,
Participatio actuosa (active participation), 507, 656–58, 662–64, 739
Paul VI, Pope (Giovanni Montini, 1897–1978), 519, 658n18, 660, 660n20, 663,
Payne, Rev. Daniel A. (1811–1893), 173, 173n14, 174–76
Peale, Rev. Norman Vincent (1898–1993), 699–700
Penn, William (1694–1718), 140
  Charter of Privileges (1701), 140
Perosi, Lorenzo (1872–1956), 507
Perfectionism, 44, 47n7, 47–48, 48n9,
Perry, Julia (1924–1979), 617
Petersburg, VA, 141, Siege of, 229–30, 234, 234n45
Peterson, John W. (1921–2006), 638–39
Pew rentals, 409n11
Pfohl, Henry Clauder (1905–2001), 616
Phillips, Philip (1834 – 1895), 417–19, 419n34, 421–22, 431–32, 553
Phillips, Sam (1923–2003), 649
Pitch pipes, 18, 52, 52n19, 337, 551, 566
Pius VI, Pope (Giovanni Braschi, 1717–1799), 115
Pius VIII, Pope (Francesco Castiglioni, 1761–1830), 309
Pius X,, Pope (Giuseppe Sarto, 1835–1914), 505–511, 511n14, 513, 515,
  Pius X School of Liturgical Music, 510, 513, 536
Pius XI, Pope (Ambrogio Ratti, 1857–1939), 518
Pius XII, Pope (Eugenio Pascetti, 1876–1958), 518, 657
Playford, John.(1623–1687), 9, 16

Pontifical Institute of Sacred Music (Rome), 309, 507, 514
Pooler, Marie (1928-2013), 632
Populism in church music (*see Cultivated and Vernacular Traditions*)
"Port Royal Experiment", 190-209
Porter, Maggie (1853-1942), 381, 393n55, 394
"Praise House" (or "Prays House"), 166-68
Pratt, Rev. James Bissett (1875-1944), 478, 478n17
Pratt, Waldo Selden (1857-1939), 312, 520-21, 521n1, 522-26, 529, 547-50, 550n70, 733, 735
Prayer Bands, 447, 454-55
Precentor, 9, 9n14, 9n17, 10, 18, 24, 101, 137, 269, 269n8
Presbyterian Association of Musicians (PAM), 635
Presley, Elvis (1935-1977), 649
Proske, Karl (1794-1861),
Psalters
  Metrical, 7- 12, 22, 97, 107, 137, 269, 269n8, 270, 276
  Pointed, 269-70, 284
Psautier de la Bible de Jerusalem (1953), 663
Purvis, Richard (1913-1994), 621, 633-34
Pusey, Rev. Edward Bouverie (1800-1882), 98, 268, 268n6, 272

Q
"Quartet (or Quartette) choirs", 306, 322, 327-36
Quartets, Gospel:
  Black Gospel Quartets: 552, 565-67, 578, 579, 583n72, 585, 589
  White Gospel Quartets and other ensembles: 552, 562-64, 588-89

R
Raikes, Robert (1736-1811), 61-62
Rainey, Gertrude "Ma" (1886-1939), 570, 573
Randoph, Rev. Peter (1825? - 1897), 169

Rauschenbusch, Rev. Walter (1861-1918), 366, 372, 374-380
  A Theology for the Social Gospel (1917), 372
Read, Daniel (1757-1836), 19, 23, 27, 27n66, 29
Recueil de Contiques (1814), 512
Reformed Judaism, Music of (19th century), 329n57
Regular singing, 5, 5n2, 6, 8-42
Repp, Raymond (1942 - 2020), 670-73, 685
Revivals, 31n76, 120n2
  1st Great Awakening, 31, 47
  2nd Great Awakening, 47, 120-21, 431
  3rd Great Awakening. 247, 287-288.
  Cane Ridge, 120n2, 121n4, 123n7, 123-25, 127, 128n27, 129-30, 130n30, 131-36, 136n43
  Gasper River and Muddy River, 120n2, 123, 126-27
  South Elkhorn, 135
  Revival of 1857-58 (Business Man's), 211-12, 407n3,
  Great Urban Revival (late 19th c), 61, 405-439, 444, 458, 553, 568
  Graham Crusades, 625, 639-643, 649, 684n67
  "Explo '72", 684, 684n67, 690
Reynolds, Isham (1879-1949), 636
Reynolds, William J. (1920-2009), 159, 611, 636
Rice, Rev. David (1733-1816), 38
  Pamphlet: *"Slavery Inconsistent with Justice and Good Policy"*, 38
Ring Shout (or "Shawt"), 168, 192,
Ritualism, 98, 98n9, 99, 119, 265-72, 272n14, 274-78, 283-85, 287, 293-94, 311, 594, 608
Rodeheaver, Homer (1880-1955), 461, 465-69, 559, 559n9, 568-69, 641-42
Romanes, George John (1848-1894), 475n8

Roosevelt, Franklin Delano (1882–1945), 480, 501, 590
Root, George Frederick (1820–1895), 80–81, 163, 345–47, 360–61, 430
Root & Cady Publishing House, 429, 433
Routley, Erik (1917–1982), 629, 632–33, 653–54, 667
Ruebush-Kieffer Company, 151n85, 554, 554n4, 558, 560n11

S

Sabatier, Charles Paul Marie (1858–1928), 476, 476n11, 659n19
Sacralization, 250–51, 452n29, 732–33
St. Gregory Society of America, 511
St. James Music Press, 720
St. John, Stephen (fl. 1815–1825), 139–40
"St. Louis Jesuits", 673
St Olaf College (Northfield, MN), 497–99
St. Olaf Lutheran Choir, 496–99
"Salt Company, The", 680
Sanctification, 35, 121n4, 451–52, 452n29, 453
Sankey, Ira David (1840–1908), 61, 122, 211, 340, 405–406, 415, 419n34, 422–23, 423n40, 424–427, 428, 430, 433, 433n60, 434–36, 438, 438n67, 439, 439n69
Sateren, Leland B. (1913–2007), 634, 634n21, 635
"Sawdust trail", 472n76
Saxton, Rufus (1824–1908), 190–92, 192n69, 201–202
Schalk, Carl (1929–2021), 633, 686, 709–710
Schaller, Lyle E. (1923–2015), 698–99, 703–704, 704n39
Schnabel, Arthur (1882–1951), 667, 667n38
Scholtes, Rev. Peter (1938–2009), 681–82
Schuler, Fr. Richard J. (1920–2007), 513, 661, 665–66

Schuller, Rev. Robert H. (1926–2015), 700–706
Schultz, Bro. Roger (1915–2005), 737
Scottish Communions (see "Holy Fairs")
Scripture Set to Music (Kelligan), 676
Sears, Rev. Edmund H. (1810–1876), 367–68, 378
Second New England School of Composers *(a.k.a. "Boston Classicists", "Boston Academics", or "The Boston Group")*, 483
Second Vatican Council of the Roman Catholic Church (1962–1965), 519, 519n34, 654–61
 Sacrosanctum Concilium (Sacred Liturgy), 519, 657–61
Seely, Rev. Raymond H. (1812–1885), 51
"Seeker Worship", 703, 703n38, 704–706
Service Men's Christian League, 622
Shackleford, Rev. John (1750–1829), 135
Shape-Note Singing and Notation, 120, 134n38, 137–38, 144, 146, 156, 161, 163, 196, 390, 558–59, 561, 569–70, 612, 730
Shaw, Henry Wheeler (A.K.A. "Josh Billings", 1818–1885), 21
Shea, George Beverly (1909–2013), 640–43
Shelley, Harry Rowe (1858–1947), 359, 531
Shenandoah Conservatory of Music/Shenandoah University, 554n4, 747
Shenandoah Seminary, 554, 554n4
Sheppard Moore, Ella (1851–1914), 382, 382n31, 383, 385–86, 388–91, 397–98
Sherwood, William H. (1854–1911), 445
Showalter, Anthony J. (1858–1924), 560, 560n11, 562–63
 Showalter Music Company, 560n11

Singenberger, John B. (1814–1924), 310–11, 505, 509, 511, 517
American Cæcilian Society, 310, 310n126, 311–12, 505, 509
Singing societies, 24, 73, 258
Slave Songs of the United States, 173, 194, 205–209
Sleeper, Henry Dike (1865–1948), 547–50
Sleeth, Natalie Allyn (1930–1992), 632–33
Smallwood, Richard (bn. 1948), 712–13
Smith, Rev. Charles Ward "Chuck" (1927–2013), 675, 691–92, 694, 694n15
Calvary Chapel, 675, 680–84, 691–92, 694, 694n15, 695–98, 704n39, 711, 714, 729–30
Smith, Gerrit, (1859–1912), 530–31, 533, 545
Smith, William (n.d.,), *See Easy Instructor.*
Society for the Propagation of the Gospel (SPG), 33, 93
Solesmes Abbey, Solesmes approach to chant singing, 308, 507, 510, 511n14, 601
Song battles, 589, 644,
Songsters, 132, 134n39, 137, 174, 210, 219, 221–23, 231, 240, 257–58, 258n32, 480
Sontag, Henriette (1806–1854), 319
Soul Stirrers, 645–48
Southern Baptist Convention, 610
Southern Baptist Theological Seminary School of Church Music (Louisville, Ky), 617, 630, 637,
Southwestern Baptist Theological Seminary School of Church Music (Fort Worth, Tx), 477, 536, 611, 636
Sowerby, Leo (14895–1968), 357, 536n35, 600, 605–606, 606n39, 607, 607n41, 608–610, 612, 634, 718
Spence, Rev. Adam K. (1831–1900), 385–86, 389

Spencer, Herbert (1820–1903), 249, 475–76
"Spurrlows, The", 704
Stamps, Virgil Oliver (1892–1940), 558–61,
Stamps-Baxter Publishing Co. and Singing Schools, 560n11, 562–63, 610, 612, 644
Stearns, Rev. Shubal (1706–1771), 37
Stebbins, George C. (1846–1945), 421–22, 425, 428–29, 429n57, 435, 438, 531
Stevens, Georgia (1870–1946), 513
Stewart, Lyman (1840–1923), 470
The Fundamentals, 470–71
Stone, Rev. Barton W. (1772–1844), 123n7, 125, 127–28, 128n27, 136n43
Storefront churches, 443, 454–57, 565, 569, 575, 579–80, 731n16
Strong, Josiah (1847–1916), 368–69, 379
Sunday, William Ashley "Billy" (1862–1935), 461–66, 469, 552–53, 568, 640
Sunday School Movement, 49, 60–64, 72, 74, 88, 230, 302, 337, 407, 409–11, 419–21, 427–28, 430–33, 553, 621
Svinin, Pavel (1787–1839), 176–78
Symbolism (Sacramentality), 101, 266–67, 277, 289, 594, 706, 725
Symmes, Rev. Thomas (1677–1725), 5n2, 8–13, 252

T

Taize, 737–39
Talmadge, Rev. T. DeWitt (1832–1902), 320, 320n25, 321
Tannenberg, David (1728 – 1804), 336
Tans'ur, William (1706–1783), 22
Taste, Musical, 4, 59, 65–70, 74–80, 92, 251, 335–36, 361, 386, 439, 477n15, 541, 596, 715, 724
Taylor, Georgia Gordon (1855–1913), 381
Taylor, Raynor (1747–1825), 116–17, 117n51,

Index 813

Taylor, Sophia Strong (1861–1936), 615
Tharpe, Rosetta (1915–1973), 552, 579–80, 585–87, 587n82, 588
Theological trends:
  Calvinism, 5n2, 7, 7n7, 31n76, 35, 44–47, 97, 112,
  "New School Calvinism", 121, 125, 128n27, 246, 269, 289, 592
  Premillennialism and Postmillennialism, 248, 250, 368, 371, 379, 405, 436, 455, 471–72, 591
  New Theology of the Nineteenth Century, 247–48, 365, 373, 378, 405
  Fundamentalism, 443, 464, 470–72, 477
  Progressive and Neo-Orthodoxy, 247, 592
  Theistic Evolution, 247
  Higher Criticism, 247
  Historicism: 247, 365, 506
Thomas, André J. (bn. 1952), 398
Thomas, Theodore (1835–1905), 251, 486, 491
Thursby, Emma Cecilia (1845–1931), 302, 319, 322–23
Tindley, Rev. Charles Albert (1856–1933), 445–49, 449n26, 450–51, 571–72
Titcomb, H. Everett (1884–1964), 600, 603–604, 604n35, 612, 618
Torrey, Rev. Reuben A. (1856–1928), 458, 470–72, 575n49
Tourjée, Eben (1834–1891), 260, 360, 417, 419–20, 420n36, 421, 498, 553
Towne, Laura M. (1825–1901), 192–93, 193n71, 194, 201, 204
Towner, Daniel Brink (1850–1919), 422, 429–30, 459
Tractarianism and "Tracts for the Times" (1833–1841), 98, 98n9, 99, 267–68, 268n6, 288, 291
Tre le sollecitudini (See *Motu Proprio*)
Trinity School of Church Music (NYC), 535–36

Trollope, Frances (1779–1863), 173
Truette, Everett (1861–1933, 481, 530, 530n25,
Tubman, Harriet (c. 1822–1913), 40, 189,
Tucker, Rev. John Ireland (1819 – 1895), 257n31, 270, 278–280, 280n32, 281, 284, 301, 601, 735
Tuckey, Willliam (1708–1781), 95–96
Tufts, Rev. John (1689 – 1750), 9, 13, 16–17, 24–25, 45, 142\
Tufts, Nancy Poore (1910–2012), 617
Tuning Forks, 18, 53, 566
Tuttle, Carl (b. 1953), 693–95, 697, 729

U

Union Theological Seminary and School of Sacred Music (UTS), 530, 533, 533n30, 537, 544–547, 602n32, 609n49, 612–14, 617, 629–30, 715, 718
United States Colored Troops (USCT), 190n61, 233, 234n45, 242
  Shaw Glee Club, 242
United States Christian Commission (USCC), 212, 220–23, 407n3, 418,
Universa laus, 663–64
"Up with People", 685

V

Van Dyke, Rev. Henry (1852–1933), 373, 378, 540
Varick, Rev. James (1750–1827), 40
Vaughan, James David (1864–1941), 554–60, 562–64
  Vaughan Publishing Company, 555
  Vaughan Quartet, 562–64
Vicksburg, Siege of (1863), 233–34, 241–42
Vested choirs, *See Boy choirs/Vested Choirs of Men and Boys.*
"Victory Vertical" (piano), 624–25
Vineyard, The and Vineyard Worship, 680n57, 690–91, 693–97, 704n39, 711, 714, 729–30
Vorsinger, 137

W

Walker, William "Singin' Billy" (1809–1875), 144n67, 149, 149n75, 154–160, 162
  Southern Harmony (1835), 149, 149n75, 156–58
Walter, Rev. Thomas (1698–1725), 13, 16, 20
Ward, Justine Bayard (1879–1975), 510, 513, 517
Ware, Charles Pickford (1840–1921), 192, 194
Warren, Rev. Richard D. "Rick" (bn. 1954), 704, 706–708
Wartburg College (Waverly, Ia), 499 (72n)
Washington, Booker T. (1856 – 1915), 185, 366n5, 400–403, 442
Washington, Ernestine (1914–1983), 589
Webb, George James (1803–1887), 81–82, 144n67
Webber, Robert E. (1933–2007), 735–37,
Wesley, Rev. John (1703–1791), 35, 120, 121n4, 131, 174, 190n59, 452, 538, 597n19
Wesley, Samuel Sabastian (1810–1876), 606n39
Westminster Assembly (1643–1653), 10
Westminster Choir College, 482n27, 537–38, 612, 614–618, 629–31, 636–37, 715, 717–18
  The Westminster Choir, 500–501, 501n75,
  Westminster Plan for Graded Choir programs, 627, 631, 636
Whalum, Wendell P. (1931–1987), 398
White, Benjamin Franklin (1800–1879), 159–161
  The Sacred Harp (1844) 159–160, 160n106, 161, 163
White, George Leonard (1838–1895), 383–395
White, Newman I. (1892–1948), 185
Whitefield, Rev. George (1714–1770), 31, 31n76, 33–35, 39, 41, 47
Whitfield, Thomas (1954 – 1992), 714
Whiting, Arthur B. (1861 – 1936), 483, 495
Whiting, George Elbridge (1840–1923), 488, 531
Whitney, Myron W. (1836–1910), 322
Whitney, Samuel Brenton (1842–1914), 295, 514, 531
Whittier, John Greenleaf (1807–1892), 368, 378
Wiley, Stephen (bn. 1956), 714
Williams, David McK. (1887–1978), 487, 600, 600n26, 602, 602n32, 608, 610, 612, 614
Williams, Rev. Don (1937–2022), 680, 680n57,
Williams, Rev. Peter (1786–1840), 40
Williamson, ,John Finley (1887 – 1954), 500–501, 537–538, 614–617, 631–32, 636
Wimber, John (1934–1997), 680n57, 693–96, 729
Winter, Sr. Miriam Therese (b. 1938), 664
Winters, Donald (1910–1989) and Frances (1908–1993), 617, 637
Witt, Franz Xavier (1834–1888), 309–10,
Wohlgemuth, Paul (1927–1987), 716–17
Women, Exclusion of from liturgical worship leadership, 299–300, 300n83, 301–304
Woodman, Raymond Huntington (1861–1943), 359
Work, John Wesley (1871–1925), 382, 386
Worship Pastor (title), 729
Wyeth, John (1770 – 1858), 134, 147–50,
  Repository of Sacred Music, 134, 148–49
Wyrtzen, Don (bn. 1942), 639
Wyton, Alec (1921–2007), 667–68

Y

Yale Institute of Sacred Music, 533n30, 718
"Youth for Christ", 622–23, 625, 640, 690, 704
Youth Musicals, Evangelical, 685

Z

Zerrahn, Carl (1826–1909), 429, 486
Zundel, John (1815–1882), 256, 314, 319, 323, 340–44, 346

www.ingramcontent.com/pod-product-compliance
Lightning Source LLC
Chambersburg PA
CBHW021216300426
44111CB00007B/335